FROM

NEW YORK STATE

JOHN FOREMAN

1990–1991

For Randi-Sue

Published by Prentice Hall Trade Division
A Division of Simon & Schuster Inc.
15 Columbus Circle
New York, NY 10023

ISBN 0-13-332462-1
ISSN 1044-2308

Manufactured in the United States of America

*Although every effort was made to ensure the accuracy
of prices and other information appearing in this book,
it should be kept in mind that prices,
policies, and facts do change in the course of time.*

CONTENTS

PART TWO

UPSTATE

MAPS

Inflation Alert

We don't have to tell you that inflation has hit New York State as it has everywhere else. In researching this book we have made every effort to obtain up-to-the minute prices, but even the most conscientious researcher cannot keep up with the current pace of inflation. As we go to press, we believe we have obtained the most reliable data possible. Nonetheless, in the lifetime of this edition—particularly its second year (1991)—the wise traveler will add 15% to 20% to the prices quoted throughout these pages.

NEW YORK STATE

I'll bet you have a few opinions about New York already, even if you've never been here. Most people do, and most of these opinions conflict. Well, it's hard to achieve a consensus on a subject so vast and diverse. Over 500 miles of highway stretch from Niagara Falls to Montauk Point. And between those two watery locales lies everything from the largest wilderness park in America to the most sophisticated urban center in the world. New Yorkers as a group don't have all that much in common. How, then, did this place ever come to be?

1. A Brief History of New York State

Algonquins, Mohawks, Cayugas, Senecas, and numerous other Indian tribes shot at and chased one another through the forests of primeval New York for millennia. That is, until the mighty Iroquois arrived at about the dawn of the 14th century. The warlike Iroquois soon put a stop to nearly all the turbulent infighting by creating a Grand Alliance of the tribes. The great Iroquois Confederation was symbolized by an eternal flame that burned in the wilderness for centuries before the European onslaught. Indeed, it burned as late as the 1870s, a reminder to any who cared to notice that organized society in New York State predated the Dutch and the English by a considerable amount of time.

The Confederation, while strong, was never exactly placid. Resentments and jealousies between various of the tribes were a constant leitmotif. The very first thing the early European arrivals did was to foment and aggravate these differences to the maximum degree possible.

EARLY TRADING MORALS

The French perhaps were the most perfidious. Or at least they perfected the tactics earliest. The first of them were traders out to make a buck without much care or respect for their Indian counterparts. The easiest and most profitable of the early trades was that in furs. French traders made a practice of promising rights to one tribe, then delivering them to another. Unhappy Onondaga braves would arrive at the trading post with canoes full of hides, only to find that the traders were gone, having already consummated a deal with competing Cayugas. The result was one local war after another, wherein resident Indians tore one another to shreds in order to secure "deals" with the elusive white men.

To be fair, it wasn't just the French who engaged in commercial double-crossing. Everybody did it. Worse luck, too, for the Indians, since they had become fatally susceptible by virtue of an acquired taste for whisky and firearms. They found themselves continually divided and conquered, and the old Iroquois order no longer seemed to work.

Of course, the Indians never had a chance. Besides newly acquired tastes, they had also to contend with newly acquired diseases. And then there were the sheer numbers of Europeans that poured across the ocean in a never-ending stream. It took a few centuries, but eventually the Native Americans of New York State were simply shoved out of the boat.

THE "HUDSON" OF HUDSON RIVER

New York traditionally considers its "discovery" to date from the voyage of Hendrik (we call him Henry) Hudson in 1609. This daring feat of exploration was undertaken at the behest of the Dutch East India Company. The purpose was to find a passage across the Americas into the spice-rich Pacific, the fabled "Northwest Passage." No such passage exists, as it happens. But Hudson did discover the beautiful river that bears his name today. The mouth of the Hudson is so broad and salty that, for a while at least, he must have thought he'd hit pay dirt. But eventually the splendid waterway into which he'd sailed grows so narrow that it can no longer be mistaken for anything but a river. Well, bad luck. But then Hudson was not a lucky man. His career ended two years later, in a rowboat cast adrift in the Arctic by a mutinous crew.

ENTER THE DUTCH

The significance of Hudson's New York adventure became clearer in the year 1621. This is the date of the charter of the Dutch West India Company (not to be confused with the Dutch East India Company). This outfit, whose name is familiar to every New York schoolchild (it should be, anyway), managed to secure a 24-year monopoly on trade along the coast of Dutch America. Having thus ensured its position, it proceeded to colonize its new property along typical Dutch feudal patterns.

The Dutch West India Company treated its New Netherlands turf with the same vague disinterest that a millionaire might treat a not terribly clever poor relation. Throughout the Dutch period in New York, the company was far more interested in trying to capture Brazil from the Portuguese and cultivate its richer colonies in the Caribbean. New Amsterdam, as New York was then called, was a stepchild that never quite lived up even to the most modest of expectations.

There was one man, however, to whom New Netherlands was a pet project. He was an Amsterdam diamond merchant named Kiliaen Van Rensselaer, and he was also a board member of the Dutch West India Company. Van Rensselaer was a tireless promoter of colonization in New Netherlands. He was quite literally a voice in the wilderness, however, since the company never had much more than a luke-warm interest in the property.

Undaunted, Van Rensselaer came up with the idea of "patroonships." Here was a concept with scale if nothing else. The idea was to allow a "patroon" to claim up to *24 miles* along any bank of the Hudson, or along the seacoast if he so desired, and it would be his. All he had to do was colonize it with a minimum of 50 settlers within a maximum of four years' time.

Sounds like a good deal, no? Interestingly, the total number of patroonships founded in the Hudson Valley during the entire Dutch period came to a measly five. And of those five, only Van Rensselaerwyck, upstate, ever succeeded for any length of time. But more about that in a moment.

While Van Rensselaer was promoting the spread of Dutch feudalism upstate, the West India Company was busy establishing its trading post at New Amsterdam. Early accounts indicate that from the outset New Amsterdam demonstrated personality traits for which New York would eventually become famous. In 1644 it was estimated that the populace of Manhattan spoke in 18 different languages. A Jesuit father named Jogues was moved to observe that the place had all the "arrogance of Babel" as well.

"We derive our authority from God and the West India Company," Gov. Peter Stuyvesant once said, "not from the pleasure of a few ignorant subjects." But this blatant tone belies the live-and-let-live quality of life in Dutch New Amsterdam. Side by side with the rowdy elements that offended Father Jogues was a prosperous and placid middle class whose nature was singularly Dutch. New Amsterdam looked like a miniature Holland, complete with step-roofed gables, winding canals, fat burghers, cows browsing in the streets, and immaculate gardens. Life was certainly milder here than it was in nearby New England. The Dutch never went in for the hellfire and brimstone of the English Puritans. To the contrary, they tolerated other people's religions, celebrated Christmas with Santa Claus and stockings full of presents (unheard of in the Puritan north), drank a lot of beer, told a lot of jokes, and were generally a warm-blooded lot.

At least such was the case down in New Amsterdam. Up north in patroon country nobody seemed to be cooperating. Indians kept raiding, settlers were almost impossible to obtain, and the Dutch West India Company was barely interested in what happened upriver, even when it affected the fur trade. And on top of it all, if the truth be known, 17th-century Holland was, quite simply, a much more wonderful place to live. It was rich, tolerant, and stable. Nobody wanted to leave. Or almost nobody.

ENTER THE ENGLISH

The Dutch era in New York trundled along with its unique blend of cantankerousness and surface calm until 1664. In that year the king of England, Charles II, decided simply to expropriate Holland's possessions in North America. Highhanded, no? Well, Dutch New Netherlands lay inconveniently between English New England and English Virginia. The king's government was vexed by the problems this created in the uniform administration of English trade and navigation acts. One supposes that the day finally arrived when some minister or other wondered aloud why His Majesty didn't just kick the Dutch out. And that's exactly what he did.

Stuyvesant wanted to fight. The citizenry, however, would have none of that. Faced with a refusal by the populace to do anything that might jeopardize their property, the Dutch governor accepted the inevitable and handed power over to the English. The terms of surrender were exceedingly generous. Property rights were fully confirmed. Religious freedom continued. Court decisions reached during the Dutch period were all confirmed. Even the apparatus of local government was left intact. Instead of the West India Company, the populace found themselves under the ultimate power and authority of the king's brother, James, the Duke of York. Day-to-day life barely missed a beat.

If the English had continued to govern as benignly as they started, there might never have been a revolution. The Duke of York was a concerned and tolerant proprietor. Alas, his new possession netted him a no better return than it had his Dutch predecessors. New York simply was not a good investment. It cost a fortune to defend and its inhabitants loathed paying taxes. It was prosperous enough as little towns in the boondocks went, but it wasn't making anyone in England rich.

A string of English governors administered New York for the next century plus. Some were better than others. One celebrated case (Lord Cornbury) conducted his administration wearing women's dresses. But the needs and wants of England grew

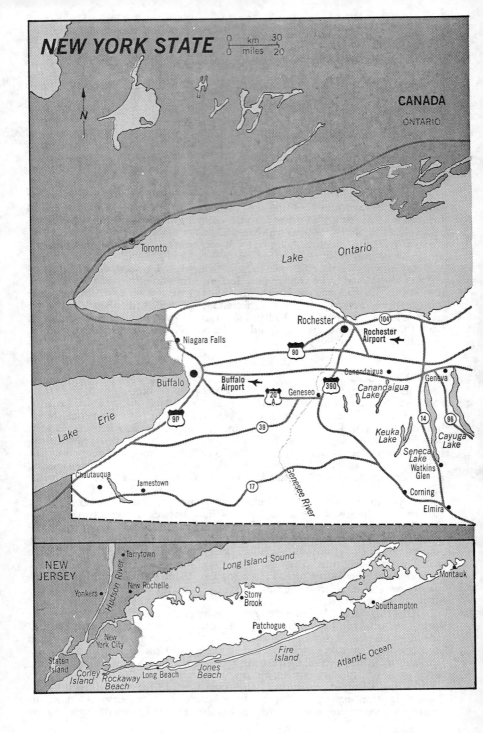

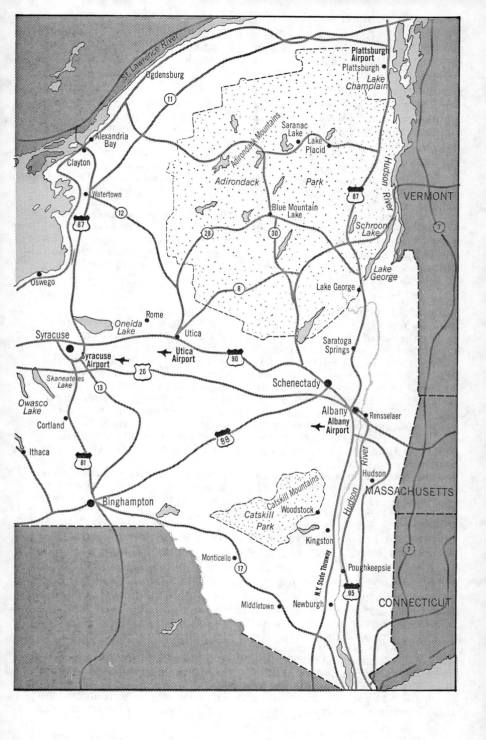

increasingly at variance with those of her colonies. On the eve of the American Revolution the English considered us, with some justification, to be a bunch of ingrates. Look at all they'd done for us! And we'd never come close to paying them back.

THE REVOLUTION

And so the deluge broke. For New York City, it really was a deluge too. It's hard to imagine the barbarism that took place in the city during those years. While major battles were fought all along the Hudson Valley, and notably at Saratoga, the city itself suffered a different fate. It was occupied by the British from the start of the war until its very end. The first thing that happened was a mysterious fire that transformed half the town into a pile of ashes. Then came long years during which houses were plundered, women were raped, husbands and fathers were beaten and branded, and the pleasant countryside of Manhattan and lower Westchester became an armed no-man's-land where law resided in the barrel of a gun.

Upstate, things were only slightly better. The Indians allied themselves with the British, putting every country settlement in jeopardy. Probably the Iroquois Confederation saw in the Revolution its last chance to reassert ancient prerogatives. Ultimately, Indian raids in the Finger Lakes district led to a devastating American retaliation led by John Sullivan and James Clinton in 1779. This dealt the Iroquois Confederation a blow from which it would never recover.

POSTWAR PROSPERITY

New York City, however, recovered from the Revolution with amazing speed. Trade in the port of New York on the eve of the British surrender equaled a big goose egg. But by 1791 the combined value of New York's imports and exports had already reached an amazing $8 million. By 1831 that figure had risen to $82 million. This kind of geometric increase in everything continued right through the 19th century.

What set New York apart from other developing cities, and as a consequence accounted for its amazing growth, was an unsurpassed natural system of transportation. It's difficult to imagine, in this era of interstate highways, airports, and railroads, the degree to which our nation once depended on rivers. Many of the streams we hardly even notice in today's metropolitan area were at one time part of a major network of natural trade and communication routes that connected the city with the rural interior.

And then, as if all those rivers weren't enough, along came the Erie Canal. Here was a navigable waterway that allowed a boat to go all the way from Manhattan to Buffalo. When the canal was opened in October of 1825, the entire state went a little nuts. A grand salute was contrived involving a battery of guns that stretched across 500 miles of countryside. At the culmination of a statewide celebration Governor DeWitt Clinton ceremoniously poured a keg of Lake Erie water into the choppy Atlantic. And history, as they say, was made.

THE FATE OF THE UPSTATE ARISTOCRACY

But what of the upstate patroons? Well, some of them went bust and slipped beneath the waters of receding history. Others had the bad luck or bad judgment to be on the wrong side in the Revolution. Result: property confiscated. But the Van Rensselaers displayed the sort of staying power that would have warmed old Kiliaen's heart. Over two centuries had passed, bringing with them war, revolution, and sweeping change. But the Van Rensselaers still presided in feudal splendor at the headwaters of the Hudson, still lords of hundreds of thousands of acres and thousands upon thousands of tenants.

In 1839 Stephen Van Rensselaer died—after which his heirs, accustomed to acting in whatever manner they chose, made a serious tactical mistake. Stephen had been a lax landlord. So lax, in fact, that he had neglected to collect rents from many of his tenants for quite a number of years. His heirs were dismayed to discover that he had left behind debts to the tune of $400,000, a staggering sum in those pre-industrial days. What did they do? Well, what would you do if you inherited all that land? They attempted to collect back rent.

Of course, one of the reasons Stephen had been so lax had to do with the extreme poverty of his tenants. The efforts of his heirs created panic across vast portions of upstate New York. Faced with a demand for accumulated rents they could never hope to pay, the tenant farmers formed farmers' committees to try to reason with the landlord. Stephen Van Rensselaer, Junior, would have none of them. Instead, he embarked on a campaign of wholesale evictions. Local marshals were being asked to evict entire townships. By 1844 Delaware County was in a state of open insurrection. Antirenters plagued rural landlords everywhere with physical violence. Finally, a concentrated antilandlord campaign in the state legislature resulted in an 1846 law that forbade future leases of agricultural land for periods in excess of 12 years. And with that, feudalism in New York State came to an end.

THE AGE OF VANDERBILT

By that time New York's old-style feudal aristocracy was on the wane anyway. Nipping at its heels were the steam age and the barons of industry. The model of the New Man of the New Age was Cornelius Vanderbilt—not just in New York but across the country. Vanderbilt started out rowing passengers across the bay to New York from his native Staten Island. By the time he was 24 he had become captain of his own steamboat. By 1828, at the age of 34, Vanderbilt had established his own network of steamboat routes. Over the next 30 years he extended these routes to New Jersey, Long Island Sound, up the Hudson, down to Panama and Nicaragua, and even back and forth across the Atlantic. This is why he was known as Commodore Vanderbilt. By 1864, having already amassed a fortune of $20 million, he turned to railroads. And then he really got rich!

It was railroads that set the stage for New York's next leap in wealth and influence. The pull of New York City's urban market became even more irresistible by virtue of its once again increased accessibility. At the same time, upstate farmers discovered that they could make the most money by selling dairy products to New York. Given the new competition from the soil-rich midwestern plains states, the switch to dairying was both profitable and prudent. To this day dairying remains the king of rural New York.

WAR WITH THE SOUTH

In 1861 New York gubernatorial candidate Edward Morgan came out strongly for Lincoln. He won by a landslide. Unfortunately, the pro-Union, antislavery sentiments that this victory suggested were largely illusory. New York business interests resented the interference with trade occasioned by the war with the South. The New Yorker in the street—and it must be noted that there was a vast and homeless underclass in the city at that time—was something less than unprejudiced when it came to black people. The low ebb in race relations came in 1863. The war was taking longer than anticipated and was devouring young men in alarming quantities. A draft lottery was established in New York to supply fresh conscripts. What it supplied instead was a full-scale insurrection.

Not many Americans realize the extent of that insurrection. During the Draft Riot of 1863 huge mobs roamed the streets of New York, murdering and mutilating any black they encountered. Even the black orphan asylum, then located on Fifth Avenue in the 50s, was besieged by a bloodthirsty mob determined to lynch the little children within. Fortunately, they escaped out the back in time and were spirited to safe hiding places. For three horrifying days there was no law in New York City at all. The mobs trained cannon down the streets. Houses were looted and burned. The populace was stricken with terror. It took the army to reassert order.

THE GILDED AGE

After the Civil War came the giddiest period of all in New York's history. A great prosperity was afoot in the country. And in New York a perfect saturnalia of greed and corruption burst upon an unsuspecting populace. The man whose name became most closely identified with the times was one William Marcy ("Boss") Tweed. Tweed was originally an alderman on the New York City Board of Supervisors. Through skillful political machinations he subsequently became school commissioner, deputy street commissioner, deputy commissioner of public works, even a state senator. All sounds on the up and up, doesn't it? However, during his tenure in these various posts Tweed managed to construct a system of patronage that enabled him to assert total personal control over the entire city government.

Between the years 1869 and 1871 the so-called Tweed Ring managed to steal the amazing sum of $45 million from the City of New York. How did they do it? Well, first they had a good front man. He was the mayor, A. Oakley Hall. Hall and Tweed had another stalwart in the person of City Chamberlain Peter B. Sweeney. And in their collective pocket (so to speak) was the last heavyweight of the "Ring," City Comptroller Richard B. ("Slippery Dick") Connolly.

These boys were common thieves, even if they did do it in a big way. They kept themselves in office through blatant vote fraud. Corrupt judges routinely "naturalized" thousands of illegal immigrants whenever votes were needed. It was the era of the "Black Horse Cavalry," those Albany legislators who sold their votes to the highest bidder. "Plunderbunds" was a term of the time, and it was applied equally to both major parties. Victory at the polls meant one thing: a chance to rob and steal.

A tale that truly captures the flavor of post–Civil War New York is that of Commodore Vanderbilt's battle with the railroad barons, Jay Gould, Jim Fisk, and Dan Drew. Vanderbilt had started buying up Erie Railroad stock in 1867, in an attempt to stamp out a rate war. Gould, Fisk, and Drew controlled Erie at the time. As soon as Vanderbilt began buying, Erie's treasurer, Drew, began issuing new stock certificates. Vanderbilt purchased $7 million worth of Erie stock in 1867 but somehow never managed to obtain a majority interest. "If this printing press don't break down," observed Drew, "I'll be damned if I don't give the old hog all he wants of Erie."

When Drew's comment was reported to Vanderbilt, the enraged commodore proceeded to obtain a warrant in the New York courts for the arrest of all three of them. The charge: illegal issuance of stock certificates. But he was too late. Hearing of the warrant, Drew, Gould, and Fisk immediately decamped to Jersey City, where they bribed a judge to set the warrant aside. Gould then left for Albany with suitcases full of cash. The plan was to bribe the Black Horse Cavalry to change the New York laws governing the issuance of stock, thereby legitimizing their maneuvers at Erie.

But since two could play this game, Vanderbilt left for Albany himself with the intention of buying Gould's men off. Some legislators began to expect millions. The collective level of greed was such that even Gould and Vanderbilt were brought up short. In fact, they decided it would be cheaper to call the whole thing off. And that's what they did. Vanderbilt abandoned the Erie Railroad to Gould, Fisk, and Drew, who stripped it of every asset, after which it entered into New York folklore as the archetypical corporate victim of a "robber baron."

REFORM

New York wasn't the only corrupt state during the latter part of the 19th century. But we certainly hit some dollar highs. The constant refrain of whichever Plunderbund was out of office was "Throw the rascals out!" And finally, to everyone's amazement, that's exactly what happened. As the century drew to a close, a new generation of honest politicians took office in New York. National figures like Samuel J. Tilden, Grover Cleveland, Theodore Roosevelt, and Al Smith all got their start in reform politics in the State of New York. They and others like them began a tradition of corruption-free government based on merit and efficiency that was to have sweeping implications both for New York State and for the nation as a whole.

Which brings us to the present. Despite all the changes of the tumultuous past, New York State remains eerily recognizable. "Sodom-on-the-Hudson" is richer and more polyglot than ever. And it still presents the same contrasts to the bucolic upstate dairylands that it has for centuries. The patroons are gone but the banks of the Hudson are still, in many places, lined with riverfront estates occupied by a squireocracy that has been in place for generations. Albany, a city that possessed only 19 bathrooms in the year 1860, is today a sophisticated state capital. And yet it's still a provincial outpost in the minds of those who live in Manhattan. As for the rest of the state, the world of the Indians is gone but the rural vastness remains. And in places like the Adirondacks, the wilderness itself still exists as it did at the dawn of time.

It is, in short, a marvelous state to explore, full of contrasts and content, rich in history and contradiction. It would take a lifetime to know even a small part of it. So on the assumption that you have only a few weeks, let's begin.

2. Getting To and Around New York State

BY AIR

For most people, the gateway to New York State will be one of the three New York City metropolitan area airports: **John F. Kennedy International Airport,** on Jamaica Bay in southern Queens; **LaGuardia Airport,** on Long Island Sound in northern Queens; or **Newark International Airport,** across New York Harbor in neighboring New Jersey. Of the three, LaGuardia is the most accessible to midtown Manhattan. There are other jetports in New York State, notably in Albany and Buffalo, but they don't handle jumbo jets.

It used to be the practice in guidebooks such as this to quote established fares from various points of origin. Well, nowadays, in the era of deregulated air fares and airline price wars, there are no more established fares. One day it costs $99 to fly from Los Angeles to New York. A month later it's twice that. Then a day after that it's down to $119.

Virtually every major carrier in the country flies into the New York City area. You can either take the phone book and start calling them in alphabetical order, or *call a travel agent* instead. The latter course is much the more sensible of the two. Travel agents cost you nothing. They receive a percentage of the fare from the carrier. And in the present age of deregulation, nobody else will be able to quote all the fares that you'll want to know.

A well-developed network of small (sometimes not-so-small) feeder airlines services many areas in upstate New York. These carriers include USAir, Precision, Command, Mall, and others. Again, for air travel arrangements upstate, you really should go to a travel agent. They're all connected with the airlines by computer these days. So wherever you live your local agent will be as informed as those right here in New York.

Having said all that, here are some local and toll-free "800" airline telephone numbers that might be helpful anyway:

American Airlines (tel. 212/431-1132, or toll free 800/433-7300)
Delta Air Lines (tel. 212/239-0700, or toll free 800/221-1212)
Eastern Airlines (tel. 212/986-5000, or toll free 800/327-8376)
Northwest Orient (toll free 800/225-2525)

SAMPLE MILEAGES BETWEEN SELECTED DESTINATIONS IN NEW YORK STATE
(Distance in Miles)

	Watertown	Tupper Lake	Syracuse	Saranac Lake	Rochester	Poughkeepsie	Plattsburgh	Niagara Falls	New York City	Ithaca	Geneva	Elmira	Buffalo	Albany
Albany	174	153	143	159	225	71	169	302	148	166	191	197	290	
Buffalo	210	309	152	330	76	361	379	21	438	155	111	147		290
Elmira	163	251	90	272	99	197	312	168	241	33	59		147	197
Geneva	121	220	53	241	46	262	280	123	280	59		59	111	191
Ithaca	130	218	57	239	90	190	279	167	234		46	33	155	166
New York City	322	301	291	307	373	77	317	450		234	280	241	438	148
Niagara Falls	219	318	164	339	85	373	384		450	167	123	168	21	302
Plattsburgh	165	71	238	50	299	240		384	317	279	280	312	379	169
Poughkeepsie	245	224	214	230	296		240	373	77	190	262	197	361	71
Rochester	134	233	87	254		296	299	85	373	90	46	99	76	225
Saranac Lake	120	21	189		254	230	50	339	307	239	241	272	330	159
Syracuse	73	168		189	87	214	238	164	291	57	53	90	152	143
Tupper Lake	99		168	21	233	224	71	318	301	218	220	251	309	153
Watertown		99	73	120	134	245	165	219	322	130	121	163	210	174

Trans World Airlines (tel. 212/290-2121, or toll free 800/221-2000)
United Airlines (tel. 212/867-3000, or toll free 800/241-6522)
USAir (tel. 212/736-3200, or toll free 800/428-4322)

BY BUS

Greyhound-Trailways (tel. toll free 800/528-0447) services nearly every city of any size in New York. It's fortunate that travel by bus is cheap, since, frankly, it's a little, shall we say, "tiring." Even its low-budget status is occasionally imperiled by those incredible airline fare wars. (Always check with the airlines to see if they are offering special fares at the time when you'll be traveling.)

It should be noted that the bus companies also offer special passes and excursion fares. An example is Trailways' 30-day "USA Pass," which entitles you to unlimited travel anywhere in the country, including New York State, for the flat rate of $350. Other fares and packages are always coming and going. If this sort of thing sounds interesting, then call Greyhound-Trailways and see what they've got when you plan to go.

BY RAIL

Also big with special fares is **Amtrak** (tel. toll free 800/872-7245), whose "All Aboard Fare," for example, costs only $182 round trip, Miami to Manhattan. Admittedly, this is cheaper than the cheapest air fare so far advertised. However, not all of Amtrak's routes are so reasonable. Indeed, cross-country rates are downright expensive, $301 one way, New York to L.A., with no stopovers. On top of this, the trip is *long*. Even in the case of the aforementioned Miami run, the train takes 24 hours instead of 3 on a plane.

Travel agents don't handle buses. But they do make Amtrak reservations. If the extra travel time doesn't bother you, ask your agent to inquire. A train trip might take a long time, but it usually provides excellent scenery, as well as departures and arrivals from the heart of whatever towns you're visiting. Not to mention the chance to get up and move around when your legs go to sleep.

BY CAR

No doubt the most American way to travel, this is by far the best way to savor the pleasures of upstate New York. If you plan to tour with a rented car, try to rent it outside the New York metropolitan area. Hertz, Avis, Budget, Econo-Car, and all the rest of them offer the same cars at their various locations. But the prices are different.

In New York City, for example, Avis's compact Chevy Cavalier costs $66 a day, with the first 70 miles free and 33¢ per mile thereafter. But in Poughkeepsie, a city on the Hudson halfway to Albany, the same car from the same company costs $63 a day, with the first 70 miles free and 32¢ per mile thereafter. By the time you get to Albany itself, Avis is down to $44 a day, with the first 75 miles free and the same 32¢ per mile thereafter. This same law holds true for all rental-car agencies, and in fact for purveyors of all manner of goods and services. If you're planning to drive a rented car upstate, rent it as far from Manhattan as you can.

For that matter, if you plan to rent a car for use in New York City, do so as far from the airport as possible. In Manhattan, as well as in most upstate cities of any size, you'll find hot competition among the cut-rate rental-car trade. It's a rule of thumb that the cheapest outfits don't maintain offices at the airports. All of them, cheap and not-so-cheap, are listed in the *local* Yellow Pages. In fact, the New York metropolitan area has dozens of possibilities. Quite a few also advertise in those airline magazines they tuck into the seatbacks underneath your tray. Rent-A-Wreck is one of my personal favorites—it's so unpretentious. Those who care to shop around will always find that there is life after Hertz and Avis.

The big companies, however, are the ones with the most offices and the toll-free "800" telephone numbers, among them:

Avis (tel. 212/593-8383, or toll free 800/331-1212)
Budget (tel. 212/807-8700, or toll free 800/527-0700)
Hertz (tel. toll free 800/654-3131)
National (tel. toll free 800/227-7368)
But enough of all this. Let's get on now to the big city.

---

3. The Purpose of This Book

The purpose of this guidebook is to enable the visitor to New York State to get the most value for each dollar spent. A very considerable amount of research has gone into the preparation of these pages. The author has personally inspected more hotels and restaurants than the average mortal will endure in a lifetime. But, of course, they all had to be looked at. What other way was there to tell whether or not they were worth the money?

This book is *not* a "budget" guide. True, many establishments have been discovered that offer tremendous value for a very low price. But just as many of the establishments described herein offer tremendous value at a very tremendous price.

The point of this guide is to provide a directory, complete with prices, of carefully researched establishments in *all* price ranges. Well, not quite all, perhaps. Those looking for soup kitchens and youth hostels will not find helpful suggestions in these pages. But almost everybody else will.

The focus of recommended establishments falls somewhere in the middle ground between very moderate and very deluxe. This middle ground naturally varies from place to place. The plushest room at a really nice upstate inn, for example, might very well cost less than a nondescript double in a commercial Manhattan hotel.

The reader may wonder as to the criteria the author has applied to the decision-making process. Let me tell you first off that nobody has paid a cent to be included in this book. If I liked a place and thought it offered genuine value, I put it in. If it was a dog, I left it out. If it was okay but the place across the street dripped with charm for the same price, then I put in the place across the street. Once again, my mission has not been to pass judgment on every single tourist establishment in New York State. Rather, it has been to provide descriptions of a recommended selection, from the moderate to the deluxe.

A FEW CAVEATS

The reader is asked not to forget that the only constant in life is change. The prices quoted in this guide were correct as this book went to press. But it can happen that by the time a reader actually gets to the XYZ Restaurant, they've dropped the filet of sole from the menu, or doubled the price, or the chef's wife has run off with the busboy and the specialty of the house now tastes like cat food. What can I say? Except that every possible effort has been made to ensure accuracy. If something has changed, let me know. But please . . . be understanding.

As to the nature of my selections, let me state from the outset that I value charm and character over bigness and modernity. Obviously I've included a lot of big new places. But there have been many times when I ruled out a given establishment simply because I didn't like the way it looked. Or because I felt somehow that it would be a pretty flat experience to patronize it.

HOW THIS BOOK IS ORGANIZED

New York has historically been divided between the city and the rest of the place. To refer to the "city" means only one thing: New York City. Upstate New

York and the more distant reaches of Long Island have been shackled to the city from the beginning of their history in a curious, sometimes abrasive, but evidently durable relationship. Some sort of symbiosis must exist—although its exact nature eludes many a New Yorker.

However, that's the way it is. In recognition of which, this book is divided between Part One, "New York City and Long Island," and Part Two, "Upstate." Please note that the still rural extremities of Long Island are purposely lumped together with New York City. That's because the island, although it does contain at its eastern end the elements of small-town life, has been totally touched by the gilded breath of New York City. Given the choice between upstate and Gotham, its affinity is clearly with the latter.

New York State has not been completely covered, as a glance at the Table of Contents will show. What you will find included in this book are only the most *interesting* areas to visit, together with places to stay and go to while visiting. As a practical matter I doubt you'll find that much has been left out. I've covered New York from Montauk to Buffalo, from Manhattan to Fort Ticonderoga, and from Millbrook to Chautauqua. This is a thorough guide for tourists. Traveling salesmen, however, may well be heading for points I've overlooked.

In addition to hotel and restaurant listings, a large part of my effort has been devoted to describing New York's sights and attractions. This has been the most enjoyable part of the whole job. Even if you have only a vague idea of what New York has to offer, after you read the pages ahead you'll be able to tell which areas will be of personal interest and which can safely be skipped.

AN INVITATION TO READERS

The publishers of this guide genuinely care about its usefulness and accuracy. We authors periodically tramp off to the hinterlands to update things. But these revisions take place at two-year intervals.

You the reader are on the scene across the state all year long. On behalf of myself and Frommer Books, we invite you to take a moment at any point during or after your trip and tell us your experiences with the guide. All suggestions are gratefully welcomed. In particular, we'd like to know your reactions to recommended establishments. Please tell us if they're still good. And for heaven's sake let us know if they aren't. If something new has opened up and you think it's terrific, we want to know about that, too. Every one of these guides contains a continually shifting constellation of recommendations. Things are always being put in and taken out. Needless to say, we appreciate good tips.

The same thing goes for sights and excursions. If you've discovered something really interesting that I've missed, by all means let me/us know. Comments can be sent to: John Foreman, Prentice Hall Travel, 15 Columbus Circle, New York, NY 10023. We'll look forward to your letters.

4. Frommer's Dollarwise® Travel Club—How To Save Money On All Your Travels

In this book we'll be looking at how to get your money's worth in New York, but there is a "device" for saving money and determining value on *all* your trips. It's the popular, international Frommer's Dollarwise Travel Club, now in its 29th successful year of operation. The club was formed at the urging of numerous readers of Guides, who felt that such an organization could provide continuing travel information and a sense of community to value-minded travelers in all parts of the world. And so it does!

In keeping with the budget concept, the annual membership fee is low and is immediately exceeded by the value of your benefits. Upon receipt of $18 (U.S. residents), or $20 U.S. by check drawn on a U.S. bank or via international postal money order in U.S. funds (Canadian, Mexican, and other foreign residents) to cover one year's membership, we will send all new members the following items.

(1) Any two of the following books

Please designate in your letter which two you wish to receive:

Frommer's $-A-Day® Guides
Europe on $40 a Day
Australia on $30 a Day
Eastern Europe on $25 a Day
England on $50 a Day
Greece on $30 a Day
Hawaii on $60 a Day
India on $25 a Day
Ireland on $35 a Day
Israel on $40 a Day
Mexico (plus Belize and Guatemala) on $30 a Day
New York on $50 a Day
New Zealand on $40 a Day
Scandinavia on $60 a Day
Scotland and Wales on $40 a Day
South America on $35 a Day
Spain and Morocco (plus the Canary Is.) on $40 a Day
Turkey on $30 a Day
Washington, D.C. & Historic Virginia on $40 a Day
($-A-Day Guides document hundreds of budget accommodations and facilities, helping you get the most for your travel dollars.)

Frommer Guides
Alaska
Australia
Austria and Hungary
Belgium, Holland & Luxembourg
Bermuda and The Bahamas
Brazil
California and Las Vegas
Canada
Caribbean
Egypt
England and Scotland
Florida
France
Germany
Italy
Japan and Hong Kong
Mid-Atlantic States
New England
New York State
Northwest
Portugal, Madeira & the Azores
Skiing USA—East
Skiing USA—West
South Pacific
Southeast Asia

Southern Atlantic States
Southwest
Switzerland and Liechtenstein
Texas
USA

(Frommer Guides discuss accommodations and facilities in all price ranges, with emphasis on the medium-priced.)

Frommer Touring Guides

Australia
Egypt
Florence
London
Paris
Scotland
Thailand
Venice

(These new, color illustrated guides include walking tours, cultural and historic sites, and other vital travel information.)

Gault Millau

Chicago
France
Italy
London
Los Angeles
New England
New York
San Francisco
Washington, D.C.

(Irreverent, savvy, and comprehensive, each of these renowned guides candidly reviews over 1,000 restaurants, hotels, shops, nightspots, museums, and sights.)

Serious Shopper's Guides

Italy
London
Los Angeles
Paris

(Practical and comprehensive, each of these handsomely illustrated guides lists hundreds of stores, selling everything from antiques to wine, conveniently organized alphabetically by category.)

A Shopper's Guide to the Caribbean

(Two experienced Caribbean hands guide you through this shopper's paradise, offering witty insights and helpful tips on the wares and emporia of more than 25 islands.)

Beat the High Cost of Travel

(This practical guide details how to save money on absolutely all travel items—accommodations, transportation, dining, sightseeing, shopping, taxes, and more. Includes special budget information for seniors, students, singles, and families.)

Bed & Breakfast—North America

(This guide contains a directory of over 150 organizations that offer bed & breakfast referrals and reservations throughout North America. The scenic attractions, and major schools and universities near the homes of each are also listed.)

California with Kids
(A must for parents traveling in California, providing key information on selecting the best accommodations, restaurants, and sightseeing attractions for the particular needs of the family, whether the kids are toddlers, school-age, pre-teens, or teens.)

Frommer's Belgium
(Arthur Frommer unlocks the treasures of a country overlooked by most travelers to Europe. Discover the medieval charm, modern sophistication, and natural beauty of this quintessentially European country.)

Frommer's Cruises
(This complete guide covers all the basics of cruising—ports of call, costs, fly-cruise package bargains, cabin selection booking, embarkation and debarkation and describes in detail over 60 or so ships cruising the waters of Alaska, the Caribbean, Mexico, Hawaii, Panama, Canada, and the United States.)

Frommer's Skiing Europe
(Describes top ski resorts in Austria, France, Italy, and Switzerland. Illustrated with maps of each resort area. Includes supplement on Argentinian resorts.)

Guide to Honeymoon Destinations
(A special guide for that most romantic trip of your life, with full details on planning and choosing the destination that will be just right in the U.S. [California, New England, Hawaii, Florida, New York, South Carolina, etc.], Canada, Mexico, and the Caribbean.)

Marilyn Wood's Wonderful Weekends
(This very selective guide covers the best mini-vacation destinations within a 200-mile radius of New York City. It describes special country inns and other accommodations, restaurants, picnic spots, sights, and activities—all the information needed for a two-or three-day stay.)

Manhattan's Outdoor Sculpture
(A total guide, fully illustrated with black and white photos, to more than 300 sculptures and monuments that grace Manhattan's plazas, parks, and other public spaces.)

Motorist's Phrase Book
(A practical phrase book in French, German, and Spanish designed specifically for the English-speaking motorist touring abroad.)

Paris Rendez-Vous
(An amusing and *au courant* guide to the best meeting places in Paris, organized for hour-to-hour use: from power breakfasts and fun brunches, through tea at four or cocktails at five, to romantic dinners and dancing 'til dawn.)

Sweep and Go—Home Exchanging Made Easy
(Two veteran home exchangers explain in detail all the money-saving benefits of a home exchange, and then describe precisely how to do it. Also includes information on home rentals and many tips on low-cost travel.)

The Candy Apple: New York for Kids
(A spirited guide to the wonders of the Big Apple by a savvy New York grandmother with a kid's-eye view to fun. Indispensable for visitors and residents alike.)

Caribbean Hideaways
(Well-known travel author Ian Keown describes the most romantic, alluring places to stay in the Caribbean, rating each establishment on romantic ambience, food, sports opportunities, and price.)

The New World of Travel
(From America's #1 travel expert, Arthur Frommer, an annual sourcebook with the hottest news and latest trends that's guaranteed to change the way you travel—and save you hundreds of dollars. Jam-packed with alternative new modes of travel that will lead you to vacations that cater to the mind, the spirit, and a sense of thrift.)

Travel Diary and Record Book
(A 96-page diary for personal travel notes plus a section for such vital data as passport and traveler's check numbers, itinerary, postcard list, special people and places to visit, and a reference section with temperature and conversion charts, and world maps with distance zones.)

Where to Stay USA
(By the Council on International Educational Exchange, this extraordinary guide is the first to list accommodations in all 50 states that cost anywhere from $3 to $30 per night.)

(2) Any one of the Frommer City Guides
Amsterdam and Holland
Athens
Atlantic City and Cape May
Boston
Cancún, Cozumel, and the Yucatán
Chicago
Dublin and Ireland
Hawaii
Las Vegas
Lisbon, Madrid, and Costa del Sol
London
Los Angeles
Mexico City and Acapulco
Minneapolis and St. Paul
Montréal and Québec City
New Orleans
New York
Orlando, Disney World, and EPCOT
Paris
Philadelphia
Rio
Rome
San Francisco
Santa Fe, Taos, and Albuquerque
Sydney
Washington, D.C.

(Pocket-size guides to hotels, restaurants, nightspots, and sightseeing attractions covering all price ranges.)

(3) A One-Year Subscription to *The Dollarwise Traveler*

This quarterly eight-page tabloid newspaper keeps you up to date on fastbreaking developments in low-cost travel in all parts of the world bringing you the latest money-saving information—the kind of information you'd have to pay

$35 a year to obtain elsewhere. This consumer-conscious publication also features columns of special interest to readers: **Hospitality Exchange** (members all over the world who are willing to provide hospitality to other members as they pass through their home cities); **Share-a-Trip** (offers and requests from members for travel companions who can share costs and help avoid the burdensome single supplement); and **Readers Ask . . . Readers Reply** (travel questions from members to which other members reply with authentic firsthand information).

(4) Your Personal Membership Card

Membership entitles you to purchase through the club all Frommer publications for a third to a half off their regular retail prices during the term of your membership.

So why not join this hardy band of international budgeteers and participate in its exchange of travel information and hospitality? Simply send your name and address, together with your annual membership fee of $18 (U.S. residents) or $20 U.S. (Canadian, Mexican, and other foreign residents), by check drawn on a U.S. bank or via international postal money order in U.S. funds to: Frommer's Dollarwise Travel Club, Inc., 15 Columbus Circle, New York, NY 10023. And please remember to specify which *two* of the books in section (1) and which *one* in section (2) you wish to receive in your initial package of members' benefits. Or, if you prefer, use the order form at the end of the book and enclose $18 or $20 in U.S. currency.

Once you are a member, there is no obligation to buy additional books. No books will be mailed to you without your specific order.

PART ONE

NEW YORK CITY AND LONG ISLAND

"BIG APPLE" ORIENTATION

1. GETTING TO AND FROM MANHATTAN

2. THE GEOGRAPHY OF THE "BIG APPLE"

3. GETTING AROUND TOWN

4. ABCs

It's not easy to pinpoint what makes New York so "New Yorkish." That it has a decided character, there can be no doubt. Yet it's a city so infinite in its effects on residents and visitors alike that its essence remains elusive.

To begin with the obvious, it's big. Indeed, it's the biggest city in North America (population within the city limits: approximately 8,000,000). If one is to believe the Convention and Visitors Bureau (I for one believe them completely!), there were almost 20 *million* additional souls who came to New York last year, just to visit. That's more people than live in many countries.

Such statistics boggle the mind. But the visitor soon learns to accept the mind-boggling as one of New York City's municipal traits. Astounding statistics abound. For example, all those aforementioned visitors spent the staggering sum of $10 *billion* while here in the Apple. Can't you just hear all that cash jingling into New York City cash registers? And that's just what came from the tourists; it doesn't even count what the locals spent.

"Spending" is probably another trait associated with New York City. We get it, and then, boy, do we spend it. How many cities, when you come down to it, contain 17,000 eating places? Or 97,000 hotel rooms? Or 12,000 licensed taxis? Not many.

Of course, people are drawn to New York City by more than a compulsion to spend for spending's sake. This place has the real goods, more so perhaps than any other spot on the globe. It is where you can buy couture clothing, high technology, pork bellies, space-age weaponry, oil tankers, and superlative pastrami. New York's great libraries and seats of learning are the places to research rare manuscripts; her 400 galleries and her almost 200 museums display art of the highest caliber; her 40 legitimate theaters present every manner of drama, and what they don't present you can still see in over 200 Off or Off-Off Broadway theaters. In fact, you can see anything in New York, and not necessarily on a stage either. New York is a place in which to become famous, to learn, to indulge one's highest aspirations, or to gratify one's lowest urges. It is a place in which to vanish into the healing anonymity of a crowd. It is the place in which to succeed. Or, for that matter, to fail.

It is, quite simply, a city with everything. Yes, I will say it categorically: there is *nothing* one cannot find in New York.

Many people will protest, however, that New York does lack one very important quality—tranquility. They will call this city the very definition of the "madding crowd" from which man must retreat from time to time for sanity's sake. Usually these people live upstate. Or out of state. (This amounts to the same thing for most New Yorkers.)

And yet anyone who has gazed upon the lighted skyline of Manhattan from, say, the heights of Weehawken, or a window high in the World Trade Center, has known, if only for an instant, the serenity of true awe. This is a sight the likes of which does not exist elsewhere on earth. To see those same towers rising pale in the dawn above the green mists of Central Park is to feel the stillness that always lies at the core of man's greatest works. Even in this mightiest of cities there is breathless beauty and peace for whomever takes the moment to look for them.

1. Getting To and From Manhattan

Visitors pour in and out of Manhattan on various forms of transportation. Here is some information on how it is done.

BY CAR

Though it is not recommended that you bring a car into Manhattan (parking is a nightmare and expensive), if you must, you should know that Manhattan is an island connected to the surrounding land masses by a number of bridges and tunnels. From the north, to get to the East Side, take the **Governor Thomas E. Dewey Thruway** (also known as the New York Thruway or I-87) or I-95 and watch for signs for the **Triboro Bridge** which will put you (if you stay to your left off the bridge) onto the southbound lanes of the **Franklin D. Roosevelt Drive** (also known as the East Side Highway). Or to get to the West Side from the north, take the **Saw Mill River Parkway** to the **Henry Hudson Parkway** over the **Henry Hudson Bridge.** From New Jersey, I-95 has signs directing you to both the **Holland** and **Lincoln Tunnels** (to lower Manhattan). From further north in New Jersey, I-80, I-95 and Route 4 also lead to the **George Washington Bridge,** which will take you to the southbound Henry Hudson Parkway (a.k.a. West Side Highway) down the West Side.

BY BUS OR TRAIN

Trains arrive at either **Pennsylvania Station** (at 34th Street and Seventh Avenue) or at **Grand Central Terminal** (at 42nd Street and Park Avenue). Buses arrive at the **Port Authority Bus Terminal** (at 41st Street and Eighth Avenue).

BY PLANE

There are three airports serving New York City—**John F. Kennedy International Airport** and **LaGuardia Airport,** both in Queens, and **Newark International Airport** in New Jersey. There are several forms of transportation serving them.

Buses

Carey Airport Express (tel. 718/632-0500) runs frequent bus service to and from Kennedy and LaGuardia airports with five separate Manhattan stops: at 125 Park Ave., between 41st and 42nd Streets; at the "Airport Transportation Center" in the Port Authority Bus Terminal on West 42nd Street between Eighth and Ninth Avenues; at the New York Hilton Hotel on Sixth Avenue between 53rd and 54th Streets; at the Sheraton City Squire Hotel on Seventh Avenue between 51st and

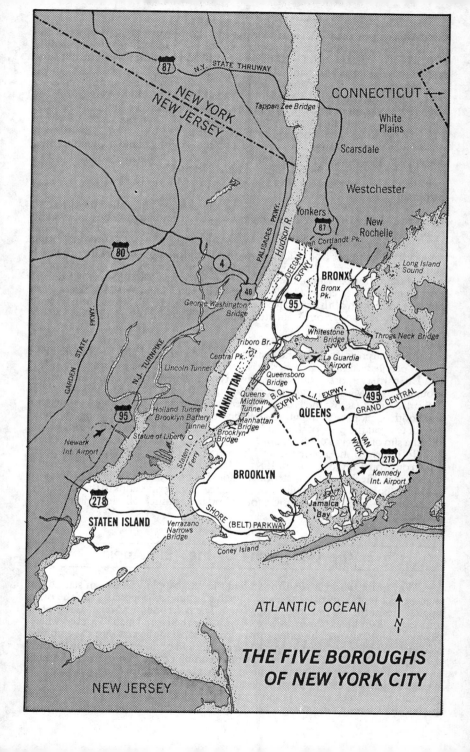

THE FIVE BOROUGHS
OF NEW YORK CITY

52nd Streets; and at the Marriott Marquis Hotel on Broadway between 45th and 46th Streets. Departures are every half hour, or less. One-way fare to Kennedy is $10; to LaGuardia, it's $8. Please be sure to call and confirm these schedules and fares as they are subject to change.

Newark International Airport service is by New Jersey Transit and Olympia Airport Express bus companies. **New Jersey Transit** (tel. 201/460-8444 or 212/564-8484) has buses running every 15 minutes to and from the Port Authority Bus Terminal from 6 a.m. to midnight. The one-way fare is $7. **Olympia Airport Express** (tel. 212/964-6233) has buses running to and from both the World Trade Center downtown every 15 minutes from 5:15 a.m. to 11:15 p.m. and a Grand Central Terminal stop at 41st Street and Park Avenue every 15 minutes from 5 a.m. to 11 p.m. The one-way fare, which you pay to the driver, is $7.

Subways

The New York City Transit Authority operates something called the **"Train to the Plane"** (tel. 718/858-7272), which is actually a combination bus-subway trip to and from John F. Kennedy International Airport that costs a total of $6.50. From JFK, there is a bus stop outside of each terminal for the free JFK Shuttle Bus. Running every 20 minutes from 5 a.m. to midnight, the bus goes to the Howard Beach subway station. There a clerk will collect the fare and direct you to the appropriate subway train. In Manhattan, the train stops at Broadway-Nassau Street, Chambers Street, and on the Avenue of the Americas (Sixth Avenue) at West 4th Street, 34th Street, 42nd Street, 50th Street (Rockefeller Center), and 57th Street (the last stop). To go out to Kennedy from Manhattan, take the train from any of these stops.

Taxis

At the airports, look for the taxi stands at each terminal. There will often be a line of people feeding in an orderly fashion into each taxi as it pulls up. From JFK and LaGuardia airports, you pay whatever is on the meter (plus tip), which will be around $30 to Midtown from JFK and about $20 from LaGuardia. If you land at Newark Airport (across the Hudson River in New Jersey), you will notice there's a taxi booth outside the terminal. You tell the clerk inside what your destination is and he will tell you the price of the trip (about $30 to Midtown) and will hand the taxi driver a slip of paper in confirmation.

To return to the airports from Manhattan, just flag a cab and tell the driver which one you want to go to. For JFK and LaGuardia, pay the amount on the meter. For Newark, the fare on the meter can be doubled once you cross the state line.

If traffic is slow the fare will be higher, since waiting time adds to the meter rate. Remember that you are responsible for all bridge or tunnel tolls, in addition to the meter charges.

---

2. The Geography of the "Big Apple"

Why in the world is New York called the "Big Apple"? The term started out among jazz musicians 60 years ago. The "big" apple, as opposed to all the other apples, meant the big-time gig in New York. The perception was then, as it is now, that if you had "made" it in New York, you had therefore "made" it everywhere. Slang terminology like this often moves from people in the arts into the common parlance. Which is just what happened here. It should be noted that during the early 1970s, when New York was suffering from a combined fiscal crisis and bad overall image, a number of people in business, the arts, and government got together to change America's perception of the place. The result was a media blitz consisting of promotional themes, television spots, musical jingles, and the like. All this municipal boosterism resulted, among other things, in a campaign to promote the city un-

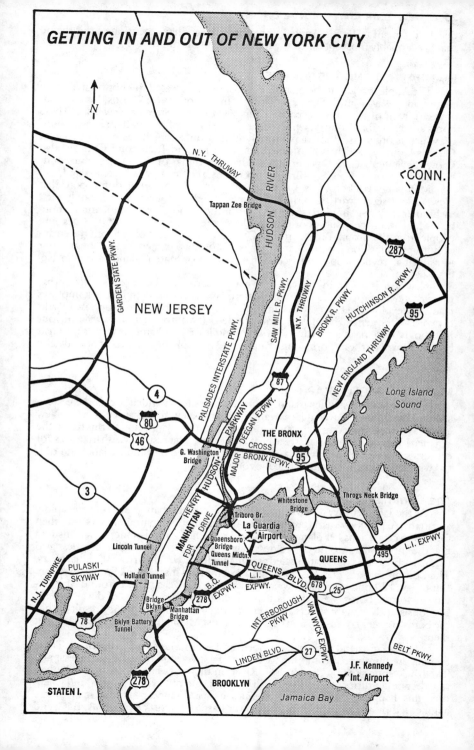

GETTING IN AND OUT OF NEW YORK CITY

N

CONN.

N.Y. THRUWAY

Tappan Zee Bridge

HUDSON RIVER

GARDEN STATE PKWY.

NEW JERSEY

287

PALISADES INTERSTATE PKWY.

SAW MILL R. PKWY.

N.Y. THRUWAY

BRONX R. PKWY.

HUTCHINSON R. PKWY.

NEW ENGLAND THRUWAY

95

Long Island Sound

4

87

80

46

MAJOR DEEGAN EXPWY.

PARKWAY

THE BRONX

CROSS BRONX EXPWY.

95

3

G. Washington Bridge

HENRY HUDSON

Throgs Neck Bridge

Whitestone Bridge

Triboro Br.

La Guardia Airport

MANHATTAN

FDR DRIVE

Lincoln Tunnel

Queensboro Bridge

Queens Midtn. Tunnel

QUEENS

QUEENS BLVD.

495

L.I. EXPWY.

N.J. TURNPIKE

PULASKI SKYWAY

Holland Tunnel

L.I. EXPWY.

678

25

78

Bridge Bklyn

B.Q. EXPWY.

278

Manhattan Bridge

INTERBOROUGH PKWY

VAN WYCK EXPWY.

BELT PKWY.

Bklyn Battery Tunnel

LINDEN BLVD.

27

J.F. Kennedy Int. Airport

STATEN I.

278

BROOKLYN

Jamaica Bay

der the theme of "The Big Apple." It has been the endless repetition of this theme that has probably most solidified the term in the public mind.

MANHATTAN AND THE "BOROS"

The Apple is big, but the first-time visitor will be pleased to know that it's easy to find one's way around. The city consists of five boroughs (or "boros," as it's often written), each of which is a separate county within the State of New York. These boros are: New York County, which occupies the island of Manhattan; Kings County, which is otherwise known as Brooklyn; the Bronx, which has no other name; Queens County, which is also called just Queens; and Richmond County, also known as Staten Island. Of course, nobody really thinks of them as separate counties. They are just the boros—Brooklyn, Queens, the Bronx, and Staten Island.

Manhattan is a boro, too. But it's so preeminently the prima donna boro that New Yorkers set it apart from the other four. People in Queens and Brooklyn tell each other they're going into the "city" when they head over to Manhattan. Snobbish Manhattan rock club doormen condemn the untrendy as "BBQs" (meaning people from the Bronx, Brooklyn, and Queens) if they don't blend with the cream of Euro-punk fashion within. Manhattan is probably as yearned for and sought after —as well as reviled and dismissed—in Brooklyn or Staten Island as it is in Nebraska.

New York is so easy for the visitor to navigate primarily because it's unlikely that the average visitor will ever leave Manhattan. Guidebook after guidebook implores readers to explore the boros, which in truth have many attractions. I suppose I'll add my voice to the general howl. I've even included a few auto tours, and a walking tour in Brooklyn, to make it easy for you. If you do leave Manhattan, except for transit back and forth to the airport, congratulations! You took the advice that nobody else did!

MANHATTAN GEOGRAPHY

Manhattan is a slender island, some 13 miles long, which forms the eastern shore of the Hudson River at its entrance to Upper New York Bay. The City of New York was once confined to the southernmost tip of this island. And to this day in the Financial District a medieval street plan still exists. The rest of Manhattan was for centuries an exceedingly pleasant countryside, traversed by winding lanes and dotted with delectable villages and bucolic country seats.

The Commissioners' Plan

As the 19th century got under way the problem of urban sprawl became rapidly apparent. A panel of distinguished and unimaginative commissioners was then formed to create a master plan. Adopted in 1811, the Commissioners' Plan ensured that the entire island would be progressively steam-rollered beneath a relentless grid of arrow-straight avenues intersected at right angles by equally arrow-straight streets. The Commissioners' Plan has nothing to recommend it save ease of transportation. But today, 170-odd years later, we must admit that it's easy to get around Manhattan. As for the boros, well, they suffered their own depredations of development, but consistently straight streets and avenues weren't among them. As a result of this, the boros are very confusing to navigate and most Manhattanites are utterly lost out there.

Manhattan Island runs roughly north and south, and so do its **avenues**. These avenues are numbered from One to Twelve, First Avenue lying far to the east and Twelfth Avenue skirting the Hudson River on the west. The shoreline of Manhattan, despite centuries of landfilling, still bulges in and out in many places, and whenever this happens those straight avenues either disappear off the map or are augmented by additions. Hence, the Lower East Side sports Avenues A, B, C, and

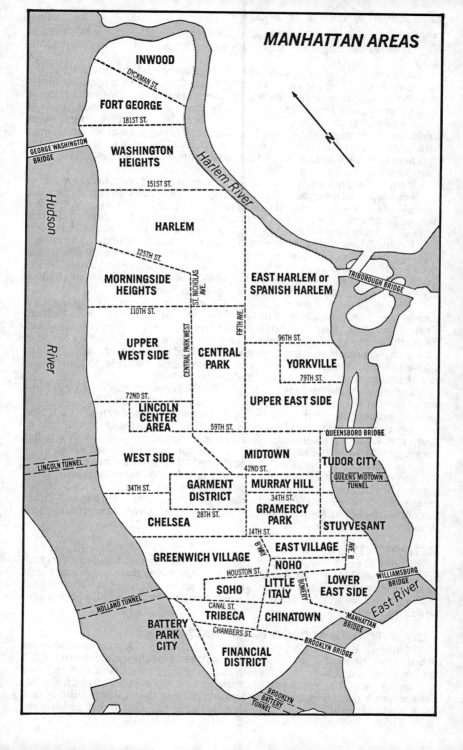

D, all of which lie east of First Avenue, while north of 155th Street in Washington Heights there is nothing at all east of Tenth Avenue (which up there is called Amsterdam).

Running in an irregular diagonal from Manhattan's northernmost tip all the way down to the Battery (a park located at the southern tip of the island) is the famous **Broadway**. Every time Broadway intersects one of the north-south avenues, a square is created. Of course, they aren't really square at all, but the intersection of broad roadways at acute angles creates open spaces that cry out for some kind of name. So at the point where Broadway crosses Seventh Avenue we have Times Square; where it crosses Sixth Avenue we have Herald Square; Madison Square is at the intersection of Broadway and Fifth; Union Square marks Broadway's transit of Fourth Avenue (now grandly called Park Avenue South); etc., etc.

Many of the numbered avenues acquired names over the years, usually as part of an effort to upgrade the image of surrounding real estate. Patrician Park Avenue, for example, is really a continuation of schlumpy old Fourth Avenue (sorry, it's Park Avenue South these days, save the short stretch from 8th to 14th Streets). Its predominant feature used to be an open railway cut that carried the tracks of the New York Central Railroad. The tracks were covered in the early part of this century, and *voilà!*—sooty old Fourth Avenue above Grand Central became swanky new Park Avenue. Other real estate booms led to other rechristenings. For example, Ninth, Tenth, and Eleventh Avenues on the Upper West Side reemerged in the 1880s as Columbus, Amsterdam, and West End Avenues, respectively.

The case of Sixth Avenue is unique. Up in Harlem, it was renamed Lenox a century ago. But down in the Midtown district the name Sixth Avenue remained. Then in the 1930s Mayor Fiorello LaGuardia, in a fit of temporary madness, saddled it with the pretentious designation of "Avenue of the Americas." No New Yorker in 50 years has called it that, except to explain to a baffled tourist where Sixth Avenue is. I am glad to note that the city has at last remounted street signs that say "Sixth Avenue" beneath those that read "Avenue of the Americas."

In the heart of the Midtown and Upper East Side districts you're going to come across another pair of avenues, namely Madison and Lexington. These thoroughfares were squeezed into the Commissioners' Plan many years after the fact and their location confuses many people searching for East Side addresses. It will help to know that *Madison Avenue runs between Fifth and Park* (which would be Fourth but for the nomenclature of fashion), and *Lexington runs between Park and Third*.

The numerical progression of the **east-west streets** starts a little irregularly in the lower part of town. Here the commissioners had to accommodate already built-up areas like Greenwich Village and the Lower East Side. But above 14th Street the progression becomes steady and remarkably regular almost all the way to Spuyten Duyvil (pronounced *Spy*-ten *Die*-vull), the ancient creek that separates northern Manhattan from the mainland.

ATTENTION WALKERS

About 20 north-south blocks make up a mile. By contrast, 6 to 10 of the much longer east-west blocks equal the same distance. Remember that the east-west blocks in the vicinity of Madison and Lexington Avenues are shorter by half than in areas without the added avenues. The blocks adjacent to Broadway, as it sidles between the various avenues, are always shorter too.

HOW TO FIND AN ADDRESS IN MANHATTAN

Addresses on the side streets are designated as either *east* or *west* depending on whether they are located east or west of **Fifth Avenue**. House numbers start with 1 and run consecutively (unless combined building lots have eliminated them) until the end of the block. When you cross the intervening avenue, however, the first number you'll come to is 100, after which you'll stay in the hundreds until the next avenue, when numbers jump to 200. Then they jump to 300 at the beginning of the next block, then to 400 at the start of the block after that, until at last you'll reach one or the other of the rivers that bracket Manhattan's east and west sides.

East Side addresses are slightly complicated by the presence of Madison and Lexington Avenues. For example, one would expect 59 East 62nd Street to be on the first block off Fifth Avenue. According to the Commissioners' Plan, it is—which is to say that it's located between the original Fifth and Fourth Avenues. But since Madison Avenue now interposes itself between those roads, 59 E. 62nd will be found on the second block off Fifth. Similar complications throw people off when they're looking for addresses around Lex. Remember, however, that the basic scheme is simple and fairly consistent.

Street Addresses

BETWEEN 14TH AND 59TH STREETS Here is a chart to help you locate street addresses between 14th Street and 59th Street.

East Side	West Side
1 at Fifth Avenue	1 at Fifth Avenue
100 at Park Avenue	100 at Sixth Avenue
200 at Third Avenue	200 at Seventh Avenue
300 at Second Avenue	300 at Eighth Avenue
400 at First Avenue	400 at Ninth Avenue
	500 at Tenth Avenue
	600 at Eleventh Avenue

59TH TO 110TH STREETS Above 59th Street, and all the way to 110th Street, things are different on the *Upper West Side only.* This is the region of **Central Park,** whose magnificent rectangle of planned rusticity has eliminated what would have been the first three West Side blocks of 51 Manhattan streets. On the Upper West Side, therefore, numbers on the streets begin at Eighth Avenue, which in this once-again fashionable quarter is called Central Park West. Number 100 is on the corner of Ninth Avenue, which up here is called Columbus, and so forth. The following chart will help you locate street addresses between 59th and 110th Streets on the Upper West Side.

1 at Central Park West (Eighth Avenue)
100 at Columbus Avenue (Ninth Avenue)
200 at Amsterdam Avenue (Tenth Avenue)
300 at West End Avenue (Eleventh Avenue)

Avenue Addresses

Addresses on the various avenues would seem to follow no consistent order save that of numerical progression. But some genius somewhere concocted a method of locating the nearest intersecting street to virtually every avenue on the island. Here is that magical method. Don't laugh—it really works.

To Find the Nearest Cross Street to a Manhattan Avenue Address

1. Drop the last number of the address
2. Divide by 2

3. Follow the directions below:

Avenue A, B, C, or D	add 3
First Avenue	add 3
Second Avenue	add 3
Third Avenue	add 9 or 10
Lexington Avenue	add 22
Fourth Avenue (Park Ave. South)	add 8
Park Avenue	add 34 or 35
Madison Avenue	add 26
Fifth Avenue	
up to 200	add 13
up to 400	add 16
up to 600	add 18
up to 2000	add 24
Sixth Avenue	subtract 12 or 13
Seventh Avenue	
below 110th St.	add 12
above 110th St.	add 20
Eighth Avenue	add 9 or 10
Central Park West	divide house number by 10 and add 60
Ninth Avenue	add 13
Columbus Avenue	add 59 or 60
Tenth Avenue	add 14
Amsterdam Avenue	add 59 or 60
Eleventh Avenue	add 15
West End Avenue	add 59 or 60
Riverside Drive	divide house number by 10 and add 72

. . . and not to be forgotten:

Broadway	
up to 750	all below 8th St.
up to 850	subtract 29
up to 950	subtract 25
above 950	subtract 31

NEIGHBORHOODS

Whereas most great cities have one major downtown area, Manhattan has two. When viewed from afar they rise like the twin humps on a camel, two glittering mountains of glass and stone towering above the city that surrounds them.

Downtown

Downtown is another name for the **Financial District,** a region of big banks and stock exchanges located at the southern tip of Manhattan. The famous World Trade Center is located downtown. So are City Hall, Police Headquarters, and all the courthouses. Not only are Financial District skyscrapers immensely high, many are arranged along former winding cowpaths with quaint names like Maiden Lane, Beaver Street, Old Slip, and so forth. Some of the canyons formed by 70- and 80-story buildings ranged along 20-foot-wide streets are quite something to behold.

Midtown

This is Manhattan's other major skyscraper district, the heart of which is probably Fifth Avenue in the 50s. The Empire State Building, down at Fifth Avenue and

34th Street, is about as far south as you can get and still consider yourself in Midtown (even then it's a stretch). Midtown is the heart of big-time corporate New York. It consists primarily of office buildings, restaurants, department stores, lots of shops, good clubs, and plush hotels. The most impressive of the Midtown modern skyscraper avenues are Third, Park, to a certain extent Fifth, and Sixth. Of course you'll find huge glass buildings on other avenues. But these in particular are lined with them, sometimes uninterruptedly for 20-block stretches in the 40s and 50s.

Central Park

New York's most famous park forms the northern boundary of Midtown. It is also the divider between two of Manhattan's famous residential districts, the **Upper East Side** (usually just called the East Side) and the **Upper West Side** (usually just called the West Side).

The East Side

This is the swankiest part of New York, a fact about which there can be no discussion. It is bracketed by Central Park and the East River, between the 60s and 96th Street. The part of it bounded by Fifth and Lexington Avenues, and extending between the low 60s and 86th Street, contains an abundance of real live palaces, dripping with gilt and marble, many of which are still private houses. And inside some of those dignified if anonymous-looking old apartment buildings along Fifth and Park are 15-, 20-, 30-, sometimes even 40-room apartments. Of course, not everybody on the East Side lives in such splendor. But a lot of people do. Their presence here has created a shopping district along Madison in the 60s and 70s that is unequaled in sumptuousness anywhere in the country, with the *possible* exception of Rodeo Drive in Beverly Hills.

The West Side

The West Side is sandwiched between the Hudson River and Central Park, and extends roughly from the low 60s to the upper 90s. It was developed in the closing years of the last century as a stronghold of the haute bourgeoisie. Block after block after block of big, ornate, and gloomy brownstones were built, usually on speculation, for the professional class of the day. After the Second World War the West Side really hit the skids. In the last ten years, however, it has become newly fashionable with a young and prosperous crowd that has swept its rooming houses, well, somewhere else, anyway. Today it's often called, not too originally, the Yupper West Side. Whatever one's political views on gentrification, the fact remains that the old brownstones are getting to look pretty swell again. And Columbus Avenue is actually sprouting branches of some of the best Madison Avenue shops.

Harlem

The whole world seems fascinated by Harlem, located on a plain to the north of Central Park. Having been at various times a select suburb, a neighborhood of city "swells," the capital of Black America, and a nearly desperate slum, Harlem seems again on the threshold of a change. The white-hot Manhattan real estate market of recent years has forced redevelopment attention even on long-neglected Harlem. When houses on Striver's Row (that's 138th Street between Seventh and Eighth Avenues) appear for sale in the *New York Times* for $450,000, as one recently did, then you know the times they are a-changin'. Harlem is very feisty, very alive, filled with astonishing contrasts as well as historic and architectural treasures. Parts of it are poor to the point of being burnt out, but 125th Street, which is the main drag, is safe enough during the day, be you black or white Generally the other big avenues are too. It's not recommended that out-of-towners venture into this neighborhood, especially at night, except with a guided tour.

Other Manhattan Areas:

There are far too many Manhattan neighborhoods to list every one. But a few other notable ones about which you'll want to know include:

SOHO The name is an acronym for *South of Ho*uston Street (pronounce that *House*-ton). It's located between Houston and Canal Streets in the middle of the island, a little below where the numbered streets begin. SoHo is full of historic 19th-century cast-iron buildings. Recently a factory and warehouse district, it now brims with ultrachic lofts, trendy restaurants, and galleries, galleries, galleries.

TRIBECA A somewhat tortured acronym, this time standing for *Tri*angle *Be*low *Ca*-nal, TriBeCa is located on the west side of the island just north of the Financial District. It has more trendy lofts, more distinguished 19th-century commercial buildings, and more galleries and boutiques. It exists because SoHo got too expensive.

THE GARMENT DISTRICT Located in the West 30s, mostly between Sixth and Seventh Avenues, it's a major manufacturing area for women's clothing and incredible traffic jams. Will you ever need to know where the Garment District is? Probably not, but it's so much a part of Manhattan I couldn't leave it out.

THE DIAMOND DISTRICT West 47th Street between Fifth and Sixth Avenues has got nothing but diamond merchants. Well, that's not quite true. But I'll bet you've never seen so many jewelry stores on one block in your life.

BROADWAY/TIMES SQUARE This is the unacknowledged porno district, a commodity that flourishes on West 42nd Street between Sixth and Eighth, and then up Eighth into the mid-40s. It won't be this way for long if the mayor and the city government have their way. The whole Times Square area is slated for major redevelopment. Of course, city administrations have been trying to clean up 42nd Street for longer than I, for one, have been alive. However, this time they've built a multimillion-dollar hotel, the Marriott Marquis, right in the middle of Times Square itself. So maybe they'll really do it this time.

THE THEATER DISTRICT Embarrassingly, it's located right in the middle of the porno district, adjacent to Broadway and Times Square. Most of the legitimate theaters are in the West 40s, generally between Broadway and Eighth. Many a midblock is lined with glittering theaters (where tickets cost $50 a shot), the streets crammed at curtain time with long black limousines, the sidewalks clogged with excited and well-dressed theater-goers from all over the world. And at the end of the same block is a flophouse and a gaggle of prostitutes. While it is perfectly safe, especially at theater time, it is best to be alert, to notice your immediate surroundings, and wear your purse or camera strap diagonally across your body.

THE BOROS

The boros are every bit as complex as Manhattan without, however, being as intense. Staten Island and much of Queens and Brooklyn are typically suburban with postwar houses on small neat lots. There are swanky parts of the boros, and horrible slums out there too. But for the visitor, there's too much on Manhattan to spend much time elsewhere.

---

3. Getting Around Town

WALKING

This is the most rewarding means of transit. Remember that a mile equals about 20 short north-south blocks and 6 to 10 long east-west blocks. The city streets teem with every human and architectural type. Walking is a feast for the senses, and really a lot of fun.

BUSES

They cost $1 a ride and require exact change or a token. They're kind of fun too, except when overcrowded during rush hour. Almost every major avenue has a bus route going whichever direction that avenue goes. The stops are clearly marked at curbside, but not every bus stops at every bus stop. Sometimes there are little route maps mounted on steel posts anchored in the sidewalk. If you can't understand the maps, you can always ask the driver if his bus is going where you want to go.

Many buses go crosstown as well, which is to say east and west on the side streets instead of north and south on the avenues.

Streets with crosstown buses include 8th (M13—eastbound only), 9th (M13—westbound only), 14th, 23rd, 34th, 42nd, 49th (westbound only), 50th (eastbound only), 57th, 59th (called Central Park South between Fifth and Eighth Avenues), 66th (westbound only), 67th (eastbound only), 72nd (this route detours down to 57th Street between Fifth and Eighth Avenues), 79th, 86th, 96th, 116th, 125th, 145th, and 155th.

Transfers from one route to another are free, but *you must ask for the transfer when you get on the bus.*

Bus maps do exist but are very hard to come by. The best idea is to request one in advance. Write to: Customer Service, New York City Transit Authority, 370 Jay St., Brooklyn, NY 11201. They're free, as long as you include a self-addressed stamped envelope. Be sure to tell them that it's the bus map you want. If you need immediate help, call 718/330-1234.

SUBWAYS

New York's underground trains provide the fastest transportation over long distances. If you're going, say, from Midtown to the World Trade Center, it'll take 15 minutes by subway as opposed to maybe an hour (or maybe two hours if traffic is bad) by bus. Many New Yorkers won't set foot in a subway because they're both noisy and dirty. Visitors from other subway cities like London, Paris, Moscow, Washington, D.C., and San Francisco will wonder how things ever came to such a pass. So, indeed, do we.

Yet for all its grubbiness, the New York City subway system is also rather magnificent. It's certainly larger than any other. Just how large is illustrated by the fact that it's possible to take one single subway train for 32.39 miles (the "C" Eighth Avenue Local from Bedford Park in the Bronx all the way through Manhattan to Rockaway Park in Queens). If you change trains just once, the longest run is an amazing 38.31 miles (from White Plains Road in the Bronx out to Far Rockaway in Queens, changing at Fulton Street in downtown Manhattan).

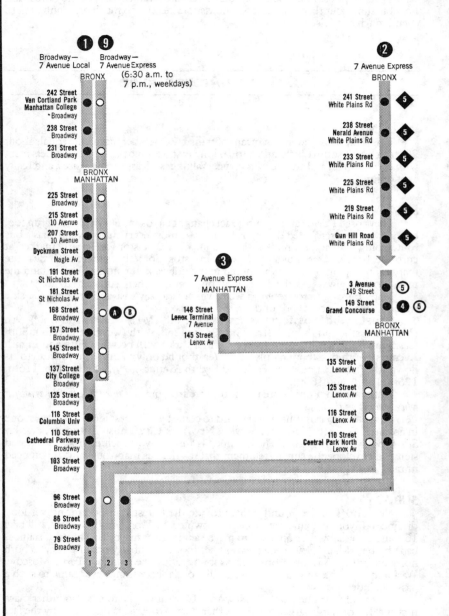

IRT BROADWAY—7TH AVENUE SUBWAY

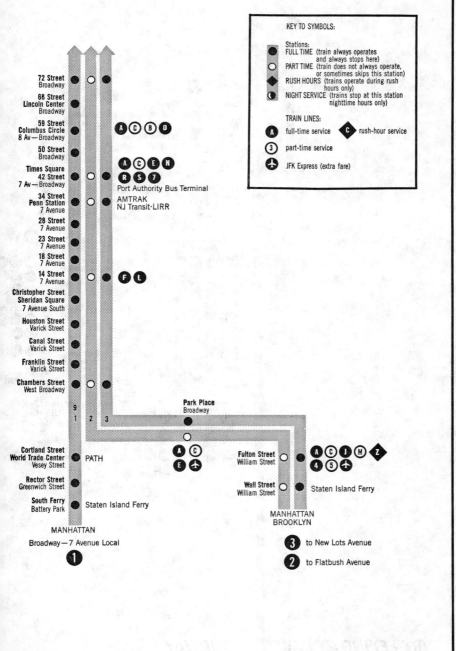

KEY TO SYMBOLS:

Stations:
FULL TIME (train always operates and always stops here)
PART TIME (train does not always operate, or sometimes skips this station)
RUSH HOURS (trains operate during rush hours only)
NIGHT SERVICE (trains stop at this station nighttime hours only)

TRAIN LINES:
Ⓐ full-time service   Ⓒ rush-hour service
③ part-time service
✈ JFK Express (extra fare)

72 Street
Broadway

68 Street
Lincoln Center
Broadway

59 Street
Columbus Circle
8 Av — Broadway   Ⓐ Ⓒ Ⓑ Ⓓ

50 Street
Broadway

Times Square   Ⓐ Ⓒ Ⓔ Ⓝ
42 Street   Ⓡ Ⓢ ⑦
7 Av — Broadway
                    Port Authority Bus Terminal

34 Street   AMTRAK
Penn Station   NJ Transit·LIRR
7 Avenue

28 Street
7 Avenue

23 Street
7 Avenue

18 Street
7 Avenue

14 Street   Ⓕ Ⓛ
7 Avenue

Christopher Street
Sheridan Square
7 Avenue South

Houston Street
Varick Street

Canal Street
Varick Street

Franklin Street
Varick Street

Chambers Street
West Broadway

                    9
                    1   2   3

                    Park Place
                    Broadway

Cortland Street   PATH   Ⓐ Ⓒ   Fulton Street   Ⓐ Ⓒ Ⓙ Ⓜ Ⓩ
World Trade Center   Ⓔ ✈   William Street   ④ ⑤ ✈
Vesey Street

Rector Street   Wall Street
Greenwich Street   William Street   Staten Island Ferry

South Ferry   Staten Island Ferry
Battery Park   MANHATTAN
                                             BROOKLYN
MANHATTAN

Broadway—7 Avenue Local
❶

③ to New Lots Avenue

② to Flatbush Avenue

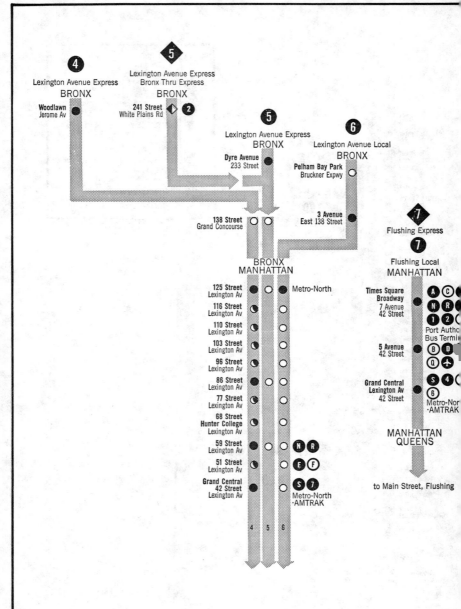

IRT LEXINGTON AVENUE SUBWAY

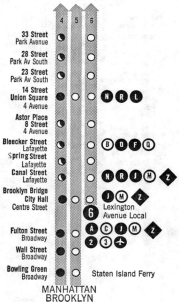

	4	5	6	
33 Street Park Avenue	◗	○	○	
28 Street Park Av South	◗	○	○	
23 Street Park Av South	◗	○	○	
14 Street Union Square 4 Avenue	●	○	○	**N R L**
Astor Place 8 Street 4 Avenue	◗	○	○	
Bleecker Street Lafayette	◗	○	○	**B D F Q**
Spring Street Lafayette	◗	○	○	
Canal Street Lafayette	◗	○	○	**N R J M Z**
Brooklyn Bridge City Hall Centre Street	◗	●	○	**J M Z**
			6	Lexington Avenue Local
Fulton Street Broadway	●	○		**A C J M Z** **2 3 ✈**
Wall Street Broadway	●	○		
Bowling Green Broadway	●	○		Staten Island Ferry

MANHATTAN
BROOKLYN

4 to New Lots Avenue

5 to Flatbush Avenue

KEY TO SYMBOLS:

Stations:
FULL TIME (train always operates and always stops here)
PART TIME (train does not always operate, or sometimes skips this station)
RUSH HOURS (trains operate during rush hours only)
NIGHT SERVICE (trains stop at this station nighttime hours only)

TRAIN LINES:
A full-time service   ◆ rush-hour service

3 part-time service

✈ JFK Express (extra fare)

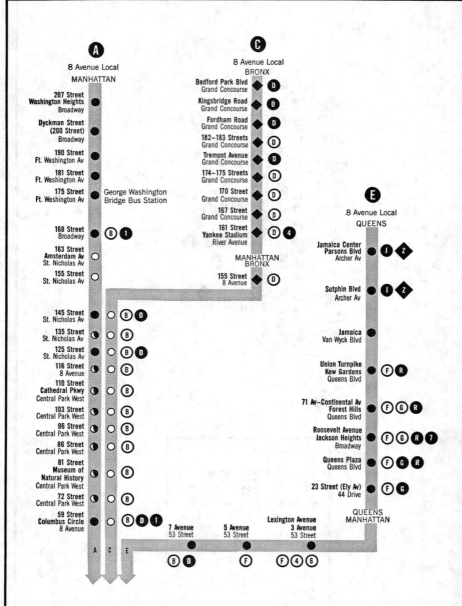

INDEPENDENT (IND) SUBWAY (8TH AVENUE)

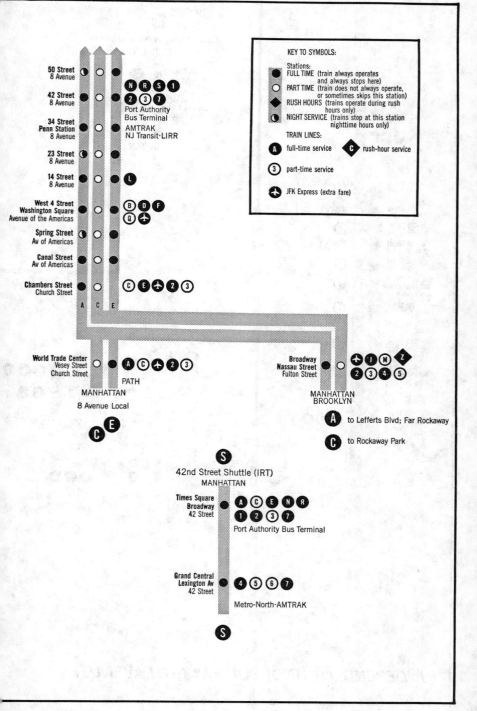

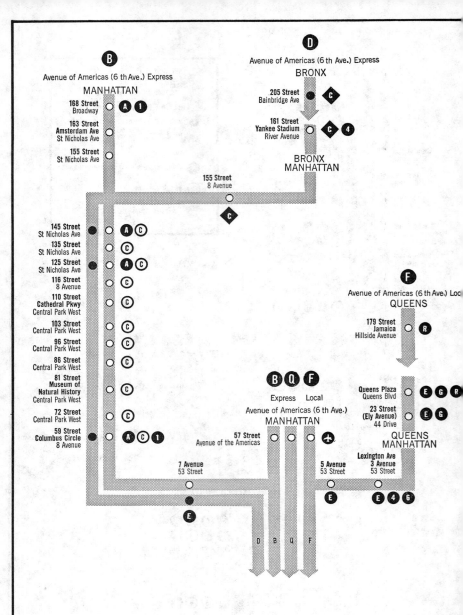

INDEPENDENT (IND) SUBWAY (6TH AVENUE)

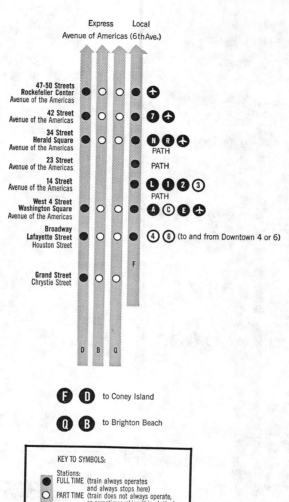

Express   Local
Avenue of Americas (6th Ave.)

47-50 Streets
Rockefeller Center
Avenue of the Americas

42 Street
Avenue of the Americas

34 Street
Herald Square
Avenue of the Americas

PATH

23 Street
Avenue of the Americas

PATH

14 Street
Avenue of the Americas

PATH

West 4 Street
Washington Square
Avenue of the Americas

Broadway
Lafayette Street
Houston Street

(to and from Downtown 4 or 6)

Grand Street
Chrystie Street

D   B   Q

to Coney Island

to Brighton Beach

KEY TO SYMBOLS:

Stations:
● FULL TIME (train always operates and always stops here)
○ PART TIME (train does not always operate, or sometimes skips this station)
◆ RUSH HOURS (trains operate during rush hours only)
◑ NIGHT SERVICE (trains stop at this station nighttime hours only)

TRAIN LINES:
Ⓐ full-time service   ◆C rush-hour service

③ part-time service

✈ JFK Express (extra fare)

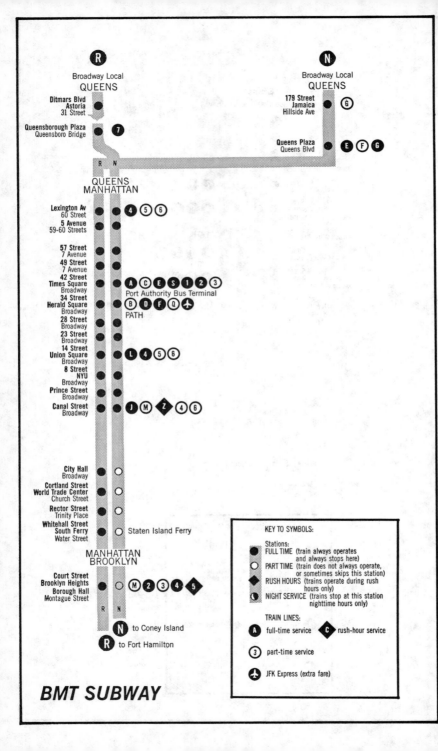

BMT SUBWAY

Over a *billion* subway tokens are sold each year, at the glass-enclosed booths located at every stop. On an average day, almost $3½ million are slipped under the cashiers' windows and an equal number of tokens are slipped back out. These tokens are then deposited into turnstiles for access to the platforms where trains stop.

Between 7 and 9 a.m., and again between 4 and 6 p.m., the subways are packed. The rest of the day it's easy to get a seat. Trains run every couple of minutes during peak hours. In the middle of the night, however, you might wait up to half an hour. Unlike those in other cities, New York's subways run 24 hours a day.

Finding your way around the subways is not too difficult—*if* you have a map. Therein, however, lies the rub. Supposedly, **subway maps** are available at every change booth. As a practical matter the booths are always out of stock. There are *four relatively dependable sources of subway maps*. The first is the Transit Authority, to which you can write in care of Customer Service, New York City Transit Authority, 370 Jay St., Brooklyn, NY 11201. Enclose a self-addressed stamped envelope, and be sure to tell them you want a subway map. They'll send you one free of charge. Alternatively, you can go to the Convention and Visitors Bureau on the ground floor of 2 Columbus Circle (that's at Eighth Avenue and 59th Street, at the southwest corner of Central Park). They'll give you one for free too. Or go to the Information Booth on the main concourse of Grand Central Terminal (Park Avenue and 42nd Street), or to the Information Booth at Pennsylvania Station over on Seventh Avenue and 33rd Street. There are also subway maps located in the subway cars themselves.

Subway maps superimpose various **numbered and lettered train routes** over a map of the city. They take a bit of studying, but anyone with reasonable intelligence can determine which train goes closest to his or her destination. Anyway, it's not a good idea to get on a train unless you know in advance where it's going.

You'll often hear New Yorkers refer to the "Lexington Avenue" or the "Broadway IRT" or the "Eighth Avenue IND" and so on and so forth. When you look at a subway map, however, these terms are nowhere to be seen. What you're hearing are the old names of various subway lines that operated independently of one another in the days when most were privately owned. Nowadays the city operates the entire system. And it differentiates only between individual train routes and no longer between former lines.

A final note: The subways get a little lonely (read that "scary") at night. Go with friends. Avoid empty cars.

TAXIS

There are a couple of kinds. The ones you hail on the streets are all painted yellow, bear a city-issued medallion riveted to the hood, and a little lighted superstructure attached to the roof over the windshield. If that thingummy on the roof is lighted, the cab is free and looking for a fare. If it's not lighted, then someone is inside the cab already or the driver is on radio call. If the off-duty lights (also located up there on the roof) are lighted, then that cab is not going to stop for you even if you get down on your knees.

Cabs cost $1.15 for the first eighth of a mile, and 15¢ additional for each eighth of a mile thereafter. "Waiting time" racks up another 15¢ for every minute the thing stands still. This sounds a bit more horrible than it really is. Most cab rides cost less than $6, including the tip, unless you're really going a distance.

Sharing a cab is perfectly legal and there is nothing that says you have to pay anything extra if one of you gets off at one address and another stays on to a second address, or even to a third. Bridge and tunnel tolls, however, are your responsibility. Hand the money to the driver when he needs it.

Taxis, like subways and buses, are crowded during rush hours. In Midtown, as a matter of fact, it's almost impossible to get one. Don't get locked into a schedule that requires catching a cab on Fifth Avenue and 48th Street at quarter to five. If you do, you'll be late.

Many visitors are uncertain how, exactly, to get the cabs to stop. Good cab-flagging form requires, above all, confidence. Don't look timid; look determined. Remember to flag only cabs with lighted roof lights! Keep the chin down, the feet firmly planted on the ground, and the right arm raised in a commanding manner. One might even mutter a little "sieg heil" under one's breath. Keep the raised arm almost rigid and the eyes steely and alert for the advance of a likely cab. Be prepared to sprint if you see one. The competition will give no quarter, nor expect it in return. And remember to keep your dignity. Points are earned for a mask-like face even when some creep darts across moving traffic to grab the cab that's veered all the way across an avenue just for you.

There are also nonyellow "gypsy cabs" on the prowl in New York. Gypsies are actually car services that aren't licensed to pick up people who don't call and make a reservation first. As a practical matter, they do a little illicit cruising anyway. "Illicit" is decidedly the buzzword on the gypsies. They not only look slightly disreputable but they have a pesky reputation for taking the unsuspecting on wild goose chases. Avoid them.

"Car services" are not all like the seediest of the gypsies. Many sport late-model Cadillacs or other perfectly clean and nice cars. They provide transportation to and from vast areas of town that yellow cabs don't frequent. If during your stay in New York you find yourself in some hinterland late at night, ask your hosts to recommend a car service, or look one up in the Yellow Pages under "Car Services." Nail down the rate before you make the reservation.

PRIVATE CARS

It's not so hard to drive in New York City. Just don't expect much politeness on the road. The big problem is parking, details of which are discussed in "Life in the Metropolis," the first section of this chapter.

---

4. ABCs

Herewith, a useful compendium of information, compiled in alphabetical order, to help you deal with New York.

AREA CODES

New York City has been telephonically Balkanized. Manhattan and the Bronx now have the area code that used to be for the whole city, **212**, all to themselves. Brooklyn, Queens, and Staten Island, although a part of the same municipality, now have a separate area code, **718**. That means if you're in Manhattan and want to dial Brooklyn, you must use the long-distance prefix 1, followed by the area code 718, and then the number.

Suburban area codes are: Westchester and Rockland, **914**; Long Island, **516**; Connecticut, **203**; and New Jersey, **201**.

BABYSITTERS

Oftentimes your hotel will be able to set you up. But if they can't, try the **Gilbert Child Care Agency,** 119 West 57th St. (tel. 212/757-7900). This reputable and well-established firm charges $6.25 an hour for kids over 9 months, plus $1.00 per additional sibling. Infants cost more. There's a four-hour minimum, plus sitters' transportation charges of $4 before 8 p.m. and $8 after 8 p.m.

BUS AND SUBWAY INFORMATION

As of this writing, they both cost $1 per ride, with free transfers at intersecting lines. Subway token booths make change, but bus drivers don't. To board a bus you'll need either the exact fare or a subway token. Bus and subway maps are hard to come by. The most dependable sources are the respective information booths at Grand Central Terminal, 42nd Street at Park Avenue, and Pennsylvania Station, Seventh Avenue at 32nd Street, or at the office of the New York Convention and Visitors Bureau, 2 Columbus Circle (which is the same as Eighth Avenue and 59th Street). For free directions on how to get from Point A to Point B using public transit, call the Transit Authority at 718/330-1234.

CLIMATE

In the depths of January New York City's average temperature is 32° Fahrenheit; in tropical July the average high is 86°. As a practical matter, these extremes vary 10° in both directions. Visitors during the winter months had better dress warmly. Bring boots too—slushy winter streets get pretty sloppy. Summer in the city is often horribly hot and humid. Add to this the extra hazard of deep-freeze air conditioning. So bring a light jacket or wrap. Spring and fall, however, are crisp and perfect during the day, and only mildly cool in the evening.

CLOTHING

In a city where rubber dresses and purple Mohawks are, if not the order of the day, at least nothing unusual, it's ironic that dressing still tends to be on the conservative side. Perhaps that's because Manhattan is all about business, and businesspeople wear suits and ties.

During the day you can sightsee in jeans and casual shirts. Tank tops, short-shorts, and flip-flops, however, are inappropriate in Manhattan, except in Central Park. When 6 p.m. rolls around, things get more formal. You'll feel painfully out of place wearing jeans in the lobby of a first-class hotel after six. Or in a midtown bar, assuming they let you in. Many very nice neighborhood restaurants are very casual about dress. But the better places are going to require, if not a tie, at least some obvious effort at dressing up. First-class restaurants and nightspots are rigid: ties and dresses are a must.

If you visit New York in the winter, bring warm clothes, especially if you'll be continuing on upstate. If you're coming in the summer, be prepared to sweat. Spring and autumn are generally pleasant during the daylight hours, but chilly at night. So take along a sweater and/or a light jacket.

CURRENCY EXCHANGE

Citibank will exchange foreign currency in Manhattan at either the Fifth Avenue and 51st Street or the Lexington Avenue and 54th Street branches. Most other banks, however, will *not* change your money into dollars. Some hotels will, but only for registered guests. The best idea is to convert money at the airport. If you need more later on, try one of the following recommended exchange bureaus in Manhattan: **Deak-Perrera,** in Rockefeller Center at 630 Fifth Ave. (tel. 212/757-6915), and also at 41 E. 42nd St., between Madison and Vanderbilt Avenues (tel. 212/883-0400); **New York Foreign Exchange, Inc.,** 26 Broadway, near Beaver Street (tel. 212/248-4700); and **Piano Remittance,** 645 Fifth Ave., at 51st Street (tel. 212/888-5891).

DOCTOR

Doctors on Call (tel. 718/745-5900), operated by the New York Medical Society, provides recommendations in a pinch (don't expect house calls). Alternatively, almost every big hospital in town maintains a 24-hour emergency room. If you can manage to walk inside, they'll take care of whatever it is.

DRINKING

The legal age for drinking in New York State is 21, so have proof of your age handy if you look younger. Bars in New York are permitted to stay open till 4 a.m., but this is not to say that all of them do. If you're on a roll and they start to close the place down at 2 a.m., know that someplace else is bound to be open. Actually, a whole category of unlicensed and at times unsavory (if exciting) establishments don't even start until 4 a.m. These are the notorious "After Hours Clubs," whose special delights lie beyond the scope of this work.

DRUGSTORES

Two good ones are the **Windsor Pharmacy,** open every day from 8 a.m. to midnight, on Sixth Avenue between 57th and 58th Streets (tel. 212/247-1538), and **Kaufman's,** open 24 hours, at Lexington Avenue and 50th Street (tel. 212/ 755-2266).

EMERGENCY

To call the **police,** dial 911—only in emergencies. For normal police inquiries, call 212/374-5000. For an **ambulance,** dial the Operator. To report a **fire,** dial 911.

EVENTS

New York City is either the scene and/or the host of a very considerable number of events and activities. For a daily listing of free city-sponsored activities, call 212/360-1333. The Convention and Visitors Bureau, 2 Columbus Circle (tel. 212/397-8222), publishes an annual calendar of events, covering everything from parades up Fifth Avenue to jogging marathons to the Japanese Cherry Blossom Festival in Brooklyn. Call them, or drop by for a copy.

MEASURES AND WEIGHTS:

In case you need to make conversions to and from the metric system, this chart will come in handy.

Length

1 millimeter = 0.04 inches (*or* less than 1/16 in)
1 centimeter = 0.39 inches (*or* just under 1/2 in)
1 meter   = 1.09 yards (*or* about 39 inches)
1 kilometer = 0.62 mile (*or* about 2/3 mile)

To convert kilometers to miles, take the number of kilometers and multiply by .62 (for example, 25 km × .62 = 15.5 miles).

To convert miles to kilometers, take the number of miles and multiply by 1.61 (for example, 50 miles × 1.61 = 80.5 km).

Capacity

1 liter = 33.92 ounces
        = 1.06 quarts
        = 0.26 gallons

To convert liters to gallons, take the number of liters and multiply by .26 (for example, 50 liters × .26 = 13 gallons).

To convert gallons to liters, take the number of gallons and multiply by 3.79 (for example, 10 gal × 3.79 = 37.9 liters).

Weight

1 gram   = 0.04 ounces (*or* about a paperclip's weight)
1 kilogram = 2.2 pounds

To convert kilograms to pounds, take the number of kilos and multiply by 2.2 (for example, 75 kg × 2.2 = 165 lbs.).

To convert pounds to kilograms, take the number of pounds and multiply by .45 (for example, 90 lbs. × .45 = 40.5 kg).

Area

1 hectare (100m²) = 2.47 acres

To convert hectares to acres, take the number of hectares and multiply by 2.47 (for example, 20 ha × 2.47 = 49.4 acres).

To convert acres to hectares, take the number of acres and multiply by .41 (for example, 40 acres × .41 = 16.4 hectares).

Temperature

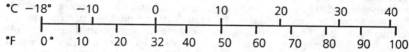

To convert degrees C to degrees F, multiply degrees C by 9, divide by 5, then add 32 (for example, 9/5 × 20°C + 32 = 68°F).

To convert degrees F to degrees C, subtract 32 from degrees F, then multiply by 5, and divide by 9 (for example, 85°F − 32 × 5/9 = 29°C).

OUT-OF-TOWN NEWSPAPERS

A famous outfit called **Hotalings,** 142 W. 42nd St., between Sixth Avenue and Broadway (tel. 212/840-1868), carries over 200 papers from all over the world.

PARKING

Everybody will tell you that parking is impossible in Manhattan. This is only partly true. There are **privately owned parking garages** all over the place, but they're extremely dear. Just how dear is illustrated by the following rates, copied recently off the wall of a typical midtown garage located in the basement of a sky-scraper near 53rd and Park:

Up to 1/2 hour	$9.21
Up to 1 hour	11.18
Up to 2 hours	13.82
Up to 3 hours	15.58
Up to 10 hours	19.74
Max. to closing	21.93

14% NYC Parking Tax extra

A sobering set of rates, no? Actually, if this had been a 24-hour garage the maximum rate wouldn't have been too bad. Most Manhattan hotels, when they do offer parking, usually offer it for $25 to $30 per 24 hours.

The farther you get from the fashionable core of Midtown or downtown, the lower the rates become. But with the exception of the occasional "early bird special," which might lure parkers in before 10 a.m. and out before 6 p.m. for $5, $6, or $7, there are few bargains among Manhattan's lots and garages.

The Kinney Corp., which is one of the big parking operators in town, runs several cut-rate **municipal garages** for the city. But be advised that the municipal garages are not particularly cheap if you want to park for days or weeks. Nor are they very conveniently located. The one in Midtown, a park-and-lock at Eighth Avenue between 53rd and 54th Streets, is the most accessible. It charges $1 per half-hour and is open 24 hours a day. The other municipals—under Police Headquarters way down at 103 Park Row; on Leonard Street between Lafayette and Centre Streets; and, remotest of all, at 113 Essex St. near Delancey—are about as convenient as parking in Pennsylvania. Besides, only the Essex Street location is open 24 hours.

A possible longer-term parking idea for visitors is an outfit in Brooklyn called **Auto Baby Sitters,** 827 Sterling Pl. (between Nostrand and Rogers) (tel. 718/493-9800). You can store your car here for $40 a week, or $80 for two weeks to a month. The Auto Baby Sitters require an appointment in advance and they charge more for vans. If the thought of searching Brooklyn for Sterling Place intimidates you, they will pick up (for $15) or drop off (for $20) your car for you in Manhattan or elsewhere in the boros. Call them between 9 a.m. and 4:30 p.m. during the week, and 9 a.m. to noon on Saturday (closed Sunday).

Free street parking in Manhattan is possible, but it's subject to an arcane set of regulations known as "Alternate Side of the Street Parking Laws." You'll only find alternate-side parking in residential neighborhoods. And it's being constantly nibbled away at by city commissioners who figure that less on-street parking means a healthier New York. One can usually forgive these well-intentioned gentlemen— that is, unless you're trying to find a parking place. Herds of prowling cars stalk Manhattan side streets in between the hours when alternate side is changing, reminding one of hunger-crazed piranhas searching for flesh in a Brazilian stream.

Alternate-side parking presumably allows street-cleaning machines to keep the city tidy by periodically clearing parked cars off alternate sides of the streets. A typical sign, say, on West 74th Street between Columbus and Central Park West will read: "No Parking 11 a.m. to 2 p.m., Mon, Wed, Fri." Signs on the opposite side have the same restrictions, except that they're in effect on "Tues, Thurs, and Sat." Sunday is a free day. Therefore, if you arrive on West 74th Street at 1:30 p.m. in the afternoon, as so many do, you can pull up to a gradually filling curb, sit in your car until 2 p.m., then get out and leave it in place until 11 a.m. two days hence. Get it?

On many East Side streets Wednesday is a free day too. A typical sign, say, on East 77th Street between Park and Madison, might read "No Parking 8 a.m. to 11 a.m., Tues and Fri." Arrive at 10:30 a.m. on Friday and you've got a legal spot for the whole weekend—in fact until Tuesday morning.

If you don't catch the alternate hours, you'll find yourself in the pack of piranhas, and at a disadvantage too, since you won't know the lay of the land. Whatever happens, do *not* park illegally. To be towed in Manhattan means a $125 towing charge, plus the cost of the ticket (another $35 to $40), plus the cost of a cab to get you to one of the city parking pounds, which are not exactly on the beaten track.

As for **metered parking,** it exists, but not in great profusion. A quarter usually buys you 20 minutes on Broadway or Madison or Third. In the really busy parts of town there are no meters.

What's the best advice? Leave your car at home.

POST OFFICE

The main branch, an enormous edifice, is at 33rd Street and Eighth Avenue (tel. 212/967-8585). It's open from 8 a.m. to 6 p.m. and operates a 24-hour emergency window for certified and express mail. Numerous branch post offices are operated throughout the city.

RAILROAD INFORMATION

Commuter lines to the northern suburbs are operated by **Metro North** (tel. 212/532-4900); trains for the whole of Long Island are run by the **Long Island Rail**

Road (tel. 718/739-4200); the toll-free number for **Amtrak** trains to other destinations is 800/USA-RAIL.

SAFETY

On the subject of **general safety,** be advised that New York is no more dangerous than most big cities. But wherever you go, keep your wits about you. Don't let a fat wallet bulge out of your back pocket or somebody is going to pick it. Beware of people who jostle or crowd in front or back of you. Don't leave your purse on the seat beside you, or worse, under the table at a restaurant, or somebody will relieve you of it. Wear a money belt and the strap of your purse or camera diagonally across your chest. Don't wear expensive jewelry on a crowded subway platform or somebody may snatch it. These are just facts of life.

As for getting mugged, which is local parlance for robbery, it won't happen to you unless you stray into some lonely area, usually at night. Wherever you go, don't dawdle on the streets. Muggers go for the slow and easy marks. Keep moving, keep with the crowds, stay alert, and you'll be perfectly safe. However, if you do get accosted, give them what they want as they may be armed.

Bicycles are thought by some New Yorkers to be the perfect solution to traffic-crowded streets. Most cyclists are the politest of souls, but many among them take a very high-handed attitude toward pedestrians. You will see bicycles streaking down one-way streets the wrong way, ignoring red lights, expecting you to hear the faint slish of skinny tires on asphalt above the roar of Midtown traffic. If you get hit, your assailant is not going to stop unless his/her precious ten-speed is rendered inoperable by the collision. *Always* look both ways when stepping off a curb. With all the one-way streets in New York, people often forget to do this. And some of us have actually been killed by bikes. At the least you're in jeopardy of having your clothes ripped and your composure severely disrupted by some little creep who lacks the common decency to stop and see if you're okay. Be careful; such little creeps abound.

Although the ranks of these card sharks are thinning, it is still possible on many street corners in this town, even in the most fashionable districts, to see sharp-eyed young men playing a card game called **three-card monte.** A player with a slick patter stands behind a cardboard box on which he deals out three cards face down. Passersby are invited to bet on the identity of these cards. Lots of money flashes back and forth and people seem to be winning. Don't get involved. This is strictly a sucker ploy.

TELEPHONES

Local calls cost 25¢ at booths, more from the phone in your hotel room (how much more depends on the hotel). Until recently the area code for all of New York City was **212.** But now Brooklyn, Queens, and Staten Island have a code of their own, **718.** That means that just to dial across the East River these days requires a 1-, then the 718 area code, and then the number. However, it is never necessary to dial a 1- before a telephone number within an area code.

As in other parts of the country, the number for **information** ("directory assistance") within an area code is 411; outside the area code, it is 1-area code needed-555-1212. The number for the **time** of day is 212/976-1616.

TIPPING

There's an old story about the girl who came to New York in August and caught pneumonia. You see, she couldn't turn off the air conditioner in her hotel room. And she was too embarrassed to call a bellman because she didn't know how much to tip. So here's how much to tip:

Restaurants: Everybody says 15% to 20%, but most New Yorkers tip closer to the 20% end. In ritzy establishments the presence of a captain inevitably raises questions. Do you have to tip this tuxedo-clad model of Manhattan urbanity simply because he led you to a table and handed you a menu? No, you don't. Stick with the regular 20% to the waiter. But what if Monsieur Marc (or whatever his name is) contrives to get you some favorite dish even though it isn't on the menu, or undertakes a successful search for your favorite wine, or arranges on the sly to surprise your spouse with a little cake for his/her birthday? Then you tip him. How much? Not a fortune; usually around 5% of the bill.

Taxis: Again, people will tell you to tip between 15% and 20% of whatever's on the meter. But something a bit on the shady side of 20% is more customary. Never give a cabby less than 50¢, unless you're parting company as avowed enemies.

Bellhops: They expect a buck per bag, unless it's a tiny little thing they can tuck under an arm. In the really elegant hotels it's more like $2 for a single bag, $3 for two bags, etc. Anytime they walk in the door, to bring something in or take it away again, plan on pressing a couple of bucks into the outstretched palm. (Don't forget, these guys live on tips.)

At the airport: If you engage a porter either to carry your things or to load them onto a trolley or to take care of your bags at curb-side-checking, plan on paying him 50¢ for each small bag and $1 for each big one.

At the theater: Ushers in American theaters do not expect tips.

TOURIST INFORMATION

This very helpful organization is located at the southwest corner of Central Park, at 2 Columbus Circle, New York, NY 10019 (tel. 212/397-8222). Helpful people at the desk will answer all manner of questions, provide maps, give useful advice, etc., etc. The C & V also publishes a free "Calendar of Events" and it would be clever of you to write in advance for this publication. New York is always hosting something or other, be it an antiques show, a dog show, an auto show, a street festival, fireworks displays, major parades, etc. The "Calendar of Events" tells you everything that's scheduled for the year.

TRAVELERS AID

This organization provides emergency assistance to people stranded in New York. It might be in the form of aid in reaching family or friends, transportation, or possibly even temporary shelter. There are two offices: one in the International Arrivals Building at JFK Airport (tel. 718/656-4870); and the other at 158-160 West 42nd Street (tel. 212/944-0013).

NEW YORK CITY HOTELS

For the purposes of hotel recommendations I've divided Manhattan into six areas: the Plaza–Fifth Avenue area, East Midtown, West Midtown, the Upper East Side, the Upper West Side, and downtown. Each of these areas has a distinct flavor that is reflected in the accommodations you'll find there.

A WORD ABOUT "PACKAGES"

New York City hotels are thronged during the week but strangely deserted on weekends. Demand for hotel rooms is overwhelming in November but lackluster in March. In order to lessen the impact of these rhythms of room occupancy, the hotel industry has created the "package."

I'm not talking about tour packages here, of the sort that include air fare, rental cars, and guided tours. But rather of the minipackages concocted by individual hotels themselves in the hopes of attracting warm bodies to otherwise empty rooms. If you're making your own hotel reservations, *be sure to ask* if there's a package rate in effect during your proposed stay. It can save you lots of money, sometimes as much as half the room rate.

The typical hotel package is aimed squarely at the libido of the New York-area suburbanite. Packages bear names like "Romance in New York," "The Suite Weekend," "Japanese Fantasy in New York," "S'Glamorous," "Weekend in the Sky," "Posh and Pampered," and so on ad infinitum.

Even though special packages are advertised all over the local press, reservation clerks won't tell you about them unless you ask. The rates quoted in the descriptions below are permanent rates in effect at press time. Packages are only temporary special deals.

Prepare yourself, before we start, for some of these prices. It is a sad truth that a decent Manhattan hotel room for under $100 is virtually unknown. And a double in the hotel you may have dreamed of staying at might well cost well over $300. Plus which, *to every price quoted below, you must add 8¼% sales tax, and another $2 per night hotel occupancy tax.*

MORE WORDS ABOUT PRICES

The recommendations in each hotel area are listed in *descending order of price.* Some areas don't have much in the way of moderate lodgings; others have nothing but. I think it's important to have some idea of neighborhood before you make a choice, which is why I've organized things this way.

1. The Grand Army Plaza–Fifth Avenue

Grand Army Plaza is an elegant small square bounded by Fifth Avenue, 58th and 59th Streets, and the east wall of the famous Plaza Hotel. This area is the very heart of fashionable Manhattan, full of expensive hotels, many of which overlook Central Park. To stay here is to be surrounded by glittering shops and skyscrapers, posh clubs, streets crowded with taxis, and sidewalks thronged with the well-heeled. It's the neighborhood of Tiffany's, Bergdorf Goodman, 57th Street, Central Park, and the Metropolitan Club. It is movers and shakers shopping at Bijan (the men's boutique where admission is by appointment only); mink-clad "ladies who lunch" heading for a swell one at La Côte Basque; gray-suited captains of industry hurrying from their limos into the august precincts of the University Club; gangs of construction workers (there's always a new skyscraper going up) whistling at long-legged secretaries during lunch; and fortunate tourists en route to and from the many first-class hotels hereabouts.

Since I'm now on the subject of hotels, let me start with the best, the **Pierre,** Fifth Avenue at 61st Street, New York, NY 10021 (tel. 212/838-8000). This graceful buff brick–and–limestone tower overlooking Central Park was put up in 1929. It's a low-key, ultraclassy hotel that prides itself on attentive service. Millionaires and movie stars have always made the Pierre home. As a matter of fact, 70% of the building consists of privately owned cooperative apartments, whose presence lends an exclusive and luxurious atmosphere that few hotels can match.

The spacious and well-proportioned lobby looks almost like the drawing room in some graceful old mansion. There are gorgeous moldings, potted palms, thick rugs, chandeliers with forests of little shaded lights, black marble floors, and glass vitrines filled with precious-looking breakables. There is also a palpable atmosphere of friendliness, geniality, grace, and self-assurance.

The Pierre has only 196 transient rooms, which makes it small as hotels go. Some 60% of its customers are repeat guests. And if you have the good fortune to stay here once, you'll want to come back too. The rooms look as though they belong in a rich aunt's town house. They are high-ceilinged, beautifully proportioned, immaculately painted and wallpapered. Here's a hotel that always seems freshly redecorated. Curtains and spreads might be done in some handsome matching chintz and the walls hung with framed floral prints. The rugs are thick and the beds firm. Everything is first-rate, right down to the little note from the manager that welcomes you to town, and the heavenly terrycloth bathrobes provided for your stay. There is a phone by the bed and a phone in the bath. There is of course a color television, as well as a shaving mirror, a scale, a clock, a huge closet with private safe inside, twice-daily maid service, 24-hour room service, even an unpacking service should you want such a thing.

Single rooms at the Pierre start at $250 per night and go all the way to $340. Most singles cost between $280 and $310. Double-occupancy rates apply to the same rooms, starting at $275 and continuing all the way up to $365 nightly. Most doubles are around $305 to $335. It should be noted that even the minimum-priced rooms are extremely attractive, as well they might be.

Downstairs you'll find a concierge who can arrange to get you a private helicopter for the evening, or telegraph a couple of thousand in cash to your daughter at the Singapore airport. Besides valet parking (about $30 a night), beauty and barber shop, and an outpost of the jeweler Bulgari, the Pierre has two swank restaurants. The Café Pierre, which doubles as the hotel bar, and the Rotunda, a domed and muraled sort of tea room adjacent to the café. For about $15 you can have the Rotunda Tea, consisting of sandwiches of the egg-and-watercress stripe, scones with Devonshire cream and fresh preserves, and any type of tea you can think of. Or perhaps just a single glass of champagne. This will cost close to $10. But to have it in this room is like *being* in a movie instead of buying a ticket to see one.

The **Park Lane Hotel,** 36 Central Park South (between Fifth and Sixth Avenues), New York, NY 10019 (tel. 212/371-4000, or toll free 800/221-4982), is a slender, 46-story glass-and-limestone high-rise that was built in 1971. It is deluxe and contemporary, and patronized by lots of movie people from the West Coast.

Everything about this place reflects the Helmsley chain's attention to detail. The lobby is chandelier city, a great vault of polished marble, crimson carpets, a sweeping staircase, and an eye-boggling display of dangling crystal. Every marble console in sight carries a spectacular spray of fresh flowers.

Care and pride are clearly in evidence upstairs in the guest rooms too. No moldings or old-mansion airs up here. Instead, the rooms have a lush contemporary suburban look. There are plenty of comfortable chairs, lots of handsome brass table lamps, little refrigerators in the bathrooms, phones in the bathrooms, full-length mirrors on the closet doors, a thermos, a clock radio, three movie channels on the color television, even ironing boards and hairdryers should you want them. The rooms aren't huge, but they are extremely appealing and comfortable. The furniture is Louis-Louis, and the views, even when you don't face the park, are quite sensational. (If a view is important, tell them you want a room above the 20th floor.)

Single rates range between $195 and $265 nightly; doubles (the same room with double occupancy) run $215 to $285. Top-end-rate rooms face Central Park; minimum-rate rooms are just as nice but without the park view. And in my opinion many of these city views are every bit as interesting as those overlooking the park.

On the hotel's second floor, at the top of the sweeping staircase, is the Park Room Restaurant, a lofty chamber that provides diners with treetop views of Central Park. Cuisine is classic French-continental and dinner will cost a good $50 per person. Adjacent to the restaurant is an appealing wood-paneled bar with a piano-chanteuse in the evening. In the basement garage your car can snooze, for $35 a night, in the splendorous company of Bentleys and Mercedeses. Room service is, of course, available 24 hours a day.

The **Ritz-Carlton,** 112 Central Park South (between Sixth and Seventh Avenues), New York, NY 10019 (tel. 212/757-1900, or toll free 800/223-7990), is a horse of a different color. To be more specific, it's a hotel that aspires to be the horsey set's home away from the country estate. The dignified limestone building with its bright-blue awnings started life in the 1920s as an apartment house. A few years back it was gutted and rebuilt, then decorated by New York society decorator Mrs. Henry ("Sister") Parrish. The result is lots of pickled pine, lacquered walls, gilt-framed pictures of dogs, Chippendale-style sofas, Chinese vases made over into lamps, and a discreet but pervasive air of unpretentious luxury.

With only 237 units, the place is not big. But of course "bigness" is just what management is trying to avoid. Owner John Coleman wants to create the air of an English country house, where an elegant informality reigns. The lobby is small and discreet—no Helmsley glitz at the Ritz. No profusion of public rooms either. Upstairs, rooms are smallish but exceedingly well tailored. They have thick dark rugs, nice wood furniture, not one but two telephone lines, marble-topped vanities bearing the usual little bottles of deluxe shampoo, hair conditioner, and so forth. There are hunt prints on the walls and free copies of the *New York Times* at doorways in the morning. Room service, as well as a concierge who is part magician, is available 24 hours.

Rates run all the way from $190 to $350 for singles, $220 to $380 for doubles; expect a standard double to cost around $280 nightly. The Jockey Club Restaurant on the ground floor has more expanses of pickled pine, including a long pine bar over which hangs a handsome painting of a hunting hound. For those who don't like flash but do like quality, this is an excellent choice. (P.S. Don't forget to ask about summer, holiday, and weekend packages!)

The Plaza, Fifth Avenue at 59th Street, New York, NY 10019 (tel. 212/759-3000, or toll free 800/228-3000), is a magnificent Edwardian pile dating from 1907. Its opulent gilt-and-marble lobbies were once the definition of New York luxury. Today its palatial ballrooms remain favorites for charity balls and society dances.

The heart of The Plaza is the Palm Court, which ripples with violin music and the tinkle of laughter each afternoon and evening. The hotel's other restaurants include the famous Edwardian Room, the somberly elegant Oak Room, the Oyster Bar, and the Tahitian excesses of Trader Vic's (which the Trumps say they will close eventually). Mirrored and marbled corridors meander this way and that, lined with shops that sell everything from evening gowns to aspirin.

Recently The Plaza was bought by real estate mogul Donald Trump, and every one of the 807 rooms has been upgraded and redecorated. All the rooms have pretty chintz flowered bedspreads and matching wallpaper. At their best they are big, handsomely proportioned, and graced with marvelous green views of Central Park.

The place has a glamour uniquely its own. Singles at the glamorous Plaza cost from $215 for an interior room to $450 for a deluxe room with a park view. Most singles are priced between $290 and $360 nightly. Double rooms start at $235 and range up to $480, the latter price being for rooms facing the park. Many of the rooms facing Fifth Avenue or 58th Street are just as nice, and more reasonably priced. Avoid the interior rooms. For another $30 nightly you can store your car in the hotel's garage.

Unquestionably the best value for the money in Midtown, and perhaps anywhere in town, is the **Wyndham,** 42 W. 58th St. (between Fifth and Sixth Avenues), New York, NY 10019 (tel. 212/753-3500). The building looks like a typical apartment house dating from sometime after the First World War. Inside is a slightly cluttered and rather pretty little lobby furnished with painted screens, a profusion of potted plants, Chinese rugs, gilt mirrors, and big comfortable sofas. It looks like someone's living room.

Which is what it is. The owners of the Wyndham, Mr. and Mrs. John Mados, live upstairs. Mr. Mados runs the business and Mrs. Mados decorates the rooms. The employees, many of whom have been here for years, are like an extended family. The Madoses' personal touch attracts many Broadway and Hollywood celebrities and savvy world travelers, as do the rooms, which are, well, unbelievably luxurious for the price.

The suites are simply huge, carpeted with thick fresh pastel-colored rugs and decorated with botanical prints in gilded frames, big comfortable sofas, Chinese throw rugs, even the occasional marble fireplace. Every piece of fabric and furniture is immaculate. All the suites have little kitchenettes; some even have dressing rooms adjacent to the bedrooms. They look like classy little New York apartments. The truth is that they are absolutely the equal of suites in the very best hotels in town. The standard rooms are just as nice. And big!

What's most amazing about the Wyndham is the price. Half the 212 units are suites, priced between $170 and $200 a night. The rest, from the ninth floor down, are standard rooms, renting for $110 to $120 single and $125 to $135 double. There is a restaurant on the main floor called Jonathan's. If you've brought a car, you'll have to take care of your own parking, but that's easy enough at nearby lots. The biggest problem at the Wyndham is fitting everybody in.

2. East Midtown

The hotels that follow are all in the East 40s and 50s between Fifth Avenue and the East River. East Midtown has a lot of the same skyscraper glamour as the Plaza–Fifth Avenue area. But as one progresses eastward the high-fashion stores and the high-elevation buildings begin to thin out and the neighborhood becomes more settled and less glitzy. To stay here is still to be in the middle of exciting and attractive Midtown neighborhoods, all of which are convenient to the attractions for which the city is famous.

First choice in the area is **The Waldorf-Astoria,** Park Avenue at 50th Street, New York, NY 10022 (tel. 212/355-3000). This 47-story, double-towered Hilton-operated limestone behemoth is the epitome of the ultralavish hotel of the art deco period. Everything is vast and satisfyingly opulent. The lobby is in the middle of a block-long progression of sumptuously rugged and chandeliered interiors. There are soaring ceilings, glittering mosaics, precious marbles, priceless furniture, and a labyrinth of corridors lined with chic boutiques and restaurants. If you stroll down Peacock Alley during the day, you're liable to hear the music of a harp; at night it'll be Cole Porter's own piano, moved from his suite to the lobby when he died in 1964. It's the glamorous lobby life of the Waldorf that, quite frankly, is one of the major reasons for staying here.

Presidents, movie stars, and the social and business elite from every continent stay at the Waldorf. Guest rooms are reached via corridors so long they seem to vanish into distant pinpoints. The suites (famous for their art deco marble bathrooms) and "special executive accommodations" are roomy and sumptuous. The standard rooms tend to be on the small side, but contain nice French reproduction furniture, marble bathrooms, and plenty of light. And after all, it's a Hilton, so everything really is first-class.

The rate structure at the Waldorf is as labyrinthine as the floor plan. Supposedly, there are rooms that go for as little as $190 single and $215 double per night. As a practical matter, you'll find most singles in the $235 to $265 range, with most doubles priced between $280 and $315. The suites are quite opulent but also quite expensive. Occupying a part of the building and managed as a separate entity is the Waldorf Towers, where rooms and suites are even more elaborate and expensive.

The hotel has a garage (for around $30 a night storage) as well as hot and cold running restaurants. There is the Bull and Bear for steaks and chops, Harry's Leopard Bar, Peacock Alley, Inagiku for Japanese food, the Cocktail Terrace, and Oscar's Coffee Shop. Besides newsstands and ticket brokers you'll find a florist, an antiques shop, several jewelers, leather goods, and clothiers tucked along the hotel's many gold-leafed passageways. How big is the Waldorf? 690,000 paying guests last year.

The Helmsley's flagship, however, is the **Helmsley Palace,** 456 Madison Ave. (between 50th and 51st Streets), New York, NY 10022 (tel. 212/888-7000, or toll free 800/221-4982). The hotel gets its name from a landmark complex of 19th-century town houses that forms its Madison Avenue streetfront. When originally built, the Villard Houses, as they are called, gave the appearance of a single Italian Renaissance palace. To a great extent they still do, even though a monolithic glass box full of hotel rooms now rises behind them.

Inside the old mansions is a series of palatial restored rooms that serve as lounges, restaurants, and a bar. The vaulted and gilded music room is now the Gold Room, where for $18.50 you can have afternoon tea to the strains of a harpist between 2 and 5 p.m. The Hunt Bar, formerly a dining room, has sumptuous dark-stained paneling plus little sofa and table groupings. The Madison Room, once a drawing room, is now a lounge with crystal chandeliers, French furniture, marble columns, and an air of St. Petersburg before the Revolution.

Most of the Helmsley Palace is located in the new structure. The block-through lobby is huge and opulently decorated with damask-covered walls, crimson velvet poufs, urns on pedestals, and mirrored wall cases filled with expensive watches and jewels. A chandelier as big as a compact car hangs above the grand stairway. The nearly 1,000 guest rooms are everything one expects from a Helmsley hotel. They have marble-topped Louis-esque furniture, hilariously monarchial gilded headboards, a soft pastel color palette, curtains bracketed by paneled valances, rugs thick enough to wade through. For all the "traditional" details, rooms still have a distinctly contemporary air.

And boy, are they comfortable. And big. And filled with Helmsley touches like satin hangers in the closet, piles of oversize fluffy towels, scales, bathroom telephones, state-of-the-art color televisions, little "amenity trays" filled with complimentary toiletries, etc.

Basic single rates range from $240 to $280 nightly; doubles run $260 to $310. Above the 41st floor is something they call the "tower," even though it's in no way structurally articulated from the rest of the building. Rooms up here are reached by private elevators, have a little private lobby in the sky, and cost $300 single, $330 double. Up here is where the suites are, including the famous triplex penthouses that rent for $2500 a night. As a practical matter, the minimum-price rooms in the Palace offer the best value for the money. The hotel restaurant, called Le Trianon, serves breakfast, lunch, dinner, and a late-night supper until quarter past midnight. Expect parking to run another $40 a night.

Not many tourists know about the ultramodern **United Nations Plaza Hotel,** One United Nations Plaza (that's East 44th Street between First and Second Avenues), New York, NY 10017 (tel. 212/355-3400, or toll free 800/228-9000), but they should. The location is a bit in the far east, but nearby 42nd Street provides easy access to the rest of town. And there is a sheltering restfulness to this hotel that's extremely appealing. Not to mention the knockout views from almost every room, and the high-floor swimming pool complete with skyline panorama.

The building is a dramatically angular affair, sheathed in tinted glass and brushed aluminum, and entered from a covered drive (the hotel entrance is the closest to First Avenue). The 21st-century lobby is a multilevel fantasy of smoked mirrors and geometric green and white marble floors. There are so many clever turns and reflective surfaces that one might well walk into a mirrored wall.

All 444 guest rooms are located between the 28th and the 38th floors (U.N. offices and the like fill the building up to there), which means superb views from every window. Accomodations have a tailored, futuristic look. There are low ceilings, mirrored tabletops, gray velvet tub chairs, remote-control televisions with HBO channels. The huge beds are equipped with chrome reading lamps and headboards upholstered in brown leatherette. The bathrooms have indirect lighting, gray tiles, and stacks of rose-colored towels. Deluxe rooms on the corners have double views.

The single-room rate runs between $190 and $225, the latter price for deluxe corner rooms. Doubles cost $210 to $245, with the top end again reserved for the corners. Parking is available for $25 nightly, and room service operates 24 hours a day. Downstairs at lobby level is the Ambassador Grill, which serves fairly expensive breakfasts, lunches, and dinners. There's a bar attached, with a piano player in the evening, and a little lounge area full of crimson plush tub chairs. Up on the roof is a complete health club, including the aforementioned swimming pool. During the week, the U.N. Plaza is basically a corporate hotel for upper-bracket traveling execs and CEOs. On the weekends it gets a lot of suburbanites in on the package deals. But for some reason it doesn't have nearly the amount of tourist traffic it would seem to merit.

The **Lyden House,** 320 E. 53rd St. (between First and Second Avenues), New

York, NY 10022 (tel. 212/888-6070), far from looking like a hotel, seems instead to be an unassuming little apartment house. The diminutive green marble lobby has no bar, no concierge, no bustle of bellmen or murmur of Muzak. It's just a pleasant entrance with a tiny desk. But upstairs are 45 transient units of superlative comfort and quality, ranging in size from single rooms to small suites.

The Lyden is one of nine properties belonging to a local outfit called Manhattan East Suite Hotels. The rooms here are stylishly decorated in tones of buff, rose, and beige. They have thick rugs, matching floral spreads and curtains, very nice traditional furniture, and immaculate white-tiled bathrooms with real tubs and showers instead of those fakey little ones you find in so much new construction. The one-bedroom suites are handsomely decorated, roomy, and immaculately clean, and even have eat-in kitchens.

Best part of all is the price: studio suites start at $155 single, $175 double. One-bedroom suites start at $200 per night for two, plus $20 per additional person.

The **Helmsley Middletowne,** 148 E. 48th St. (between Lexington and Third Avenues), New York, NY 10017 (tel. 212/755-3000, or toll free 800/221-4982), is an old tapestry brick building, 17 stories tall, with 194 rooms. It also has no restaurant, no bar, no concierge, and no parking (although a lot down the street charges about $20 for 24 hours). In many ways it's just a bigger, more centrally located version of the Lyden. Except for one major difference: the Helmsley touch.

That touch is apparent the minute you set foot in the cozy little gray marble lobby. Fully half of the ceiling is covered with a crystal chandelier. Upstairs, the halls have nice striped wallpaper and more chandeliers. All rooms feature a little kitchenette, which many times is the first thing you walk into. Never mind, because the quality of everything is so good. There are thick pile rugs, handsome-looking chairs, desks to write at, and plenty of lamps to see by. There are lots of closets, marble tops on the bureaus, and gleaming white-tiled bathrooms. And then there are the many personal touches, like the shaving mirror, the oversize towels, the tray of complimentary toiletries.

Room decor is neither old-fashioned nor modern; it looks somehow "traditional" and yet not in any recognizable historical context. The prices for these cheerful and extremely comfortable accommodations range between $125 and $135 for singles, between $135 and $145 for doubles, and run $195 to $370 for suites. Once people find it, they always come back.

People don't expect many family-run hotels in Midtown Manhattan, but the **Hotel Beverly,** Lexington Avenue at 50th Street, New York, NY 10022 (tel. 212/753-2700, or toll free 800/223-0945), is yet another. It is a slender brick tower dating from the 1920s, ornamented with stone gargoyles and protruding air conditioners, and radiating an unpretentious aura of comfort. The redecorated lobby is actually rather elegant with its new mirrored columns, leather sofas, potted palms, and dignified woodwork. There's even a uniformed concierge, unusual for a modest hotel.

Of the 200 units, 175 are either one-bedroom suites or what they call "junior suites," which are oversize rooms with separate seating areas and kitchenettes. These suites are enormously appealing. They have lots of windows and unusual floorplans, big rooms, wall-to-wall carpeting, rice-papered walls, nice modern tile baths, and matching curtains and spreads, and the kitchens usually have new appliances. Suites on even floors from the 16th up have terraces too. They're all bright, clean, and comfortable, and often have great views of the surrounding skyscrapers. Even the standard rooms have little refrigerators, comfy old blond furniture, framed prints, and huge beds.

Standard rooms cost $139 to $149 single, $149 to $159 double; junior suites are priced between $149 and $169; the one-bedroom suites cost between $180 and $255 nightly, single or double. The higher prices apply to the higher floors. Additional persons pay $10 apiece per night, with a maximum of four persons per suite. Kenny's Steak and Seafood Restaurant, located off the lobby, provides breakfast, lunch, and dinner in a family atmosphere. Valet parking is available for about $20 a night.

The **Pickwick Arms Hotel,** 230 E. 51st St. (between Second and Third Avenues), New York, NY 10022 (tel. 212/355-0300, or toll free 800/PICKWIK), is a great bargain. Built as a men's club 60-odd years ago, it has been much renovated with uneven aesthetic results. The Spanish tile roof of the Torremolinos Restaurant lends a south-of-the-border touch to an otherwise dignified facade. And inside, the original quasi-English lobby has been disguised with new mirrored walls, a modern marble reception desk, and piped-in rock and roll.

The atmosphere is youthful but certainly engaging. And the rates are hard to beat: $40 to $52 single and $75 to $85 double. Rooms are reached via diminutive self-service elevators paneled in simulated rare wood. Bottom rates apply to rooms with shared bathrooms located in the halls. These rooms are small but fairly cheerful, and have little sinks in the corners and the same color televisions contained in the better rooms. Higher-priced accommodations are bigger and sometimes better furnished. But even if the furniture is scuffed here and there, the place does seem clean. And a bargain here on the East Side is far more desirable than one in some questionable corner of Times Square.

The Pickwick also offers "studios," which another hotel might call a junior suite. These cost $75 and up, will sleep four, and are mentioned here only on account of their low price. Parking is available at a nearby lot for about $20 nightly.

3. West Midtown

This section contains hotels in the West 40s and 50s. Most of the streets hereabouts are not quite so glamorous as their East Side counterparts. And yet here's where you'll find cultural attractions like Carnegie Hall, business meccas like the awesome glass canyons of Sixth Avenue, the art deco beauties of Rockerfeller Center, as well as New York's famous Theater District and the legendary bright lights of Times Square. West Midtown is a very central and certainly a very exciting part of New York in which to stay. And its accommodations cater to a very considerable range of tastes.

First choice in the area is **Le Parker Meridien Hotel,** 118 W. 57th St. (between Sixth and Seventh Avenues), New York, NY 10019 (tel. 212/245-5000, or toll free 800/543-4300). This architecturally spectacular (at least on the inside) new tower is owned by American industrialist Jack Parker and operated by Meridien Hotels. The lobby signs are in French and English, the restaurants specialize in nouvelle cuisine, and an international atmosphere permeates the place from basement health club to rooftop pool.

The location on 57th Street is a hop, skip, and jump from Central Park, and adjacent to some of the best shopping and sightseeing in New York. And then there's the lobby. Featured on the cover of the December 1981 issue of *Interior Design,* it combines 65-foot ceilings, classical columns and arches, gleaming sweeps of marble flooring, and a soft palette of roses and creams. It's so glorious as to put to rest permanently those old mutterings about how "they don't make them like they used to."

There are 600 rooms and 100 suites in the Parker-Meridien. Accommodations have the low ceilings typical of new construction, but the furnishings and textiles are stylish and very handsome. There are thick, plush carpets, big beds, plenty of light from wide modern windows, and marble bathrooms complete with telephones, scales, and amenity trays. Deluxe rooms are L-shaped and have handsome wood shelf units that divide sitting areas from sleeping areas, making them almost like little suites.

In the basement is Club La Raquette with piped-in rock and roll, Nautilus equipment, squash courts, and plenty of mirrors in which to admire yourself. On the 42nd floor is a swimming pool with fabulous city views, as well as an outdoor jogging track. Down at lobby level are Maurice, the elegant main restaurant, and Le Patio Montparnasse for informal (but still pricey) buffets and drinks. There is 24-hour room service, as well as valet parking for about $25 nightly.

The price for all this style and comfort is $195 to $235 single, $220 to $260 double. Minimum-priced rooms are every bit as nice as the others—they're just on lower floors. Top prices are for "deluxe" rooms, meaning those with the clever divider units.

The **Marriott Marquis,** 1700 Broadway (between 45th and 46th Streets), New York, NY 10019 (tel. 212/398-1900), represents one of the critical first steps in the plan to revitalize Times Square. Designed by Atlanta architect John Portman, it's a brand-new 50-story behemoth of poured concrete and smoked glass bulging out over Times Square. The Marriott contains 1,876 guest rooms arranged along balconies overlooking a 37-story atrium that, quite frankly, looks like something that landed from Mars. This is primarily a convention hotel and as such it features things like a 28,800-square-foot ballroom, easy access to New York's new convention center, and special deals for corporate customers.

Everything about the Marriott is huge. You must make your way to the eighth floor just to find the lobby. Rooms are reached via vertiginous glass elevators that rise through the middle of the atrium (those with weak stomachs had better keep their eyes tightly closed). The rooms are big and bright, nicely furnished with curiously traditional-looking pieces. They feature subdued peach and plum color schemes, clock radios, sitting areas, even a video checkout wherein your bill is presented for approval on the screen of your television set.

Prices at the Marriott are steep: $255 single and $285 double. Package deals can soften the blow somewhat. And staying here is certainly an exciting experience that will appeal to many. There are various restaurants on the premises, among them the Encore and the Atrium Café, as well as a great field of sofas and chairs in the atrium through which attractive young women circulate taking drink orders. Up on the roof is a three-level revolving restaurant called the View. Room service is available around the clock, and you can stash your car in the basement garage for about $30 a night.

The **Sheraton Centre,** Seventh Avenue at 52nd Street, New York, NY 10019 (tel. 212/581-1000, or toll free 800/325-3535), is the flagship of the Sheraton chain. Built 20-odd years ago, it's a 50-story Las Vegas transplant, complete with dramatic angular architecture and lots of marble and glass. The lobby is a sprawling modern affair, full of bustling bellmen, hurrying conventioneers, and the sounds of laughter and silverware from the Café Fontana. Arriving guests stand in velvet-roped lines as they approach a desk the size of a ticket counter at a major international airport.

Upstairs, behind doors graced with Sheraton crests and computer-card locks, are some 1,800 guest rooms. The decor is motel plush, which is to say coordinated spreads and curtains, marble-topped vanities, full-length mirrors, piles of fluffy Sheraton towels, and color televisions with pay movie channels. Not deluxe perhaps, but the place really is very nice. The top several floors are called, rather grandly, the "Sheraton Towers." Rooms here benefit from a private elevator, special check-in on the 46th floor, and a few additional amenities (like bathrobes) in the rooms.

Single rates range from $145 to $190 ($215 to $230 in the Towers); doubles cost between $175 and $220 ($245 and $260 in the Towers). All the rooms are very similar; the higher prices are charged for the better views. Besides the aforementioned Café Fontana, the Sheraton has a deluxe restaurant called Raniers, a disco called La Ronde, and the Columbian Coffee House overlooking Seventh Avenue. There is also a swimming pool, free to guests, located across the street at—

The **Sheraton City Squire,** Seventh Avenue at 52nd Street, New York, NY 10019 (tel. 212/581-3300, or toll free 800/325-3535). This latter establishment is a motor-hotel that has been associated with the skyscraper Sheraton Centre since the days when they were both part of the Americana chain. The City Squire is nondescript on the outside, but contains 720 comfortable modern rooms that are the equal of those across the street at considerably lower prices.

The auto entrance is on 51st Street between Seventh Avenue and Broadway. The lobby itself opens onto Seventh Avenue across from the immense new Equitable Building. The lobby is marble-clad, thickly rugged, done up in an anonymous "modern international hotel" style. The upstairs halls are wide and indirectly lit. And the rooms are, well, very Sheraton. The building isn't tall, so there are no great views. But there is plenty of light, nice thick rugs, lots of towels, FM radios, alarm clocks, direct-dial phones, marble sinktops, and amenity trays full of little shampoo bottles and shower caps and shoe cloths. There are free ice and soda machines on every floor, and on-site parking for about $20 daily.

Rates are $145 to $190 single and $175 to $220 double, with most singles priced around $160 to $175 and the typical double costing either $190 or $205. Considering the quality of the rooms and the excellent central location, these are good buys. Also on the premises are The Restaurant and the Croissanterie, the latter being a take-out place for baked goods and sandwiches. Nor can we forget the famous pool, where beautiful stewardesses recline on chaises and the air is filled with the soothing hum of filtration machinery and the warm smell of chlorine.

So much has been written about the celebrated **Algonquin Hotel,** 59 W. 44th St. (between Fifth and Sixth Avenues), New York, NY 10036 (tel. 212/840-6800), that one is almost intimidated to write more. In a nutshell, it's a small (172 rooms) Edwardian hotel in the heart of Midtown, greatly celebrated in the world of letters as the site of the "Round Table." It was here during the 1920s that a group of witty young journalists met for lunch almost every day, among them Dorothy Parker, Ring Lardner, Robert Benchley, Heywood Broun, and Edna Ferber, to name only a few. Their bequest to the Algonquin is its continued identification with the world of wit and literature. It is a New York institution, much beloved, with enormous atmosphere and a devoted clientele.

It is a sign of the times that the long-time family owners of the Algonquin have recently sold it to the Aoki Corporation of Tokyo. The highly decorated brick-and-stone façade; the marvelous old lobby with its dark woodwork, heavy moldings, and lofty ceiling; and the 165 rooms aloft—all, at this writing, are in the midst of extensive restoration. By the time you read this, everything will likely be in pristine Edwardian condition.

The charm of the Algonquin lies in its lobby and its famous (and pricey) restaurants. The former is filled with plush sofas and comfy wing chairs grouped around little oak tables whose attached bells enable you to summon a waiter for drinks. The place is filled with low laughter and the murmur of conversation from people sitting over cocktails, as well as from those in the restaurants that open directly onto the lobby. The Rose Room and the Oak Room, with its adjoining Chinese Room, do a thriving lunch and dinner business. Many a fashionable literary lunch still takes place in the former. In the evening the latter is a stronghold of ultrasophisticated cabaret.

The rooms upstairs aren't small, they're snug. They are being redecorated with nice antique reproductions, paisley spreads and curtains, and glazed or freshly papered walls hung with original drawings, watercolors, and prints. All rooms have immaculate little bathrooms, color televisions, and a complimentary copy of the *New Yorker,* the magazine made famous by the members of the Round Table.

The Algonquin attracts many people in the arts, plus a goodly share of youthful travelers who simply like places with atmosphere. Room rates are still reasonable for Manhattan: $140 to $150 single, $150 to $160 double. One-bedroom suites cost between $280 and $300.

I loved **The Royalton,** 44 West 44th Street, New York, NY 10036 (tel. 212/633-9500), which is unlike anything I've ever seen in my life. Interior designer

Philippe Starck has created a luxury hotel for the Jetsons, via the 1950s, within the shell of a vintage Midtown hotel building. Everything is sleek, sculpted, frosted, glazed, and custom-made.

The multilevel lobby with its enormous mirrors aspires to be a living room for New York's new wave *beau monde*. The main floor features avant-garde seating areas, a circular bar, fish tanks, living art, horn-shaped Daum crystal wall fixtures and vases, and The Royalton Grill, a trendy installation run by Jeffrey Choderow of the China Grill.

Upstairs there are 205 rooms decorated with more sophistication and wit than you are likely to find in any other hotel in town. Every single item in these rooms — stainless-steel postcard stands, slate floors, the arched slate fireplaces (in 40 of the rooms) — has been custom-designed by Philippe Starck. The overall effect is something like the streamlined luxury of a 1930s first-class passenger train.

Singles cost between $190 and $285; doubles will run you between $215 and $310. Weekend rates are great, $140 single or double; $180 for a suite.

The **Salisbury Hotel,** 123 W. 57th St. (between Sixth and Seventh Avenues), New York, NY 10019 (tel. 212/223-0680), has a great location — practically across the street from Carnegie Hall and but two short blocks from Central Park. It's a sedate former apartment house, dating probably from the 1920s. The postage-stamp-size lobby is quiet and distinguished, decorated with handsome dark paneling, crystal chandeliers, and an ornate plaster ceiling. Although there's nothing deluxe about the Salisbury, it does have a decided air of refinement.

The 185 rooms are rather spacious and nicely furnished with attractive chenille spreads, pictures in gilded bamboo frames, and muted color schemes. Most rooms also have small serving pantries with miniature sinks and refrigerators. Room rates are very attractive: $98 to $108 for singles, $108 to $118 for doubles, $175 to $200 for one-bedroom suites, plus $15 per additional person in a roll-away bed. The Terrace Café adjoining the lobby serves breakfast, lunch, and dinner. There is an abundance of other restaurants in the immediate area.

The **Milford Plaza,** 270 W. 45th St. (between Times Square and Eighth Avenue), New York, NY 10036 (tel. 212/869-3600, or toll free 800/221-2690, 800/522-6449 in New York State), is a great buy located smack in the center of the Theater District. This looming brick skyscraper also dates from the building boom of the 1920s. Inside, however, the Milford is entirely new.

The lobby is an immense double-level contemporary space, paneled in snowy-white marble and hung with contemporary crystal chandeliers. It is abustle with traveling families, foreign tourists, and groups of every description. Besides shops selling souvenirs, airline tickets, haircuts, and sightseeing tours, there are several good restaurants. The Stage Door Canteen offers drinks and light snacks, the Celebrity Deli is for burgers and sandwiches, Mamma Leone's features more elaborate lunches and dinners, and a delicious-looking breakfast buffet is served every morning on the lobby mezzanine.

The Milford is the only hotel in this book where rooms on higher floors cost less than those below. This is because they're smaller; however, the views up there are sensational. None of the 1,300-odd rooms is very big, in fact, but all of them are immaculately clean, and decorated with textured wall coverings, big mirrors, spanking-new furniture, chrome reading lights above the beds, color television sets, thick carpets, and gleaming white-tiled bathrooms. The daily tariff is between $95 and $135 single, $110 and $150 double. West 45th Street adjacent to the hotel entrance contains a half dozen of New York's most famous legitimate theaters. Eighth Avenue around the corner, besides small shops and restaurants, contains a sprinkling of porno theaters. Security at the Milford is excellent, however, and the place does offer good value and a central location.

The **Hotel Wellington,** 871 Seventh Ave. (between 55th and 56th Streets), New York, NY 10019 (tel. 212/247-3900, or toll free 800/652-1212), has about 700 medium- to low-priced rooms distributed between two elderly buildings on

Seventh Avenue. The lobby has a big-city look, with double-height ceilings and broad carpeted expanses. It's well used, but comfortable enough.

The same could be said of the rooms, which are small, adequately furnished, and clean. What most recommends the Wellington is not its aesthetics, but its low (for Manhattan) rates and excellent Midtown location. Singles pay $86 to $99 nightly; double rates range from $96 to $109. The Alpine Tavern adjoins the lobby and features giant burgers and a college-bar atmosphere.

4. The Upper East Side

This is Manhattan's premier residential district. The side streets are lined with houses, not office buildings. And while the avenues have shops, they are often of a rarified nature ($2,000 dresses, $100,000 rugs, etc.). The East Side is beautiful, the more so in the sections closest to Central Park. The typical hotel in these parts has great style and atmosphere . . . and prices to match. If you want to sample real New York elegance, this is the part of town in which to stay.

Perhaps the hotel most associated with the stylish East Side is the **Carlyle,** Madison Avenue at 76th Street, New York, NY 10021 (tel. 212/744-1600). It's in the absolute epicenter of Madison Avenue's most fashionable shops and galleries, and its distinctive tower, actually best seen from the West Side, has been a neighborhood landmark since 1931.

The main entrance to the Carlyle is on 76th Street and it leads to a perfectly splendid little lobby with gorgeous moldings and marble pilasters. It's furnished with gilt rococo mirrors, marble-topped consoles, crystal chandeliers, thick rugs with floral medallions, enormous sprays of fresh flowers, and rare-looking paintings and tapestries. This was the New York White House during the Kennedy years, and the hotel continues to host presidents and pundits from around the world.

The rooms, once again, look less like hotel rooms than elaborate guest rooms in somebody's very fine private house. There are only 225 units, of which two-thirds are available to transients. The typical standard room is big, silent (due to double-glazed windows), and furnished with flowered curtains pulled back on swags, and has parquet floors, high molded ceilings, perhaps a little tented foyer with a marble-topped console. The walls might be decorated with framed prints from a Piranesi or an Audubon folio. The bathroom will have marble walls, various sizes of soap, stacks of towels (changed twice daily), a tray of amenities created by Givenchy, a scale, even a hairdryer.

The price for all this luxury is $225 to $280 daily for singles, $245 to $300 daily for doubles, more for one- and two-bedroom suites. It's worth noting that these rates are less than those charged by many a Midtown hotel in the same category, even though the Carlyle offers a good deal more class. Also on the main floor are: The Restaurant, serving breakfast, lunch, and dinner in dim, hushed, and swank surroundings; the famous Café Carlyle, a piano bar often presided over by the celebrated Bobby Short; and Bemelman's Bar, named after the artist responsible for its whimsical child-like murals.

The **Lowell,** 28 E. 63rd St. (between Madison and Park Avenues), New York, NY 10021 (tel. 212/838-1400), is in an enviable location just steps from Midtown business offices to the south and the elegant Madison Avenue shops and art galleries to the north, and yet it is surrounded by fine private mansions on a quiet residential block. There are only 68 units here, housed in a 1928 mid-rise with glazed rose and beige tiles decorating the first floor.

The lobby is a small tour de force of updated classicism. It has a marble floor, gilded pilasters, Empire furniture covered in sumptuous yellow satin, and a small but rather dramatic black marble reception desk. The impression is one of luxury, intimacy, and well, money Only 8 of the 68 units are what they call "studios," which means standard rooms. They are roomy, beautifully furnished with high-quality upholstered pieces, lacquered cabinets, framed 18th-century prints, and lush carpets. The bathrooms are marble-clad and ultramodern, with gold towel bars and tons of towels. The look is one of "no cost spared," and the level of taste is irreproachable.

Room rates for the studios are $240 single, $260 double; junior suites, which are overscale studios with separate seating areas, cost between $330 and $360; one-bedroom suites are priced from $420 to $450; bigger suites cost more. The one-bedroom suites have wonderful city views, immaculate full kitchens, real books on the bookshelves, luxuriant potted plants, oftentimes even a woodburning fireplace (there are 34 of these in the building). Note that the prices of the suites are the same as those charged for single park-view rooms in other hotels nearby.

The Lowell serves breakfast, tea, and dinner only in a creamy paneled restaurant called the Pembroke Room; guests can also sign for their meals at the Post House next door. Valet parking is available, for $30 nightly.

The **Mayfair Regent,** 610 Park Ave. (at 65th Street), New York, NY 10021 (tel. 212/288-0800), is about as swanky looking as New York hotels can get. It's a fine old limestone-and-brick building that looks much like one of the aristocratic apartment houses for which Park Avenue is famous.

A cluster of Rolls-Royces and stretch Caddies always seems to gather by the 65th Street entrance. The dignified lobby features a polychrome wood ceiling, marble floors, muted rugs in geometric patterns, Chinese bowls with sprays of hothouse flowers, upholstered sofas, and antique chairs. Both this room and the Mayfair Lounge beyond are suffused with a creamy rose glow. It's all terribly elegant, and very specifically in the Park Avenue vernacular.

The Mayfair is a hotel for affluent vacation and business travelers who naturally gravitate to traditional surroundings. The elevators are run by uniformed attendants. The halls upstairs are extremely wide. The guest rooms, of which there are only 200, are decorated in pale pinks and salmons and beiges. They're wonderfully big, as one would expect from an older hotel. The updated bathrooms have white marble counters and monogrammed towels; the closets have satin hangers; the bedrooms themselves contain comfortable painted furniture and usually little pantries too.

Room rates are the same for singles or doubles: from $230 to $250 for standard rooms, and $360 for "junior suites," which are oversize rooms with separate seating areas. Larger suites start at $370 and head off into the stratosphere. A famous gourmet restaurant called Le Cirque is located adjacent to the lobby; the aforementioned Mayfair Lounge also serves breakfast and tea; parking is the responsibility of your chauffeur.

Paris marries the East Side in the **Hotel Plaza Athénée** (that's "At-en-*ay*," if you please), 37 E. 64th St. (between Madison and Park Avenues), New York, NY 10021 (tel. 212/734-9100, or toll free 800-CALL-THF), with predictably glittery results. The building's been a distinguished hotel since 1927. But it's been the Plaza Athénée only since 1984, when it emerged dripping with marble and ormolu from a Cinderella transformation.

Inside the smallish lobby you'll see gleaming black and cream marble floors, bronze cupids clutching ormolu torchières, Louis XVI–style chairs upholstered in supple green leather, and a check-in area that looks like a small sitting room in a French palace. Everything in this hotel is bright, small, quiet, and shiny. Management's clearly delineated policy is to provide as much service as is humanly possible without at the same time being intrusive.

The 160 rooms are arranged along rather fabulous hallways carpeted with faux-marbre-patterned rugs, prints in gold-leaf frames, and Chinese porcelain ashtrays. All rooms have safes, tie bars, hairdryers, scales, lit mirrors, bathrobes, pastel color schemes, and marble-walled bathrooms. The building may be oldish, but everything inside it is brand spanking new. Stylish as it may be, there is no feeling of age or tradition in this place.

"Superior" rooms cost $235 to $265 single, $265 to $295 double; "deluxe" rooms are priced from $305 to $335 single and $345 to $375 double. Suites go up . . . and up. The difference between "superior" and "deluxe" has to do with size and location, not with the basic quality of the furnishings or amenities. La Régence serves meals in an atmosphere evocative of Versailles before the Revolution; a small bar replete with green leopard poufs and Brazilian mahogany provides alcoholic refreshment for thirsty plutocrats.

The **Surrey Hotel,** 20 E. 76th St. (between Fifth and Madison Avenues), New York, NY 10021 (tel. 212/288-3700), is another Manhattan East Suite Hotels property, this time located on a block of splendid East Side mansions. Indeed, it's hard to imagine a more elegant New York address. The building was a dignified prewar residential hotel whose small marble lobby is brightened with huge bouquets of flowers, Louis XVI–style chairs, a grandfather clock, and the obligatory crystal chandeliers. It's quiet, refined, and serene, another of those places that do not at all seem like hotels.

Upstairs, the rather opulent halls with their green and white paneled doors and thick rugs lead to a mere 117 units. Studios and suites are surprisingly big and beautifully furnished with upholstered sofas and chairs, thick new carpets, enormous beds, crystal lamps with pleated shades, and attractive framed prints on the walls. Virtually every unit has walk-in closets and a kitchenette. The bathrooms are solid old black-and-white-tiled affairs with full-length mirrors and tubs in which you can actually take a bath. Many a New Yorker would kill to live in an apartment like these.

Prices for these attractive accommodations have risen since the last edition; however, the Surrey does offer discounted rates for extended stays. Singles in studio units pay $165 to $185 a night. For doubles the rates rise to $175 to $205. One-bedroom suites are priced from $245 to $315; two-bedroom suites run from $275 to a top end of $475.

The **Hotel Wales,** 1295 Madison Avenue (between 92nd and 93rd Streets), New York, NY 10028 (tel. 212/876-6000), has been in continuous operation since 1901. This old painted brick building has a new owner and has just undergone a $5-million renovation. The lobby now sports painted marble walls, plush carpeting, elegant striped wallpaper, a grand marble fireplace, and a reception desk at the far end.

The entire building has been renovated with keen attention to aesthetic detail. There are ten floors of rooms, all of which have wonderfully restored woodwork, fine deep-pile carpeting, reproduction mahogany furniture, oil paintings, and lots of old-world charm.

Single or double rooms, as of this writing, are a very excellent buy at $95. Suites, which usually consist of two rooms and oftentimes a vintage fireplace, cost between $145 and $175. Sarabeth's Kitchen, under separate management, provides meals in cheerful rooms adjacent to the lobby.

5. The Upper West Side

The West Side is a trendy, newly gentrified quarter of renovated brownstone town houses and a new and growing rash of boutiques and cafés. It lies to the west of Central Park, just north of the Midtown business district. Transportation to the rest of town is quite convenient as there are lots of subway and bus lines. It's a very interesting and dynamic residential area, full of prosperous young professionals and older people who've lived here for a lifetime. For all the new glitz, West Side hotels are still quite modest. Although not luxurious, they offer a lot of value in a good location.

First choice in the area is the **Hotel Olcott,** 27 W. 72nd St. (between Central

Park West and Columbus Avenue), New York, NY 10023 (tel. 212/877-4200). The Olcott is part of a fairly massive palisade of buildings that lines this side of 72nd Street. At the foot of its brick-and-limestone façade is a modern anodized-aluminum awning sheltering automatic doors that slide apart automatically as you approach. Inside is a surprisingly elegant old lobby with gilded moldings on the ceiling, black marble pilasters, broad expanses of soft brick-colored carpeting, antique carved chairs along the walls, and a couple of fabulously ornate old brass elevators. Next to the small marble reception desk is a copy of a 1925 magazine ad that announced the Olcott's opening as a select residential hotel.

The Olcott has pleasant, modest "studios" (which are just standard rooms) with tiled baths, old moldings on the walls, motel modern furniture, and small cooking pantries; it has many more one-bedroom suites, also simply and pleasantly decorated and equipped with full kitchenettes. About 75% of the place is rented full time; the rest has a 1% vacancy rate—because of the prices: $75 a night for singles or doubles in a studio room, $105 for two in a suite that will sleep four (add $15 nightly per extra person). Weekly rates are even better: studios are $450 single and $500 double, and the suites are $625 plus $70 weekly for additional persons beyond two. Color TV and cable are included. No credit cards accepted.

Needless to say, rates like this make the Olcott an item in much demand. The sooner you make reservations the better. Single-night stays are discouraged, but it is possible to catch an unexpected vacancy at the last minute. No harm trying. Your fellow guests are visiting parents and children, United Nations auditors, Japanese and Israeli educators, lots of opera and ballet people (Lincoln Center is quite nearby), as well as Tiny Tim, who lives here with his mother. A great cheap restaurant, the Dallas Bar-B-Que, is located off the lobby.

Nine blocks to the north, and located directly across the street from the Museum of Natural History, is the **Excelsior Hotel,** 45 W. 81st St. (between Central Park West and Columbus Avenue), New York, NY 10024 (tel. 212/362-9200, or toll free 800/368-4575). The neighborhood hereabouts is sedate and residential, convenient to Central Park, Columbus Avenue shopping, and transportation to the rest of town. The Excelsior is some 60-odd years old, and features an attractive traditional lobby with wood paneling and an elaborate molded ceiling. About half the lobby has been partitioned off for a coffeeshop, popular with neighborhood people and serving breakfast, lunch, and dinner. Eight clocks beside the reception desk tell the time everywhere from Tokyo to Tel Aviv. A sign on the desk informs visitors that the hotel meets criteria established by the United States Travel Service for providing basic services in English, Spanish, French, and German.

This hotel is particularly popular with foreign tourists and airline personnel. The 175 transient rooms (125 others are occupied by permanent residents) are clean, carpeted wall to wall, equipped with television sets and kitchenettes, and have old-fashioned modernized bathrooms with colored towels. No frills or undue aesthetics here, just a good cheap deal on a clean and decent room. Prices are $75 a night, single or double. Suites with one separate bedroom cost $94, $101, or $108 nightly, depending on whether occupancy is by two to three, four, or five persons, respectively. There are two-bedroom suites as well, going up in price to a top end of $150 a night for six. Some of the higher-floor rooms facing 81st Street have skyline views, or pleasant prospects of the park surrounding the museum across the street. There is no difference in rates between rooms facing the street or facing the back.

When the **Hotel Empire,** Broadway at 63rd Street, New York, NY 10023 (tel. 212/265-7400), opened its 500 rooms in 1929, the West Side was a select neighborhood of private town houses. But the years that followed saw storms of neighborhood change. Today the neighborhood is fashionable again. And here's the Empire, still with us, and even undergoing a substantial renovation.

The old brick building now has modern smoked-glass windows, a location right across the street from the world-famous performing arts complex known as

Lincoln Center, and trendy restaurants and shops for neighbors. The lobby is quite sumptuous for a moderately priced hotel. They've kept all the good stuff—like marble walls and brass railings—and added subtle indirect lighting, low leather benches, rose-colored carpets, and brushed brass.

Some rooms are renovated and some aren't. The renovated models are smallish, but very nicely done with demurely textured wall coverings, new color televisions, leather armchairs, flowered curtains on swags, and nice shiny bathrooms. Unrenovated rooms are simpler, with motel modern furniture, curtains that don't quite meet the windowsills, and darker color schemes. But they're still clean and comfortable.

Singles cost $95 to $140, depending on whether the room is new or old; doubles are $110 to $155. Valet parking is available for $20 nightly. Adjacent to the lobby is O'Neal's Baloon, a popular neighborhood spot for luxury burgers.

---

6. Downtown

My first recommendation really is in the part of town New Yorkers call "downtown." The other two are in Murray Hill, a residential enclave in the East 30s, just to the south of Midtown.

Staying at the **Vista International New York,** 3 World Trade Center (the entrance is on the west side of the Trade Center complex, on West Street just above Liberty Street), New York, NY 10048 (tel. 212/938-9100), is a novel way to visit New York. This is because most New Yorkers, unless they work here, never even get to this part of town. Which is too bad, since downtown is the oldest and in many ways the most interesting part of Manhattan.

The Vista is a sleek brushed-aluminum and glass structure pressed against the knees of the stupendous World Trade Center towers. The view across West Street is no longer much of a vista, however, as the new World Financial Center now sits smack between the Vista and its former unobstructed view of the river. But there is a lot of exciting modern architecture to look at around here, as well as the fabled skyscraper Gothic canyons of the 1920s.

The Vista's lobby is large and hushed, very modern, and outfitted with dark paneling, thick rugs, and dramatic indirect lighting. It contains shops providing everything from ritzy curios to rental cars. The 829 rooms are operated by Hilton International, so quality is predictably high. Guest rooms are smallish, but have a handsome tailored look. There are thick rugs, blond modern furniture, brass lamps with pleated shades, big windows, bathrooms with marble sinktops, lots of light, and piles of towels. Some computer somewhere probably devised the muted color schemes, but no matter, since they're very restful and sophisticated.

Rates are $190 to $240 for a standard single, $215 to $265 for a standard double, the higher-priced rooms being those on the higher floors. As a practical matter, minimum-rate rooms are just as appealing. The 20th and 21st floors are titled the "Executive Floors." Here, as in many hotels these days, the rooms have a special lounge/reception area, a few more amenities, and an air of privilege. They cost $255 single, $280 double. A marvelous restaurant called the American Harvest is located off the second-floor lobby and draws people from all over town. There are also the Tall Ships Bar and the Vista Lounge, as well as a more informal restaurant called the Greenhouse. The Vista also has a beautiful enclosed rooftop swimming pool (kept at a constant 80 degrees), a quarter-mile indoor jogging track, a sauna, and a set of exercise machines.

Why do they call it **Morgans,** 237 Madison Ave. (between 37th and 38th Streets), New York, NY 10016 (tel. 212/686-0300, or toll free 800/344-3408)? Because J. P. Morgan himself once lived down the block in a big brownstone still standing at 37th and Madison. Morgans has a good pseudo-Midtown location, and a trendy postmodern look that's very '80s. Everything in this place seems to be black, white, or gray, from the diamond-patterned rug in the coolly elegant little lobby (where flower arrangements consist of three twigs and two blossoms) to the fashionable uniforms on the doormen. These fellows must be actors, they're so good-looking. But then again, so is everybody else. The entire staff is friendly, intelligent, and apparently overqualified.

Morgans' owners are none other than Steve Rubell and Ian Schrager, of Studio 54 fame. They've created an upmarket little hotel here aimed at younger businesspeople, young jet-setters, and young Hollywood types. They're luring them here with extra service (fresh flowers in the bathrooms, Christmas cards to everyone who's ever registered), and rooms with highly sophisticated decor.

The 112 transient units are a bit small, but so Milano-deluxe it hardly matters. They have gray-green carpets, built-in furniture, AM/FM stereo cassettes, VCRs, color televisions, unusual gray-stained bird's-eye maple wall panels, individual refrigerators, handy reading lights, and telephones in the bathrooms. Those bathrooms have an intriguing 1930s retro look that's the result of black and white tiles, stainless-steel sinks with a slightly surgical air, flowers, and glass-doored showers. Everything is gray, gray, gray, and terribly fashionable. Some rooms are hi-tech fantasies, like the cathedral-ceilinged room with the bathtub next to the bed, or the penthouse duplex with its spiral staircase and huge potted plants.

Singles cost $160 to $195; doubles are $175 to $215; weekend rates are $130, single or double; one-bedroom suites cost $270 to $380, or a flat $170 nightly on weekends. There's a bar in the basement, and a two-level restaurant with the dining room below and a grill on the mezzanine. Bring money and be chic.

Also in Murray Hill is the **Shelburne Murray Hill,** 303 Lexington Ave. (between 37th and 38th Streets), New York, NY 10016 (tel. 212/689-5200). This is another of the Manhattan East Suite Hotels, several of which have been recommended already. The Shelburne is a very nice small hotel with a dignified façade, located close to Midtown. It has an awning on Lexington Avenue and little trees in white pots. Inside is a smallish but elegant lobby, very much in the established style of the owners. It has French-looking furniture sprinkled with a few genuine antiques, opulent multi-arm wall sconces with pleated shades, marble floors, handsome patterned wallpaper, and crystal chandeliers.

There are 248 units available, either nightly or for extended periods. The typical room is very nicely decorated with textured wall coverings, matching spreads and curtains, good-quality traditional-style wood furniture, Chinese lamps, gold-framed prints, new bathrooms, and fully equipped modern kitchenettes. Everything is immaculately clean and of a very high quality. Some of the rooms look like luxurious living rooms with queen-size beds in the corner.

These accomodations are an excellent value too. Singles cost $120 to $160; doubles run $140 to $180; junior suites (oversize rooms with seating areas) cost between $140 and $180; one-bedroom suites are $160 to $180; two-bedroom suites go for $280 to $320 nightly. Billy Budd's Chop House, located off the lobby and run by separate management, serves reasonably priced meals in a congenial bar atmosphere.

---

7. Bed-and-Breakfast Choices

Another way to stay in the Big Apple is a bed-and-breakfast. An outfit called **Urban Ventures,** P.O. Box 426, New York, NY 10024 (tel. 212/594-5650), has been successfully lodging visitors in this way since 1979. Today they handle 700 apartments, and the prices are cheap.

Urban Ventures has two types of accommodations. The first is a spare bedroom in somebody's apartment, sometimes with a private bath but usually without. The host is on hand to give advice and make breakfast. The second type is a whole apart-ment, temporarily vacated by some out-of-town owner. You're on your own for breakfast, but there's no host to get in your hair.

For example, for $45 a night one individual can stay in a new building in the East 60s with a planted garden and a doorman. For $85 a night there's a two-bedroom apartment in an East Side doorman building where the room for rent comes with its own private bath. Or you might like a West Side brownstone with great period details and a $68 room for two, again with shared bath.

Sample apartments include a large Midtown studio in an elegant doorman building, priced at $120 a night double; or a two-bedroom/two-bath spread up on West End Avenue that will sleep four for $165 nightly.

Urban Ventures considers cleanliness, location, aesthetics, and the personality of the host before listing anything. Many applicants are turned down. Prospective guests are advised to write or phone as far in advance as possible. Urban Ventures gets very nice feedback from 99% of the people they place.

NEW YORK CITY RESTAURANTS

Let me spare you the typical guidebook gush about New York, the Fabulous Gastronomic Capital. Suffice it to say that it is. After all, a city with 17,000 eating places is by definition a city that caters to a lot of demanding eaters.

HOW THIS CHAPTER IS ORGANIZED

The recommendations that follow are divided into five separate sections.

The first three sections correspond approximately to the geographic areas in the hotel chapter. It seemed to me that after a busy day sightseeing you'd want to know first which restaurants are within easy walking distance of your hotel.

The fourth section contains recommendations in parts of town you're likely to be visiting.

The fifth section contains recommended special excursions to selected citadels of haute cuisine, plus a potpourri of places that for one reason or another are worth a special trip, including Chinatown.

Every section contains cuisines of all sorts, and is organized in *descending order of price*. With few exceptions the restaurants in this chapter have been around for 5, 10, sometimes even 20 or more years. There are no astonishing new discoveries here; rather, this is a list of New Yorkers' favorites, places with good track records and a high likelihood of being here when you come to visit.

Now then, let's get something to eat.

1. Midtown East and West (Including the Theater District)

Lello, 65 E. 54th St., between Park and Madison Avenues (tel. 212/751-1555), is the nickname of the owner of this very elegant little Midtown restaurant specializing in northern Italian cuisine. People come back again and again for pasta, veal, and fresh fish, beautifully served in an intimate little room with thick rugs and shaded chandeliers. Try the angel-hair primavera, or the veal boscaiola (prepared with marsala wine, wild mushrooms, and prosciutto). Delicious. Everything is à la carte: pastas range between $15 and $18; fish and meat dishes cost $20 and up per plate. Undeniably expensive, but the meals are memorable and the intimate ambience is unsurpassed. Lello is open for lunch Monday through Friday from noon to 3 p.m.; dinner is served Monday through Saturday from 5:30 until about 11 p.m.; closed Sunday. Jackets and reservations required.

The **Russian Tea Room,** 150 W. 57th St., between Sixth and Seventh Avenues (tel. 212/265-0947), is the place for shashlik, Stroganoff, caviar, and blinis. Located next door to Carnegie Hall in its own little town house, the RTR is a longtime favorite with theater types and showbiz celebrities. Beyond its etched-glass doors is a dazzling interior done up in crimson red and highlighted with gleaming brass. Lunch runs the gamut from red caviar omelets to chicken Kiev. Figure $35 per person, plus drinks. Dinner might be something like half a roast duckling with cherry sauce, eggplant à la Russe, or the special fish of the day. Typically, dinner runs $32 to $47 per person, plus drinks, tip, and tax. The RTR is bright and lively, and open every day of the year from about 11:30 a.m. to 11:30 p.m.

Christ Cella, 160 E. 46th St., between Lexington and Third Avenues (tel. 212/697-2479), is the place for a "power" lunch. Or dinner, for that matter. It's a steakhouse primarily, but serves fresh fish and a range of other items too. Since 1926 it has been a favorite of New York's titans of business and industry. The atmosphere is purposely unglitzy: acoustical-tile ceilings, a bare wood floor, bright lights, and simple tables with crisp white cloths. The effect is that of a downtown restaurant in some small midwestern city. A white-aproned waiter will recite the menu at your table. Dinner might be filet mignon, London broil, sirloin steak, pepper steak, broiled lobster, bluefish, or red snapper. The menu is extensive and everything is à la carte. Most entrees cost between $18 and $30. A full dinner with appetizer, salad, dessert, and a drink or two can easily run $55 to $70. However, you may never again taste a steak this good. Open Monday through Friday from noon to 10:30 p.m., on Saturday from 5 to 10:45 p.m.; closed Sunday and holidays. Reservations required. By the way, "Christ Cella" is pronounced "Kris-*sell*-uh" and derives from the founder's name, Christopher Cella.

The **Palm,** 837 Second Ave., between 44th and 45th Streets (tel. 212/687-2953), is a lot like Christ Cella in that it's a luxury-price steakhouse with a purposely funky decor. Places like this raise unpretentiousness to the level of fine art. The Palm is located in an old tenement building and comes complete with sawdust on the floor, a scuffed little bar tucked away in the corner, and cartoon caricatures painted on the walls. People are loyal to the Palm like you wouldn't believe. Taste the food and you'll believe it. Steak, filet mignon, roast beef, lamb chops, etc., are the order of the day, with à la carte entrees priced at $24 or so per plate. Open Monday through Friday from noon to 11:30 p.m., on Saturday from 5 p.m.; closed Sunday. Reservations required.

Il Nido, 251 E. 53rd St., between Second and Third Avenues (tel. 212/753-8450), is in the basement of an undistinguished old brownstone. Inside, however, it's rather elegant with its stuccoed walls, stained timbering, and sprays of hothouse flowers. Il Nido specializes in northern Italian cuisine, especially veal. The à la carte menu is very extensive and features all kinds of pasta, fish, and meat, with typical entrees priced from $20 and up. There are immaculate white cloths on the tables, comfortable chairs and banquettes, soft lighting, and an air of sophisticated rusticity. Very much a New York favorite. Open Monday through Saturday from noon to 2:30 p.m. for lunch, and 5:30 to 10:30 p.m. for dinner; closed Sunday. Reservations required.

Smith & Wollensky, corner of Third Avenue and 49th Street (tel. 212/753-1530), is a big (seating capacity: 400), old-fashioned green and white wooden

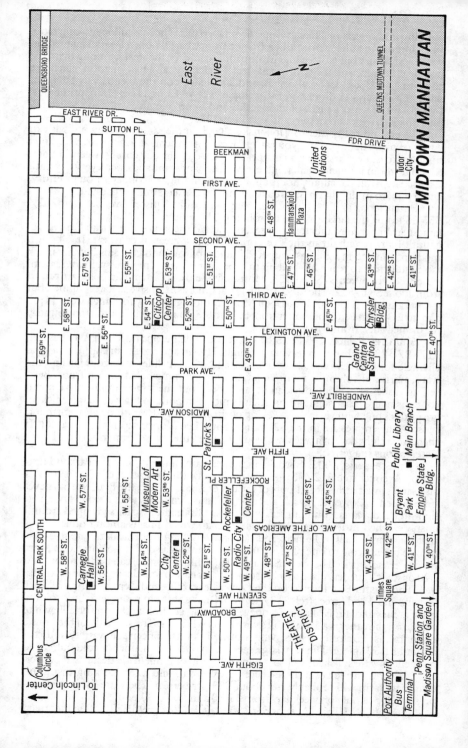

MIDTOWN MANHATTAN

East River

QUEENSBORO BRIDGE

EAST RIVER DR.

SUTTON PL.

BEEKMAN

FDR DRIVE

United Nations

QUEENS MIDTOWN TUNNEL

Tudor City

FIRST AVE.

E. 48TH ST.

Hammarskjold Plaza

SECOND AVE.

E. 57TH ST.

E. 55TH ST.

E. 53RD ST.

E. 51ST ST.

E. 47TH ST.

E. 46TH ST.

E. 43RD ST.

E. 42ND ST.

E. 41ST ST.

THIRD AVE.

E. 58TH ST.

E. 56TH ST.

E. 54TH ST.

Citicorp Center

E. 52ND ST.

E. 50TH ST.

E. 45TH ST.

Chrysler Bldg.

E. 40TH ST.

LEXINGTON AVE.

E. 59TH ST.

E. 49TH ST.

Grand Central Station

PARK AVE.

VANDERBILT AVE.

MADISON AVE.

St. Patrick's

Public Library Main Branch

FIFTH AVE.

Museum of Modern Art

ROCKEFELLER PL.

Rockefeller Center

Bryant Park

Empire State Bldg.

CENTRAL PARK SOUTH

W. 57TH ST.

W. 55TH ST.

W. 53RD ST.

W. 46TH ST.

W. 45TH ST.

AVE. OF THE AMERICAS

W. 58TH ST.

Carnegie Hall

W. 56TH ST.

W. 54TH ST.

City Center

W. 52ND ST.

Radio City

W. 50TH ST.

W. 48TH ST.

W. 47TH ST.

W. 43RD ST.

W. 42ND ST.

W. 41ST ST.

W. 40TH ST.

SEVENTH AVE.

W. 51ST ST.

W. 49TH ST.

Times Square

BROADWAY

THEATER DISTRICT

EIGHTH AVE.

Columbus Circle

To Lincoln Center

Port Authority Bus Terminal

Penn Station and Madison Square Garden

N

building in the heart of Third Avenue skyscraperland. The masculine-looking renovated interior includes a marble bar, framed prints, bare wooden floors, stamped-tin walls, and an airy big-city feeling. Most people come for the steaks, among them the double chateaubriand for two, sliced steak Wollensky, and filet mignon. There are also things like scallops, veal dishes, and lamb chops on the menu, plus the usual satisfying desserts. A dinner of, for example, S & W Famous Pea Soup, prime ribs, two glasses of wine, a piece of cheesecake, and a cup of coffee will run about $50, plus tip. Skip wine and dessert and you'll save $10.

Go around the corner to **Wollensky's Grill**, in the same building but with an entrance on 49th Street, and you can enjoy a lighter menu at lesser cost. Sliced filet mignon, roast beef hash, lemon pepper chicken, etc., usually cost between $14 and $19. The room is much smaller, but every bit as handsome and open every day until 2 a.m. The main restaurant hours are noon to midnight Monday through Friday, and 5 p.m. to midnight on Saturday and Sunday. Reservations suggested.

Hatsuhana, 17 E. 48th St., between Fifth and Madison Avenues (tel. 212/355-3345), is the largest single customer of the Fulton Fish Market, contains the largest sushi bar in Manhattan (48 seats), and has the largest American Express account of any restaurant in the five boros! This is a great place to eat. It is bright, modern, paneled in light oak, carpeted in deep purple, and contains butcher-block tables sufficient to seat 128. Full dinners of the teriyaki, tempura, sushi, or sashimi variety cost between $18 and $25. Most individual à la carte menu items are priced from about $8 to $17. The lunch menu is not quite as extensive as that at dinner, but it costs a couple of dollars less. Open Monday through Friday for lunch from 11:45 a.m. to 2:30 p.m., and for dinner from 5:30 to 9:30 p.m. Open Saturday and Sunday for dinner only, from 5 to 9:30 p.m.

Shun Lee Palace, 155 E. 55th St., between Lexington and Third Avenues (tel. 212/371-8844), has been serving top-flight Hunan and Szechuan cuisine to a loyal clientele for over 15 years. It's very sleek and glossy inside, with gold fans on the walls, mirrored columns, multiple levels, and a chrome-railed bar up front. Best-selling dishes are Peking duck and orange beef, but the large and inventive menu contains many other suggestions, such as moo shu pork, Wang's amazing chicken, crispy duckling with vegetables, Peking pork omelet, etc. Everything is à la carte and most of the entrees are in the $20 range. Shun Lee is open seven days a week ("If there were eight days in a week, we would be open then too") from noon to 11 p.m. Reservations suggested.

The **Brasserie,** 100 E. 53rd St., in the Seagram Building between Park and Lexington Avenues (tel. 212/751-4840), resonates with the aesthetics of the 1960s. It also serves great meals at all hours of the day or night. In fact, the Brasserie has never once closed in 26 years. It's a high-ceilinged, modern room with a stone floor, soft lighting, and a large counter area, plus flocks of rattan café chairs grouped around crisply clothed little tables. Cuisine is Alsatian, which means among other things that the menu's half in French. You can have anything from steak tartare to salade niçoise to fettucine to one of "les hamburgers de la maison" to an entrecôte. Most menu items are priced between $10 and $15, while a full meal can be had for around $20 or so. It's an ideal place to meet someone, or have an omelet at 3 in the morning.

The **Oyster Bar,** located on the Lower Level of Grand Central Terminal, Park Avenue and 42nd Street (tel. 212/490-6650), is a vast old room with buff-colored brick arches and a tiled floor. To one side is a big counter with comfortable white chairs; on the other is a sea of tables with checked cloths. The specialty of the house, of course, is ultrafresh oysters, which come in every conceivable variety and cost around $1.50 apiece. The very large menu also offers all manner of cold buffet plates, delicious fresh fish, as well as a wide selection of homemade desserts. The average à la carte entree costs somewhere between $18 and $25, meaning that a full dinner with tip will probably run about $35 per person. The wine list is quite impressive. Open only on weekdays from 11:30 a.m. to 10:30 p.m.

Clarke's, 915 Third Ave., at 55th Street (tel. 212/759-1650), often incorrectly called "P. J. Clarke's," is an original Third Avenue Irish saloon that has miraculously survived in near-original condition. There they are, the old tiles and the sawdust on the floor, the ornate Victorian bar stained almost black with time and tobacco smoke, the beveled mirrors, the stained glass, and the ebullient atmosphere. The big carved bar is up front, with a few tables beyond it for the burgers and fries listed on a blackboard menu. In the back is a large dim dining room with the blue-checked cloths, yellow shaded lamps, walls full of Victorian framed stuff, and sometimes live music. Clarke's is the place for drinks and burgers, and occasionally chicken, spaghetti, or steak if the spirit moves you. It's loud, congenial, informal, packed after work, and cheap. Few menu items cost over $10. If you do run up a bill it's because you drank a lot. Open seven days a week from about noon until the wee hours.

The **Siam Inn,** 916 Eighth Ave., near 55th Street (tel. 212/489-5237), is an intimate little place with a bar up front and a cluster of little pink-clothed tables to the rear. Thai cuisine is notable for dishes like chicken Masamen, prepared with avocado, coconut milk, peanuts, spices, and chili; or pla lad prig, a deep-fried fish with a spicy Thai sauce; or salmon broiled with green curry, ground shrimp, coconut milk, chili, and spices. The food at Siam Inn is exotic, very reasonably priced, and absolutely delicious. People come regularly from all parts of town. The average dinner, exclusive of tip and tax, will run about $20 per person, and that includes a drink. Lunch with a drink will probably cost around $10. Open seven days a week for dinner, from 5 to about 11:30 p.m.; lunch is served only on weekdays, from noon to 3 p.m.

The **Hard Rock Café,** 221 W. 57th St., between Seventh Avenue and Broadway (tel. 212/459-9320), is a clone of the London establishment of the same name. The rear end of a 1960 Cadillac is embedded in the building wall over the shiny brass doors, its backup lights aglitter. But if the car's in reverse, the café is not. They line up on the sidewalk to get inside here. Not to dance either, but simply to enjoy burgers, ribs, and sandwiches to the accompaniment of taped rock and roll in an atmosphere that really is fun. The room is huge and consists of various levels decorated, well, with just about any old thing. Religious statues stand cheek by jowl with neon signs proclaiming "Victims Wanted." An immense black horseshoe hangs on a wall decorated with every whatnot you can imagine. There's an $18 steak, but the menu emphasis is on things like the "pig" sandwich (that's smoked pork), barbecued chicken, chiliburgers, "country club" chicken salad, ribs, etc., none of which cost over $10. All manner of soda-fountain desserts and sundaes are available as well. They have the same menu at both lunch and dinner, and meals are served between 11:30 a.m. and 2 a.m. daily. Handsome bar personnel behind an immense curvaceous bar pour drinks for a youthful clientele until 4 a.m.

Now for a few delis, starting with the **New York Delicatessen,** 104 W. 57th St., between Sixth and Seventh Avenues (tel. 212/541-8320). The vintage building looks like an enormous jukebox with windows full of hanging salamis. Behind the bowed glass walls overlooking 57th Street is a huge multilevel room dominated by a gilded statue of a girl who holds aloft a globe of light. Judging from her figure she hasn't been eating at the New York Deli, where stupendous portions are the order of the day. Salad platters, overstuffed sandwiches, half-pound burgers, omelets, hot open sandwiches, blintzes, etc., all run in the neighborhood of $6 to $9. Full meals like chicken-in-the-pot, pastrami or corned beef platters, the "top of the line fish platter," etc., are usually between $14 and $16. Open 24 hours a day, every day.

The **Carnegie Deli,** 854 Seventh Ave., between 54th and 55th Streets (tel. 212/757-2245), has a flashing neon sign outside and more hanging salamis in the window. Up front they make the sandwiches, in the back the crowds sit, talking, laughing, and eating and eating and eating. The menu is one long gag of oxymorons: "Bacon Whoopee" (get it?) is a chicken salad club, "The Mouth That Roared" is a roast beef sandwich with sliced onion, etc. Actually, the food is of legendary quality and almost everything is priced between $9 and $15. Seems like a lot, but one sandwich can feed two people. Open "22 out of every 24 hours," seven days a week.

Sarge's Deli, 548 Third Ave., between 36th and 37th Streets (tel. 212/679-0442), is a neighborhood favorite that's slightly out of the way, but worth the trip. There's plenty of comfortable seating in two brightly lit rooms. Patrons are mostly individuals and families from the area, though many make longer trips to shop in the attached gourmet shop. Sarge's has nobly proportioned sandwiches of every imaginable type priced around $8 to $9. Generous full dinners like goulash, filet of sole, London broil, fried shrimp, etc., run from around $13 to $18. Often these are featured as "Complete Family Dinners," at which time they include salad, soup, entree, beverage, and even dessert. They even have frozen yogurt. Open 24 hours daily.

THREE IN THE THEATER DISTRICT

Restaurants all over the place serve pre- and post-theater suppers. But it's convenient to know a place that's only steps from the theater itself. The following three are personal favorites, heavy on atmosphere and value, and not even particularly expensive.

Café Un Deux Trois, 123 W. 44th St., between Sixth and Seventh Avenues (tel. 212/354-4148), serves hearty bistro fare to an eclectic crowd of business people and theater-goers. It's in a large old-fashioned room with quite a fantastical decor. The columns holding up the lofty ceiling have been voluptuously painted to resemble veined marble. Large murals of clouds surround flocks of white-clothed tables and comfortable red banquettes. The menu lists à la carte items like onion soup, country pâté, escargots, steak tartare, roast chicken, steak au poivre, lamb curry, omelets of choice, etc., all at reasonable prices. A typical lunch with appetizer, main course, and a glass of wine will run close to $25, plus tip and tax. If you skip the appetizer and just have an omelet, it'll be closer to $15. The dinner menu offers similar fare for slightly higher prices. Open seven days a week until 1 a.m.

Cabana Carioca, 123 W. 45th St., between Sixth Avenue and Broadway (tel. 212/581-8088), is a Brazilian seafood house with a big local following. It occupies the basement of a former brownstone, a long, low room with stucco walls, romantic lighting, a bar up front, and crisply clothed tables and hacienda chairs in the rear. The menu lists daily specials like broiled chicken "gaúcha" style, codfish "Carioca," Portuguese paella, Brazilian fish stew, etc., all priced between $10 and $15. Other daily entrees run the gamut from roast suckling pig to shrimp "Paulista," all priced in the same range. So popular was Cabana Carioca that the owners took over the second floor of the building. And so inadequate in the face of demand did that second floor prove that they then opened a nearly identical Cabana Carioca II, practically next door at 133 W. 45th St. The original is open for lunch and dinner seven days a week until 11 p.m.; Carioca II is closed Sunday and open for dinner only on Saturday.

Charlie's, 705 Eighth Ave., between 44th and 45th Streets (tel. 212/354-2911), has just moved to this new location after having been around the corner on 45th Street for almost 15 years. The new place, still in the middle of the Theater District, is virtually identical to the old. There's a blackboard menu outside, a long old-fashioned carved oak bar with mirrors, walls decorated with pictures of Broadway and movie stars, and an atmosphere that's lively and informal. The food includes things like chicken fingers, Chinese ribs, hamburgers, fresh pasta, and a fabulous chocolate cake. The staff is extremely genial and the place gets packed before the theater. Lunch or dinner will probably run in the vicinity of $18 to $22 a head, including one drink. Charlie's is open seven days a week until 1:30 a.m.

DON'T FORGET THE HOTEL RESTAURANTS

Many of the big Midtown hotels have luxury restaurants that are famous in their own right. Particularly worth remembering, if you're looking for a memorable and elegant Midtown dinner spot, are the **Edwardian Room** and the **Oak Room** at the Plaza, the **Café Pierre** at the Pierre, and the **Rose Room** at the Algonquin Hotel. Refer to the hotels in the Grand Army Plaza–Fifth Avenue area (in Chapter II) for telephone numbers and addresses.

2. The Upper East Side

Le Veau d'Or, 129 E. 60th St., between Lexington and Park Avenues, practically opposite Bloomingdale's (tel. 212/838-8133), has been in business for over 40 years. It's a small, softly lit room whose polished wood walls are decorated with photos of the Paris meat market and posters of French châteaux. A little padded bar stands just inside the door, while white-clothed tables extend to a mirrored wall in the back. It's all very tidy and Gallic, and the food is fabulous. Lunch might be chicken in tarragon sauce, steamed mussels in white wine, veal kidneys with mustard sauce, or an omelet with herbs, priced from about $18 to $20. For dinner you might try roast duckling with cherry sauce and wild rice, tripe in the style of Caen, veal medallions in a cream-and-mushroom sauce, or perhaps grilled lamb chops with watercress, priced variously from $25 to $30. The menu also lists all manner of traditional French appetizers and desserts. Open from noon to 2:30 p.m. for lunch, from 6 to 10:15 p.m. for dinner; closed Sunday. Reservations suggested.

Auntie Yuan, 1191 First Ave., between 64th and 65th Streets (tel. 212/744-4040), must be the most stylish-looking Chinese restaurant in New York. A tuxedo-clad captain greets you at a special desk, then conducts you to one of the immaculately white-clothed tables distributed around a striking black-walled room. Decorations are limited to framed calligraphy and dramatically spotlighted arrangements of fresh flowers. Most popular items on the menu are Peking duck, salmon steamed with black beans, crisped orange beef, and the homemade dumpling appetizers. Most dishes cost between $18 and $22; soups and appetizers run about $4 to $9. A special complete "tasting dinner" has a little bit of everything and costs about $45. Not cheap, but superbly good. Open seven days a week from noon to midnight (except Thanksgiving, when they close for lunch). Reservations suggested.

Il Monello, 1460 Second Ave., between 76th and 77th Streets (tel. 212/535-9310), has been serving satisfying northern Italian cuisine at this location for 11 years. Its low-ceilinged interior is plush, handsomely decorated with gilt-framed oils, thick carpets, padded booths, a flocked ceiling, and an almost palpable hush ideal for intimate conversations and private business deals. Lunch might be spaghetti alla bolognese, broiled striped bass, grilled veal steak, veal scaloppine sauteed with wine and lemon, or boneless chicken in garlic and wine. Luncheon entrees run from $14 to $27. The à la carte dinner menu is more extensive and features specialties like fettuccine Il Monello, crostacei (shellfish) marinara, valdostano (a veal chop stuffed with prosciutto and cheese), and breast of chicken marsala. The typical dinner entree costs between $18 and $32. Salads and appetizers cost another $10 to $14. Open from noon to 3 p.m. for lunch and 5 p.m. to midnight for dinner; closed Sunday. Reservations required.

Petaluma, 1356 First Ave., corner of 73rd Street (tel. 212/772-8800), is a dramatic, ultracontemporary establishment that gets its name from the owners' California hometown. The floors are natural wood, the ceiling is blue, and there are potted cacti and architectural-looking columns painted shiny gray and brick red. Up front is an inviting bar, and in the rear is the open kitchen, mesquite coals aglow on the grill. Up to 244 persons can dine on various levels to the strains of piped-in classical music. À la carte dinner entrees include things like butterflied baby chicken with new potatoes, Louisiana crab cakes, fried calamari, black-bean chili, wok-fried vegetables, even a hamburger, all priced at a very moderate $7 to $15. There are additional long lists of inventive appetizers and side dishes, as well as a very extensive and reasonably priced wine list. Prices at lunch are one or two dollars cheaper. Open seven days a week from 11:30 a.m. to 3 p.m. for lunch, and 5 p.m. to midnight for dinner. Reservations suggested.

Mezzaluna, 1295 Third Ave., between 67th and 68th Streets (tel. 212/535-9600), is named after a kind of knife used in Florentine and northern Italian cuisine. This engaging and informal little place has pink marble tables, rock-and-roll music, black folding chairs, walls covered completely with pictures, and an exuberant international clientele. They come for taglioline (a kind of square pasta) with shrimp and radicchio, pizza Mezzaluna (with four different toppings), and carpaccio (paper-thin slices of beef topped with things like avocado and heart of palm or parmesan cheese). Best desserts in the house are a creamy cheese concoction called tirame su (literally "keep me up") and the tricolore tropicale, which is papaya, pineapple, and kiwi with zabaglione. A typical complete meal will run somewhere between $18 and $22 per person. Open seven days a week: for lunch from noon to 3 p.m. and dinner from 6 p.m. to 1 a.m.

J.G. Melon, 1291 Third Ave., at 74th Street (tel. 212/744-0585), is an old-fashioned Irish bar with a veneer of East Side chic. It's full of dark woodwork, the obligatory carved Victorian bar, lots of little tables covered with blue-checked table-cloths, a jukebox with rock and roll, walls covered with framed pictures of melons, and plenty of neighborhood patrons who come for the convivial surroundings and cheap eats. The blackboard menu lists hamburgers, chili, club sandwiches, a chef's salad, a turkey sandwich, and a few more filling items for prices mostly in the $5 to $10 range. Great atmosphere; open daily from about 11:30 in the morning till 4 a.m.

Ray's Pizza of East 76th, 1330 Third Ave., at 76th Street (tel. 212/988-3337), is one of the numerous Ray's around town. It's a typical corner pizza joint where you can watch 'em bake it, then take it with you to a Formica table and eat it. Ray's pizza is justifiably famous. Slices cost about $2 or so, depending on what's on them. Various full pizzas, from cheese to health to the "monster," cost between $10 and $20. Open daily from about 10:30 a.m. until 3 a.m.

Three restaurants bear the name **First Wok,** and they're located at 1384 First Ave., at 74th Street (tel. 212/772-2435); 1374 Third Ave., at 78th Street (tel. 212/861-2600); and 1570 Third Ave., at 88th Street (tel. 212/410-7747). Each serves the same Hunan-Szechuan cuisine, has the same menus, and even the same tables and chairs. These places are great for cheap lunches and dinners or take-out food. Crispy whole fish, house beef in special sauce, seafood delight, General Tso's chicken, moo shu pork, baby shrimp with black-bean sauce, and ten-ingredients pan-fried noodles are but a few items chosen from an extremely extensive menu. Almost nothing costs over $8, and most dishes cost much less. The weekday luncheon special includes rice, tea, and any dish you want from a list of 17 alternatives, for about $5. All three locations are open seven days a week from noon to 11 p.m.

BUDGET HINT FOR EAST SIDE HOTEL GUESTS AND SIGHTSEERS

First, Second, and Third Avenues are literally lined with restaurants in the 70s and 80s. Not all are distinctive, but you can always find something reasonable. In the more rarified neighborhoods closer to Central Park it's very tough to find a simple sandwich or a quick bite. There is, however, a cluster of modest coffeeshops near the Whitney Museum on Madison Avenue between about 74th and 76th Streets. They are clean, have low (for the area) prices, and are good to know about.

3. The Upper West Side

Tavern on the Green, inside Central Park, adjacent to the intersection of Central Park West and 67th Street (tel. 212/873-3200), is a local institution as popular with New Yorkers as it is with tourists. Built in the 19th century as a sheepfold, it's currently decorated with ankle-deep carpets, acres of gleaming brass, and more chandeliers than are contained in most medium-size cities. The restaurant is big and has a complex plan. The Chestnut Room has massive green plush chairs, a beamed ceiling, and huge chandeliers; the Park Room has a 52-foot mural depicting Central Park at the turn of the century; the Crystal Room is surrounded with walls of glass, contains more chandeliers than a maharaja's palace, and is the room where everyone wants to sit. Indeed, sitting in the dazzle of the Crystal Room and gazing at the trees outside, their limbs lined with tens of thousands of tiny lights, is an experience not soon forgotten. The extensive à la carte menu is the same wherever you sit. At lunch it features things like broiled halibut steak with five greens, smoked chicken crêpes with mushrooms, veal blanquette, and many other dishes, mostly priced between $10 and $20. You can always get a hamburger or the Tavern's Classic Club Sandwich for about $10. Many of the same items appear on the dinner menu, priced $3 or $4 higher. A huge and varied à la carte brunch is served on Sunday. Open daily for lunch from 11:30 a.m. to 4 p.m. and for dinner from 5:30 p.m. to 1 a.m. Reservations are a must.

What could be more romantic than dinner (or lunch) at the **Café des Artistes,** 1 W. 67th St., off Central Park West (tel. 212/877-3500)? This intimate Edwardian-era room was muraled in 1933 by the famous Howard Chandler Christy. Today his rosy naked nymphs and satyrs are as much a draw as owner George Lang's continental cuisine. One enters through the paneled and marbled lobby of the residential Hotel des Artistes. Inside the café are deep-green rugs, small booths and tables covered with pristine white cloths, and everywhere those appealing images of gilded youth cavorting with its clothes off. The luncheon menu includes a wide selection of à la carte appetizers and entrees like sliced fresh peppered duck liver, snails sautéed with onions, avocado stuffed with curried mussels, swordfish with mustard sauce, and fabulous desserts. Main courses at lunch cost between about $15 and $23. Dinner might be salmon with lobster and rosemary sauce, green pepper steak, pot-au-feu, duck with raisins in pear brandy, or any number of other things, priced mostly between $20 and $25 per entree. The house also serves a prix-fixe lunch and dinner, priced as of this writing at about $20 and $30, respectively. Lunch is served Monday through Saturday from noon to 3 p.m.; brunch is served on Sunday from 10 a.m. to 4 p.m.; dinner hours are 5:30 p.m. to 12:30 a.m. Monday through Saturday and from 5 to 11 p.m. on Sunday.

Fiorello, 1900 Broadway, between 63rd and 64th Streets (tel. 212/595-5330), serves terrific Italian trattoria fare in updated art nouveau surroundings directly opposite Lincoln Center. The place has just been redone and now sports a profusion of etched-glass partitions, wood panels, and red leather booths. In the summer the sidewalk café is great for people-watching over cappuccino or drinks. Any time of year this is a good choice for "visionary versions of the plebeian pizza" as they call it, all manner of pastas, wonderful cold salads, and Italian main courses like veal piccata and chicken parmigiana. À la carte luncheon entrees usually cost between $10 and $12. At dinnertime you might try the special fish of the day, or perhaps "vitello, vitello, vitello," which is three types of veal on one plate, or the cold chicken salad milanese. Specials change every day and dinner entrees are priced from around $10 for pasta up to $20 or so for one of the meat dishes. Open from noon to midnight, seven days a week (Sunday nights they close a little early).

La Mirabelle, 333 W. 86th St., between West End Avenue and Riverside Drive (tel. 212/496-0458), is a real neighborhood find. Cuisine is classic French and reservations are a must. There are three small pink and white dining rooms with modern chairs and mirrors on the walls; everything is crisp and immaculate. Only dinner is served, between 6 and 10 p.m. nightly. It might consist of bay scallops Provençale, veal with a light mustard sauce, shell steak with green-peppercorn sauce, lamb chops with fresh herbs, etc. À la carte main courses range from $15 to $20. Closed Sunday.

Amsterdam's, 428 Amsterdam Ave., between 80th and 81st Streets (tel. 212/874-1377), is a former liquor store transformed by the soldiers of gentrification into the epitome of the *New* West Side restaurant. Or more correctly, "rôtisserie," which is to say that everything is cooked on open fires in an open kitchen located between the bar up front and the dining mezzanine in the rear. No burgers, omelets, or quiches around here. Rather, this is the place for smoked brook trout, gravlax with dill mustard sauce, half a roast chicken with green herb sauce, or a sliced sirloin sandwich. They go through 3,000 pounds of chicken a week. Go at peak dinner hour when the rôtisserie is spinning nonstop and the chicken is freshest. Lunch entrees are priced mostly from $5 to $10; at dinner they go up to about $10 to $16. Decor is High West Side: white-painted brick walls, burgundy tablecloths, black chairs, strip oak floors, a lofty ceiling, black and white tiles around the rôtisserie. There is rock and roll in the air at all hours. The place is packed with a good-looking younger crowd, so much so that lines form outside for weekend tables. Open seven days from noon to 2 a.m. No reservations accepted.

Dobson's, 341 Columbus Ave., between 76th and 77th Streets (tel. 212/362-0100), has the classic Columbus Avenue restaurant look. That means high ceilings, big plate-glass windows, a restored vintage bar, dimly lit dining rooms connected by natural brick arches, art deco light fixtures, huge potted plants, and wheat-colored tablecloths. Service couldn't be friendlier, and the food is tasty and reasonably priced. Lunches like eggs Benedict, a chef's salad, sliced steak platter, or a burger cost in the $6 to $12 range. Dinners like broiled bluefish, ginger chicken, and combination platters of shrimp, chicken, and steak are priced mostly from around $10 to $14. They have all sorts of salads and great desserts as well. It's been a neighborhood favorite for over ten years. Open seven days a week from 11:30 a.m. to 12:30 a.m., to 1:30 a.m. on Friday and Saturday.

Cherry Restaurant, 335 Columbus Avenue, between 75th and 76th Streets (tel. 212/874-3630), has been a neighborhood favorite for at least 20 years. It has a basic coffeeshop menu, one of those huge ones with everything from tuna fish sandwiches to seafood specials. They also have oriental specialties, favorite being tonkatsu (breaded pork chop) served with salad and white rice, for $7. Prices are very reasonable; plenty of sandwiches for $3 to $5. The place is clean, with a counter up front and a large dining room in back. The Cherry is open for breakfast, lunch, and dinner from 8 a.m. to 11:30 p.m. Closed Monday.

Perretti Italian Café (or just "Perretti's"), 270 Columbus Ave., between 72nd and 73rd Streets (tel. 212/362-3939), is located at the spiritual epicenter of the New West Side. It has red-checked tablecloths covered with paper sheets upon which the wine list is stamped by passing busboys, a (very) small counter (only four seats!), modern industrial hanging lamps, black fake tiles on the walls, and crowds of neighborhood families and singles who like the unpretentious style and good solid food. Meals include fresh pasta in every style from bolognese to primavera; frittati made of eggs, sausage, eggplant, peppers, onions, or any combination thereof; veal; lasagne; ziti; pizza; and so on. Almost everything costs between $8 and $12. Open from noon to midnight weekdays, to 1 a.m. on Friday and Saturday.

Los Panchos, 71 W. 71st St., between Central Park West and Columbus Avenue (tel. 212/874-7336), creates a south-of-the-border atmosphere by means of stuccoed walls, glittery sombreros on the walls around the bar, pierced metal lanterns, and piped-in mariachi music. It's a long, low room, occupying the ground floor of a former private brownstone. In the back is a perfectly delightful outdoor terrace filled with umbrella tables and strings of colored lights. For lunch the menu offers chiles rellenos, carne asada (sliced marinated steak), all manner of Mexican casseroles, as well as combination plates of burritos, tostados, tacos, and tamales. Luncheon items typically cost between $5 and $10. The dinner menu is not much more expensive, with a slightly larger selection of combinations and entrees. Open seven days a week from 11:30 a.m. to midnight.

Right next door is **Café La Fortuna,** 69 West 71st St., between Columbus Avenue and Central Park West (tel. 212/724-5846), a real Italian café/bakery that's been in the neighborhood for a long time. You walk down a few stairs, past the sign that says "Children welcome, no strollers please," into a long room that goes all the way to the back of the building where it opens onto an outdoor café. The oldtime decor includes green lace curtains, framed pictures of Italian opera singers, a photo tribute to John Lennon (who lived in the neighborhood), and a big display case full of wonderful desserts. There's a good selection of sweets like homemade cannoli, Sachertorte, strawberry shortcake, and tray after tray of biscotti—Italian cookies. At La Fortuna you can have a cup of cappuccino, or iced cappuccino, with Italian ice and a plate of biscotti for about $7. It's a great place to take a break from a day of shopping on the West Side. They're open daily from noon to 2 a.m. Closed Monday.

Dallas BBQ, 27 W. 72nd St., between Central Park West and Columbus Avenue (tel. 212/873-2004), used to be the catering hall of the recommended Hotel Olcott. It's a cavernous old room with a lush multilevel decor installed sometime in the 1970s. Although this is a budget restaurant, it abounds with amenities associated with much pricier establishments. There is, for example, a pianist in the evenings at a grand piano by the bar. There are dramatic modern tapestries on the walls, comfortable upholstered chairs, and free platters of cut vegetables at cocktail hour. This is the place for half a chicken with cornbread and french fries, a fresh-fruit entree with a mountain of frozen yogurt, hamburgers, ribs, or a loaf of onion rings. What does it matter if the menu is limited when a Texas size portion of ribs with all the fixin's costs $8.95? Open seven days a week from noon: Sunday through Thursday they close at midnight; on Friday and Saturday they stay open until 1 a.m.

La Sarten, 564 Amsterdam Ave., between 87th and 88th Street (tel. 212/787-6448), is a tiny restaurant with exposed brick walls, butcher-block tables, and authentic Spanish-style Caribbean food. Everything here is home-cooked by chef/owner Victor. Lunch is served Monday through Saturday, with three or four different specials for each day of the week. Wednesday, for example, might bring thick Dominican soup with tropical vegetables, or a sandwich Cubano. Lunch entrees are priced between $3 and $5. The dinner menu is more extensive and often offers spicy seafood specials like shrimp à la Sarten, simmered in special red sauce with peppers and onions ($11.95). Try the fried yellow plantains as a side dish ($1.75). La Sarten is family run and service can be leisurely, but the food is great. Dinner entrees are priced mostly between $9 and $15. Open for lunch and dinner from 11:30 a.m. to 11 p.m.; closed Sunday.

---

4. SoHo and the Village

Here now are a few recommendations in areas you're likely to be visiting during your stay.

SOHO

The name of this famous district of art galleries and boutiques is a contraction of "*So*uth of *Ho*uston." It's not a very big area, being bounded by Houston Street on the north and Canal Street on the south. The main drag is called West Broadway, and one of our walking tours will take you through it. Herewith, a few recommended restaurants for those in SoHo at mealtime.

New Deal, 152 Spring St., between West Broadway and Wooster Street (tel. 212/431-3663), offers artistic and inventive cooking in a stylish "retro" atmosphere. The room is narrow, moodily lit, and muraled with overscale black-and-white scenes of dancers, construction workers, fields being harvested, crates being off-loaded, etc. It's supposed to look like WPA art from the '30s (in fact, the place used to be called WPA). Lunch might be pasta primavera, fettuccine with fresh seafood, any of various omelets, or a pâté sandwich. Most menu items seem to cost between $8 and $14. À la carte entrees at dinner include salmon baked in a garlic crust, grilled tuna with a citrus soy sauce, chicken "New Deal," veal with wild mushrooms, rack of lamb with mustard and basil sauce, etc., and are priced mostly at $15 to $18. Open for lunch Monday through Saturday from 11 a.m. to 3:30 p.m.; dinner is served everyday from 5 p.m. to 9 p.m. There's a jazz pianist at the bar nightly.

The **Spring Street Bar and Restaurant,** 162 Spring St., at West Broadway (tel. 212/219-0157), is a sleek, modern place with lots of sharp angles, big windows, pale-pink walls, and single flowers in spotlighted vases. It consists of several medium-size rooms radiating from a glossy black bar by the front door. There's always a good luncheon special for around $10 or $12, things like veal scaloppine or breast of chicken with artichoke. Regular à la carte lunch entrees include an omelet of the day, broiled swordfish, sautéed calves' liver, club steak with fries, or a simple hamburger. Prices are mostly in the $7 to $12 range. There is similar fare at dinner, when the average entree price zeroes in at about $15 or so. Jazz and mellow rock on the box; open seven days a week from about noon to 4 a.m. (the kitchen closes at midnight).

The **Broome Street Bar and Restaurant,** 363 West Broadway, at Broome Street (tel. 212/925-2086), on the next block down from the Spring Street Bar, has more of an oldtime New York saloon atmosphere, seen through the eyes of fashionable SoHo. This is a good place for informal meals of sandwiches, burgers, and beers. Very possible to get out for under $10 a head. Open seven days a week from 11 a.m. to 1:30 a.m.

THE VILLAGE

Greenwich Village was a rural hamlet until it was engulfed by urban sprawl in the 1830s (there's nothing new about urban sprawl). What people today call the "West Village" contains the site of the original town. What people call "The Village," however, is usually meant to be the region around Washington Square, from 14th Street to Houston Street.

Presiding for the last 37 years over a Village street off Washington Square is the **Coach House,** 110 Waverly Pl., which would be 7th Street if it had a number, between Washington Square East and Sixth Avenue (tel. 212/777-0303). Once the carriage house for a nearby mansion, it's now a spacious, comfortable restaurant serving big and expensive American meals. The decor is airy, handsome, and traditional, with high ceilings, modernistic chandeliers, a collection of framed oil paintings on the walls, red leatherette chairs, big white-clothed tables, and a rear mezzanine reached by a flight of crimson-carpeted stairs. Only dinner is served and the menu focuses on just those things they do with superlative skill. House specialties like American chicken pie, brochette of beef and lamb, and a boneless sirloin cost from about $20 to $30. Additional à la carte entrees such as prime rib, baby lobster tails, roasted red snapper, poached striped bass, etc., cost from $30 or so all the way up to about $40. Appetizers like fresh oysters, prosciutto and melon, or baked clams will run another $5 to $12 apiece. People come from around the world to eat at this restaurant and reservations are a must. Open from 5:30 to 10:30 p.m. only; closed Monday, holidays, and the entire month of August.

John Clancy's, 181 W. 10th St., at Seventh Avenue (tel. 212/242-7350), is the famous seafood grill where mesquite cooking was introduced to New York. Mesquite, in case you haven't heard, is a desert shrub whose charcoal imparts a tangy and distinctive flavor to whatever's on the grill. Clancy's is on the first two floors of an old Village house. About 100 patrons can be accommodated within its sleek, gray-walled interior. The tables are covered with pink-and-white cloths, the lighting is dim, and fresh flowers seem to be everywhere. The menu contains grilled seafood such as sea scallops on a skewer, Dover sole, filet of striped bass, Norwegian salmon, etc., all prepared over mesquite coals and priced between about $18 and $28. Appetizers like oysters on the half shell, mushroom stuffed with crab, or smoked trout with horseradish will run another $7 to $9. As of this writing, dinner only is served, from 6 to 11:30 p.m. daily. Reservations required.

Il Mulino, 86 W. 3rd St., between Thompson and Sullivan Streets (tel. 212/

673-3783), is the classic little Village restaurant that people love to brag about finding. Rock singers, grandmothers, movie stars, sports personalities, and people from all over town beat a regular path to its discreet gray-and-white awning. Inside is a not-very-large dining room with a bar up front, a profusion of healthy potted plants, lush Muzak in the air, and a flock of white-clothed tables in the back. The à la carte menu is the same at lunch and dinner. It lists things like sautéed veal in cream and champagne, veal in lemon and butter, pastas from spaghettini to tortellini, morsels of chicken braised in wine and artichokes, breast of chicken in cream and Calvados, etc., all priced from around $15 to $30, with most entrees falling somewhere in the middle. This is the place for a rich, classic Italian meal where calories don't count. Open daily except Sunday and holidays from noon to 2:30 p.m. for lunch and 5 to 11:30 p.m. for dinner. Reservations required.

Cent' Anni, 50 Carmine St., between Bleecker and Bedford Streets (tel. 212/989-9494), is a Florentine trattoria described by management as "not fancy but good." The name is an Italian toast meaning "May you live for a hundred years!" The white walls are hung with art and lit by track lights, and there are crisp cloths on the tables. A spirited neighborhood crowd is sprinkled with tourists and uptowners. Lunch might be green and white fettuccine in a sauce of cream and smoked salmon, angel-hair pasta in herbs and butter, sautéed veal kidney, shrimp and scallops scampi, sautéed calves' liver, etc., chosen from a menu where typical à la carte entrees cost about $10 to $23. For dinner you might try a mixed grill (rabbit, lamb, sausage, and quail), veal chop sautéed in wine and sage, grilled porterhouse steak, or angel-hair pasta in a sauce of lobster meat and clams. Nighttime entrees will cost between about $13 and $25 per person. Open for lunch Monday through Friday from noon to about 2:30 p.m.; dinner is served seven days a week from about 5 to 11 or 11:30 p.m.

The **Corner Bistro**, 331 W. 4th St., at Jane Street just off Eighth Avenue (tel. 212/242-9502), is an old corner bar with a loud jukebox and lots of youthful (and not-so-youthful) West Village types on low budgets. It has a stamped-tin ceiling, brick walls, dark wooden booths, a big carved bar up front, a menu on the wall, and a postage-stamp-size kitchen that cranks out really tasty burgers, grilled cheese sandwiches, chicken, french fries, and the like for under $5 a plate. Very unpretentious, but at peak hours you won't be able to get a table. Open seven days a week from about noon to 4 a.m.

---

5. Special Excursions

Some restaurants, of course, are worth going to no matter where they're located. The following "Special Excursion" recommendations are divided into three groups.

First is "Haute Cuisine," consisting of world-famous citadels of cuisine-as-art. One could write an entire book about these, but for our purposes the field has been limited to four of the most representative.

A second group has been collected under the loose heading of "Atmospheric Cuisine." These establishments come in all price ranges and some, by virtue of style and atmosphere, offer dining experiences that might well constitute the high point of your vacation.

Last of all is Chinatown, where almost all the restaurants are good—and my recommendations in particular are terrific.

HAUTE CUISINE

The best restaurant in New York is **Lutèce**, 249 E. 50th St., between Second and Third Avenues (tel. 212/752-2225), which for all its grand and glorious reputation is the most welcoming, unsnobbish, delightful place imaginable. Lutèce has occupied its pair of connected East Side brownstones for 25 years. It's a warren of corridors and stairways connecting a diminutive downstairs bar with several dining rooms on two levels. The big garden room in the back has potted palms, lattice walls, an arched glass ceiling, and sprays of hothouse flowers. Upstairs are a pair of smaller rooms, with lofty ceilings, framed oils, hanging tapestries, small chandeliers, more dramatic sprays of flowers, and an air of intimate luxury. Cuisine is modern French, and very inventive. The prix-fixe lunch, which runs about $35 per person, might start out with a brioche aux trois poissons (pike, sole, and salmon in a brioche with a watercress sauce), move on to veal scallop Vosgienne (which is a sort of Cordon Bleu), and end with a frozen raspberry soufflé. Dinner is also prix-fixe and costs $58. The menu contains appetizers like a duckling mousse with juniper berries, and blanquette de pêcheur (a sort of seafood stew); main courses such as médaillons de veau aux morels (veal with morels), and a caramelized rack of lamb for two; and desserts like the heavenly gâteau chocolat à l'orange. Open for lunch Tuesday through Friday only from noon to 2 p.m.; dinner is served Monday through Saturday from 6 to 10 p.m.; closed every Sunday as well as the entire month of August. Reservations are required.

There are at least another half dozen "haute French" restaurants in New York, all of them with an air of "grand luxe" and a reputation for exquisite cuisine. But since I must choose among them, my choice will be **La Côte Basque,** 5 E. 55th St., between Fifth and Madison Avenues (tel. 212/688-6525). Classic French cuisine reigns within this spacious and famous room tricked up to look like a seaside inn. There are timbers on the ceiling, stucco on the walls, and "faux" windows opening onto "faux" perspectives of the French coast. Of course, it looks about as rustic as Marie Antoinette's "village" at Versailles. But charm is the order of the day here, as well as famous food. Lunch and dinner are both prix fixe, with courses chosen from an extensive menu. A sample lunch might start with pheasant en croûte or perhaps pea soup, move on to something like poached bass in butter and herbs or "cassoulet du Patron Toulousain," and end up with something from the dessert "chariot," perhaps mousse au chocolat with Grand Marnier. Dinner is basically more of the same: for example, you might start with lobster terrine, move on to an entree like roast rack of lamb, and end it all with something incredible from the "chariot." Lunch costs about $32 per person; at dinner the tab is closer to $60. Many menu items have separate prices in parentheses and choosing these adds substantially to the final bill. Open for lunch from noon to 2:30 p.m., for dinner from 6 to 10:30 p.m.; closed Sunday. Reservations required.

At **The Four Seasons,** 99 E. 52nd St., between Park and Lexington Avenues (tel. 212/754-9494), everything—the menus, the potted trees, the waiters' jackets, even the matches and the ashtrays— changes four times a year. The location is at the foot of the famous Seagram Building. When built in 1959 this was the epitome of ultramodern international-style swank. Today, over a quarter century later, both the building and the restaurant remain unchanged, a testament to the good parts of a now-unfashionable school of architecture. But besides shallow stairs and immense ceilings, shimmering gold-chain curtains and huge modern paintings, burnished bronze columns and travertine marble floors, there is also the matter of food. The same people eat here every day—and these people could eat anywhere they wanted. They are the captains of industry, the barons of communications, and a fair cross section drawn from the Social Register. The lunch menu contains appetizers from beluga caviar to game bird pâté; entrees like shrimp with mustard fruits, lemon sole with crayfish and dill, sirloin steak, veal scallop with ginger, or a trio of lamb chops; as well as desserts such as a macadamia and bourbon soufflé for two. Dinner offers the same broad range of choices at about the same prices. Expect to pay upward of $14 for an appetizer and $30 and up for most à la carte entrees. Vegetables are extra too, albeit exquisite. At both lunch and dinner you have the option of "spa cuisine" (entrees from $32 to $42), which consists of main courses with ultralow calorie counts. Above the bar in the Grill Room is an amazing hanging sculpture composed of thousands of slender rods of burnished bronze. In the Pool Room is a startlingly large and tranquil reflecting pond. Reservations are imperative; try to get the Pool Room. Open for lunch from noon to 2:30 p.m., for dinner from 5:30 to 11:30 p.m.; closed Sunday.

Barbetta, 321 W. 46th St., between Eighth and Ninth Avenues (tel. 212/246-9171), celebrated its 80th anniversary in 1986. It's located in a pair of old brownstones that look, on the inside, not unlike a small palace. From the street, one passes through a progression of intimate wood-paneled rooms filled with old paintings, needlepoint chairs, little chandeliers, and an air of Euorpean elegance. In the back is a fine large dining room with Venetian curtains on the arched windows, a splendid chandelier, old giltwood wall sconces, and French doors opening onto one of the most delicious formal outdoor dining patios in New York. The cuisine is northern Italian—Piedmontese. Lunch might be wild hare in civet, pheasant of the day (!), tagliarini verdi alla bolognese with wild Porcini mushrooms, broiled fresh sole, or veal chop in parsley sauce. Everything, of course, is à la carte. Most main lunch courses cost between $25 and $30. Dinner entrees are pretty much in the same price range, and include things like beef braised in red wine, bolliti misti piemontesi (a mixture of beef, chicken, and vegetables), or veal tonne (thin-sliced veal with tuna and caper sauce, a summertime special). Open for lunch from noon to 2 p.m., for dinner from 5 to 11:30 p.m.; closed Sunday. Reservations are required; and if you come in the summer, reserve a table in that garden.

ATMOSPHERIC CUISINE

A number of city skyscrapers have restaurants on top, and the most famous of them all is **Windows on the World,** 107th Floor, One World Trade Center (tel. 212/938-1111). Get ready for your ears to pop on the way up to this one. But once you're there, the view is truly awesome, especially looking south across the harbor and out into the Atlantic. The Statue of Liberty looks like a toy. To the north the towers of Manhattan appear to be intricate scale models wrought by a race of watchmakers run amok. The 107th floor has a number of separate eating areas, each with its own name and menu. Only dinner is served in the "Restaurant," whose cool champagne color scheme and multiple-level seating set the view off quite nicely. The room is big and hushed and golden, and offers several table d'hôte dinners priced from $32 to $36, as well as à la carte items like grilled scallops with white basil butter, roast veal tenderloin, sautéed fresh venison, salmon steak, filet mignon, and fricassee of lobster and crayfish, all priced between about $23 and $25. Appetizers like fresh salmon marinated in dill, pesto agnolotti in cream, or mussel bisque will add another $4 to $9 to the bill. The "Cellar in the Sky" features a $77 prix-fixe haute cuisine dinner for a maximum of 36 people. This room has no view; one supposes patrons are too busy with the food. The "Hors D'Oeuvrerie" is the best deal in the place. No reservations are needed, there's piano music and dancing every evening (cover is a mere $3 or so per person), and the menu consists of all manner of light appetizer-type fare at relatively low prices. Examples: deep-fried mozzarella, crab fritters, Korean short ribs of beef, all for about $5 to $8. The full Sunday brunch features things like cold barbecued chicken breast, baked seafood pot pie, and grilled baby chicken with ratatouille, mostly priced between $13 and $18. Immediately adjacent is the "City Lights Bar," which provides conversation-stopping views of bridges and Brooklyn from its mustard leather armchairs. Hours for the dinner-only Restaurant are 5 to 10 p.m. Monday through Saturday; the Hors D'Oeuvrerie and the City Lights Bar open at 3 p.m. and close at 1 a.m. (on weekends they open at noon). The bar is open seven days a week; on Sunday the Hors D'Oeuvrerie opens only for brunch. Got all that?

The **River Café,** 1 Water St., Brooklyn (tel. 718/522-5200), is situated on a barge moored practically underneath the Brooklyn Bridge. The view across the glittering surface of the East River toward the downtown skyline is something never to be forgotten. The lacy spans of the Brooklyn Bridge loom overhead, all manner of shipping from yachts to barges passes majestically back and forth, and the city from this angle looks like Oz. It's quite a wonderful place for either lunch or dinner. Cuisine here is "New American," which means things are lightly basted, "deep-frying" is a dirty term, and nothing is too heavy. Lunch might start with the American charcuterie (newly styled pâtés and terrines) or fresh duck foie gras with warm apple brioche, then move on to an entree like fruitwood-grilled pork tenderloin with apples or swordfish steak with grilled shrimp. Figure $20 to $30 per person for a luncheon appetizer and a main course. The prix-fixe $55 (at this writing) dinner might start with eggplant and pesto terrine or select oysters, move on to sautéed Maine lobster or pan-fried red snapper, and end up with a ginger pecan flan or perhaps a warm strudel with two cheeses. The smallish dining room, reached by a cute enclosed gangplank, contains a bar, a grand piano, pencil spotlights trained on dramatic flower arrangements, and a wall of windows overlooking the river. There are excellent views from every seat. Lunch is served Monday through Friday from noon to 2:30 p.m.; Saturday and Sunday brunch (basically the lunch menu with a few egg dishes) also runs from noon to 2:30 p.m. In the evening, dinner is served from 6:30 to 11 p.m. Sunday through Thursday and from 7 to 11:30 p.m. on Friday and Saturday. Management is a stickler about reservations, which they advise you to make two weeks in advance, and then reconfirm (on pain of cancellation) by 3 p.m. on the afternoon of your proposed visit. Last-minute reservations can sometimes be gotten, however, during the week. Parking is free, and most taxis know where the place is. For the trip back to your hotel, management will call you a cab.

Another good river-oriented excursion is a meal aboard one of five floating luxury restaurants operated by **World Yacht Enterprises,** Pier 62 at the foot of West 23rd Street (tel. 212/929-7090). A cruise on one of these boats is a pretty lively affair, since each sails with a live band and a clientele that likes to sing and dance. There is considerable drama in arriving at the pier, picking up your tickets, and boarding the boat. The menu offers a choice of several alternative appetizers, main courses, and desserts. For dinner, there's a fresh fish, chicken, and a filet of beef entree, each artistically prepared and served with considerable skill. With tax and service charge, dinner Friday and Saturday evenings will cost close to $65 per person, not including drinks. The Sunday brunch cruise will run about $40 per person, the lunch cruise about $30. The whole undertaking takes some three hours, during which you'll line up for appetizers, sit for course after course of food (except those times you're climbing up and down the sweeping staircases to the crowded dance floor), and oh yes, admire the view. No place for an intimate evening, but lots of fun for those in a celebrating mood. Lunch cruises board at 11 a.m. and depart at noon; Sunday through Thursday dinner cruises board at 6 p.m. and sail at 7 p.m.; Friday and Saturday dinner cruises board at 7 p.m. and sail at 8 p.m.; Sunday brunch cruises board at 11:30 a.m. and depart at 12:30 p.m. Reservations are required.

Jezebel, 630 Ninth Ave., at 45th Street (tel. 212/582-1045), serves high-class soul food in a lofty room filled with hanging beaded dresses, lace tablecloths, art deco chandeliers, potted palms, fringed lampshades, and an attractive urban crowd of people in the arts and theater. Only a small metal plaque marks the door, which is easy to miss. À la carte main courses, such as spicy honey chicken with yams, hot-and-spicy shrimp, hamhocks with rice and greens, and smothered chicken, cost mostly between $15 and $22. A bowl of Jezebel's cowpea soup or a piece of sweet-potato pie will add another $5 to $7 to the tab. The food is authentic and delicious. The atmosphere is a suave combination of down-hominess and big-city sophistication, very much an "only in New York" combination. The patroness is usually on hand. Open only for dinner from 5:30 p.m. to 12:30 a.m.; the bar stays open to 2 a.m.; closed Sunday. Reservations required.

Ozeki, 158 W. 23rd St., between Sixth and Seventh Avenues (tel. 212/620-9131), serves superlatively good and reasonably priced Japanese food in an atmosphere of Asian calm. The room is long and narrow, paneled in clean natural wood and highlighted with potted plants. Lunch might be shrimp tempura, sashimi, miso scallops, or oyako-don (chicken, vegetable, and egg with sauce and rice) for around $8 to $11. Combination dinners, allowing a choice of items like ginger pork, chicken teriyaki, or chicken tonkatsu, cost about $12.50. Noodle dishes and various other à la carte items like yakizakana (fish broiled in teriyaki sauce) or spiced salmon are priced from around $8 to $18. Open Monday through Friday from noon to 2:30 p.m. for lunch and from 5:30 to 10:30 p.m. for dinner. On Saturday and Sunday dinner only is served, from 5 to 10:30 p.m. Very informal; no reservations needed.

America, 9 E. 18th St., between Fifth Avenue and Broadway (tel. 212/505-2110), is a restaurant that wants to make an American statement. This big and trendy place occupies the entire ground floor of a restored 19th-century loft building. It has huge plate-glass windows overlooking 18th Street, strings of red, white, and blue neon wiggling across the ceiling, acres of strip oak flooring and white clothed tables, a raised bar area under a skylight in the rear, and immense pastel wall murals with American motifs (farms, mountains, the Statue of Liberty, etc.). Both lunch and dinner are chosen from the same extensive menu. Omelets (from wild mushroom and brie to smoked ham and pear chutney), salads (from applewood-smoked chicken to fresh tuna in ginger and misu), entrees (from shrimp jambalaya to Tex-Mex fajitas), pastas, sandwiches, pizzas, and desserts are almost all priced between $6 and $15. Changing monthly specials like fresh salmon filet or free-range chicken or a classic country club sandwich are usually priced from about $12 to $17. The extensive wine list is entirely domestic (who knew there were wines native to Hawaii or New Jersey?). Very popular, very appealing, and quite informal. Open daily from 11:30 a.m. to 1 a.m.; the bar pours until 2 a.m.

Positano, 250 Park Ave. South, at 20th Street (tel. 212/777-6211), is one of those sleek hi-tech places so popular with successful young professionals from the worlds of publishing, advertising, and business. It has a very imposing entrance on the corner of an old limestone office building. Inside, everything is ultranew and white, from the walls and floors to the curtains on the plate-glass windows. Seating is on several levels arranged above and below a central bar. There is soothing jazz in the air and a modulated murmur of prosperous patrons enjoying the Italian cuisine. The antipasti include dishes such as eggplant with pomodoro and provolone cheese, and sliced mozzarella with grilled mushrooms and fresh basil, priced around $8 each. Pasta dishes like risotto with seafood or farfalle alla calabra (bow-tie pasta with broccoli) run around $15 to $18. Meat and seafood dishes, such as boneless rabbit with celery and onions, Italian broccoli simmered with sweet sausage, or butter-fried whiting, cost from around $15 all the way to $28 or so. Open for lunch Monday through Friday from noon to 3 p.m.; dinner is served Monday through Saturday from 5:30 to 11:30 p.m.; closed Sunday. Reservations suggested.

Indochine, 430 Lafayette St., south of Astor Place, which in turn is quite close to East 8th Street (tel. 212/505-5111), serves French-Vietnamese cuisine in tropical Saigon-ish surroundings. There are murals of banana palms on the walls, lazy fans rotating on the ceilings, potted trees, soft lighting, a few pieces of vintage rattan, fresh flowers on the tables, and recorded violin and piano music in the air. Dinner only is served in one not terribly large room. It might be a salad of fresh pineapple and shrimp, squid with fresh mint and red peppers, steamed whole fish with ginger, brochette of whole prawns, spareribs with lemon grass, to name but a few, all priced from about $10 to $16. Open seven days a week, from 6 p.m. to 12:30 a.m. Reservations suggested.

"TriBeCa" is the name recently given to a neighborhood of trendy loft conversions, as well as chic shops and restaurants, spawned by the prohibitively high prices in nearby SoHo. The word stands for "*Tri*angle *Be*low *Ca*nal" Street. And whatever your opinion on the issue of gentrification, the fact remains that several excellent restaurants have accompanied the phenomenon around here.

Most famous, perhaps, is the **Odeon,** 145 West Broadway, between Thomas and Duane Streets (tel. 212/233-0507). This place affects a high style by virtue of its humble beginnings. Once a cafeteria (the large neon sign survives on the wall outside) with chrome-and-vinyl kitchen chairs and other fairly standard 1930s fittings, it has, by means of some strange alchemy, been rendered "chic." The room is big, high-ceilinged, and filled with flocks of white-clothed tables and a vaguely art deco–looking bar at one end. Magazine racks by the door provide single diners with periodicals like *Interview, Time,* and *Trucks.* Lunch might be chicken and linguine; a smoked salmon, cream cheese, and onion sandwich; a cheeseburger; or maybe an omelet—variously priced between about $7 and $17. Dinner entrees include smoked Norwegian salmon, grilled paillard of chicken, a pasta of the day, etc., priced from $18 to $24. Brunch and late-night supper are served as well. Open daily from noon to 3 p.m. for lunch, and from 7 p.m. to 12:30 a.m. for dinner. Reservations are "pretty necessary."

CHINATOWN

A decidedly foreign air pervades the short blocks on either side of Mott Street between Canal Street and Chatham Square. This is the heart of New York's famous Chinatown, a compact district where the phone booths have pagoda roofs, the street signs have subtitles, and the crowded sidewalks could just as well be in Shanghai. The visitor senses immediately that this is another world, and one which he is unlikely to get to know in any depth. Mott Street, although it has an Asian ring to it, is actually named after an old New York family. It's crooked and narrow, and lined with elderly walk-up tenement houses whose ground floors are filled with Oriental grocery stores, souvenir shops, and one restaurant after another. New Yorkers rarely come to Chinatown for any other reason than to eat. The atmosphere on the streets provides an exotic counterpoint to the food.

It's pretty hard to get a bad meal in Chinatown, but here now are several particularly good recommendations, each of which is open seven days a week. The first is located on a tiny dogleg street off Mott. It's called **Yun Luck,** 17 Doyers St. (tel. 212/571-1375), and it's a collection of brightly lit little rooms with low ceilings and plastic furniture. The menu provides a choice of everything from lo mein to foo young to chop suey to very tasty beef, pork, chicken, and shrimp dishes.

Also good is **Bo Ky,** 80 Bayard St. (tel. 212/406-2292), at whose crowded, communal-style tables you can get a very good meal for about $12 a person, including tax and tip.

Nice Restaurant, 35 East Broadway (tel. 212/406-9510), is famous for its dim sum as well as its enormous Cantonese menu where practically nothing exceeds $10.

Finally, there's the **Silver Palace,** 52 Bowery, just south of Canal Street (tel. 212/964-1204), which occupies a vast second-floor room accessible via a mirrored escalator. It too offers all manner of dim sum (for instance, steamed dumplings, crabmeat delight, chicken bundle, Chinese popcorn, etc.), plus a huge selection of traditional Cantonese dishes. At any of these places, it's going to take an effort to spend more than $10 a head per meal.

SIGHTSEEING IN NEW YORK CITY

1. THE FAMOUS SIGHTS
2. DO-IT-YOURSELF WALKING TOURS
3. MUSEUMS AND GALLERIES

New York City possesses an expected abundance of famous sightseeing attractions. The first section of this chapter contains a baker's dozen of the most important, profiled briefly to give you a sense of each at a glance. After reading this section you should have a pretty good idea which will interest you and which won't.

The second section contains do-it-yourself walking tours that will enable you to explore New York's most fascinating neighborhoods at your own speed. Walking is far and away the best way to see the city. Again, glance through them and pick those you think will be the most fun.

Many people come to New York City for the sole purpose of enjoying its famous museums and galleries. The third section of this chapter is a descriptive list of these, and of the sorts of things you're likely to see in them.

A GOOD NUMBER TO KNOW

The **City of New York's Department of Parks** (tel. 212/360-1333) sponsors a considerable agenda of concerts, special events, and regular programs in all the boros and at all times of the year. Dial the above number and you'll get a recording of a hale and hearty individual whose accent could only come from one city in the world. He will tell you about swimming programs in city-owned pools, ice skating on city-owned ponds or rinks, concerts in churches, bands in the parks, movies at the many branches of the New York Public Library, etc. All events are sponsored by the city, many are specifically designed for children, and most are free.

THE NEW YORK CONVENTION AND VISITORS BUREAU

This helpful and highly professional organization dispenses advice, encouragement, brochures, and (usually) subway and bus maps from a street-level lobby at 2 Columbus Circle, where Broadway crosses Eighth Avenue at Central Park South (tel. 212/397-8200). Have a travel-related problem? Call them up or drop by; they're there to answer questions and to make your visit more pleasant.

ORGANIZED TOURS

It's quite possible, of course, to see New York via one of the many standard bus tours run by various sightseeing companies. **American Sightseeing/Short Line**

Tours, 166 W. 46th St., at Seventh Avenue (tel. 212/354-4740), has city tours that last from two to eight hours and will take you to all different parts of town. No advance reservations are needed; just show up at the terminal. Another major bus tour operator is **Gray Line of New York,** 900 Eighth Ave., at 54th Street (tel. 212/397-2600). Again, no advance reservations are necessary, but it's wise to call ahead for the day's schedule. Expect prices to start at about $14 or so per person, at either Gray or Short Line, for a basic two-hour-plus city tour.

---

1. The Famous Sights

Here they are, listed in order of my own preference.

THE EMPIRE STATE BUILDING

This is the Marlene Dietrich of Manhattan skyscrapers. There may be younger, taller girls in town, but there's only one Marlene. The building is a tour de force of art deco design and decoration. Wait till you see this lobby with its matching imported marbles and angular decorative motifs. Happily, the building's present owners are fully aware of its quality and historic importance, so maintenance is first-rate and alterations have been handled sensitively.

The Empire State Building was conceived in the frenzied days of the late 1920s. The site at Fifth Avenue and 34th Street was originally that of Mrs. William B. Astor's New York town house, and later that of the original Hotel Waldorf-Astoria. When the Empire State opened in 1931, it was the tallest building in the world, a distinction it maintained for almost two generations (the World Trade Center, downtown, and the Sears Tower in Chicago are both taller, albeit not by a lot).

All sorts of things have happened here. King Kong blazoned it into the national consciousness in the 1930s; a plane crashed into it in the 1940s; the top 30 floors were illuminated in color in the 1970s; the New York Road Runners staged footraces up the stairwells in the 1980s. The slender and elegant mast that forms the building's very pinnacle was intended as an aerial mooring in the days when transatlantic dirigibles seemed the coming thing. Of course, it's so windy up there no dirigible was ever able to tie up. One try was made, but a sudden updraft stood the thing on end, terrifying everybody. The captain only managed to dump the water ballast before abandoning 34th Street for New Jersey, in the process drenching scores of unsuspecting pedestrians below.

The view from both the 86th- and 102nd-floor observation decks is truly awesome. Management estimates that over two million people come up here every year to have a look. If the weather's clear it's possible to see Massachusetts and Pennsylvania. But it is the vistas of the city itself that are the most fascinating. Both observation decks have just been redone. You can go outside on the 86th floor; the enclosed area on the 102nd floor resembles the interior of a spaceship.

The Empire State Building is located at Fifth Avenue and 34th Street (tel. 212/736-3100). The observation decks are open from 9:30 a.m. to midnight, seven days a week (they close early on Christmas Eve, Christmas Day, and New Year's Day). Admission is $3.50 for adults, $1.75 for seniors and children under 12.

THE WORLD TRADE CENTER

The Empire State Plaza in Albany and the World Trade Center at the tip of Manhattan embody New York State's style of big government and big public works as it was in the 1960s. Already the era is beginning to seem (dare I say it?) antique. The WTC, which opened in 1970, is also very much in New York City's own tradition of being/having the "biggest." What it is, by the way, is an immense office complex (ten million square feet!) that belongs to a quasi-public organization called the

Port Authority of New York and New Jersey. It occupies 16 acres at the edge of the Financial District, and it has not one but two 110-story buildings, numerous other not-so-lofty but stylistically unified high-rises (one of which is a first-class hotel), a plaza the size of four football fields, an underground shopping mall, dozens of restaurants and banks, and a major terminus for trans-Hudson commuter travel via a subway called the PATH (short for Port Authority Trans-Hudson) Tube. It's tenanted by a roster of firms, mostly engaged in international trade, that employs almost 50,000 people. It also houses the New York Commodities Exchange, the famous Windows on the World (see Chapter III, "New York City Restaurants"), as well as an observation deck.

It is this latter "Deck at the World Trade Center" that draws most tourists (about a million and a half a year). You buy your tickets on the mezzanine level of Two World Trade Center (that's the southernmost of the twin towers), then take a special elevator (1,377 feet in 58 seconds) to the 107th floor. The view is entirely different from the one uptown at 34th Street. There's a much greater sense of port activities and industrial vastness, less of a sense of Manhattan. On the 110th floor is the open-air promenade, the "highest in the world" (even if the building isn't).

The World Trade Center is located at the southern end of Manhattan, not far from City Hall Park, on a site bounded by Church, Vesey, West, and Liberty Streets.

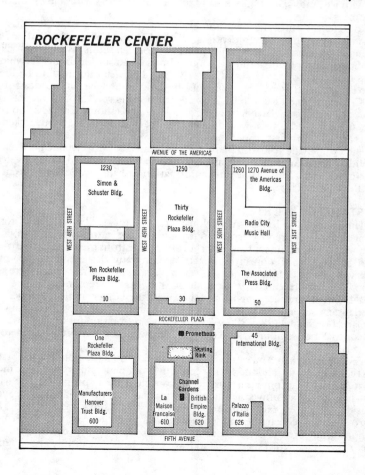

Observation facilities (tel. 212/466-7377) are open every day from 9:30 a.m. to 9:30 p.m. Admission is $3.50 for adults, $1.75 for seniors and children under 12, free for kids under 6.

ROCKEFELLER CENTER

In the late 1920s megamillionaire John D. Rockefeller planned to build a great opera house on a midtown site he'd acquired adjacent to Fifth Avenue. Then the stock market collapsed and the deal went sour. Rockefeller, however, was determined to build. And instead of an opera house, New York got Rockefeller Center, one of the first (and surely one of the grandest) multiple-use urban developments in the nation.

Rockefeller Center is both beautiful and photogenic. It's a collection of stone-clad skyscrapers in high-1930s drag, augmented in recent years by a string of lordly glass boxes along Sixth Avenue. The original structures are embelished everywhere with almost Mayan-looking art in the form of statuary, murals, and monumental reliefs. At the heart of it all is a landscaped pedestrian mall whose plantings change with the seasons. Called the **Promenade,** it creates a sort of triumphal approach to 30 Rockefeller Plaza, a soaring office tower straight out of Flash Gordon. A famous sunken plaza with a gilded statue of Prometheus stands at its foot. In winter it's filled with ice skaters; in summer, gaily colored umbrellas shelter tables full of outdoor diners.

Rockefeller Center is also the home of the world-famous **Radio City Music Hall** (for details on programming and prices, refer to Chapter V, "New York After Dark," Section 3, "Music and Dance Performances"). You can see its fascinating backstage and fantastically opulent auditorium and lobbies on a tour for about $6 (which is a lot less than the cost of a ticket). Call 212/632-4041 for information. Besides the Music Hall, Rockefeller Center contains the radio and television broadcast studios of **NBC,** located at 30 Rockefeller Plaza. Regular tours run through the sets of the "Today Show," "Saturday Night Live," and local news shows. Call 212/664-7174 between 9 a.m. and 5 p.m. weekdays for details, or drop by the lobby ticket desk. Tickets are sold on a first-come, first-served basis.

The Promenade at Rockefeller Center is located at Fifth Avenue between 49th and 50th Streets. An interesting and informative brochure titled "Walking Tour of Rockefeller Center" is available at the information desk just inside the main entrance to 30 Rockefeller Plaza.

THE STATUE OF LIBERTY

These days she looks "mahvelous," thanks to a zillion-dollar restoration scheme financed entirely by private contributions. The statue herself sits atop Liberty Island, a former sandbar located a short ferry ride from the southern tip of Manhattan. She is made of copper mounted on an iron frame designed by Gustave Eiffel, the very man who did that famous tower in Paris. Skin and framework were assembled in Paris and presented to the people of America at a ceremony in France on July 4, 1884. The statue and supporting frame were then disassembled, shipped across the Atlantic, reassembled in New York Harbor, and dedicated by President Grover Cleveland on October 28, 1886. As with today's restoration funds, the costs of design, construction, shipment, and reassembling were borne entirely by generous individuals.

Few structures in America evoke the same emotional response as the Statue of Liberty. It's beautiful, and the setting certainly is dramatic. But its symbolic message —that there is a welcoming haven on this continent where people can live without fear—has the sort of universal import that touches every one of our lives. Symbolism aside, it's a great excursion. You'll probably take a subway either to the South Ferry or Bowling Green station (depending what line you take), then find your way the short distance to the Circle Line pier (tel. 212/269-5755) at the southern end of Battery Park. Boats for Liberty Island leave every half hour in July and August between 8:30 a.m. and 5 p.m. and every hour the rest of the year between 10 a.m. and 4 p.m. Round-trip fare is $3.50 for adults, $1.50 for children.

THE UNITED NATIONS

U.N. Headquarters occupies a 16-acre campus on First Avenue between 42nd and 48th Streets. People's perceptions of the U.N. have changed considerably since it was founded 40-odd years back. A signature air of dedicated idealism clings to the place, however, and it remains an ever-hopeful symbol of the possibility of a better world.

As a sightseeing attraction, it has a lot to offer. Physically, it's quite impressive, with its sweeping lawns and soaring marble-and-glass buildings done up in the high modern style of the late 1940s. Its interior meeting rooms are quite stupendous. The meetings where issues of peace, justice, and human well-being are discussed by representatives of 159 member states are occasionally open to the public. Free tickets are issued on a first-come, first-served basis. Call 212/754-1234 for schedules (no kids under 12 permitted).

Hour-long guided tours of U.N. buildings and activities leave about every 15 minutes from the General Assembly Building. They cost $4.50 for adults, $2.50 for students (no kids under 5). The tour information number is 212/963-7713. You can, if you wish, stroll around the grounds for free.

THE CIRCLE LINE

"America's Favorite Boat Ride" has been operating since 1945. It's a three-hour, 35-mile cruise around Manhattan Island, passing under 20 famous bridges and over four tunnels and 73 transit tubes. The Circle Line fleet includes eight snackbar-equipped sightseeing yachts, each of which holds between 400 and 600 people. Interestingly, most of these boats were built for the U.S. Navy as LCIs (Landing Craft Infantry), and destined for the beaches of Normandy and Okinawa. One ship, as it happens, was the first American craft to return to Corregidor.

Few views compare to that of Manhattan's Financial District on a sunny day, rising from the sparkling waters of the harbor. Other parts of the cruise are just as interesting, especially up in the region of sheer cliffs known as the Palisades above the George Washington Bridge.

The Circle Line is located at Pier 83, at the foot of West 42nd Street. If you drive, on-site parking is available for $8. The three-hour cruise costs $15 for adults and $7.50 for children under 12. Call 212/563-3200 for current sailing schedules. Between June and September the Harbor Lights Cruise leaves every night at 7 p.m. and returns at 9:30. There is no guide and the price is the same as the daytime cruise. Circle Line also operates the **Hudson River Day Line,** which runs excursion boats farther up the Hudson one day each month. Day Line cruises are nine-hour undertakings that include stops at Bear Mountain and West Point before the boat turns around at Poughkeepsie for the return to Manhattan. The trip provides some of the best scenery in the East, plenty of time ashore, and a convenient opportunity to see the U.S. Military Academy (for an extra $3) at West Point. Round-trip passenger fares on the *Dayliner* are $15 for adults and $7.50 for kids.

THE NEW YORK STOCK EXCHANGE

This gorgeous Roman temple, designed in 1903 by George B. Post, contains an immense interior trading floor and overhanging galleries that can be toured for free. A visit to the Stock Exchange is actually quite interesting. You'll learn how stock is traded, how brokers communicate, how prices are set, plus other seemingly logical and orderly processes that hardly seem possible in the cacophonous roar below you. The atmosphere of financial might—this is, after all, one of the most important financial centers on earth—is worth experiencing.

Visually, the trading floor is a wild combination of beaux arts magnificence and state-of-the-art communications equipment populated by hordes of men and women in a perfect frenzy of activity. Up in the galleries are multi-image slide shows and tricky technological displays that explain what's really afoot downstairs.

The Exchange is located at 20 Broad St., between Wall Street and Exchange Place (tel. 212/656-5167). Tours can be had from 9:30 a.m. to 3:30 p.m. Monday through Friday. This is a good site to include on the Financial District walking tour.

SOUTH STREET SEAPORT

There's so much going on down here that it's a tough place to comprehend. Basically, the seaport is a restored fragment, encircled by glass towers, of what was once the heart of Manhattan's waterfront in sailing-ship days. Half of it is operated by something called the South Street Seaport Museum as a sort of mini-Williamsburg; the other half is run, with considerable flash and efficiency, as a sort of theme-park-cum-shopping-mall by the Rouse Organization.

The seaport's centerpiece is the old Fulton Fish Market, now a multilevel complex of gourmet food stalls and restaurants. Surrounding this are restored historical buildings (almost embarrassingly perfect and clean), several fantastic old sailing ships that you can walk around on, and an enormous new pier (Pier 17) that is essentially a large enclosed shopping mall. Some condemn the seaport as the new "mesquite coast," an allusion to the trendy cookery served in its many restaurants. But in fairness, much has been saved hereabouts that would otherwise have been lost. And the theme-park atmosphere, while hardly an authentic re-creation of the rowdy past, happens to be enormously appealing.

It's possible just to browse around the seaport for free, peeking in the windows and strolling through the Fulton Market or Pier 17. A much better idea is to buy a ticket at one of the many clearly marked booths: $5 for adults, $3 for seniors, and $2 for kids entitles you to any (or all) of three basic guided tours, plus admission to the Seaport Museum's exhibition halls, print shop, photo galleries, film events, and restored sailing ships. These ships, and the stories surrounding them, are perhaps the most intriguing part of a visit here. The tour guide's tales of New York's sailing past are definitely worth the cost of a ticket.

For one price you can tailor your day to include as much guided tour and free exploration as you like. As if there weren't enough to see, the Rouse Organization keeps the cobbled streets full of jugglers, concerts, fashion shows, strolling musicians, and whatever else they can think of. To find out what special events Rouse has cooking, call 212/732-7678.

The South Street Seaport is located downtown at the eastern end of Fulton Street, an easy walk from Wall Street or City Hall Park. The nearest subway stops are at Fulton Street. There are plenty of places to eat (to say the least); fast, economical meals in a wide range of cuisines can be had on the top level of Pier 17. Carry your tray to the terrace overlooking the river; it's hard to think of a finer place for a sandwich.

LINCOLN CENTER

America's first performing arts center certainly is grandiose. The complex was erected in the 1960s and includes: the New York State Theater, home of the New York City Ballet and New York City Opera; Avery Fisher Hall, home of the New York Philharmonic; the Metropolitan Opera House; the Vivian Beaumont Theatre; the famous Juilliard School of Music; an outdoor bandshell; a Museum of the Performing Arts; a branch of the New York Public Library; plus assorted smaller halls and theaters. The heart of the complex is a broad travertine marble plaza graced with a large fountain and surrounded by 1960s-vintage performance halls.

Lincoln Center is a busy place and its performance schedule is a full one. For current information, call 212/877-2011. Even if you don't attend a performance you can still tour the buildings and perhaps catch a glimpse of rehearsals in progress. The interiors of the various theaters, particularly the Metropolitan Opera House with its Chagall murals, are sumptuous in the modern manner. Tours operate daily

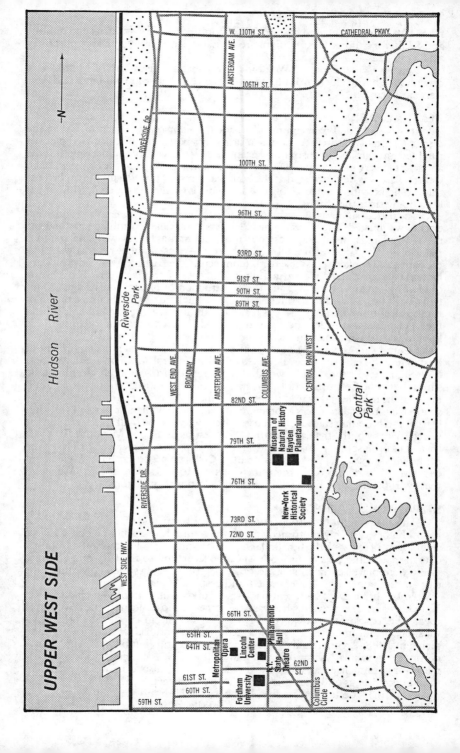

from 10 a.m. to 5 p.m. and cost $6.25 for adults, $5.25 for students and seniors, and $3.50 for children. Reservations are advisable, since groups are kept purposely small; call 212/877-1800, ext. 512.

Lincoln Center is on the West Side of Manhattan, just north of Midtown. It occupies the entire blocks from 62nd to 66th Streets between Columbus and Amsterdam Avenues.

CENTRAL PARK

It may seem odd to recommend a park as a sightseeing attraction. But in the case of Central Park, an exception is in order. It's both a highly calculated piece of rural-seeming art and a consummate example of 19th-century engineering. It is the ancestor of every picturesque park in America, and a great gift to the common man. Central Park was designed so that the beauty and restorative effects of unsullied nature would be within the reach of all. Its purpose is to nurture the soul, which it has been doing since the 1850s.

The park design was the result of a competition won by Calvert Vaux and Frederick Law Olmsted. The "Greensward Plan," as it was called, combined pastoral vistas of woodlands, meadows, rocky outcrops, and tranquil lakes, with an ingenious traffic plan. This latter feature allowed elaborate systems of walkways, roadways, bridle paths, and sunken transverse roads (connecting the East and West Sides of Manhattan) to coexist without once getting clumsily in one another's way. The 20 years of blasting, grading, planting, and the construction of picturesque bridges, fountains, pavilions, lakes, and so on, transformed a blighted wasteland into a dream of rural perfection. When the park was first built, the low-rise city was invisible behind the trees, a fact that added greatly to the intended effect. But even today, with the looming city skyline so often visible, the effect of tranquility remains.

Central Park is worth leisurely exploration and is quite safe during the day, at least in heavily trafficked areas. Be sure to visit the **Central Park Zoo** at 5th Ave. and 64th St., newly restored and a wonderful destination for a leisurely afternoon. Be sure to visit the **Bethesda Fountain,** too, and its romantic lakefront plaza. You'll find it in the middle of the park, about on the line of 72nd Street. Immediately to the south of it is the **Mall,** a fine Victorian promenade lined with multiple alleys of stately trees and brooding statues of literary figures. Between the Mall and Tavern on the Green (over by 67th Street and Central Park West) is the **Sheep Meadow.** This vast lawn, a favorite spot for Frisbees and sunbathing, provides spectacular views of the Midtown skyline. The park also contains a **Children's Zoo** (at Fifth Avenue and 64th Street), and a formal garden (the **Conservatory Garden,** at Fifth Avenue in the low 100s), to name but a few of its many additional attractions.

ST. PATRICK'S CATHEDRAL

This magnificent limestone cathedral was the brainchild of the Right Reverend John Hughes, a highly motivated Irish immigrant who became the first Catholic archbishop of New York. In 1850 Hughes announced his intention to build a church that would be a credit both to Catholicism and to the City of New York. These were brave sentiments at the time, as Irish Catholics then constituted the city's most impoverished, uneducated, and despised underclass.

Notwithstanding 19th-century New York's anti-Catholic prejudices, St. Patrick's was duly erected in what was to become the most elite residential section of town. The structure was designed by James Renwick, Jr., in an eclectic Gothic Revival style. Begun in 1858, it was dedicated in 1879 and had its twin towers completed in 1888. Architectural experts may get a few grins out of St. Patrick's, since it's not a very scholarly essay on European Gothic. However, the rest of us can only marvel at its immense scale and gorgeous decoration. It also forms a nice contrast to the art deco doings of Rockefeller Center across the street.

St. Patrick's occupies the entire block between Fifth and Madison Avenues, and 50th and 51st Streets. Be sure to go inside; the silence and majesty are memorable.

U.S.S. *INTREPID* SEA-AIR-SPACE MUSEUM

This is a real live navy aircraft carrier. What's more, it's a historic carrier. Construction started on the *Intrepid* a mere six days before the bombing of Pearl Harbor. Between August 1943 and the end of the Second World War she saw almost continuous duty in the Pacific. She survived three direct hits by suicide kamikazes and played a major role in the Battle of Leyte Gulf, a forerunner to the liberation of the Philippines.

After total modernization in the early 1950s, the *Intrepid* continued active duty. This was the ship that plucked returning astronauts Scott Carpenter, Gus Grissom, and John Young from the choppy Atlantic in the mid-1960s. A few years later she was in the Gulf of Tonkin off the coast of North Vietnam. It wasn't until 1974, after a stint of antisubmarine duty with the Sixth Fleet, that she was finally decommissioned.

Today the *Intrepid* is a floating museum containing one huge military exhibit hall after another. These contain audiovisual presentations, special films (repeated every 20 or so minutes), artifacts of war and aviation, galleries devoted to aircraft design and space exploration, as well as a considerable number of parked aircraft, all of which can be examined at your own speed.

The *Intrepid* is tied up in the Hudson at Pier 86, located at the foot of West 46th Street (tel. 212/245-0072). Admission is $4.75 for adults and $2.50 for children. Open Wednesday through Sunday from 10 a.m. to 5 p.m. (last admission sold at 4 p.m.).

CHINATOWN

New York's exotic Chinatown section has been drawing ethnic Chinese since the 1850s. For the visitor, it's an undeniably colorful quarter, characterized by tiny shops filled with esoteric goods and foodstuffs, dozens upon dozens of restaurants, phone booths and the occasional building topped with a brightly painted pagoda roof, narrow crooked streets, and sidewalks teeming with Chinese. For the people who live here it's an overcrowded ghetto, reeling from recent waves of moneyless immigrants, high rents, and substandard housing.

But it certainly is picturesque, as well as being a superior place for delicious cheap meals (see Chapter III, "New York City Restaurants," section 5, "Special Excursions"). The busiest day in Chinatown is Sunday, when everything's open and former residents from all over town come back to stock up on things Chinese. Also memorable is Chinese New Year, celebrated with fireworks and dancing dragons on the first full moon after January 21.

The heart of Chinatown is Mott Street between Canal Street and the Bowery. In recent years the Bowery itself, between Chatham Square and Canal Street, has become a full-fledged part of the neighborhood instead of just its eastern boundary. There's no architectural or urban grandeur hereabouts, nor is the area particularly large. But yes, it is exotic.

---

2. Do-It-Yourself Walking Tours

The following itineraries contain easy-to-follow directions, ample descriptions of what there is to see, and the approximate time it takes to walk each from start to finish at a leisurely pace.

TOUR NO. 1: MIDTOWN–FIFTH AVENUE

Start: Grand Army Plaza, Fifth Avenue and 59th Street. *Finish:* Seventh Avenue and Central Park South. *Time required:* Approximately 1½ hours.

Grand Army Plaza, or simply "The Plaza," is one of New York's most hand-some outdoor spaces. Its centerpiece is a fountain atop stacked reflecting pools, do-nated to the city in 1916 by publishing czar Joseph Pulitzer. At its summit is a graceful statue of *Pomona,* Roman goddess of bounteous gardens. Some of the finest private mansions in New York once overlooked this square, notably the 138-room château of Cornelius Vanderbilt, grandson of the original Commodore Vanderbilt. This lamentably long-demolished house once occupied the entire Fifth Avenue blockfront from 57th to 58th Streets. The site has been occupied since 1928 by **Bergdorf Goodman.**

Bergdorf's is one of the ritziest stores in New York, and the facial expressions and body language of its display mannequins are a ready barometer of fashionable attitudes. Also overlooking the Plaza is the august **Metropolitan Club,** designed in 1893 by McKim, Mead, and White and located on the corner of 60th Street and Fifth Avenue. Supposedly, this club was organized by J. P. Morgan to accommodate friends who couldn't get into the nearby University Club on Fifth and 54th. What-ever its origins, it is about as magnificent a building as one can imagine.

If you're interested in magnificence, you should take a quick look at the gilt and marble lobbies of **The Plaza** hotel, on the western boundary of the Plaza between 58th Street and Central Park South. Designed by Henry Hardenbergh in 1907, it is some gorgeous place. Also worth a look inside is the **General Motors Building,** which is the white marble tower directly across Fifth from the Plaza Hotel. Built in 1968 the G.M. Building provides showroom floors full of brand-new cars so that carless New Yorkers can see what the rest of the country is driving around in.

The Plaza is a divider between business districts to the south and fancy residen-tial areas to the north. Northward from this spot Fifth Avenue was once called "Mil-lionaires' Mile." It was literally lined with the ornate châteaux and brownstone palaces of the merchant elite. Today, most are gone (others like them survive along the side streets), replaced by swank apartment houses. But I'm saving the upper-crust East Side until later. For now we're heading south down Fifth Avenue.

Between 58th and 59th Streets, on the same side of the street as the G.M. Build-ing, is **F.A.O. Schwarz,** the famous luxury toy store. You may not have realized that toys could be so opulent. When you're done browsing at Schwarz, hop across Fifth and take a look around the pastel and perfumed interior of Bergdorf's. This is what every fancy department store in the world wants to look like.

The corner of 57th Street and Fifth Avenue is perhaps the best retailing address in Manhattan. Two of New York's world-class jewelers, **Tiffany & Co.** and **Van Cleef & Arpels,** overlook this intersection and provide nuclear-proof-looking windows full of heart-stoppingly amazing gems. Glance up at the Crown Building too, on the southwest corner of 57th and Fifth. All that glittery yellow stuff on the stonework is real gold leaf.

Stay on the Tiffany side of Fifth for another half a block. About midway be-tween 56th and 57th Streets is the entrance to **Trump Tower.** This glittery mixed-use cooperative has commercial tenants on the lower floors and million-dollar-plus apartments upstairs. Real estate developer Donald Trump is New York's "wunder-kind" for the 1980s, a successor to rock-and-roll idols of the past. Push the huge gold Ts mounted on the doors and you'll enter a posh shopping atrium with an 80-foot waterfall and more pink marble than you would have supposed was in all of Italy. Shops here sell antiques, Paris fashions, jewels, and all sorts of other good stuff. After a few exhilarating breaths of Mr. Trump's world, follow the sign to the left of the escalator that says "To IBM Plaza and Madison Avenue." You'll cross through a little bit of **Bonwit Teller,** a superior-class department store adjoining Trump Tow-er, before emerging in yet another dramatic enclosed atrium.

IBM Plaza, where you are now, is nothing less than a glass-enclosed bamboo forest. It's a great place to sit and have a light snack from the refreshment kiosk (crowded, however, at lunchtime). There are tables and chairs, aromatic floral plant-ings that change with the seasons, and an impressive sense of space. If you're fortunate there may even be a little concert (chamber music or some such) in progress beneath the bamboos. IBM deserves high marks for this one.

Leave IBM Plaza by the 57th Street door, then cross Madison Avenue. That good-looking art deco office tower on the northeast corner of Madison and 57th is the **Fuller Building,** built in 1929. If you stand at the foot of the Fuller Building and look south down Madison, you'll get a fine view of Philip Johnson's new **AT&T Building.** It's the big granite number that looks like a Queen Anne highboy standing on the east side of Madison down at 55th and 56th.

Continue walking on **57th Street** now, eastbound in the direction of Park Avenue. This is one of the most splendid and cosmopolitan shopping districts on earth. The shop windows are filled with museum-quality antiques, precious crystal and jewels, and the latest fashions.

When you reach Park Avenue, pause for a moment. That slender and elegant building across the avenue on the northeast corner of Park and 57th is the **Ritz Tower.** Built in 1925, it is best known as the former home of Le Pavillon, once the most famous French restaurant in New York. Now look to the south down Park Avenue. Straddling the roadway is the guilded **Helmsley Building,** formerly the New York Central Building. Its famous silhouette was severely injured in 1963 by the construction of the egg-crate-like **Pan Am Building** right behind it.

Stroll down the west side of Park to 56th Street, then glance down 56th toward Madison Avenue. The new **Park Avenue Tower,** which isn't on Park Avenue at all but rather on the south side of 56th Street, gives the appearance of twisting at the strangest angle. Ah, modern architecture. Now continue down Park to 55th and cross to the east side of the street. The green-roofed tower down the road, by the way, belongs to **The Waldorf-Astoria** hotel at Park and 50th Street.

Continue eastbound on 55th Street for one block to the corner of Lexington Avenue. The block from Park to Lex, with its dignified town houses, gives a good idea of what this neighborhood looked like before the era of the mighty glass office building. The onion-domed structure at the southwest corner of Lex and 55th looks like a little bit of old Moscow. Actually it's the **Central Synagogue,** the oldest synagogue building in continuous use in New York City. The structure was designed by Henry Fernbach, New York's first practicing Jewish architect. It was erected in 1871.

Continue south one block on Lex to 54th Street. That huge complex on the east side of Lex between 53rd and 54th is the **Citicorp Building.** Inside is yet another atrium, this one called the Market. It contains the obligatory incredible interior space, plus lots and lots of places (many of them quite reasonable) to eat. Most sell food that you can carry out with you to one of the many tables and chairs beneath a very lofty skylight. If you're temporarily full of atriums, turn right (west) on 54th Street back in the direction of Park Avenue. You might note **11 E. 54th St.** as you pass. This former private home was built in the architectural style fashionable just before this neighborhood turned commercial.

At Park Avenue and 54th Street, look downtown at that low building on the west side of Park between 52nd and 53rd Streets. This is the **Racquet and Tennis Club,** a patrician stronghold containing one of the handful of court tennis courts in the country. (Court tennis, by the way, is more difficult and complicated than regular tennis and was played by Henry VIII at Hampton Court Palace on a 90-by-30-foot court still in use there.) Several years ago the Racquet Club assured its future finances by selling valuable air rights to the developer of the glass office tower that now looms behind it.

Stay on 54th Street, cross Park Avenue, and continue one block west to Madison Avenue. Now cross to the west side of Madison Avenue and go one block south to 53rd Street. You might do a bit of window-shopping while you're here in the chic shops at the foot of the angular **Continental Illinois Building.**

Turn right on 53rd Street and head west one block toward Fifth Avenue. The East 50s were once New York's most exclusive and opulent mansion district. A survivor is **12 E. 53rd St.,** no longer a residence but still complete with battlements, balconies, and leaded windows. On the north (right-hand) side of this block, just before Fifth Avenue, is **Paley Park,** a delectable little cobbled enclave furnished with lacy locust trees, climbing ivy, metal chairs and tables, and a wall of falling water at its far end. Built in 1967 on the site of the famous Stork Club, it's a wonderful place to sit and meditate on life, or maybe have a sandwich.

Leave Paley Park and go to the corner of Fifth Avenue. To your right, up at the northwest corner of Fifth and 54th Street, is the lordly **University Club,** McKim, Mead, and White's 1899 homage to the Italian Renaissance. We're going the other direction, however, one block south to 52nd Street. Note **Cartier's,** housed in a former private palace on the southeast corner of Fifth and 52nd. A now-forgotten millionaire named Morton Plant was induced by the Vanderbilt family to build this house in 1904. The Vanderbilts, many of whom had houses on Fifth in the 50s, were trying desperately to keep the area residential. They failed, and all their houses are gone. Mr. Plant's remains. It has been occupied by the jewelry firm of Cartier since 1917.

Continue south on Fifth Avenue for another block to 51st Street. The big brown glass tower on the northeast corner of Fifth and 51st is the **Olympic Tower,** another fashionable multiple-use building. **St. Patrick's Cathedral** occupies the east side of Fifth between 51st and 50th. It rates a separate discussion (see Section 1 of this chapter, "The Famous Sights"). The towers were topped off in 1888, and the inside is well worth a look.

Continue south to 50th Street and cross Fifth Avenue. Now you're in the region of **Rockefeller Center** (also described separately in Section 1 of this chapter). Facing the famous Promenade, which leads off Fifth, and occupying the entire eastern blockfront from 49th to 50th Streets is **Saks Fifth Avenue,** one of New York's great department stores. Save Saks for a later browse and turn right (west) into the Promenade, also located midway between 49th and 50th Streets.

Rockefeller Center is one of the most handsome urban complexes in New York, perhaps in the nation. As you turn off Fifth into the Promenade, you'll see the slender tower of the **RCA Building** (known also by its address, 30 Rockefeller Plaza), looking like something out of H. G. Wells. At Christmastime the Rockefeller Center tree stands before it. Stroll down the Promenade, admire the beautiful plantings, and have a look at the sunken plaza. In the good weather, meals can be had under brightly colored umbrella tables; in the winter you can rent ice skates (about $5 for the skates; under $10 for admission to the rink).

Walk around the sunken plaza and have a look inside 30 Rockefeller Plaza. The lobby is the epitome of high style à la 1933 (the building's completion date). Above the black marble floors and walls are monumental sepia-toned murals depicting the unending labors of Michelangelo-esque men and women. They were painted by José Maria Sert. Originally, a highly political mural by Diego Rivera faced the building's front door. Rather than remove images of Lenin and venereal germs hovering over a tableau of rich people playing cards, Rivera insisted the mural be destroyed. The Rockefellers willingly obliged.

Walk all the way down the lobby of the RCA Building to the exit onto **Sixth Avenue.** Now turn right (north) and start walking back uptown. There used to be an elevated train on Sixth Avenue, which for most of the neighborhood's history exercised a fairly depressing influence. A building boom in the 1960s and 1970s transformed the dreary blockfronts into an astonishing canyon of 50-story glass skyscrapers. Although this is just another Manhattan business district and the buildings individually aren't of great note, taken together they form an urban environment of considerable grandeur.

At 56th Street, turn left (west) toward Seventh Avenue, and go a few steps to the entrance to **Le Parker Meridien Hotel,** located on the north side of the street. Enter the lobby doors and walk straight across the reception area toward the big hanging tapestry on the wall ahead. Bear to the right into the atrium court. This is a public area, not restricted to guests. And the atrium, with its columns and balustrades and palette of pale peach, coral, and cream, is quite beautiful. Exit the atrium via the door market "57e Rue" (which means "57th Street" in French). You'll pass through another spectacular interior space with marble floors and an immensely high polychrome ceiling. Its sole purpose is to serve as a passageway to 57th Street.

Outside on 57th, turn left (west) toward Seventh Avenue. At the end of the block, on the southeast corner of 57th and Seventh, is **Carnegie Hall,** built in 1891 and saved from demolition by a hairsbreadth in the early 1960s. It recently underwent total restoration.

Now cross 57th Street and continue north (uptown) on Seventh Avenue. This neighborhood is really an extension of the apartment-house district along Central Park South. Most of the buildings hereabouts are anonymous enough, with the blinding exception of **Alwyn Court.** Built in 1909 on the southeast corner of Seventh and 58th Street, its façade is a frenzied tour de force in terracotta ornamentation. Descriptions cannot do it justice; it must be seen to be believed.

The next block of Seventh, between 58th and Central Park South, contains the **New York Athletic Club,** famous for its prosperous ambience. And the corner ahead, that of Seventh Avenue and Central Park South, marks the end of our tour.

TOUR NO. 2: GREENWICH VILLAGE

Start: "West 4th Street, Washington Square" subway station, whose entrances are at Sixth Avenue and West 3rd Street and at Sixth Avenue and Waverly Place. *Finish:* Same as start. *Time required:* Approximately one hour and 10 minutes.

It's erroneously believed, even by many New Yorkers, that Greenwich Village centers around Washington Square and two honky-tonk strips on Bleecker and West 3rd Street between Sixth Avenue and LaGuardia Place. Actually, this is not at all the case.

The original Greenwich Village, the separate town that once lay beyond the boundaries of New York, is located someplace else. Today people sometimes refer to that area as the "West Village," and it occupies the region between Greenwich Avenue and the Hudson River, bounded on the south by West Houston Street. Greenwich Village was one of the earliest settlements on Manhattan. It remained a bucolic hamlet during and after the Revolution, then experienced explosive growth in the 1820s. Its sudden prosperity was largely a function of the poor quality of the drinking water in the neighboring city of New York. It those days epidemics of typhoid and smallpox were almost annual affairs. As soon as the new season's plague struck New York, everyone who could afford to decamped immediately to healthful semi-rural, and nearby Greenwich.

Greenwich possessed its own network of built-up streets well before burgeoning New York City engulfed it. They still exist, radiating at bewildering angles from the grid plan that dominates the rest of Manhattan. The old Village surveyors must have been a little weak when it came to right angles. Original Village blocks are almost, but not quite, square. Many are parallelograms. The block plan is further complicated by subsequent swaths slashed through it for the construction of Seventh and Eighth Avenues. On top of all this, some of the old named streets have been given numbers supposedly corresponding to adjacent numbered streets. The results are baffling intersections, such as that point where West 4th Street, West 12th Street, and Eighth Avenue all converge. Even native New Yorkers get lost in the Village, at least without a map.

Our tour starts at **Sixth Avenue and Waverly Place,** an intersection located one block south of 8th Street and quite near the uptown exits from the Washington Square–West 4th Street subway stop. Proceed east from Sixth Avenue toward Washington Square Park. Waverly Place is a typical Village street lined with well-used brick town houses from the early 19th century, as well as buildings of more recent vintage. At the end of one block you arrive at Macdougal Street and **Washington Square Park.**

In 1789 the park you see before you was designated a pauper's burial ground. It was an unprepossessing patch of land then, not terribly close to New York, not wanted by anyone else. But by 1826 fashion was on the march. The paupers were unceremoniously removed and the former graveyard became a parade ground. Soon fine Greek Revival houses began to appear along the southern boundary. Every one of these has disappeared, victims of time and the encroaching building programs of New York University's campus.

The brick houses that still stand on the park's northern boundary, however, give a vivid idea of what the whole square once looked like. Known collectively as **The Row,** they enjoyed their day (in the 1830s) as the home of New York's elite. Like good neighborhoods everywhere they were eventually abandoned for palmier addresses, this time farther up Fifth Avenue. Henry James and Edith Wharton, incidentally, both lived and worked at 1 Washington Square North. Today many of these old mansions are only façades masking new apartments inside. But a few have survived almost intact.

Now let's make a short detour. Turn to your left (north) and head away from Washington Square Park up Macdougal Street. After a few steps you'll see **Macdougal Alley** on your right. This little street, lined with former carriage houses, is typical of the sort of small enclave that makes the Village such an appealing place to live. You might stroll up to the end of Macdougal Street (the Alley is private) and have a look at **West 8th Street** while you're here. It's a wilderness of shoe stores, clothing stores, poster shops, and copy centers. It's hard to believe that its mutilated buildings were ever aristocratic private houses. And yet that is precisely what they were.

Now return to Washington Square, turn left (east) and walk along the Row toward Fifth Avenue. Note the double house at no. 20, built in 1828 as a freestanding suburban mansion for one George P. Rogers. The very air on this block is redolent with the gentility of the past. One can almost imagine the clip-clop of horses and the creak of carriage springs as the ladies climb out to make their calls.

At Fifth Avenue, turn left (uptown). On the east side of the avenue you'll see **Washington Mews,** another alley lined with former carriage houses now converted to residences. Although the original town houses along this stretch of Fifth were long ago replaced with apartment houses, the street preserves a dignified residential air.

Three blocks north of Washington Square at 10th Street is the **Church of the Ascension,** a pleasant old place set back from the street behind an antique iron fence. It's been here since 1841, although the interior dates from a renovation in the 1880s by the celebrated McKim, Mead, and White. Turn left off Fifth Avenue onto **West 10th Street.** This is one of the nicest blocks in the Village, lined with fine city houses. Note no. 12, a particularly capacious old manse once owned by Bruce Price, the architect of Tuxedo Park and the father of etiquette expert Emily Post. The row of once identical "English-front" (meaning no high stoop) town houses between no. 20 and no. 38 tells the whole sorry history of brownstone "modernization." No. 38 has been shamefully stripped of ornamentation; no. 26 is in perfect original condition. There's no debate as to which is the better looking.

At the end of the block you'll reach the corner of Sixth Avenue. And here you'll have a fine view of the **Jefferson Market Courthouse,** located across Sixth and now a branch of the New York Public Library. This exuberant Victorian castle, dating from the 1870s, was once considered one of the half dozen most beautiful buildings in the United States. Subsequent generations considered it a horror. Concerned Villagers saved it from demolition in the late 1960s after it had stood vacant for over 20 years. When built, it was part of an innovative multiple-use complex that included a jail, a market, a courthouse, and a prison.

Cross Sixth Avenue for a closer look at it. Note how 10th Street now angles off to the south, following old Village road lines. The lovely garden (lovely except for a perfectly awful chain-link fence that surrounds it) occupying the rest of the court-

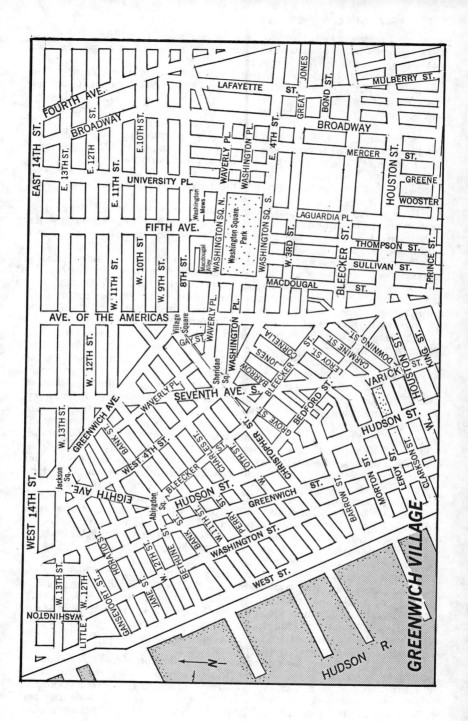

house block replaces a 1931 House of Detention for Women. Until its demolition in 1974, evenings on this block were characterized by husbands and boyfriends down on the street howling up to their womenfolk behind bars.

Across 10th Street from the Jefferson Courthouse is another little enclave of the sort that so typifies Greenwich Village. Called **Patchin Place,** it contains but ten modest brick houses facing one another across a leafy cul-de-sac. Theodore Dreiser, Jane Bowles, and e.e. cummings were among Patchin Place's illustrious residents in the days when the Village was America's "bohemia."

Now continue walking west on 10th Street away from Sixth Avenue. The corner ahead is **Greenwich Avenue,** a busy local shopping street. Originally it was called Monument Lane after a pre-Revolutionary obelisk that stood at its northern terminus. Note the bathroom-brick behemoth at 33 Greenwich Ave. This is the sort of building that won't be built anymore (thank goodness!) in landmark Greenwich Village.

Cross Greenwich Avenue and keep walking west on 10th Street. The modest-looking tenements that line the street contain apartments as pricey as those on the elegant block between Fifth and Sixth. Why? Because they're on West 10th Street, a premium New York address.

Continue straight across the intersection of 10th Street and Waverly Place. After one more short block you'll come to **Seventh Avenue South,** slashing brutally through the venerable Village blocks. Seventh Avenue used to stop up at 11th Street. It was extended south about the time of the First World War, over the protests of the entire Village. Before we move on, glance downtown (to your left) and you'll see the gleaming twin towers of the World Trade Center down on Vesey Street.

Crossing Seventh Avenue is something of a hazard. You want to get over to where West 10th Street picks up on the other side. When you regain West 10th, go just a few steps to the intersection of West 10th and West 4th Streets, one of those conceptually bizarre intersections for which the Village is famous. Now turn right and start walking northwest up West 4th. Now we're getting into the real Village, or "West" Village as it's called. The next couple of intersecting streets—Charles, Perry, West 11th, and Bank—are filled with old brick houses, shady trees, a smattering of better shops and galleries, and a great feeling of calm. Note the brick house at the corner of West 11th and West 4th. It must have looked just as it does now for over 100 years, which is no mean feat in New York.

When you reach **Bank Street,** turn left (west). During a particularly virulent smallpox epidemic in the 1820s, so many New York banking institutions set up temporary offices on this street that the Village of Greenwich named it after them. Note the ancient wisteria growing on no. 60. This is the sort of tenement house that invaded the Village as it became less fashionable in the latter part of the 19th century. Today even the tenements have an appealing patina of age. Many fine old Greek Revival houses remain on this block of Bank, making it one of the Village's nicest.

At the end of the block, Bank intersects **Bleecker Street** adjacent to Abingdon Square. Turn left (south) and continue down Bleecker. This is a street of antiques shops whose windows display Dutch chests and French chandeliers. There are occasional boutiques, interesting bookstores, cracked sidewalks, and some pretty blowsy looking modern-ish buildings. The narrow tree-lined side streets, however, are absolutely delightful. Continue south on Bleecker for five blocks to **Christopher Street** and turn right (west toward the Hudson). Ahead in the distance you can see New Jersey across the river. On the street around you'll see gay New York in full flower, as Christopher Street is more or less its spiritual center.

Stay on Christopher for one short block to **Bedford Street** and turn left (south). At the end of the block, on the corner of Grove Street, is a nest of particularly picturesque wooden houses. No. 17 Grove St., on the corner of Bedford and Grove, was built by a Village sash-maker in the 1820s. It sags wonderfully and evokes the past quite vividly. No. 100 Bedford St., located midblock between Grove and Christopher, is a Grimm's fairytale concoction of stucco, timbers, and crazy angles. This individualistic renovation was paid for in 1925 by financier Otto Kahn. Called **Twin Peaks,** it is the design of Clifford Daily, who thought the Village was becoming too dull, architecturally anyway, for the proper stimulation of its artistic population. During a wild housewarming party in 1926, Princess Anna Troubetzsky climbed atop one peak to make an offering of burnt acorns to the gods, while screen star Mabel Normand climbed atop the other and smashed a bottle of champagne on the ridgepole. Kahn's daughter lived in the house for many years, hence her father's willingness to foot the bill.

Make a right on Grove Street in the direction of the Hudson. The road makes a dogleg turn just a few steps from Bedford. Right at the angle of the turn you'll see a little gate set into a brick wall. Although it's private beyond, you can step up to the gate and look over it into **Grove Court.** Built for blue-collar tenants about 1830, and originally called Mixed Ale Alley, this tree-shaded enclave of little brick houses is the sort of Village spot many New Yorkers would kill to live in.

After you've admired the Federal houses in Grove Court, continue another half block to the end of Grove at **Hudson Street.** The old church across Hudson is **St. Luke's in the Fields,** also built in the 1820s when so much of this part of the Village was going up. The original St. Luke's was destroyed by fire, but the restoration preserves its rural look, despite the enormous Victorian-era warehouses looming behind it.

As you leave Grove Street, turn left (south) on Hudson for one block to **Barrow Street,** and turn left again. The first corner you'll come to is called **Commerce Street.** The intersection sports an interesting pair of identical houses, no. 39 and no. 41 Commerce St., which were built in the 1830s and "modernized" in the 1870s with matching mansard roofs. Turn right off Barrow into tiny Commerce Street. This crooked little thoroughfare used to be called Cherry Lane until the big smallpox scare of 1822 sent so many businesses up here from New York that the name was changed. When you reach the end of the block, you'll be back on Bedford Street. Turn right (south) again, and then look to your right for 75½ Bedford St. This 9½-foot-wide house holds the distinction of being the narrowest house in Greenwich Village, as well as the one-time residence of poet Edna St. Vincent Millay.

Keep walking south on Bedford. In another block you'll come to one of the violent intersections wrought so many years ago by the extension of Seventh Avenue. Immediately on your right is Morton Street. Don't turn here, but continue another block south on Seventh Avenue to **St. Luke's Place.** Now turn right.

Although the south side of St. Luke's Place is occupied by a modern playground, the north side preserves a terrific old row of houses from the 1850s. No. 6 St. Luke's Pl. was the residence of a former mayor of New York, the popular James J. ("Gentleman Jimmy") Walker. Although a crook and a scoundrel, Walker managed to epitomize the glamour of the 1920s. Incredibly enough, he is remembered quite fondly to this day.

After you've admired Jimmy Walker's digs, return to Seventh Avenue and continue straight across it on the line of St. Luke's Place. Once across Seventh you'll note that St. Luke's becomes **Leroy Street.** Stay on Leroy, past the continuation of Bedford Street for one block to the corner of Bleecker Street. Just before this intersection, note 7 Leroy St., a nearly perfect circa 1810 house, complete with alley entrance and original dormers.

When you get to Bleecker, you'll find a local shopping area with enterprises such as Rocco's Pastry Shop, the Bleecker Street Fish Market ("If It Swims, We Have It"), a record shop called Discorama, and assorted souvenir shops. Turn left on Bleecker for two very short blocks to **Jones Street.** Turn right onto Jones and take a quick look at no. 17 to see what usually happens to old houses like the one at no. 7 Leroy. A pity, no? At the end of the block, you'll be back on West 4th Street. Turn right for another short block and presto, here you are again back on Sixth Avenue, a mere two blocks south of Waverly Place where our tour began.

TOUR NO. 3: THE UPPER EAST SIDE HISTORIC DISTRICT

Start: Grand Army Plaza, Fifth Avenue at 60th Street. *Finish:* Madison Avenue and East 91st Street. *Time required:* Approximately one hour and 20 minutes.

It was predicted over a century ago that fashion would settle permanently along the verges of Central Park. And that prediction has turned out to be true. Fifth Avenue north of Grand Army Plaza was called the Millionaires' Mile in the era of private palaces. Judging from old pictures, it was something to behold. Today it's lined with apartment houses interspersed with the occasional remaining mansion. But let's not believe for an instant that the age of imperial living is over. Some of the buildings on Fifth (as well as on Park and elsewhere on the East Side) contain apartments that are every bit as palatial as the now-vanished mansions. Even New Yorkers are surprised to hear of apartments with 20, 30, or even 40 rooms. But they do exist, and probably in no fewer numbers than the great houses they replaced.

Before we start you might take a look at Augustus Saint-Gaudens' equestrian **statue of General William Tecumseh Sherman,** which stands at the northern end of the Plaza between the lines of 59th and 60th Streets. It was Sherman, of course, whose Civil War "March to the Sea" dealt the Confederacy such a staggering blow. The Plaza is officially called Grand Army Plaza in honor of the Grand Army of the Republic, or the Union Army. Saint-Gaudens' statue was shown in Paris in 1900 and erected here in 1903. It's more in tune with the area's residential past than the traffic and tumult that surround it today. But it remains a welcome aesthetic touch, and very much in the spirit of the "City Beautiful" movement of the early 20th century.

We're going to go north (uptown) on Fifth Avenue. Cross the extension of 60th Street that doglegs into the corner of Central Park and stay on the park side of Fifth. If the weather is good the **bookstalls** lining the sidewalk near 60th Street will be open. This is a bit of a self-conscious touch of Paris, but it's still rather nice. After browsing through a few old books, glance back at the gaggle of deluxe hotels crowding around the Plaza. They serve as a sort of conceptual buffer between midtown businesses to the south and uptown residences to the north.

Also in the immediate vicinity are several of Manhattan's classiest clubs. That painted-stone Italian palace on the corner of Fifth and 60th Street is the **Metropolitan Club,** designed by the celebrated (and ubiquitous) McKim, Mead, and White. If you like this sort of thing, you might detour across the street for a look at the main entrance on 60th Street. At 4 E. 60th St., right across from the Metropolitan, is the **Harmonie Club,** an elite Jewish social club also designed by McKim, Mead, and White in 1905, a little over ten years after the Metropolitan. These two fine buildings purposely complement one another (if only more new construction did the same).

Go back to Fifth and keep walking uptown. At the corner of 62nd Street is the Georgian brick **Knickerbocker Club,** which looks a lot like the sort of big private house that once characterized the avenue. The Knickerbocker, built in 1914, was the work of a firm called Delano and Aldrich, a favorite of society in the early years of this century. It retains a very pedigreed image.

The next block up is 63rd Street and on the corner you'll see **820 Fifth Ave.** Built in 1916, this is one of the earliest apartment houses hereabouts, and also one of the best. There is but one apartment on each floor, with five fireplaces and seven bathrooms.

Go back to Fifth and continue northward to 64th Street. Just inside Central Park, facing 64th, is the **Arsenal,** built in 1848 as an arms depot when this neighborhood was distant and deserted. The **Central Park Zoo** is right behind it. Across Fifth Avenue on the southeast corner of 64th Street is the former mansion of coal magnate Edward Berwind. If you've been to see the mansions at Newport, Rhode Island, you've probably already seen Mr. Berwind's summer house, "The Elms" on

Bellevue Avenue. His New York residence dates from 1896 and has been preserved as cooperative apartments.

Turn right (east) off Fifth onto 64th Street and proceed toward Madison Avenue. This is a particularly handsome East Side block, lined with architectural extravaganzas of the sort that formerly stood on Fifth Avenue. Note in particular **3 E. 64th St.,** an opulent beaux arts mansion built in 1903 for the daughter of Mrs. William B. Astor. The house was designed by Warren and Wetmore, the firm responsible for Grand Central Terminal. Also worthy of admiration on this block are nos. 11, 19, and 20. No. 19, which looks more antique than its 1932 construction date, was built not as a house but as the art gallery it is today.

At the corner of **Madison Avenue** and 64th, turn left and proceed two blocks north to 66th Street. Madison is lined with fashionable shops and boutiques catering to the carriage trade. Note the rather fantastical apartment house built in 1900 on the northeast corner of 66th and Madison, then turn left (west) off Madison onto 66th Street, heading back in the direction of Fifth Avenue. Among the many notable houses on the block is 5 E. 66th St., now the **Lotos Club,** but built in 1900 as the city residence of William J. Schiefflin. The architect was Richard Howland Hunt, and the style is Manhattan Magnificent, courtesy of the French Second Empire.

Now return to Madison Avenue and continue northward for two more blocks to 68th Street. At 68th Street, turn right (east) toward Park Avenue. Now you're on a block with lots of private houses, even though most people don't quite realize that fact. I myself would certainly like to live on this elegant street. One of the best of these houses is **58 E. 68th St.,** on the south corner of the block at Park Avenue. Now occupied by the Council on Foreign Relations, the house was originally built in 1920 for Harold I. Pratt, son of Rockefeller partner Charles Pratt. Its construction signaled a major departure for this member of the famously close-knit Pratts. His three brothers all built mansions in Brooklyn opposite their father's. Virtually the entire family summered together in a complex of adjoining estates at Dosoris near Glen Cove, Long Island. But 58 E. 68th St. is in Manhattan, with no other Pratts in sight.

Across 68th Street from the Pratt house is a fine brick-and-marble mansion built in 1909 for banker Percy Pyne. This house, whose address is **680 Park Ave.,** once belonged to the Soviet Delegation to the United Nations. Khrushchev waved to curious crowds from its Park Avenue balcony during his famous shoe-banging visit to the U.N., now many years ago. In 1965 this house was saved from demolition at the 11th hour by the Marquesa de Cuevas (born a Rockefeller), who bought it and donated it to the present occupant, the Center for InterAmerican Relations. The entire west side of Park Avenue from 68th to 69th is lined with refined brick-and-marble Georgian Revival houses like that of Percy Pyne. It's a surprise they're all still here!

Go north on Park to 69th Street, then turn right and cross Park Avenue, and continue eastbound on 69th Street toward Lexington Avenue. No. 101 E. 69th St. on the corner of Park is the patrician **Union Club,** designed in 1932 to house New York's oldest club. On the other side of 69th Street, and occupying the entire block from 68th to 69th and Park to Lexington, is **Hunter College.** Continue toward Lexington, soaking up the East Side atmosphere. Note 117 E. 69th St., a prototypical not-so-small private East Side house.

When you arrive at **Lexington Avenue,** turn left (north) and go one block to 70th Street. Then turn left again (to the west) and continue down 70th back in the direction of Park Avenue. Note **125 E. 70th St.,** a post–World War II mansion built for Paul Mellon in a sort of French Provincial style. **East 70th Street** presents a succession of elegant houses, one more beautiful than the other. Some consider this the finest street in New York.

When you arrive at the Park Avenue end of the block, note the modern building housing the **Asia Society** with its changing exhibits as well as its Asian-focused bookstore and gift shop. Then look across the street at **720 Park Ave.,** on the northwest corner of the intersection. This is a premier example of the sort of swanky Park Avenue building that lured former mansion dwellers away from their private houses. The complex upper floors of buildings like no. 720 often contain apartments with three or four floors and dozens of rooms.

Cross Park Avenue and continue west toward Fifth Avenue on 70th Street. The mansion at 46 E. 70th Street now houses the famous **Explorers Club.** The one at 32 E. 70th, built in 1910, is hard to beat for pure East Side class.

At the end of this block, cross Madison Avenue and continue on 70th toward Fifth Avenue. At the corner of Fifth is the famous **Frick Collection,** housed in the 1914 mansion of coke and steel magnate Henry Clay Frick. The beautiful classic garden overlooking 70th Street was built in 1977 and landscaped by Russel Page. It's a good fake; it looks definitely like something from the guilded age. Inside the Frick is a notable collection of paintings, as well as many original furnishings. Frick intended that the house, an 18th-century palace occupying a full blockfront on Fifth Avenue, be converted to a museum after his death. Huge as it is, this is not the biggest house still standing on Fifth. (Otto Kahn's is, farther up Fifth.)

Turn right at the corner of Fifth and 70th and continue three blocks north to the corner of Fifth and 73rd Street. Now turn right onto 73rd in the direction of Madison Avenue. Note **11 E. 73rd St.,** a particularly sumptuous house built in 1903 by (who else?) McKim, Mead, and White for Joseph Pulitzer, publisher of a once-famous but long-vanished newspaper called the *New York World*. Pulitzer rarely lived in this house because of an extreme sensitivity to sound. At one time it contained a special soundproofed room (mounted on ball bearings, no less) to prevent vibrations. The house today contains cooperative apartments.

Continue to the end of the block at Madison Avenue and turn left (north). Now stroll up Madison for six blocks to 79th Street. This is the heart of Madison Avenue Gallery Country, presided over by the elegant **Hotel Carlyle** at 76th Street. That weird-looking box on the southeast corner of Madison and 75th, by the way, is the **Whitney Museum of American Art,** designed in 1966 by Marcel Breuer in the appropriately named "brutalist" style of architecture. The Whitney now wants to expand and, wonder of wonders, people are stepping forward to protest alterations to the original Breuer design. Of course, perhaps they're just afraid of more of the same.

At **79th Street,** turn left (west) and return to Fifth Avenue. The south side of 79th is a landmark block, designated too late, alas, to prevent the senseless demolition of the house on the Madison Avenue corner. More than enough remains, however, to provide a pretty good idea of how Fifth Avenue looked in its heyday. There's everything here, from Loire Valley châteaux to neo-Georgian town houses.

When you reach the corner of Fifth, turn left for a look at the block between 78th and 79th. No. **972 Fifth Ave.** is now the French Embassy's Cultural Services Office. But it was built in 1906 as a wedding present for one Payne Whitney by his doting (and childless) rich uncle, Col. Oliver Hazard Payne. This McKim, Mead, and White opus cost $1 million and was the talk of the town in its day. Next door, on the corner of 78th Street, is the classic French-style mansion of tobacco millionaire James B. Duke. His daughter, Doris, occupied the house intermittently until 1957, when she donated it to New York University. NYU now operates it as a fine arts institute.

Now turn around and walk north on Fifth until you reach 82nd Street. On your left is the imperial-scale entrance to the **Metropolitan Museum of Art,** one of New York's greatest cultural resources. The block of 82nd Street that faces the museum's mammoth staircase almost acts as a sort of formal court. The sumptuous brick-and-limestone mansion at **1009 Fifth Ave.** is another old house preserved as cooperative apartments.

Turn right off Fifth onto 82nd and head toward Madison Avenue again. This is another fine East Side block, lined with elegant old town houses. The modern brick

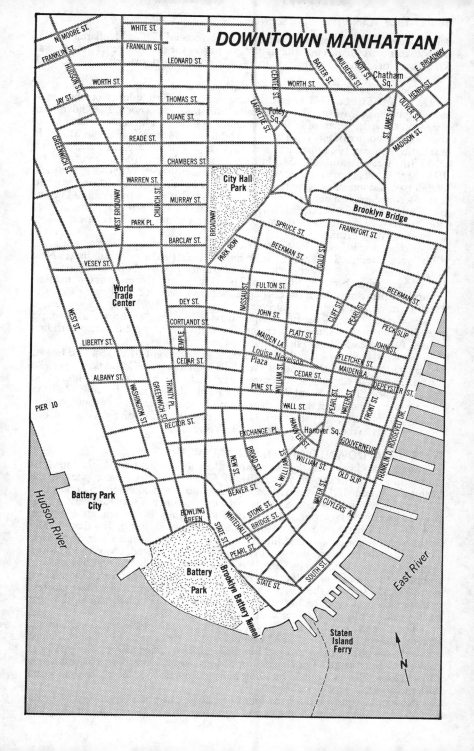

DOWNTOWN MANHATTAN

school across Madison between 81st and 82nd Streets is **P.S. 6,** a Manhattan public school whose excellent reputation is a major reason for the high rents hereabouts. Walk two blocks north on Madison to 84th Street and then turn left (west) toward Fifth Avenue.

When you reach Fifth, turn right (north) and continue uptown for two more blocks to **86th Street.** This is a big dividing line on the East Side, a fact which may not be apparent to visitors. It's a measure of the snobbery of some East Siders that they won't even *go* north of 86th Street. The big brick-and-limestone mansion on the southern corner of Fifth and 86th was built in 1914 for William Star Miller. It was to this house in 1944 that Mrs. Cornelius Vanderbilt retreated when her famous 640 Fifth Ave. was sold. No. 640 Fifth was located down on 51st Street, and by 1944 Mrs. V. was pretty much alone down there, surrounded by ghosts of the Vanderbilt past and lots of noisy traffic and new office buildings. No. 640 Fifth was the first of a concentration of Vanderbilt family houses that at one time caused Fifth in the 50s to be called "Vanderbilt Alley." The exile to 86th Street appears, at least from the look of this house, to have been comfortable, anyway. Today the building houses the Yivo Institute.

Two blocks farther up Fifth is the **Guggenheim Museum,** between 88th and 89th Streets. Designed by Frank Lloyd Wright in 1959 (it's his only building in New York), it's as architecturally controversial today as it was when built. One block past the Guggenheim, between 90th and 91st Streets, are the enormous enclosed grounds of the former **Andrew Carnegie Mansion,** now occupied by the Cooper-Hewitt Museum of Design and Decorative Arts. Built in 1901 this Georgian-esque palace originally shared the neighborhood with squatters' shanties and roaming pigs. By the time the squatters were gone and the streets were built up with fine houses, Carnegie was dead. His widow lived on in the house until 1949.

Across 91st Street from the Carnegies' is the **Convent of the Sacred Heart,** occupying the largest private house ever built in Manhattan. Constructed in 1918 for financier Otto Kahn, it survives in pretty original condition. Other houses on this block, notably nos. 7 and 9 E. 91st St., are almost as grand. By now, Madison Avenue is approaching in the near distance, and that's the end of our tour. No subways are around here, but you can easily catch a downtown bus on Fifth Avenue, or a crosstown bus to the West Side down on 86th Street.

TOUR NO. 4: DOWNTOWN–FINANCIAL DISTRICT

Start: Broadway and Chambers Street (half the subways in Manhattan must stop within a block or so of this intersection). *Finish:* Bowling Green (adjacent to the Lexington Avenue IRT station). *Time required:* About one hour and 15 minutes.

Broadway and Chambers Street is at the upper corner of **City Hall Park,** a 250-year-old greensward surrounded by landmark buildings. Before you go anywhere, look east on Chambers Street toward the **Municipal Building.** It's that slightly Stalin-esque wedding cake straddling Chambers Street on the other side of the park. This is really the best vantage point for admiring McKim, Mead, and White's monumental city office complex built in 1914. It cleverly utilizes an awkward site and combines functionalism with beauty in a manner too often forgotten by modern architects. The statue at the very pinnacle of the thing represents *Civic Fame,* whatever that might be. Certainly she (he?) is high enough to overlook the corruption that has historically plagued this region of Manhattan.

Those interested in beaux arts architecture should walk east on Chambers Street to the end of the block. At 31 Chambers St., at the corner of Park Row and just across the street from the Municipal Building, is a Frenchified palace built in 1911 as New York's **Surrogate's Court.** The stupendous marble lobby of this place is surely worth a look. Here is a public building built to impress, not merely to drag along with the drab duties of civic life.

Now turn around and retrace your steps along Chambers Street back in the direction of Broadway. That dull-gray and capacious old 1872 Italianate building just inside City Hall Park on your left is the famous **Tweed Courthouse.** Actually, it is officially called the New York City Courthouse. But William Marcy ("Boss") Tweed, during whose tenure on the Board of Supervisors it was built, stole so much of its construction funds that it has evermore borne his name. When the cornerstone was laid in 1861, the city had budgeted $250,000 for its construction. By the time it was finished ten years later, the total cost had approached $14 *million.* Tweed and his cronies (described in the introduction of this book) induced every subcontractor to present padded bills. For example, one Andrew Garvey, subsequently known in the press as the "Prince of Plasterers," was paid $45,966.89 by the city for a single day's work. An estimated $10 million went into the pockets of Tweed and his pals. The ensuing scandal would eventually end Tweed's career. He died in jail four years later, without a penny to his name.

When you reach Broadway again, turn left and continue south for two blocks to Murray Street. Now we're going to enter City Hall Park and head for the front door of **City Hall,** which faces the parking area in the middle of the park, about on the line of Murray Street. In what historian T. A. Janvier termed a "shrewd thrust of prophetic sarcasm," New York City originally housed both convicted felons and city officials in the same building down on Wall Street. The present City Hall is a rather fragile-looking gem, considering the hardball that's been played here since 1811. The design is clearly 18th century, an amalgam of French and British antecedents cooked up as part of a city-sponsored contest. The winning architects were Joseph Mangin, a Frenchman who had worked in Paris on the Place de la Concorde, and a Scot by the name of John McComb. When completed in 1811, this was practically the northernmost structure in town. As a result the rear wall was faced with brownstone (cheaper than the limestone used on the rest of the place) on the theory that since hardly anybody would see it, why not save the money? In subsequent years the brownstone was replaced. Parts of City Hall are open to the public on weekdays from 10 a.m. to 4 p.m. It's a beautiful place, but one constantly wonders how such a big city can be managed from such a small city hall.

Before leaving City Hall, stop for a moment on the steps to admire the **Brooklyn Bridge,** looming impressively in the east. Built in 1883, it was the world's first steel suspension bridge. It's possible, if you are so inclined, to walk all the way across it to Brooklyn. The walkway is free, and the views are truly superb. Let's leave it for another day's excursion, however, and continue with our tour.

Return now to Broadway at Murray Street, noting Frederick MacMonnies' **statue of Nathan Hale,** located just inside the park opposite Murray. Noble, isn't it? (Guess who designed the base? Stanford White.) Turn left on Broadway and continue south for one block to Park Place. On the west side of Broadway, occupying the block between Park Place and Barclay Street, is the **Woolworth Building.** Five-and-dime czar Frank W. Woolworth ponied up $13 million in *cash* back in 1913 to pay for his new headquarters. During the opening ceremonies President Woodrow Wilson himself pressed a button in Washington that illuminated 80,000 bulbs in the tower. The Rev. S. Parkes Cadman, witnessing the scene, declared the building to be a "Cathedral of Commerce," the sight of which provoked "feelings too deep even for tears." For 17 years this architectural marriage of Gothic Europe and the American skyscraper was the tallest building in the world. It still ranks as one of New York's handsomest. By all means, go inside the lobby. With its marble walls and domed ceiling it's certainly as ornate as most cathedrals.

Leave the Woolworth Building and pause for a moment on the sidewalk outside. The other side of City Hall Park is bounded by a street called **Park Row** which, in the early years of this century, contained the offices of 12 New York City newspapers. In those days the area now containing the approaches to the Brooklyn Bridge was known as Printing House Square. Today the entire industry has scattered to various other parts of town.

Go another block down Broadway from the Woolworth Building, past Barclay Street, to Vesey Street. On your right, occupying the western blockfront of Broadway between Vesey and Fulton Streets, is **St. Paul's Chapel.** This delicious old Georgian church dates from 1766, although the steeple wasn't added until after the Revolution in 1794. George Washington worshipped here; Pierre L'Enfant, the planner of Washington, D.C., designed the gilded sunburst above the altar; the graveyard outside contains the picturesque tombs of now-forgotten city squires and ladies. The building is an incredible contrast to the huge towers of the World Trade Center scraping the sky behind it. You're free to wander inside for a look. And if the interior layout seems confusing, bear in mind that St. Paul's was originally designed to face the river. That's the side with the steeple. But as Broadway grew to become the town's most important thoroughfare, it was decided to erect a new portico here instead of on the original front.

Leave St. Paul's, turn right, and continue south again on Broadway. Across Fulton Street on the next block, occupying a site that extends from Fulton south to Dey Street, is no. 195 Broadway, the original **AT&T Building.** If you're in the mood for another taste of the majesty of capitalism, have a look at the lobby. It's a perfect forest of immense columns. Indeed, the exterior of this building has more columns than any other stone structure in the world. Built in 1917, it was recently abandoned by AT&T for a new headquarters up on Madison and 56th.

When you've marveled sufficiently at what long-distance rates hath wrought, exit 195 Broadway and turn right (south) to the corner of Dey and Broadway. Turn right again onto Dey Street and continue west to the corner of Church Street. Before you is the $700-million **World Trade Center** (described in detail in section 1 of this chapter, "The Famous Sights"). If you wish, you can detour to the Observation Deck on the 110th floor of Two World Trade Center, the tower to your left as you face the complex from the other side of Church Street. Alternatively you can just take a spin around the immense plaza at the foot of the twin towers, save the deck for later, and continue with our tour.

After you've checked out the Trade Center, retrace your steps back up Dey Street to Broadway. Now cross Broadway and continue east on **John Street** (which is just Dey Street with its name changed). This canyon-like thoroughfare is so narrow that it's closed to traffic at lunch hour. Note the modern skyscraper castle, complete with crenelated turrets, at the corner of John and Nassau.

Cross Nassau, keeping on John, and continue east. The simple, steeple-less church at 44 John St. (in the shadow of the huge new tower) is the **John Street Methodist Church.** The present building was erected in 1841, but the congregation has owned and worshipped at this address since 1768, making it the oldest Methodist society in America.

Keep going east on John Street for 4½ more blocks. It's a short walk, down an 18th-century street lined with towering 20th-century buildings. On the last of these blocks, between Pearl and Water Streets, is **127 John St.,** a 1969 office building with a street-level concourse filled with 1960s nonsense. There are an astonishingly complicated digital clock, blue neon-lined tubes leading to the elevators, and all manner of whimsical constructs for seating and shelter. Not beautiful, but very evocative of the '60s.

Pearl Street, by the way, was originally called Mother-of-Pearl Street, because it was once the beach that ran along the shore of the East River. Water Street, a block farther east, was built on landfill, as was everything beyond it.

Turn left off John onto Water Street, skirting the perimeter of 127 John, and continue north for one block to Fulton Street. The corner of Fulton and Water marks the entrance to the **South Street Seaport** (also described separately in Section 1 of this chapter). From this point to the East River Fulton Street has been transformed into a cobbled pedestrian mall. Between Water Street and South Street it's lined with restored buildings, Seaport Museum galleries, pricey shops, and "intriguing" restaurants. The seaport is definitely worth a day unto itself. For now, you might stroll the two short blocks down Fulton to South and admire the sailing ships at berth in the river. After which you might get a snack at one of the restaurants or food stalls in Pier 17, and then return one block up Fulton to Front Street and turn left (south).

Keep south on **Front Street** for six short blocks. Until recently this area was filled with ancient brick buildings similar to those in the seaport. Their sudden disappearance and replacement by the modern behemoths that line the street today were a principal factor leading to the founding of the Seaport Museum.

The sixth intersection you'll come to is that of Front Street and **Wall Street,** and here you'll turn right. As you may already have heard, Wall Street follows the line of a crude palisade erected in the 17th century by the Dutch to deter Indian attacks. It was never put to a test, even though the Indians did almost as much mischief as the Dutch in other regions of Manhattan. Start walking west on Wall Street, past Water and Pearl Streets. Ahead you'll see the slender spire of **Trinity Church,** located at Broadway and Wall. It's hard to believe that this tiny antique, cringing at the bottom of a Grand Canyon of concrete, was once the tallest structure on Manhattan, a landmark visible from far out in the harbor.

On the left side of the next block, just past Hanover Street, is the entrance to **55 Wall St.** This was the site of a Merchants' Exchange destroyed in the great New York fire of 1835. The exchange was rebuilt in 1836, and the first three floors of it still exist right here in 55 Wall. In 1907 the place was remodeled for the National City Bank, and its size was doubled in the process. The building now belongs to Citibank, and its banking floor is well worth a look. This interior resembles nothing so much as an imperial Roman bath. Beneath the soaring marble walls and columns are perfectly ridiculous-looking modern banking islands. We should be glad, however, that nobody has tried to tear the place down.

Exit 55 Wall, turn left (west), and continue in the direction we've been heading. Stay on Wall past the intersection of William Street until you see on your right the statue of George Washington standing above the steps to **Federal Hall National Memorial.** This museum, located at the corner of Wall and Nassau Streets, occupies a very fine Greek Revival building erected in 1842. New York's City Hall, before being relocated to the present City Hall Park, formerly stood at this site. In 1789 the father of our country took the oath of office on the balcony of the old building, which at that point had been remodeled by Major L'Enfant and rechristened Federal Hall. There's a free museum inside the present Federal Hall, with exhibits pertaining to the building, the Revolution, Washington, etc.

Federal Hall stands at the head of **Broad Street,** down which we're now going to turn. Just south of Wall, on the right (west) side of Broad Street, is the gratifyingly magnificent columned façade of the **New York Stock Exchange,** at 3 Broad St. There's been a stock exchange in New York since 1792, when a group of brokers started meeting under a buttonwood tree near Wall and William Streets. The initial purpose of the exchange was to sell government bonds to pay off the debt left over from the Revolutionary War. The market grew in power and importance throughout the 19th century. In 1903 it moved to the present building, which can be visited for free (refer to Section 1 of this chapter for details).

The next intersection to the south is that of Broad and **Exchange Place.** Turn left (east) onto Exchange and behold the popular image of "Wall Street" before your very eyes. This street is so narrow you want to turn sideways to walk down it. And the buildings along its sides are so tall that direct sunlight probably hasn't hit the pavement since 1917. Continue to the end of the block and cross William Street. Then continue on Exchange to the end of the next block (these are very short blocks by the way) and turn right onto **Hanover Street.** It's only about 30 feet to the corner of **Beaver Street,** where you'll turn right again for another 30 or 40 feet until you arrive at the corner of **William Street.** And here, with Delmonico's Restaurant facing you across the street, you'll turn left onto William for another 50-odd feet until you arrive at **Hanover Square.**

This is quite a historic corner of old New York. Like so many other districts, Hanover Square had its day in the sun as an elite residential enclave. The premier householder was none other than Captain Kidd, a notorious pirate abroad (the English caught him and hanged him in 1701) but a respected citizen of New York City and a contributor to Trinity Church. The first newspaper in town, the *New-York Gazette,* was also printed in Hanover Square, in 1725 by William Bradford. The great Fire of 1835 started with a gas explosion in Hanover Square. The ensuing conflagration engulfed 20 acres and destroyed 650 buildings, including everything that had survived until then from the Dutch period. **India House,** that charming old brownstone building on the south side of William at the corner of Pearl, was built in 1854 as the Hanover Bank. It is today a private club.

Now turn around and go back on William Street to Delmonico's. When you reach the corner of William and Beaver, take a sharp left onto **South William Street.** The wall of Delmonico's will be on your right as you walk down South William. There are wonderful opportunities hereabouts for pictures of twisting narrow streets and huge soaring skyscrapers. South William continues for one block only, until it joins Broad Street. When you get to the corner, turn left (south) onto Broad for two blocks to **Bridge Street** and pause for a moment on the corner.

That old brick building just ahead of you down at Broad and Pearl is **Fraunces Tavern.** Samuel Fraunces was a black man whose "Queen's Head Tavern," as the place was originally called, figured in several passages of American history. The New York Chamber of Commerce was founded here in 1768. In 1783 the tavern was the scene of DeWitt Clinton's gala celebration of the British evacuation of occupied New York. It was here, also in 1783, that George Washington (Fraunces was his chief steward) bade farewell to his officers and announced his retirement to Mount Vernon. The building had fallen pretty low by the end of the 19th century. In 1904 it was lovingly restored by the Sons of the Revolution, although the authenticity of its present appearance is questionable. Today it is again a restaurant with a small museum attached.

Turn right off Broad Street onto Bridge Street and walk one block to the corner of Whitehall Street. Cross Whitehall and continue another short block to **State Street,** where you'll turn right. The huge building to your right was until 1973 the **U.S. Customs House.** It's a shame Customs moved to the World Trade Center. Nothing could match the magnificence of this 1907 beaux arts masterpiece, which has stood vacant ever since.

The main entrance to the Customs House is at the head of State Street facing **Bowling Green.** This little park was once a Dutch cattle market, and later a green for bowls. The iron fence around it has been there since 1771, and was erected originally to protect an equestrian statue of King George III. On July 9, 1776, a rowdy crowd, excited by a reading of the Declaration of Independence, descended upon Bowling Green, tore the statue down, and broke it into pieces. Legend has it the lead was melted into bullets that subsequently felled 400 British soldiers.

The greensward that faces the side wall of the Customs House on the other side of State Street is **Battery Park,** named after a gun emplacement that once stood along the line of present State Street. Usually just called the Battery, this very pleasant park is constructed entirely on landfill. It's an ideal place for strolling and admiring unobstructed views of New York Harbor.

At the northern end of the Battery, located directly on the waterfront, is **Castle Clinton.** This old fortress started life in 1807 as another gun emplacement. Before the waterfront was filled in, it sat about 300 feet offshore on a pile of rocks. In the 1820s the federal government ceded it to the city, which converted it to a civic reception hall. Lafayette, President Jackson, and the Prince of Wales were all officially greeted here by the City of New York. By 1850 it was called Castle Garden and operated as a concert hall. This is where P. T. Barnum first presented Jenny Lind, "The Swedish Nightingale," to an adoring American audience. Five years after that the building was converted to the Immigrant Landing Depot. Almost eight million future Americans were processed at Castle Garden before Ellis Island was completed in 1892. After its immigrant era it became the New York Aquarium, which it remained until that institution moved to Coney Island in 1941. Vacant and threat-ened with demolition in the years thereafter, it was eventually rescued and restored in 1976 by the National Park Service to its present somewhat dry appearance.

And with that, we come to the end of another tour.

TOUR NO. 5: TIMES SQUARE–42ND STREET

Start: 42nd Street and Seventh Avenue. *Finish:* 42nd Street and First Avenue. *Time required:* About one hour and 30 minutes.

An advertising man by the name of O. J. Gude is credited as being the first to call **Times Square** the "Great White Way." This was back in 1901, when the golden age of electrically lighted billboards was just beginning. These billboards, whose suc-cessors still dominate the intersection of Seventh Avenue and Broadway, reached their apogee in the 1940s and 1950s. There was once an immense sign for Camel cigarettes over Times Square that blew real smoke rings (as long as the wind o-bliged), another for Gilbey's gin that featured a 40-foot simulated waterfall of hootch, and yet another consisting of a monumentally scaled image of Little Lulu clutching a Kleenex.

The days of fabulous signs on this strip of honky-tonk, running roughly from 42nd Street to 47th Street, are hardly over. Instead of smoke rings we have block-long billboards of models wearing jeans and hilarious expressions of postcoital bore-dom. We also have computer-run extravaganzas that present mesmerizing and ever-changing advertisements on huge boards of multicolored lights. And we have the old familiars, like Coca-Cola and Castro Convertibles, glaring benignly over Broadway, day in and day out. It's bright enough to read a newspaper here at mid-night, a state of affairs that seems unlikely to change any time soon.

Occupying a small triangular block on the north side of 42nd Street—Broadway is on one side of it, Seventh Avenue is on the other—is the first attraction on our tour. Unfortunately, it's a really hideous building, made ugly by an uncomfortable-looking white marble skin affixed to it in 1966. This was once the **Times Tower,** headquarters of the world-famous *New York Times.* At the turn of the century *Times* publisher Adolph Ochs set a daring precedent by moving his paper out of Printing House Square, adjacent to City Hall, downtown, and up to what was then called Longacre Square, a backwater dominated by harness and carriage shops. However, Longacre Square lay directly on the route of the new IRT subway. And Ochs, in a stroke of public relations genius, got the Longacre station renamed Times Square.

Times Square has always had a slightly seedy/voluptuous reputation, as if some combination of artistic exaltation, luxury, and human degradation was endemic to the very locale. People will tell you about the "lobster palaces" that once thrived here, places with names like Shanley's and Rector's where swells like Lillian Russell and Diamond Jim Brady laughed and drank and spent freely. But at the same time the sporting set was quaffing champagne at the Café de Paris or in the roof garden of the old Astor Hotel, people were being routinely mugged a few blocks south in the heart of the Tenderloin.

Even with the arrival of the *Times,* together with a coincident influx of legiti-mate theaters (most were converted to movie palaces in the 1920s), the area never really lost its slightly dicey air. The proliferation of pornography in the 1970s was nothing new for Times Square. During the 19th century, but a few blocks away, prostitutes openly displayed themselves in windows overlooking the tracks of the Sixth Avenue Elevated Railway. The present drive to "Clean Up Times Square" is nothing new either. It's just the latest round in an ongoing battle between vice and virtue that some unseen deity has seen fit to stage at the intersection of Broadway and Seventh Avenue.

Anyway, let's get moving (always a prudent idea on Times Square). Head north (uptown) for two blocks from 42nd Street to 44th Street. Now turn back and look at the old Times Tower. A quite fantastic computer-driven sign called **The**

Spectragraph dominates the narrow uptown prow of the old joint. If you want, you can buy space on that sign and have a personal message displayed for a loved one (who'd better be there for the expensive moment it appears). Every New Year's Eve at midnight, the famous electrically lighted ball (in more recent years an apple) descends a mast attached to the top of this same building, launching the sea of people below into a frenzy of excitement.

At 44th Street you're right in the epicenter of Times Square. Actually, the north end of the place, up at 47th Street, is called **Father Duffy Square** after the "Fighting Chaplain" who accompanied New York's 69th Regiment into World War I. Up there at 47th Street is the day-of-performance outlet for half-price theater tickets, known as **TKTS** (details are in Chapter V, "New York After Dark"). On the west side of Broadway between 43rd and 44th Streets is the **Paramount Building,** at 1501 Broadway. The famous Paramount Theater, one of New York's premier movie palaces, once occupied the south side of this place until it was gutted and replaced with offices.

Walk up to **45th Street** and turn left (west). Before you, occupying the blockfront from 45th to 46th Streets, is the new **Marriott Marquis Hotel,** a pricey behemoth catering mostly to the convention trade. One hesitates to call the Marriott beautiful, but the 37-story interior atrium is certainly amazing to behold. To take a look, find the hotel's midblock vehicular entrance on 45th Street, go inside, and take the glass-walled elevator to the eighth-floor lobby. Stroll around, look up (nothing like this in Kansas), and when you've had enough, check out the Broadway Lounge, a lobby-level bar overlooking Times Square. There's an excellent view from here, especially at night when all the signs are lit.

Leave the Marriott via the 45th Street exit, cross 45th Street, and find **Shubert Alley,** the little lane that connects 45th and 44th Streets. This is pretty much the heart of New York's legitimate **Theater District,** which since the 1920s has been located on the side streets flanking Broadway. On your left, as you proceed down Shubert Alley toward 44th Street, is the back wall of **One Astor Plaza.** This huge and curious-looking modern skyscraper has a roofline reminiscent of the tail fins on a 1959 Plymouth. It occupies the site of the old Astor Hotel, spiritual forebear of today's Marriott.

On the right (west) side of Shubert Alley are two of the district's approximately 40 theaters, notably the Shubert Theater on 44th Street. The Shubert brothers and their many theaters became such a powerful force on Broadway, and indeed throughout the country, that the federal government brought an antitrust suit against them. A decree in 1956 compelled them to sell off 12 theaters in six cities. They still remain a major theatrical power.

When you reach 44th Street, turn left (east) and return to Times Square. Then turn right and proceed two blocks south to the northwest corner of Seventh Avenue and 42nd Street. To your right, according to the big sign across the street, is the "Greatest Movie Street in the World." The lineup of movie marquees stretching from Seventh to Eighth Avenues on 42nd Street certainly gives credence to the claim. All of these theaters were built originally for legitimate stage shows. Many, especially the New Amsterdam, are incredibly opulent inside, despite the ravages attendant on decades of Viking movies and porno flicks. All sorts of sharpies make this block their home, so don't let anybody see the corn behind your ears.

Turn left on 42nd Street, cross Seventh Avenue, and then continue on across Broadway. On the south side of the street, at 142 W. 42nd St. on the corner of Broadway, is the old **Knickerbocker Hotel,** built in 1902 for John Jacob Astor IV. Now an office building, the Knickerbocker has the same sort of Astorian brick-and-limestone elegance that characterized the now-vanished Hotel Astor. Maxfield Parrish's famous mural of King Cole, located uptown nowadays in the Sheraton St. Regis, once hung in the bar of this hotel.

Keep walking east toward Sixth Avenue. This part of 42nd Street has been considerably sanitized of late. Perhaps by the time you read this there won't be an

X-rated bookstore left. This seems hard for some of us to believe, but change, they say, is inevitable. The New York Telephone Building, a black-glass and white-marble high-rise box at the southwest corner of Sixth Avenue and 42nd Street, is presumably a harbinger of things to come.

Cross Sixth Avenue and everything changes. Suddenly seedy old Times Square is gone and fashionable Midtown surrounds you. That lush patch of greenery running south along Sixth from 42nd to 40th Streets is **Bryant Park,** named in 1884 after the famous poet William Cullen Bryant. In 1822, after the city removed the buried paupers from Washington Square, a new potter's field was established here on Sixth Avenue. It didn't last for very long, however, for by 1842 the Croton Reservoir (a four-acre lake with walls in the style of an Egyptian tomb) was erected on the Fifth Avenue end of the site (where the New York Public Library stands today). And in 1853, a famous exhibition hall called the Crystal Palace was built at the other end. Constructed entirely of iron and glass, the Crystal Palace was widely touted as being completely fireproof. At least until it burned to the ground in 1858. The Bryant Park we saw until recently was designed in the 1930s. However, at present it is being renovated and will probably be closed for awhile.

When you've contemplated Bryant Park, return to 42nd Street and continue east toward Fifth Avenue. The slope-sided black-glass tower on the north side of the block at 41 W. 42nd St. is the **W. R. Grace Building,** an atypical skyscraper design of the mid-1970s.

You'll notice that the neighborhood gets more solid with every step you take. At the corner of Fifth Avenue you'll be right alongside the **New York Public Library,** whose main entrance faces Fifth between 40th and 42nd Streets. This 1911 beaux arts palace is one of the finest buildings in New York, a fitting place for the repository of knowledge. Make a one-block detour to the right (south) on Fifth Avenue to the library's main entrance. The famous stone lions out front make good backdrops for snapshots. The building's interior is worth exploring too. "Imperial" is about the only word that really describes it.

Fifth Avenue in the 40s bears absolutely no resemblance today to the quiet residential quarter it was at the turn of the century. The mansions and the clubs have all been swept away, victims of a runaway tide of rising real estate prices. At one time the intersection of Fifth and 42nd marked the very center of New York domestic fashion, being located midway between Mrs. Astor's house at Fifth and 34th and Mary Mason Jones's Marble Row in the "hinterlands" at Fifth and 57th. How hard it is even to imagine those days, surrounded now by the roar of traffic, the crush of the sidewalk crowds, and the giddy heights of today's tall buildings.

Before crossing Fifth, you might note the good view uptown to your right. In the distance at 50th Street is St. Patrick's Cathedral, silhouetted fetchingly against the brown-glass wall of the Olympic Tower. Now cross Fifth and continue east toward Madison Avenue. Cross Madison when you get there and keep going east. The handsome office building at 60 E. 42nd St., on the south side of the street, is the **Lincoln Building,** built in 1939. In another moment you'll be at Vanderbilt Avenue, a short street that starts on the north side of 42nd Street. The great railroad station before you is **Grand Central Terminal.**

Commodore Vanderbilt himself named the place "Grand Central" in the late 1860s, notwithstanding the fact that it was then way out in the boondocks. The original station underwent more or less continuous alterations until the present structure replaced it in 1913. Besides being visually magnificent, it's an engineering tour de force, combining subways, surface streets, pedestrian malls, vehicular viaducts, underground shopping concourses, and 48 pairs of railroad tracks together with attendant platforms and concourses into one smoothly functioning organism.

Turn left on Vanderbilt Avenue and go one block north to the 43rd Street entrance to Grand Central. Inside these doors is a perfectly breathtaking sight. The main concourse of Grand Central is one of America's most impressive interior spaces—125 feet high, 375 feet long, and 120 feet wide. It's decorated with fine stone carvings, gleaming marble floors, sweeping staircases, and a blue vaulted ceiling decorated with the constellations. Compare this to the Marriott. In 1960 the owners proposed that this space be divided into four levels, the top three being devoted to bowling alleys. Since 1965 it has been a city landmark. Today much of it is being restored as part of deal worked out with developer Donald Trump for bonuses on an adjacent site.

Descend the cascading staircase to the main concourse. Then cut diagonally to your left across the floor toward the bank of escalators on the north wall. Ride the escalators up, admiring the wonders of the old terminal as you go. Note the chandeliers (how *do* they change those bulbs?). The escalator will deposit you at the south end of the **Pan Am Building,** also known as 200 Park Ave. Just keep walking north, away from Grand Central, and you'll eventually emerge on 45th Street between Vanderbilt and Lexington Avenues.

Walk directly across 45th Street and into the ornate doorway of **230 Park Ave.** This handsome structure is now known as the Helmsley Building, after its current owner, real estate magnate Harry Helmsley. Built in 1929 as the New York Central Building, it is a triumph of the business-palatial style. When the fortunes of the railroad began to falter, the place was sold and the sign on the wall was changed to the New York General Building. The Helmsley interests have changed the name again and decorated the façade with a considerable amount of gold leaf. Walk straight through the lobby, notable for its sumptuous marble and bronze work. At the far end you'll emerge on 46th Street, right in the middle of Park Avenue.

Turn right, cross over the northbound roadway of Park Avenue, and head toward Lexington Avenue. Don't go all the way to Lex, but look instead on your right for the doorway to the **Park Avenue Atrium.** This new building is worth a detour for a look at its handsome multistory atrium, furnished with plush burgundy carpeting, polished granite benches, chromium walls, and silent exterior-mounted elevators that whoosh up and down past an immense and dramatic hanging sculpture made of golden metal bands. A pretty restaurant surrounded by potted ficus trees occupies the area adjacent to the soaring central space. It looks like a nice place for a glass of wine and a refined lunch. Next to it is a more informal bar called Charley O's that serves sandwiches and big drinks.

Take the Lexington Avenue exit from the Park Avenue Atrium and turn right (south). Three blocks ahead, on the east side of Lexington Avenue between 42nd and 43rd Streets, is the famous **Chrysler Building.** This was the tallest building in the world when completed in 1930, at least for a couple of months until eclipsed by the Empire State Building. The exterior demonstrates all that's right about oldtime skyscrapers. It's an ornament to the skyline. Notice the huge winged radiator caps that mark the base of the tower. The lobby inside has lots of brown-veined marble and a signature art deco angularity. It's so glamorous you almost expect Jean Harlow to whiz around the corner in a satin dress.

Exit the Chrysler Building via the 42nd Street door, turn left, and continue east on 42nd toward Third Avenue. At 220 E. 42nd St., between Third and Second Avenues, is the **Daily News Building.** This modern brick tower, also built in 1930, was the inspiration for the Daily Planet Building, where Clark Kent worked when he wasn't being Superman. The exterior was ahead of its time for 1930. Even today it hardly looks 59 years old. The lobby contains a huge revolving globe sunk in the floor and surrounded with little plaques bearing messages like: "If the sun were the size of this globe and placed here, then comparatively the moon would be one-third inch in diameter and placed at the main entrance to Grand Central Terminal." Elsewhere in the lobby are gauges disclosing wind direction, humidity, temperature, etc., plus blowups of news photos, famous front pages, etc.

When you're done with the News Building, return to 42nd Street and turn right. Continue east across Second Avenue, then cross 42nd Street to the north side of the block. That slab-like building beyond the big Tudor City sign is the **United Nations Secretariat Building** (described in Section 1 of this chapter). Midway between Second and First Avenues, on the north side of the street, is the brownish granite fortress of the **Ford Foundation Building.** Built in 1967, it contains an early atrium that has yet to be surpassed in terms of beauty. There's a little pool with water gurgling into it, brick paths wandering through terraces of greenery, and a great sense of calm. Well, why shouldn't the Ford Foundation be calm?

Return to 42nd Street and, if the mood seizes you, walk up the brick stairs flanking 42nd Street to **Tudor City.** This very large apartment complex dates from the 1920s and is done entirely in the sort-of-Tudor style so popular after the First World War. When built, it was surrounded by slums and slaughter houses so that by necessity the project included its own park, shops, restaurants, and post office, as well as some heart-stoppingly beautiful apartments, many of which rent today for absurdly low controlled prices. Gaze up at those walls of double-height leaded windows on the upper floors. It looks almost as if a series English country mansions had been grafted onto the top of a row of apartment towers.

When you've had enough of Tudor City, return to 42nd Street. The crosstown bus stops at the corner of First Avenue. Don't forget to ask the driver for a free transfer if you're eventually heading north or south of 42nd.

TOUR NO. 6: SOHO GALLERIES AND THE CAST-IRON DISTRICT

Start: West Broadway and Houston Street. *Finish:* Sixth Avenue and Houston Street. *Time required:* About one hour and 25 minutes.

Until the late 1840s what we now call SoHo (a fractured acronym for *So*uth of *Ho*uston Street) was a quiet residential quarter of the northern edge of town. Starting in about 1850 a commercial building boom (petering out finally in the 1890s) totally transformed the place into a neighborhood of swank retail stores and loft buildings for light manufacturing. All this activity coincided with the development of cast iron as a building material. Columns, arches, pediments, brackets, keystones, and everything else that once had to be carved in stone could now be mass produced at lower cost in iron. The result was a commercial building spree that gave free rein to the opulent architectural styles of the day.

But after the spree came long generations of neglect. By the late 1960s the area was dismissed as too dismal for words. And for that precise reason it began attracting impoverished artists. Back then you could rent huge spaces in SoHo's former sweatshops (considerable exploitation went on behind these handsome façades) for next to nothing. But restless fashion was not about to ignore a developing new brew of art and historic architecture. By the early 1970s the land boom was on. Today West Broadway is literally lined with rarified boutiques, avant-garde galleries, and trendy restaurants. SoHo lofts now appear in the pages of *Architectural Digest* and they're more likely to be inhabited by art patrons than artists.

Yet one cannot dismiss SoHo as a travesty of art sold out to commerce. Its concentration of galleries soon made it a major force in world art markets, and as such a major force in the very shape of today's art. The intellectual and artistic ferment in SoHo had strong parallels to what was happening in Paris and Berlin between the wars or in Greenwich Village at the turn of the century. The rediscovery of the old buildings is somewhat ironic (no pun intended) as they are about as spiritually distant from modern art as it is possible for buildings to be.

Admittedly, SoHo doesn't look too promising from our departure point at Houston and West Broadway. Back in the 1920s Houston was widened as part of the construction of the IND subway line. It seems somehow or other never to have healed.

Proceed south from Houston down **West Broadway** in the direction of the World Trade Center towers that loom so picturesquely in the distance. Although this street is the center of the gallery world and SoHo's most famous thoroughfare, it does not by a long shot contain the best cast-iron buildings. Top honors in that category probably belong to Broome Street, which we'll visit further on.

What makes West Broadway so famous, besides lots of places to shop for chic

clothes, is its concentration of galleries. You don't need an appointment to go in and look. And what you'll see could be anything from the highly representational to the intensely personal, from neo-impressionist landscapes to sculpture to constructions that challenge your entire definition of "art." In between galleries bearing names like Vorpal, Circle, Germans Van Eck, and Nancy Hoffman are shops like Filippo, Cicciobella, Rizzoli, and Benetton, selling everything from books to clothing designed in Milan. The streetside atmosphere is exciting and cosmopolitan in a very particular way: SoHo is a local lifestyle, and a stylish one at that.

When you reach the end of the fourth block south of Houston Street you'll be at the intersection of West Broadway and **Grand Street.** Turn left on Grand and head east. Now we're really getting into cast-iron country. Note the newly renovated building at the end of this block, on the corner of Grand and Wooster Streets. This marvelous Victorian façade is typical of what's been rediscovered down here. Structurally speaking, cast-iron buildings were not particularly innovative. They were usually supported by the same brick walls and timber floors as the buildings they replaced. The cast iron was merely mounted on the façades as a substitute for carved stone. Nor did it necessarily cover an entire façade.

But it did have a definite "look." And the next block of Grand, between **Wooster and Greene Streets,** shows this look to best advantage. Iron pillars seem to line the street into infinity. A century ago these sidewalks were crowded with shoppers. The ground floors of the buildings contained all manner of dry-goods emporia, while the upper levels were jammed with immigrants crouched over sewing machines for 12 hours a day. The building at the southwest corner of Greene and Grand (the one that says 1873 on top) sums up the commercial aesthetic of those times. It is a real iron palace, lifted direct from the Italian Renaissance as interpreted by some 19th-century architect. The exclusive Chanterelle Restaurant, in a cast-iron building at the southeast corner of the same intersection, sums up the SoHo of today: innovative, visually arresting, and expensive. Before we move on, glance up Greene Street for more cast-iron vistas. Historical footnote: During the cast-iron heyday of SoHo, Greene Street was one of New York's premier red-light districts.

Continue another block east on Grand to the corner of **Mercer Street.** The old Empire Safe Company Building on the south side of the street shows how cast iron was combined with other building materials. In this case, it's been confined to the first floor façade, which doesn't look as if it's changed one bit in the last century. Turn right and continue one block south to the corner of Mercer and **Howard Street.** Overlooking the intersection at 11 Mercer St. is the **Museum of Holography** (described in Section 3 of this chapter), worth a look for those interested in laser imaging.

From the Museum of Holography, proceed east on Howard Street (it's the only direction you can go, since Howard begins at Mercer Street) and go one block to the corner of Broadway. Note the extravagant **Dittenhofer Building** (built in 1870) on your right at the near corner of Howard and Broadway. These are the sorts of buildings we 20th-century Americans have traditionally been trained to ignore. And what a pleasure it is to rediscover them under our very noses.

Turn left on Broadway and walk uptown for one block to Grand Street. That wonderful old building on the corner of Grand and Broadway shows the heavy hand of modernization on its first floor. (Who could have really thought the modernish mess they've made of the street level was better than what was there in the first place?)

Continue north up Broadway for another block to **Broome Street.** At 488 Broadway, on the northeast corner of Broadway and Broome, is the many pillared **Haughwout Building.** Among other things this building is noted for its original 1857 Otis elevator, still in service. The street-level showrooms of 488 Broadway were once filled with the silver, chandeliers, and crystal goods of one Eder Haughwout. While the original cream-colored paint job is a distant memory, the structure remains essentially unaltered, an evocative reminder of Broadway's former commercial glory.

Turn left onto Broome Street and continue two blocks west to the intersection of Broome and Greene Streets. Much of SoHo, as you can see, remains pretty gritty and industrial notwithstanding its historic buildings and trendy new art culture. And yet a critical mass has definitely been achieved. Today the dirtiest SoHo Street corner manages somehow to look "fashionable," at least in the eyes of a downtown New Yorker.

Turn right onto Greene Street and proceed two blocks north to the corner of Prince Street. Before you reach Prince you'll see examples of just about everything that's happening in SoHo these days. There are cast-iron buildings—some gloriously renovated, some still grotty—another clutch of galleries, a new condominium (in a renovated iron building at 97 Greene that's clearly not being marketed to starving artists), various unglamorous oldtime tool and rag businesses, and a nightclub called Greene St.

Pause for a moment at Prince and Greene and look up at the eastern wall of **114 Prince St.,** also called the SoHo Center. This cleverly painted blank brick wall re-creates the cast-iron street façade, complete to the painted cat in the painted open window.

Turn left off Greene onto Prince Street and walk west for two blocks to West Broadway. Chic shops and restaurants proliferate the closer you draw to that celebrated thoroughfare. Cross West Broadway, keeping on Prince, and continue for another block to **Thompson Street.** The cast-iron district is behind you now; this is tenement country. The next street you'll cross is Sullivan Street, shortly after which you'll see **203 Prince St.** on your right. This perfectly beautiful restored Federal house holds out hope for every mutilated building in town. If they can be brought back to this, then no damage is beyond repair. The next street that crosses Prince is Macdougal, and a few steps farther is the great swath of widened Sixth Avenue hurtling south from Greenwich Village.

Directly across Sixth Avenue, angling a little to the south of the course of Spring Street, is **Charlton Street.** That's where you want to go, although crossing Sixth Avenue can be daunting. Charlton Street is the center of a small historic district notable for its concentration of intact Federal-period houses. The site was originally a country estate located midway between New York and Greenwich. The mansion, built in 1767 and named Richmond Hill, surveyed the surrounding countryside from the top of a sizable hill, leveled in 1817, when John Jacob Astor developed the property into building lots. Illustrious inhabitants of Richmond Hill have included Vice-President John Adams, whose wife Abigail described the view south to New York as "delicious," and Aaron Burr, who lived here at the time of his fateful duel with Alexander Hamilton.

After its hilltop was sliced from beneath it, the Richmond Hill mansion was moved to a new site on the southeast corner of Varick and Charlton. It became a theater, then a tavern, and was finally torn down in 1849. Despite the towering loft buildings standing in the background, the block of Charlton between Sixth Avenue and Varick Street retains much of the flavor of early 19th-century New York. It gives you a good idea, too, of what SoHo looked like before the cast-iron invasion.

When you reach Varick Street, turn right for one block to **King Street** and turn right again. King Street is less intact than Charlton, but it still contains its share of old houses. Nos. 32 and 34 King St., on the south side of the block near Sixth Avenue, tell interesting stories for the student of architecture. No. 34 King St. is in near original condition; 32 King St. obviously started life as a Federal house and was then "modernized" in the 1860s or 1870s. It now sports a Second Empire mansard roof and Italianate door and window hoods.

At the end of King Street you'll be back on Sixth Avenue (a major uptown bus route), one block south of Houston Street.

3. Museums and Galleries

Herewith, in alphabetical order, is a list of some of the city's most important and/or unusual museums. Each listing includes a brief description of the sorts of exhibits presented.

THE AMERICAN CRAFTS MUSEUM

This handsome museum, located at 40 West 53rd St. (tel. 212/956-3535), offers exhibits of American contemporary crafts: glass, wood, fiber, and ceramics. Admission is $3.50 for adults, $1.50 for students and seniors, and children under 12 are free. It is open Wednesday through Sunday from 10 a.m. to 5 p.m.; Tuesdays from 10 a.m. to 8 p.m. (admission free from 5 to 8 p.m.); closed Mondays.

AMERICAN MUSEUM OF NATURAL HISTORY

Known to every kid in New York as the museum with the dinosaurs, this noble institution has been in existence for well over a century. It's immense, containing within its four-square-block campus over 35 million specimens and artifacts arranged artfully, and at times dramatically. The 40 separate exhibition spaces, bearing names like the Hall of Ocean Life, The Hall of Man in Africa, the Hall of Oceanic Birds, the Hall of Minerals, etc., contain everything from lifelike dioramas to enormous reconstructed dinosaur skeletons to the fabulous Star of India sapphire. Adjoining the museum is the Hayden Planetarium, which presents computer-automated sky shows projected on a dome-like ceiling.

The museum's main entrance is at Central Park West and West 79th Street. Doors are open daily from 10 a.m. to at least 5:45 p.m., and on Wednesday, Friday, and Saturday evenings until 9 p.m. On school days nobody under 18 is admitted unless accompanied by an adult (presumably as an antitruancy measure). Admission is $3.50 for adults, $1.50 for children, free on Friday and Saturday evenings after 5. The Planetarium show costs another $3.75 for adults and $2.00 for kids. For further information, call 212/769-5100; for Planetarium schedules, call 212/769-5900.

COOPER-HEWITT MUSEUM OF DESIGN AND DECORATIVE ARTS

Three granddaughters of local philanthropist Peter Cooper founded this museum in 1897 to provide visual information for the study of design. What that means is that they collected examples of decorative art—drawings, prints, silverware, glass, fabrics, furniture, metalwork, jewelry, etc.—so as to preserve them for future study. Since 1968 this venerable New York institution has been a part of the Smithsonian. In 1976 the collection was installed in the former Andrew Carnegie mansion on Fifth Avenue and 91st Street, a fitting display case for decorative arts if ever there was one. Recent exhibitions have included the "Arts and Crafts Movement in America," "Weimar Ceramics," the architectural drawings of Erich Mendelsohn, and "L'Art de Vivre: The Design Arts in Paris 1789–1989." The Cooper-Hewitt additionally runs lectures, workshops, and tours. It's worth a visit just to see the Carnegie mansion.

The museum is located on the corner of Fifth Avenue and 91st Street (tel. 212/860-6868). Hours are Tuesday through Saturday from 10 a.m. to 5 p.m. (on Tuesday until 9 p.m.), on Sunday from noon to 5 p.m.; closed Monday and major holidays. Admission is $3 for adults, $2 for seniors and students over 12.

THE CLOISTERS

This museum of medieval art is located in northern Manhattan in the middle of Fort Tryon Park. It's quite a place up there on its hilltop, surveying the Hudson and the Palisades. Both the museum and the park were given to the city in 1938 by John D. Rockefeller. The museum building, which looks for all the world like an ancient

Italian monastery, contains rare tapestries (particularly a famous series called the *Unicorn Tapestries*), 13th-century stained glass, 12th-century wooden religious statuary, rare armor, paintings, precious small objects, tomb ornaments, etc. A cloister is a covered walkway, usually surrounding an open courtyard. Several ancient European cloisters were moved here and incorporated into the present structure, hence the museum's name. All in all it's a grand place, its inherent erudition counterbalanced by a dramatic location and the imposing scale of many of its exhibits.

The Cloisters is actually an adjunct of the Metropolitan Museum of Art (see below). Its location in Fort Tryon Park is accessible either by the IND Eighth Avenue A train to 190th Street and Overlook Terrace (from which you walk through the park to the museum), or by the Madison Avenue no. M4 bus, which will take you to the door. Open daily (except Monday) from 9:30 a.m. to 5:15 p.m. March to October, to 4:45 p.m. November through February. Admission is by contribution, the amount suggested being $5 for adults, $2.50 for students and senior citizens. Kids under 12 are admitted free. For information, call 212/923-3700.

FORBES MAGAZINE GALLERIES

This is not a terribly large gallery, but its collection reflects the panache of *Forbes* magazine and the family that owns it. Perhaps most exciting are the precious objects and bibelots made of gold, enamel, silver, and rare gems. Forbes owns ten Fabergé Easter Eggs originally made for the Russian imperial family, plus cases of exquisite Fabergé "stuff" (music boxes to decanter stoppers), constituting the largest private collection of it in the world. Also on display are rare letters from American presidents, models of *Forbes* magazine yachts, and a collection of trophies commemorating forgotten events (there's a moral to this, as you'll see if you get down here).

The Forbes Gallery is located at 60 Fifth Ave., between 12th and 13th Streets (tel. 212/620-2389), and it's open Tuesday through Saturday from 10 a.m. to 4 p.m. Admission is free.

THE FRICK COLLECTION

When industrialist Henry Clay Frick died in 1919, his will stipulated that his Fifth Avenue house be eventually opened to the public "for the study of art and kindred subjects." In 1935, after certain alterations, this wish was carried out. The Frick contains old master paintings by Renoir, Boucher, Holbein, El Greco, Vermeer, Rembrandt, and Gainsborough, among others, plus sculpture by Houdon, furniture by Boulle, and painted 16th-century enamels from Limoges. Much of the Frick family's original furniture remains. The Fragonard Room, decorated with a series of painted canvases entitled *The Progress of Love,* is the apotheosis of a New York society, pre–World War I, French-style reception room. This museum is a place of great elegance and beauty, a visit to which will be a memorable event.

The location is 1 E. 70th St., at the corner of Fifth Avenue (tel. 212/288-0700). The hours are 10 a.m. to 6 p.m. Tuesday through Saturday, and 1 to 6 p.m. on Sunday; closed Monday and assorted major holidays. Admission is $3, $1.50 for students and senior citizens.

THE GUGGENHEIM MUSEUM

Designed by Frank Lloyd Wright (his only building in New York City) for any other site than the one in which it stands, the controversial Guggenheim houses a famous collection of modern masterpieces. French impressionists and postimpressionists like Manet, Bonnard, Cézanne, Gauguin, Seurat, etc., dominate the permanent collection, which also includes Picassos, Modiglianis, and other recognizable names. The principal gallery space occupies one side of a long winding ramp that hugs the interior of a snail-shaped stucco structure plopped down in the very midst of dignified Fifth Avenue. The constantly changing roster of temporary exhibits concentrates exclusively on 20th century artists.

The Guggenheim is located at 1071 Fifth Ave., between 88th and 89th Streets (tel. 212/360-3500). Museum hours are 11 a.m. to 5 p.m. Tuesday through Sunday (to 8 p.m. on Tuesday night only); closed Monday. Admission is $4.50 for adults, $2.50 for students and seniors with valid ID.

THE JEWISH MUSEUM

Housed since 1947 in the Fifth Avenue mansion of financier Felix Warburg, this is one of the three largest collections of Judaica in the world. The permanent collection contains over 14,000 objects inspired by the Jewish experience, among them paintings, graphics, sculpture, and religious artifacts. Every year the museum mounts two or three major exhibitions, plus four or five smaller ones. Shows in recent years have borne titles such as "Danzig 1939: Treasures of a Destroyed Community," "The Jewish Heritage in American Folk Art," "The Dreyfus Affair: Art, Truth and Justice," and, opening in September 1989, "Gardens and Ghettos: The Art of Jewish Life in Italy."

Located at Fifth Avenue and 92nd Street, the Jewish Museum (tel. 212/860-1888) is open on Monday, Wednesday, and Thursday from noon to 5 p.m., Tuesday to 8 p.m., and on Sunday from 11 a.m. to 6 p.m.; closed Friday, Saturday, and major holidays.

THE METROPOLITAN MUSEUM OF ART

The "Met" is one of the great cultural resources of New York City. It also happens to be the largest art museum in the Western Hemisphere. The permanent collection consists of over three million works of art representing almost every epoch in the history of man. There are treasures from ancient Egypt, classical Rome, the Islamic Empire, the Far East, and particularly Europe from medieval times to the 20th century. Besides its famous collections of sculpture, painting, period rooms, bronzes, an Egyptian tomb, etc., the Met mounts continuous changing exhibits. Recently these have included a 600-year survey of the art of India, 60 paintings by the Hudson River School painter John Frederick Kensett, an exhibition of 18th-century American furniture, the "Costumes of Royal India," and 80 sculptures by Rodin from the collection of B. Gerald Cantor. With 1½ million square feet of space to play around with, and an annual budget of $83 million, you can imagine the scope and quality of these exhibits.

The entrance to the Met is on Fifth Avenue opposite 82nd Street (tel. 212/535-7710). Hours are Tuesday through Sunday from 9:30 a.m. to 5:15 p.m. (to 8:45 p.m. on Tuesday night only); closed Monday. Admission is by contribution, the suggested amounts being $5 for adults and $2.50 for students and seniors. Kids under 12 are admitted free.

THE MUSEUM OF AMERICAN FOLK ART

Devoted exclusively to American folk art, this museum displays a charming array of paintings, sculpture, textiles, and decorative art objects from the eighteenth through the twentieth centures. To see everything from stunning old weather vanes to the primitive paintings of Grandma Moses go to 2 Lincoln Square opposite Lincoln Center anytime between 9 a.m. and 9 p.m. seven days a week.

MUSEUM OF THE CITY OF NEW YORK

This place has been collecting artifacts and memorabilia connected with New York City since 1923. In those days it was located over in Gracie Mansion, before that pleasant old house became the residence of New York City's mayor. The present building was erected in 1932 and contains everything from antique fire engines, Tiffany silver, Duncan Phyfe furniture, and historical portraits to entire historic rooms (notably John D. Rockefeller's bedroom rescued from his demolished town house on West 54th Street), hundreds of antique toys, and some truly incredible antique dollhouses. There are many, many old pictures as well, chronicling the march of time across the City of New York.

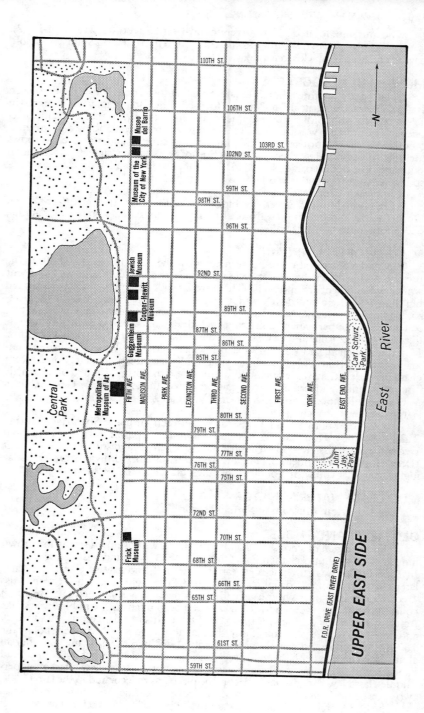

The museum, located at Fifth Avenue and 103rd Street (tel. 212/534-1672), is open Tuesday through Saturday from 10 a.m. to 5 p.m., and on Sunday and holidays from 1 to 5 p.m.; closed Monday.

MUSEUM OF HOLOGRAPHY

A hologram is a three-dimensional image that looks exactly like a solid object. But if you try to touch it, all you'll find is focused light. Holography was invented in 1947, but it wasn't until the development of lasers in the 1960s that it became practicable. The museum was founded in 1976 to promote understanding and advancement of this revolutionary new medium. Some current and prospective shows include "Illusion," described as a collection of works that "challenge perceptual skills and pose optical paradoxes"; and "Planning for Human Nature: Society's Responsibility for Its Actions and How We Affect the Future."

Our walking tour of SoHo goes right past the museum's front door at 11 Mercer St., opposite Howard Street, one block west of Broadway (tel. 212/925-0581). Open Tuesday through Sunday from 11 a.m. to 6 p.m. Admission is $3 for adults, $1.75 for seniors and kids under 12.

MUSEUM OF MODERN ART

"MOMA'S" collection of modern art spans the period from the 1880s to the present, and includes the masterpieces of Van Gogh and Cézanne as well as recent works by Rauschenberg and Stella. There are 20 galleries in the recently renovated building, as well as a quite lovely sculpture court (decorated with the works of Picasso, Rodin, and Lachaise), a theater showing film classics, a museum store, and two restaurants. The permanent collection includes architectural drawings by people like Mies van der Rohe and Le Corbusier; photographs taken by people like Stieglitz, Man Ray, Steichen, and Walker Evans; paintings by Matisse, Pollock, Miró, etc.; engravings and etchings of artists like Dubuffet, Klee, and Munch; etc. Some recent changing exhibitions have included a survey of the printed work of Henri de Toulouse-Lautrec; advertising photographs taken in the 1930s by W. Grancel Fitz; a Mies van der Rohe centennial exhibition; "Vienna 1900: Art, Architecture, and Design"; to name but a few.

You'll find MOMA at 11 W. 53rd St., between Fifth and Sixth Avenues (tel. 212/708-9500). Hours are 11 a.m. to 6 p.m. (to 9 p.m. on Thursday); closed Wednesday. Admission is $6 for adults, $3.50 for seniors and students with current ID, free for children under 16. Films are free with museum admission. On Thursday nights, pay what you wish. For film schedules, call 212/708-9490.

MUSEUM OF NATURAL HISTORY

See "American Museum of Natural History."

OLD MERCHANT'S HOUSE

This little gem of a house was built in 1832 on what is now a seedy downtown industrial block. But back then East 4th Street was a select and aristocratic quarter. In 1835 the lot was purchased by Seabury Tredwell, and it wasn't until a century later that his youngest daughter finally died. Throughout all those years Miss Tredwell kept her father's house virtually unchanged. When she died in 1933, a rich cousin bought the place, endowed it, and it's been open to the public ever since. Actually, not many people visit this part of town. It's not dangerous, but it's ugly and out of the way. As a matter of fact, the neighborhood was pretty well shot by the 1870s, three generations before Miss Tredwell finally died. One imagines her all alone down here in her father's house, watching the world pass her by from behind hand-blown window panes. This is an unusual opportunity to view intact an upper-middle-class New York domestic decor (the place was redecorated in the late 1860s, two years before "papa" died). Even Miss Tredwell's clothes are still in the closets.

The Old Merchant's House is located at 29 E. 4th St., between Lafayette Street and the Bowery (tel. 212/777-1089), and is open only on Sunday from 1 to 4 p.m. Admission is $2 for adults, $1 for students and seniors, and free to children under 12.

STUDIO MUSEUM IN HARLEM

The Studio Museum's handsome Harlem gallery is devoted to the collection and documentation of the art of Black America and the African Diaspora. The institution is young, a mere 18 years having passed since it was founded. But it's ambitious, heartfelt, and professional. Its growing collection includes painting, sculpture, drawing, prints, posters, photographs, artifacts, etc. The Studio Museum is a concerned member of the Harlem community too, sponsoring artist-in-residence programs, conducting seminars for aspiring collectors, exposing school-children to art, presenting lectures, and mounting a changing series of exhibits. It has been described as the foremost center for the study of Black art in America.

The museum is located at 144 W. 125th St., between Lenox Avenue and Adam Clayton Powell Boulevard, as Sixth and Seventh Avenues are called uptown (tel. 212/864-4500), and is open Wednesday through Friday from 10 a.m. to 5 p.m., on Saturday and Sunday from 1 to 6 p.m.; closed Monday and Tuesday. Admission is $2 for adults, $1 for seniors, students, and children.

WHITNEY MUSEUM OF AMERICAN ART

Gertrude Vanderbilt Whitney, herself a sculptor, was the leading patron of American art from 1907 until her death in 1942. By the late 1920s she had acquired so many works of art that she attempted to give them to the Metropolitan Museum, but the Met turned her down. So in 1930 she founded the Whitney Museum of American Art and a year later installed her collection in an old house on West 8th Street. Today's Whitney, housed in a startling-looking stone building built on the East Side in 1966, presents the full range of American art from colonial times to the present. The overwhelming emphasis, however, is on the work of living artists. The permanent collection includes names like Ralston Crawford, George Sugarman, Alexander Calder, Eric Fischl, etc. Typical exhibits are challenging, to say the least. Yet for those passionate about modern American art, this is a museum that cannot be missed.

The Whitney is at 945 Madison Ave., between 74th and 75th Streets (tel. 212/570-3600). It's open on Tuesday from 1 to 8 p.m., Wednesday through Saturday from 11 a.m. to 5 p.m., and on Sunday from noon to 6 p.m.; closed Monday. Admission is $4.50 for adults, $2.50 for seniors, free for children (and free for everybody on Tuesday night between 6 and 8 p.m.).

NEW YORK AFTER DARK

My daughter, at the age of four, once explained to me why there are such big crowds on the streets of New York at night. She said that since all the houses were filled up, there was no place else for the people to go. Perhaps she was right, which would also explain why New York has so much nightlife.

Herewith, some suggested after-dark activities, from sedate to devil-may-care.

1. Movies

To find out what's playing where, do one of the following: buy the *New York Times* or the *New York Daily News* and look at the ads on the inside pages for current first-run features. Both papers also carry a smattering of advertising for less mainstream stuff. There used to be a magazine in town called *Cue,* which listed every single movie house and what it was showing that week. *Cue* was absorbed by *New York* magazine some years back and now appears in abbreviated form as a back-page supplement to each issue of *New York.* The Cue section has capsule reviews of many (but by no means all) of the pictures playing around town.

The *New Yorker* (not to be confused with *New York* magazine) is a glossy international publication that also has a sophisticated local entertainment guide. The *New Yorker* provides capsule reviews too, for a selective list of the films it deems of interest. These include as many foreign releases and revivals as new Hollywood offerings. Manhattan movie houses show many fascinating films you're not liable to see elsewhere, and the *New Yorker* is a good way to track them down.

The above publications are all available at the sort of well-stocked newsstand you'll find at major street corners, big subway stops, and large hotel lobbies. Also available (at least in the subways and on the streets) is the *Village Voice*, a thick liberal weekly paper, which also covers the entertainment scene, but specializes in its downtown area and includes many of the more off-beat presentations that might not make it into the uptown press. It hits the stands on Wednesdays.

Manhattan has a couple of movie-house concentrations, but none really qualifies as the center of local moviedom. Third Avenue in the low 60s has a bunch of first-run houses; Loew's 84th Street, up on Broadway and West 84th, has six theaters under one roof; 42nd Street between Seventh and Eighth Avenues is a block of solid marquees, but the titles include a preponderance of words like "lust" and "chainsaw." The majority of Manhattan's movies, be they first run or revival houses, are just scattered around the residential districts.

Every autumn since 1963 the Film Society of Lincoln Center, at Broadway and 65th Street, has sponsored the **New York Film Festival.** This is one of the most important annual film events in the U.S. The Film Society does not run a theater all year long, but at festival time it sponsors an intensive series of screenings featuring films from around the world. Most screenings are open to the public, although tickets are limited. If it's autumn and you're interested, call the society at 212/877-1800 for program information.

OLD CLASSICS

The **Museum of Modern Art,** 11 W. 53rd St., between Fifth and Sixth Avenues, runs a variegated film program all year. Museum admission includes the cost of a ticket, but if it's a popular show they're liable to run out of seats early. The program may consist of a fabulous old comedy classic from the museum's archives or videomakers discussing and showing their work; or it may be a part of a series of films from India, West Germany, Italy, or wherever. Call 212/708-9490 to find out what's on.

There are also a number of movie houses that specialize in old films. Among them are the **Biograph** at 225 W. 57th St. (call 212/582-4582), the **Film Forum Twin Cinema** at 57 Watts St. (call 212/431-1590), and the **Thalia Soho** at 15 Vandam St. (call 212/675-0490). They show a variety of such glories from the past as *Wuthering Heights* with Laurence Olivier and Merle Oberon and *Springfield Rifle* with Gary Cooper or such silents as *Tumbleweed* and *Riders of the Purple Sage* (with live piano accompanying as in the old days).

---

2. Theaters

There are about 40 big-time legitimate Broadway theaters in New York. Added to that are another 300 or so Off-Broadway theaters, many offering shows that are at least as exciting (occasionally more so) as anything on the Great White Way. The same papers and magazines that list the movies (described above) also list and describe shows at the theaters. Box office prices ain't cheap; expect to pay $45 or more per ticket on Broadway. Prices are considerably less by the time you get to Off-Off-Broadway, which might be a theater in a loft, a church, somebody's basement, a storefront, or anyplace else the rent is cheap. Ticket brokers can often supply otherwise-impossible-to-obtain tickets to hot shows, either on or Off-Broadway. If you use one, expect to pay a service charge

Alternatively, you might try to get day-of-performance, half-price tickets from the Times Square Ticket Center, called simply **TKTS** and located on the traffic island between Broadway and Seventh Avenue at 47th Street. Every day but Sunday, from 11 a.m. to 5:30 p.m., TKTS sells surplus tickets to that evening's performances. Occasionally you can buy a ticket one day in advance for a Wednesday matinee or a Sunday performance, but these are limited. Everything is first-come, first-served, and there's usually a line (though it moves quickly). If your heart is set on a particular show, come early.

3. Music and Dance Performances

Various halls around town specialize in music and dance, but none is so well known as **Carnegie Hall,** at the corner of Seventh Avenue and 57th Street. Built a century ago by industrialist Andrew Carnegie, this lovely old landmark was blessed with perfect acoustics. It presents world-famous virtuosos of keyboard and string, philharmonic orchestras, great singers in recital, competition winners, chamber music, even the occasional benefit performance by Frank Sinatra. Call 212/247-7800 for program and ticket information.

Lincoln Center, at Broadway and 65th Street, possesses three of the city's foremost halls, arranged around a broad plaza with a big fountain in the center. The **New York State Theater,** whose stage was partly designed by George Ballanchine, is the home of the New York City Ballet and the New York City Opera. To find out the current program, call the box office at 212/870-5570. The **Metropolitan Opera House** is home to a company that's over 100 years old. The box office number is 212/362-6000. **Avery Fisher Hall,** the third in the fountain plaza triumverate, bears the name of the stereo equipment czar who paid for its renovation some years back. It's the home of the New York Philharmonic, and the location of all manner of music concerts from symphonic to rock. Call the box office at 212/580-8700 to find out what (if anything) will be on during your visit. For plays, Lincoln Center has the **Vivian Beaumont Theater** and the smaller **Mitzi Newhouse Theater** (212/362-7600), located behind the plaza between Avery Fisher Hall and the Met. Across 65th Street is **Alice Tully Hall,** a concert hall whose programs range from chamber music to experimental theater to screenings of the New York Film Festival. The box office number is 212/362-1911.

The **Brooklyn Academy of Music** (often abbreviated as BAM), at 30 Lafayette Ave. near Atlantic Avenue in Brooklyn, is a bit of a trip by subway or bus. But BAM's presentations of dance, theater, and music are always ambitious and usually first-rate. This landmark hall began to acquire its experimental reputation in the early part of the century when people like Isadora Duncan and Sergei Rachmaninoff appeared in between engagements of the New York Philharmonic and the Metropolitan Opera. Today's programs range from Pina Bausch and Robert Wilson to productions by Ingmar Bergman and Peter Brook. Some performances are in the newly restored **Majestic Theater** nearby. Call the box office at 718/636-4100 for program information (and directions).

Radio City Music Hall, 1260 Sixth Ave., at 50th Street, was the last of the Manhattan movie palaces presenting a full stage show and a new Hollywood movie. It's a gloriously glitzy art deco palace of awe-inspiring proportions, a mere glimpse of whose golden interior is worth the price of admission. Threatened with demolition in the late 1970s, it was rescued, landmarked, and reopened with what management calls a "multifaceted entertainment policy." That means they don't show movies anymore. The stage shows are now ultralavish productions, twice as long as they used to be. They bear names like *Manhattan Showboat, Gotta Getaway!,* and *America,* and still feature the famous 32-girl precision dance team known as the Rockettes. Big-name entertainers frequently give concerts at the Music Hall these days. Linda

Ronstadt, Stevie Wonder, Diana Ross, Lionel Richie, and Peter Allen have all appeared here in recent years. The holiday shows, particularly the "Magnificent Christmas Spectacular," really are fun. For prices and program information, call the box office at 212/757-3100. For information on backstage tours, call 212/632-4041.

The *New York Times* and the *Village Voice* both carry considerable advertising for music and dance events. There is also a day-of-performance, half-price ticket booth for music and dance, the **Bryant Park Music and Dance Half-Price Ticket Booth.** You'll find it at the 42nd Street and Sixth Avenue corner of Bryant Park. It carries tickets for performances at Lincoln Center, Carnegie Hall, and the **City Center** (a famous hall on 55th Street between Sixth and Seventh Avenues), among other places, and is open Tuesday, Thursday, and Friday from noon to 2 p.m. and 3 to 7 p.m.; on Wednesday and Saturday from 11 a.m. to 2 p.m. and 3 to 7 p.m.; and on Sunday from noon to 6 p.m. The booth is closed on Monday. For information call the WOR Artsline at 212/382-2323.

4. Rock Clubs

Nell's, 246 West 14th Street (tel. 212/675-1567), has the atmosphere of a private club. Upstairs the room is like a hotel lobby, with overstuffed club chairs and comfortable sofas, a long crowded bar, and a dining room in back. You'll hear soft jazz music playing and sometimes there are live performances. Downstairs is where they play current Top 40 music leaning toward New Wave. The small dance floor is usually packed. Nell's is open every night from 10 p.m. to 4 a.m. Admission is $10 on Friday and Saturday, $5 Sunday through Thursday.

M.K., 204 Fifth Avenue at 25th Street (tel. 212/779-1340), is in a former bank building. It occupies four stories and is definitely decorated to shock, judging by the giant stuffed Dobermans standing guard at the bar and the huge filled aquarium. Popular music is heard every night from 10 p.m. to 4 a.m. Admission is $15 on weekends, $5 during the week.

CBGB, 315 Bowery, at the end of Bleecker Street (tel. 212/982-4052), is not for dancing, but for seeing ultranew live bands. What's been "new" lately? Stealin' Horses, So Are You, Harley and the Highway Men, etc. Sunday afternoons are for "hardcore," which is ultraheavy fast rock. Admission varies between $5 and $10, depending on who's there.

Limelight, 660 Sixth Ave., between 20th and 21st Streets (tel. 212/807-7850), occupies a former church. If this isn't titillating enough, there's very hot new recorded dance music every Friday and Saturday night for an $18 admission charge. This is a place you've got to see. It's open seven nights a week from 10 a.m. to 4 p.m.

The Bottom Line, 15 W. 4th Street at Mercer Street (tel. 212/228-7880), is a long-established Village nightspot featuring a wide range of entertainment from New Wave to old rock. Recent acts have included the Lounge Lizards, Janis Ian, Fairport Convention, and Kenny Rankin. Again, it's for watching, not for dancing. Admission varies from act to act and typically runs $13 to $15. Food and drink are available; there's no minimum.

Roseland, 239 W. 52nd St., between Broadway and Eighth Avenue (tel. 212/247-0200), is an immense old place that caters to quite a wide variety of types. On Thursday from 2:30 in the afternoon until midnight it's strictly ballroom dancing with two live orchestras (one American, one Latin). Admission is $10. On Friday it's disco from 10 p.m. to 4 a.m. On Saturday afternoons the orchestras are back for ballroom dancing from 2:30 to 11 p.m. After that they change over to disco. And on Sunday it's ballroom again, from 2:30 p.m. all the way until midnight. Admission on Friday, Saturday, and Sunday is about $12, unless there's a special act or group.

Regine's, 502 Park Ave., at 59th Street (tel. 212/826-0990), is actually a swanky club that sells one-night "memberships" at the door. The crowd is older and richer, and has more than likely just finished a big French dinner right here at Regine's. The dance floor is very small. The disco music features "hits" you may never have heard, from France and South America, as well as the U.S. Admission Monday through Thursday is $15; on Friday and Saturday it's $25.

---

5. Jazz Clubs

The **Village Gate,** 160 Bleecker St., between Thompson and Sullivan Streets (tel. 212/475-5120), is a New York landmark. It actually consists of three separate clubs: the Top of the Gate, the Terrace, and Downstairs at the Village Gate. At any one of these locations you can hear the likes of Millie Jackson, Nell Carter, the Lounge Lizards, or Ruben Blades. The Downstairs is really a cabaret theater, except on Monday night when "Salsa Meets Jazz" (Latin dancing for $15 admission). The Terrace features a pleasant bar with a different jazz duo every other week. Admission for the bigger acts can be as much as $25. Open every night.

The **Blue Note,** 131 W. 3rd St., between Sixth Avenue and Macdougal Street (tel. 212/475-8592), usually has two complete shows every night of the week. Top-name entertainers like Sarah Vaughn, Dizzy Gillespie, The Modern Jazz Quartet, and Nancy Wilson play regularly. On weekend afternoons there's usually a special brunch. Admission is usually somewhere between $15 and $30, depending on who's appearing. Add to that a $5 food and/or drink minimum.

The **Angry Squire,** 216 Seventh Ave., between 22nd and 23rd Streets (tel. 212/242-9066), is an atmospheric place with a two-drink minimum and a small music charge that rarely tops $8. Mainstream jazz quartets are the order of the day. Shows start at 10 p.m.; the kitchen is open nightly till midnight.

Fat Tuesday's, 190 Third Ave., between 17th and 18th Streets (tel. 212/533-7902), is an intimate jazz club located below a restaurant called Tuesday's. Management books top-name talent like the Les Paul Trio on Monday nights, George Coleman, and Scott Hamilton. The music charge ranges from $12.50 to $25, and there's a $7.50-per-person drink minimum.

New Deal, 152 Spring St., between West Broadway and Wooster Street (tel. 212/431-3663), is a trendy SoHo restaurant with great 1930s-looking murals, an ambient bar, and a jazz pianist every night of the week. No cover or minimum; an interesting place to hang out. Open for lunch and dinner every day, plus brunch on Sunday.

Sweet Basil, 88 Seventh Ave. South, near Bleecker Street (tel. 212/242-1785), is also open every day of the week, and presents two and sometimes three separate shows. People like Art Blakey, McCoy Tyner, and Doc Cheatham perform regularly. The music charge is $12 to $15, to which you add a $6-or-so drink minimum. Reservations are required.

The **Hors D'Oeuvrerie,** part of the Windows on the World Restaurant at One World Trade Center (tel. 212/938-1111), provides piano music and dancing on a small floor 107 stories above the city. The views are, well, out of this world. Lots of delicious small appetizer things can be purchased here in addition to drinks. There's no minimum, and a very modest $4-or-so cover charge.

---

6. Country and Western Clubs

The **Lone Star Roadhouse,** 240 West 52nd Street (tel. 212/245-2950), with a façade that resembles a bus, is probably the best place in New York City to hear live country music. Their lineup includes bands like NRBQ, Levon Helm and the All Stars, Dan Hicks and the Acoustic Warriors, and Arthur Prysock. There's a bar up front, while in the back is the stage with a big dance floor and lots of tables where you can enjoy dinner and the show. The Lone Star Roadhouse is open for lunch and dinner, and the menu includes home-style favorites like chicken fried steak with gravy ($10.50), mesquite burgers served with cole slaw and fries ($7), and Cajun popcorn, which is spicy "crawfish" tails deep-fried and served with spicy hot sauce ($5.50). The music charge is $5 to $20 depending on the group. Open noon to 3 a.m. daily. Reservations advised; credit cards accepted.

O'Lunney's, 915 Second Ave., between 48th and 49th Streets (tel. 212/751-5470), is a pretty laid-back spot featuring country acts like Nancy Liker and Tommy Joe White six nights a week. No cover and no minimum, unless you sit at a table, and then the minimum's only $5 per person. Closed Sunday.

---

7. Cabaret and Supper Clubs

What has been fully restored to 1934 splendor, is two stories high, and has dozens of floor-to-ceiling windows overlooking one of the most magnificent skyline views in Manhattan? Answer: The newly renovated **Rainbow Room,** 30 Rockefeller Plaza, 65th floor (tel. 212/632-5000). Dining here is quite literally a theatrical experience—waiters in pastel tails; a 32-foot revolving dance floor; terraced seating on three levels; a 12-piece live orchestra; aubergine silk walls; oodles of 30s glamour. Even the food is good. Full dinners, with main courses like steak with béarnaise sauce, lobster thermidor, or rack of lamb for two, are apt to cost $100 per person. But there's also a prix fixe, pretheater dinner for about $40 a head, and a Sunday brunch priced at about $35. Besides dinner, one can also enjoy dancing nightly and/or a cabaret called Rainbow and Stars ($35 cover). The Rainbow Room is open until 1 a.m. Tuesday through Thursday; until 2 a.m. on Friday and Saturday; and until midnight on Sunday. Closed Monday. Reservations a must.

The Ballroom, 253 W. 28th St., between Seventh and Eighth Avenues (tel. 212/244-3005), is part established restaurant, part cabaret presenting noted vocal and instrumental acts in a separate room. Peggy Lee, Martha Raye, Blossom Dearie, and Larry Adler are typical of the acts that have played here. Admission to the cabaret runs from $15 to $25 (occasionally higher), depending. Add to that a two-drink minimum, which can, however, be spent on "tapas" (small, Spanish-style appetizers). There are two to three shows a night, Tuesday through Saturday.

The **Oak Room** at the Algonquin Hotel, 59 W. 44th St., between Fifth and Sixth Avenues (tel. 212/840-6800), is the nighttime home of Julie Wilson, stylist and cabaret singer extraordinaire. Her material is very sophisticated stuff—Kurt Weill, Noël Coward, etc.—presented in elegant surroundings. She does have a marvelous touch. The music charge is $10, to which you add a $15-per-person minimum. Shows are Tuesday through Saturday.

The **Café Carlyle** in the Hotel Carlyle, entrance on Madison Avenue between 76th and 77th Streets (tel. 212/570-7189), is smallish and elite, and usually presents the famous Bobby Short or someone of similar stature at the piano. Cover charge is $35 for Bobby Short Tuesday through Saturday, to which you'll usually add the cost of a deluxe dinner. Right across the hall is **Bemelmans Bar,** with more of the same Upper East Side atmosphere, plus a jazz pianist and a modest $5 cover Monday through Saturday. The café is closed on Sunday and Monday nights.

Last, but certainly not least, is **Chippendale's,** 1110 First Ave., near 61st Street (tel. 212/935-6060), whose "For Ladies Only" show has been packing 'em in since 1983. Chippendale's amusing print ads ("New York, where some men still take off their hats for a lady") tell only part of the story. These men take off a good deal more than their hats. Open from 6:30 p.m. four days a week. Admission is $25, seating is on a first come, first served basis. There's an extra charge for ring and rail seating.

After 10:30 p.m. men are admitted. But during the show it's ladies only—and they mean it.

8. Comedy Clubs

Improvisation, 358 W. 44th St., between Eighth and Ninth Avenues (tel. 212/765-8268), is a showcase for new comics who haven't yet made it to the big time. Richard Pryor, Jerry Stiller, Anne Meara, David Brenner, Joe Piscopo, and many, many others have had their moments on the funky stage of the Improv. Food is available and cheap: Monday through Thursday the cover and minimum are each $8; on Friday, Saturday, and Sunday they're $11 and $9, respectively.

Catch a Rising Star, 1487 First Ave., between 77th and 78th Streets (tel. 212/794-1906), is a similar concept, with more-established comedians onstage. Open all week with a two-drink minimum and cover charge of $8 Sunday through Thursday and $12 on Friday and Saturday. Reservations must be made a day in advance.

Dangerfield's, 1118 First Ave., between 61st and 62nd Streets (tel. 212/593-1650), presents comedians from all over the country performing seven nights a week. You may or may not see comic-proprietor Rodney Dangerfield himself. Figure the regular two-drink minimum, plus a $10 cover Sunday through Thursday, $15 on Friday and Saturday.

9. Atmospheric Bars

For Edwardian-era plush, dark wood paneling, and an atmosphere of oldtime big-city grandeur, try the **Oak Room** in the Plaza Hotel, at Fifth Avenue and Central Park South. One side is a restaurant; the other is a bar with numerous tables and leather chairs. This dimly lit and exceedingly popular watering spot is an appropriate place to linger over drinks and contemplate the majesty of the Big Apple.

The lobby of the **Algonquin Hotel,** 59 W. 44th St., between Fifth and Sixth Avenues, is like a baronial living room in some English country mansion. It's filled with fashionable people in the arts and theater, coming and going. There are comfortable sofas and chairs scattered around, all within easy reach of little tables with attached bells for summoning the drink waiter. A superb place to meet your friends, have a nightcap after the theater, or soak up the sophisticated Manhattan atmosphere.

The **Hunt Bar** (not to be confused with Harry's Bar) in the Helmsley Palace Hotel, Madison Avenue between 49th and 50th Streets, used to be the wood-paneled dining room in a New York millionaire's mansion. It's small, elegant, and very comfortable. Its little groupings of upholstered furniture and atmosphere of grand luxe invite intimacy.

The **Four Seasons,** at 99 E. 52nd St., between Park and Lexington Avenues, is an enormous deluxe restaurant with a splendorous modern bar. Suspended above it are zillions of gleaming bronze rods that together form a fairly startling piece of modern sculpture. Lots of leather banquettes and chairs for those who don't like to sit on stools. Very sleek and sophisticated.

Celebrity-watchers might try their luck at **Elaine's,** 1703 Second Ave., near 88th Street (tel. 212/534-8103), a nice but not particularly fancy Second Avenue bar/restaurant. On certain nights, however, luminaries from the literary and film worlds flock to Elaine's to see and be seen. The small bar by the door provides a good perch if this is your sort of thing. Alternatively, you might drop by **Sardi's,** 234 W. 44th St., between Broadway and Eighth Ave. (tel. 212/221-8440). This elegant restaurant with adjacent bar is practically synonymous with New York theater folk and big-name entertainers.

The **Top of the Tower,** atop the Beekman Tower Hotel, 3 Mitchell Pl. (which is actually the corner of First Avenue and 48th Street), provides great city vistas from almost every table. It's actually an enclosed terrace surrounding the building's art deco pinnacle. Only open in the evening.

A number of Manhattan skyscrapers have rooftop bar/restaurants, but many don't have much of a view from the bar. Not so at the **City Lights Bar,** which is part of the Windows on the World Restaurant at One World Trade Center. It's located right next to the Hors D'Oeuvrerie (described earlier under "Jazz Clubs"), whose live music permeates the evening air. The sleekly modern City Lights is a small bar and every seat provides a glorious view of the Financial District.

Clarke's (also known as "P.J. Clarke's"), 915 Third Ave., at the corner of 55th Street, is a boisterous upscale saloon, complete with sawdust on the floor, carved woodwork that's black with age, a loud jukebox, and café tables with blue-checked cloths. Lots of singles here too, seemingly from the professional classes.

The **White Horse Tavern,** 567 Hudson St., at the corner of 11th Street, is an oldtime bar with lots of funky atmosphere and considerable Greenwich Village literary associations, notably with Dylan Thomas. It's especially nice if it's warm enough to sit outside at picnic tables and cool off with one of seven different draft beers. Or **McSorley's Old Ale House,** 15 E. 7th St., near the Bowery, whose 19th-century saloon policies were intact to the point of prohibiting women until only a few years ago. And finally **Chumley's,** 86 Bedford St., at Barrow Street, a dark, smoky pub hidden away in a courtyard that attracts oldtime Villagers and young movie stars.

All of these are good spots to hang out and, well, drink.

10. Gay Bars

Last, but certainly not least, a few good suggestions for our readers who have, as they say, "sampled both sauces."

The **Monster,** 80 Grove St., immediately east of 7th Avenue (tel. 212/924-3557), is the famous namesake of the original Monster in Key West, Florida. This is a big sleek modern place, with a downstairs disco and a huge bar. The crowd is upscale and good-looking, as liable to be dressed in English-tailored suits as tight jeans. On weekends, there's a doorman who insures a certain panache to the clientele inside. All ages come to the Monster, with perhaps a preponderance of people who at least look like they're in their thirties. Open weekdays from 4 p.m. to 4 a.m., Saturday and Sunday from 2 p.m. to 4 a.m. Best time to visit: Thursday night.

A similar-looking crowd gathers at the **Company,** 265 Third Ave., between 26th and 27th Streets (tel. 212/532-5222). Actually, this is a restaurant as well as a bar, and in the former you're likely to see both women and men at either dinner (served Monday through Saturday from 6:30 p.m.) or Sunday brunch. The decor is muted and modern, and the bar attracts convivial crowds or what might, for lack of a better word, be termed "Guppies." Open daily till 4 a.m.

Finally, for something a little different, you might try **The Works,** 428 Columbus Ave., near 80th St. (tel. 212/799-7365). No food, no women, and no dancing (even though the music's hot). The typical customer is maybe twenty-five, has lots of muscles, and wears clothing that shows them off accordingly. The room in the back has videos and chain-link fencing on the walls. But this is still pretty mainstream, considering how far this sort of thing can go. Open daily from 2 p.m. to 4 a.m.

Besides recommendations from the people you meet, you can find out about other gay bars, plus activities, restaurants, movies, and so on, of interest to gays, in one of the give-away guides often stacked in handy piles in gay bars. "Michael's" is a good one that contains all matter of useful information.

CHILDREN'S NEW YORK

1. EXCURSIONS AND ACTIVITIES
2. SHOWS AND TOURS
3. MUSEUMS

Traveling with kids means coming up with things that they're interested in too. The following list of suggestions contains something of interest for *every* kid, from the nursery school four-year-old to teenaged Mr./Ms. Cool.

1. Excursions and Activities

THE STATUE OF LIBERTY
Getting to **Liberty Island** most decidedly is an excursion, which accounts for the fact that so many New Yorkers have never been there. The first leg is by subway to the Battery, a small city park near many subway lines. Unless you're staying in the Financial District, the trip is too long by bus and awfully costly by cab. Once at the Battery you'll have to find the Liberty Island Ferry Pier, located near Castle Clinton. Boats are supposed to leave every hour from 10 a.m. to 4 p.m., but you should reconfirm this schedule by calling the ferry ticket office at 212/269-5755. The trip costs a couple of bucks; the statue is free. As soon as you board the ferry it's guaranteed that everyone will be having fun. The trip across the harbor is new and exciting for most people. The statue itself, as you probably know, was completely refurbished for its 1986 centennial, although it was great-looking even when run-down. The symbolism is quite moving and the views are superb. There's a museum in the statue's base, filled with informative exhibits.
It's possible to combine a trip to the Statue of Liberty with one to the nearby **Ellis Island National Monument.** This was the former immigration station through which so many of our forebears passed. It is being restored as a museum dramatizing the story of immigration.

CENTRAL PARK
The park has numerous playgrounds filled with swings and jungle gyms and small children howling around under the watchful eyes of mothers and nurses. A good one is the **Heckscher Playground,** which would be at 61st Street and Seventh Avenue if such an intersection existed in the wooded regions of the park. There's

also a **carousel** in the park, and quite a grand old-fashioned one too. You'll find it just west of Park Drive North, where 65th Street and Seventh Avenue would be. Perhaps of greatest interest to kids is the **Belvedere Castle**, where the National Weather Station takes the New York City temperature readings. The building is a Victorian-era stone folly perched on a cliff above an ornamental lake. Inside, in addition to the Weather Service, is a "discovery chamber" where visiting school groups engage in educational projects. Most kids just like the castle, which also provides very good backdrops for pictures. It's located close to where Seventh Avenue and 79th Street would be. Just wandering around the park is lots of fun. It contains a **zoo** at Fifth Avenue and 64th Street, the **Wollman Ice Skating Rink,** near the hypothetical intersection of 62nd Street and Sixth Avenue, plus many other attractions some of which are more fully described below. On warm sunny days when there are plenty of people afoot, it's as safe as anyplace in this uncertain world of ours.

To find out the times and locations of city-sponsored cultural and recreational activities in all the city parks, call the recorded events number at 212/360-1333.

Bikes

Central Park is a fabulous place to ride a bike. It's scenic, it's big, and on many days it's closed to traffic. Between March and November you can rent a bike either at the **A & B Bikes'** main store at 663 Amsterdam Ave., at 92nd Street (tel. 212/866-7600), or at their in-park location at the Central Park Boathouse, where Sixth Avenue and 74th Street would be. The cost is $4 for the first hour and 75¢ for each additional half hour. ID required.

Boats

Also between March and November you can rent a boat and row around Central Park's scenic chain of ornamental lakes. The **Boathouse,** which has a restaurant and snackbar on a wonderful porch overlooking the lake, is located on the northbound Park Drive just above the 72nd Street transverse (tel. 212/517-4723). You may rent either wooden or aluminum models. The cost is $6 an hour and each boat holds a maximum of five persons. A refundable $20 deposit is required, and adults must accompany children 16 years of age and younger. You can rent boats Monday to Friday from 10 a.m. to 5:30 p.m. and on Saturday and Sunday from 10 a.m. to 6:30 p.m.

Ice Skating

After years of bureaucratically directed inaction you can again actually skate at Central Park's beautiful **Wollman Rink,** thanks to the intervention of local real estate mogul Donald Trump. The cost is about $5 for adults, $2.00 for kids. Add $2.50 for skates and skate as long as you like. Open daily and most evenings from October to April. Phone 212/517-4800 for precise hours. Location is between Fifth and Sixth Avenues approximately on the line of East 63rd Street.

Roller Skating

Starting in the spring, you can roller skate at Wollman Rink. They're open daily and most evenings May through September. Skate rentals are $5 for adults; $2.50 for kids under 12. Call 212/517-4800 for information and to find out when "cheapskate" night is.

THE MARKET AT CITICORP

"The Market" is the name of an immense enclosed atrium in the glossy new Citicorp Building at Lexington Avenue and 53rd Street. The place is a sort of updated version of the Hanging Gardens of Babylon, croissants and quiche being substituted for the flowering plants of antiquity. If you call 212/559-2330, you'll reach a recording that describes the day's free entertainments, sponsored by Citicorp for

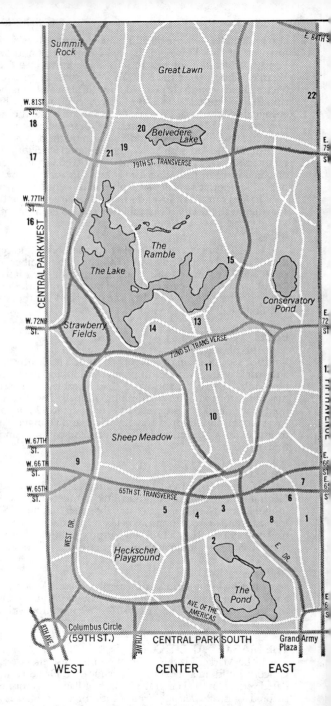

CENTRAL PARK

1. Arsenal
2. Wollman Rink
3. Dairy
4. Chess and Checkers
5. Carousel
6. Delacorte Clock
7. Children's Zoo
8. Zoo
9. Tavern on the Green
10. The Mall
11. Naumburg Bandshell
12. Frick Museum
13. Bethesda Fountain
14. Cherry Hill Fountain
15. Loeb Boathouse
16. New-York Historical Society
17. American Museum of Natural History
18. Hayden Planetarium
19. Shakespeare Gardens
20. Delacorte Theater
21. Swedish Cottage
22. Metropolitan Museum of Art

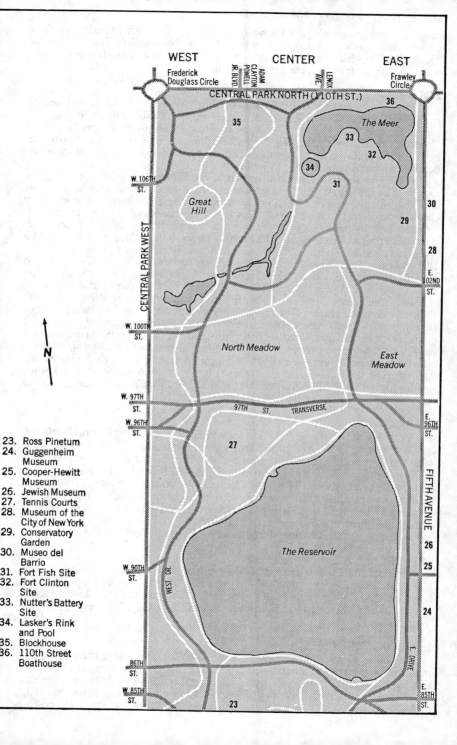

WEST   CENTER   EAST

Frederick
Douglass Circle

ADAM CLAYTON POWELL JR. BLVD

LENOX AVE.

Frawley
Circle

CENTRAL PARK NORTH (110TH ST.)

36
The Meer
35
33
32
34
31
W. 106TH ST.
Great Hill
30
29
28
E. 102ND ST.
W. 100TH ST.
North Meadow
East Meadow
N
W. 97TH ST.
97TH ST. TRANSVERSE
E. 96TH ST.
W. 96TH ST.
27
FIFTH AVENUE
W. 90TH ST.
The Reservoir
26
25
WEST DR.
24
E. DRIVE
86TH ST.
W. 85TH ST.
E. 85TH ST.
23

CENTRAL PARK WEST

23. Ross Pinetum
24. Guggenheim Museum
25. Cooper-Hewitt Museum
26. Jewish Museum
27. Tennis Courts
28. Museum of the City of New York
29. Conservatory Garden
30. Museo del Barrio
31. Fort Fish Site
32. Fort Clinton Site
33. Nutter's Battery Site
34. Lasker's Rink and Pool
35. Blockhouse
36. 110th Street Boathouse

the pleasure of whoever happens to be in their atrium. These can include magicians, mime artists, bee-bop bands, etc. Sometimes (but not always) Saturday is designated "Kid's Day," at which time little ones can have their faces painted, learn origami, or watch a miniplay featuring Hagar the Horrible.

ZOOS

The newly renovated **Central Park Zoo** (Fifth Avenue and 64th Street) has animals from around the world. It's open April through October from 10 a.m. to 5 p.m. Call 212/439-6500 for information. Close by the Central Park Zoo is the **Central Park Children's Zoo.** The animals are primarily refugees from the barnyard, but there are amusing animal-motif playhouses to crawl around in/on, and an unbeatable admission price of one thin dime.

A far grander experience can be had at the **Bronx Zoo,** which at 265 acres weighs in as the largest city zoo in America. The Bronx Zoo has a lot in common with big theme parks. It features monorails, jungle habitats, a participatory children's zoo, and "Wild Asia." This latter attraction is a 37-acre compound, viewable only by monorail, wherein Far Eastern beasts roam around uncaged in ignorance of the fact that they're in the Bronx. The zoo is open daily from 10 a.m. to 5 p.m., and until 5:30 p.m. on Sunday and holidays. To get there by subway, take the IRT–Seventh Avenue no. 2 train to the Pelham Parkway station, a 45-minute trip from Midtown. Alternatively, there's a bus from various corners along Madison Avenue. Call Liberty Lines, the operator, at 212/652-8400 for fares and schedules.

If anyone in the family is of a horticultural bent and you're already up at the Zoo, then consider visiting the nearby **New York Botanical Garden,** located within (not-impossible) walking distance to the north. Besides many beautiful plantings, it contains a spectacular restored Victorian greenhouse, really a crystal palace, called the Enid A. Haupt Conservatory. The Botanical Garden can be reached via a Metro-North train from Grand Central, which might be more pleasant than the subway. Alternatively, the IRT–Lexington Avenue no. 4 train to 200th Street and Jerome Avenue, or the IND–Sixth Avenue D train to Bedford Park Boulevard, will each get you pretty close.

ICE SKATING

Probably the most enjoyable spot for winter visitors to skate is at the **Rockefeller Center Rink,** at the foot of the Promenade, located on Fifth Avenue between 49th and 50th Streets. A session beneath Rockefeller Center's famous gilded statue of *Prometheus* costs $7 for adults, $6 for kids, and the skates (if you haven't brought your own) cost another $3.50 to rent. Open usually from late October to mid-April, weather permitting. At Christmas time when the gigantic Christmas tree dominates the scene and the mall leading from Fifth Avenue is decorated, it is a veritable wonderland. For further information, call 212/757-5731. Slightly less expensive, but just as aesthetic, is the **Wollman Rink,** described above under "Central Park."

THE CIRCLE LINE

The famous boat ride around Manhattan Island provides great views and a genuine sense of adventure. Some children will find the trip very exciting. Be aware, however, that it takes three hours. (For full details on the Circle Line's various cruises, refer to Chapter IV, "Sightseeing in New York City," Section 1, "The Famous Sights.")

HELICOPTER FLIGHTS

If you're a family of high rollers, you might consider taking the kids (not to mention yourselves) on a pricey, but intensely exhilarating, helicopter tour of the skyscraper district. **Island Helicopters** keeps a collection of ready birds at the East River Heliport, located at the foot of East 34th Street on the East River (tel. 212/683-4575). There are three basic tours, lasting from 7 to 17 minutes, and costing from $35 to $55 per person. Between 6 and 11 people can fit into a helicopter, depending on how big it is. No reservations are needed; just show up at the heliport. Open daily except Christmas and New Year's Day.

U.S.S. *INTREPID*

This is a full-size aircraft carrier, complete with jet planes on the deck. It's moored on the Hudson River and open to the public as a sea-air-space museum. The ship is a historic one, and the effort to preserve it is commendable. Some kids are really going to get off on this one; others won't be moved. (Refer to Chapter IV, "Sightseeing in New York City," section 1, "The Famous Sights," for full details.)

THE SOUTH STREET SEAPORT

There are almost daily events, often aimed specifically at children, staged on the cobbled streets of the seaport by the Rouse Corporation. Besides these, there are museum galleries, films, and historic buildings, plus the fascinating old sailing ships moored across South Street just begging to be explored. (See Chapter IV, "Sightseeing in New York City," Section 1, "The Famous Sights," for full details.) You and the kids can easily spend a full day at the seaport savoring New York's seafaring past.

THE STATEN ISLAND FERRY

This miniature sea voyage takes you from the southern tip of Manhattan to the north coast of Staten Island on the other side of Upper New York Bay. Gulls cry; tugs toot; waves lap and spray. The views of the Statue of Liberty and Lower Manhattan are "to die." Best of all is the cost: one humble quarter will get you all the way down to St. George on Staten Island, and all the way back too. The ferries are constantly crisscrossing the harbor, leaving every half hour from 9:30 a.m. to 9:30 p.m., and every hour for the rest of the day. Three major subway lines will take you to within a short walk of the South Ferry Terminal: the IRT–Lexington Avenue no. 4 or 5 train to the South Ferry station; the BMT local to the Whitehall–South Ferry station; and the IRT–Seventh Avenue no. 1 local train to the South Ferry station.

GIDDY HEIGHTS

Most kids love to go to the top of tall buildings. In Midtown, consider an excursion to the observation deck of either (or both) the **Empire State Building** or **30 Rockefeller Plaza.** These are both fully described in Chapter IV, "Sightseeing in New York City," Section 1, "The Famous Sights." Don't forget the **World Trade Center** either, whose deck is described in the same section of Chapter IV.

---

2. Shows and Tours

RADIO CITY MUSIC HALL

Years ago Marshall McLuhan told us that the medium was the message. Certainly this has become the case with Radio City Music Hall, the former movie palace at Sixth Avenue and 50th Street that now conducts guided tours of itself. The one-hour backstage tour costs about $6 and includes production areas, the impressive auditorium, and the several sumptuous lobbies. Call 212/632-4041 for reservations. An even better idea is to attend a Music Hall performance and see the stage for yourself. Quite spectacular but check to make sure the program being presented is appropriate for the age of your child. Call 212/632-4000 for ticket and program information.

CHILDREN'S THEATER

The On-Stage Children's Company at the **Hartley House Theatre,** 413 W. 46th St., between Ninth and Tenth Avenues (tel. 212/666-1716), presents Saturday-afternoon kids' shows throughout the year, but not on a regular basis. The production, as of this writing, was called *The Alice in Wonderland Game,* and tickets cost $5 for kids, $7 for adults. Call them when you're in town to see what's scheduled.

The **Children's Improv Company** is a division of something called the New Media Repertory Company, 1462 First Ave. (tel. 212/734-5195). Every Saturday, as of this writing, young teenaged actors are presenting *Alfred the Dragon Solves Another Mystery.* The show is suitable for ages 4 to 8 and takes place in St. Peter's Lutheran Church, which is at Lexington Avenue and 54th Street, adjacent to the Citicorp Center. Prices are $5 for adults and $4.50 for kids. Of course, by the time you read this Children's Improv may be performing elsewhere, so be sure to call the number above for schedules and information. Best time to call is on Friday between 3 and 6:30 p.m.

THE HAYDEN PLANETARIUM

This New York institution is a part of the American Museum of Natural History on Central Park West, but it has a special entrance on West 81st Street, between Central Park West and Columbus Avenue (tel. 212/873-8828). Planetarium shows feature special effects like supernovas, black holes, clouds, and thunderstorms, projected on the inside of a huge domed ceiling. Recent presentations have borne titles like *Star Quest, The Violent Universe, Encounter: The Search for Extraterrestrial Life,* and *Is Anyone Out There?* Admission is $3.75 for adults, $2 for kids (ages 2 to 12), and $2.75 for students and seniors. There are shows every day and your ticket will also admit you to the Museum of Natural History.

NBC TOUR

The National Broadcasting Company conducts regular tours of its television and radio broadcast facilities at 30 Rockefeller Plaza, in the middle of the block bounded by Fifth and Sixth Avenues and 49th and 50th Streets (tel. 212/664-4000). Tours leave every 15 minutes six days a week (except Sunday). Admission is $7 per person, first-come, first-served; no kids under 6. In high summer, better get here early because they do sell out.

---

3. Museums

THE CHILDREN'S MUSEUM

It's misleading to call this collection of participatory exhibits, art activities, theatrical performances, and nature and science shows a "museum." Located at 314 W. 54th Street, between Eighth and Ninth Avenues (tel. 212/765-5904), it's guaranteed to delight and fascinate small children (optimum age is probably about 4). Admission Wednesday through Friday is $2 for kids and $1 for adults. On Saturday and Sunday it's $3 for kids and $2 for grownups. Closed Monday.

AMERICAN MUSEUM OF NATURAL HISTORY

The main entrance is at Central Park West and 79th St. (tel. 212/873-4225), around the corner from the aforementioned Planetarium. The museum houses an amazing collection of stuff from reassembled dinosaur skeletons to rare and incredible gems. Most people remember the dinosaurs and the dioramas providing lifelike glimpses of exotic beasts in natural habitat. Open daily from 10 a.m. to 5:45 p.m. (until 9 p.m. on Wednesday, Friday, and Saturday nights). Admission is $3.50 for adults, $1.50 for students and children, and it's free on Friday and Saturday nights.

MUSEUM OF THE CITY OF NEW YORK

Located on Fifth Avenue at 103rd Street (tel. 212/534-1672), this museum contains a unique and distinguished gallery devoted entirely to antique toys and dollhouses. There are 12 historic dollhouses on display, the biggest being about five feet tall. One is a replica of a 19th-century New York brownstone house, complete with period decoration. Lots of period rooms, antique silver, old photo exhibits, etc., to interest grownups too. Open Tuesday through Saturday from 10 a.m. to 4:45 p.m., on Sunday from 1 to 4:45 p.m.; closed Monday. Admission is $3 for adults, $1 for children.

THE FIRE MUSEUM

This establishment contains two floors of rare equipment such as a pumper used in 1820, a hand-pulled hook and ladder, and a wooden fire hydrant. It traces the history of fire fighting from volunteer days in the 1820s all the way to 1933. The museum is downtown at 278 Spring St. (tel. 212/691-1303). It's open Tuesday through Saturday from 10 a.m. to 4 p.m. Admission is by donation.

CON EDISON ENERGY MUSEUM

You can see what a kitchen looked like in the 1890s; climb through a simulated manhole into the world of gas, water, telephone, steam, and sewer lines that lurks beneath the Manhattan streets; learn all about Thomas Alva Edison and his ingenious inventions; even pick up a few energy-saving tips from the hands-on demonstration exhibits. The museum is at 145 E. 14th St., between Irving Place and Third Avenue (tel. 212/460-6244). Open Tuesday through Saturday from 10 a.m. to 4 p.m. Admission is free.

NEW YORK TRANSIT MUSEUM

This is a substantial exhibit of old photos, classic subway cars, buses, and all manner of working equipment housed in a vintage subway station that's no longer on a line. It tells the entire history of the development of New York City's complicated subway system, complete with exhibits you can climb into and walk through. Kids and adults alike may find it extremely interesting. Located in the former Court Street Station, on the northwest corner of Boerum Place and Schermerhorn Street in downtown Brooklyn. Call 718/330-3060 for information and directions. Open Monday through Friday from 10 a.m. to 4 p.m., Saturday from 11 a.m. to 4 p.m. Admission is one token ($1) for adults, half price for kids under 17

NEW YORK CITY SHOPPING

Any Western city as rich and populous as New York has got to have good shopping, almost by definition. On top of its wealth and size New York is also a major international port, a gateway to all the other consuming citizens of America. Many people come to New York for the sole purpose of shopping for things that are unavailable elsewhere. Perhaps you're one of these and know precisely where you're going as soon as you get off the plane.

This chapter, however, is for those who don't know much about New York City shopping. As such, it's an abbreviated orientation designed for visiting tourists, not a thorough directory for dedicated shoppers in search of rare or specialized goods. It's organized as follows:

The first section provides an overview of nine famous department stores, both in terms of what they've got and to whom they cater. The second section provides block-by-block tours of four of Manhattan's most celebrated shopping avenues. The third section is a guide to discount stores. The fourth section contains recommended antiques shops and flea markets. The fifth and last section is a directory of selected museum shops whose fine reproductions and giftwares make them good shopping destinations in and of themselves.

1. The Big Stores

BLOOMINGDALE'S

It's high-class without being swanky, deluxe without being exclusive, enormously large but still very stylish. Bloomingdale's local reputation rests on its fashionable clothing for men and women. It was the first store to present Ralph Lauren, Perry Ellis, Halston, Calvin Klein, and Yves St. Laurent in on-site shops of their own. It has pioneered "country promotions," wherein the whole place is periodically inundated with goods from China, Ireland, Japan, India, or whoever else is on deck in the promotion department. The main floor teems with people hurrying this way and that, especially up the glittering black and white marble-floored alley lined with opulent cosmetics counters. Other departments sell home furnishings, Waterford and Lalique crystal, gourmet foods, sportswear, telephone answering machines, etc. Interpreters are on hand for foreign shoppers. And there are even three restaurants: the deluxe Train Bleu, Forty Carrots for health-food aficionados, and the Showtime Café for self-service snacks.

The main entrance to Bloomingdale's is on Lexington Avenue, between 59th and 60th Streets (tel. 212/705-2000). Open from 10 a.m. to 6:30 p.m. on Tuesday, Wednesday, Friday, and Saturday, to 9 p.m. on Monday and Thursday, and from noon to 6 p.m. on Sunday.

SAKS FIFTH AVENUE
Saks has got a different atmosphere than Bloomies. It's deeper, more conservative, but somehow more lushly luxurious. Again, it's known primarily for its high-quality clothing for men and women. But unlike Bloomingdale's it doesn't even contain departments unrelated to clothing. Actually, that's not quite true—you can also buy things like gourmet chocolates, fine crystal, stationery, and a few other odds and ends. But the overwhelming emphasis is on deluxe clothing and accessories, from sportswear, designer clothes, and Vuitton luggage to lingerie, shoes, furs, and so on and so forth. No matter what it's on, a Saks label is certainly a flattering one to have in one's closet.

Saks' huge and glamorous Manhattan store is located right in the middle of Midtown, on Fifth Avenue, between 49th and 50th Streets (tel. 212/753-4000). Open Monday through Saturday from 10 a.m. to 6:30 p.m. (to 8 p.m. on Thursday night); closed Sunday.

B. ALTMAN & CO.
Altman's is a very proper, old-line Fifth Avenue department store with a fairly dizzying assortment of goods. There is quality clothing, of course, with all the big-name designers for men and women represented. But there's also a famous rug department noted for rare Orientals. There are shoes and children's clothing and shops for the bath and closet, but there are also a rare-book department, a portrait studio, and a travel desk. Altman's landmark store occupies an entire block, and has eight floors full of quality merchandise, as well as a palpable atmosphere of good service and tradition. It's a great place to shop for gifts.

The store is located at Fifth Avenue and 34th Street (tel. 212/679-7800). Open Monday through Saturday from 10 a.m. to 7 p.m. (to 8 p.m. on Thursday nights). Open Sunday 11 a.m. to 5 p.m.

MACY'S
This is the largest store in the world, each of whose nine floors contains three *acres* of retailing space. Not too many years ago Macy's reputation had sunk to that of a borderline bargain basement. But it has been substantially revamped and upgraded in recent years. Nowadays it has departments that are as upscale as anything in Bloomingdale's.

And boy, do they have a lot of stuff! You can buy gourmet cheeses, antiques, a fur coat, a home computer, toys, cosmetics, housewares, linens, shoes, luggage, sporting goods, rugs, and clothes, clothes, clothes, for men, women, and children. This doesn't even begin to suggest the exceptional range of merchandise. One good measure of Macy's size is the fact that it contains six separate restaurants.

The main entrance is on Broadway between 34th and 35th Streets (tel. 212/695-4400). The store is open daily from 9:45 a.m. until 6 p.m. on Saturday and Sunday, until 6:45 p.m. on Tuesday and Wednesday, and until 8:30 p.m. on Monday, Thursday and Friday

LORD & TAYLOR

There are now something like 45 Lord & Taylors across the country. But they all take their inspiration from the landmark store on New York's Fifth Avenue. This is the home of what management calls the "American Look," which is their way of describing prosperous conservatism. The majority of the merchandise consists of high-quality clothing for women, even though there are departments for men and children. You can also buy antiques and furniture at Lord & Taylor, as well as outfits for posh country weekends, and of course, cosmetics. If you arrive at 9:30 a.m., you'll be treated to a preshopping complimentary cup of coffee. At 10 o'clock sharp, the "Star Spangled Banner" is played over the loudspeaker, everyone stands at attention, and only when the music is over does the shopping begin.

Lord & Taylor is on Fifth Avenue between 38th and 39th Streets (tel. 212/391-3344). It's open daily from 10 a.m. to 6:45 p.m. (on Monday and Thursday nights until 8:30 p.m.).

BONWIT TELLER

The old peach-colored-stone Bonwit's was razed a few years back for the construction of Trump Tower on Fifth Avenue. But a new store has arisen, phoenix-like, on a site adjacent to (and connected with) the old. Bonwit's is an elite establishment with perfectly exquisite merchandise. One imagines that most of its customers are privileged women shopping for designer clothes, furs, accessories, fragrances, elegant shoes, watches, and the like. There's also a men's shop that carries clothing bearing the labels of Valentino, Uomo, Battistoni, Ralph Lauren, etc. The six floors are suffused with an air of luxury found only in world-class cities.

Bonwit's is at 4 E. 57th St. (tel. 212/593-3333). Open from 10 a.m. to 7 p.m. Monday through Friday (on Thursday to 8 p.m.), to 6 p.m. on Saturday, and from noon to 5 p.m. on Sunday.

BERGDORF GOODMAN

Bergdorf's, the *ne plus ultra* of New York department stores, is not the sort of place to bother with branch locations. It's a perfectly gorgeous establishment filled with the most extravagant clothing and accessories money can buy. It's the only place in New York where, for example, you can purchase Turnbull & Asser shirts, Angela Cummings jewelry, or Penhaligon's cologne. Also available are the clothing designs of Issey Miyake, Geoffrey Beene, Anne Klein, Chanel, etc., each housed in a little boutique of its own. Bergdorf's has something for every rich person that he or she finds it impossible to live without.

The brand-new main entrance to Bergdorf Goodman is on Fifth Avenue between 57th and 58th Streets (tel. 212/753-7300). Store hours are Monday through Saturday from 10 a.m. to 6 p.m. (to 8 p.m. on Thursday).

HENRI BENDEL

This small store intends to be everything to one customer, rather than a little bit of something to a lot of customers. That one customer, in the words of Bendel's former president Geraldine Stutz, is a "hip, big-city woman." She is also small (only sizes 2 to 10 are carried in the store), adventurous, and pretty rich. Bendel's (pronounced *Ben*-dels) was the first store to bring Chloe, Sonia Rykiel, and Dorothee Bis designs to New York. It has a reputation for deluxe avant-garde merchandise, most of which is women's clothing. Also in stock are gloves, bags, tableware, jewelry, linens, scarves, and stationery. It's a very inventive and exciting store.

Bendel's address is 10 W. 57th St., between Fifth and Sixth Avenues (tel. 212/247-1100). Open Monday through Saturday from 10 a.m. to 6 p.m. (to 8 p.m. on Thursday).

BARNEY'S

This is a very big, very stylish, and very attractive department store that has been family run at this same location for a very long time. Barney's carries men's and women's designer clothes representing every American and international designer you can think of—Calvin Klein, Ralph Lauren, Perry Ellis, Giorgio Armani, and so on. This store has traditionally been a great place to buy a men's suit, and now they have just about anything else you can think of too. Even their own parking lot across the street.

Barney's is located at 106 Seventh Ave., between 16th and 17th Streets (tel. 212/929-9000). Hours are Monday through Thursday from 10 a.m. to 9 p.m., Friday and Saturday from 10 a.m. to 8 p.m., and Sunday from noon to 6 p.m.

---

2. Four Famous Shopping Avenues

MADISON AVENUE

From about 59th Street to about 86th Street, Madison Avenue offers the sort of shopping associated with world-class cities. It is primarily a street of exclusive designer clothing, antiques, and art, and the stores hereabouts obviously cater to the carriage trade. But even if you're not in the luxury league, a stroll up Madison will provide unsurpassed window-shopping opportunities. In fact, with the possible exception of the much shorter Rodeo Drive in Beverly Hills, there is no other street like this in the United States. Dedicated shoppers won't want to miss it. Besides, great buys are always to be had at sales, one or more of which may well be under way at the time of your visit.

We'll start our walk at Madison Avenue and 60th Street, at the point where the glass skyscrapers of Midtown give way to the low-rise buildings of the East Side Historic District. On the northeast corner of Madison and 62nd Street is **The Limited,** the new New York showcase for the national chain of women's clothiers that bears the same name. Before you reach 63rd Street you'll also see **Furla,** full of deluxe handbags, and **Floris,** traditional English bath products and perfumes.

Between 63rd and 64th Streets is a typical potpourri of Madison Avenue shops. **Laura Ashley** is filled with her signature "pretty" things; **Descamps** sells luxury sheeting and towels; **La Bagagerie** has top-of-the-line luggage and bags; and **M. J. Knoud** carries hunting and riding clothes and paraphernalia. The next block, from 64th to 65th Streets, offers more of the same. Of particular note is **Isabel Canovas,** featuring jewelry and accessories in a very dramatic boutique. **Rodier** has sporty Paris fashions; **Betsey, Bunky, and Nini,** serendipitous clothes; and **Andrea Carrano,** luxe shoes and bags.

The parade continues a block north with **Charles Jourdan,** the luxury shoe shop at the southeast corner of Madison and 66th, and **North Beach Leather,** which carries high-style leather clothes. Between here and 67th Street you'll encounter gorgeous jewelry at **Fred Leighton;** clothes for privileged tots and their moms at **Christian de Castelnau;** luxury sportswear at **Henry Lehr;** elegant clothes for "ladies and gentlemen" at **Jacques Bellini;** elegant table settings at **Thaxton & Co.;** and designer dresses at **Sonia Rykiel.**

Crossing 67th Street you begin to encounter more and more shops bearing the name of one famous designer or another. Before you reach 68th Street you'll pass **Pierre Balmain,** purveyor of exceedingly fine suits for men, and **Emanuel Ungaro** of women's fashion fame. Between 68th and 69th Streets is a real thicket of them. **Gianni Versace, Joan and David** (exceedingly high-class shoes), **Giorgio Armani, Veneziano, Sr. David, Jaeger,** and **Kenzo** are all on this one block.

Cross 69th Street and you'll come to the New York **Missoni** store, filled with high-fashion women's clothing from Italy. Also on the block between 69th and 70th are **Pratesi,** makers of sheets and towels for royalty; **Piaffe,** a fashionable boutique devoted entirely to small sizes; and **Lanvin** of Paris, the famous French couture house.

From 70th to 71st Streets is quite a block, even by Madison Avenue standards. **Saint Laurent Rive Gauche,** featuring the unexcelled designs of Mr. Big himself, is located here. So is **Arche** (trendy shoes); **Brigitte Cassegrain** (luggage, bags, and accessories); **Matsuda** (fashionable clothes for men); **T. Jones** (equally fashionable clothes for women); and **Pierre Deux** (famous for French country arts and accessories). After a clutch of smaller shops selling all manner of notions and clothing, you'll come to the corner of 72nd Street and **Ralph Lauren.** This latter establishment, occupying the former Rhinelander mansion, is the concrete realization of the "Polo" image.

Although the famous Parke Bernet auction gallery (now merged with, and known only as, Sotheby's) is no longer located at Madison and 76th Street, the adjoining district of art galleries that it spawned still exists and flourishes. The block between 72nd and 73rd contains several interesting emporia. **Philip W. Pfeifer** sells antique telescopes and decorative scientific objects d'art from the past; **Hymore Hodson Antiques, Ltd.,** has antique English furniture and clocks.

Cross 73rd Street and you'll come to **Devenish & Co.,** specializing in furniture for palaces. The block from 74th to 75th Streets, besides being home to the famous Whitney Museum of American Art, also contains **Antiquarium** (filled with fine ancient art) and **Len & Gerry Trent** (a source of art nouveau objets and glass).

The next block, that between 75th and 76th Streets, is dominated by art and antiques. **Delorenzo** has extravagant early 20th-century furniture; **Florian Papp** is known for its fine English antiques; **Time Will Tell** is a shop full of antique wristwatches; **Vito Giallo** is more of a unique gift shop, again with emphasis on antiques; **Koreana** offers arts and antiques from Korea; and **Leo Kaplan** has antique glass objects.

That big modernish building between 76th and 77th Streets, opposite the Carlyle Hotel, used to be Parke Bernet. Now both it and the ground floor of the Carlyle contain exclusive art galleries. The **Davlyn Gallery** (modern art), **William H. Wolff** (Far Eastern antiquities), **Marvin Kagan** (rare Oriental rugs), and **Michael Weisbrod** (Chinese porcelain) are only some of the establishments on this single block.

Other galleries of interest as we head northward from 77th Street are **Weintraub** (modern art and sculpture) and **Navin Kumar** (more Far Eastern art). Between 78th and 79th Streets are **Perls Galleries** (painting and sculpture), **Jacob Frères** (more furniture for palaces), **Kenneth Lux** (fine European paintings), and **E. & J. Frankel** (Chinese and Oriental fine arts).

After 79th Street, Madison loses a bit of its intense edge. But the parade of galleries continues right up to 86th Street. Notable among them is **Jay Johnson** ("America's Folk Heritage Gallery," between 79th and 80th), **Eeyore's** (books for children, between 80th and 81st), **Ballantrae** (fabulous and dramatic antique furniture, between 81st and 82nd), the **San Francisco Model Ship Gallery** (great models, scrimshaw, paintings of the sea, etc., between 82nd and 83rd), **Lucien Goldschmidt** (rare books, prints, and drawings, between 83rd and 84th), **Marco Polo Antiques** (gorgeous silver objects, etc., between 84th and 85th), and **Carlyn Gallery** (contemporary American arts and crafts, between 85th and 86th).

Admittedly, I've skimmed the last seven blocks. But the flavor and content of the avenue should certainly be apparent.

FIFTH AVENUE

The very name is synonymous with luxury clothing and jewelry. But over the last 15 years most of the fashionable shops have moved to Madison Avenue. Great stores still remain on Fifth, but only on a relatively short stretch from the Plaza at 59th Street to the region of Rockefeller Center at 49th Street. We'll start at the top and work our way downtown. At the corner of Fifth and 59th Street, on the ground floor of the Sherry Netherland Hotel, is **A la Vieille Russie,** a place for malachite urns, satinwood marquetry commodes, and Fabergé eggs. Just looking in the windows is a treat if you're partial to small exquisite objects. Cross 59th Street heading south. The block from 58th to 59th on the east side of the street is occupied by the huge white marble General Motors Building. The sunken plaza out front never quite developed into the exclusive plaza G.M. must have had in mind. Today it contains outposts of **Christine Valmy** (the skin-care specialists) and **Vidal Sassoon** (of haircutting and cosmetics fame). **F.A.O. Schwarz,** the luxury toy store famous for its displays, recently moved into the GM building.

Between 58th and 57th Streets, Fifth Avenue is at its best. The east side of the block has chic shops like **Leron** (lingerie), and the soon-to-be opened **Bergdorf's for Men Shop.** That elegant building across Fifth Avenue on this same block is **Bergdorf Goodman,** perhaps the most luxurious department store in New York (see Section 1, "The Big Stores," above, for a description of Bergdorf's). On the corner of 57th Street, at the southern end of the Bergdorf building, is **Van Cleef & Arpels,** a famous jewelry store whose windows are also worth a look.

Speaking of windows, across 57th Street is **Tiffany & Co.,** the world-famous jeweler whose small (and seemingly nuclear-proof) windows hold the sort of jewels worn by the haute monde, displayed with the most artistic elegance. Also on the block between 57th and 56th are **Salvatore Ferragamo** (designer clothes for men), **Doubleday** (a huge and fascinating bookstore), **Bulgari** (famous jewelry), **Fendi** (Italian leather shop), and last but not least, the **Trump Tower.** This latter structure contains an immense and glittery atrium filled with luxury shops.

Between 56th and 55th Streets is, first of all, another **Salvatore Ferragamo,** this one catering to women. By the way, the **Steuben Glass** Building, which is that sleek green glass skyscraper set slightly back from the southeast corner of Fifth and 56th, has an interesting gallery of glass objects. You're free to go in and browse around. Also on this block are **Harry Winston** (jewels for plutocrats; can't just browse around in here), **Beltrami** (designer for women), another bevy of chic little shops purveying everything from shoes to eyeglasses, and finally **Nat Sherman,** the luxury tobacconist.

The block from 55th to 54th sports more than a few merchandising heavy-weights. **Fred** is the sort of jeweler who inflames revolutionists; **Godiva** sells the sorts of chocolates Marie Antoinette might have tried giving to the mob; **Bijan** is a men's boutique so exclusive that you must phone ahead for an appointment; **Wempe** is the place to buy a $10,000 Rolex watch; and **Gucci** is, well, the prince of luxury leather goods (closed during lunch hour, since all its regular patrons are busy at swanky restaurants).

Between 54th and 53rd Streets is, first of all, the annex to **Gucci.** After that is the big **Fortunoff** store selling everything from silver to jewelry to fabulous gifts. Fortunoff calls itself "the source," and for good gifts and durable luxuries, it's exactly that. **Carrano** next door has trendy shoes; **The Peninsula** is a fairly extraordinary-looking jewelry and Chinese arts store that looks transplanted from a street in Hong Kong; and **Doubleday,** on the corner of 53rd, is a cousin to the store on 56th Street and also a good browse.

Books are the order of the day too at **B. Dalton,** at 666 Fifth Ave. between 53rd and 52nd Streets. There aren't too many bookstores in the world that are quite this huge. Across 52nd Street is the limestone palace built for Morton Plant, but occupied for almost 70 years by the fine jeweler **Cartier.** In an adjoining building on 52nd Street, between Fifth and Madison, is **Les must de Cartier,** selling little things you *must* have (like silver picture frames, bits of jewelry, little trays, amusing boxes, lighters, etc.). If you've detoured over to Les musts, you might as well duck into the pedestrian passage of the brown-glass Olympic Tower. This enclosed walkway, complete with potted palms, splashing waterfall, benches, florist, and café/restaurant, connects 52nd and 51st Streets. It's a good place to stop and rest, and perhaps contemplate the commercial glories around you.

Between 51st and 50th Streets are St. Patrick's Cathedral on one side of Fifth and a section of Rockefeller Center on the other. The shopping picks up again on the block between 50th and 49th, where you'll find **Saks Fifth Avenue** (this great New York department store is described above in Section 1, "The Big Stores").

The corner of 49th Street is really the termination of ultrafashionable Fifth Avenue, at least as far as shopping is concerned. Great stores (like **Lord & Taylor** and **B. Altman**) do, of course, exist south of here. But the street lacks the intensity of those blocks in the 50s through which we've just strolled. In fact, even in the 50s a process of attrition is under way. New York has always been like this; the day will also come when fashionable retailers desert Madison Avenue too.

Before leaving Fifth Avenue, book-lovers should have a look at **Barnes & Noble,** between 49th and 48th Streets. It's really a huge supermarket for books. Besides cut-rate bestsellers, this is a good place to pick up remainders of lavish coffee-table books for a fraction of the cover prices.

South of 48th Street, Fifth Avenue begins literally to get "shiny patches" like a too-old suit. These are in the form of too brightly lit discount houses, often with banners proclaiming a "Going Out of Business" sale. The curious thing is that this type of establishment never actually seems to close permanently. Instead it continues "Going Out of Business" indefinitely.

At the corner of Fifth and 47th Street is the **International Jewelers Exchange,** which forms the portal to 47th Street, New York's fabled **Diamond District.** Extending only from Fifth Avenue to Sixth Avenue, this block contains hundreds upon hundreds of individual dealers whose sole business is buying and selling diamonds, gold, and silver. Picturesque Hasidic Jews, in beaver hats, long coats, and flowing beards, bustle back and forth across the crowded pavements. Unobtrusive plainclothes police will swoop out of nowhere if a known criminal has the bad judgment to set foot on this block.

57TH STREET

From Third Avenue to Sixth Avenue, 57th Street offers some of New York's most sophisticated shopping for clothes, precious antiques, and gifts. There is definitely a "57th Street Style," epitomized by stores like Bendel's, Bonwit's, and Hammacher Schlemmer. The "real" thing is the only thing you'll find on 57th Street. The rents are too high for anything else.

The crosstown blocks on 57th Street are considerably longer than the short blocks on the avenues. For that reason, addresses are provided in parentheses after each shop name.

On the north side of the block between Third and Lexington Avenues is **Hammacher Schlemmer** (147 E. 57th), source of James Bondian adult toys, poolside elves, luxe sporting goods, lawn chairs, etc. With a few exceptions, the rest of the block is not so interesting.

At Lexington Avenue, consider detouring two blocks north to 59th Street, then a half block toward Park Avenue to **Fiorucci** (125 E. 59th). This New York branch of the famous Milan store is full of fabulous far-out clothing and accessories. Even the salespeople are an experience. Meanwhile, back on 57th Street on the block between Lexington and Park Avenues, is a growing diversity of shops. **Phone City** (126 E. 57th) has models featuring everything from Garfield the Cat to something from the French Empire period; **Norsk** (114 E. 57th) is filled with Scandinavian furniture and accessories for the home; **Countess Mara** (110 E. 57th) sells lush ties and accessories; **S. J. Shrubsole** (104 E. 57th) has a window full of antique English silver that's almost beyond imagination.

The block between Park and Madison Avenues is the epicenter of fashionable 57th Street shopping. **Madler** (on the southwest corner of Park) has luxe ladies' handbags; **Sherle Wagner** (60 East 57th) deals in fantasy bathroom fixtures; **Orrefors** (58 E. 57th) is a gallery of crystal; **Arthur Ackerman** (50 E. 57th) deals in old English furniture and paintings of museum caliber; **Alfred Dunhill** (65 E. 57th) is the British haberdasher transplanted here to New York; the silversmith **Buccellati** (46 E. 57th) might have a life-size boxer dog made of sterling in the window; **Dalva Bros.** (44 E. 57th) sells French antiques; **La Marca** (41 E. 57th) sells fabulous expensive shoes; **Guy Laroche** (36 E. 57th) has sports couture for women; **Louis Vuitton** (41 E. 57th) is headquarters for top-of-the-line luggage; **Victoria's Secret** (34 E. 57th) is famous for luxury lingerie; **Maud Frizon** (41 E. 57th) means fancy (and very high-style) shoes; and **Sheridan** (on the northeast corner of 57th Street) has a big selection of designer linens, quilts, and bedspreads.

After a block like that it's hard to summon the energy to continue. Yet 57th between Madison and Fifth is still quite fabulous. A few of the highlights would include **Laura Ashley** (21 E. 57th) for clothing and accessories with her English country accent; **James Robinson** (15 E. 57th) for more extraordinary English silver, table settings, etc.; **Hermès** (11 E. 57th) and its famous leather goods; the properly elegant furnishings for men and women at **Burberry's** (9 E. 57th); **David Webb's** (7 E. 57th) windows full of real jewelry; plus the designer clothes for women at **Ann Taylor** (3 E. 57th); not to mention **Bonwit Teller** and **Tiffany & Co.,** two famous New York institutions that also happen to be on this block.

Fifth Avenue and 57th Street is no longer the geographical heart of Manhattan's elite retail district, whose center of gravity has shifted northward up Madison. But it remains a mighty glittering intersection, with Tiffany's and Bergdorf's commanding its opposite corners.

Now then, on to the block between Fifth and Sixth Avenues. The stores closest to Fifth are much like their counterparts on the Madison-Fifth block. **Van Cleef & Arpels** (in the Bergdorf building) sells incredible jewels; **Yves St. Tropez** (4 W. 57th) is a sophisticated clothing boutique for women, as is **Lillie Rubin** (22 E. 57th). Other establishments not to miss include **Henri Bendel** (12 W. 57th, described above in Section 1, "The Big Stores"); **Bolton's** (29 W. 57th), the Midtown branch of a very big women's discount clothing concern; and **Rizzoli** (31 W. 57th), the famous and beautiful international bookstore.

Sixth Avenue marks the western boundary of the fashionable shopping district on 57th Street. But worth a look, since you've gone this far, is the **Ritz Thrift Shop** (107 W. 57th), just a few steps off Sixth Avenue. The sign says it all: "Slightly Used Furs at a Fraction of Their Original Cost." It's doubtful anyone could tell the difference.

COLUMBUS AVENUE

More than a dozen years ago Columbus Avenue was the very definition of the word "dreary." Since then the surrounding blocks have been renovated and gentrified, and Columbus Avenue itself has emerged as a street of expensive clothing boutiques and trendy café-restaurants. It doesn't rival Madison Avenue, but it's breezy and youthful. The interesting stores start roughly at 67th Street, peak around 79th Street, and extend to 84th or so.

Starting on the block from 67th to 68th, you'll see a typically eclectic Columbus Avenue duo. **Furla** has beautiful and expensive purses and leather goods; **Trocadero** is really three stores filled with L.A.-style fun clothes and accessories and loud rock music.

From 69th to 70th Street there's the **General Store** with Fiesta ware and kitchen gadgets; **Banana Republic,** clothes for big-game hunters; **GapKids,** great cotton clothes for kids; and **Nautica,** polo-type clothes for men.

From 71st to 72nd Streets things get seriously under way. **Shu Uemura** has makeup; **Betsey Johnson** features her own unique designs for women; **Kenneth Jay Lane** sells costume jewelry; **To Boot** is an ultrachic shoe store; and **Charivari** sells the sort of drop-dead clothing that every fashion-conscious West Sider wants.

You might have noticed that every other storefront seems to be a restaurant. This phenomenon continues unabated on the next block, between 72nd and 73rd Streets. Between the eateries you'll see **Sock Express,** which sells just that—socks; **Savage,** costume jewelry that lives up to the store's name; and the **Silver Palate** for gourmet take-out.

From 74th to 75th you'll encounter far-out clothes at **Parachute; Cotton Ginny** handles only natural-fiber clothes from Canada; and **ACA Joe** has more Columbus Avenue–look clothes for either sex.

The shops between 75th and 76th Streets are a riot of cross-cultural references ranging from **The Limited,** a national chain that carries stylish women's clothes and accessories; to **Crabtree & Evelyn,** items for elegant bathrooms with English accents; to **Putumayo,** folk fashions from around the world; to **Ecco,** Italian-styled shoes and boots for women; to **La Merceria,** sporty tailored clothes for women.

Things are fairly quiet (retailing-wise) from 76th to 77th, with the exception of **Kenneth Cole's** shoes for men and women in a challenging environment. Between 77th and 78th is a novelty store called **Mythology,** which you shouldn't miss (six-foot inflatable dinosaurs, mechanical toys from China, unusual postcards, etc.).

From 78th to 79th Streets the range of shopping is from the pseudo–flea market clothing and accessories at **Alice's Underground;** to the luxury lingerie, antique and reproduction jewelry (all with hearts on them) at **Only Hearts;** to **Belle France** with its pretty French-made clothes for women.

The block between 79th and 80th Streets is unquestionably the most amazing, at least for those who remember Columbus Avenue in its humbler days. **Laura Ashley** is here, in even more splendid digs than she has on 57th Street; **Vittorio Ricci** offers very slick shoes; **Beau Brummel** sells clothes for the fashionable men who hang around with the women shopping next door at **Henry Lehr; Courts & Sports** has sports-oriented clothing and accessories; **Mishon** sells costume jewelry; and **Botticelli** has exquisite shoes and boots. This is the block that's closest to rivaling Madison Avenue.

Between 80th and 81st things calm down a bit. Of note, however, are **Street Life,** mostly black clothes for women; and **Central Carpet** (a long-established source of Oriental carpets at not-unreasonable prices).

There's a second wind of fashionable activity between 81st and 82nd Streets. Another branch of **Charivari** provides clothes for the West Side "dress for success" look; **Schweitzer Linens** stocks fine robes, towels, and bath accessories; **Frank Stella** sells men's and women's outfits for swanky weekends; **Greenstones et Cie.** is an unusual children's clothing store; **Penny Whistle Toys** is for upscale tots; and **Salou** has exotic flowers; **Descamps on Columbus** is full of linens.

Then things taper off again. Between 82nd and 83rd you'll find **Bellissima II,** presenting beautiful shoes and bags on a block full of restaurants and bars, and 83rd to 84th features **Handblock** (crafts, sweaters, and clothing), **Screaming Mimi's** (wild vintage clothes for both sexes), and **Nice Stuff** ("where you can afford the clothes you can't afford" according to the sign outside).

The **Down Quilt Shop** (quilts, sheets, comforters, wool blankets) is on the next block up, between 84th and 85th. By the time you approach 86th Street you've pretty well "done" Columbus Avenue. Appropriately for the times, the west side of the avenue sports a take-out fried-chicken counter called **Poulet Take-A-Way.**

3. Discounts

LOEHMANN'S

The Bronx flagship store of this famous nationwide chain has recently moved from Fordham Road to Riverdale. It's a bit of a trek from Midtown, but worth the trip. Loehmann's is a fabulous source of bargains, filled with high-fashion designer clothes for women, minus the labels, and priced at a fraction of their original cost. Knowledgeable shoppers will be in heaven. The store is located at 5740 Broadway at the corner of West 236th Street in Riverdale. You can take the #1 train to the West 238th Street stop (or take a fairly pricey taxicab). The hours are Monday through Saturday from 10 a.m. to 9 p.m., on Sunday from 11 a.m. to 6 p.m. Credit cards accepted.

DEALS

Deals offers the best values in town for upscale basics like 100% cotton shirts, Paul Stuart shoes, and other preppy-type items of clothing for men and women. They specialize in natural fibers, and carry everything in a full line of colors and sizes.

It's located at 81 Worth St., near Broadway (tel. 212/966-0215), is open Monday through Saturday from 9 a.m. to 6 p.m.

RICHARDS ARMY-NAVY

This place stocks military-surplus stuff like regulation pea jackets, plus "military-chic" items like flight jackets and camouflage fatigues, as well as jeans, fashion swimsuits, sports footwear, etc. Lots of good ideas, if you're an original dresser.

The store is at 233 W. 42nd St., between Seventh and Eighth Avenues (tel. 212/947-5018), and the hours are Monday through Wednesday from 9:15 a.m. to 7 p.m., Thursday through Saturday to 7:30 p.m.

BOLTON'S

This is the biggest discount chain for women's clothing in New York. The clothing is all new, of good quality, and in perfect condition. The most convenient branches for visitors are probably the two on 57th Street: at 225 E. 57th St., between Second and Third Avenues (tel. 212/755-2527); and at 27 W. 57th St., between Fifth and Sixth Avenues (tel. 212/935-4431). There's another branch at 1180 Madison Ave., at 86th Street (tel. 212/722-4454), as well as others all around town. Hours vary from store to store, but most are open from 10 a.m. to 7 p.m. Monday through Saturday (to 8:30 p.m. on Thursday) and from noon to 5 p.m. on Sunday.

UNIQUE CLOTHING WAREHOUSE

If you want costumes, clothes by underground designers, cotton basics, military chic, or anything else that no one back home has ever seen, this is the place. It's cheap too (or relatively so). The location is downtown at 726 Broadway, near 8th Street (tel. 212/674-1767). They're open Monday through Thursday from 10 a.m. to 9 p.m., Friday and Saturday to midnight, and Sunday from noon to 8 p.m.

CANAL JEAN

Besides tons of discounted jeans, they've got sportswear, T-shirts, hiking boots, vintage sunglasses, beach towels, knit sweaters, etc. It's at 504 Broadway, between Spring and Broome Streets (tel. 212/226-1130), and the hours are 10 a.m. to 8 p.m. daily.

ORCHARD STREET

Every Sunday, a half dozen blocks of Orchard Street (located on the Lower East Side, parallel to and five blocks east of the Bowery, between Houston and Grand Streets) are closed to traffic. The street is lined with little discount clothing shops on the ground floors of old tenement buildings, and on Sunday the goods spill right out onto the sidewalk, creating an open-air bargain bazaar. Every conceivable item of clothing, from jeans to exotic designer dresses, appears to be available. The crowds are huge, the competition stiff, and the haggling intense. The stores are open on other days as well. But a visit on Sunday will be as much a sightseeing experience as an excursion for high-fashion bargains.

4. Antiques and Flea Markets

MANHATTAN ART AND ANTIQUE CENTER
Most Manhattan antiques stores are scattered around the city in no particular district. This center brings together 120 dealers, each occupying his/her own shop on the main floor and two basement levels of a Midtown high-rise. There is everything here from rare paintings to antique jewelry, from bronze sculpture to quilts, from Tiffany glass to Oriental rugs. Prices range from $10 to $300,000. At the very least it's a good browse.

The center is located at 1050 Second Ave., at 56th Street (tel. 212/355-4400). It's open Monday through Saturday from 10:30 a.m. to 6 p.m., on Sunday from noon to 6 p.m.

BLEECKER STREET
The six blocks of Greenwich Village's Bleecker Street between Abingdon Square and Seventh Avenue South contain a fair collection of antiques shops. Some are not too expensive. Starting at Abingdon Square, **Hamilton Hyre Ltd.** (413 Bleecker) sports windows full of faux bamboo desks, Empire chandeliers, and unusual bibelots; **Treasures and Trifles** (409 Bleecker) has lots of crystal chandeliers, Louis XVI bergères, and bronze and crystal objects; **Susan Parrish** (390 Bleecker) has unique American quilts, folk art, and American Indian art; **Cynthia Beneduce** (388 Bleecker) also displays Americana, old signs, and quilts; **Peter Spielhagen** (372 Bleecker) offers pictures, bronze statues, and Biedermeier furniture; **Pierre Deux** (369 Bleecker), home of the French country look, has scrubbed pine chests and long country tables, Provençal fabrics, and home accessories; **Kelter/Malce** (361 Bleecker) specializes in quilts and has a great collection of cotton Pendleton and Beacon blankets; **Niall Smith** (344 Bleecker) offers busts, statues, urns, and bronzes; **Dorothy's Closet** (335 Bleecker) is full of vintage clothes and 1950s dining-table accessories; **The Antique Buff** (321½ Bleecker) has tons of "smalls," from cases full of antique jewelry to crystal perfume bottles to little things made out of silver and glass and porcelain; and **Tim McKay** (318 Bleecker) sells statues, gargoyles, and other dramatic architectural elements in wood and stone. There are plenty of other stores as well, but this should give an idea of the area's flavor.

THE ANNEX
This unlikely name attaches itself to an outdoor flea market and adjacent antiques bazaar. Both are held every Saturday and Sunday, year-round, from 9 a.m. to 5 p.m. in a parking lot on the corner of Sixth Avenue and 26th Street (tel. 212/243-5343). Dealers from all over the place come with furniture, Oriental rugs, antique dolls, bric-a-brac, bronzes, silver, jewelry, you name it. A small entrance fee is charged to the antiques fair, mostly to discourage marauding kids.

I.S. 44 FLEA MARKET
At Columbus Avenue, between 76th and 77th Streets (tel. 212/316-1088), this is one of the best flea markets around, especially if you love to browse. There are about 300 or so vendors, many of them regulars, with a wide variety of antique "stuff." One dealer specializes in watches from the '20s, '30s, and '40s. There are lots of large collections of old jewelry—Victorian earrings, huge '40s brooches and necklaces, lots of Bakelite jewelry, and radios too. Another dealer has Amish quilts, country quilts, quilt tops, antique tablecloths, linens, lace pillows, and on and on.

The variety is wide and the prices go anywhere from $5 to $5,000. Hours are Sunday from 10 a.m. to 6 p.m.

5. Museum Shops

Almost every big museum in town has a lobby gift shop stocked with reproductions of items in the collections, plus posters, prints, books, and so forth. One of the finest and largest is that of the **Metropolitan Museum of Art,** Fifth Avenue at 82nd Street (tel. 212/879-5500). This place has perfectly beautiful things, plus an especially inventive collection of children's books. The **Museum of Modern Art, 11 W.** 53rd St., between Fifth and Sixth Avenues (tel. 212/708-9700), has a shop that's not as large but still pretty extensive. This is a great place for beautiful art publications relating to MOMA's collection. Also intriguing is the shop at the **Cooper-Hewitt Museum,** Fifth Avenue at 91st Street (tel. 212/860-6868), whose merchandise reflects the museum's commitment to preserve and disseminate fine designs.

It's a good idea to explore the museum shop at every museum you visit. They're all interesting, if only for postcards. These three are worth special trips.

VIII

LONG ISLAND: ONE-DAY TRIPS TO CLOSE-IN DESTINATIONS

1. THE SORTS OF THINGS TO SEE AND DO

2. SELECTED CLOSE-IN ATTRACTIONS

3. RECOMMENDED RESTAURANTS (PLUS A FEW HOTELS)

Long Island is a wonderful place laboring under a bad reputation for being overdeveloped. I say "bad" in lieu of "unfair" because in truth the island really is overdeveloped. The traffic is horrible. Worse, it's capricious. One expects tie-ups on the Long Island Expressway at rush hour. But at 3 a.m.? How in the world could all those cars be at a standstill then? However, they just might be.

Nonetheless, the aggravation associated with traveling around, plus the often-depressing effect associated with certain tractless suburban wastelands, pale in comparison to the island's peculiarly attractive flavor and its abundance of attractions. Fortunately for New York City–based visitors, many of these latter constitute ideal day-trip destinations.

1. The Sorts of Things to See and Do

One end of Long Island actually faces Manhattan across the East River. However, the people over there in Brooklyn and Queens never think of themselves as being on Long Island. No, first one must travel the approximately 14 miles to the Nassau County line, cross over it on parkway (the local name for restricted-access highway), path, or foot, and only then will one have arrived on Long Island. So even though the island technically contains four counties (Brooklyn or Kings County, Queens, Nassau, and Suffolk), only two (Nassau and Suffolk) are considered by the locals to be on Long Island. Curious, but that's the way it is.

So what is there to do out there? Well, first of all there are the beaches, some of which actually lie within the borders of New York City. It comes as a surprise to many out-of-towners to learn that broad expanses of white sand and Atlantic surf are readily accessible by public transit. So even though a day at the beach isn't on your typical New York City itinerary, you can have it if you wish. Details follow below.

After the beaches I'd have to say that the so-called Gold Coast along the north shore of Nassau County qualifies as the next greatest attraction. This region, to use a recognizable term, is "Gatsby country." Of course, Fitzgerald's Gatsby was a poor boy turned gangster who tried to woo a rich girl by throwing big parties in a big house. Most of the real people who built great estates on the North Shore were more substantial individuals. It is accepted doctrine that all the great houses of the era between the turn of the century and the Stock Market Crash have been either razed or turned into schools. Not true. More than you think are still in private hands. And many others are open to the public as house-and-garden museums that provide vivid glimpses of just how sweet life can be. The northern section of Nassau County is exciting territory indeed for anybody interested in big old houses. It doesn't matter that a lot's been lost. A lot's still there.

Finally, there are the museums. As a matter of fact, there are more close-in museums than one could possibly hope to see. It would take an avid historian indeed to plow through most of them. But some are quite unusual. One, for example, is an entirely preserved farming village where costumed "inhabitants" trudge around hauling butter churns or spinning thread or shoeing horses. You'd never know it, standing in the middle of this place, that beyond the crests of the nearby sandy hills lie Levittown and Massapequa, places not noted for their rural associations. Other museums contain artifacts from Long Island's daredevil whaling days, another houses an immense collection of carriages, and yet another contains a millionaire natural historian's cache of marine life specimens housed in his former baronial home.

An area as rich and populous as close-in Long Island obviously supports major classical and pop cultural events, shopping on a grand scale, and sports facilities catering to a huge and sophisticated market. But with due respect to all these prosperous suburban pleasures, this chapter has been limited just to the sorts of attractions one can only find on Long Island.

---

2. Selected Close-In Attractions

This is not a comprehensive list of everything there is to see. But it does cover the highlights and give you a good cross-section view of what's out there for a day trip.

THE BEACHES

As mentioned earlier, there are a number of them actually within New York's city limits. In fact, every boro but Manhattan has at least a couple. They vary widely in desirability, however. Of the bunch, my favorites are Rockaway Beach and Riis Park, both located in Queens on a sandy, slender finger of land that forms the southern border of Jamaica Bay.

Perhaps the most appealing—and on weekends the busiest—part of **Rockaway Beach** adjoins the neighborhoods of Belle Harbor and Seaside, between about Beach 88th and Beach 118th Streets. These are comfortable middle-class areas that don't look a lot different from many inland tracts in Queens. You can take a subway practically to the line of the surf: it's the Eighth Avenue IND A train, whose last stop is Beach 116th Street. And there are plenty of facilities for snacks and seaside diversions.

About a mile and a half to the west is **Riis Park,** now part of the Gateway National Recreation Area. Gateway is operated by the federal government, patrolled by park rangers in Smokey the Bear hats, and comprises a hodgepodge of rescued undevel-

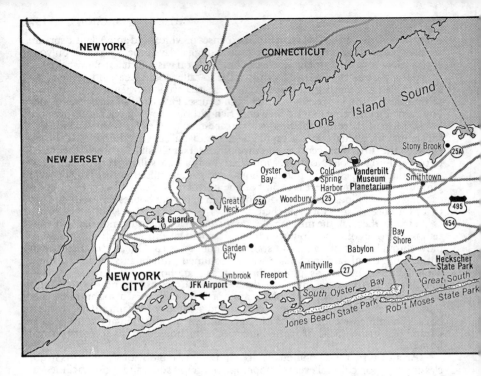

oped tracts situated at or near the entrance to New York Harbor. Riis Park has been a public beach for a lot longer than Gateway's been around. Indeed it includes a noble (if tattered) bathhouse in high-1930s style. The beach is broad and sandy, and instead of adjacent bedroom communities there's parking for 9,000 cars. The western fringe of Riis Park, close to Fort Tilden, is what the local press calls the "land of the total tan," in case that's of interest. You can reach Riis Park by car via the Belt Parkway, which follows the bulge of the Brooklyn shoreline, to the Riis Park–Marine Parkway Bridge exit. If you take the Eighth Avenue IND A train to Beach 116th Street in Rockaway, you'll have to transfer to a Q-35 bus for the mile-or-so trip to Riis.

But beaches on the Rockaway Peninsula, albeit close and nice, are mere antipasti to New York's big beach experience. That's **Jones Beach,** located about 25 miles from Midtown as the crow flies, in the southeastern corner of Nassau County. Jones Beach, open from May 24 to September 1, is a state park surrounded by sand dunes instead of housing projects. It's also huge, with six parking fields holding a total of 23,000 cars, eight Atlantic beaches, two Olympic-size swimming pools, snackbars, restaurant, cocktail lounge, ball fields, pitch 'n putt golf, lockers, showers, etc. There's even the **Jones Beach Theater,** which throws rock concerts during the summer. Recent acts have included Julian Lennon, the Pointer Sisters, the Cure, and the Beach Boys. Call 516/221-1000 for current program information.

Fortunately, the beach is magnificent enough not to be overpowered by all this stuff. If you want easy access to hot dogs and the boardwalk, park in Field 4 or 5. The crowds are thinnest over by Field 6 at the eastern end of the beach. A half mile past Field 6 is, unless people complain, the local no-swimsuit land. Wherever you settle, the sand is gorgeous and white, and the surf is at times pretty big.

Two major parkways, the Wantagh State and the Meadowbrook State, connect Jones Beach State Park to two of Long Island's major east-west arteries, namely, the

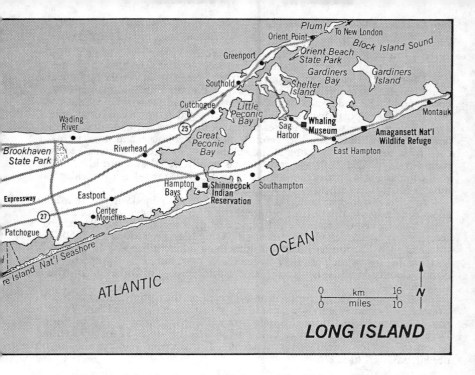

LONG ISLAND

Southern State and the Northern State Parkways. The drive would be short and simple, were it not for the traffic. How long does it take to drive 25 or so miles across Queens and Nassau Counties on a sunny Saturday in July? That's a question with no answer. If you drive during the week, at least the beach won't be crowded. But be prepared for traffic delays. After all, this is Long Island.

Alternatively, you can take advantage of the Long Island Rail Road's summertime Jones Beach excursion fare. Round trip from Penn Station (32nd Street and Seventh Avenue) costs $8.50 for adults and $5 for kids under 11. Actually, you just take the regular train to Freeport, a former fishing village engulfed by postwar suburbia, where you pick up a shuttlebus to the beach. During July and August trains leave almost every half hour, at least on weekends. The trip takes something under an hour and a half each way. There's no charge to use Jones Beach once you get there, but it does cost 50¢ to swim in the pools. For exact train times, call the Long Island Rail Road's 24-hour information number, 718/454-5477. Be prepared for it to be busy.

If you've come by car, a few other (and at times less crowded) beaches can be found just to the east of Jones Beach down Ocean Parkway. **Gilgo Beach** is a surfer beach in an undeveloped state park four or so miles from Jones. If you hanker for the full state park complement of bathhouse/snackbar/ballpark and so forth, you might also check out **Robert Moses State Park,** about six miles farther on. Like Jones, Moses is open daily between May 24 and September 1, and charges $3.50 per car. It's located on the westernmost tip of auto-free Fire Island and its parking lots are about the only place on that island where cars are permitted.

OLD BETHPAGE VILLAGE RESTORATION

It may sound funny, but there's something almost eerie about Old Bethpage Village Restoration. A moment may come during your visit, as it did during mine, when no tourists are in sight, when there are no sounds other than the rustle of crops or trees, and when not a single trace of the 20th century intrudes. For a fleeting instant you just might wonder if you really have stepped across the barriers of time.

The restored village is wisely and effectively isolated from its parking fields and visitor center. You tramp down a sandy road, of the sort Walt Whitman must have known and loved, and presto, there before you is an antique farming village, complete with rural population in antique clothing engaged in typical rural occupations, depending on the season. With the exception of the Powell farm, sections of which have been here since the late 18th century, all the other houses and stores were rescued from the clutches of Long Island subdividers and road wideners. Each was then moved to Old Bethpage and painstakingly restored and furnished. What you're looking at is a pretty thorough reconstruction of a pre–Civil War village, although strictly speaking no such village ever really stood here.

All sorts of things are going on in Old Bethpage Village and you'll want to allot about three hours to do the place properly. If you come in June, you'll see a Union Army training center beside the village; in August competing teams play baseball according to 1860 rules; October means the Long Island Fair, done à la 1860. The village is open 12 months a year, and something different happens every month. Incidentally, this is not a privately owned theme park, but rather a property of the Nassau County Museum Division. There's a total absence of Disney glitz—this is all the real stuff.

Old Bethpage Village Restoration is located on the eastern border of Nassau County, on Round Swamp Road, just south of Exit 48 on the Long Island Expressway. It is open Tuesday through Sunday from 10 a.m. to 5 p.m. (to 4 p.m. during December, January, and February). Admission is $4 for adults, $2 for children and seniors ($1 less for Nassau County residents). The telephone number, should you need it, is 516/420-5280.

OLD WESTBURY GARDENS

Less than ten miles from the border of Queens is one of the most fabulous estates ever developed on Long Island's North Shore. Incredibly, it has survived virtually in its entirety and is now open to the public.

Originally called Westbury House, this was the Long Island residence of John S. Phipps (1874–1958) and his wife, Margarita Grace Phipps (1876–1957). He was the son of Carnegie partner Henry Phipps; she was one of the Graces of shipping line fame. The house they built in 1906 is about the most sumptuous Georgian Revival mansion one can imagine. It still has all its original gilt-framed oils, English antiques, brocaded curtains, crystal chandeliers, and overscale chintz-covered furniture. But more incredible than this truly palatial house is the magnificent grounds that so beautifully complement its formal architecture. There are a two-acre walled garden complete with ornamental pools and statues, a boxwood garden, a temple of love, a woodland walk, a cottage garden with a little girl's thatched cottage, even a ghost walk complete with bronze peacocks with topiary tails. The view from the rear of the house across a huge lawn and down an allee of linden trees is the sort of vista one associates with Versailles.

The above description does not at all do justice to Westbury House. It's an extraordinarily beautiful place, and talk about providing good backdrops for pictures! Besides the house and grounds, there's a busy schedule of lectures and concerts held pretty much throughout the year. The estate is open from 10 a.m. to 5 p.m. Wednesday through Sunday from April 29 to November 5. Admission to the gardens is $4.50 for adults and $1 for children aged 6 to 12. To tour the inside of the house you'll pay an additional $3 for adults and $1.50 for kids 6 to 12. House and garden combination tickets are available to seniors for $3.50; there's no charge for kids under 6.

Old Westbury Gardens is located on Old Westbury Road, just south of the Long Island Expressway. Get off the expressway at Exit 39 and continue for about a mile on the eastbound service road. You'll see Old Westbury Road on your right. For information about the estate or the concerts, call 516/333-0048.

SAGAMORE HILL

This rambling stone-and-shingle Victorian mansion was the summer home of Theodore Roosevelt, former assistant secretary of the navy, lieutenant colonel of the Rough Riders, governor of New York State, president of the United States, and life-long proponent of the "strenuous life." Here Roosevelt, his wife, and their six children spent the summers hiking, swimming, shooting, riding horseback, and entertaining important personages of the day.

The house and grounds are administered by the National Park Service and have been open to the public since the early 1960s. The interior boasts dramatic rooms paneled in swamp cypress, mahogany, and black walnut, and furnished with big-game trophies and Victorian antiques. Yet it's an eminently livable house, and most evocative of the dynamic and patrician American family that built it and loved it for so many years.

Sagamore Hill is located on Cove Neck Road just outside the village of Oyster Bay. Take the Long Island Expressway to Exit 41 North, then follow Rte. 106 north to Oyster Bay. At the third traffic light, turn right and follow the signs to Sagamore Hill (tel. 516/922-4447). The estate is open daily from 9:30 a.m. to 5 p.m. between Memorial Day and Labor Day; during the rest of the year it's open from 9:30 a.m. to 4:30 p.m. and closed on Monday. There is a $1 donation.

Oyster Bay retains a slightly ramshackle country look in spite of all the postwar development on Long Island. It's still surrounded by fine country estates tucked away behind impressive walls and magnificent gates. The forests hereabouts are lush and mature, and the roads narrow and canopied with green.

Right in the middle of Oyster Bay, at 20 W. Main St. (a stone's throw from the intersection of South Street, which is also N.Y. 106), is **Raynham Hall.** At the time of the Revolution this house was owned by one Samuel Townsend, whose secret identity as the spy "Culper Jr." wasn't revealed until 1939. Townsend's patriot politics, however, were no secret. And as a reward for same, the occupying British Lieutenant Colonel John Simcoe expropriated Townsend's house for the headquarters of the Queen's Rangers.

Townsend's sister, Sally, stayed behind, however, and charmed the British with her wit and grace. She kept her ear to the door too, for it was Sally Townsend who overheard Major John André and Colonel Simcoe discussing Benedict Arnold's planned betrayal of West Point. She conveyed the message to her brother and the treachery was thwarted. Such is Raynham Hall's claim to fame. (Another variation of the story credits Samuel's son instead of his sister with the discovery of the plot.) The house was considerably altered over the years to suit Victorian tastes, then restored to a late-18th-century appearance in the late 1940s. It's not a big museum, but if the Revolutionary period interests you and you're already in Oyster Bay, you should stop in for a look. The hours are 1 to 5 p.m. Tuesday through Sunday. Admission is $1 for adults, free for kids under 12. The phone number is 516/922-6808.

PLANTING FIELDS ARBORETUM

The unpretentious Indian name of Planting Fields was given by one William Robertson Coe to his drop-dead estate just west of Oyster Bay. Coe, an English immigrant who became a millionaire insurance executive, developed the property between the end of the First World War and his death in the early 1950s. The main entrance to the property is through a set of perfectly exquisite 18th-century English wrought-iron gates, located on a country lane with the amusing name of Chicken Valley Road. Alas, the public isn't allowed to enter this magnificent property through the main gates, the way the owner and the architect intended. Today's visitors must detour around to the back and enter via an anonymous side drive.

This is a small price for the opportunity to see one the North Shore's grandest and most beautifully maintained estates. Mr. Coe was quite a garden nut. When advised to start a collection of camellias, he built a pavilion for them the size of a small railroad station. His other greenhouses are equally impressive, as are the gorgeous flowering shrubs (particularly the azaleas and rhododendrons) and the sunken gardens, all of which really are in extraordinary condition. The main house, now referred to as Coe Hall, is open to visitors from 1 to 3:30 p.m. on Tuesday, Wednesday, and Thursday only. It's an immense and elaborate stone mansion in a somewhat severe Elizabethan Revival style. The original Coe family furnishings are gone, but the place is filling up with suitable antiques. If you liked Old Westbury Gardens, you'll adore Planting Fields. Despite architectural differences, they're both cut from the same expensive cloth.

The entrance to Planting Fields Arboretum is located on Planting Fields Road outside the village of Oyster Bay. To get there, take the Long Island Expressway to Exit 39 North (Glen Cove Road). Go north on Glen Cove Road to N.Y. 25A; turn right (east) and continue to Wolver Hollow Road (the Old Brookville Police Station is on the corner of 25A and Wolver Hollow). Turn left on Wolver Hollow and continue to Chicken Valley Road; then turn right, admire those gorgeous if no-longer-operable gates, and follow the signs to the arboretum entrance. The arboretum is open daily from 9 a.m. to 5 p.m., and there's a $3-per-car admission charge. If you need further information, call the arboretum at 516/922-9200.

WHALING MUSEUM AT COLD SPRING HARBOR

This charming little colonial village still retains a rural air, abetted by lovely views of green hills, blue water, and bobbing boats from Harbor Road. Between 1836 and 1862 Cold Spring supported no fewer than nine whaling vessels, each engaged in the business of bringing back sperm oil for pre–petroleum era illumination and lubrication. Whaling expeditions could last up to five years, and the adventure and bravery associated with whaling are part of the mainstream of American folklore.

Cold Spring's Whaling Museum started in 1936 with the modest donation of a whaleboat and a collection of whaling implements. Today the collection includes 10,000 whaling artifacts; thousands of journals, letters, and logs; and 700 pieces of scrimshaw, which is the name given to the carvings on whalebone or whale ivory made by patient seamen on the trail of the great whales. Some 42,000 visitors explored the Whaling Museum last year, a statistic quoted with considerable pride by the staff. It's not a big place physically, occupying a smallish but picturesque one-story building on Main Street with a whale atop the cupola. But it's a treasured community resource. Besides permanent exhibits like the miniature replica of Cold Spring in the 1840s and "Mark Well the Whale," there are constantly changing displays that tell the story of whaling. Walking tours, scrimshaw workshops, and lectures and films pertaining to whaling are offered throughout the summer, usually on Sunday at 3 p.m.

The Whaling Museum is located just across the Suffolk County line, at 25 Main St. in the middle of the village of Cold Spring Harbor. The best way to get here from town is via the Long Island Expressway again to Exit 41 North. Take N.Y. 106 north to N.Y. 25A, then 25A east to Cold Spring Harbor. Museum hours are daily from 11 a.m. to 5 p.m.; closed Monday. Admission is $1.50 for adults and $1 for children and seniors. The telephone number is 516/367-3418.

SANDS POINT PRESERVE

This was the Guggenheim estate, developed over a number of years and possessing several formidable mansions that belonged to various Guggenheim family members. Actually, railroad heir Howard Gould did the original planning. In 1902 he erected a perfectly enormous crenellated stone parade stable known today as **Castlegould.** This is currently a visitors' center and museum of Americana. The main residence, called **Hempstead House,** went up in 1910 to the designs of Hunt

and Hunt. During the war this immense stone mansion suffered serious depreda-
tion at the hands of the U.S. Naval Training Device Center. It has been partly
patched up in recent years, but is closed to the public except on special occasions.
You can walk around the outside, however, and marvel that something so big could
be the private house of a man whose grandfather came to America as a peddler.

Daniel Guggenheim bought Hempstead House and the surrounding 200-or-so
acre estate in 1917. His son, Capt. Harry Guggenheim, subsequently built a house
of his own on the property in 1923. Captain Guggenheim and his wife, Alicia Patter-
son, were the founders of *Newsday*, a major Long Island paper. His Norman-style
château, called **Falaise**, is considerably smaller than Hempstead House but, still and
all, imposing atop its cliff overlooking Long Island Sound. Falaise is in original condition, chock-a-block with European antiques and carved moldings, and open to the
public. The guides and brochures here make much of Captain Guggenheim's friend-
ship with Charles Lindbergh, who wrote a book called *We* while staying here in
1927. Lindbergh's later flirtation with the Nazis is conspicuously ignored by the
present-day guardians of his Jewish host's estate. Yet another family house on the
property, a suave French affair called **Mille Fleures,** is, like Hempstead House,
closed up and unfurnished.

The entrance to the Sands Point Preserve is on Middleneck Road, which is the
extension of N.Y. 101 or Port Washington Boulevard. Take Exit 36 from the Long
Island Expressway and proceed north on Searingtown Road, which runs directly
into Port Washington Boulevard. The estate, which was willed to Nassau County by
Captain Guggenheim in 1971, comprises about a mile of shoreline on Long Island
sound, plus enormously atmospheric estate buildings, woods, fields, and a wonderful old iron fence along Middleneck Road. There's a $2 fee for the tour of Falaise.
The preserve is open May to mid-November from 10 a.m. to 5 p.m., on Saturday
through Wednesday only. Tours of Falaise are operated Monday through Wednesday from 10:30 a.m. to 3:45 p.m., and on Saturday and Sunday from noon to 3:45
p.m. The whole place is very romantic and beautiful. The telephone number is 516/
883-1612.

THE VANDERBILT MUSEUM

William K. Vanderbilt II, great-grandson of the famous Commodore Vanderbilt, developed this 43-acre North Shore estate between 1908 and 1934. An avid
natural historian, Vanderbilt designed special private museum wings for his Spanish
baroque mansion and filled them with wildlife dioramas and artifacts picked up in
the course of family travels all over the world. In the high tide of his enthusiasm he
even had a separate **Marine Museum** constructed on the Little Neck Road border of
the property. Done up with the same florid architectural flourishes as the main
house, it contains everything from an antique deep-sea diving suit to an Egyptian
mummy.

When Vanderbilt died in 1944 he willed **Eagle's Nest,** as the estate is called, to
the people of Suffolk County, "for the education and enjoyment of the public." In
1971 a planetarium was built on the site of the former tennis courts, a logical extension of Vanderbilt's lifelong curiosity about the natural world.

Eagle's Nest is a sumptuous estate but nowhere near as grand as Planting Fields
or Westbury House. The main residence is a rambling, romantic concoction, over
half of which is and always was a museum. It's massed around a central courtyard
entered via a bridge through a belltower. The effect is rather like a set from a 1926
production of *Zorro*. Original Vanderbilt furniture remains throughout, as do the
marble and wood fireplaces, elaborate ceilings, and a 1918 Aeolian Duo-Art pipe
organ. Besides the main house and the Marine Museum, visitors can explore a romantic **boathouse** down on Northport Harbor, as well as lovely lawns and gardens,
all still maintained quite beautifully. The **Planetarium** is one of the most sophisticated in the country and presents sky shows throughout the year.

The Vanderbilt Museum is located on Little Neck Road in Centerport, on the

North Shore of Long Island not quite 40 miles from Midtown. You can tour the main house daily except Monday between May 1 and October 31. Hours are 10 a.m. to 4 p.m., and noon to 5 p.m. on Sunday and holidays; call for their winter hours. Admission is $4 for adults and $3 for seniors and kids under 12. Call 516/262-7878 for further information. The Planetarium also charges $4 for adults and $3 for seniors and kids (no children under 6 admitted to the sky shows). The phone number for program information is 516/262-STAR.

THE MUSEUMS AT STONY BROOK

The village of Stony Brook, located on the North Shore of Suffolk County 50-odd miles from Midtown Manhattan, bears the indelible mark of a man named Ward Melville. In 1940, already alert to the aesthetic damage being wrought in other parts of the island, Melville instigated an ambitious plan to rebuild the village along 18th-century lines and protect the surrounding area with strict zoning. Today's Stony Brook, with its eliptical row of clapboard shops, rolling lawns, and big trees, doesn't exactly look 18th century. But it certainly is neat and pretty in a sort-of-colonial way.

Besides being civic-minded, Melville was a major collector of antique carriages. His personal collection now constitutes the major attraction of what has come to be called the Museums at Stony Brook. Over 250 carriages are displayed in a brand-new exhibition hall. It's the largest and best collection of horse-drawn vehicles in the country, and possibly in the world. Besides carriages, there are also collections of 19th-century genre painting, notably the work of a Long Island artist (and native of Stony Brook) named William Sidney Mount; changing exhibits of period costumes, tools, toys, etc.; 15 fully furnished miniature rooms; several restored 19th-century buildings; and a museum store with good reproductions of many of the objects on display.

The museums, located at 1208 on N.Y. 25A just outside Stony Brook Village, are open year-round: Wednesday through Saturday and most Monday holidays from 10 a.m. to 5 p.m., and on Sunday from noon to 5 p.m. Admission is $4 for adults, $3 for seniors and students, $2.75 for kids over 6, and free for kids under 6. Telephone them at 516/751-0066 for information on current exhibits and special events.

Stony Brook really is a pretty spot with several pleasant inns nearby for dining or staying over (see below). The area close to Long Island Sound hereabouts has, thanks to Ward Melville and others like him, in great part preserved its rural charm. The back roads warrant exploration, especially those around the little village of Setauket, located a few miles east of Stony Brook. A few miles to the southwest, down N.Y. 25A, is the **St. James General Store,** a National Historic Landmark that has been in continuous operation since 1857. It's a modest clapboard structure in a bucolic spot at 516 Moriches Rd., half a mile north of 25A. There is a wooden Indian on the porch, a wagon wheel leaning on the wall, and an atmospheric clutter of goods within. No longer is this a rural post office, notions store, and grocery. Today the shelves are filled with stone pears, soap, sachet, postcards, books on Long Island, jams, and homemade baked goods. In short, it's a gift shop, but a historic and atmospheric one. If you're going to Stony Brook, it's right on the way and worth a stop.

---

3. Recommended Restaurants (Plus a Few Hotels)

The following recommended restaurants are all convenient to one or more of our day-trip destinations. They're listed below by locality; find the one that sounds the best and/or is closest to where you're going. It should be noted that close-in Long Island is literally crawling with restaurants, many of which are every bit as good as those suggested below. The task at hand, however, is not to evaluate every single restaurant in Nassau County, but rather to put forward a recommended selection.

ROSLYN

This is a pretty little village with delightful restored colonial houses and a distinguished stone clock tower. Its countrified air belies the fact that it is but five miles from the border of Queens and surrounded by densely built-up suburbs. Roslyn, which incidentally was the home of William Cullen Bryant, is quite close to the Sands Point Preserve and Old Westbury Gardens, and only a short trip from the attractions around Oyster Bay.

In the heart of the village opposite the clock tower is the **George Washington Manor,** 1305 Old Northern Blvd. (tel. 516/621-1200), so called because General Washington did indeed stop by here. The date was Saturday, April 24, 1790. "Left Mr. Young's before six o'clock," the president's diary goes, "and passing Musqueto Cove, breakfasted at a Mr. Underdunck's at the head of a little bay; where we were kindly received and well entertained. This Gentleman works a Grist & two Paper Mills, the last of which he seems to carry on with spirit, and to profit."

Today the Pine-Onderdonk-Bogart House, as the plaque on front describes it, has been much enlarged into a rambling, clapboarded structure with green shutters, valet parking, and begonia borders along the drive. There are many restaurants of this sort across America, big, comfortable, attractive, filled with prosperous patrons, and basking in some sort of historical glow. Inside the George Washington are large dining rooms done up in colonial style and bearing names like the Thomas Jefferson Room and the Nathan Hale Room. You couldn't really call it authentically old-fashioned, but it's awfully good looking and the food is good too.

The lunch menu has jazzy sandwiches like the Clocktower (a triple-decker club) for around $8, plus numerous à la carte entrees (filet of sole, veal fantasia, Yankee pot roast, seafood linguine, etc.), mostly priced between $9 and $18. At dinnertime the selection of entrees increases substantially (crisp roast duckling, roast leg of lamb, etc.) and so do the prices (mostly about $16 to $25 or so). Lunch is served daily from 11:30 a.m. to 4 p.m., and dinner from 4 p.m. to 10 p.m.; the $12.95 Sunday brunch is available from 11:30 a.m. to 3 p.m. Open seven days a week.

EAST NORWICH

Rothman's East Norwich Inn, at the intersection of N.Y. 25A and N.Y. 106 (tel. 516/922-1500), is just a little over two miles south of Oyster Bay. The intersection is a big one, even though there don't seem to be too many buildings around. Rothman's (formerly Burt Bacharach's) is right on the corner, a low, much-altered building with a tasteful new stucco and timber motel (sorry, "inn") behind it. There's an atmospheric tap room with a brick floor, low ceilings, and an Olde English look about it, plus a big dining room with brown wallpaper, print curtains, linen tablecloths, and restful Muzak, and a smiling maître d' at the door.

The clientele and the food both resemble those at the George Washington Manor. At lunch, burgers, big sandwiches, and hot entrees mostly run between $6 and $10. At dinner you can choose from a list of appetizers like clams on the half shell, melon in season, and shrimp cocktail (mostly $4 to $8), then move on to à la carte steaks and chops and seafood entrees priced in the $15 to $20 range. There are specials too, which change periodically.

Rothman's is open daily from noon to 3 p.m. for lunch and 5 to 11 p.m. for dinner.

OYSTER BAY

In the village itself is an inexpensive sandwich and soda place called the **Sweet Shop,** 128 South St. (tel. 516/922-2600), just a few steps south of West Main Street and Raynham Hall. It's a bright storefront in the middle of the village, with fake wood paneling, orange leatherette seats, and a small-town air. Sandwiches, burgers, sundaes, etc., are the order of the day, available either at a counter or at tables. Good place for a cheap (under $5) lunch; they close at 5 p.m., and don't open at all on Sunday.

COLD SPRING HARBOR

This very attractive village, located just across the Suffolk County line, is the home of the Whaling Museum described above. It's also a quick scenic drive on country roads from Old Westbury Gardens, Planting Fields Arboretum, Sagamore Hill, Old Bethpage Village, and even the Vanderbilt Museum. **Wyland's Country Kitchen,** 55 Main St. (tel. 516/692-5655), located right in the middle of it, is therefore the most centrally located restaurant on this list.

As far as I'm concerned, it's about the most appealing too. Wyland's is an informal, lunch-only, small-town establishment occupying a dark-shingled, modernish building with blue awnings. There are a pair of small, connected dining rooms, each filled with wood tables and paper placemats. There is a cozy family atmosphere, enhanced by terrific smells emanating from the kitchen. Lunch might be chopped sirloin on toasted French bread, ham diablo with potato salad, a Monte Cristo club, or a fruit salad with sherbet or cottage cheese, all priced at about $4 to $5.

Wyland's serves lunch from 11 a.m. to 4:30 p.m., Tuesday through Friday, from 11 a.m. to 3:45 p.m. on Saturday. Closed Sunday and Monday.

CENTERPORT

This is the village by the Vanderbilt Museum. Actually, it's something less than a village, but it does possess several restaurants conveniently located for those who've made the trip to the museum. My favorite is the **Mill Pond Inn,** right on N.Y. 25A close to Little Neck Road (tel. 516/261-5353). It's a modest roadhouse, painted red and situated at water's edge. There's a bar up front with a silver-flecked red acoustical ceiling, and an old-fashioned dining room beyond with picture windows overlooking boats in the harbor. The place is friendly, unpretentious, and very neighborhoody. Dinner might be New York shell steak, broiled scallops, linguine marinara, cioppino, or various pasta dishes priced generally from $13 to $18. Open daily for dinner only from 4 to 10 p.m. (until midnight on Friday and Saturday).

STONY BROOK

If you've come all this way to see the Museums at Stony Brook, you'll need not only a restaurant but perhaps a place to stay over as well. Fortunately, there are two good places in the immediate area.

The first is the **Three Village Inn,** 150 Main St., Stony Brook, NY 11790 (tel. 516/751-0555), which is both appealing restaurant and delightful country inn. It's a leafy, lawny place right in the middle of orderly and crisply painted Stony Brook. The central building is an old rambling house built in the mid-18th century by a family named Hallock. It sits well back from the road, shaded by immense trees, and graced by stone terraces, precisely clipped beds of ivy and colorful tubs of flowers. Despite the languid country look, there's a slight air of formality about the place. Jackets and ties, while not required in the dining rooms, are nonetheless clearly in evidence.

The dining rooms are all modern, but with traditional touches like rush-seat chairs, wallpaper, scenic plates on the walls, and old fireplaces. There is almost a Williamsburg atmosphere, enhanced by waiters in 18th-century costume. The salad and sandwich menu has things like Oriental chicken salad, salad Nissequogue (fruit, avocado, sherbet, and nut bread), a hamburger, and a turkey club, priced from about $8 to $12. A larger, table d'hôte lunch menu is also available. The dinner menu, which changes daily, contains broiled fish and seafood, all manner of roasts and grills, and prices from about $20 to $30 per meal, including the day's selection of homemade desserts. Meals are served seven days a week.

Besides the dining rooms are 32 highly individual rooms, of which my favorites are those located in the inn itself. Tiny stairways and labyrinthine passages lead to these pleasant accommodations, decorated with chenille bedspreads, spool beds, beamed ceilings, and small patterned wallpapers. No two rooms are alike, but they all have private baths (some of which are surprisingly huge) and lots of character. Newer motel units are located in the "cottages" behind the original inn. These are a little bigger and a bit less atmospheric. Those called the "porch rooms" have views of Stony Brook Harbor and more elaborate furnishings. Overnight rates are $65 to $75 single, $85 to $95 double. Between April 1 and October 31 a two-night minimum stay is required on weekends.

PORT JEFFERSON

About five miles east of Stony Brook is the village of Port Jefferson, a bright, beachy former whaling town beyond which the farm fields at last begin to outnumber the housing tracts. Right on the harbor is **Danford's Inn,** 25 E. Broadway, Port Jefferson, NY 11777 (tel. 516/928-5200). This is an enormous place with endless balconies, brick walls, and boutiques. Although it's completely new, the style is Victorian and the effect isn't bad at all.

The restaurant is really terrific, a big bright room overlooking the harbor, paneled in tongue-and-groove stained wood, lit with faux Tiffany lamps, and graced with an outside porch just perfect for warm-weather dining. The lunch menu lists hot and cold sandwiches (roast beef, turkey, shrimp salad, etc.) for about $4.50 to $8, entrees (broiled scrod, marinated steak, sautéed shrimp, etc.) from around $8 to $12, and various styles of burger from $5 to $6 or so. The dinner menu features entrees like shrimp and scallop casserole, broiled seafood platter, roast Long Island duckling, filet mignon, etc., priced from about $14 to $20.

Also located at Danford's, above all those boutiques (and a lobby with a portrait of Washington labeled "I Never Slept Here"), are 50 particularly nice hotel rooms. All of these have balconies, 80% of which face the water. The "executive doubles" are really quite lordly with their Victorian accent pieces, canopied beds, lavish bathrooms, and rattan balcony furniture. But even the standard rooms are pretty terrific. They have wall-to-wall carpeting, very nice framed prints on the walls, color televisions, Queen Anne benches with damask upholstery, and gilt-framed mirrors. Five of them even have fireplaces. The quality throughout is top-notch. Singles pay $100 to $125 nightly; doubles, $125 to $150. There are suites too, priced from $150 to $200 a night.

IX

LONG ISLAND: THE SOUTH SHORE, FIRE ISLAND, AND THE HAMPTONS

The South Shore is composed of a great many worlds. Between the union men in Massapequa, the working stiffs in Brentwood, the gay vacationers in Cherry Grove, the socialites in Bellport, the arrivistes in Southampton, and the bluebloods in East Hampton, there's not a great deal of common ground. Yet this entire crew has gravitated to the flatter, ocean side of the island, where the views are longer and the variety of special pleasures is broader.

1. Deciding What to See and Do

Southern Long Island's greatest natural asset is its beaches. And resort towns up and down the coast each cater to the divergent tastes of their respective summer populations.

For example, the Hamptons (a generic term encompassing a half dozen adjacent villages) combine beautiful beaches with fashionable inns and restaurants, fast-track nightlife, streets full of fancy cars and socialites (real and aspirant), exclusive clubs, and elaborate mansions. Southampton has been a society resort for a long time. It's beautiful and it knows it. Other villages in the Hamptons don't have the same hard glitter. It's possible, for instance, to be quietly elegant and relaxed in East Hampton, or plain relaxed in Amagansett. Like it or not, wherever you go in this most easterly part of the island, the genie of fashion will always be nearby. Of course, that may be the point of the entire exercise, in which case you will have come to the right spot.

It's also possible to have a quiet "inn" experience in this part of the world. Quogue, for example, is a patrician little beach resort with very little going on, a gorgeous village beach, and big nifty old shingled houses. Sag Harbor is a handsome old whaling town with wonderful 19th-century architecture and a very appealing restored hotel. Even swank Southampton has a good guesthouse.

Other types of experiences can be had on Fire Island, a 32-mile-long strip of barrier beach that parallels much of the route to the Hamptons. Fire Island's National Seashore status hasn't interfered with the existence of 17 separate communities here, reachable by ferry only (cars are prohibited on the island). The atmosphere in each little town varies widely, to say the least. While singles bay at one another (and occasionally at the moon) in Davis Park, beautiful and nearly naked men cast flirtatious looks at one another in Fire Island Pines and Cherry Grove; while working families alternate between the beach and the barbecue in Ocean Beach, low-profile WASPs enjoy select little parties in mansions (well, not quite) in Point 'O Woods; and so it goes. Most people either own or rent a house on Fire Island, which is both a function and a cause of the high ferry rates and parking fees that confront the day-tripper. The few communities that do have overnight accommodations are divided about equally between gay and straight.

Though most of what's doing on the South Shore is doing on or in relation to the beach, other attractions do exist. You can break the trip from New York to Southampton at historic villages, parks, and appealing restaurants. If you don't, the non-stop trip to the Hamptons with no traffic (a not-unheard-of event) can take less than two and a half hours. If everything goes wrong and you wind up creeping bumper to bumper all the way to Smithtown, it still takes only four hours. Most of the traffic you see on the road is intending to skip everything between the Hamptons or the Fire Island ferry. The next section briefly details what they're missing.

2. The South Shore Route to the Hamptons

From the outset, it should be repeated that the *fastest* route to the Hamptons is via the Long Island Expressway to Exit 70 at Manorville. Proceed south on N.Y. 111 to the Sunrise Highway Extension (also called N.Y. 27). Take Sunrise Highway eastbound (like the expressway and N.Y. 111 it's a high-speed road) right across the Shinnecock Canal and you'll be within striking distance of Southampton. Sunrise Highway actually runs parallel to the Long Island Expressway all the way from town. But it's a heavily traveled local artery for much of its length, and offsetting its multitude of lanes is a multitude of traffic lights.

Here's another bit of advice: no doubt there are explorers out there who see the old Montauk Highway on their map. Don't be tempted by that tantalizingly snakey route through all the old villages. Montauk Highway is disfigured by commercialism virtually all the way to Southampton. It's the one dependably overbuilt road even in the South Shore's remaining rural regions.

Although the lion's share of Long Island's great country estates went up on the North Shore, there were enclaves of aristocratic country living on the South Shore as well. One of these was around **Oakdale,** a somewhat anonymous area nowadays but one that still provides evocative glimpses of the gilded past. William K. Vanderbilt, grandson of the commodore, one-time husband of flamboyant social climber and suffragette Alva Vanderbilt, father of William K. Vanderbilt, Jr. (whose Eagle's Nest in Centerport is now the Vanderbilt Museum), proprietor of Marble House in Newport, was once a resident of Oakdale. His spectacular residence, Idle Hour, still stands on Idle Hour Boulevard just south of the Montauk Highway in Oakdale. The grounds have been chopped to pieces for split-levels, and the mansion is now part of Dowling College. But at least it's still standing, and boy is it immense!

Vanderbilt's one-time neighbor was a fellow named Frederick G. Bourne, whose place immediately to the east of Idle Hour is often called the largest house on Long Island. The walls and gates along Montauk Highway are certainly impressive, if no longer perfectly manicured. The property has been owned for many years by the LaSalle Military Academy and is not open to the public.

Facing Idle Hour across the little Connetquot River is another sumptuous former private estate called Westbrook. It was developed in the 1880s by a railroad man named William Bayard Cutting (1850–1912). When his 94-year-old widow died in 1949, she left it to the Long Island State Park Commission. Today the mansion, designed by Charles C. Haight, and the grounds, laid out by the famous Frederick Law Olmsted (he designed New York City's Central Park), are called **Bayard Cutting Arboretum** (tel. 516/581-1002) and are open to the public. Hours are Wednesday through Sunday from 10 a.m. to 5 p.m. during Daylight Saving Time, to 4 p.m. during Eastern Standard Time. There is a $3-per-car admission charge.

Mr. Cutting's house is a rambling "shingle style" mansion with Tudor-timbered gables and a forest of chimneys. Inside is an appealing snackbar on the enclosed porch, plus a small natural history museum. The grounds contain scenic walks and specimen trees. It was Mrs. Cutting's hope that through her gift the public would gain "a greater appreciation and understanding of the value and importance of informal planting."

Also in Oakdale was a famous millionaire's shooting preserve called the Southside Sportsmen's Club. Today the grounds are preserved as the **Connetquot River State Park** and open to the public. The important early Shingle Style clubhouse, designed in the late 1880s by Isaac H. Green, is in the process of restoration.

To be truthful, a detour to Oakdale is not going to appeal to everyone. I personally was excited as could be to discover that Idle Hour, about whose colorful owner I'd read so much, was still standing and even visible from a public road. But not everyone will be so moved. Likewise, even though the Cutting mansion is a splendid place and the arboretum grounds quite beautiful, it takes a taste for old mansions and social history to warrant the special trip. But if you like this kind of stuff, take Exit 57 (Veterans Memorial Highway) from the expressway, then Connetquot Road south to Great River Station, at which point you'll be practically in the arboretum. Oakdale and Idle Hour are less than two miles east on Montauk Highway.

The South Shore of Long Island is very densely built up all the way to Patchogue, a bustling town six or seven miles beyond Oakdale. In fact, except for the state parks and the National Seashore, there's hardly a square foot of land south of the expressway that doesn't have somebody's house standing on it. After Patchogue, things begin to open up. The land is mostly pine barrens, still in a primeval state yet perilously close to the cutting edge of suburbia.

Another good detour for those not in such a hurry to get to the Hamptons would be to the fashionable village of **Bellport,** located about four miles east of Patchogue on N.Y. 36. Bellport has a society feel to it, and boasts many fine restored colonial and Edwardian houses. There are picket fences galore, all gleaming under fresh coats of white paint, tall leafy trees, views of the Great South Bay, a pretty village center, and two very good restaurants.

The more modest of the two is the **Bellport Kitchen** (or simply the BK, as it's called), 159 Main St. (tel. 516/286-1681). This enormously appealing small establishment has the look of a fashionable saloon. There's a tile floor, dark tongue-in-groove paneling, potted plants, a small bar surrounded by little tables with crisp green cloths under glass. The atmosphere is informal and extremely friendly. There are reasonably priced daily lunch specials on a blackboard menu (the club sandwich is great). At dinner the printed à la carte menu runs the gamut from roast duckling to a shrimp, scallop, or chicken étouffée to sauerbraten, all prepared very much in gourmet style. Dinner entrees are priced between $11 and $16, with most falling somewhere in the middle. The Bellport Kitchen is open Tuesday through Sunday from noon to 3 p.m.; dinner is served from 5:30 to 10:30 p.m. Closed Monday.

A more elegant dining experience can be had at the **Old Inlet Inn,** 108 S. Country Rd., which is the extension of Main Street (tel. 516/286-2650). This is a very Bellport sort of place, located in a wonderfully pretty restored colonial house, complete with local historical associations and duly listed on the National Register of Historic Places. Beyond the manicured gravel lot and the manicured green lawn is, in the summer season, a delicious outdoor terrace for al fresco dining. Just inside the door, a leather-padded bar shares the front room with a very handsome staircase. Beyond lies an intimate dining room with low ceilings, leaded-glass windows, leather chairs, an elegant fireplace mantel, and a flock of tables set with crisp linen and silver. At dinner the à la carte menu offers a large selection of seafood, plus things like roast Long Island duckling in raspberry sauce, for about $17 to $23 per plate. Open for dinner only from 6 to 10 p.m. (to 11 p.m. on Friday and Saturday); closed Monday. Tag line on the menu: "The favor of a jacket is requested of all gentlemen."

If you like exploring pretty villages, continue east another mile on South Country Road to the village of **Brookhaven.** Not much happening here, but it's a nice-looking place.

At Brookhaven you have several options. The first is to rejoin Montauk Highway for the short hop to the (by-now-traffic-light-less) Sunrise Highway Extension. It's less than 30 miles from here to Southampton. If you're up for another big country estate, this one with notable Revolutionary War connotations, consider detouring around Bellport Bay to Mastic and the **William Floyd Estate.**

William Floyd, a craggy and thin-lipped patriot, judging from old paintings, was one of the signers of the Declaration of Independence. His huge plantation at Mastic was originally run (at least partly) by slaves. Although the original acreage was reduced over the years, an incredible 613 acres of fields, forests, marshlands, historic outbuildings, and a large mansion survived in family hands until the late 1970s. The year before her death in 1977 Cornelia Floyd Nichols transferred the estate to the National Park Service. It's now open to the public as part of the Fire Island National Seashore.

The 25-room mansion started modestly enough in 1724 as a three-room farmhouse. It was renovated five times after that, getting bigger and grander like a rolling snowball. The Floyd estate was developed as a working farm, not as a badge of social advancement. Consequently, the house, while large and full of interesting furniture, isn't one of those Long Island showplaces dripping with crystal, gilt, and damask.

And 613 acres is big enough to convey a sense of a rural place even though all the adjacent land is closely developed with tract houses. Besides the main house, 11 outbuildings and a family cemetery are open to visitors. There's no charge for either the guided tours of the house or the self-guided tours of the grounds. The estate is open April 6 to October 31, 10 a.m. to 4:30 p.m. (tel. 516/399-2030). The shortest route, either from nearby Brookhaven or from the Long Island Expressway, is via the William Floyd Parkway (Exit 68 on the expressway) to Havenwood Drive. Take a left at Havenwood and follow the signs.

An alternative to the Hampton Experience exists on the shores of Shinnecock Bay, a few miles outside the village of East Quogue. It's called the **Caffrey House,** Squires Avenue, East Quogue, NY 11942 (tel. 516/728-1327), and bills itself as the last Victorian seaside inn on eastern Long Island. I'm not really sure that's true, but after having seen the Caffrey myself, I will attest to the fact that there's nothing else like it on Long Island.

It's a not-very-rambling, painted-shingle rooming house, or rather two rooming houses connected by an outside porch overlooking the water. The approach is via a narrow sandy drive, past the backyards of nearby split-levels. The lobby, if that's what you call it, is appealingly run-down and furnished with antique jukeboxes, a Weber grand player piano, a deer head with a Halloween mask, dusty framed pictures, piles of books and newspapers, a stuffed bobcat with a squirrel in its mouth, glimpses of wallpaper on those few portions of the walls where something isn't hanging, and a sexy state-of-the-art television with attached VCR. Outside is a not exactly manicured lawn with unmatched chairs scattered about. The rooms are small and very basic, but bright and close to seaside-cottage-type shared baths. The whole place looks like a Booth cartoon, if that conjures a recognizable image. If not, then let's just say it's extremely long on atmosphere, but not for the fastidious.

The room rates are really a tangle and probably subject to a degree of negotiation. On summer weekends there's a two-night minimum for double rooms, most of which cost around $80 to $95 if you share the bath, and $110 to $120 if you have one of your own. Rates are about half that during the week.

Squires Avenue is located off Montauk Highway, about a mile from East Quoque in the direction of Southampton. Just take Squires all the way to the bay. There's a pretty private beach right in front of the Caffrey, and the hotel is close to the fashionable village of Quoque if you like exploring ritzy summer places.

This, then, brings us to the close of Section 2. Throughout our explorations we've been paralleling Fire Island. Now let's take a quick look at what's going on over there.

---

3. Fire Island

I guess I'd have to call Fire Island "legendary" in every sense of the word. It has managed to combine vivid images of dazzling beaches and sexual abandon and root the result firmly in the public consciousness. With good cause too. But like many complex places (and people, and situations), there's considerably more to Fire Island than meets the eye.

All 32 miles of it is now designated as a National Seashore and administered by the National Park Service. Yet over a dozen beachfront communities continue to exist much as they always have. The same people come back to the same communities year after year, usually to the same houses. Some communities are quite chic, others are staid and stuffy, some cater to yuppies, others cater to gays, some are fairly drunken, others are just plain ramshackle, and some remain completely private and virtually unknown save to members of their respective property owners' associations.

At the extreme western end of Fire Island is **Robert Moses State Park,** which has been a public beach since 1898. Unlike almost every other part of Fire Island, you can drive a car to Moses State Park. It's readily accessible from the Long Island Expressway (Exit 52), the Southern State Parkway (Exit 40), and via the Ocean Parkway from nearby Jones Beach. It's not exactly isolated—there are parking facilities for over 8,000 cars, beach shops, boat basins, pitch and putt golf, comfort stations, etc.—but it's less crowded than Jones Beach. The same $3.50-per-car fee charged at Jones is also charged here, and the beach is open daily from May 24 until September 1. Is it really a beautiful beach? Yes, without question. Is it better to drive here or to take one of the ferries to other parts of Fire Island? In my opinion, there's little point in paying steep ferry and parking fees if the point of your trip is to spend a day on a beautiful Atlantic beach.

Well, perhaps there's an exception to that statement. About a third of the way down the island is a place called Sailors Haven, adjacent to which is something called the **Sunken Forest.** This is in the middle of the auto-free section of Fire Island, and its only connection to the rest of Long Island is via a ferry from Sayville (departure information number: 516/589-8980). The Sunken Forest is a pretty choice spot, an unspoiled primeval forest shielded from the ocean by tall dunes. The trees aren't very big, but they form an unbroken green canopy over a network of lovely boardwalks that snake through sun-dappled silence. There are decks and places to sit and meditate deep in leafy hollows. Everything is green and clean and hushed. The only sound is the distant crash of breakers on the beach. One might also call this lovely spot the Sunken Poison Ivy Forest. Visitors are repeatedly warned not to stray from the walkways, and with good reason. Stay on those walks and you'll be physically safe and spiritually refreshed.

The ferry stop for Sunken Forest is the same as that for **Sailors Haven,** the adjacent beach run by the National Park Service. Here you can buy snacks and ice, rent an umbrella, take a shower, or attend activities at the "interpretive center" (one of my favorite terms in park service-ese). The beach is just as magnificent (and even less crowded) than any of those so far mentioned. Lifeguards are on duty from June 19 through September 5 from 10 a.m. to 5 p.m. daily. It's also free, but the ferry from Sayville isn't. Adult fare each way is $3.50; children under 12 pay $2 each way. The Sayville Ferry operates between late June and September 1 from 9 or 10 a.m. to about 6 p.m. Call 516/589-8980 for exact schedule information. Dockside parking in Sayville costs $5 per weekday, $6 on weekends.

There are two other National Park Service–administered beaches on Fire Island. One is at **Watch Hill,** located about as far east of Sailors Haven as Sailors Haven is from Moses State Park. The other is **Smith Point West,** situated near the island's undeveloped eastern point. Watch Hill is connected to civilization via the Patchogue ferry (departure information number: 516/475-1665); Smith Point is connected to the William Floyd Parkway, which is to say that you can drive your car right to the beach. Expect to pay a $3.50 parking fee and ferry rates similar to those mentioned above. The Watch Hill facility also has 25 free campsites, available by advance reservation only, and open from May 15 until October 15. Call 516/281-3010 for information.

Alternatively, you might like to sample one of the oceanfront **communities accessible only by ferry.** The ferry from Bayshore (departure information number: 516/665-2115) serves, among other places, Ocean Beach and Ocean Bay Park. After stashing your car in the dockside lot ($6 daily during the week, $8 on weekends), you'll join a throng of holiday makers on the pier. There are crowds of kids, shouting mothers, piles of groceries, boxes full of household goods, and an easy relaxed atmosphere. The ferry charges $4.75 one way and $9.50 round trip for adults, $3 one way and $6 round trip for kids under 11. Who takes a one-way ticket, you may ask? People who intend to return via another ferry. The three separate ferry companies, located in Bayshore, Sayville, and Patchogue, respectively, do not honor one another's tickets.

All the ferries are essentially metal barges, covered down below, open up top, at times piloted by surprisingly youthful captains. The trip across Great South Bay takes a little over half an hour. Sparkling whitecaps break over the prow of the boat and a holiday air prevails.

At **Ocean Beach** you'll disembark in the midst of an unpretentious summer colony composed of clean but anonymous commercial buildings, behind which extends a low forest filled with tiny cottages on postage-stamp-size lots. There are no cars and no tall buildings. The beach is about ten minutes away on the ocean side of the island.

Several modest hostelries offer overnight accommodations in Ocean Beach. I liked **Jerry's Accommodations,** P.O. Box 425, Ocean Beach, Fire Island, NY 11770 (tel. 516/583-8870), the best. Also known as Jerry's Rooms, it's a collection of very modest buildings clustered on a pedestrian lane near the ferry. The rooms, all of which share hall baths, have a summer camp look. They're furnished with new fake wood paneling, new carpeting, brightly colored spreads, and random pieces of motel-modern furniture. They are beachy and functional. Rates are $65 per person on weekends, $40 per person between Sunday and Thursday; a minimum two-night stay is required on weekends. There are also one-bedroom apartments for $950 a week ($250 a night on weekends), as well as two-bedroom apartments for $1,050 a week, $295 a night. Open May 1 through September 15.

Up the beach in **Ocean Bay Park** is the **Fire Island Hotel,** P.O. Box 334, Ocean Beach (the address is Ocean Beach but the hotel is in Ocean Bay Park), Fire Island,

NY 11770 (tel. 516/583-8000). This is a collection of converted Coast Guard buildings moved to the site at various times since 1930. There are 50 rooms, furnished with nice flowered curtains, fresh towels and bathmats folded neatly on the beds, and hotel pieces from the 1920s and 1930s. The rooms are small but bright, some paneled in pine, about a third with shared bath. The hotel is not quite on the beach despite the name. But the surf is only a stone's throw away. A clean, modest, family air prevails. Weekday rates are $50 single and $80 double; weekend stays have a two-night minimum and cost $120 single and $225 double. There are additionally all manner of midweek and weekly specials. The hotel also operates a large and popular restaurant on the bay side of the island. There's a live DJ in the bar on Friday nights and Saturday afternoons, at which time things get pretty rousing. À la carte dinner entrees run $15 and up.

A very different sort of experience is to be had at **Cherry Grove** and **Fire Island Pines**, served by the same Sayville Ferry that docks at Sailors Haven (ferry information number: 516/589-8980). These two towns might well be the premier gay resorts on the East Coast. The Pines especially is a very physically attractive place, architecturally and otherwise. Dramatic modern houses crouch between the dunes and the ocean-bent pine trees. Glittering private pools abound in addition to the magnificent beach. The **Cherry Grove Beach Hotel,** Cherry Grove, Fire Island, NY 11782 (tel. 516/597-6600), has one of those pools (Olympic-size, no less), as well as a piano bar, discothèque, drag shows, contests, movies, and more. It's the biggest hotel on the island (which is not to say it's very big) and charges between $100 and $160 per person per night, depending on the day and the month you visit. There are all sorts of special, midweek, combo, and holiday rates; you'd best phone for specifics. Alternatively, you could try the **Fire Island Pines Botel,** Fire Island, NY 11782 (tel. 516/597-6500), so called because of its adjacent docking facilities. It's also a nice-looking place, with a tangle of rates that basically range between $45 and about $125 nightly per person, depending on time of week and period of the season. There's a pool here too, as well as a number of rooms with private bath.

Party girls and boys in their late 20s and early 30s might find **Davis Park** the most interesting part of Fire Island. The beach here, as elsewhere, is simply magnificent. Davis Park itself is no Fire Island Pines, aesthetically speaking anyway. But who's looking at the buildings? The **Leja Beach Motel,** P.O. Box 18, Patchogue (the address is Patchogue but the motel is on Fire Island), NY 11772 (tel. 516/597-6905), rents clean, twin-bedded motel-type rooms in a long, low gray building near the casino for $80 nightly during the week and for $165 nightly on weekends. It's clean and modest and certainly in the middle of what's happening. To get here, take the ferry from Patchogue (departure information number: 516/475-1665).

The above will provide a fair superficial overview of Fire Island. Good to have before you go to the National Park Service's "Fire Island National Seashore" brochure. Park Service headquarters, at 120 Laurel St., Patchogue, NY 11772 (tel. 516/289-4810), will send you one free. It includes an excellent map and all manner of useful visitor information. Sections of Fire Island, especially the eastern half from Watch Hill to the Moriches Inlet, are virtually in wilderness condition. Between Watch Hill (whose free camping facilities are described above) and Smith Point are about seven miles of deserted beach that haven't changed since the first European settlers stepped ashore over 400 years ago.

---

4. Touring the Hamptons

The South Fork of Long Island, on which are situated the famous "Hamptons," is an approximately 35-mile-long spear of randomly bulging land stretching from the Shinnecock Canal in the west to Montauk Point in the east.

Strictly speaking, there are "Hamptons" on both sides of the canal. The traveler heading east from New York City will, for example, pass **Westhampton, Westhampton Beach,** and **Hampton Bays** before even reaching the bridges at Shinnecock Hills. But it is to the towns beyond the canal that most visitors are heading. And with good reason, since that's where the most Hampton-ish attractions lie.

The South Fork is a very old part of New York State. In fact, the town of Southampton claims to be the state's first English settlement (although Southold on the North Fork disputes this claim). Farms and villages were well established here as long ago as the 17th century. A surprising number of old buildings survive from those days, lovingly cared for by the various villages. Actually, you could spend an awful lot of time climbing around enormously picturesque windmills and peering at fully furnished houses that were built in the 1660s. There are enough of them around here to sate the appetite of the most dedicated antiquarian.

The South Fork's agrarian look persists in spite of a century of fashionable summer people and the intense development pressure of the past two decades. Adjoining the summer traffic jams on Montauk Highway are huge fields of potatoes, serenely ablossom under the June sun. Away from the beachfront mansions are sparsely trafficked country lanes twisting through empty-seeming pine barrens and placid abundant farms.

There is, however, a human current on the South Fork—really more of a riptide—that's as impossible to ignore as the seasons. It flows first east on Friday and Saturday, then west on Sunday and Monday, always back and forth on Montauk Highway. The other roads on the South Fork are barely affected by this lemming-like ebb and flow. But since Montauk Highway is about the only way to go east or west, it's a hard flow to avoid. Longtime residents, including longtime summer people, blame it (rather acidly) on New York City. Weekend people, who are the source of the problem, seem unfazed by four-hour one-way jaunts to or from the city at peak hours. Drivers hereabouts have developed a level of derring-do unmatched in other parts of the state. One needs the bravery and abandon of a kamikaze pilot just to pull onto Montauk Highway on a summer Saturday. If you want to make a left turn, better add to that the patience of Job.

Of course, if this state of affairs ever altered, the local economy would go straight down the drain. Free movement and commerce were once before restricted on this part of Long Island—by the British blockade and occupation at the time of the Revolution. The result was hunger, depopulation, and general misery. Like it or not, the South Fork is married to the tourist industry, despite its occasional agricultural posturing.

SOUTHAMPTON

The closest Hampton past the Shinnecock Canal is Southampton, settled in 1640 by a group of disgruntled pilgrims from Lynn, Massachusetts. They landed at a place called Conscience Point, a region now enlivened by a discothèque of the same name, and proceeded to form a small republic. Practically nothing remains of colonial (or Republican) Southampton, a notable exception being the **Halsey Homestead,** (tel. 516/283-3527). This delicious little shingled cottage has stood on South Main Street just a few blocks from the center of town since 1648. It hugs the side of the road, oblivious to the tall clipped hedges, broad lawns, and white mansions all around it. The interior is open to the public from mid-June through mid-September, Tuesday through Sunday from 11 a.m. to 4:30 p.m.

But the Halsey house is not representative of Southampton today, or even 100 years ago. Rather, it's the spacious and manicured mansions and grounds that radiate on tree-lined roads from the center of town to the beach. Sometimes all you can see of these houses are glimpses of chimneys or upper stories at the ends of long drives, or above ten-foot-tall privet hedges. Even along the beach, the lawns are vast and rolling and the houses secluded from one another by generous amounts of expensive beachfront space. Southampton's summer houses are real showplaces, running the architectural gamut from Shingled Behemoth to Norman Château to Giant WASPy Colonial to Victorian Monsteresque with almost every other architectural stop in between duly noted. Head straight down South Main Street and you'll be right in the thick of them.

The center of the village itself is the intersection of Job's Lane and Main Street. This is a sophisticated shopping district filled with extravagant stores and boutiques, many bearing the same names you've seen on Fifth or Madison Avenue and catering to a similar clientele. It's a very nice-looking downtown, not too big, but running a couple of blocks in several directions. The streets are broad, tree shaded, and full of expensive cars, slim women with pulled-back blond hair, tanned older men in expensive sports clothes, and lots and lots of attractive younger people with blue eyes and tennis manners.

You're going to find it difficult at least, and probably impossible, to use the beach in any of the Hamptons. Of course, America's beaches are free once you get onto them, and finding a public access even in Southampton isn't too difficult. The problem is what to do with the car. Free legal parking spots do exist, but they're unmarked and pitifully few. Park illegally and you'll be fined and/or towed. People staying in the various villages can usually get low-cost day passes from their hotels. Others will pay $15 a day on weekends and $6 on weekdays to park at town beach lots.

Worth a visit in addition to (or possibly in lieu of) the Southampton beach is the **Parrish Art Museum,** 25 Job's Lane (tel. 516/283-2118). Founded in 1898 by a prosperous summer resident who paid for the building and donated his collection, the Parrish has grown into a noted museum of 19th- and 20th-century American art. It's a delightful spot, with a cool garden full of beautiful statuary and sculpture, a busy schedule of special events, and regular summer programs of music in the garden, film, and theater. Even if you're not a museum goer you'll doubtless find something of interest. Open Tuesday through Saturday from 10 a.m. to 5 p.m., Sunday from 1 to 5 p.m. A donation is suggested.

Southampton also has terrific places to stay, but more about that below, under "Where to Stay and Eat in the Hamptons." For now, let's continue our tour of the South Fork.

WATER MILL

Until a little beyond Southampton, twisting two-lane Montauk Highway is designated as N.Y. 27A, while larger roads have borne the larger designation of N.Y. 27. All that ends in the fields east of Southampton. Much of Southampton's semi-suburban sprawl ends too. So that by the time you reach Water Mill, a totally perfect-looking little hamlet a mere three miles from Job's Lane and Main Street, you'll feel truly in the country, except for the insane summer traffic. That big windmill in the center of town isn't the 1644 model that gave the place its name. Today's mill is a relative newcomer, dating only from 1800. Actually, it was built in Sag Harbor, a former whaling center somewhat to the northeast of here, and moved to Water Mill in 1814. If you're a mill nut you'll no doubt be interested to learn that the only regularly functioning wind-driven gristmill on Long Island is right here at the **Water Mill Museum** on Old Mill Road (tel. 516/726-9685). Freshly ground cornmeal and wheat flour are actually for sale, as are various other items in the mill museum shop. The museum is open Wednesday through Monday from 10 a.m. to 4 p.m.; on Sunday from 1 to 4 p.m.; closed Tuesday. Admission is $1. Water Mill, despite its name, is considered to be one of the Hamptons. As such, it's surrounded by attractive weekend homes, the nicest ones being closest to the beach. Many former potato fields hereabouts have in recent years sprouted dramatic, geometrically shaped houses sheathed in glass and weathered wood. But the potatoes still grow too—at least as of this writing.

BRIDGEHAMPTON
Montauk Highway continues east from Water Mill through farm fields, past some great restaurants (more about these later too), antique stores, farm stands, and the occasional shopping center. After about five miles you'll come to Bridgehampton, another attractive town with an established summer colony. Pretty much all the land around here, at least that which lies south of the highway, has been developed for summer and weekend houses. Former farming hamlets like **Sagaponack, Mecox,** and **Wainscot** dot the flat and formerly rural fields, all of which seem to be bordered no longer by trees or fences but by angular modern summer houses. It's a characteristic of much of the South Fork, and the North Fork too, that still-active farmland runs to the very edge of the summer-house lawns and that farm machinery shares narrow back roads with flotillas of Mercedes Benzes. This peculiar situation is, in large part, the result of Suffolk County's aggressive and ingenious efforts to preserve its open farmland by means of the transfer of development rights. In some places these efforts have come too late. But in others they haven't, and the visual results—like working farms encircled by trendy summer homes—are often quite pleasant, if a tad anomalous.

At Bridgehampton you have the option of continuing east toward Montauk, or detouring 4½ miles to the north up N.Y. 79. This picturesque country road is also called the Sag Harbor Turnpike, as it leads directly into the bustling town of Sag Harbor. It's a nice drive and chances are you'll be glad to get off N.Y. 27 for a while.

SAG HARBOR
Sag Harbor likes to style itself the "Un-Hampton Hampton," which I suppose means that it has the class without the congestion. Certainly it's removed from the horrid traffic jams on N.Y. 27, even though unless you live here you'll have to face them eventually. The village is bigger than most of the other Hamptons, excepting Southampton itself. While the towns along the Atlantic beaches attracted vacationers throughout the last century, the old whaling port of Sag Harbor up on Shelter Island Sound just languished. Whaling, which began here in the 1760s, peaked in the 1840s. Then came the California gold rush of 1849, followed by the long and inexorable decline of the whaling industry. By the 1870s Sag Harbor was dead. It remained more or less moribund until the real estate boom of the last decade brought it back to life. Even today, its streets again crowded, its shop windows full, its extremely charming old buildings restored, the population is only about two-thirds of what it was in 1845.

Sag Harbor isn't so intimidating as Southampton, despite the new glamour. It certainly is pretty, with its profusion of leafy streets and wonderful mid-Victorian houses. One of the most fabulous of these is the **Sag Harbor Whaling and Historical Museum,** on Main Street just before the center of town (tel. 516/725-0770). This elegant Greek Revival mansion houses memorabilia and artifacts from the days when Sag Harbor was home port to 31 whalers. The museum charges $2 for adults, 75¢ for kids aged 6 to 13, and is open daily mid-May until October from 10 a.m. to 5 p.m. (1 to 5 p.m. on Sunday). Across the street is **The Custom House** (tel. 516/725-0250), dating from the late 18th century. The house was the home of the custom master when Sag Harbor was a federal port of entry to New York State. It is open to the public from 10 a.m. to 5 p.m. except on Monday. Admission is $1.50 for adults, $1 for children, and there are guided tours and children's activities.

Lunch and dinner suggestions, plus a description of Sag Harbor's very attractive American Hotel, appear below. Besides strolling around, peeking in antique shops, and soaking up the 19th-century ambience, there's not much else to do. As soon as you're ready, climb back in the car, find N.Y. 114 (it's at the very top of Main Street, within sight of the American Hotel), and head back south for about seven miles to Montauk Highway and the village of East Hampton.

EAST HAMPTON

East Hampton is perhaps the most gorgeous-looking village in the Hamptons. It's a manicured little world of great sweeping elm trees, rambling colonial mansions, velvety lawns, clipped hedges, picturesque ponds, and occasional pockets of ancient 17th-century buildings. The central business district has fashionable shops and restaurants, and even an adjacent windmill. The beach areas near East Hampton sport a collection of Southampton-type summer mansions, many of which are quite breathtaking. Also here is the exclusive Maidstone Club, a high-class beach and golf club whose very name is synonymous with Hampton-style luxury. The most interesting areas to explore are down Ocean Avenue toward Apaquogue and along Further Lane in the vicinity of the Maidstone.

East Hampton's favorite attraction, as far as the locals are concerned, is the **"Home Sweet Home" Museum,** facing the Village Green at 14 James Lane (tel. 516/324-0713). "Home Sweet Home" rings a bell with almost everybody, but it's the rare individual who knows quite why. It's a song (right!—now you remember), first performed on the stage of Covent Garden in 1822, but written and performed by an American named John Howard Payne. Payne, a music hall sensation who by the time of his death had become the American consul at Tunis, was a native East Hampton boy. His father had settled here in the late 18th century to teach at the **Clinton Academy,** a historic early prep school whose building at 151 Main St. (tel. 516/324-1850) is also open as a museum. In 1907 a fellow named Gustav Buek and his wife purchased and occupied the Payne house. For the next 20 years the Bueks painstakingly restored and furnished it with 18th-century antiques. After Buek's death the village of East Hampton bought both house and contents. And since 1928 the place has been open year-round as a museum. It's not a big house, nor is it an elaborate one. Built in 1660, it's a shingled saltbox full of country treasures whose look has only recently become fashionable. Outside on the lawn is another windmill, also rescued, moved, and restored by Mr. Buek.

Besides historic houses and posh estates, East Hampton offers good shopping for gifts and antiques and a great bar called O'Malley's, about which more later.

AMAGANSETT/SPRINGS

A few miles east of East Hampton on N.Y. 27 is the next Hampton, a village called Amagansett. This place showed great commercial promise back in the 18th century as a farming and manufacturing center, but it never recovered from the British Revolutionary War blockade. Today's Amagansett looks like a junior version of East Hampton, pretty but neither as plush nor as big. To the north of it lies a hilly, piney area whose spiritual center is a hamlet (really a crossroads) called **Springs.** No big mansions, posh clubs, magnificent beaches, museums from the 1600s, or any similar Hamptons-type attractions are associated with Springs. Yet, ironically, it's a very fashionable area. To drive through it, you'd never know. In fact, you'd probably get lost in the spaghetti tangle of narrow roads through dense but low pine forests. There are many lovely little beaches, modest crescents of golden sand lapped by the low waves of Gardiners Bay, all around this area. The problem again is the lack of legal parking. Actually, the parking situation is exactly what preserves the delicate charms of Springs. This woodsy enclave on the crowded South Fork is as appealing as it is precisely because there's no place to park.

Beyond Amagansett the look of the land changes suddenly. Gone are the lush trees and green fields. Gone, too, is pretty much of the land on either side of Montauk Highway. After **Beach Hampton,** a dot on the map about a mile beyond Amagansett, is an area called **Napeague,** notable for its open sand dunes upon which a community of condominium/hotel complexes is rising. The presence of **Hither Hills State Park** is the only insurance that the whole beach won't become built up.

MONTAUK

The closer you draw to Montauk Point (it's about 16 miles from the center of Amagansett to the Montauk Lighthouse) the more barren and windswept the landscape becomes. Even on hot days there's a stiff breeze off the ocean and not much onshore to slow it down. The windswept moors around the present village of Montauk were used to pasture cattle as long ago as the 1660s. The present lighthouse was constructed in the 1790s on orders from George Washington himself. In the late 19th century Stanford White designed a few small but suave shingled cottages for vacationing sportsmen. And in 1909 Teddy Roosevelt's Rough Riders, 30,000 strong, briefly recuperated hereabouts after the Spanish-American War. Otherwise, not much happened.

But in 1926 things took a bizarre turn. That was the year that Carl Fisher, the famous Miami Beach developer, bought up most of Montauk with the intention of developing it into the Miami Beach of the north. He built a village center complete with art deco office tower, shops, and roads, improved the harbor facilities, and erected an enormous Tudor-style luxury resort hotel called the Montauk Manor. Shortly after all this the Florida land bubble burst, and then in 1929 the stock market collapsed. Fisher went bankrupt and Montauk entered a long and eerie period of desolation. The office tower, never occupied, stood vacant for over 50 years. The Montauk Manor remained in operation for quite a while, all things considered, but eventually it, too, went under. A collection of modest beachfront motels developed adjacent to the village, but otherwise the place was dead.

Today Montauk is riding the same crazy real estate boom that has galloped over all of Long Island, and indeed over most of the Northeast. There must be nearly 100 motels lined up today along the windy, surfy beach or scattered in and around the village center. The former office tower is now a glossy condominium. Even the old Montauk Manor molders no longer. It, too, is in the process of a multimillion-dollar conversion to vacation condos. But despite a handful of restored and newly constructed buildings, the majority of Montauk's built environment is not exceptional.

Standing in the shadow of the Montauk Lighthouse, one certainly has the feel of being at the edge of the world. Actually, much of New England lies considerably east of this point. But that inconvenient fact is not what detracts from the beauty of the spot. To be sure, there *is* a particular beauty to Montauk, stemming from an almost-otherworldly air of desolation. Montauk's original atmosphere of weird and mysterious remoteness has been preserved in pockets at Hither Hills State Park, and within the boundaries of two back-to-back parks both called **Montauk Point,** and administered respectively by New York State and Suffolk County. The real problem is that Montauk just isn't remote anymore. To the contrary, it's a very developed place. And its development will undoubtedly conflict with some people's romantic preconceptions.

GARDINERS ISLAND

Last but not least in this part of the world is Gardiners Island, a private manor that's remained in the hands of the Gardiner family for over three centuries. There is no way out to the island save by boat or plane. And since it's private you'd have to be a guest of the Gardiners to even contemplate the trip.

Yet Gardiners Island is a singularly romantic vestige of the past, complete with windmill, farm, and manor house. King Charles I of England granted the island, as well as considerable additional tracts in other sections of Long Island, to Lion Gardiner in the early 17th century. Shopping centers, expressways, and tract houses now stand on other Gardiner manors. But the 16th Lord of Gardiner's Island still rules a realm untouched even by 18th-century democracy. The island lies low and mysterious on the horizon, cradled by the curling sandy arm of Montauk. It's like the American class system itself, whose greatest charm lies in the fact that so few people realize it exists.

5. Where to Stay and Eat in the Hamptons

Collectively the Hamptons occupy a small region, so if you explore one you'll probably wind up exploring them all (or at least several). Village-shopping is an accepted pasttime hereabouts, even among full-time residents. Therefore I have collected together all my recommended restaurants and hotels into a single section, divided it by village, and listed the individual villages alphabetically. In this manner you can find a good restaurant wherever in the Hamptons you happen to be, and a good hotel in whichever Hampton sounds most to your liking.

AMAGANSETT/NAPEAGUE

Gordon's, on Main Street in Amagansett (tel. 516/267-3010), has operated out of its diminutive white and brown building in the center of the village for over ten years. It's a nice small-town restaurant, with a lofty little dining room decorated with hanging plants, gold-colored tablecloths, and a crystal chandelier hanging from a brown-painted acoustical ceiling. The menu is limited but the food is really good. Lunchtime specialties include things like broiled sea trout, veal marsala, minute steak, or cannelloni au gratin, priced from about $12 to $18. At dinner you'll pay between $18 and $22 for things like filet mignon, veal piccata, beef bordelaise with wild rice, Long Island duckling, etc. Everything is à la carte. Lunch is served from noon to 2 p.m., dinner from 6 to 10 p.m.; no lunch at all is served during the months of July and August (everybody's at the beach). The restaurant is closed Monday, as well as the entire months of January and February.

Less expensive and more homey is **The Stephen Talkhouse,** located on Main Street (tel. 516/267-3117), which features music and comedy in an intimate setting. Though the menu is plain (burgers and sandwiches), it's good. The Talkhouse is open daily year-round.

Out on Napeague Beach a few miles to the east of Amagansett is the **Lobster Roll,** on Montauk Hwy. (tel. 516/267-3740), recognizable by its big blue sign that says "Lunch." This is a reasonably priced old-fashioned roadhouse with a family atmosphere and fabulous seafood. It has an outside porch whose plastic screens block the wind, boxes full of geraniums, checked plastic tablecloths, and an adjacent sandy lot crammed with cars bound to or from nearby Montauk. The house specialties are seafood salads made from lobster, crab, shrimp, or combinations thereof. They come either on rolls or platters, or in bowls. In addition to these are all manner of burgers, fried clams, fish-and-chips platters, chowders, and special broiled fish. The menu's the same at lunch and dinner, and prices range from around $4 to $6 for most lunch items, and up to about $10 to $12 for the special seafood platters. Open daily from 11:30 a.m. to 10 p.m. from Memorial Day to Labor Day; weekends only in May, September and October; closed during the winter.

Within sight of the Lobster Roll are numerous vast beachfront resort/condominiums. They're new, perfect, right on the ocean, and not cheap. Their angular "clean" design reflects the modern taste in architecture seen in cities across the country. They are the polar opposites of the old-fashioned country inns back in East Hampton and Southampton. Instead of ancient charm they offer tennis courts, swimming pools, private beaches, cable color televisions, and kitchenettes—and everything is new, new, new. This is precisely what many travelers want.

If you count yourself among this number, you'll doubtless like the **Hermitage,** Montauk Hwy. (P.O. Box 1127), Amagansett, NY 11930 (tel. 516/267-6151).

All the units here have two bedrooms and are housed in very white squared-off buildings facing the beach, the dunes, or the pool. They really are quite nice inside, with contemporary furnishings, glass-topped tables, and tasteful beachy color schemes. If you're visiting between June 23 and September 11, they require a one-week minimum stay. Weekly rates range from $1,290 to $1,590, depending on location and view. It is sometimes possible to stay for a single night during the season, if a suite would otherwise be vacant, for between $195 and $240 double. But you shouldn't count on it.

A very similar sort of place is the nearby **Windward Shores,** Montauk Hwy. (P.O. Box L), Amagansett, NY 11930 (tel. 516/267-8600), where a double-occupancy studio room with kitchenette costs between $830 and $900 a week during the season. However, if it would otherwise be empty they'll let you have it for a single night for between $125 and $150. Two-bedroom duplexes with two baths cost between $1,350 and $1,680 weekly, or $200 to $250 nightly if that can be arranged. Both these establishments, as well as their competitors up and down the beach, have significantly reduced off-season rates.

BRIDGEHAMPTON/WAINSCOTT

HSF, on Montauk Highway in Bridgehampton (tel. 516/537-0550), is the fanciest-looking Chinese restaurant I've ever seen, and a cousin of the famous Manhattan HSF in Kips Bay. The place is easy to miss, as the black sign on the south side of Montauk Highway (just before the light at Caldor's on the way to Bridgehampton from Southampton) is so low-key and tasteful as to be almost invisible. Inside HSF are tailored gray banquettes, linen tablecloths, a mirrored ceiling, and an ultrasleek black bar by the door. Lunch might be black-bean chicken Hong Kong style, barbecued roast duck, prawns and scallops in a love nest, or a seafood casserole, drawn from a list of chef's suggestions priced between about $9 and $17. The early-bird dinner, called a Sunset Special and served from 5 to 6:45 p.m., includes soup, appetizer, choice of main course, rice, and dessert, and costs only $14. The main à la carte menu contains the usual steamed, roast, and crispy Chinese dishes and runs the gamut from beef and pork to chicken and seafood. People in the Hamptons rave about HSF, which is open daily from noon to 3:30 p.m. for lunch, and 3:30 to 11 p.m. for dinner (until midnight on Friday and Saturday).

Located on the west side of the Wainscott post office is **Bruce's,** Montauk Hwy., Wainscott (tel. 516/537-3360). This little red cottage by the roadside, adjacent to vast rolling fields, is a real gourmet restaurant serving things like broiled halibut with roasted green pepper sauce, marinated tuna steak, veal sautéed with mushrooms and fresh thyme, bourbon pot roast with fresh horseradish cream, blackfish broiled with lemon butter, etc., at prices ranging between $16 and $20 per plate. Additionally there are original salads and soups, a pianist at the bar on weekends, and a list titled "Our Suppliers" enumerating the source of every strawberry, lemon, coffee bean, and piece of fish and meat on the menu. Patrons sit in a collection of English pub–like rooms with stucco walls, beamed ceilings, crisp linens, shaded pewter chandeliers, and gleaming dark floors. Open for dinner only from 7 to 11 p.m.; closed Monday.

EAST HAMPTON

Down a little alley in the very center of town, directly opposite the traffic light at Main Street and Newtown Lane, is **O'Malley's Saloon,** 11 East Main Street (tel. 516/324-9757). Actually, this is a pretty gentrified alley, what with its pots of geraniums, umbrella tables, sculpture of giraffes, and chic boutiques. O'Malley's has a boisterous Irish-saloon atmosphere and a collection of little rooms decorated with ceiling beams, brass rails, leather-lined booths, and an assortment of decorative junk. There's a bar up front and a garden room with a glass roof and hanging green shades in the back. Every conceivable burger on earth is served here, made with mozzarella cheese, smoked barbecue sauce, western chili, onions, spinach, mushrooms, you name it. There's even a diet burger, and a jogger's burger (topped with carrot, celery sticks, a lemon wedge, and lettuce). They all come with french fries and cost about $5. Also available are a few additional sandwiches, daily blackboard specials, some great heavy desserts, and a 14-ounce marinated steak served with Irish potatoes and priced at a reasonable $11. For value, location, and congenial atmosphere, this is a hard place to beat. Open daily from 11 a.m. until 3 a.m.; the kitchen stays open until 11:30 p.m.; until 1 a.m. on weekends.

Set amid lawns and ancient trees is the old Huntting Inn, home of a luxurious restaurant called **The Palm**, 94 Main St. (tel. 516/324-0411). The Palm has a small bar adjacent to several intimate lounges, one furnished with huge green plush sofas, the other with brass-railed mezzanines, a piano, and flocks of little tables lit by art-glass lamps. The large dining room has low painted-tin ceilings, crisp white cloths, and an adjacent enclosed porch with additional tables. The Palm is the Hamptons branch of the famous New York City establishment of the same name. Unsurprisingly, the entire place has a big-time New York City atmosphere. Primarily it's a steakhouse, serving dinner only, seven days a week during the season from 5 to 11 p.m. Filet mignon, prime rib, lamb chops, sirloin, plus a few items like swordfish, veal piccata, and shrimp sauté cost about $15 to $25 per plate. Dinner here, á la carte of course, is a very handsome experience and you certainly won't leave hungry.

There is two truly wonderful old inns in East Hampton and it's a toss-up as to which is the more appealing. The **1770 House**, 143 Main St., East Hampton, NY 11937 (tel. 516/324-1770), is a roomy old center-hall colonial with black shutters and a picket fence out front. Shaded by majestic trees, surrounded by other historic houses, and overlooking East Hampton's lovely Village Green, it's about the nicest-looking place one could imagine. The interior is a warren of cozy old rooms, chockablock with wonderful antiques, big leather sofas, a grandfather clock clinging picturesquely to a tiny landing on the stair, beams, old pine paneling, and a delightful profusion of nooks and crannies. Each room has air conditioning, a private bath, antique furnishings, pretty wallpaper, sometimes even a fireplace. Frankly, the Chippendale highboys, canopied beds, and marble-topped vanities in the guest rooms are worth the absence of a pool or a tennis court. Besides, you've got the fantastic East Hampton beach.

During July and August management requires a four-night minimum stay on weekends. Nightly double-occupancy room rates range from $95 to $145 and include a continental breakfast. The rest of the year there's a minimum weekend stay as well, but it's only two nights. Rates are the same, but the breakfast is full instead of continental. There are only seven rooms in the inn, but another three are down the street in a fairly fabulous mansion, called the Philip Taylor House, belonging to the proprietors. Rooms there have fireplaces and even air conditioning, and cost $185 a night. The perfectly beautiful formal garden behind the Taylor House is a soothing wonder to behold.

The **1770 House Restaurant,** located in the main inn, serves breakfast to guests only, lunch to no one at all, but dinner to any and all comers. It's a $32 prix-fixe affair providing appetizer (soup, shrimp casino, Oriental scallop salad), salad, main course (like lobster stuffed with crabmeat, stuffed breast of veal, fresh swordfish), and vegetable. Dessert and beverages are extra. The beamed dining room is filled with antique tables, rose medallion plates, pale-strawberry-colored linen napkins, and an enormous number of antique clocks ticking away on the pink-painted walls. Dinner is served from Thursday to Sunday in the summer, but on Saturday night only in the winter.

Just down the street is the **Maidstone Arms**, 207 Main St., East Hampton, NY 11937 (tel. 516/324-5006). It is two old white houses joined on the first floor and overlooking Main Street and the tranquil lawny expanses of the Village Green. You walk onto a painted porch with a green-and-white-striped awning, through a handsome front door flanked with leaded sidelights, and into what seems for all the world like an elegant colonial house. An inn since the 1870s, the Maidstone has 19 rooms, furnished with Chinese rugs, some fabulously ornate Victorian furniture, fireplaces, old rockers, flowered wallpaper, and curtains on tie-backs. All rooms have private baths, phones, and air conditioning. Between Memorial Day and Labor Day the nightly rate ranges from about $100 to $175, with a three-night minimum stay required on weekends. A continental breakfast, served in a sunny wicker-filled porch overlooking the green, is included in the room rates. During the week a double can be had for between $85 and $105 nightly, including continental breakfast.

The **Maidstone Arms Restaurant** (tel. 516/324-2004) is in the back of the first floor. Under separate management, it consists of a dark, clubby-looking tap-room, beyond which is a 20-table, low-ceilinged restaurant decorated with green carpeting, brown walls, and crisp white tablecloths. Continental-French cuisine is the order of the day, with sample à la carte entrees including things like Norwegian salmon, veal Prince Orloff, calves' liver lyonnaise, and a local bouillabaisse, priced between $16 and $24. Dinner is served nightly except Tuesday from 6 to 10 p.m. The restaurant is closed in January and February.

MONTAUK

The Anchorage, 271B W. Lake Dr. (tel. 516/668-9394), is a good, family-style seafood restaurant that makes an ideal part of a day trip to Montauk Point. Located on Lake Montauk in a little mustard-colored building set far back from the road, it's decorated with tanks full of live lobsters, tables with paper placemats, a big bar with a television, and open windows overlooking water views. Typical menu items include crabs' legs, softshell crabs, fried oysters, flounder filet, and lobsters (ranging from one to five pounds). Expect to pay between $10 and $20 for a typical platter. Open daily from noon until 10 p.m.; "lobster lover" specials (whole lobsters from one to three pounds for about $8 to $22) are available until 5 p.m. Open from April through Halloween.

Another excellent place, also informal and family oriented but considerably bigger, is **Gosman's,** at the end of Flamingo Road right by the entrance to Lake Montauk (tel. 516/668-5330). Gosman's Dock, where the restaurant is located, is a sort of mini theme shopping center, the accent being on seafood and seafaring. It's an attractive, modern, multilevel complex of gray-sided buildings arranged around odd-shaped courtyards and patios overlooking the water. A constant procession of gleaming-white fishing boats passes back and forth in and out of Lake Montauk. Whitecaps fleck the surface of the Atlantic, gulls cry, and the wind blows. Gosman's Restaurant is a big airy place with lots of windows, beamed ceilings, and a forest of wooden tables and chairs. Typical menu items include swordfish, cold steamed Montauk lobster, fried clams with coleslaw and fries, and all manner of fresh broiled fish, mostly costing between $10 and $16. Open from noon until 10 p.m. seven days a week from mid-April until mid-October. Gosman's does not take credit cards, but does accept personal checks with the proper I.D.

If Montauk somehow captures your imagination to the point that you want to stay here, the best advice is to proceed to the chamber of commerce building on the oval in the middle of the village opposite the tower. The chamber acts as a sort of central booking office for the many, many, many motels in town, and if there's space available they'll find it for you. Expect minimum-stay requirements and rates comparable to those of other parts of the South Fork. I'll see you later in East Hampton.

SOUTHAMPTON

My favorite hotel here is the **Village Latch Inn,** 101 Hill St. (the extension of Job's Lane), Southampton, NY 11968 (tel. 516/283-2160). At first glance the place looks like an old mansion pressed into modern-day service as an inn. It has tall hedges, big lawns, a green-shuttered colonial façade, and aristocratic-looking gates on Hill Street. Actually, it used to be the annex to the Irving Hotel, a famous and now-demolished Southampton hostelry that stood across the street. You enter the building from the rear, at the end of a long, dim hallway adjacent to a postage-stamp-size office. At the distant end of this hall is a collection of bright public rooms filled with overstuffed furniture, hanging plants, bright pillows in floral prints, and random antiques. There's a cheery breakfast porch, as well as a sun porch filled with white wicker and blue floral fabrics. Everything is quite atmospheric and rather lush.

The 70 guest rooms are distributed among the inn, a shingled annex in the back, and several former estate buildings rescued and moved to the property by the present owners. All accommodations are quite nice and equipped with things like thick rugs, stripped-oak furniture, tweed-covered chaises, lazy ceiling fans, private baths, easy chairs, and the occasional fireplace. They look somehow sleeker than the typical "country inn," which is perhaps the inevitable result of being in fashionable Southampton. Unlike so many other inns, the Latch also has a pool (quite a pretty one too), a tennis court, and a former conservatory in the back that now contains a hot tub. Parts of the Latch are open only from Memorial Day to Labor Day; other parts stay open all year. The price of a regular double room ranges between $95 and $115 nightly during the week, and between $125 and $160 on weekends, plus a 10% service charge. A three-day/two-night minimum is usually required on summer weekends.

Much smaller (only seven rooms) but just as attractive is the **Old Post House Inn,** 136 Main St., Southampton, NY 11968 (tel. 516/283-1717). This is a really charming old building, added to over three centuries, and located adjacent to the hub of Southampton's chic Main Street shopping area. The old wooden structure has three stories, shuttered windows, and a big ivy-clad tree by the front door. Beyond the wicker-filled porch is a small lobby with a beamed ceiling and ladderback rush-seated chairs. The rooms upstairs are small but quite luxurious. Each has a private bath, tastefully papered walls, charming old-fashioned bedroom furniture, and surprisingly thick rugs. Once again there's an indefinable Southampton lushness about this place; it's just somehow extra nice. The room rates rise and fall with the mean monthly temperature. At the height of the season you can expect to pay between $90 and $150 nightly, with a two-night minimum required for weekend stays. Rates are slightly less in the spring and fall, and about a third less during the winter. Continental breakfast, included in the room rates, is served by an ancient fireplace downstairs in a room with a hooked rug, English pine furniture, and low ceiling beams.

The **Hill Guest House,** 535 Hill St., Southampton, NY 11968 (tel. 516/283-9889), occupies a comfy old shingled house painted white and screened from the street by high private hedges. There's a grassy parking lot in the back, between the house and the barn. Scattered here and there on the clipped grass are lawn chairs and plastic chaises. Beyond the wooden-floored porch with its obligatory wicker is a cheerful and modest guesthouse, run for the last 24 summers by Mr. and Mrs. Salerno of Queens, N.Y. The six rooms have window shades, painted furniture, and vintage metal beds, and are neat and clean as a pin. It's a great old-fashioned place and you'll be lucky if you can get in. Weekday rates range from $50 to $60 nightly, double occupancy, the highest rate applying to rooms with private bath. On weekends, when there's a three-night minimum, the rates range from $60 to $75 per night, double occupancy. Continental breakfast is served downstairs in the dining room between 9 and 11 a.m. for an additional $1.50. Open during the summer season only.

There's a terrific restaurant right downtown, attached to the Old Post House Inn, and called the **Post House,** 136 Main St. (tel. 516/283-9696). The shady slate-floored terrace out front, with its pink and white linen and views of the action on Main Street, is a great spot for a summer meal. Inside, the colonial era meets the 1990s, in decor anyway. There's a big bar, beyond which stretches a largish dining room with pink walls and tablecloths. Lunch, served from noon to 3:30 p.m. daily, might be an omelet, the pasta du jour, broiled flounder, a grilled chicken paillard etc., priced in the $7.50 to $10 range. The dinner menu, available from 5 to 10 p.m. daily (to 11 p.m. on weekends), features appetizers like chevre baked in puff pastry and entrees like grilled loin lamb chops, grilled swordfish, filet mignon with béarnaise sauce, or the fish du jour, and costs around $16 to $24 per à la carte entree.

For a fast, inexpensive sandwich, try the **Sip 'n' Soda,** 40 Hampton Ave., a half block east of Main Street, near the Old Post Inn. "Since 1958," it says on the menu, and indeed it looks as though Lucy herself might come spinning through the door at any moment, wearing a poodle skirt and shouting for Ricky. This is a place for good luncheonette-style sandwiches, salads, burgers, and homemade ice cream (a house specialty). Expect lunch to cost $7 or less. Open daily until about 5 or 5:30 p.m.

The most venerable, and perhaps venerated, eatery in Southampton is **Silver's Famous Restaurant,** 15 Main St. (tel. 516/283-6443). Silver's is a family-owned and -operated candy store-newsstand-cum-restaurant, festooned with Mexican-yellow walls. There is a real soda counter in the middle of the place, as well as an excellent newspaper and magazine section by the front door that stocks practically everything. Garrett Wellins, the self-styled "philosopher chef," welcomes smart conversation regarding the world's pleasures and pains. You'll welcome his Russian borscht and vegetable gumbo, (about $4) and marvel at his lighter-than-air omelet soufflés that range from $7 to $10. The rest of the menu consists of sandwiches, assorted pastas and salads, and rich desserts (try the pecan tart). Truly a Southampton landmark. Open Monday to Friday, 10:30 a.m. to 4:30 p.m.; Saturday and Sunday, 10:30 a.m. to 5:30 p.m.—later in summer, if busy.

SAG HARBOR

There's a wonderful and reasonably priced little Italian place in Sag Harbor, open for dinner only, called **Il Capucino,** on Madison Street (tel. 516/725-2747). It's in a small red building with a hanging picture of a monk outside, and located within sight of the commercial center of Sag Harbor just two blocks south of the American Hotel. Inside is a collection of small rooms with hanging chianti bottles, whitewashed shingles, and unstained pine on the walls, and flocks of little tables with red-and-white-checked cloths. The menu offers antipasti (steamed clams, mussels, calamaretti in bianco, etc.) for between $5 and $8, pasta dishes mostly priced at $9 or $10, and main courses (such as fettuccine Alfredo, cappelleti al pistachio, baked lasagne, and shrimp Fra Diavolo) for between $12 and $15. Open seven days a week from 5:30 until 10 p.m. (on Friday and Saturday until 11 p.m.).

For a quick and inexpensive lunch in Sag Harbor, try the **Paradise Restaurant,** on Main Street (tel. 516/725-2110) almost opposite the American Hotel. This is a busy modern luncheonette, with tables, a long counter, fake wood paneling, and big windows overlooking the street. Sandwiches cost around $4 to $5; triple deckers run up to $6 or so; burgers are in the $4 to $5 vicinity. Breakfast is served all day, and homemade desserts and ice cream are a specialty of the house here too. It's a busy place, filled with pretty waitresses and hungry locals. Open from 7 a.m. to 5 p.m.; closed Wednesday.

You might also consider taking a meal in the restored Victorian precincts of the **American Hotel,** Main Street, Sag Harbor, NY 11963 (tel. 516/725-3535). This old three-story brick landmark has a lacy white porch tacked onto its front, stone tubs full of flowering rhododendron, antique blue wicker porch chairs, and people's bikes leaning casually against the walls. The dining areas are divided by a plushy Victorian lobby filled with Oriental rugs, dark carved furniture, and paisley wallpaper. It's small, but plummy. The bar just beyond it has a sensational moosehead on the wall, great old dark wood paneling, and a collection of little café tables. The atmosphere is terrific.

Smokers who want to eat here are banished to a narrow cinderblock-walled former passageway, painted white and tricked up with a greenhouse ceiling, and called all too accurately the "Alley." The nonsmokers' dining room is considerably nicer, decorated with old-fashioned gilt-framed pictures, patterned wallpaper, and crisp white linens. Lunch, served from noon to 3 p.m., might be sliced filet mignon au poivre, duck and quail salad, roast chicken, filet of weakfish meunière, eggs Benedict, or a French bread sandwich, priced generally between $8 and $12. The dinner hour, running from 6:30 until about 10:30 p.m. nightly, features slightly heavier fare with entrees like seafood vol au vent, Norweigan salmon sautéed in dill, roast duckling, sirloin steak, veal sweetbread "bonne maman," and chateaubriand, priced mostly between $15 and $25 per à la carte selection.

Upstairs at the American are eight hotel rooms, each with private bath, and all quite perfectly restored (reconstructed really). They are furnished with wall-to-wall carpeting, sleigh beds, flowered curtains, gilt-framed pictures, and miscellaneous antiques. They're pretty big too, as "inn" rooms go. Winter room rates are $75 per person during the week, and $100 per person on weekends, with a three-night minimum on holiday weekends. In the summer (Memorial Day to Labor Day) you'll pay $90 per person during the week and $130 per person on the weekend, with a two-night minimum weekend stay.

A WORD ON NIGHTLIFE

There are plenty of hot clubs in the Hamptons where you can drink and dance and generally have a howl of a time. They're open dependably on summer weekends, and occasionally on summer weekday nights. As in the city, the clubs out here don't get going until late. Don't expect much action until at least after 11 p.m. As of this writing, the typical cover charge is about $15 per person, plus whatever you spend for drinks. Most places cater to people in their mid to late 20s.

Here now are the names of three establishments that were good at the time this guide went to press. **Bay Street** (not to be confused with a café of the same name), on Long Wharf in Sag Harbor (tel. 516/725-2297), has dancing, occasional shows, and a live DJ. **Conscience Point,** north of Southampton on North Sea Road in Noyac (tel. 516/283-2992), has plenty of people in their 30s. **Danceteria,** on Montauk Highway in the middle of the village of Water Mill (tel. 516/726-7606), is great for disco dancing.

What's good this year, as we all know, may be the pits next year. Almost everywhere in the Hamptons you'll see a free tabloid-size paper, usually with a picture of some glamorous and slightly reckless-looking girl on the cover, called *Hamptons*. This sheet is chockablock with ads for all manner of summer services, including nightclubs. So if the above ideas poop out, have a look here.

X

LONG ISLAND: THE NORTH FORK AND SHELTER ISLAND

1. AN INTRODUCTION TO THE NORTH FORK
2. WHERE TO STAY AND EAT ON THE NORTH FORK
3. SHELTER ISLAND

The North Fork is that complementary spit of land that balances Long Island's South Fork. The tips of their respective tines dandle Gardiners Island between them. A little deeper down their throat lies fashionable Shelter Island. And at the bottom of the split, where both forks originate, lies the little city of Riverhead, seat of Suffolk County.

1. An Introduction to the North Fork

The North Fork, geography aside, is nothing at all like the South Fork. Besides the glittering waters of Great Peconic Bay, Little Peconic Bay, Shelter Island Sound, and Gardiners Bay, a very considerable antipathy (some persist in calling it local pride) has traditionally divided their respective populations. In recent years the real differences between these two water-girt worlds have begun to blur. What's happening is that the North Fork, traditionally rural, agricultural, and unpretentious, is beginning (*just* beginning, mind you) to get a wee bit Hampton-ish.

What's the North Fork like? Well, it's rather like a former virgin on the morning after her wedding night. She looks the same and she feels the same, but somehow she just isn't the way she used to be. The most obvious change is that old Long Island bugaboo, heavy traffic. But that's only on summer weekends. During the winter, and on rainy summer weekdays, the North Fork looks like any other farming region in rural America. Planted fields stretch away toward the horizon; pretty (albeit slightly ramshackle) villages, each with a nice white church and a single stoplight, cluster around the main road (N.Y. 25) at respectable distances from one another; diner lots and gas stations are full of pickup trucks and battered sedans; there's no suburban sprawl but there are plenty of modest split-level houses dotted around the countryside. As for flashy mansions and startlingly modern condo complexes of the sort that dominate the South Fork, there is (as yet) nary a trace.

Oh, but it's coming. And everybody knows it. The locals have read the proverbial handwriting on the wall with a curious mixture of outrage and excitement. True, it's getting hard to drive around during the summer. True, that slightly blowsy lot next door that one neglected to pick up five years ago for $16,000 just sold to some city people for $130,000. But on the other hand there's a curious new prestige associated with the North Fork, something that was never a part of earlier local equations. And most important, the old homestead, especially if it should happen to be a farm with maybe 100 acres, is suddenly worth millions. This latter fact should be enough to comfort all but the most curmudgeonly.

The North Fork, like its larger and glossier sister to the south, also contains its requisite complement of 17th-century churches and houses. If old colonial stuff is your cup of tea, there's at least one interesting building to look at in almost every village. Out in **Orient,** for instance, there's a small complex of them, administered by the **Oysterponds Historical Society,** on Village Lane (tel. 516/323-2480). An 18th-century house and an adjoining Victorian-style inn, both with special exhibits, are just two reasons to visit. Open on weekends from June through September (and Wednesday and Thursday too during July and August), Oysterponds warrants inclusion in any excursion out to Orient. Admission is $2 for adults and 50¢ for kids.

Greenport, opposite Shelter Island, has several modest attractions, among them the **Stirling Historical Society's restored village house** on Main Street (tel. 516/477-0099). Admission is 50¢ for adults, children free, and it is open from July 4 until Labor Day, Wednesday, Saturday, and Sunday, 1 to 4 p.m.

But perhaps the most notable in the area is the aptly named **Old House,** on the Village Green in Cutchogue, midway between Riverhead and Orient Point. Maintained by the Cutchoque-Suffolk Historical Society (tel. 516/734-7122) this structure, built in 1649, claims the distinction of being the oldest English house in New York State. Its weathered boards and shingles were restored in 1940, but it still manages to look older than Time itself. Note the rather aristocratic chimney, which would look quite as comfortable on an East Hampton mansion. The Old House is also part of a small complex that includes the Wickham House (the apotheosis of the charming shingled Long Island farmhouse) and a little white schoolhouse complete with ca. 1840 desks, blackboard, and maps. Open July and August from Saturday to Monday; admission is $1 for adults, 50¢ for kids under 12.

Despite advances in room rates and property prices, plus the recent arrival of handsomely maintained horse farms and vineyards (established, one suspects, more as a result of tax laws than out of any love for horseflesh or wine), you mustn't think that the North Fork has completely lost its rural, laid-back appeal. Driving through the fields along Sound Avenue or gazing off into the ocean distances from Orient are still soul-soothing experiences. There are a number of charming places to stay and eat, and prices are still not as high as they are on the South Fork. The villages are unpretentious but fun to explore. There are abundant farm stands where you can select the freshest imaginable produce right by the side of the field in which it grew. And there are other fields, marked by hand-lettered signs on big pieces of cardboard, where you can still go out and pick your own fresh produce.

It's less than 30 miles from Riverhead all the way to Orient Point, so exploration of the North Fork is not a major undertaking. What with Shelter Island lying where it does, you can easily head out to the end of one fork and return via the other.

Probably the prettiest parts, scenically speaking, of the North Fork are out around Orient. Also quite beautiful are the seemingly endless farmfields that flank North Road and Sound Avenue parallel to N.Y. 25. The beaches hereabouts are lovely, but much smaller and more tranquil than those facing the Atlantic. The North Fork is going to appeal to people who like beautiful country—and have the luck or sense not to land up there on a weekend.

2. Where to Stay and Eat on the North Fork

The North Fork is smaller and less developed than the South Fork. Accordingly, the range of hotels and restaurants is more limited. Here's a run-down on some of the best deals for your money.

HOTELS

Greenport, the biggest town on the North Fork, isn't very big. It's a fishing village full of old, ungentrified buildings and a harbor crammed with fishing boats and pleasure craft. Greenport is also the terminus of the Shelter Island Ferry and the end of the line for the North Fork branch of the Long Island Rail Road.

It's also the home of the **Townsend Manor Inn,** 714 Main St. (N.Y. 25; between Broad and Webb), Greenport, NY 11944 (tel. 516-477-2000), a collection of old houses arranged around a very appealing swimming pool and overlooking a marina on Stirling Basin. The main building is a wonderful old pillared Greek Revival house dating from 1835. Inside is a collection of wallpapered dining rooms (the inn operates a fairly big, moderately priced restaurant), a cozy parlor with a fireplace, a cocktail lounge and a small modern paneled office containing the reception desk.

The hotel rooms are located elsewhere, in the Waterfront Cottage, the Gingerbread House, and the Captain's House, respectively. Minimum-rate rooms in the Waterfront Cottage are sparkling clean, and have wall-to-wall carpeting, modestly appointed full baths, venetian blinds, curtains on tie-backs, and the vacation smell of a seaside cottage. The Gingerbread House, a neighboring Italianate mansion absorbed by the Townsend complex, has bigger rooms with nonperiod touches like pecky paneling and brightly colored carpeting. The Captain's House contains deluxe rooms fitted out with still newer decor and little private balconies. High-season double-occupancy rates (July 15 through August 21) range mostly from $65 to $85 during the week and $95 to $125 on weekends. During this same period there's a two-night minimum stay required on weekends. Overnight rates decline gradually on both sides of the peak season to a midwinter low of about $50 nightly.

The **Sound View Inn,** North Road, Greenport, NY 11944 (tel. 516/477-1910), seems like it's about ten blocks long. That's because it's only one room wide and every room faces the water across a private sandy beach. The place must be 30-odd years old. Really, it's just a big motel, each of whose units has sliding glass doors to a private balcony, two double beds, and modern motel furnishings. Also on the premises are a blindingly bright swimming pool protected from brisk breezes by glass windbreaks, a quartet of tennis courts across the road, and a popular moderately priced restaurant. Daily peak-season (June 30 to September 6th) double-occupancy rates are about $90 for standard rooms, and from $95 to $140 for variously sized suites with cooking facilities. Off-season (October 15 to May 10), double rooms cost about $65 a night.

The **Silver Sands Motel,** Silvermere Road (which intersects N.Y. 25 on the western edge of Greenport), Greenport, NY 11944 (tel. 516/477-0011), is a small, mint-condition, period-piece 1950s resort motel. It combines the seaside flavor of Greenport before the current real estate boom with amenities like a delightful private beach, a tranquil location well away from noisy traffic, and well-maintained rooms. The inner courtyard is flamingo pink; the outer walls below the stylized seahorse "S" are swimming-pool blue; the views across the beach are of Shelter Island and boat traffic on the shining waters. All rooms have color televisions, little refrigerators, and coffee makers. Double-occupancy rates, which include complimentary continental breakfast, range from $80 to $100 nightly (the latter being for a room with kitchenette) during the season (June 20 to September 15), and $70 to $90 in the spring and fall. There's a special price of $160 for any consecutive three nights during the spring and fall, with complimentary wine and cheese when you check in. Closed in January. Management "requests" a one-week minimum stay during the season. But if they've got a room that would otherwise go vacant, a shorter stay can be arranged.

Two North Fork guesthouses struck me as particularly appealing. The **Bartlett House Inn,** 503 Front St. (N.Y. 25), Greenport, NY 11944 (tel. 516/477-0371), is a roomy shingled house on the corner of 5th Street close to downtown Greenport. Built at the turn of the century by John Bartlett, a former New York State assemblyman, today it's a bed-and-breakfast with nine rooms. The interior is surprisingly elegant, with its big formal staircase, fluted columns with Corinthian capitals, parquet floors, and brass gasoliers. For a peak-season (June 17 to September 5) double with private bath and continental breakfast you'll pay about $69 a night; for $10 more you can have a fireplace room with a queen-size bed! Rates decline in further stages during the rest of the year, hitting a midwinter low of $57.

Alternatively you might try the **Gandalf House,** N.Y. 25, Laurel (a hamlet about 2½ miles west of Mattituck), NY 11948 (tel. 516/298-4769). This pink-towered Victorian house has no sign and but three rooms for rent. But it has a nice swimming pool, an appealing farm-country location, and bed-and-breakfast rates ranging from $45 to $60 a night double. The stylishly modernized interior boasts a grand piano, a profusion of potted plants, huge sofas, and a delicious Victorian country atmosphere.

It should be noted that almost all of the above recommendations offer special deals for extended or off-season stays.

RESTAURANTS

Don't forget the restaurant at the **Sound View Inn,** described above. Also fun is the **Jamesport Manor Inn,** Long Island's equivalent of the prairie-girt Victorian manse in the movie *Giant.* Located on Manor Lane (which runs between Sound Avenue and N.Y. 25) outside the village of Jamesport (tel. 516/722-3382), it's a highly wrought and heavily mansarded former sea captain's house plopped in the middle of farm fields. The interior has a bit of red-flocked wallpaper, a touch of Tudor timbering, and flocks of little tables covered with crisp pink cloths and clustered around atmospheric fireplaces. The food is fabulous. Luncheon dishes like fried shrimp, lobster Newburg, filet mignon en brochette, and a club sandwich cost between $6 and $9. À la carte dinner entrees, like broiled flounder amandine, sautéed bay scallops, seafood crêpes, stuffed sole, or a New York strip sirloin are priced mostly in the $10 to $15 bracket. Open for lunch from noon to 2 p.m. Monday through Friday; for dinner from 4 to 9 p.m. Monday through Friday, until 10 p.m. on Saturday; and on Sunday from noon to 8 p.m.

Also highly recommended is **Puerto Verde** ("green port," get it?), in the Stirling Harbor Yacht Basin (directions below), Greenport (tel. 516/477-1777). The place is all the way at the back of the marina, surrounded by docks full of gleaming boats. The room, which has a vague country-clubbish air to it, is large, modern, carpeted in deep blue, and surrounded with picture windows overlooking the boats. Cuisine is Spanish, and very comprehensible. At lunch there are gazpachos, tortillas, and various summery entrees (filet of sole, chicken in garlic, minute steak, seafood salad), priced from about $8 to $15. There's also a great "Special Complete Lunch" that changes daily, includes two courses (plus vegetable and coffee), and costs only about $8. The à la carte dinner menu is, of course, more extensive. Broiled salmon with hollandaise, scallops in onion and lobster sauce, veal in dry sherry wine, seafood in green sauce, etc., cost mostly between $12 and $20. Lunch is served daily from noon to 2:30 p.m.; dinner hours are 5 to 10 p.m. Sunday through Thursday, to 11 p.m. on Friday and Saturday. To get to Greenport's Stirling Harbor Yacht Basin, take Main Street (N.Y. 25) to the 900 block and turn east on Champlin Place. Follow Champlin to the end (only a couple of blocks) and turn right onto Manhanset Avenue. The entrance to Stirling Harbor will be immediately on your right.

You'll find more traditional American fare at the **Poop Deck,** Meeting House

Creek Road, Aquebogue (tel. 516/722-4220). This is a modern little seafood restaurant whose graveled parking lot is edged by the obligatory pilings and ropes. There's a wood-paneled cathedral-ceilinged bar up front and several pleasant dining rooms decorated with nautical pictures and brown tablecloths. In the back is a screened patio with a view of a small marina, the ideal place for a warm-weather meal. The lunch menu offers things like a chef's salad, omelets, fried scallops, burgers, and club sandwiches for around $5 to $10. At dinnertime you can choose from a list of à la carte entrees including broiled lobster tails, fresh broiled flounder, fisherman's platter, marinated New York sirloin, boneless Long Island duckling, etc., priced mostly around $15 to $20. Lunch is served daily from 11:30 a.m. to 3 p.m., and dinner from 5 to 10 p.m.; closed Monday after Labor Day. Aquebogue is less than four miles east of Riverhead on N.Y. 25. Look for the intersection of Edgar Avenue and N.Y. 25, take Edgar south following the signs to Peconic Bay Boulevard, cross the railroad tracks, pass the boatyard, and the restaurant will be on your right.

Also in Aquebogue, right on N.Y. 25, is a really good family-style diner called the **Modern Snack Bar** (tel. 516/722-3655). You can't miss the big old-fashioned sign with the swooping arrow. People come from all over the North Fork to enjoy seafood plates, "Dry Land Favorites" (as they call pot roast, meatloaf, fried chicken, and the like around here), and all manner of sandwiches. Particularly good are the seafood salads. This is the place for a $5 lunch or a $10 dinner, in cheery dining rooms attended by bustling young waitresses in white. Open Tuesday through Saturday from 11 a.m. to 9 p.m., and on Sunday from noon to 9 p.m.; closed Monday.

3. Shelter Island

Much too poised to get mixed up in the hullabaloo down on the South Fork (rather too refined in the opinion of many of its North Fork neighbors), Shelter Island pursues its own handsome and quiet path. The place really is pretty, and graced with lovely old 19th-century vacation "cottages" (some of which are quite grand), delightful Victorian villages, heavily wooded hills, pretty beaches, and a luxurious air of upper-middle-class isolation.

The biggest contributor to Shelter Island's air of remove is the ferry—or more correctly, the two ferries. These picturesque little boats steadily plow back and forth from 5 a.m. until about midnight. The trips aren't long; in fact, the south ferry is barely more than a puddle jump. But the fares are high. To get your car across the southern arm of Shelter Island Sound, which blocks N.Y. 114 from Sag Harbor to Greenport, costs $4 ($5 for a same-day round trip). It honestly looks as though a man with a good arm could throw a rock across this same stretch of water. When you reach the village of Shelter Island Heights on the north side of the island it'll cost another $3.50 to get over to Greenport ($5.50 for a same-day round trip). But the result of the high tolls and ferry-line waits is a delightful absence of heavy traffic throughout the island, even at the peak of the summer season.

Shelter Island's history is another version of New England's familiar litany of English pirates, religious settlers, dissenting Quakers, manorial land grants, hardworking farmers, enterprising Prohibition-era bootleggers, and suave vacationers from the city. The lovely summer houses of the latter, some of which have been passed from generation to generation, give the place considerable *ton*. Shelter Island's original manor house, started in the mid-17th century and significantly enlarged in the 18th, still stands. Called **Sylvester Manor,** it's located on the approximate center of the island (gates on N.Y. 114). It remains in private hands, on reduced but still extensive acreage.

Essentially, Shelter Island is a place where nothing happens, and everybody likes it just that way. The midnight curfew on the ferry does a great deal to keep the lid on things. No wee-hour carryings-on at Southampton discos, if you please. That is, not if you expect to get back here for the night. The southeastern portion of the island, occupying about a quarter of its total acreage, is an untouched nature conservancy called the **Mashomack Preserve.** The rest of the place is characterized by country roads, vacant meadows bordered by huge old trees, a handful of delightful Victorian villages with crooked streets and gingerbread cottages, dark forests, and lots of summer houses. There are also a couple of old-fashioned hotels, plus numerous boarding houses and inns, nearly all of which are within sight of some body or other of glittering water.

Worth exploration on foot is the village of **Shelter Island Heights,** located adjacent to the Greenport ferry. Lack of sustained traffic, perhaps more than anything else, contributes to the distinct feeling here of other times. The village is like a miniature San Francisco, its twisting roads decorated with little wooden gingerbread wedding cakes, and shaded by massive trees. Eastward across a small bay is the village of **Dering Harbor,** a quaint place notable for its tony waterfront houses. Midway along the southwestern coastline is **Nostrand Parkway,** a region of capacious old shingled mansions enjoying delicious sunset views across the bays. And everywhere in between are fresh, rural, and unspoiled vistas. Though many summer on Shelter Island, the place still seems remarkably uncrowded.

WHERE TO STAY AND EAT ON SHELTER ISLAND

Whether you're passing through or staying over a few days, try a meal at the **Clam Digger** in Shelter Island Heights. Sitting at a linen-covered table out on the terrace of a summer afternoon, in the lee of the wonderful old clapboard hotel, savoring sea breezes, listening to the rustle of leaves in the spreading maples, admiring the village view, is close to heaven itself. Fortunately, the food is good too. Lunch is served daily from noon to 3 p.m. and features things like local flounder, nachos, burgers, fish and chips, smoked turkey, avocado delight, etc., for mostly around $5, with some items ranging as high as $8 or so. Dinner is reasonable too; served from 6 to 9:30 p.m., it might be deep-fried jumbo shrimp, Tex-Mex ribs, seafood gumbo, chicken marsala, or whole crispy bass, priced mostly between $13 and $16. Open May 1 to September 15.

The old **Chequit Inn,** Shelter Island Heights, NY 11965 (tel. 516/749-0018), has great porches, antique rattan sets, and 38 old-fashioned rooms (26 with private bath) furnished with pieces that have seen many, many summers by the sea. Rates run from $45 to $80 a night. There are two restaurants and a bar that features nightly entertainment during the summer.

The **Ram's Head Inn,** Shelter Island Heights, NY 11965 (tel. 516/749-0811), despite its mailing address, is not in the Heights at all, but way out on Big Ram Island. This diminutive sandy hump is connected to the northeast portion of Shelter Island by flat, narrow causeways overlooking Coecles Harbor. The inn is an utterly charming shingled mansion, built actually as an inn on the eve of the great Stock Market Crash, in the Colonial Revival style. It has crisp white trim, shaped juniper trees by the front door, snappy green shutters, pots of geraniums and climbing roses alongside a crisp gravel circle out front. Inside, all is light, airy, and handsomely done up with fresh colonial wallpapers and glistening painted trim. There are but 17 rooms, all located on the second floor and furnished with flowered wallpaper, shipwheel mirrors, simple wooden furniture, and no TV or telephone. The look is very 1930s, which is to say that it's not exactly modern, but neither is it old. The inn is open from May 1 through October 31, during which time you'll pay $80 for a double with shared bath and $105 for a double with private bath; there's a two-bedroom suite with an adjoining bathroom for $165 a night. A very excellent deal.

Downstairs is a big restaurant dining room that looks as if it was lifted right out of a good sorority house at a Big Ten school. It has a handsome fireplace, lots of painted woodwork, and French doors overlooking a lawn and distant glimpses of water. It's open only for dinner, and the menu lists à la carte entrees such as boneless breast of duckling with cherries, baked Norwegian salmon, New York strip steak, breast of chicken, etc., for about $15 to $22. Also a great Sunday brunch for under $10. The inn additionally provides guests with the use of two 13-foot O'Day sloops and an on-site tennis court. This was my favorite place on Shelter Island. Closed during the winter.

There's a very different atmosphere at the **Dering Harbor Inn,** P.O. Box AD, Shelter Island Heights, NY 11965 (tel. 516/749-0900). This is not an inn at all but a stylish condominium within walking distance of both Dering Harbor and Shelter Island Heights. Besides an excellent central location there's a saltwater pool and a restaurant off the lobby. What does it look like? A Long Island country club, with a big ca. 1962 stone/wood/glass clubhouse looking across the parking lot at a slew of tennis courts. Inside is a two-story lobby with gold furniture and huge picture windows, the aforementioned restaurant, and rice-papered corridors leading back to a complex of newer shingled buildings that contain a total of 30 condominium units. Now each of these units belongs to somebody who's decorated it and furnished it to his own personal taste. Basically, the look is pale wood paneling, wall-to-wall carpeting, color TVs, and nice contemporary furniture. Units range in size from a two-bedroom/two-bath waterfront "cottage" to a "studio room", which is essentially a standard hotel room. Of the 30 units, probably about 15 to 17 are available to transients at any given time. The basic high-season double-occupancy rate for the studio is $95 nightly, $650 weekly. Rates go up, depending on unit size and view, to a top end of $220 daily and $1,500 weekly for two people in the cottage described above. Additional persons are charged $10 nightly, and there's a $25 nightly surcharge on Friday and Saturday nights. The rates decline in stages to an off-season (early spring or late fall) low of $50 to $130 nightly, double occupancy. Closed from November through March.

PART TWO

UPSTATE

XI

THE HUDSON RIVER VALLEY

1. DECIDING WHAT TO SEE AND DO
2. THE LOWER HUDSON
3. THE MID-HUDSON REGION

The alert reader scanning the headings above will doubtless wonder what in the world has happened to the "Upper" Hudson. Well, the upper portion of the river north of Albany, while pleasant enough, is just not on any tourist trail. Important destinations lying close to the Hudson's upper reaches, notably Saratoga Springs, are fully described elsewhere.

Three-quarters of the Hudson River Valley—148 miles' worth of it—lies south of Albany anyway. It's an area rife with legend, rich with history, and quite beautiful despite over three centuries of civilization (read pollution, visual and otherwise). Actually, water quality in the Hudson has been steadily improving for at least a decade. These days people actually swim in many parts of it. I have myself, and on numerous occasions.

Not only swimmers but fishermen are gradually returning to this most beautiful of American rivers. So what if a few species are too permeated with mercury or PCBs, or whatever continues to spew from the pipes of unreconstructed upriver "employers"? The important thing is that fewer fish glow (or whatever polluted fish do) now than in many ages past. A really "clean" river seems eminently possible . . . someday. And whereas one would certainly think twice before taking a dip off, say, West 79th Street, moms and tots frolic in the water as close as Croton, not 30 miles from Midtown. From Poughkeepsie north to Hudson, save for the immediate environs of a few cement plants, people swim and waterski all the time.

But enough of this aquatic pep talk. The visitor will want to know what else lies in these leafy hills and why one should bother driving up here to have a look.

1. Deciding What to See and Do

The Hudson Valley's biggest attraction is probably the scenery. It's a perfectly beautiful place in which to drive around. The visual range—from the sheer and mighty drops of the Palisades to the subtle rolling hills of Westchester to the dramatic chasms of the Hudson Highlands and the startling Catskill vistas north of Hyde Park—is as wide as it is satisfying. So that's one thing.

If you're big on historic houses and/or architecturally magnificent old mansions, then that's another reason to explore the Hudson River Valley. It has tons of them, from pre-Revolutionary manors to Edwardian palaces. Happily a great number of these are open to the public. The valley has been a favored locale for country estates for centuries. During the last one, romantic-minded plutocrats graced more than one river-view mountaintop with pinnacled and crenelated castles. Many of these old mansions still stand and are highly scenic, to say the least. They have even provoked frequent characterization of the Hudson as "America's Rhine." This particular notion may be ambitious, but the castles really do look grand.

Antiquing is another pastime (compulsion? vice?) that draws considerable numbers of people up the Hudson. Indeed, the economy of many a village in these parts would seem to rest entirely on its collection of antiques shops. Opportunities for browsing are considerable. I don't know about bargains, but there sure is a lot of old stuff for sale between New York and Albany.

Complementing everything mentioned above is the valley's abundance of sophisticated inns and restaurants. The fact is, no excursion to a historic mansion, scenic park, or quaint antique district would be complete without a good meal at someplace quaint. This fact of touristic life has not been lost upon the locals, and they have acted accordingly.

Many roads lead up and down the Hudson, some very fast and some very ugly. As much as possible I've suggested routes along scenic roads. Not every city or attraction has been included. But I think you'll find the highlights are here, plus an ample selection of places to stay and eat. Now then, let's begin.

2. The Lower Hudson

Everything in the Lower Hudson can be seen on a day trip. Which is just as well, since there aren't very many interesting hotels in the area. We're dealing here with a bit less than 50 miles of river valley, stretching from New York City in the south to the Hudson Highlands in the north. The Highlands, if you've never been, are a treat. They're notable for romantically gloomy mountains with very high, cliff-hanging, serpentine roads. These roads are cut out of the sheer faces of rock. One bears the wonderful name of **Storm King Highway,** and from its every curve you're confronted alternately with vistas of mountaintops and the spectacle of the Hudson curling along the bottom of a stone chasm. The scenery is almost Swiss, albeit in a gentler Hudson Valley idiom. And of course the Highlands are also the site of the famous U.S. Military Academy at West Point, most excellent of day-trip destinations.

STARTING OUT: NEW YORK CITY TO TARRYTOWN

Wherever you are when you get into your car, plan on leaving town via the West Side Highway. This river-edge parkway, actually part of a Depression-era beautification project for Riverside Park, sits atop the formerly open tracks of New York Central's Hudson Division. Throughout recent memory it has been criticized as cutting the public off from the water's edge. This is quite true. You have to be a pretty laid-back individual to find real rest and refreshment (the supposed point of urban parks) with six lanes of traffic howling back and forth behind you.

But for the people in the *cars,* the West Side Highway (or Henry Hudson Parkway, as most of it is properly called) is quite another matter. As a matter of fact, it's about the most visually impressive approach to and from a great metropolis that one could imagine. The sheer size of everything, which after all is New York's hallmark,

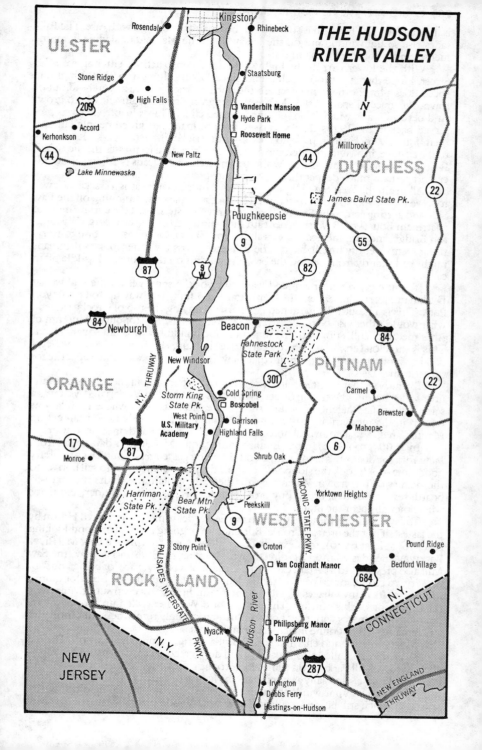

THE HUDSON RIVER VALLEY

ULSTER

Kingston
Rosendale
Rhinebeck
Stone Ridge
Staatsburg
High Falls
209
Accord
Kerhonkson
44
New Paltz
Lake Minnewaska

Vanderbilt Mansion
Hyde Park
Roosevelt Home
44
Millbrook
DUTCHESS
22

James Baird State Pk.
Poughkeepsie
9
55
87
9W
82

84
Newburgh
Beacon
84
New Windsor
Fahnestock
State Park
PUTNAM
22
301

ORANGE
Storm King
State Pk.
Cold Spring
Boscobel
Carmel
West Point
Garrison
Brewster
**U.S. Military
Academy**
Highland Falls
Mahopac
17
Shrub Oak
6
Monroe
87

Harriman
State Pk.
Bear Mtn.
State Pk.
Yorktown Heights
Peekskill
WEST CHESTER
9
Stony Point
Croton
Pound Ridge
Van Cortlandt Manor
Bedford Village
684
ROCK LAND
N.Y.
CONNECTICUT

Nyack
Philipsburg Manor
Tarrytown

NEW
JERSEY
287
NEW ENGLAND
THRUWAY

Irvington
Dobbs Ferry
Hastings-on-Hudson

is inescapable. The Hudson is so wide—it holds aircraft carriers with ease. The Palisades rise so high and grand on the Jersey side. The Manhattan skyline is so immense, and it goes on for so long.

With the lower part of the highway under reconstruction, enter above 57th Street. Hope there isn't too much traffic, since tooling along smoothly at highway speed does a lot for the total effect. To the north in the distance as you head out of town, the graceful span of the George Washington Bridge begins slowly to grow. And beyond it are, what? Wild-looking forested cliffs! This valuable view was preserved back in the 1920s thanks to the efforts of many farsighted people (among them John D. Rockefeller, Jr.) who established a series of interstate parks. It suggests to the city eye, in a vivid manner, the possibility of the rural fastnesses that lie ahead. It declares to Manhattan that the world to which this river leads is different, far older, and perhaps much deeper than city types are prepared to admit.

All in all, the West Side Highway/Henry Hudson Parkway is a crackerjack way to leave New York. So don't be tempted by the faster parkways spinning off the East Side and cutting across the Bronx. Take the parkway instead, past the curling miles of apartment houses on Riverside, beneath the whining spans of the George Washington Bridge, and into the deep forests above Fort Tryon. Once past the bridge everything seems weirdly uninhabited. The Palisades across the water look as if Indians might pad silently from behind the broken boulders on the shore and paddle off in canoes.

If you're good with maps and want to savor the spot, get off the highway at Dyckman Street (the last exit in Manhattan) and find your way up to **Fort Tryon Park.** This is a beautifully gardened city park occupying the top of a rocky ridge in what would otherwise be the West 190s. It contains the Metropolitan Museum of Art's medieval collection, housed in a monastic building with a tall square tower. This is the **Cloisters,** to which you can drive right up, climb out of your car (legal parking spots abound), and admire that view. It certainly does whet the appetite for the road ahead.

By the way, that forested hill to the north of Fort Tryon, on the other side of the little valley holding Dyckman Street, is **Inwood Hill Park.** In Victorian days it was a select countrified neighborhood of suburban estates, some of whose foundations remain in the modern-day park. Inwood Hill is about as lonely as you can get on Manhattan. On that equivocal note, let's get back in the car and press northward.

In 1800 it took the famous English tourist John Maude four days to sail from New York to Albany in a sloop with 24 other paying passengers. Four days was pretty good time too. It took the sloop *Sally* a whole day, for instance, just to sail upriver to the vicinity of Tarrytown. When they got there, the captain tossed the anchor overboard, sent a boat to shore to buy provisions for his passengers' dinner, and that's where they all spent the night.

Today it takes 25 minutes to get to the East Side from the Tarrytown Hilton by the fastest, if not the prettiest, route. But since we're going to travel on good-looking roads (or at least try to), my next advice is to leave New York via the **Saw Mill River Parkway.** Besides connecting directly with the Henry Hudson Parkway, the Saw Mill also preserves to a certain extent the illusion of woodsy space, of being "out" of the city. Actually, lower Westchester is densely developed and has been for quite a long time. Its many villages had for all intents and purposes been suburbanized by the beginning of this century. The post–World War II era filled up a lot of the remaining open spaces with tract houses. But a broodingly romantic 19th-century air still remains—if not quite intact—in many places.

Most romantic and charming are the villages right along the Hudson. The old Albany Post Road, called also Broadway and designated on road maps as U.S. 9, parallels the Saw Mill Parkway on a line closer to the river's edge. It's a slow road with a lot of local traffic, especially as it traverses the length of the city of Yonkers. But from northern Yonkers up it winds through a series of leafy and appealing old suburbs, several of which still possess a village-like charm. A good place to leave the Saw Mill and cut over to Broadway/U.S. 9 would be either at Odel Avenue in Yonkers, or Farragut Parkway in Hastings, both of which are exits on the Saw Mill.

Interestingly, Broadway/U.S. 9 is an extension of the same Broadway that runs the length of Manhattan Island. Long stretches of it, even as far south as Yonkers, are still lined with ornate stone walls, mute witnesses of the vanished 19th-century suburban estates that once proliferated hereabouts. There are lots of old mansions still along U.S. 9, as well as new suburban developments, all sorts of old Victorian buildings, splendid churches, big trees, great river views, and littlish shopping centers. This is not the land of the mega-mall. But even though the area's developed, it still manages to preserve a faint but very evocative countrified air.

Hastings-on-Hudson is the first town north of Yonkers. In many ways it's just another old suburb, but once it was the home of famous newspaper publisher Horace Greeley ("Go west, young man!") and Admiral David Farragut (Civil War hero of Mobile Bay and namesake of Farragut Parkway). Just north of the village, overlooking the river at 71 Broadway, is a terrific old castle designed ca. 1850 by the famous Alexander Jackson Davis for one E. B. Strange of New York. It was converted years ago to a school, and none too delicately. However, it's still a pretty astonishing-looking old house.

The next village, less than two miles distant, is **Dobbs Ferry,** notable for a swanky girls' prep school called the Masters School. At the center of the Masters campus is a wildly ornate and highly typical (for the area) mansion called Estherwood. You might want to detour the block or so off Broadway onto Clinton Avenue and take a look. Estherwood was built by a businessman named McComb and given to the school in the 1890s. Clinton Avenue is just south of the shopping center in the middle of Dobbs Ferry.

Broadway grows ever leafier and lawnier as one continues north from Dobbs Ferry into the ritzy precincts of **Ardsley** and **Ardsley-on-Hudson.** Romantic gatehouses can be seen along the verges of Broadway now, leading occasionally to subdivisions of split-levels beyond which Tudor mansions glower over reduced acreage. A few of the old estates are still intact, albeit in sometimes heavy institutional hands. Their open spaces still lend to the neighborhood an air of roominess and luxury. A particularly gorgeous one is Nevis, at 136 S. Broadway, the Stanford White remodeled mansion of Alexander Hamilton's grandson. It now belongs to Columbia University. It's not open to the public, and only partly visible from the road, but the rolling fields and forests of Nevis still conjure vivid images of an older Broadway.

In another mile you'll be in the village of **Irvington.** Until recently, wild woods and a romantically ruined gate stood at the top of Irvington's Main Street, at the intersection of U.S. 9. Now the site contains a very big condo, its "townehome" complexes draped artistically over rocky outcroppings, its tall trees preserved, its air of mystery and the past utterly expunged. Main Street descends steeply from U.S. 9 down the river. It's really very charming, without being a major attraction. The buildings are old and the views are great. A 19th-century atmosphere prevails, particularly on the side streets.

By the time of the First World War, Irvington was arguably the most opulent and fashionable of the close-in Hudson River suburbs. Chauncey Depew, president of the New York Central, lived here; so did Cyrus Field, the man who developed the first Atlantic cable; so did Louis Comfort Tiffany, of art-glass fame, and Albert Bierstadt, the renowned landscape painter; and so did Madame C. W. Walker. This latter lady was a black millionairess whose fortune stemmed from a patented hair straightener. Her very fine mansion, which she called **Villa Lewaro,** is a neoclassical affair with a semicircular columned portico. It still stands on Broadway, a bit north of the Irvington light at the corner of Fargo Lane. Madame Walker's house was designed in 1917 by Vertner Tandy, the first black member of the American Institute of Architects. A close family friend was Enrico Caruso, who coined the word "Lewaro" from the name of Madame Walker's daughter, Lelia Walker Robinson. The place today is an old folks' home, clearly visible from the road.

Irvington got its name from a devoted local resident whose famous and historic home is now, by a stroke of zoning irony, located in the adjoining village of Tarrytown. I refer of course to Washington Irving, perhaps America's first celebrated man of letters. His delectable Dutch cottage, called **Sunnyside,** is located at the foot of Sunnyside Lane and open to the public. Actually, the original Dutch house was burned by the British during the Revolution on the orders of Gen. Sir John Vaughan. Pesky patriots had made a hangout of the place and Vaughan was out to teach them a lesson. Irving bought the ruins in 1835 and converted it into a highly romantic small estate reflecting the romantic architectural tastes of the time, as well as his own interest in the Dutch antecedents of the region.

In Irving's day Sunnyside was the object of pilgrimages by statesmen and literary lions alike. The master of the house was, after all, the famous chronicler of Diedrich Knickerbocker, Rip Van Winkle, and Sleepy Hollow's Headless Horseman. Thackeray, Louis Napoleon, and Oliver Wendell Holmes were all guests at Sunnyside. While the house isn't large, it certainly does have charm. Irving's descendants "mansionized" it considerably after his death. But all Victorian accretions have since been systematically demolished, leaving the place exactly (one supposes) as it looked to Irving. Today costumed guides lead visitors through period rooms filled with Irving memorabilia. Outside, you're free to wander around really pretty grounds with great views of the river.

Sunnyside (tel. 914/591-8763) belongs to an outfit called **Historic Hudson Valley,** which owns and operates other historic sites on the Hudson, some of which are described below. A single-visit ticket to Sunnyside costs $5 for adults, $4.50 for seniors, and $3.50 for juniors. Sunnyside is open daily from 10 a.m. to 5 p.m., with the last tour starting at 4 p.m. Closed Thanksgiving, Christmas, and New Year's. For further information, call Historic Hudson Valley at 914/631-8200.

The next stop, not even a mile distant, is also a major attraction in the region. It's **Lyndhurst,** the crenellated castle of robber baron Jay Gould, donated in 1961 to the National Trust for Historic Preservation by Gould's daughter, Anna, Duchess of Talleyrand-Périgord. What a lot of distance there is between that aristocratic title and Gould's days of manipulating Erie Railroad stock. Literature available at the site takes rather a revisionist position on Gould. But then again, one doesn't expect to see pamphlets for sale in his own house branding him as a liar and a thief.

The main gate to Lyndhurst is on a stretch of Broadway that's lined with impressive walls and leafy old forests. One of the last estates in private hands hereabouts is immediately south of, and contiguous to, the Lyndhurst property. Called Belvidere, it's the residence of the mysterious Rev. Sun Myung Moon. The fortified gates are impossible to miss.

The National Trust describes Lyndhurst as "the beginning and culmination of residential Gothic Revival architecture in America." Put more simply, it's the be-all and end-all of authentic American-born castles. Of course, it's a whole lot smaller than a great English country house. But it's still a fabulous-looking place, pretty big as American mansions go, and of great historic and architectural significance. The original portion of the house was built in 1838 for one William Paulding in the then highly new and fashionable Gothic style. The architect was Alexander Jackson Davis, and this commission helped establish him as a major new force in American architecture. A fellow named George Merrit bought the place in 1864 and had Davis expand it to its present proportions. It's a neat job and you'd hardly know the whole house wasn't built of a piece. Gould became the owner in 1880. He cherished Lyndhurst throughout his tenancy, preserving the house and adding only to the outbuildings, which in themselves are fairly fantastic.

About 60-odd acres remain around the Gould mansion; the hilly portion of the estate on the inland side of Broadway has, alas, become a housing development (albeit not a huge one). Lyndhurst includes, besides the mansion and its original furnishings, a bowling alley, an immense greenhouse (currently under restoration, it must be seen to be believed), various cottages, a stable complex, a noble indoor swimming pool, and views of the Hudson and the Tappan Zee that are, as they say, to "die" from. Lyndhurst is also the scene of numerous events, such as the Antique Auto Show, the Lyndhurst Dog Show, the Craft Show, the Outdoor Antique Show, etc. The grounds are open between May 1 and October 31, Tuesday through Sunday from 10 a.m. to 4:15 p.m. Between November 3 and December 31 the estate is only open on weekends, from 10 a.m. to 3:30 p.m. Admission is $5 for adults, $4 for seniors, $3 for students; kids under 6 are free. The entrance is via the original main gatehouse on Broadway. For information about events, etc., the number to call is 914/631-0046.

Just north of Lyndhurst is the village of **Tarrytown,** which has over the years become a town of some size. A big General Motors plant shares the shoreline with new condominiums and a very pleasant "downtown" area of older low-rise buildings. Steep hills immediately to the east are covered with mature trees and old houses. The view from here is of that great broadening of the Hudson known as the Tappan Zee, bordered in the distance by the cliffs of the Nyack Range. Tarrytown is where, on September 23, 1780, a trio of locals captured Major John André, the British spy who contrived with Benedict Arnold to betray West Point. For most of its history it was the eastern terminus of a ferry, rendered obsolete by the huge new Tappan Zee Bridge. Actually, the bridge is not so new anymore, having been opened back in 1955. Its construction was a sore point with Anna, Duchess of Talleyrand-Périgord at Lyndhurst, whose view it substantially altered.

Towering on a hilltop overlooking the multilaned approaches to the Tappan Zee Bridge is another picturesque castle. This is **Carrollcliffe,** a local landmark since 1900. Built by Brigadier General Howard Carroll, it has been an office building since 1941. The architecturally incompatible town houses crouching at its feet are relatively new intrusions. Picturesque gatehouses and walls still survive along the original property line, particularly the impressive main gate house on White Plains Road (N.Y. 119).

About two miles north of the New York State Thruway/Tappan Zee Bridge intersection with U.S. 9 is **Philipsburg Manor,** (tel. 914/631-3992), a 20-acre compound located just north of the intersection of N.Y. 448 and Broadway/U.S. 9 in the village of North Tarrytown. This is a painstaking reconstruction of the 17th-century manor house, mill, dam, kitchen garden, granary, wharf, and mill pond of Frederick Philipse. Today it's a property of the aforementioned Historic Hudson Valley. The Philipse family was a major landholder in pre-Revolutionary New York. This modest-looking manor house was once the nerve center of a 52,500-acre estate, a considerable spread by anyone's standards. Frederick Philipse III made the personally honorable but strategically lamentable decision to side with the Brits during the Revolution. Result: Postwar arrest and confiscation of his property.

More costumed guides will take you around and describe life in colonial times. The place has been restored to its appearance ca. 1750. Although luxurious for the wilderness, it is quite simple even in comparison to little Sunnyside. Occupied as a private house until 1940, it was saved by John D. Rockefeller, Jr., and opened in its restored state in 1969. Daily hours are 10 a.m. to 5 p.m.; admission is $5 for adults, $4 for seniors, and $3 for students. Those interested in the Revolutionary period will love the place.

Perhaps you've noticed the name Rockefeller cropping up repeatedly around here. That's because nearby Pocantico Hills, just northeast of Tarrytown, is the Rockefellers' home turf. It's not where the first John D. was born, but it's where he built his great mansion **Kykuit** (still standing, still private) and where considerable numbers of his descendants have, over the years, built a compound of adjoining estates in the midst of a greenbelt of some thousands of acres. When Gov. Nelson Rockefeller died, he willed his share in Kykuit to the National Trust for Historic Preservation. As yet there are no provisions for the public to see the place. From the air it's stupendous indeed. N.Y. 448 (here known as Bedford Road), which starts at U.S. 9 in North Tarrytown, winds its way through the very heart of the Rockefeller compound. You can't see Kykuit from the road, or much of any of the other houses either. But you can admire the picture-perfect village of **Pocantico Hills,** really a company town for the Rockefeller estates, and savor the undiluted air of privilege that drips from the very trees.

Where to Eat and Where to Stay Near Tarrytown

Benny's, just south of the Irvington light on U.S. 9 at 6 S. Broadway, Irvington (tel. 914/591-9811), is a great little local seafood house with an informal atmosphere, moderate prices, and excellent food. There is a bar just inside the door, a small front dining room with captain's chairs and plastic tablecloths, and a larger dining room in back decorated with murals of fishing boats, white-painted paneling, and harpoons on the walls. Lunch might be something like fried scallops with french fries and slaw, fried oysters, a hot roast beef sandwich, or a chicken salad plate, priced anywhere from $5 to $7. At dinner the à la carte entrees are mostly in the $12 to $20 range and include broiled swordfish, bluefish, flounder, veal and pork chops, steak, etc. Open Monday through Saturday for lunch from 11:30 a.m. to 2:30 p.m. and for dinner from 5 to 10 p.m. Only dinner is served on Sunday, from 1:30 until 10 p.m.

The **Gallery Restaurant and Wine Bar,** at 24 Main Street (just off U.S. 9) in Tarrytown (tel. 914/631-4409), has a wonderful art deco/modern decor. Lunch, from salads to hot dishes, is served Monday through Friday from noon to 3:30 p.m. and costs $2.50 to $9. Dinner features unique American cuisine and is available Monday through Thursday from 6 to 9:30 p.m., and until 10:30 p.m. on Friday and Saturday. The dinner will range in cost from $15 to $22, with a Sunday champagne brunch offered between noon and 3:30 p.m. for a fixed rate of $13.95. In keeping with the wine bar theme, the Gallery offers an extensive selection by glass or bottle of *only* American wines.

A grander experience can be had in nearby Tarrytown, in a former mansion called **Tappan Hill,** Highland Avenue, Tarrytown (tel. 914/631-3030). Mark Twain once owned this property, but it was a banker named Jacques Halle who in 1915 built the stone mansion that is today's restaurant. Despite modern additions, it's still a pretty zowie old house, complete with an unforgettably vast circular marble hallway. Meals are served in various modern rooms as well as in the former drawing room, library (my favorite), and on an immense enclosed terrace. Some, but not many, tables have river views. The à la carte luncheon menu features things like casserole of rock Cornish game hen, sautéed chicken breast, Norwegian smoked salmon, filet mignon, double lamb chops, etc., priced between about $15 to $25. Many of the same items appear on the evening menu, along with things like medallions of lamb with mint sauce, Atlantic salmon steak, baked saddle of rabbit, a steamed vegetarian plate, etc., mostly priced at about $15 to $30. Tappan Hill serves lunch daily from noon to 2:30 p.m., and dinner from 5:30 to 9:30 p.m. On Saturday and Sunday there's a special brunch for about $17 served from noon to 3 p.m. The big trick might be to find the place. If you can get to Benedict Avenue, which intersects U.S. 9 a half mile north of the Thruway, and then turn right, you'll be close. Go up the hill on Benedict and watch for the signs to Tappan Hill. It's an experience; you'll like it.

I'm not a fan of mass-produced hotel accommodations. But the **Tarrytown Hilton,** immediately south of the Thruway on U.S. 9 at 455 S. Broadway, Tarrytown, NY 10591 (tel. 914/631-5700), must be the exception that proves the rule. This is an amazingly nice place, amazing mostly because of all the things they didn't do. The pool, for example, is not located right next to the highway. Instead, it's surrounded by gardens, overlooked by a delightful awninged restaurant, and nowhere near the noisy road. The rooms, instead of being stacked up in a tacky modern highrise, are arranged in three tasteful low-rise wings. Besides the expected Hilton quality furnishings and color televisions, accommodations all have little private terraces or sliding glass doors that lead to shady lawns furnished with yellow plastic chaises. What a difference from the hermetically sealed overnight environments of the competition. There are also tennis courts, a fitness club, a coffeeshop, a big restaurant, a little bar with dancing, babysitters on call (kids are free in your room regardless of age), even a jogging course around the flower-filled property. I was prepared not to like it, and to my surprise discovered that it was hands down the nicest (not even the most expensive) place to stay in all of lower Westchester. Rates for single occupancy range from about $105 to $145 nightly; doubles pay $20 more; special weekend rates available. Management also offers good weekend and package deals, usually including discounts at Sleepy Hollow Restoration properties, maybe a champagne brunch, a complimentary *Times,* a deluxe room, stuff like that, for a less than normal tariff.

Equivalent accommodations in town would cost twice as much. But town, it should be repeated, is only half an hour away on the Thruway.

ANTIQUES-LOVERS' DETOUR—THE TAPPAN ZEE BRIDGE TO NYACK

Flanked by Tarrytown on the east and Nyack on the west, the Tappan Zee is a widening of the Hudson measuring about 2½ by 12 or so miles. The word "Tappan" is an Indian term for "cold spring." "Zee" is Dutch for "sea." "Nyack" possibly means "antiques shoppe" in some obscure Lenni-Lenape tongue.

Nyack can be a day trip all by itself. From New York, a good scenic route would be via the West Side Highway to the George Washington Bridge (upper level, if possible). As soon as you cross the bridge, take the first exit onto the **Palisades Interstate Parkway.** The scenic overlooks shortly after you join this parkway are definitely worth a stop. The panorama of Manhattan, the George Washington Bridge, the Hudson, and, on a clear day, even Long Island Sound, is memorable. Continue on the Palisades Parkway to Exit 9. Then take the New York State Thruway eastbound to Exit 11, "Nyack." Go left at the foot of the exit and you'll be on Main Street.

To get to **Nyack** from Tarrytown (and if you like antiques shops, you're going to want to go), return to the intersection of U.S. 9 and the New York State Thruway. Follow the signs to the Tappan Zee Bridge, which is in sight of the intersection. Crossing the Tappan Zee is visually quite spectacular. Behind you are the scenic shores and mansion-crested hills of Irvington and Tarrytown. The castellated towers of Lyndhurst loom picturesquely on a lawny slope. If the day's clear, you'll have a fine view of the George Washington Bridge and the spiky Manhattan skyline beyond. Ahead of you on the left are the steep cliffs of Grandview. And to the right is the village (really a little city) of Nyack.

In order to get into the right part of Nyack, detailed directions are again in order. Take the first exit after the bridge, follow the signs to Nyack (a spaghetti-like intersection, but just keep following those Nyack signs) until you come to the red blinker at the bottom of the Nyack ramp. You now should be on South Franklin Street. Proceed straight to the second traffic light, which should be Main Street. Turn right and proceed a couple of blocks toward the river until you reach the light at Broadway. There are some antiques shops on Main, but the bulk of them lie about four blocks south on South Broadway.

At the center of the district (the block with the Vintage Car Store) there must be a dozen antiques shops on a single block. The streetscape is Victorian and small scale. There are lots of trees and glimpses of the river. Parking on or adjacent to South Broadway isn't too difficult.

What sort of antiques shops? Well, they're filled to their rafters with wood and metal and rust and lots of paintings. Don't expect Louis Louis or George the Whatever; do expect a fair number of crafts stores (some entrepreneurs evidently have begun to hedge their bets). Most of the merchandise in Nyack seems to be American in origin, the bulk dating from the last century and the early part of the present one. The sight of old ladies exclaiming, "Why, I *gave* one just like that to Mabel!" is commonplace. But of course, that particular remark is part of antiquing everywhere.

Besides buying old stuff there isn't an awful lot to do in Nyack. Exploring the village itself is pleasant if you like quaint old houses and an updated Victorian village atmosphere. Broadway continues southward through old, leafy districts, with a great air of calm. Some of the houses are very gingerbready. Taken the other direction Broadway will bring you to Upper Nyack, a modest westbank version of the glories of Irvington. Helen Hayes lives in Upper Nyack.

Getting a Bite to Eat in Nyack

There's a good, oldtime-looking bar–cum–burger joint smack in the middle of the antiques on South Broadway. It's the **Old Fashion,** 83 S. Broadway (tel. 914/ 358-8114), and it serves burgers, quiches, salads, sandwiches, and full meals at dinnertime to the accompaniment of rock-and-roll music. Busy bar against the side wall; attractive youthful clientele; open seven days a week until 4 a.m. Also good is the **Skylark,** 84 Main St. (tel. 914/358-7988), a typical, moderately priced small-town family restaurant/coffeeshop. The lights are bright; there are plenty of seats at the counter, as well as at flocks of small tables; open for breakfast-lunch-dinner until 8 p.m. daily (until 5 p.m. on Sunday).

A very stylish alternative to the above (for dinner only) is **Raoul's,** 134 Main St., at South Franklin Street (tel. 914/353-1355). This swell-looking place is housed in Nyack's former Village Hall, now renovated and fitted out with demure red banquettes, a great mural of the Tappan Zee, elaborately stamped tin ceilings, mirrored walls, and beautiful sprays of fresh flowers. It's dim and cool and romantic, and very French/Alsatian. On Thursday, Friday, Saturday, and Sunday, there is only a prix-fixe menu offering three different complete meals priced from $14 to $20. On Saturday night there is live music from 10 p.m. to 2 a.m. Another menu lists numerous and inventive hot and cold appetizers priced from about $5. The food is great, and the atmosphere manages to be elegant and relaxed at the same time. Open from 6 to 10 p.m. for dinner only (from noon to 3 p.m. on Sunday); closed Monday, Tuesday, and Wednesday. Check out the wine cellar in the back; it occupies a former jail cell.

Boulderberg Manor is located some 15 miles north of Nyack on U.S. 9W in Tomkins Cove (tel. 914/786-5386). This Gothic Revival mansion was constructed in 1858 of cast-in-place concrete and is considered the earliest cement building in the state. Its ornately detailed interiors now house a fine restaurant, which offers lunch from noon to 3 p.m. for $7 to $12, and dinner between the hours of 5 and 10 p.m. for about $13 to $22. Dinner may include such dishes as fruits de mer Fra Diavolo, chicken Cordon Bleu, steak Delmonico, etc. Sunday champagne brunch is available from noon to 3 p.m. at a $14.95 fixed rate. Closed Monday.

Back on the Road

South Broadway will take you back to the New York State Thruway. From there you can recross the river on the Tappan Zee Bridge, and then either return straight to New York (if it's been a day trip) or continue up the valley.

NORTHWARD TO BEDFORD

One of Westchester County's most enjoyable attractions is the schedule of outdoor summer concerts at **Caramoor,** the former Katonah estate of Mr. and Mrs. Walter Tower Rosen. Started 40 years ago in memory of a son lost in World War II, the **Caramoor Music Festival** has grown into a world-famous event. The greatest names and finest talents in classical music perform in the Spanish Courtyard and the Venetian Theater (the mansion is Mediterranean in style) every season from late June until the end of August. Concert programming runs the gamut from chamber music to solo recitals, to symphony, to opera. Says the *New York Times,* "Caramoor is one of the few [outdoor festivals] that makes a persistent effort to present something different from what we have been having indoors all the rest of the year."

On top of which, the Rosen estate itself is also something to see. Built in the 1930s, it incorporates whole rooms removed from sundry European châteaux and palazzi. The furnishings, all original, are equally sumptuous. As are the manicured grounds. The admission to the "museum" (the Rosens' house) is $4 for adults and $2 for kids under 12. It's open from mid-May until the end of October, Wednesday through Saturday from 11 a.m. to 4 p.m., and on Sunday from 1 to 4 p.m. Concert prices vary depending on who's appearing. For concert information, telephone Caramoor at 914/232-5035. Alternatively, write to them at Caramoor, P.O. Box R, Katonah, NY 10536, and ask for a current program.

The best way to get to Caramoor from Tarrytown is via I-684 (I-287 from the Tappan Zee Bridge connects directly with I-684 near White Plains). Get off I-684 at Katonah; take N.Y. 35 for about a quarter of a mile to N.Y. 22 and turn right (south). Stay on N.Y. 22 (also called Jay Street) for about three miles to Girdle Ridge Road (N.Y. 137). Go left onto Girdle Ridge; the gates to Caramoor are half a mile farther on your right.

Caramoor is located in an estate-filled neighborhood whose easeful countrified look is maintained at the cost of considerable real estate taxes. A little over three miles south of Girdle Ridge Road on N.Y. 22 is **Bedford Village,** a bit of New England hardly over an hour from New York City. There are Bedfords all around here (Bedford Hills, Bedford Center, Bedford Village), but the nicest one is Bedford Village. At its center is the **Bedford Green,** a rolling manicured triangle surrounded by restored 18th- and 19th-century buildings. Among these is a courthouse dating from 1787, and 1838 post office, and a carpenter Gothic Presbyterian church erected in 1872. Also present are many very attractive big old houses. If you're an explorer, roads of note in the area include Guard Hill Road, Broad Brook Road, and McLean Street, as well as numerous leafy and exclusive lanes that run in between. By the way, N.Y. 22, from Bedford all the way down to Valhalla, is a pleasant alternative to I-684.

There's another historic house in the Bedford area which you might also like to see. It's the **John Jay Homestead State Historic Site,** located on Jay Street just north of Girdle Ridge Road (tel. 914/232-5651). To refresh your memory, John Jay served as first chief justice of the Supreme Court, president of the Second Continental Congress, minister to Spain, and two times as governor of New York State. His spacious gambrel-roofed country house was built here in 1797, and occupied by Jay descendants until 1954. Today it's been restored to its appearance in Jay's day, and is open to the public free of charge from Memorial Day to Labor Day, Wednesday through Saturday from 10 a.m. to 5 p.m., on Sunday from 1 to 5 p.m.

Good Places to Eat Near Bedford

Herewith, three unusual recommendations. The first is **La Camelia,** located in nearby Mount Kisco on N.Y. 117 just north of the center of town and quite close to Guard Hill Road (tel. 914/666-2466). It's an old clapboard house with an early American look, tucked up on a hillside away from the commercial excesses on the highway. There's an awning out front and a profusion of blooming bushes. Inside is a collection of charming small rooms with low ceilings, antique fireplaces, old rugs, and flocks of tables covered with crisp white cloths. The place is very popular, both at lunch and at dinner. Cuisine is nouvelle Spanish. At lunch diners choose from a reasonably priced menu that includes things like mussels with saffron, chicken with spring vegetables, paella valenciana, chef's salad, etc., priced mostly between $8 and $14. At dinner a typical main course such as duckling with dry prunes, fish of the day, chicken and lobster with vegetables, veal scallop, etc., will run only from $13 to about $20. Lunch is served Tuesday through Friday from noon until 3 p.m.; open for dinner Tuesday through Saturday from 6 to 9:30 p.m.; only the dinner menu is available on Sunday, from 1 to 9 p.m.; closed Monday.

About equidistant from Bedford (four or so miles), but located in the opposite direction, is the **Inn at Pound Ridge,** on N.Y. 137 in Pound Ridge (tel. 914/764-5779). Valet parking sets a tony note, as does the black and white awning and the old colonial architecture. Inside are two dining floors: the lower has slate floors, heavy beams, barnboard siding, a big bar, and window walls overlooking lawns and gardens; the upper is somewhat roomier, very "Westchester" looking, with more barn siding, crisp linen, etc. It's a classy place with a horsey atmosphere; what more can I say? Lunch might be calves' liver sautéed with Calvados, cold curried chicken salad, chicken crêpes au gratin, or any of a number of special fish and veal dishes priced mostly from $8 to $15. At dinner be prepared to pay between $17 to $24 or so for à la carte entrees like steak au poivre, filet of sole, and prime rib. Open for lunch Wednesday through Saturday from noon until 2:30 p.m., for dinner Wednesday and Thursday from 6 to 9:30 p.m., and on Friday and Saturday until 10:30 p.m. There's a brunch on Sunday (prix fixe at $13, served from noon to 3 p.m.) as well as dinner, served until 8:30 p.m.; closed Monday and Tuesday.

About five miles north of Pound Ridge, via N.Y. 124 and N.Y. 35, is the bucolic hamlet of **South Salem**, in the middle of which is the **Horse and Hound**, Spring Street at Main Street (tel. 914/763-3108). Built in 1721, this picturesque old place is unique for a menu (dinner only) that concentrates on fresh game. Typical à la carte entrees include stuffed baby pheasant, caviar soufflé, venison steak (one of the few places it's available), roast wild boar, roast duckling flambé, plus sirloins, porterhouses, and filets of buffalo steak. Blackboard specials on any given night might include Kodiak bear, alligator gumbo, or braised rabbit. Entree prices hover in the $15 to $24 range. The dining rooms are about as romantic as you could hope for: primitive furniture, candlelight, napkins in wine glasses, etc. Open at 5 p.m. daily (on Sunday from noon to 6 p.m.); a complete prix-fixe dinner is offered on Saturday nights for a bit under $45 per person.

There are only three bedrooms at the Horse and Hound, and chances are they'll be booked until six months after your next birthday. Anyway, we've strayed far enough from the Hudson. Unless you're returning to New York for the night (not much more than an hour from Bedford), find N.Y. 35 (the principal east-west secondary road hereabouts) and head westbound toward Peekskill, the southern gateway to the Hudson Highlands.

THE HUDSON HIGHLANDS AND WEST POINT

This is one of the most scenically beautiful stretches of riverfront anywhere in America, and it has been acclaimed as such by travelers for centuries. The Highlands are so called on account of the extremely steep and picturesque mountains which at this point hem the Hudson into a very deep and narrow watercourse. It's not that the mountains are so high, but rather that their slopes are so sheer. Most of the crests of these towering hills are only about 800 or 900 feet above sea level. But their wild and rocky look, plus their dramatic verticality, makes for impressive views and a general air of mystery.

The Highlands stretch from **Dunderberg Mountain** opposite Peekskill on the south to **Storm King Mountain** at the entrance to Newburgh Bay on the north. The distance from one end to the other is something on the order of ten miles. Right in the middle the river makes a hairpin turn around **West Point**. From the military academy atop the cliffs at West Point there's an unobstructed view both up and downstream. Every ship that passes on the Hudson must do so under the guns of West Point, which fact rendered the fortifications here so important during the Revolution.

A number of battles were fought in the Highlands during 1776 and 1777 as part of a British effort to dominate the Hudson Valley. The Americans prevented the capture of West Point itself, foiling Benedict Arnold's treason before he was able to simply hand the fort over to the enemy. But elsewhere in the Highlands the British generally managed to get the upper hand. They successfully took Forts Clinton and Montgomery in the vicinity of today's Bear Mountain Bridge. By doing so they were able to dismantle a famous "chevaux-de-frise," or iron chain across the Hudson between Bear Mountain and Anthony's Nose. The Americans had wanted for some time to interdict military transport on the river by means of a chain. The original hope was to install it downriver at Fort Washington in northern Manhattan.

However, the Continental Army was forced to abandon Manhattan before anything could be done. The chain at Bear Mountain, installed in 1776, cost the patriots a quarter of a million dollars. The British dismantled it in 1777, took it back to Europe, and used it for many years to protect their harbor at Gibraltar.

Through much of 1777 the British General Burgoyne was surrounded by American forces near the headwaters of the Hudson at Saratoga. In one of the war's major tactical blunders, the British high command never relieved him. Burgoyne was finally forced to surrender, shortly after which the British withdrew from the Highlands and the focus of the war moved south.

Peekskill is an old and troubled Hudson Valley town dominated by the unhealed scars of "urban renewal." It can be bypassed via the scenic **Bear Mountain Parkway,** which intersects N.Y. 35 just east of town. After about three miles of curvy, woodsy parkway, you'll come to a light beside a causeway. Turn right and follow the signs to the Bear Mountain Bridge and N.Y. 6 and 202 West. Soon you'll be on an incredibly serpentine road, climbing the cliffs above the river. Below you is **The Race,** one of the narrowest and fastest-moving parts of the Hudson channel. Across the river are the picturesque and craggy slopes of Dunderberg Mountain.

Everyone exclaims over the beauty of the nearby **Storm King Highway,** located on the other side of the river north of West Point. In point of fact, this section of N.Y. 6 and N.Y. 202 is almost as scenic. About 3½ miles from the causeway at Peekskill is the **Bear Mountain Bridge,** site of the famous Revolutionary War chevaux-de-frise. Once the longest suspension bridge in the world, this slender lovely thing was built in 1924 as a private profit-making venture by the Harriman family. The State of New York bought it in 1940. Our eventual path lies to the north, along N.Y. 9D. But for now we're going to detour across the river for a look at two of the region's principal attractions.

The first is **Bear Mountain,** whose 1,305-foot summit can be reached via N.Y. 6 westbound about 2½ miles to the Seven Lakes Parkway; then left on Seven Lakes for maybe a mile to Perkins Memorial Drive. The distant views from the summit of Bear Mountain are superb. Considerable wilderness seems to extend in almost every direction. The bulk of it, to the southwest, lies in the Harriman State Forest, an area of some tens of thousands of acres given to the people of New York State by the late Governor Averell Harriman. Originally this land was all part of **Arden,** the Harriman family estate. Arden House, located on a mountaintop above the village of Harriman on N.Y. 17, is now a conference center owned by Columbia University.

The barrenness of Bear Mountain is one of many explanations put forth to explain its name. From what I've read, no one seems seriously to suggest that there were ever many "bears" in these parts. The Dutch called it by various different names. Why it's come down to us as "Bear" Mountain is just a mystery.

At the foot of the mountain, along the riverfront to the immediate south of the traffic circle on this side of the Bear Mountain Bridge, is a complex of recreational facilities centered around the old **Bear Mountain Inn** (tel. 914/786-2731). Besides assorted playing fields, there is a roller rink, an ice skating rink, a swimming pool, a little zoo, the remains of Fort Clinton (conjuring images of a not-very-bright day in the American Revolution), and a shady walk around the verges of **Hessian Lake.** In the last century this little body of water was owned by the Knickerbocker Ice Company. Huge chutes delivered cut ice down the cliffsides to warehouses on the water's edge. For a century before that it was called Bloody Pond. After the fall of Fort Clinton, the bodies of so many of the dead were thrown into it that the water turned red. The Bear Mountain Inn rents rooms (almost all of which are in modern motel-style satellites) and serves meals. The cafeteria is cheap; the main restaurant is moderately priced and quite grand-looking in an Adirondack-loggy sort of way. Bear Mountain State Park is a great favorite with busloads of city dwellers.

Some 5½ miles north of the Bridge Circle (on N.Y. 318 in Highland Falls) is the **United States Military Academy,** better known by the name of the rocky eminence atop which it sits, **West Point.** Although the academy was not formally authorized by Congress until 1802, cadets were attached to a permanent artillery corps here as early as 1794. During the Revolution, West Point was but one, albeit the most strategic, of numerous fortifications in the Highlands. In 1779, well after Burgoyne's surrender at Saratoga and the subsequent waning of the British threat to the Hudson, another chain was stretched across the river, from here to Constitution Island. It was never put to a test. In 1780 the British almost succeeded in playing on the frustrations and grievances of Benedict Arnold, then commander of West Point. Had British Major John André not been captured in Tarrytown with incriminating papers, Arnold might well have succeeded in turning over the fort to the Britis' without a fight. Had that happened, yet another chain might have wound up Gibralter.

Above West Point is the site of **Fort Putnam,** partly restored around 1910 an. now a part of the grounds of the military academy. In 1832 the English actress Fanny Kemble took a steamboat up the Hudson. Like today's Day Liners, Miss Kemble's boat stopped at West Point. She and her father climbed to Fort Putnam, which even then was famous for its view. "I was filled with awe," she says in her *Journal of a Residence in America,* "The beauty and wild sublimity of what I beheld seemed almost to crush my faculties. . . . I felt as though I had been carried into the immediate presence of God."

Compared to the secrecy that shrouds military installations in other countries, West Point is astonishingly open. Thayer Road (N.Y. 318) cuts right across the middle of the campus. There are cadets at the various gates waving traffic into and out of the grounds. Once inside, you're free to wander at will. In fact, the best way to see West Point is on a self-guided tour.

Your first stop should be the **Visitor Center,** located just south of the **Thayer Gate** on N.Y. 318 in Highland Falls. It's well marked; you won't miss it. This sophisticated facility features exhibits, a gift shop, a helpful information desk, even movies on cadet life and the history of the academy. Here also is where you can pick up a "Visitors Guide," which serves as an itinerary for self-conducted tours of the campus. The guide includes a detailed map of the grounds, plus brief details on the academy buildings, historic sites, scenic overlooks, etc. Also available at the Visitor Center is the "Arts and Entertainment Calendar," a listing of theater groups, band concerts, and specialty shows scheduled throughout the year. You can request these publications in advance, and/or inquire as to what events, games, etc., are scheduled during the time of your visit, by writing to the Public Affairs Office, United States Military Academy, West Point, NY 10996. Alternatively, you can call them at 914/938-2006.

Presidents Grant and Eisenhower, Generals Patton and MacArthur, and Astronauts Aldrin and Borman are but a few of West Point's many celebrated graduates— Edgar Allan Poe was a dropout. Currently there are about 4,400 cadets enrolled in a four-year program combining college curricula with intensive military training. The culmination is a Bachelor of Science degree and a stint (usually a career) in the army. Applicants must be between 17 and 22, morally and physically fit, either male or female, and be recommended by a congressman.

Also on the grounds of West Point is the **Hotel Thayer,** named after Major Sylvanus Thayer, superintendent of the academy from 1817 to 1833. The Thayer is a good place to eat and to stay. It's described in full below.

After West Point you might want to savor the scenery along the **Storm King Highway.** This cliffhanger of a road (also designated as N.Y. 218) is located immediately north of the academy, and as it's the only route along the river, you can't very well miss it. The scenery is most dramatic, the corners are veritable hairpins, and the pavement is exceedingly narrow. It's a fun couple of miles, at the northern terminus of which is the village of Cornwall on Hudson and the end of the Highlands. Here you should probably turn around and take N.Y. 218 back south. Keep going past the north gates to the academy until you reach U.S. 9W. Then take 9W south to the Bear Mountain Bridge and cross back over the river to the eastern shore.

The road up the east bank of the Highlands is called N.Y. 9D. You'll see signs for it at the eastern end of the Bear Mountain Bridge. It is a woodsy winding road that passes a couple of charming villages and a number of big estates. One of the latter is **Castle Rock,** the pinnacled mountaintop mansion above Garrison that's clearly visible from the road and from West Point across the river. It was built in the early 1880s for railroad man William H. Osborn, brother-in-law of J.P. Morgan. It remains in private hands.

About four miles north of Castle Rock, just below the village of Cold Spring, is **Boscobel,** N.Y. 9D, Garrison-on-Hudson. NY 10524 (tel. 914/265-3638). This exquisite Adam-style mansion is filled with priceless furniture and surrounded with sumptuous gardens, possesses great river views, and is open to the public. It was built in 1806 by one States Morris Dyckman in what was then the highest London fashion. However, it wasn't built here. Until 1955 Boscobel stood 15 miles to the south in Montrose, on a site adjacent to (and eventually engulfed by) the Franklin D. Roosevelt Veterans' Administration Hospital.

Although the present location is similar to the original, and the furnishings contemporary to Dyckman's era, what we have here is not a historic house as much as an inspired interpretation of aristocratic American country life in the Federal era. The place, however, is extremely beautiful, and if nothing else, full of good ideas on Federal-period decorating. Of particular note are the carved swags above the river-front porch, the graceful main staircase, and the many fine examples of Duncan Phyfe furniture. Boscobel is open April through October from 9:30 a.m. to 5 p.m., to 4 p.m. during the months of November, December, and March. Admission is $4 for adults and $2 for children 6 to 14.

Just north of Boscobel is the pretty village of **Cold Spring,** notable for its 19th-century atmosphere, interesting antiques shops, and good inns and restaurants, about which more below.

Where to Stay and Eat in the Hudson Highlands

This is the land of country inns. At most of the following recommendations you can either enjoy a meal, stay overnight, or both. Most are quite small, however, so travelers on summer weekends will need advance reservations. We'll start first on the west bank, then cross the river and continue on the other side.

Many people don't realize that the **Hotel Thayer,** just inside the Thayer Gate on the grounds of the U.S. Military Academy, West Point, NY 10996 (tel. 914/446-4731), is open to the public as well as to the military. It's an imposing (almost fore-boding) brick edifice dating from 1926, with 210 rooms, a crenellated roofline, and an excellent restaurant. The spacious double-height lobby has marble floors, iron chandeliers, huge ceiling beams (actually made of plaster painted up to look like wood), potted palms, crimson leather sofas, and over the fireplace a big portrait of Colonel Sylvanus Thayer, the "Father of the Military Academy." Everything is extremely well kept, the location is grand and exciting, and the atmosphere couldn't be friendlier. The rooms are smallish and not elaborate. They all have colored tile baths, antique reproduction furniture, television sets, and occasionally a good view. The prices, however, are very reasonable: $60 to $70 for a double, depending on size. Both tennis and swimming at military academy facilities can be arranged for registered guests.

The dining room serves breakfast, lunch, and dinner, the latter two meals served from 11:30 a.m. until 4 p.m. and 5:30 until 9 p.m. respectively. It's quite a grand room, with gilded reliefs of parrots and rabbits on its stucco columns, thick rugs, chandeliers, an adjacent terrace room overlooking the Hudson, and beyond that an open-air patio for al fresco dining. Typical full dinners cost under $20. A Sunday champagne brunch, served from 10 a.m. until 2:30, is priced at about $16. Lunch can be done for under $10 per person. Even if you don't stay at the hotel, it's worth stopping by for a meal.

Now let's cross the river and see what's good on the other side, starting with the

Hudson House, 2 Main St. (all the way at the foot of the street, on the other side of the railway tracks), Cold Spring, NY 10516 (tel. 914/265-9355). This is the second-oldest inn in New York State, although it has been so totally renovated that the interior architectural fabric is no longer antique. It's a two-story frame building with a mansard roof and a tranquil location right at the river's edge. The main floor is a restaurant, divided into several simple, airy rooms, with low ceilings and wonderful river views. There are wide-plank floors, print wallpaper, framed views of the Hudson River, blue-painted chairs, and a little bar across the lobby—the modern "country inn" look par excellence. On a fine day, with the windows open and cooling breezes wafting off the Hudson, you'd be hard-pressed to imagine a nicer spot. Lunch, served daily from noon to 2:30 p.m., might be, for example, a hamburger, or chicken breast in mustard sauce, or seafood "palette" (crab, salmon, and sole in aspic), or catfish fry, or maybe a surprise omelet. À la carte prices run from about $8 to $16. At dinner, available seven days a week from 6 until 9 p.m., typical entrees include blackened Cajun steak, shellfish assembly, duck and coriander salad, nesting chicken, etc., costing mostly between $14 and $20.

The Hudson House has but 15 guest rooms, priced from $70 to $85 single and $80 to $95 double. They're small, wallpapered, decorated with bunches of dried flowers, "primitive" wood furniture, and pretty iron beds; they have individual private bathrooms. They're quite nice and some have terrific river views. But essentially these are modern rooms housed in a building that, from the inside anyway, also looks brand-new.

A few miles east of Cold Spring on Old Albany Post Road, in a little valley traversed by U.S. 9, is the ultimate hideaway, the **Bird & Bottle Inn,** U.S. 9, Garrison, NY 10524 (tel. 914/424-3000). First opened in 1761, the Bird & Bottle Inn is an ancient-looking yellow house with a steep shingled roof, brick walls, tall trees, a double porch with square columns, and an air of great seclusion and tranquility. Fortunately, it's a bit off U.S. 9, so the roads around it are all of dirt, and the only sound is the music of a little brook and the whispering of wind in the stately trees. Inside are low ceilings, more wide-plank floors, big old fireplaces, and the low gleam of well-maintained early Americana. The first floor is a veritable warren of small, picturesque rooms. You step down into the "Drinking Room," which is tiny and dark, with clusters of little tables and a collection of guns mounted over the mantel. The ceilings are beamed; the walls are decorated with framed pictures of ducks; get the picture?

The French-continental cuisine here is famous. Saturday lunch might be anything from a chicken tarragon sandwich to the croissant du jour, to a quiche Lorraine, priced from $7. The $35 prix-fixe dinner includes a selection of entrees such as medallions of veal Cecile, baby rack of lamb, filet of sole, roast pheasant, etc. Luncheon is served Saturday from noon to 2:30 p.m. Dinner is served Tuesday through Sunday from 6 to 9 p.m. The Sunday brunch costs about $15 and is available from noon until 2:30 p.m.

There are only a few guest rooms at the Bird & Bottle, but they're wonderfully atmospheric. Each has its own working fireplace, a canopied bed, hooked rugs, clock radios, private baths, old-fashioned framed prints and paintings on the walls, and an abundance of ancient nooks and crannies. They look like guest rooms in the "simple" country house of a rich and sophisticated New Yorker. Overnight rates range from $185 to $205 for two persons, including dinner and breakfast, the latter price applying to a suite or cottage. To get to the inn, take N.Y. 301 (the extension of Main Street in Cold Spring) east over the hill through Nelsonville to U.S. 9, then turn right (south) for just a few miles.

Back on N.Y. 9D, immediately south of the village of Cold Spring, is the **Plumbush** (tel. 914/265-3904). You'll recognize the place by the long stone wall surmounted by a white picket fence. Beyond the gates is a rambling clapboard Victorian house, painted brown, graced with a wisteria-clad porch, and surrounded by old shade trees. Inside is a warren of rather opulently decorated small dining rooms called variously the Rose Room, the Oak Room, the Lemon Room, etc. They have potted palms, heavy curtains pulled back on swags, old wood paneling, and wallpaper for which I personally would kill. Lunch might be smoked sausage with sauerkraut, shrimp in beer batter, veal à la Suisse, Maryland crab cakes, etc., priced mostly from $9 to $14. There's a prix-fixe dinner for about $30, plus an à la carte dinner menu with selections like roast quail, veal chop, tournedos of beef, roast duckling, steak au poivre, etc., most of which cost around $23 to $25. Lunch hours are noon to 2:30 p.m.; dinner is served from 5:30 until 10 p.m. or so; closed Monday and Tuesday. Upstairs are three very appealing guest rooms, decorated either with antique Victorian pieces or new wicker furniture, floral wallpaper, and new bathrooms. They cost either $100 or $125 nightly, double occupancy, and are really very nice.

Back in the village of Cold Spring is a terrific bed-and-breakfast with a twist. It's called the **Olde Post Inn,** 43 Main St. (just before the railroad tracks), Cold Spring, NY 10516 (tel. 914/265-2510), and the twist is that it's a combination country inn and jazz tavern. The building is a diminutive 19th-century house, painted yellow and white, with a porch right on the sidewalk. The airy main floor has a little desk, an adjoining breakfast room, and a few comfortable chairs and sofas. Upstairs are six rooms sharing two hall baths. Accommodations are small and immaculately clean, decorated with hooked rugs, antique bureaus, and framed prints. On Friday and Saturday the overnight double-occupancy room rate is about $65; the rest of the week it's $55. The basement tap room is the province of part-owner George Argila, a jazz musician himself who has attracted the likes of Junior Mance, Ray Bryant, and Bucky Pizzarelli up from the city to play here. No meals are served, just drinks in the evening. All in all, a very appealing place.

A good spot in Cold Spring for reasonable lunches and dinners in atmospheric surroundings is the **Depot,** located practically across the street from the Olde Post Inn in Cold Spring's former railway station (tel. 914/265-2305). The tall-ceilinged passenger waiting room has been transformed into an atmospheric combination bar-restaurant. The menu (full of railroading puns) offers a full range of omelets, burgers, sandwiches, and things-in-the-basket, for about $4 to $8 at lunch. During dinner hours you can still get burgers if you want, plus barbecued chicken, filet of flounder, steak, a seafood combination platter, etc., for around $8 to $12 per plate. Open daily for lunch from noon to 5 p.m., and dinner from 5 to 11 p.m.

Last but by no means least is **Xavier,** located in the middle of the golf course in Garrison, just south of the intersection of N.Y. 9D and 403 (tel. 914/424-4228). The Osborn mansion, Castle Rock, is on a mountaintop almost directly overhead, and indeed the elegant little building that houses Xavier was built originally by the Osborn family as a pavilion for large parties. It's a huge room with tall windows giving onto views of rolling golf links. There is an outdoor terrace under a striped awning and vases everywhere filled with sprays of fresh flowers. Lunch might be fettuccine with seafood, filet of beef with green peppercorns, Norwegian salmon, etc., priced mostly under $12. At dinner the à la carte entrees include Dublin bay prawns, fresh quail, Norwegian salmon again, etc., this time costing between $17 and $24 per plate. Open for lunch from noon to 2:30 p.m., and for dinner from 6 until 9 p.m.; closed Monday. This is a particular local favorite.

3. The Mid-Hudson Region

What I'm calling "Mid-Hudson" is that portion of the valley between the city of Poughkeepsie and the state capital at Albany. The area is in many ways like the lower Hudson, except that it's far less crowded and more agricultural. The scenery, however, is just as good. And there are lots of wonderful places to explore and interesting establishments at which to stay and eat.

We'll start with a detour inland for the benefit of antiques fanatics.

AN EXCURSION TO MILLBROOK

The attractive village of Millbrook sits at the absolute center of Dutchess County, named in honor of the wife of the Duke of York. The most aesthetic route from the Highlands is from Cold Spring via N.Y. 301 eastbound to the intersection with the **Taconic State Parkway,** a distance of about 8 miles. Get on the Taconic (a very pretty parkway) northbound for 20 or so miles to the exit marked for U.S. 44, Poughkeepsie and Millbrook. Millbrook is about 4 miles east of the parkway on U.S. 44.

This little village has been fashionable since its inception in the late 19th century. The so-called Millbrook Colony once supported a fine resort hotel known as the Halcyon. The hotel later became Bennett College for girls, and although it has been empty now for many years, it may soon again be opened as a hotel. The village remains much as it's always been, the service center of a bucolic area noted for very large estates and horse farms. One of the most magnificent of these is **Thorndale,** whose columned portico is visible just before the Millbrook light. This extremely elaborate and formal estate has been in the Thorne family for well over a century. Numerous equivalent properties are tucked out of sight among the manicured rolling hills that surround the village.

Low-profile Millbrook achieved brief and totally uncharacteristic notoriety during the 1960s. For about four years Timothy Leary operated his League for Spiritual Discovery in a rambling and gloomy Victorian mansion that 50 years before had been a local showplace. Long hair, beads, and curious aromas mixed for a period with the plaid pants and streaked hair of the locals. But all that's over now, and in its place Millbrook has become known for antiques. There are three separate antiques malls within a block of one another on Franklin Avenue—the **Millbrook Antiques Mall,** the **Millbrook Antiques Center,** and the **Village Antiques Center**—plus several independent shops. All told, there must be close to 100 individual dealers, every one of whom is constantly bringing in new stuff. There's enough to look at here—from glorified tag-sale junk to decidedly pricey French and English antiques to pre-Revolutionary Americana—to keep you busy for hours.

A few miles west of Millbrook on Tyrrel Road is **Innisfree Gardens** (tel. 914/677-8000), an elaborate Oriental "cup garden" that was once the site of an estate belonging to one Walter Beck. The fine Tudor-style house has, alas, been taken down. But the garden, upon which the Becks labored for generations, has been preserved under the auspices of a private trust that opens it to the public between May and October. It's called a "cup" because of its location in a small valley hemmed in by landscaped hills surrounding a jewel-like lake. The original focus of the property was the vanished mansion, which stood on a site across the lake from the parking area. There are abundant manicured lawns, terraces of stone, Oriental gates, ornamental waterfalls, beautiful flowerbeds, and old-fashioned wooden chairs situated to take advantage of carefully thought-out views. This is a great spot for a picnic, especially during the week, when almost nobody else is around. Open Wednesday through Friday from 10 a.m. to 4 p.m., and on Saturday, Sunday, and holidays from 11 a.m. to 5 p.m. There's a $2 admission on weekends. To find Tyrrel Road, look for the Innisfree sign on U.S. 44 just west of the Dutchess Home and Farm Center near N.Y. 44A.

Meals and Lodging in Millbrook

If you'd like to picnic at Innisfree, good sandwiches to go can be obtained at the **Millbrook Deli,** on the corner of Church and Franklin Streets in the center of the village (tel. 914/677-9391). Half the people who work in Millbrook seem to line up at the counter here every noontime. Another excellent idea, if like me you have a taste for good small-town sandwich shops, is **Jamos,** a stone's throw from the deli on Church Street (tel. 914/677-5108). This is the spot for inexpensive sandwiches (love that chicken salad), hot dogs, sundaes, ice cream sodas, shakes, and homemade soups. Open only for breakfast and lunch; closed Sunday. Just a block away on Franklin Avenue is the **Millbrook Diner** (tel. 914/677-5319), where dependable eggs are served up in vintage stainless-steel-sided surroundings.

There's a horsier atmosphere a half block up Franklin Avenue at the **Millbrook Town House** (tel. 914/677-9763). This charming ivy-covered cottage contains several intimate dining rooms decorated with prints of horses and maps of the Millbrook Hunt, plus a small bar that's a favorite haunt of the locals. The lunch menu offers a range of sandwiches from roast beef and Swiss to Monte Cristo, to Reuben, to tuna melt on a croissant, etc., priced mostly between $4 and $7. At dinner there's an extensive à la carte menu listing such items as lamb chops, stuffed shrimp, tenderloin of beef, and liver with onions, plus numerous chicken dishes, costing around $10 to $18. The food is great and the atmosphere is very "Millbrook." Open for lunch Monday through Saturday from 11:30 a.m. to 2:30 p.m.; dinner is served Monday through Thursday from 5 to 9:30 p.m.; and on Friday and Saturday until 10 p.m.; on Sunday they open at 1 p.m.

The best restaurant in Millbrook, both from the standpoint of food and country atmosphere, is **Allyn's,** located four miles east of the village of Millbrook on U.S. 44 (tel. 914/677-5888). Allyn's features "cross-cultural cuisine" with an ever-changing menu of French, Italian, Oriental, and Spanish dishes. This local favorite is open daily except Tuesday for lunch from 11:30 a.m. to 3 p.m., and for dinner from 5:30 to 9:30 p.m. (to 10:30 p.m. on Friday and Saturday). Lunch costs between $4 and $9; dinner is in the $10 to $20 range. A champagne Sunday brunch is offered at a fixed rate of $11.95; patio dining is available in the summer months.

For an exclusive hideaway retreat, try **Troutbeck,** Leedsville Road, Amenia, NY 12501 (tel. 914/373-9681). This English country–style estate is secluded amid 450 acres of parklike grounds and woodlands, and is graced with such amenities as an indoor pool, sauna, exercise room, tennis courts, large outdoor pool, and gourmet dining. The antiques-filled Tudor-style manor offers 35 rooms, many with fireplaces, and houses a 13,000-volume library. A couple can experience the luxury of Troutbeck—including three meals—for between $325 and $475 daily, depending on the room.

Just a half mile from the village center of Millbrook is **The Cat in Your Lap,** a bed-and-breakfast located at the junction of Old Route 82 and the monument (tel. 914/677-3051). This great 1840s farmhouse offers three double rooms with private baths, as well as one studio apartment. Cost ranges from $55 to $95 a night for double occupancy.

POUGHKEEPSIE—THE "QUEEN CITY" OF THE HUDSON

This is the seat of Dutchess County, located on the Hudson about 14 miles from Millbrook on U.S. 44. The Dutch settled the area in the late 17th century. In 1788 a crucial state convention, attended by Alexander Hamilton and John Jay, was held in Poughkeepsie. The result was an historic vote to accept the nation's new federal Constitution. The railroad came through in 1849, bringing with it a great prosperity that lasted until the Second World War. But Poughkeepsie's salad days of manufacturing might have been over for a long time. "Urban renewal" has done a considerable amount of damage. The postwar growth of the suburbs, especially the shopping centers south of town along U.S. 9, essentially finished off the job. Yes, Poughkeepsie has been "malled."

To be fair, the "Queen City" of the 19th century is not completely down for the count. It is still the home of **Vassar College,** founded by local magnate Matthew Vassar. The college's reputation for educational excellence is worldwide, and its campus, located on Raymond Avenue south of U.S. 44 and N.Y. 55 near the eastern boundary of town, is quite impressive. The home office of **IBM** is located in (actually just outside) Poughkeepsie too, down among the shopping centers on U.S. 9. This is a very lucky thing, since otherwise the local economy would really be dead.

The city's extremely rich 19th-century architectural heritage is also being belatedly rediscovered. There are now several "historic" districts in the city. The region along the river immediately north of the Mid-Hudson Bridge is in the process of becoming a miniature Georgetown, complete with restored old buildings, brick sidewalks, and gas street lamps. Many of the ornate wooden mansions on nearby Academy Street have been restored as well, with fairly spectacular results. Maybe one day even Main Street will be freed from its ersatz pseudo-modern identity as the desolate "Main Mall" and returned to the Victorian street that it was intended to be, complete with life-giving traffic.

In the heart of downtown Poughkeepsie is the **Bardavon 1869 Opera House,** 35 Market St. (tel. 914/473-2072). Rescued from demolition (unlike so many of its worthy neighbors), the Bardavon has been restored to its original splendor and now presents a varied program of theater, music, and dance. If you're staying overnight anywhere near Poughkeepsie, you'd be well advised to give them a call and see what's on. Typical presentations have ranged from the San Francisco Western Opera's *La Bohème,* to Rita Moreno in a one-woman show, to the Vietnam veteran drama *Tracers* mounted by Joe Papp's New York Public Theater, to a festival of Mozart performed by the resident ensemble of Lincoln Center. Poughkeepsie is fortunate to have a resource like the Bardavon and it deserves support.

Of the assorted historic houses in and around town, the most interesting is probably **Locust Grove,** the Italianate villa of Samuel F.B. Morse, inventor of the telegraph and accomplished portraitist. This great old Victorian mansion overlooks the Hudson from a site on U.S. 9, two miles south of the Mid-Hudson Bridge. A family by the name of Young bought it from the Morse estate in 1901, maintained it lovingly until 1975, then endowed it with a trust and opened it to the public. The famous Alexander Jackson Davis collaborated with Morse on the mansion's design. The interior is full of great Victorian stuff, some of it Morse's own. The house is still surrounded by its original 150-acre estate, which contrasts dramatically with the surrounding malls and garden-apartment complexes. The exact address is 370 South Rd., Poughkeepsie (tel. 914/454-4500). Open Memorial Day through September, Wednesday through Sunday from 10 a.m. to 4 p.m. Admission is $4 for adults, $1 for kids 7 to 16, free to kids under 7.

Other than that, there's not much reason to tarry in Poughkeepsie. That is, unless you're tired and/or hungry. In which case see below.

A Restaurant and Good Hotel

A good Poughkeepsie suggestion, both for dining and overnighting, is the **Vassar College Alumnae House,** located opposite the Vassar campus on large leafy grounds bordered by Raymond, Fulton, and College Avenues, Poughkeepsie, NY 12601 (tel. 914/437-7100). This great big old slate-roofed, half-timbered Tudor building looks like nothing so much as a big country mansion. Since 1924 it has served not just as a center of campus life but also as a full-scale country inn open to the public. It's quiet and handsome inside, with spacious wood-paneled rooms, carved fireplaces, and an air of stately calm. The main dining room is big and cool, flanked by French doors, lit by huge iron chandeliers, and ornamented by a baronial fireplace. It's elegant without being in the least formidable. The adjoining Pub is much smaller, with varnished wooden booths lining the walls and a series of perfectly wonderful murals (painted years ago by somebody named Anne Cleveland) depicting willowy Vassar girls studying beside piles of books, dashing with dates through the rain, dressed to the nines for long-forgotten formals, etc.

Lunch at the Alumnae House might be a Reuben sandwich, pasta salad, salade niçoise, a turkey club, chicken teriyaki, hamburgers (of course), or any of numerous other items priced mostly between $6 and $10. During dinner hours you can still get sandwiches in the Pub, or enjoy more elaborate entrees in the dining room, like pecan chicken, pork dijonaise, scallops with pesto, lobster Alfredo, etc., most of which cost between $10 and $12. Lunch is served daily from 11 a.m. to 3 p.m., and dinner from 5 to 9 p.m. The Pub stays open till midnight.

The upstairs floors contain 30 rooms with shared baths (they call them "cubicles" but they're somewhat better than that), and another 16 units with individual private baths. The former are utterly functional, with leafy views beyond leaded windows and big institutional bathrooms across the halls. The latter are big and old-fashioned, furnished with floral slipcovers, full-length mirrors, flowered curtains on brass rods, writing desks, twin beds with chenille spreads, and bathrooms with tub/shower combinations. They have just the touch of unpretentious gentility that one would expect from Vassar. Room rates are extraordinarily low. The so-called cubicles rent for only $35 a night double; the private rooms cost about $60 a night double. All in all, a great bargain.

Poughkeepsie has other good places to stay and eat, but we won't be staying here long enough to need them. Before heading north, however, you may want to explore a few unusual sights on the other side of the Mid-Hudson Bridge.

A SIDE TRIP TO NEW PALTZ

The steel Gothic **Mid-Hudson Bridge** was officially opened to traffic on August 25, 1930. Eleanor Roosevelt cut the ribbon while a crowd of notables, including FDR, looked on approvingly. This good-looking bridge carries U.S. 44 and N.Y. 55 across the river between Poughkeepsie and Highland.

The west bank of the Hudson has traditionally existed somewhat in the shadow of the swankier east bank. Perhaps this is because you don't have the same sunset and Catskill Mountain views from the western shore. Whatever the reason, the towns over here are more modest, the big estates less frequent, and land is less expensive and more frequently devoted to agriculture.

A great deal of this local agriculture is devoted to the raising of grapes for wine. This part of the Hudson Valley is notable for over a dozen different wineries, the great majority of which are within a short drive of the western terminus of the Mid-Hudson Bridge. They're all extremely proud of their produce, and they're glad to have you sample it on their various individual winery tours.

One of the more elaborate of the local wineries is the **Hudson Valley Wine Company.**, located on U.S. 9W just south of the Mid-Hudson Bridge near Highland (tel. 914/691-7296). An investment banker named Aldo Bolognesi bought the property in 1900 and established the vineyard as a hobby. Ruined by the Stock Market Crash, he retired to the country and survived despite Prohibition as a producer of "sacramental wine."

About 50 of the 300 or so acres here are devoted to the raising of Catawba, Delaware, Iona, and Bacchus grapes. Plants on the premises produce chablis, white burgundy, pink catawba, sauterne, and various other wines, including champagne. There's an attractive "manor house" used for group tours and special events, a landmark clock tower overlooking the city of Poughkeepsie across the river, a wine "shoppe," a press room for crushing grapes, facilities for bottling and storing "sleeping wines," a champagne room with high-pressure champagne tanks, etc.

Tours of the facilities operate all year long, several times daily, and include wine tasting, parking, breadsticks and cheese, nonalcoholic juice for the kids, and on weekends a complimentary wine glass. Weekday admission is $3 for adults and gratis for kids; on weekends the adult tariff is $5 and the kids are charged $1 each. Tour times vary throughout the year, but generally they're between 11 a.m. and 5 p.m. Better call for the exact schedules at the time of your visit. In addition to tours, the company operates a full and varied program of special weekend events, such as the Champagne Tasting Weekend, the Marriage Weekend (present your certificate for free admission), the Country Bakeoff, Karate Exhibitions, Grape Stompers, the Antique Show, etc. Call the number above for details.

If winery tours are your sort of thing, there are 14 other vineyards within easy driving distance. A "Winery Tours" brochure, available among other places from the Hudson Valley Wine Company, lists the names and addresses of the other wineries.

About eight miles northwest of the Mid-Hudson Bridge, via U.S. 9W and N.Y. 299, is the village of **New Paltz,** notable for a branch of the State University of New York, plus **Huguenot Street,** the oldest street in America with its original houses. The latter is quite a remarkable local attraction, encompassing nine restored 17th- and 18th-century buildings distributed among similar compatible structures along an ancient and aesthetic little street adjacent to the heart of New Paltz.

The Huguenots were French Protestants, hounded across Europe by intolerant princes until they emigrated to America. The village of New Paltz is named after "die Pfalz," a temporary refuge in the Rhine-Palatinate that was their last European address. In 1677, 12 Huguenot family heads, known locally as the "Duzine," struck a deal with the local Esopus Indians for about 40,000 acres of land. By 1692 they were sufficiently established to start building stone houses. Incredibly, some of these houses remain today in original condition, right down to the original furnishings.

To drive through New Paltz on N.Y. 299 you'd never dream that Huguenot Street even existed. Most of the village is a fairly typical agglomeration of renovated Victorian-era buildings mixed with modern supermarkets and gas stations. It's not ugly, but neither is it particularly noteworthy. Craft stores, beer bars, and hamburger stands cater to the college population. It's just an average small town with a state college adjacent.

But turn north off N.Y. 299 (Main Street) onto N.Y. 32, find North Front Street, and in another moment you'll enter another world of huge trees, ancient stone buildings, and gentle lawns with glimpses of the Wallkill River. Huguenot Street is an enchanted island unto itself, quite oblivious to the rest of New Paltz.

The Huguenot Historical Society was founded in 1894 to preserve an architectural heritage that was already beginning to disappear. Since then the society has been slowly acquiring properties, improving the ones it owns, and opening them to the public. The **Jean Hasbrouck House,** at the intersection of North Front and Huguenot Streets, is perhaps the most interesting. It's the primary example of medieval Flemish stone architecture in America. The Deyo House, built originally in 1692 and enlarged with fashionable additions in 1894, marries Edwardian elegance to medieval antecedents. The French Church is actually a painstakingly accurate 1972 duplication of the 1717 original. The elegant brick LeFevre House shows how prosperous the Huguenots had become by 1799. And so on and so forth.

There's quite a lot to be gotten from Huguenot Street just by driving down it and admiring the steep roofs and the ancient stonework. But anyone really interested in the period will want to tour the interiors with one of the society's guides. The complete **guided tour** takes 2¼ hours, includes all the houses, leaves at 10 a.m. and again at 1:30 p.m., and costs $5 for adults, $4 for seniors, and $1 for children under 12. The "Short Tour" takes 1¼ hours, includes two houses and the church, and costs $2.50. Some houses can be visited individually for $1.50.

Whatever you decide, first present yourself at **Deyo Hall** (not to be confused with the Deyo House), located on Brodhead Street between N.Y. 32 and Huguenot Street (tel. 914/255-1889 or 914/255-1600). All tours leave from here. Also at Deyo Hall is a gift shop and a museum on the second floor. If you'd like brochures or further information, write to the Huguenot Historical Society, P.O. Box 339, New Paltz, NY 12561.

A Bite to Eat in New Paltz

The DuBois Fort, 81 Huguenot St. (tel. 914/255-1771), is located right in the middle of Huguenot Street in (what else?) a stone house. Built in 1705, it is ivy-clad, surrounded by tall trees, and sports a double porch supported by white columns. The look inside is very colonial, with patterned wallpaper, corner cupboards, wooden tables with rush-seated chairs, and gauzy curtains. It's spare, simple, and clean.

The menu changes daily and features complete prix-fixe meals (appetizer to dessert) priced at around $9 for lunch, and between $9 and $12 for dinner (price varies depending on the entree). A typical lunch would start with sherbet and fruit cup, move on to a smothered breast of chicken with a choice of vegetable, and end off with apple betty. Dinner might be something like cream of carrot soup, followed by roast leg of lamb, and ending with chocolate cream cake. Coffee is included. DuBois (pronounced Du*Boyce)* is notable for authentic Huguenot Street atmosphere and good home-cooking. Open Tuesday through Saturday for lunch from noon to 2 p.m., and for dinner from 5:30 to 7:30 p.m.; open Sunday from noon to 4 p.m.; closed Monday.

Also on Huguenot Street, located a mile or so out in the country, is the **Locust Tree Inn,** 215 Huguenot St. (tel. 914/255-7888). The restaurant is in an old house that was occupied by the Elting family from 1759 until 1954. Today it's at the center of a golf course and reached via a winding drive through a deep pine forest. If you like charming unspoiled country inns, you're going to love this place. It's a rambling farmhouse with lots of gables and angles, banked by huge old shrubs and shaded by specimen trees. Inside is a delightful collection of atmospheric dining rooms decorated with heavy beams, ancient fireplaces, silk-shaded lamps, and vases of flowers — quaint with a capital "Q." Lunch entrees include omelets, bay scallops, chef's salad, tenderloin sauté, burgers, etc., priced between $5 and $7. During dinner hours à la carte entrees like the fisherman's platter, veal Oscar, roast duckling, chicken Stroganoff, and filet mignon will run from around $12 to $16. Lunch is served Tuesday through Friday from 11:30 a.m. to 2:30 p.m.; dinner is available Tuesday through Saturday from 5:30 to 10 p.m.; there's a Sunday brunch from 11 a.m. to 2 p.m., and regular Sunday dinner from 3 to 8 p.m.; closed Monday.

And Just Outside New Paltz . . .

One of the last great mountain resorts of the 19th century still stands in magnificent condition a mere six miles west of New Paltz. This is the **Mohonk Mountain House,** a National Historic Landmark whose official address is Lake Mohonk/ New Paltz, NY 12561 (tel. 212/233-2244 and 914/255-4500). An astonishing stone-and-wood Victorian castle perched on the rim of an alpine lake, Mohonk in years past welcomed such guests as Andrew Carnegie, Teddy Roosevelt, Rutherford B. Hayes, and William Howard Taft. The unspoiled countryside, the awesome views, the crystal lakes and charming Victorian pavilions, the manicured formal gardens, the huge wood-paneled lobbies and wonderful double-height dining room that charmed people in the last century are all still here. There are facilities for golf, tennis, swimming, fishing, hiking, boating, carriage rides, and in winter for cross-country skiing and ice skating. Mohonk was founded in 1870 by Quakers as a family resort for people who like clean living in the fresh air. To a very great extent it has remained true to that original ideal. Smoking is prohibited in the lobbies and the dining room; there is no bar or cocktail lounge, and alcoholic beverages have only recently become available at dinner and lunch.

The Mountain House is absolutely huge (it can accommodate up to 500 guests) and far more picturesque than words can convey. It's a place to explore, and a place in which to relax. Rooms vary considerably in size but they all have old-fashioned charm. Some have fireplaces and fabulous views. Others are small, simple, and have shared baths. Double-occupancy rates include three meals a day and range from an off-season low of $158 in a bathless room to a high-season peak of $307 in one of the special tower rooms. Midweek package plans are available, as are special monthly rates.

It's also possible—and highly recommended—to visit Mohonk just for a meal. The midday buffet costs $18 and is served from 12:30 to 2 p.m.; the evening meal runs $22 and is available from 6:30 to 8 p.m. Advance reservations are required. The immense wood-paneled dining room is something you'll never forget. Alternatively, for $4 during the week and $6 on weekends you can purchase a day pass that will entitle you to explore the grounds. The pass does not, however, entitle you to enter the Mountain House.

The Mohonk Gatehouse is on Mountain Rest Road: take Main Street (N.Y. 299) out of New Paltz and follow the Mohonk signs.

For close to a century Mohonk's neighbor and competitor was a pair of huge Victorian hotels that shared adjacent clifftops above neighboring **Lake Minnewaska,** in Lake Minnewaska (tel. 914/255-6000). Both hotels are gone today, but the property remains open year-round as a day park. The biggest attraction is probably Lake Minnewaska itself, an azure-blue, sheer-sided mountaintop lake that's hugely dramatic and a great place to swim. There are docks on which to sun yourself, tables at which to picnic, and canoes that can be rented for $5 an hour. The lake is very popular on summer weekends, but during the week you're likely to have it almost all to yourself. Also on the property are picturesque waterfalls and endless miles of woodland paths. Adults pay $6 on weekends ($5 during the week) for an unlimited pass; for children 6 to 12 the tariff is $1 at all times. A swim at Minnewaska and dinner in New Paltz are a hard combination to beat for a hot summer afternoon. The entrance to Minnewaska is located about ten miles west of New Paltz via N.Y. 299 and U.S. 44.

THE EAST BANK ROUTE TO ALBANY

Return to Poughkeepsie via the Mid-Hudson Bridge and pick up U.S. 9 north. Our next stop, only a few miles upriver, is the historic town of **Hyde Park.**

This aristocratic name was first applied to the locality in 1741, when Peter Fauconier, private secretary to Edward Hyde, Viscount Cornbury, bought land here. Cornbury was the English governor of New York who perplexed contemporary observers by wearing dresses in public. Hyde Park marks the beginning of the **16-Mile Historic District,** which runs northward along the eastern shore of the river. Listed on the National Register of Historic Places, the district contains a nearly unbroken string of fine riverfront estates, many of which have played important roles in American history.

Perhaps most important, and certainly the most famous of these estates, is **Springwood, the Home of Franklin D. Roosevelt National Historic Site,** U.S. 9, Hyde Park (tel. 914/229-2501). This formal and elegant country mansion has been preserved just as it was in 1945, when President Roosevelt died. Actually, the place almost burned down in 1982, but it has been so painstakingly restored that you'd never know. The house is typical of the country places maintained by the Dutchess County squirearchy to which the Roosevelts belonged. It sits on a beautiful estate with fine views of the river. FDR was born and raised here, and throughout his life he returned as often as possible. Many famous personages have been guests at Hyde Park, including King George VI and Queen Elizabeth on a weekend in 1939, and Winston Churchill upon several occasions during the war.

Springwood was originally a not-too-large clapboard Victorian country house, the outlines of which are still visible on the river façade. But in 1916 FDR and his mother decided to "mansionize" the place in high Classical Revival style. Now it's got 35 rooms and nine baths. The interiors reflect the traveled, luxurious life of its privileged owners. But more than that, these lovely rooms preserve a palpable air of FDR himself. He was a remarkable, albeit controversial, man. And he saved America not once but twice: first from the catastrophe of economic collapse, and then from the menace of Nazi Germany. FDR looked 80 when he died, even though he was only 63. Greatness takes its toll.

The grounds around the house include architecturally unusual outbuildings, an enchanting rose garden maintained in perfect order and containing the graves of President and Mrs. Roosevelt, a greenhouse dating from 1906, woodland trails, and the **Franklin D. Roosevelt Library Museum.** This latter structure was erected in 1939 to house presidential papers and archives. Today it's a major study and research facility, as well as a museum devoted to the lives of Franklin and Eleanor Roosevelt.

Springwood is open seven days a week April through October from 9 a.m. until 5 p.m. From November through March the site is open only Thursday to Monday. Admission is $3 for adults and free to kids under 16 and seniors over 62.

The **Eleanor Roosevelt National Historic Site** is at her former summer and weekend retreat **Val-Kill**, 249 Albany Post Rd. (tel. 914/229-9115). After President Roosevelt's death in 1945, Val-Kill became Eleanor's permanent home. The site, very evocative of its interesting owner, is open seven days a week, April through October, from 9:30 a.m. to 5 p.m.; in November, December, and March the hours are 10 a.m. to 4 p.m.; closed January and February.

The price of admission to the FDR house and library and Val-Kill also entitles you to visit the nearby **Vanderbilt Mansion National Historic Site**, U.S. 9, Hyde Park (tel. 914/229-7770). This spectacular beaux arts estate was developed in the 1890s as the country home of Frederick W. Vanderbilt, grandson of the commodore and something of a black sheep (he married an older woman). McKim, Mead, and White designed the house, which was originally the centerpiece of a 700-acre property. The views of the Hudson and the Catskills are superb. The mansion, which contains all its original furniture, is the sort of house you see in Newport. In other words, it's a palace, from its marble-clad double-height entry hall to its 18th-century French paneled reception room.

The Roosevelts, the Vanderbilts, and the Rogers (whose immense mansion is now in the hands of a religious order) were once quite the princes of little Hyde Park. Nowadays commercialization and the proliferation of tract housing have blurred the feudal configurations of the place somewhat. Yet on the Vanderbilt property the past is quite clearly preserved. Besides the house there are elaborate formal gardens (not fully restored as of this writing), an old carriage house (complete with vintage limousines), a pavilion that once served as a guesthouse (it's now the visitors' center), a half mile of riverfront to explore, and, of course, the unbelievably beautiful view. The public owes the late Margaret Van Alen Bruguiere a vote of thanks for donating her uncle's house and 212 acres to the U.S. government in 1940. She had tried to sell the place in 1938 and 1939, first for $350,000, finally for $250,000. But there were no takers. In lieu of auction, demolition, and subdivision, she gave it to us.

The Vanderbilt Mansion is open daily April through October from 9 a.m. to 5 p.m.; from November through March the hours are the same but the house is open Thursday through Monday. Admission is $2 for adults and free for individuals under 16 and over 62. And remember, if you already purchased an admission ticket at the FDR house, it's good here too.

Meals and Lodging in Hyde Park

Easy Street, on U.S. 9 at the southern end of the Hyde Park "strip" (tel. 914/229-7969), is a great place for lunch. For that matter, dinner is good too. Both are served in a shopping-center/Wild West-style edifice with a false front; inside is a long convivial-sounding bar, lots of booths and tables, abundant hanging plants, and a youthful clientele many of whom are students at the neighboring Culinary Institute of America. At lunch, quiches, crêpes, salads, burgers, and huge sandwiches cost around $3 to $5. Dinner entrees, like grilled pork chops, strip sirloin, crab Mornay, and pot roast, cost about $9 to $14 and include salad, vegetable, and potato. The lighter luncheon menu is available all day long. Meals are served Monday through Saturday from 11:30 a.m. to 10 p.m., on Sunday from noon to 10 p.m. Fast service, friendly atmosphere, and cheap food: it's a hard combination to beat.

One of the Hudson Valley's most famous educational institutions—and one of its greatest cultural resources—is the **Culinary Institute of America,** on U.S. 9 about half a mile south of Hyde Park The CIA, as it's called locally, occupies an imposing former seminary building overlooking the Hudson where 1,850 full-time students attend classes in cooking, baking, and hospitality management. Of particular concern to us are four superb restaurants, operated by CIA students, located on the campus, and open to the public. Eating at the CIA really is fun, and if you can arrange to have a meal here, by all means do so.

The most informal of the restaurants is the **St. Andrew's Café** (tel. 914/471-6608), where $10 or so will buy you a lunch of medallions of pork with red onion confit, or baked salmon filet, or broiled tuna steak, etc., plus dessert and beverage. Dinner is hardly more expensive, sample entrees including tenderloin of beef with bleu cheese and herb crust, duck ravioli, pan-smoked breast of chicken, etc. Open Monday through Friday from 11:30 a.m. to 1 p.m. for lunch, and from 6 to 8 p.m. for dinner. Reservations are suggested. The café is located behind the main building, close to the big parking lot.

The award-winning **American Bounty Restaurant** specializes in American regional cuisine. The restaurant has received a three-star rating from *The Mobil Travel Guide* and the prestigious Ivy Award for excellence in foodservice from *Restaurants & Institutions Magazine*. Specialties include things like pan-fried crab cakes with smoked-pepper butter sauce served with creamed sweet potatoes and leek soup, roasted pheasant with forest mushrooms and kiln-dried cherry sauce, and grilled black Angus beef tenderloin with roasted garlic glaze. The American Bounty is open Tuesday through Saturday, with lunch served from noon to 1 p.m., dinner from 6:30 to 8:30 p.m. À la carte entrees range in price from $11.50 to $14.50 at lunch and from $16.50 to $21 at dinner. Jackets are required. Reservations are requested and can be made by calling the Institute's Reservations Office at 914/471-6608.

The **Escoffier Restaurant** offers traditional French cuisine served in elegant surroundings overlooking the scenic Hudson. Its à la carte and prix-fixe menus feature such specialties as salade au confit de canard, consommé au quenelle de beurre, coquilles St-Jacques grillées au romarin, and filet de boeuf à la moelle gratinée et noix. Known on campus as the "E-Room," the Escoffier has been awarded four stars by *The Mobil Travel Guide*, three stars by the the *New York Times*, and is a recipient of the prestigious Ivy Award from *Restaurants & Institutions Magazine*. Lunch is served Tuesday through Saturday from noon to 1 p.m., with à la carte entrees ranging from $11.50 to $16 and the prix-fixe costing $20. Dinner is served from 6:30 to 8:30 p.m. and priced from about $16.50 to $24 for à la carte selections and $40 for the prix fixe. Jackets are required. Reservations are requested and can be made by calling the Institute's Reservations Office at 914/471-6608.

Last, but by no means least, is the **Caterina de Medici,** which features regional Italian cuisine. The menu includes risotto alla Sbirraglia, mille cosedde, osso bucco alla milanese, and zabaglione. Open Monday through Friday for a single luncheon seating at 11:30 a.m., with one seating for dinner at 6 p.m. The prix-fixe lunch is priced at $16; the prix-fixe dinner is $24. Jackets and reservations are required. For reservations, call 914/471-6608.

Hyde Park has been a tourist destination for over 40 years, ever since FDR died. There is a well-established village infrastructure of motels, movies (including a drive-in), small shopping centers, and restaurants. The motels are all quite nice, not too big, and not too new. My favorite of the bunch is the **Golden Manor,** U.S. 9, Hyde Park, NY 12538 (tel. 914/229-2157), a perfectly spotless 1950s-vintage establishment whose white columns and brick wings face the Roosevelt site across a spacious lawn. There are 40 rooms here, furnished with modern imitation wood paneling, brown rugs, modern motel furnishings, easy chairs, color televisions, and framed pictures of mountain scenery. Nothing fancy, but very pleasant and comfortable, and very clean. Double-occupancy room rates vary from around $40 to $50 nightly, depending on season and room location. Also on the premises is a very fine-looking swimming pool, surrounded by Astroturf and shielded from the road by the lobby wing.

Northward to Staatsburg and Rhinebeck

A few miles north of the Vanderbilt Mansion on U.S. 9 you'll see a turnoff to the left opposite the sign for **Staatsburg.** Not much to see in this sleepy little village, save the pleasant stone Episcopal church designed in 1891 by Richard Upjohn. Inside are a pair of 13th-century stained-glass windows from Chartres Cathedral, the gift of Ogden Mills, one of the local riverfront seigneurs.

And it is to the **Mills Mansion State Historic Site,** Old Post Road, in Staatsburg (tel. 914/889-4100), that we are headed next. The house is another McKim, Mead, and White extravaganza dating from 1896. It was built for Ogden and Ruth Livingston Mills and decorated quite as opulently as the Vanderbilt house to the south. Mills died in 1929 and his daughter donated the property to the State of New York in 1937. The mansion's basement has been the headquarters of the Taconic Region of the New York State Office of Parks Recreation and Historic Preservation ever since.

The Mills house has suffered considerable depredations at the hands of the weather and low state maintenance budgets. Leaking roofs have on occasion caused much of it to be closed. But progress is being made and the ceilings at least no longer drip. Interestingly, the 1896 construction encases a much older house. The views from the lawns are superb, the lawns themselves are immense, and the river is beautiful here. The house is quite palatial, and if you like this kind of thing you shouldn't miss it. Between May 1 and Labor Day the mansion is open Wednesday through Saturday from 10 a.m. to 5 p.m., and on Sunday from 1 to 5 p.m. From Labor Day until the last Sunday in October, the Wednesday through Saturday hours are noon to 5 p.m., and the Sunday hours are 1 to 5 p.m. Admission is free. Closed the rest of the year with the exception of Christmas, even though the beautiful grounds remain open.

The Old Post Road rejoins U.S. 9 about a mile above the Mills house. And from here it's only another four or five miles to **Rhinebeck,** one of the Hudson River Valley's most appealing little towns.

Just exactly what makes Rhinebeck so nice? The tree-lined streets? The delightful Victorian buildings? The abundance of excellent restaurants? The fine country properties that surround the village? The interesting shopping? The lovely rural surroundings? All of the above, no doubt, plus proximity to the sights down in Hyde Park and Staatsburg. And the **Old Rhinebeck Aerodrome** (tel. 914/758-8610), located about three miles north of town near the neighboring village of Red Hook.

The aerodrome is part museum (three hangars full of antique planes, cars, motorcycles, etc.) and part air show spectacular, and it's open daily from 10 a.m. to 5 p.m., May 15 to October 31. On weekend afternoons, besides the museum exhibits, you can also see either the Saturday "History of Flight Show" (World War I and Lindbergh-era planes) or the Sunday "Melodrama" (a staged air battle between the Black Baron and the good guys). Air shows take place every weekend from mid-June to mid-October. Either before or after the show you can also go "barnstorming" in an open-cockpit biplane. Admission is $7 for adults and $3 for kids. Barnstorming costs about $20 per person, takes about 15 minutes, and is on a first-come, first-served basis. Admission on non–air show days is $3 for adults and $1 for kids (ages 6 to 10).

Meals and Lodging in Rhinebeck

Rhinebeck is famous as the home of America's oldest inn, the **Beekman Arms,** U.S. 9, Rhinebeck, NY 12572 (tel. 914/876-7077). The Beekman's columned façade surveys the very center of the village across a smallish manicured lawn. It's a wonderful old whitewashed building, rambling this way and that, parts of which date to 1766. Beyond the beamed and ancient-looking lobby is a popular restaurant with several separate rooms and a delicious air of country elegance. Meals can be taken either in an atmospheric tap room complete with dark booths and colonial-era fireplace, or in an early American dining room, or amid hanging plants in the new "greenhouse." Lunch specialties include seafood pot pie, beef Stroganoff, quiche, country omelet, etc., and usually cost between $6 and $8. At dinner you might settle on something like prime rib, duck breast, blackened salmon, grilled swordfish, or one of the daily specials such as braised veal shanks or fresh salmon with béarnaise sauce. Expect to pay between about $13 and $20 for an à la carte entree.

The Beekman Arms is also a hotel offering 54 rooms housed in several different buildings. By far the nicest of these is the Delamater House, a textbook example of Hudson River Gothic architecture located a long block north of the inn. Built in 1844 for the founder of the First National Bank of Rhinebeck, it was completely restored/renovated by the Beekman only a few years ago. The rooms are spacious, have tasteful pastel color schemes, antique-reproduction furniture, color TV's, and modern bathrooms. They are extremely handsome and cost but $65 to $85 nightly, double occupancy. The architecturally compatible Delamater Courtyard and Carriage House are located immediately to the rear. Rooms here are even bigger and most have working fireplaces. Although not located in historic buildings (the courtyard is new, save for one old house in the middle of it), accommodations have the same tasteful traditional interior decor as the Delamater House. Double-occupancy rates back here range from $75 to $95 nightly. There are pleasant and less expensive rooms in the inn itself, but value-wise the best and most atmospheric deal is chez Delamater.

The **Rhinebeck Village Inn,** P.O. Box 491, Rhinebeck, NY 12572 (tel. 914/876-7000), is a new motel with an arts-and-crafts look, located on U.S. 9 at the southern edge of town. For $58 a night double occupancy ($48 on weekdays) you get a very large new room furnished with suave gray carpeting, twin double beds, color television, individual air conditioning, a very nice bright white bathroom, even a complimentary continental breakfast. This is a most excellent bargain. There are antlers on the walls, stained wooden headboards and desks, and ropes holding the hanger bars. Whatever the owners couldn't make themselves they got at the Rhinebeck Crafts Fair. Only 16 units, each of which is fresh, clean, new, and very aesthetic. Also on the premises is a Jacuzzi room, which turns out to be a marbleized California fantasy complete with cathedral ceilings and potted plants.

Rhinebeck has a disproportionate number of good restaurants for such a small town. Herewith are three personal favorites.

Foster's Coach House Tavern, 22 Montgomery St. (tel. 914/876-8052) is a two-story brick Victorian building that once was indeed a coach house. Today there's a strong horse motif running through the decor, from the phone booth (it's an old coach on springs) to the horseshoe door pulls to the framed prints of horses on the walls. In the backroom thousands of patrons have tucked their business cards between cracks in the barnside paneling. Curious, isn't it?—even though looking them over is rather interesting. Foster's has great burgers and innumerable sandwiches priced at $3 to $4, plus salad plates, Italian dishes, and standbys like fried chicken, broiled scallops, open steak sandwich, red snapper, etc. Most dinner plates cost around $8 or $9. The same menu is available all day, from 11 a.m. to 11 p.m. for hot foods and until midnight for cold foods. Closed Monday. Foster's is so popular there's often a line at the door at peak hours. Don't be discouraged; it moves fast.

Across the street in an old rambling Baptist church is **La Parmigiana,** 37 Montgomery St. (tel. 914/876-3228). The restaurant consists of an 1825 original church later engulfed by a much larger Queen Anne–style addition. The older part of the structure is the principal dining space and also the location of the wood-fired baking ovens. All the pizzas and calzones are baked with wood heat and deliciously flavored with hickory and apple smoke. Creative pizzas, calzones, and a great selection of homemade northern Italian pasta dishes are available for both lunch and dinner. Lunch is served from 11 a.m. to 4 p.m. and costs in the $3 to $6 range. Dinner runs from $5 to $14 and is available from 4 to 11 p.m. daily. Closed Tuesday.

I cannot, unfortunately, include every worthy restaurant in little Rhinebeck. So I'll conclude with **Mariko's,** north of town, about a mile above the intersection of U.S. 9 and 9W (tel. 914/876-1234). Management has succeeded by dint of sheer will in making this little roadhouse actually appear Japanese. There are vertical wood slats over the windows, banners decorated with prints of glowering samurai, and curtains which you must push aside, Japanese style, to enter. There's a bar up front and a roomy, simple, and appealing dining room beyond. A sign on the inside of the front door asks, "Are you a weekender? How about getting a free dinner by helping us bring fresh fish from New York City?" Dinner is the only meal served: Thursday through Saturday from about 5 to 10 p.m., and on Sunday from 4 to 9 p.m. Cuisine is "Francasian," which is to say it mixes French touches with the classic Japanese. Sample menu entrees include Tokyo steak, sukiyaki, sushi, various teriyakis, plus specials like the broiled sea scallops in a blanket, or the crab and avocado parfait. Typical à la carte entrees cost between $13 and $19.

Two Touring Notes

Rhinebeck is a good jumping-off point for an excursion west to the **Catskills.** Just above town on U.S. 9 you'll see signs for N.Y. 9G and the **Kingston-Rhinecliff Bridge.** Chapter XIII describes the Catskills in detail. If you'd like to interrupt your tour of the Hudson Valley, this is a good place to do it.

The second note harks back to my promise about "scenic" routes. After Rhinebeck, our east-bank route to Albany will take us first to **Clermont,** ancestral home of the legendary Livingstons, and then to the old city of Hudson. The most direct road is N.Y. 9G, which you pick up just north of Rhinebeck. A vastly more picturesque route is via the old **River Road,** which winds its way through the 16-Mile Historic District on a route that roughly parallels 9G. You'll pass beneath canopies of old trees, alongside the stone walls and imposing gatehouses of old riverfront estates, past a sleepy village or two, plus some old houses, lots of woods, and the attractive campus of Bard College. There's practically no traffic and it's a really pretty drive.

To find River Road from the center of Rhinebeck, take Market Street (N.Y. 308) westbound from the light at the Beekman Arms toward **Rhinecliff** (a hamlet with an Amtrak station on the water's edge). River Road is just a little over a mile west of the center of Rhinebeck, on the right side of N.Y. 308 as you head toward Rhinecliff.

The Road to Hudson

There are stretches of River Road on which one can easily imagine patriots in tricorn hats galloping this way and that, or carriages full of 18th- and 19th-century gentry riding from one estate to another. Many famous people have lived along this stretch of the Hudson, which has not yet lost its rural residential atmosphere.

Soon after turning onto River Road you'll see signs for **Ferncliff,** now the site of a modern nursing home but once the country estate of William B. Astor, Jr. Gore Vidal's novel *1876* has a scene set in Ferncliff during the days of *the* Mrs. Astor. This is the woman whose house on Fifth Avenue and 34th Street contained a ballroom that could accommodate only 400 persons. Her aide de camp, a social-climbing Southern lawyer named Ward McAllister, commented at the time that since there were only 400 people worth knowing in New York society, small ballrooms made no difference. Ferncliff is where these exquisite snobs spent parts of each spring and autumn. Portions of the estate, including a fabulous marble "casino" building designed by Stanford White, remain in private hands.

A bit north of the intersection of N.Y. 199 and River Road is **Rokeby,** identified by a historic marker by the roadside. Built by a Revolutionary War general named Armstrong, Rokeby was for many years the home of William B. Astor, Sr., father of the developer of Ferncliff. Astor Sr.'s granddaughter married a man named Chanler, had eight children, and then, along with her husband, suddenly died. In the closing years of the 19th century the so-called Astor Orphans grew up at Rokeby all by themselves (with governesses, servants, and tutors, of course) and went on to become adventurers, noted artists, socialites, intimates of American presidents, etc. Theirs is a fascinating tale, in which there's much of the flavor of the Hudson River Valley.

Just before Annandale is **Montgomery Place** (tel. 914/758-6667), an estate named in honor of Revolutionary War hero General Richard Montgomery by his widow. The exquisite old house was purchased in 1985, contents intact, by Historic Hudson Valley. The mansion was built in 1804–1805 by Janet Livingston Montgomery, widow of the general. The original house, an outstanding example of Federal architecture, was later transformed into a beautiful Classical Revival country home by the great 19th-century architect Alexander Jackson Davis. Visitors today can tour restored rooms and roam the more than 400 acres of land at Montgomery Place, savoring the beauty of the woods, streams, and gardens and enjoying the magnificent views of the Hudson River and the Catskill Mountains. In the fall, the estate's orchards offer pick-your-own apples. Montgomery Place is open daily except Tuesday from 10 a.m. to 5 p.m. from April through October; open weekends only in November, December, and March from 10 a.m. to 4 p.m. (grounds only, Thursday and Friday, 10 a.m. to 4 p.m.); closed January and February.

The picturesque campus of **Bard College,** a four-year liberal arts institution, straddles River Road north of the hamlet of Annandale. A mile or so beyond Bard, River Road rejoins the highway (N.Y. 9G).

About five miles to the north, on the west side of the highway, you'll see a sign for **Clermont State Historic Site,** located in the town of Clermont (tel. 914/537-4240). Clermont was the home of seven generations of the famous Livingston family. The Clermont mansion stands on a part of the original Manor of Livingston, whose charter was obtained by Robert Livingston in 1686 and which originally encompassed over 160,000 acres. It was built by Robert's son, known rather grandly as Robert of Clermont, in 1730. It was Robert of Clermont's grandson who, during the years leading to the Revolution, was chancellor of New York. He was also a strong advocate of independence, a member of the Second Continental Congress, and one of the five men who drafted the Declaration of Independence.

In 1777 Clermont was burned by the British in retaliation for its owner's political sentiments. But it was rebuilt after the war and flourished along with its distinguished owner's career. Chancellor Livingston went on to become America's first minister of foreign affairs, after which he became minister to France. It was Livingston who negotiated with Napoleon for the Louisiana Purchase. And Livingston again whose partnership with Robert Fulton led in 1807 to the first successful steamship, known as the *Clermont.*

Livingstons still live all around this area. Indeed they lived right here until 1962, at which time the state acquired the property. The house is perhaps a bit modest compared to some of its riverfront neighbors. But it literally drips with history, the grounds are quite lovely, and all the furnishings are original. It's open to the public between May 1 and October 31, Wednesday through Saturday from 10 a.m. to 5 p.m. and on Sunday from 1 to 5 p.m. Admission is free. The grounds are open year round from 8:30 a.m. until sunset.

About ten miles farther north on N.Y. 9G, just before the little city of Hudson, is **Olana** (tel. 518/828-0135). This is the extravagant Persian-style home of Frederic E. Church, famous landscape painter and notable member of the Hudson River School, America's first indigenous art movement. From the threshold of Olana it's easy to see where he got his inspiration. The view from this mountaintop Victorian aerie is absolutely awe-inspiring. "About one hour this side of Albany is the center of the world," wrote Church about his property. "I own it."

The house itself is a curious confection of Moorish arches, towers, loggias, and pinnacles. It's filled with Church family belongings, including canvases by its celebrated owner. Olana is another case of a historic old house being rescued and preserved at the 11th hour. It certainly deserved to be saved, but whether or not it's beautiful is a moot point. You can tour it and make up your own mind anytime between May 1 and Labor Day, Wednesday through Saturday from 10 a.m. to 5 p.m. and on Sunday from 1 to 5 p.m. From Labor Day through October 31 the hours are noon to 5 p.m. Wednesday through Sunday. The charge is $1 for adults and 50¢ for kids. On weekends you may need reservations. The grounds, open all year from 8 a.m. until sunset, are perfect for picnics (no cooking). For a good place for take-out sandwiches, etc., see below.

The nearby city of **Hudson,** located a mere 30 miles from Albany, is the capital of Columbia County. Hudson was once a famous boom town. In 1784 it had but one house, but within three short years a mob of settlers (many from Rhode Island) had built over 150 dwellings, plus factories, barns, storehouses, wharves, etc., and the town supported a population of 1,500 souls. By 1790 Hudson had a 25-ship whaling fleet. But the Erie Canal nipped development in the bud, and the advent of the railroad finished off the job. When Hudson ceased to be a major trade terminus, it entered a long, slow period of decline that has not completely ended.

As in many other places, economic adversity has served to preserve Hudson's remarkable architectural heritage. The length of Warren Street, the main drag running uphill from the river, is an architectural textbook of changing historical styles. There is everything from chaste Greek Revival temples to effulgent early Victorian mansions. There's been a great deal of preservation restoration work in recent years and the results are obvious. Hudson still has problems, but at least it's nice-looking. At the foot of Warren Street is Parade Hill, a public park with a fine view of the river and the mountains beyond. If you like exploring old riverfront towns, you should drive down here for a look. Also interesting is the early Victorian residential district that is bordered on the west by N.Y. 9G and on the north by Warren Street.

Restaurant Suggestions in Hudson

The **Mouse House Cheeses & Café,** 701 Warren St. at the corner of South 7th Street (tel. 518/828-4840), is the sort of hole-in-the-wall sandwich shop for which I have a great weakness. Run by smiling ladies, it offers a range of gourmet foods and cheeses, plus a changing menu of lunch items like smoked-turkey sandwiches, cream of chicken and vegetable soup, roast beef sandwiches, croissants and bagels, and excellent chicken salad. Prices are cheap (most sandwiches are $3 to $4), and they'll either make things up to go or you can enjoy lunch at one of a half dozen little tables in the back. Open Monday through Saturday from 9 a.m. to 4 p.m., on Saturday from 9:30 a.m. to 4 p.m.; closed Sunday and Monday.

More substantial meals are obtainable at a terrific local restaurant a mere five miles from town. Take Columbia Street in Hudson (near the Mouse House) to N.Y. 66 eastbound (Columbia runs right into it); stay on 66 for four miles until the intersection of N.Y. 9H. Turn left (north) and go about a mile to **Kozel's,** N.Y. 9H, in Ghent (tel. 518/828-3326). This family-style restaurant in the middle of farm country has been a local institution for 50 years. It's a big, modernized roadhouse with pots of flowers by the door and old New Orleans-type iron posts holding up the porch. Inside is a collection of roomy "modern" dining rooms grouped around a big central bar. Prices are very reasonable and portions are generous. The lunch menu lists all manner of sandwiches, priced mostly from $4 to $5, plus special plates like fried chicken, ham-and-egg plate, turkey with gravy, and a club sandwich, costing about $5 to $7. Dinner entrees such as roast sirloin with gravy, brook trout, lobster tails, lamb chops, ham steak Hawaiian, red snapper, roast turkey, etc., are priced mainly from $8 to $20. And these prices include soup, salad, bread, and potato. Kozel's serves lunch from 11 a.m. until closing; the dinner menu is available from 5 p.m. onward; the bar stays open late so there's no set closing hour. Open daily except Tuesday.

Some Final Attractions Before Albany

Those up to their gills with historic houses may consider themselves excused and proceed directly to Albany. The more determined tourist and historian may want to proceed to **Lindenwald,** the former country home of Martin Van Buren, president of these United States from 1837 to 1841. The neighboring village of Kinderhook is Van Buren country, and Matty Van is no joke around here. The Martin

Van Buren National Historic Site, in Kinderhook (tel. 518/758-9689), was established by another somewhat anonymous president, Gerald Ford, in 1974. The astonishing exterior of this much-altered and Victorianized mansion is fully restored. The interior may be done too by the time you get there. It's a great old house, with a $1 admission fee. And you never know when tidbits about Martin Van Buren will come in handy. Open daily from mid-April through October, Wednesday through Sunday during November and to around December 5, from 9 a.m. to 5 p.m. Lindenwald is right on N.Y. 9H about ten minutes north of Kozel's.

In Kinderhook itself is the graceful and elegant Federal mansion of lawyer James Vanderpoel, known locally as the **House of History,** on U.S. 9 in Kinderhook (tel. 518/758-9265). This is a lovely old place, in need of a bit of paint but full of period furnishings and administered by knowledgeable members of the Columbia County Historical Society. Admission is $2 for adults, $1.25 for children over 12, and free to kids under 12. The house is open from Memorial Day to Labor Day, Tuesday through Saturday from 11 a.m. to 5 p.m., on Sunday from 1 to 5 p.m.

Last of all, in nearby Old Chatham (eight miles east of Kinderhook), is the **Shaker Museum,** on Shaker Museum Road (tel. 518/794-9100). The Shakers, officially called the United Society of Believers in Christ's Second Appearing, were a Protestant monastic order that reached a peak about 1850. Even at that date there were only about 6,000 Shakers altogether, living in 18 separate communities (only two of which survive today). The Shakers believed in equality of the sexes and celibacy. Their communities were models of industry that produced items notable both for their beauty and their simplicity. The Shaker Museum comprises three buildings that display the sorts of things the Shakers made and the sorts of places in which they made them. Furniture, crafts, textiles, period rooms, plus a café and a gift shop, are among the many exhibits. There is a certain purity and beauty to the things the Shakers made. This museum is dedicated to promoting an understanding of the heritage they bequeathed to us all. The museum is open daily, May through October, from 10 a.m. to 5 p.m. Admission is $5 for adults, $4 for seniors, $3 for students aged 8 to 17, and free to little ones under 8.

XII

THE CATSKILLS

1. CATSKILL ORIENTATION
2. THE CATSKILL FOREST PRESERVE
3. THE RESORTS

The wild peaks of New York State's Catskill Mountains have inspired wonder and longing in the hearts of men since time began. They aren't very tall—Slide Mountain, the tallest, tops out only at 4,204 feet above sea level—but they possess a lion's share of the picturesque steepness that so typifies the Hudson River Valley. The great names of America's 19th-century landscape movement, the Hudson River School, painted their dense forests, rocky chasms, tumbling streams, and awesome views again and again. Men like Frederic Church, Thomas Cole, George Inness, Asher Durand, and Jasper Cropsey all struggled to capture the exquisite dazzle of light and color on the "divine architecture" of the Catskills. Their great canvases show mists and mountains and colors and sky in a way that can't help but move the imagination.

1. Catskill Orientation

The Indians called them Onteora, or "Land in the Sky." They were closely associated with the magic and legends surrounding the "Great Spirit" who was said to dwell there. And as such, everybody gave them a wide berth. When the practical Dutch arrived on the scene, they named them the Katsbergs in acknowledgment of the large population of wildcats. Somehow over the centuries this latter name evolved into Catskills, "kill" being the Dutch word for stream.

In the early part of the 19th century the first of the great mountain hotels went up in the Catskills. They bore names like the Laurel House, the Catskill Mountain House, and the Kaaterskill. All of them are gone today, victims of changing tastes and fashions. But there was a time when these opulent pillared palaces were oases of luxury in the very heart of the wilderness. They were originally accessible only by long carriage rides through wild valleys and up the sides of craggy cliffs. The sense of primeval nature contrasted with Victorian engineering must have been exciting indeed. Especially against the inevitable backdrop of a view that might stretch from Albany in the north to the Berkshires in the east to the Hudson Highlands in the south.

The Catskill Mountains are located on the west bank of the Hudson about two-thirds of the way from New York to Albany. The majority of the mountains are contained within the boundaries of the **Catskill Forest Preserve,** a New York State–administered wilderness park measuring over 50 miles across at its widest point. State land coexists with private property throughout the Catskill Preserve. A light network of high-speed roads and not-very-prosperous villages crisscrosses the area from one end to the other. There is also an elaborate network of hiking and horseback-riding trails, clearly marked, and maintained by New York State's Department of Environmental Conservation. To be out on these trails is to savor the wild and romantic atmosphere that drew the first vacationers. To be on the roads is to see a fair amount of junk in the foreground with mysterious peaks sulking in the distance.

Recommended for hikers is the "Catskill Trails" waterproof five-map series for $9.95 from the **New York–New Jersey Trail Conference,** GPO Box 2250, New York, NY 10116 (tel. 212/696-6800). They also have map sets for the West Hudson trails ($5.95), Harriman–Bear Mountain ($5.95), East Hudson trails ($5.95), and Shawangunk trails ($6.95).

West of the forest preserve, and to a greater extent to the southwest toward Pennsylvania, is a region of resort hotels known colloquially as the **Borscht Belt.** This is the home of enormous establishments like the Concord, Kutsher's, and Grossinger's. Big hotels in "the mountains" combine Miami Beach high-rise architecture with nonstop activities, including every imaginable daytime sport plus "name" entertainment at night. These places may be in the middle of nowhere, but "solace" and "wilderness" are not part of their mental equation.

Footloose sightseers with a taste for exploration and its attendant change of scenery should probably limit their Catskill excursion to precincts of the forest preserve. The scenery is the best and there are plenty of interesting things to see and places to stay. Those who like a resort atmosphere where every moment is planned will be happier in the Borscht Belt. You pick a hotel, you go there, you stay there. And that's that.

But first, a diversion.

EXCURSION TO STONE RIDGE

If you like unspoiled country villages, lush rural scenery, untrafficky roads dotted with an interesting selection of antiques shops, a handsome and luxurious old inn, and a famous country restaurant that rates four stars from the *New York Times,* postpone your trip to the mountains and head instead for **Stone Ridge.** This is a modest ten-mile detour to the southwest of Kingston via N.Y. 209, which intersects N.Y. 28 just west of Thruway Exit 19. There's not a great deal to see down here, but the area is just so pretty. Stone Ridge is the sort of hamlet where dogs sleep in the streets. There are a few 18th-century houses, some very big old trees, and clipped lawns and capacious old houses on the outskirts. Absolutely nothing is happening anywhere nearby. But aesthetically speaking, it's an irresistible detour.

The most irresistible part of it is dinner at the **DePuy Canal House,** N.Y. 213 in High Falls (tel. 914/687-7700). This restored landmark building started life in 1797 as a tavern. Today it's a quietly luxurious restaurant with an early American accent. Gourmet dining is the order of the day, conducted in several restored rooms on two floors. Only dinner is served, Thursday through Sunday, from a prix-fixe menu priced either at $38 for the three-course meal or at $48 for the seven-course alternative. A sample meal might start with brisket beef consommé with tiny spinach leaves and poached quail egg, continue with baked gnocchetti with chicken livers, move on to an entree such as salmon filet in tarragon lemon egg sauce, and end up with a choice from the dessert tray. There are numerous alternative appetizers, pastas, entrees, etc., and the menu changes regularly. Open for dinner from 5:30 p.m. on Thursday, Friday, and Saturday, and from 3 p.m. on Sunday. Sunday brunch is served between 11:30 a.m. and 2:00 p.m. for $25. Reservations are a must.

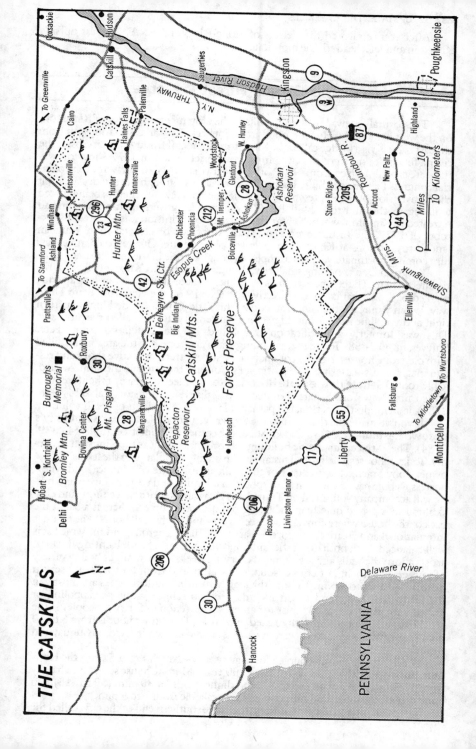

THE CATSKILLS

N

Croxsackie
Hudson
Catskill • Hudson
To Greenville
Cairo
N.Y. THRUWAY
Palenville
Haines Falls
Hensonville
Hunter
Tannersville
Windham
Ashland
296
23
Hunter Mtn.
To Stamford
42
Belleayre Ski Ctr.
Prattsville
Roxbury
30
Burroughs
Memorial
Mt. Pisgah
28
Bovina Center
Bromley Mtn.
Hobart • S. Kortright
Delhi
206
206
30
Hancock

Saugerties
Hudson River
Kingston
Poughkeepsie
9
9W
87
Highland
New Paltz
10
0   Miles   10
0   10   Kilometers
44
209
Accord
Stone Ridge
Ashokan Reservoir
Ashokan
W. Hurley
Woodstock
Glenford
28
Mt. Tremper
212
Chichester
Phoenicia
Esopus Creek
Boiceville
Big Indian
Catskill Mts.
Forest Preserve
Shawangunk Mtn.
Ellenville
Margaretville
Pepacton Reservoir
Lewbeach
55
17
Liberty
Fallsburg
To Middletown
To Wurtsboro
Monticello
Roscoe
Livingston Manor
206
30
Delaware River
PENNSYLVANIA

After you've savored the charms of Stone Ridge, take N.Y. 28 west outside Kingston and let's head for the mountains.

2. The Catskill Forest Preserve

The natural gateway to the Catskills is the aforementioned city of **Kingston,** on the west bank of the Hudson opposite Rhinebeck. Easy access to Kingston from the east bank is via a bridge called the **Kingston-Rhinecliff Bridge,** which crosses the river a few miles north of the city limits. For a brief period in 1777 Kingston was the state capital. Driven from New York by the British in 1776, New York's provincial congress fled first to White Plains. There it had just enough time to declare itself the Convention of the Representatives of the State of New York before being forced to flee again, this time to Fishkill. By 1777 the so-called government-on-the-run had retreated to Kingston, where New York's first state constitution was adopted. By October of 1777, the British were again at the door. Major General John Vaughan landed royal troops at Kingston and set the place on fire. Our representatives saw him coming, fortunately, and decamped to Poughkeepsie in the nick of time.

Kingston is an appealing small city, though in truth there's not much of touristic interest here. The center of town is conveniently accessible via a four-lane arterial, marked N.Y. 28, that connects directly with Exit 19 on the New York State Thruway. When you reach the Kingston end of this little spur of divided highway, turn right and you'll be right at the edge of a 17th-century district called the Stockade. This was formerly a fortification established by the Dutch governor, Peter Stuyvesant, in 1658. Today the defending walls are gone but the area is still filled with old stone houses, narrow colonial-gauge streets, trees, attractive shops and restaurants, and a smattering of historic sites. Among the latter is the stone-walled, gable-roofed **Senate House State Historic Site,** the meeting place of the aforementioned first New York Senate. Located at 312 Fair St., Kingston (tel. 914/338-2786), it's a modest attraction, but perhaps of interest to students of the Revolution.

If you've made the detour into the Stockade, a good place to eat is **Anthony's Uptown Restaurant,** 33-35 Crown St., at the corner of John Street (tel. 914/339-2184). The 18th-century stone building was originally built as the Kingston Academy. Today it houses a delightful restaurant justifiably popular with the locals. Chef/owner Tony Fraenkel, a graduate of the Culinary Institute of America, and wife/hostess Debbie have created an atmosphere that is quiet and elegant. Live piano music will accompany your meal on Thursday, Friday, and Saturday evenings, and classical music is played quietly in the background at other times. There is a bar at the back of the house where conversation seems easy and lively at all hours. The menu is international and creative, the portions are more than generous, and the wine list is well balanced, with both domestic and imported wines on hand. Paintings by local artists adorn the walls and are changed every six weeks. Lunch might be any variety of burger, sandwich, hot entree, soup, or salad, priced from $5 to $9 and served from 11:30 a.m. to 3 p.m. Tuesday through Saturday. Dinner entrees are mostly in the $9 to $17 range and might include poached salmon, scallops cappolini, or grilled baby lamb chops. A must for an appetizer (enough for two people) is the artichoke and jalapeño dip with toasted pita bread. The dinner hour is from 5 to 10 p.m. Tuesday through Saturday; reservations are recommended; closed Sunday and Monday.

For lighter fare just a couple blocks away, at 94 North Front St., try the **Hoffman House** (tel. 914/338-2626). This 300-year-old stone house serves lunch daily from 11:30 a.m. to 5 p.m. ($5 to $7) and dinner until 10:30 p.m. ($9 to $15). On Sunday both the lunch and dinner menu are available from 1 to 9 p.m.

The most interesting part of Kingston is the southern end of the city, called the

Roundout. The historic 19th-century waterfront hereabouts was known as Kingston Landing until 1828, when the completion of the Delaware and Hudson Canal made the Roundout into a vital terminal port on the Hudson River. By the 1870s the Roundout had become a congested commercial center with canalboats, steamboats, and trains transporting Pennsylvania coal, Ulster County bluestone, cement, and locally manufactured bricks.

Today this lively and much-restored neighborhood where the Roundout Creek and the Hudson River meet offers a number of interesting activities. Your first stop should be the **Hudson River Maritime Center,** Roundout Landing (tel. 914/338-0071). The center is an outdoor and indoor museum featuring a wooden boat–restoration shop. It's open daily from 11 a.m. to 5 p.m. (closed Tuesday) from May through October, with programs through December. The museum charges $2 for adults, $1 for children (6 to 12, under 6 free), and $1.50 for senior citizens. Across the street is the **Trolley Museum of New York,** 98 East Strand St. (tel. 914/331-3399). This one features trolley rides, a selection of antique trolleys, and a visitors' center, which is open daily during July and August, noon to 5 p.m., and weekends from Memorial Day to Columbus Day. Admission is $1 for adults and 50¢ for kids.

If you want to get out on the Hudson River itself try the *Rip Van Winkle,* a 500-passenger vessel based out of the Roundout. This boat makes a number of different excursions, including one to West Point and a Poughkeepsie minicruise, plus various lunch, dinner, and music cruises. Contact **Hudson River Cruises,** 524 North Ohioville Rd., New Paltz, NY 12561 (tel. 914/255-6515) for schedule and price information.

For riverside dining, try **Mary P's,** 1 Broadway (tel. 914/338-0116). Named after a day steamer out of Kingston to New York, the restaurant features northern Italian cuisine and is open daily for lunch from 11 a.m. to 4 p.m. ($4 to $10), for dinner from 4:30 to 10 p.m. ($9 to $20). Mary P's also offers a summer brunch and seasonal outside patio dining. Just around the corner you'll find the **Armadillo Bar and Grill,** 97 Abeel St. (tel. 914/339-1550). This establishment specializes in Southwestern cuisine like fajita steaks and shrimp-stuffed jalapeños. The grill is open for lunch from 11:30 a.m. to 3:30 p.m., for dinner from 4:30 to 11 p.m. Closed Tuesday.

Just one mile south on Route 32 is **The Hillside Manor,** 240 Boulevard (tel. 914/331-4386). This elegant northern Italian restaurant is one of the few in the Hudson River Valley to rate four stars from the *Mobile Travel Guide.* It boasts fresh seafood and homemade pasta. The interior is furnished with Mediterranean-style furniture, and the bar area is an open atrium filled with plants, gleaming brass, and polished wood. Not only is there a roomy dining area with crisp white linens and black-tie service, but there is also a new 14,000-square-foot banquet facility offering white-glove service. Dinner is in the $7 to $19 range and might include homemade pastas like paglia e fieno, or red snapper pescatora, fresh salmon alla griglia, and chicken dijonnaise. Open Tuesday through Friday from 5:30 to 9:30 p.m.; Saturday until 10 p.m.; Sunday from 1 to 9 p.m.; closed Monday. Reservations are required.

On the outskirts of Kingston on N.Y. 28, a stone's throw from Thruway Exit 19, is the obligatory **Howard Johnson's Motor Lodge** (tel. 914/338-4200) and **Ramada Inn** (tel. 914/339-3900). Hojo's has double-occupancy rates ranging from about $60 to $70. Do check the Ramada Super Saver rates of $39 to $69. I mention these just in case.

Kingston is the point of origin for a logical circular scenic route that swings through the very heart of the Catskills. The road is fast and the total round-trip distance is under 90 miles. Although I'll recommend numerous hotels and restaurants along this route, it's possible to swing right through it all on a day trip.

Of course, to do that is to lose considerable local flavor. What lured people to these mountains in the first place was a peculiar combination of remoteness and otherworldliness. The high-speed roads have changed all that. True, the scenery along these highways is at times absolutely gorgeous—clean serpentine pavements, frowning peaks, pine forests with rivers rushing over rocky shallows, etc. But the real scenic treats lie deeper in the forest. For those you have to get out of the car and walk.

The rub is, how do you know where to walk? How do you find Kaaterskill Falls (a 260-foot drop; quite a sight) or Inspiration Point or Jimmy Dolan Notch or the Pine Orchard? To be honest, you need advance preparation that lies beyond the scope of this book. The New York State Department of Environmental Conservation publishes a booklet called "Catskill Trails," which contains maps and brief trail descriptions of three- to eight-mile hikes in the northern and central Catskills. Contact the DEC Catskill Area Office, Region 4 Subregion Office, 439 Main St., Catskill, NY 12414 (tel. 518/943-4030), and ask for a copy. I suppose you c-ould also pick it up in person, as the town of Catskill is only 20 miles upriver from Kingston. This booklet doesn't describe things in much detail, however. Full-length books exist for that purpose, a good one being *Fifty Hikes in the Hudson Valley,* by Barbara McMartin and Peter Kick, published in 1985 by Backcountry Publications, Woodstock, VT 05091. This fascinating little tome will lead you knowledgeably to and around places like Vernooy Kill Falls, Mount Tremper, Giant Ledge, Black Dome, etc. The typical hike takes four to five hours, and the accompanying text and maps are easy to use and most informative. These hikes, by the way, require neither pitons nor native guides. Wear good shoes, don't go alone, take matches, and be sure somebody knows where you're going (in case you get lost), and you'll be sufficiently prepared.

ARTISTIC WOODSTOCK

This attractive village, located just across the boundary of the Catskill Park about ten miles from Kingston, is only now reacquiring a New England look. For many years in the wake of the famous 1969 rock festival Woodstock assumed a sort of tie-dyed disguise. Old wooden porches and gables around town turned purple and lavender, shop windows sprouted displays of unusual art and paraphernalia not often associated with upstate towns.

Woodstock, however, had a bohemian reputation long before anyone ever thought of rock and roll. In 1902 a pair of American artists named Bolton Brown and Hervey White met up with a fellow named Ralph Radcliffe Whitehead, known as the "wealthiest commoner in England." Brown and White brought Whitehead up to Woodstock and sold him on the idea of founding an artists' colony true to the aesthetic of Whitehead's idols, John Ruskin and William Morris. The result was **Byrdcliffe,** a 1,500-acre complex of 30 arts-and-crafts-ish buildings and a mile and a half of roads. By 1903 over 100 artist-types were busy laboring over looms and kilns, taking pictures, carving wood, and throwing pots. Many distinguished people have been associated with Byrdcliffe over the years, from author Thomas Mann to FDR's confidante Harry Hopkins. The place still exists, on its now heavily wooded hillside a short drive outside Woodstock. Many shops in town have stacks of free "Byrdcliffe, A Brief History and Walking Guide" brochures, usually right next to the cash register.

Woodstock is also the home of one of the oldest chamber music concert series in the United States. This was a 1916 undertaking of the busy Hervey Smith. Artists and creative people have been homing in on Woodstock for so long that it's little surprise the Woodstock Festival wound up here too. Today, although the village has a new Massachusetts-style serenity (a function of the rekindled interest in white clapboards and dark-green shutters), it is still home to a broad and sophisticated range of shops and galleries. These are quality establishments, dealing primarily in arts, crafts, and fashionable clothing. Girls with electric hair and tie-dyed shirts are not completely gone from the streets, but the new Woodstock is better known for its diminutive but trend-setting emporia with names like Laughing Bear Batik, Woodstock Chimes, White Mare, Crabtree & Evelyn, and Homecoming. Serious shoppers for women's clothes should take note: if you like a particular high-style casual look, you're going to *love* shopping in Woodstock.

The environs of the village are a favorite locale for weekend houses of people from the city, which fact helps explain how Woodstock can support not one but several summer theaters. The **Woodstock Playhouse,** P.O. Box 427, Woodstock, NY 12498 (tel. 914/679-2436), just west of the intersection of N.Y. 212 and 375, is the oldest stock theater in the country. Their schedule usually offers 10 to 12 different shows over approximately 19 weeks, on every day but Monday. There are even Saturday-morning children's productions. Call for program information. **River Arts Repertory** features revised original productions of the classics plus new American plays during the summer season at the Byrdcliffe Theatre in Woodstock. Contact them at P.O. Box 1166, Woodstock, NY 12498 (tel. 914/679-2100), for information on forthcoming productions.

Woodstock even has a great radio station, **WDST** (100 on the FM dial) whose programming ranges from classical to rock, a neat trick carried off with exemplary skill.

Meals and Lodging in Woodstock

Woodstock has a lot of restaurants, not one of which is really bad. Burgers on outdoor terraces with a bar somewhere in the back is a familiar summer theme in town. Something a little different would be **The Little Bear,** 295 B Tinker St., Bearsville (tel. 914/679-9497), located on N.Y. 212 one mile west of Woodstock. This is probably the best Chinese food I've had in upstate New York. House specialties include wok-cooked foods from all the major regions of China—Peking, Hunan, Szechuan, Canton, and Shanghai. The restaurant is rustic and simple, with wooden floors and tables located in a porch dining area overlooking the rambling Saw-Kill Creek. Chef Sha-Wu is not just a masterful cook but also a swell fellow and something of a regional celebrity. His extensive menu is available daily from noon to 10 p.m. and almost everything is in the $4 to $11 range. Try the no-name chicken ("no-name" because it's not on the menu). Reservations recommended.

If you've got a taste for fast, hot, inexpensive fried food, try **Duey's,** on N.Y. 212 at 50 Mill Hill Rd. (tel. 914/679-9593), whose umbrella tables and potted flowers flank the sidewalk a block or so from the Village Green. Inside is a modern pine-paneled room with a lofty ceiling, a dozen or so tables, and a short counter. Cheeseburgers, buckets of chicken, grilled sandwiches, fries, and homemade desserts are almost all priced under $5. Most of the burgers, in fact, cost less than $2. It's nonchain fast food, but it's good. Open seven days from 6:30 a.m. until 9 p.m.

There aren't any hotels in Woodstock, but there is an appealing guesthouse. It's called **Twin Gables,** located adjacent to the center of town at 73 Tinker St., Woodstock, NY 12498 (tel. 914/679-9479). "We're 50 years behind the times" boasts the rate sheet, and indeed they are. Claudette Colbert and Clark Gable might well have stayed in a place like this in some madcap Metro comedy from 1936. It's a modest old yellow frame house, with a porch overlooking Tinker Street and a "Catskill Grandma" interior filled with flowery wallpaper, flowery rugs, and immaculately clean little rooms. Share-the-bath doubles pay only about $40 nightly. A double with a private bath costs but $5 to $10 more.

SHANDAKEN, THE HEART OF THE CATSKILLS

Shandaken is the name of both a village and a township. The village is located on N.Y. 28 about 30 miles from Kingston. But when people say Shandaken, they usually refer to an area that also includes Mount Tremper, Phoenicia, Big Indian, and several other mountain hamlets spread out along a 20-mile stretch of N.Y. 28.

The township dates from 1804, when the tanning industry was getting under way. There were once seven big leather tanneries hereabouts, cumulatively requiring the bark of 20,000 cords of hemlock trees . . . *every year.* The hillsides were denuded with a ferocity that would warm the heart of many a modern-day strip miner. So many skinned hemlocks were produced in the course of the first half of the 19th century that a wooden road, complete with toll booths, was laid all the way from Pine Hill to Kingston, a distance of 40 miles. When the last standing hemlock was debarked, the locals, as is so often the case, turned to tourism. There were never any great mountain hotels out here, as was the case closer to the Hudson. Instead, there were rooming houses, some of which still stand, in varying states of repair and devoted to varying different uses.

Once in a while even the most jaded traveler stumbles upon an experience that is the more surprising and delightful for being so unexpected. Such is the Shandaken area, which is often referred to as the **French Catskills** and truly represents a French rural mountain culinary retreat. It is a modern anomaly that spectacular French bourgeois cooking, as good as anything in Paris or Lyons, is available in the middle of the Catskills. The *patrons* seem collectively to have acquired a taste for modern American building materials. Most of their restaurants occupy structures decorated on the outside with textured panels and on the inside with fake wood paneling. But the dining rooms at night are charming withal, and the food is famous.

You could easily spend several days here, hiking in the woods, and sampling a different excellent local restaurant every night. Or you could combine a single meal with a day trip from Kingston.

Restaurants and Lodging in Shandaken

My favorite French retreat is the **Auberge des 4 Saisons** on N.Y. 42 (½ mile from N.Y. 28), Shandaken, NY (tel. 914/688-2223). During my last visit the modest inn was hosting a birthday party for a chef from one of the other French restaurants. The simple, unpretentious meals might include entrees like filet mignon with sauce béarnaise, veal in madeira sauce, rabbit in white wine, etc. They cost about $11 to $16. Dinner is served from 6 to 10 p.m. daily in the summer, and from 5 to 9:30 p.m. on Friday, Saturday, and Sunday in the winter. Not only does the Auberge boast a fine French restaurant, but it also includes a pool, a tennis court, facilities for bocci, badminton, volleyball, and croquet—not to mention a variety of lodging options. The "Chalet" features spacious motel-style rooms with private baths, TV, and balconies. Cabins with private baths are located near the pool, and additional very simple rooms are available in the inn itself. The entire experience, which includes accommodations, two meals, and all the facilities, costs from $55 to $80 per day per person.

La Duchesse Anne, 4 Miller Rd., Mount Tremper, NY 12464 (tel. 914/688-5260), occupies an untouched, antique rooming house by the side of a river in a woody glen. It's complete with ancient wallpaper, floors that creak and sigh, and wood stoves that still produce heat. The big old-fashioned dining room has low ceilings supported by dark-wood columns, dark-green wallpaper, an elaborate old wood stove, and flocks of tables covered with crisp white cloths. Luncheon entrees like rabbit provençale, pork with mushrooms, veal scallop, grilled entrecôte, and filet of sole mostly cost between $6 and $10. Also available are numerous crêpes and quiches. At dinner, duck flambé, veal scallop normande, poached trout with white butter sauce, etc., will typically run between $12 and $19. Lunch is only served on weekends, from 10 a.m. to 2 p.m. on Saturday, to 4 p.m. on Sunday. Dinner is available from 6 until 9:30 p.m. on most weekdays, and until 11 p.m. on Friday, Saturday, and holidays. Closed Tuesday during the summer, and Tuesday and Wednesday during the winter. Above the dining room are 17 rudimentary bedrooms that share baths (one bathroom per three bedrooms). These cost between $40 and $45 per night double occupancy. Children and pets are welcome.

Yvonne's, on N.Y. 28, Phoenicia, NY 12464 (tel. 914/688-7340), is a wonderful French roadside café. Originally a drive-in offering quiches, roast duck, and the traditional hamburger, Yvonne's has become a very popular café; it seats up to 60 patrons. The waitressess all wear traditional clothing from the Périgord region in

France. The food is highly acclaimed and includes such dishes as a venison plate with truffles, wild boar, rabbit, salmon rillettes, French marinated herrings, etc. Dinner is in the $15 range and can be enjoyed any summer evening (except Tuesday and Wednesday) from 4 to 10 p.m. During the fall and spring the restaurant is open on weekends only; closed in the winter.

The **Val D'Isère,** on N.Y. 28 in Big Indian, NY (tel. 914/254-4646), is located in an old Victorian house that's been Swiss-alpined on the outside. The dining room is bright and cheerful, with acoustic ceilings, faux beams, a mirrored fountain wall on one side, lots of windows on the other, abundant hanging plants, and a capacity of 65 persons. Only dinner is served, year-round, daily except Tuesday. Typical entrees include grilled salmon, sautéed tournedos of beef with bordelaise sauce, grilled filet of beef with green peppercorn sauce, chicken with raspberry vinegar sauce, etc., priced from about $10 to $16. With an appetizer and dessert, neither of which you'll want to skip, dinner will cost about twice that. There are also six guest rooms available with shared baths for $40 a night.

Rudi's Big Indian, on N.Y. 28 in Big Indian (tel. 914/254-4005), is something completely different. It sits in solitary splendor just outside the two-building town of Big Indian. The restaurant is a modern place with a Frank Lloyd Wright look to it. Diners have a choice of several appealing places to eat. There's a great outdoor deck with awnings and umbrella tables, a plant-filled "conservatory," and a cathedral-ceilinged main dining room furnished with antique Victorian tables facing walls of glass. The lunch menu offers quiches, burgers, chicken wings, pot pies, omelets, etc., for about $5 to $9. À la carte dinner entrees such as hot broccoli salad, turkey scaloppine, broiled sirloin, fresh salmon, grilled pork chop, etc., mostly run from $13 to $19. Open noon to 9:30 p.m. seven days a week from July 4 until Labor Day; closed Tuesday and Wednesday the rest of the year, plus the month of November and part of December.

Sweet Sue's, on Main Street in Phoenicia (tel. 914/688-7852), is an old-fashioned small-town restaurant whose house specialty is pancakes. Blueberry, peach, whole-wheat, or apple varieties of same cost about $3.50 per stack. Alternatively, you might try the spiced-fruit-bread french toast. There are also sandwiches of turkey, roast beef, tuna, etc., plus chili and homemade soup, priced at under $3. Only breakfast and lunch are served, in a little room with flowered cloths and plastic chairs. Open from 7 a.m. to 3 p.m.

My first choice in the area for accommodations is the **Mount Tremper Inn,** on N.Y. 212 and Wittenberg Road, Mount Tremper, NY 12457 (tel. 914/688-5329), a rambling clapboard boarding house whose big front porch is hung with baskets of flowers and supported by ornate brackets. The decor inside includes crimson crushed-velvet wainscoting, rococo revival furniture, curtains on swags, dropped ceilings, and the genteel strains of recorded classical music. Of the 12 rooms, 10 share three hall baths; two rooms have baths of their own. The room decor includes cheery tiny pattern wallpaper, random antiques, and fluffy comforters. Although not precisely a Victorian period piece, the Mount Tremper has a particular charm all its own. Double-occupancy rates include a full breakfast and range from $60 for a standard room, to $75 for one of the private-bath rooms, to $90 for the "suite." Complimentary evening sherry, served on the porch, is a good way to meet your fellow guests. La Duchesse Anne is just across the road.

The **Shandaken Inn,** on N.Y. 28 just west of the intersection of N.Y. 42, Shandaken, NY 12480 (tel. 914/688-5100), is a beautiful old vine-clad building nestled amid lawns and gardens just outside the village of Shandaken. This former golf club, built in the 1920s, sports a delightful pool, a tennis court, a rushing brook, lovely stone-flagged terraces furnished with umbrella tables and chairs, and inside a handsome lodge-like living room complete with fireplaces, wing chairs, pine paneling, and an adjacent bar. There are but 12 rooms, all spotlessly clean, cozy, decorated with random antiques and looking like the comfortable guest rooms in someone's house. During the week that's exactly what the place is. But on Friday and

Saturday nights two people can rent one of the attractive rooms for between $185 and $210 nightly ($160 if there's no private bath), including breakfast and dinner. Cuisine is French (as is the proprietress), and the Saturday-night meal is like an elegant country house party. It usually ends up with dancing in the bar. This is the best-looking place in the area. Reservations required; no children.

Right on N.Y. 28 in the steep valley that leads from Mount Tremper to Phoenicia is the **Mount Pleasant Lodge,** N.Y. 28, Phoenicia, NY 12464 (tel. 914/688-2278). This is actually a little complex of log-cabin-style buildings that includes a 12-unit motel, 20 duplexes ($120), a bar/restaurant, a ski shop, even a swimming pool. The guest rooms are well kept, surprisingly big, with shag carpets, natural-log walls, private bathrooms, and color television sets. They're really quite good-looking. Double-occupancy rates are a reasonable $70 nightly, $15 less during the week. The moderately priced café serves home-cooked breakfast, lunch, and dinner, and includes a very congenial bar. On Saturday nights there's even live music.

My favored non-French restaurant in this neck of the woods is the **Catskill Rose,** on N.Y. 212, Mount Tremper (tel. 914/688-7100). The last time I was there they had a full brass Dixieland band that followed one of the best smoked duck–with–plum sauce dinners I've ever had (the only one, but I'd go back for more). The folks here have wonderful vegetarian dishes, as well as their own smoked fish, fowl, and meat. The menu is sort of American eclectic, and is served Tuesday through Sunday from 5 to 10:30 p.m., with a Sunday brunch offered from 10:30 a.m. to 3 p.m. Dinner will cost between $11 and $16, with brunch in the $9 to $11 range.

THE ROUTE BACK VIA HUNTER

After you've explored the Shandaken area to your satisfaction, find N.Y. 42 (it intersects N.Y. 28 at the village of Shandaken) and head north toward Lexington. This is a particularly scenic road with lovely prospects of rushing rivers and craggy mountaintops. The village of **Lexington,** 11 miles from Shandaken, is a nice-looking hamlet with some fabulous old unrenovated Victorian buildings. In the middle of it you'll cross a bridge over the Schoharie Creek, shortly after which you'll arrive at the intersection of N.Y. 23A. Get on 23A eastbound toward Hunter.

Before coming into Hunter, you'll see the **Baptist Ukrainian Church** on the north side of the road. This wooden confection is straight out of a Russian fairy tale. It's also about the last good-looking building you'll see for the next couple of miles. **Hunter,** it would seem, has been infected with a dangerous strain of the "Cutesy Swiss" virus. It's the rare house or store that has escaped a Swiss-ish modernization characterized by absurd cut-out eaves, shutters with heart-shaped holes in them, and half-timbering that is all too plainly concocted of one-by-fours tacked onto the façade with roofing nails. The ubiquitous accompaniment to all this seems to be untidy parking lots and dispirited-looking malls.

Things do look better in the winter with three feet of snow on the ground. That's when the famous **Hunter Mountain Ski Area** is in full swing. Whatever the aesthetic drawbacks of the village of Hunter, there's no doubt that Hunter Mountain has the best skiing in the Catskills. The facilities include 37 trails, a 1,600-foot vertical drop, 17 lifts with a capacity of 17,000 skiers per hour, base and summit lodges, plus rentals, a nursery, package deals, etc. The entrance to the ski area is smack in the center of the village. For complete information on skiing at Hunter, contact Hunter Mountain, Hunter, NY 12442 (tel. 518/263-4223, or toll free 800/FOR-SNOW). There are other ski areas in the Catskills, information on which can be obtained by writing to Greene County Promotion Dept., P.O. Box 527, Catskill, NY 12414 (tel. 518/943-3223). The *I Love New York Greene County Travel Guide* describes them all.

During the summer you can ride up Hunter Mountain on the **Hunter Mountain Skyride,** the longest, highest chair lift in the Catskills. The views are pretty spectacular and the cost is a reasonable $5 for adults, $2.50 for kids 6 to 12, and 50¢ for little ones 5 and under. The Skyride operates daily (weather permitting) from

June 28 to Labor Day, and on weekends only in the spring and fall. Hours are 11 a.m. to 4:30 p.m. Call 518/263-4223 for further information.

Hunter is also widely known for its **Summer Festivals,** which run the gamut from the German Alps Festival to the National Polka Festival, to the Mountain Eagle Authentic Native American Indian Festival, to the International Celtic Festival, with several stops in between. Program and ticket information can be obtained from Exposition Planners, Bridge Street, Hunter, NY 12442 (tel. 518/263-3800).

Ten or so more miles on N.Y. 23A will bring you to the little village of **Tannersville,** a town of false-fronted Victorian buildings with an almost Western look. After the age of the tanneries this area became a center of upscale summer development, much of which still exists. Several private residential parks, their roads barred to nonmembers, are clustered around Tannersville. The swellest is **Onteora Park,** a former artists' colony that became almost posh around the turn of the century. Fine mansions still line Onteora Road, north of the Tannersville light. The park itself, centered around a clubhouse, golf links, and a private lake, is filled with picturesque cliff-hanging dwellings designed in rustic mountain style. However, it's not open to the public. Neither is **Twilight Park,** located east of the nearby village of Haines Falls on steep slopes overlooking Kaaterskill Clove. Twilight isn't quite as luxe as Onteora, but some of its houses have wonderful views of **Kaaterskill Falls.** You can't see the falls from the road, even though they're only half a mile from 23A. The access trail joins 23A beside a hairpin curve about a mile east of Haines Falls. It's marked, but first-timers might have trouble finding it.

Instead of hiking you might want to rent a horse. The **Silver Springs Ranch,** on N.Y. 16, Tannersville (tel. 518/589-5559), can include you on a guided trail ride anytime from 9 a.m. to 5 p.m. The cost is about $12 per hour. There is another stable between here and Woodstock called the **Circle Tee Stable,** Lower Glasco Turnpike, Woodstock (tel. 914/679-8909). Again, guided trail rides are the order of the day, at about $10 hourly.

Meals and Lodging in the Hunter/Tannersville Area

Best idea for an informal meal in the area is the curiously named **Last Chance Cheese and Antiques Café,** Main Street (N.Y. 23A), Tannersville (tel. 518/589-6424). They do actually *sell* antiques, and the place is full of them. In fact, there's not an inch of wall space that isn't covered with some item of Victorian-era bric-a-brac, a gilt-framed picture, a hunk of imported cheese, a barrel of something-or-other, or a package of gourmet food. Like Tannersville itself, this establishment has a faint Western atmosphere, reminiscent of a general store in some 19th-century Colorado boom town. Besides gourmet items, the Last Chance has a varied menu that includes cheese fondue, pot pie, pastrami sandwiches, nachos, French onion soup, yogurt fruit salad, fresh pressed cider, chili, melted brie on raisin pumpernickel, etc., at reasonable prices. Expect to pay about $5 for a hefty sandwich, and up to about $8 for a house specialty. Usually the cheesecake's terrific. A narrow porch out front is ideal for summer dining. Open daily from 10 a.m. until 7 p.m.

The nicest spot in the area for dinner, and indeed for staying overnight, is the **Redcoat's Return,** Dale Lane (off Platte Clove Road, N.Y. 16), Elka Park, NY 12427 (tel. 518/589-6379). This square four-story clapboard building surrounded by broad porches was built as a rooming house in 1912. The present English owner (hence the name Redcoat's Return) has revamped and redecorated the place into a quite cozy and singularly comfortable inn/restaurant. The Victorian eclectic lobby is decorated with rich dark colors, a moosehead over the fireplace, a Chinese screen, books aplenty, a piano, and a fish tank. The 14 rooms upstairs are small, but nicely turned out with painted iron beds and pretty patterned wallpaper. About half have private bathrooms and rent for $100 nightly including a full breakfast. Skip the private bathroom and the double-occupancy rate drops to $85. On holiday and winter weekends there's a minimum stay, so better inquire about that in advance. Alternatively, you might make a reservation just for dinner. Roast duckling with orange sauce, broiled sirloin, poached filet of sole, etc., served in atmospheric surroundings will cost between $15 and $18 à la carte. To find the Redcoat's, follow N.Y. 16 south from the Tannersville light for about four miles to Dale Lane on your right. You can see the inn from here, sharing its meadowy valley with an aluminum-sided family resort which, once you pull into Redcoat's, becomes magically invisible.

Also useful to know about in the Hunter/Tannersville area is the **Hunter Mountain Lodging Bureau,** on N.Y. 23A, Hunter, NY 12442 (tel. 518/263-4208), is a free central booking agency located in a small shopping plaza opposite the entrance to the ski area. They can book you into any one of 20 participating area hotels/motels/inns, plus a collection of private chalets that rent to transients. Expect to pay about $80 to $100 nightly, double occupancy, often with a minimum stay required. There's someone at the phone every day from 10 a.m. until 6 p.m.

A Scenic Route Home

N.Y. 23A from Tannersville to Palenville is a very pretty road. It twists along the bottom of the steep-sided Kaaterskill Clove, crossing and recrossing the rocky bed of Kaaterskill Creek. But N.Y. 16, known as Platte Clove Road (the road from Tannersville to the Redcoat's Return), is far more scenic. It's also incredibly twisty, and so narrow in places you'll wonder if you're on a real road at all. If you follow Platte Clove Road east to the end, you'll emerge on N.Y. 212 only a few miles from Thruway Exit 20 at Saugerties.

3. The Resorts

South of the Catskill park, near the towns of Monticello, Ellenville, and Liberty, are the famous Catskill resorts. In many minds these huge establishments are synonymous with the very name Catskill. In point of fact they aren't in the Catskill Mountains at all.

To be sure, the terrain around Monticello is hilly and quite beautiful. There was a boarding-house era up here too, at the end of the 19th and in the early 20th centuries. Except that these boarding houses, instead of closing down as the present century progressed, kept growing bigger and bigger. After the Second World War they blossomed into modern Miami Beach–style behemoths with private golf courses, private lakes, sometimes a dozen tennis courts, indoor pools, outdoor pools, ice rinks, steamrooms, riding stables, bike trails, ski slopes, health clubs, planned activities for tots, planned activities for teens, and in fact any- and everything else they could think of to attract guests.

Woody Allen's movie *Annie Hall* begins with a great gag about two elderly Jewish ladies at a Catskill resort. "The food is so bad!" complains the first. "And they don't give you enough!" replies the second. This joke, which is actually the exact opposite of the true situation, still serves as an amusing introduction to those specific hallmarks of the Catskill resort experience. The first is the hotel nightclub with the Catskill comedian. Some of these clubs really do feature first-rank talent, names everyone's heard. The second is the hotel dining room where you can (and indeed you are urged to) eat everything that isn't nailed down. Food is something of a preoccupation in this neck of the woods (certainly it's no place to go on a diet). The third is socialization. Hotel blurbs all tout a fairly dizzying array of activities that will keep you, your kids, your parents, and all your friends busy from the instant you set foot on the manicured grounds.

In recent years the big resorts have suffered declining popularity. They are not, I'm sorry to say, particularly beautiful. To many people this makes no difference. As long as the place is well kept and has a ton of facilities, they won't mind. But the national resurgence of interest in historic preservation and finer craftsmanship, plus the development of nearby Atlantic City, New Jersey, into a casino center, has left many of the Catskill resorts in the wrong court. Some have turned themselves into part-time "conference centers," others have begun developing bits of their land into vacation condominiums, while still others have turned into religious or meditation centers, and many have just gone belly-up.

It still remains possible, however, to enjoy a traditional Catskill resort holiday, complete with more food than you dreamed you could eat, daytimes filled with poolside lounging and planned activities, and nighttimes spent in a glitzy nightclub chortling over Borscht Belt gags. It's estimated that there are still 198 holes of golf in the immediate environs of Monticello, plus 32 swimming pools (of the immense Olympic variety) and 154 tennis courts.

Since the last edition of this book, two more resorts have fallen by the way. Most of the hotels that remain are still managed by the families that founded them. These are **Grossinger's** (800/431-6300), the **Concord** (800/431-3850), the **Nevele Hotel** (800/647-6000), **Kutsher's Country Club**, (800/431-1273), **Fallsview Resort and Country Club** (800/431-0152), the **Raleigh Resort and Country Club** (800/446-4003), the **Villa Roma Resort and Country Club** (800/533-6767), **The New Brown's Hotel** (800/3-BROWNS), the **Pines Resort Hotel** (800/36-PINES). Grossinger's and the Concord are probably the most elaborate of the bunch. Typical daily rates, including three full meals, range between $80 and $100 per person, with significant discounts for five-night or weekly stays. These rates are discounted by another 10% to 20% during the autumn, winter, and spring.

If this all sounds interesting, I suggest that you phone one or more of the above establishments direct (they all have toll-free 800 numbers) and request individual brochures and rate sheets.

THE CAPITAL DISTRICT

New York City may not be the "real" New York. But Albany most certainly is. Besides containing the capitol itself, the so-called Capital District boasts fine shopping, many historic sightseeing attractions, plus exotic Saratoga Springs, cash-rich home of racing touts and dancing tutus.

1. Greater Albany

Henry Hudson never made it to China, but in the fall of 1609 he did make it to Albany. Today's charming little city (pop. 110,000) holds the distinction of being both the capital of New York State and the oldest permanent settlement in the 13 colonies. From its early days as an important trading post, Albany has evolved into a major regional financial center as well as the eye of New York's hurricanes of political power and influence.

Ten years ago Albany had fallen pretty low. The story is a familiar one of post-war population shifts, boom development in adjoining suburban areas, and destructive downtown "urban renewal." But if ever a city has had magic dust sprinkled on it, that city is Albany. It seems like three-quarters of the downtown area, blocks rich with 19th-century architectural fabric, is now protected by local landmark laws. I've never seen so much restoration under way in one place in my life. The result is an exceedingly attractive and livable urban setting, graced with magnificent architecture and considerable amenities. The city isn't expensive, doesn't sprawl, and is fun and easy to explore.

ALBANY ORIENTATION

Albany is disproportionately sophisticated for its size, a fact best illustrated by the skyline of the **Governor Nelson A. Rockefeller Empire State Plaza.** This immense complex of 1960s marble-clad government buildings is clearly visible from many miles away. You'd never expect anything so big in a city of 110,000 people.

The Empire State Plaza and the **State Capitol** sit right at the heart of the town.

State Street runs about a half dozen blocks from the Capitol steps to the Hudson. On State and adjacent cross streets is where you'll find the biggest and finest commercial buildings, as well as the local Hilton hotel and the heart of the downtown business district.

Albany is situated on the west bank of the Hudson River and connected to the other shore by a free bridge, which is part of I-90. A spur of the Interstate system, **I-787** runs right along the Hudson shoreline, depriving the city of its waterfront but delivering traffic from I-90 in the north and I-87 (the New York State Thruway) in the south to the very center of town with amazing efficiency. There is ample parking underneath the Empire State Plaza. As a matter of fact, there is free street parking all over the city, including angle parking right on State Street. Driving a car around is actually a cinch, at least when the state legislature isn't in session.

Immediately bordering the business center are tree-lined residential streets consisting of small-scale 19th-century brick and brownstone rowhouses. There are six separate historic districts adjoining downtown, about which more later. Behind the Capitol itself, located on an extension of State Street, are the finest of the in-town mansions. Then comes **Washington Park,** an 84-acre preserve designed by the ubiquitous Frederick Law Olmsted. Beyond the park the city becomes more architecturally modest and soon tapers off into suburbs.

Today's elite live north of I-90 in neighboring **Loudonville.** The huge discount shopping malls for which Albany is famous are located in the environs of **Wolf Road,** a few miles west of town at the intersection of I-90 and I-87. Interesting restaurants and bars are scattered all over the city. The roster of interesting hotels, alas, is not extensive.

I loved the street names in Albany. For roadways running north and south they went in big for birds: Quail, Partridge, Lark, Dove, Swan, etc. The east-west streets today bear the names of the founding fathers (Jefferson, Washington, Hamilton, Madison, Jay, etc.), but before the Revolution they bore names like Mink, Otter, Snipe, Lion, and Tiger. Elk Street is about the only one left.

THE SIGHTS OF ALBANY
Herewith, brief descriptions of those attractions that make the city unique, starting with:

The Governor Nelson A. Rockefeller Empire State Plaza
It cost $1 billion (in the 1960s) to construct this multibuilding office plaza situated smack in the center of town. The first impression is of blinding light, a result of acre upon acre of pure-white marble gleaming in the sun. The plaza has an outdoor pedestrian concourse that extends a full quarter mile south from the side of the State Capitol. Lining it is a series of stylistically unified white marble office buildings, dazzling reflecting pools, trees clipped into cubes, occasional outdoor art, and nice views of the city and the forests beyond. Actually it looks a lot like the capital of some Third World country determined to prove its worth in the modern world. The architecture may be a little sterile, especially in contrast to the older stone confections nearby, but it sure is impressive.

The tallest building on the plaza is the **Corning Tower,** notable for its free 42nd-floor **observation deck.** Below grade is the **Indoor Concourse,** an awesomely long enclosed mall lined with striking modern art of the 50-foot-long-canvas school and numerous shops and offices.

A walk up and down the plaza is an absolute must for all visitors. A free map of the place, with detailed descriptions of the buildings and all that goes on within them, may be obtained at the **Visitor Assistance Office** (tel. 518/474-2418), located at the north end of the main Underground Concourse (which is actually just across the street from the State Capitol Building). Among the buildings described in the Empire State Plaza Guide is:

ESIPA at the Egg

ESIPA stands for **Empire State Plaza Institute for the Performing Arts;** the Egg is that peculiar sort-of-egg-shaped concrete structure next to the Corning Tower. The Egg has been acclaimed as the most accessible theater in the United States. Which means, I suppose, that the programming appeals to a very broad spectrum of the population. Inside its curvaceous concrete walls is a 900-seat auditorium where anyone from Alvin Ailey to Chuck Mangione, from Wynton Marsalis to the Boys Choir of Harlem, from Bobby Short to the cast of *Les Miserables* is quite likely to be performing. Ticket prices vary but are quite reasonable by Manhattan standards. For information on current productions, call the Visitor Assistance Office at 518/ 474-2418.

The New York State Museum

The days of museum corridors lined with cases full of historic "artifacts" are over, at least here. The New York State Museum is more of an entertainment experience than anything else. Located in a self-consciously modern building covered with marble louvers and located at the south end of the Empire State Plaza, it consists of two very large halls devoted respectively to the "Adirondack Wilderness" and the "New York Metropolis." A third hall, dedicated to New York's "Upstate," was not yet open at this writing.

This is a very slick installation indeed, one consisting of artifacts, photos, dioramas, scale reconstructions, filmclips, etc. Visitors advance through the huge darkened exhibition halls like Hansel and Gretel in the forest. Around every corner there's another exhibit bathed in dramatic light, and augmented as often as not with sound effects from bird calls to clanking subway trains. In one upholstered corner, called the "Blowdown Theater," you can stand in the dark and listen to an Adirondack windstorm complete with crashing trees and shrieking winds. From another point you can admire 20-foot-tall color slides of fall foliage. A life-size diorama depicts a logjam in a mountain stream, right down to real water. Over on the New York City side is an astonishing cutaway scale model of Grand Central Terminal, a 1925 Fifth Avenue bus, an entire subway car with nearby monitors that show a video called *Working the A Train,* and a collection of antique fire engines.

The museum has additional exhibits, but these are the highlights. It's open daily from 10 a.m. to 5 p.m. and admission is free. For further information, call 518/ 474-5877. The main entrance is on Madison Avenue, which is one floor below the open-air concourse at the south end of the Empire State Plaza. Plenty of parking is available in the museum's adjacent lot.

The State Capitol

This fantastical pink-granite monster was started in 1869 and completed in 1898. It then burned in 1911, but was restored by 1914 to even greater grandeur. It sits at the head of State Street, the apotheosis of everything that's wrong but still lovable about Victorian architecture. After years of neglect and abuse, it's undergoing a piecemeal restoration.

The State Capitol has more types of arches and columns and pilasters than you can name. Its interior is the definition of Edwardian opulence, especially the restored **Senate Chamber,** the faintly Byzantine **Assembly Chamber,** and the famous **"Million Dollar Staircase."** This latter feature is located on the western side of the building, and is a perfect maze of intricately carved granite stairs and landings. They crisscross their way upward in a most leisurely fashion inside a splendid interior space lit by sinuous old bronze fixtures.

Free tours of the Capitol leave daily on the hour from 9 a.m. until 4 p.m. from the **tour reception area** located on the north side of the main floor. Alternatively,

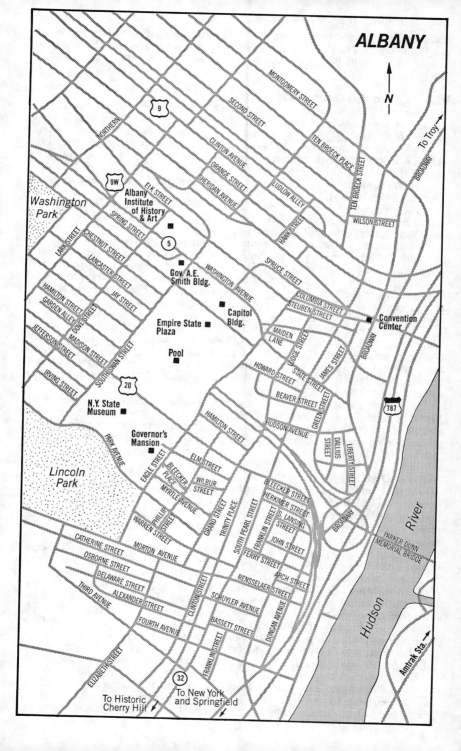

you can pick up a tour leaving from the Visitor Assistance Office at the north end of the Empire State Plaza's Main Underground Concourse. You can also just poke around by yourself. For more information, call Visitor Assistance at 518/474-2418.

Walking Around Downtown

The year 1986 was Albany's tricentennial, an event celebrated among other things by publication of an excellent small guidebook titled *Albany, Still Making History, 1686–1986*. If you can't find a copy in bookstores (admittedly it was a promotional piece without traditional bookstore distribution), you might try the aforementioned Visitor Assistance Office in the Empire State Plaza Main Concourse or the "I Love New York" office (tel. 518/474-4116) on the mezzanine of One Commerce Plaza (a modern office building adjacent to the State Capitol on the corner of Washington and Swan).

The point of having this guide is its excellent walking tours. The chapter by Judith Botch of the Historic Albany Foundation divides downtown Albany into three tours: State Street Hill, Capitol Hill, and Residential State Street. They're informative, easy to follow, and lots of fun. If you are unable to locate a copy of *Albany, Still Making History,* you can still stroll down State Street and admire its provincial grandiose. Perhaps most grandiose after the Capitol itself is the Flemish palace at the foot of the hill at State and Broadway. It's now the Central Administration Building of the State University of New York but it was built as the central office of the Delaware and Hudson Railroad. Its picturesque tower is one of Albany's most appealing landmarks.

Immediately to the north of the Capitol building, radiating from the intersection of Eagle and Elk Streets, is **Capitol Hill.** This area abounds with fine 19th-century rowhouses and public buildings. Elk between Eagle and Hawk is particularly interesting. The 1883 **Albany City Hall** on the corner of Eagle and Pine is architect Henry Hobson Richardson at his "most Romanesque." It sports yet another of Albany's famous towers.

You should also take a stroll along the three-block stretch of **Upper State Street** between Swan and Northern Boulevard. This is an upper-class late-Victorian district of attached town houses. Not many are used as private houses anymore, but the streetscape is wonderfully intact and gives a good sense of the texture of upscale provincial life a century ago.

Historic Districts

Downtown Albany boasts not one but *six* historic districts, which is enough to warm the cockles of every preservationist heart. The positive impact of Albany's current landmark policy cannot be overstated. A beautiful city has been saved, and what makes it so attractive today is not the new construction but the salvaged and restored architectural fabric from the past.

The five districts vary in quality but each has interesting lessons for those concerned with urban planning and restoration. The most intact and elaborate is Capitol Hill, a region distinct from that in the Albany Guide walking tour mentioned above. The **Capitol Hill Historic District** is located on the other side of the Capitol building between Swan Street and Washington Park. Its grandest street is upper State Street; the best-preserved blocks lie between State and Jay. Architecturally, it has much in common with Brooklyn Heights. It also seems to have many of the same prosperous middle-aged joggers wearing expressions of pain.

The **Pastures Preservation Historic District** takes its name from the old Schuyler estate, also called the Pastures (the Schuyler mansion still stands; see below). It's separated from the downtown business district by the big exit ramps that connect I-787 with the Empire State Plaza garages. The district is small, comprising only 13 blocks bounded by Pearl, Bleecker, South Ferry, and Dongan Streets. There's been a tremendous amount of work done here. Practically every house has undergone a gut renovation, and new brick sidewalks and street trees are everywhere in evidence. Even the empty lots are covered with mowed grass. A new infrastructure of parking lots and green areas has been superimposed on an early to mid-19th-century building stock. It needs time to age now, but the results are very interesting.

The other four districts are called **South End, Mansion, Clinton Avenue,** and **Arbor Hill,** respectively. South End ironically occupies land adjacent and to the south of the Schuyler mansion, the Pastures; the Mansion District takes its name from the Governor's Mansion on Eagle Street near Elm. Arbor Hill is the most interesting of the three. It's bounded on the south by Clinton Avenue and its principal thoroughfare is Ten Broeck Street. There's still serious poverty along Clinton Avenue and in Arbor Hill, plus crudely lettered signs that protest (rather desperately) "No Houses for Sale!" It seems, however, that just about every other house along the former has scaffolding out front. And when built, Ten Broeck Street in Arbor Hill was surely one of the most attractive late-Victorian thoroughfares in the northeast.

The Albany Institute of History and Art

Set back on a lawn two blocks from the Capitol building, this elegant old-fashioned museum eschews the glitz and showmanship of new-style display "environments." What it offers instead is a jewel-like collection of local portraits, silver, furniture, and the like, served up in an atmosphere of patrician calm. There is some really exquisite stuff in here, from Dutch period chests and chairs to pictures of the imperious old aristocrats who owned them. It's quite interesting to look at the faces of all the Ten Broecks, Schuylers, Van Rensselaers, Wendells, and so forth who ran the world hereabouts in centuries past. Total gallery area isn't too big, but lovers of beautiful things can spend many hours in this justly famous local institution at 125 Washington Ave. (tel. 518/463-4478). Hours are Tuesday through Friday from 10 a.m. to 4:45 p.m. and on Saturday and Sunday from noon to 5 p.m. Admission is free.

The Albany Urban Cultural Park

This ambitious little museum is really an Albany city family album. It's a photo museum of what Albany used to look like, and if you've enjoyed exploring today's city and already gotten the feel of it, then you'll doubtless get a kick out of this collection of old maps and photos. There are great shots of the old D&H Building, the State Street banks during the 1920s, Union Station as it looked when trains still stopped there (current rail service to Albany terminates on the other side of the Hudson in Rensselaer), Richardson's City Hall upon completion in 1883, plus the current renewal districts as they looked before they needed renewal. The display is cleverly mounted complete with moving parts that visitors can operate. But for me, it was the old pictures that really made it fun.

The Urban Cultural Park (quite a handle for a small place) is located in Quackenbush Square, the rather grand name of a cluster of restored commercial buildings located on Broadway immediately north of the exit ramp from I-787. The closest city cross street is Clinton Avenue. The museum is free and open Tuesday through Saturday from 10 a.m. until 4 p.m., on Sunday from 1 until 4 p.m.; closed Monday. For information, call 518/434-5132.

Four Historic Mansions

The first is the **Schuyler Mansion,** called originally the Pastures and built in 1761 by the aristocratic Philip Schuyler. Alexander Hamilton married a Schuyler daughter in this house; General James ("Gentleman Jimmy") Burgoyne was a houseguest-cum-prisoner after the British debacle at Saratoga; Washington and Franklin were guests in their time, as were most of the prominent people who passed through Albany. The house is Georgian, beautifully restored, filled with original furnishings, and owned by the State of New York. Admission is free. Hours are

Wednesday through Saturday from 10 a.m. to 5 p.m., on Sunday from 1 to 5 p.m.; closed Monday and Tuesday and open weekends only during January, February, and March. The location is in a rather shabby district south of the downtown area at 32 Catherine St. (tel. 518/474-0834), on the corner of Clinton Street (not to be confused with Clinton Avenue on the other side of town).

Less than a dozen blocks to the south is **Historic Cherry Hill,** a capacious old clapboard house with a gambrel roof and an interior full of beautiful furniture, silver, crystal, and paintings. Built in 1787 by Philip Van Rensselaer, this comfortable old country seat remained in the hands of family descendants until 1963. It was once the hub of a 900-acre farm; today its pretty grounds are surrounded by featureless industrial and residential suburbs in the lee of I-787. Cherry Hill is at 523½ S. Pearl St. (tel. 518/434-4791). Hours are Tuesday through Saturday from 10 a.m. to 3 p.m., on Sunday from 1 to 3 p.m.; closed Monday and the month of January.

The **Ten Broeck Mansion** is a patrician brick mansion in the Federal style, built in 1798 by one Gen. Abraham Ten Broeck. It was once called Arbor Hill, a name that now applies to the gentrifying neighborhood that surrounds it. The house is screened from the neighborhood (not all of which is so very wonderful) by a dense leafy park. It was donated to the Albany County Historical Association in 1947 by the Olcott family, various members of which had occupied it for a century. A trip up here is a good excuse to take a look around Arbor Hill. You'll find the entrance to the grounds at 9 Ten Broeck Pl., a one-way lane that runs perpendicular to Ten Broeck Street (tel. 518/436-9826). To get on it going in the right direction you'll have to drive up to North Swan Street, then turn right down Ten Broeck Place toward Ten Broeck Street. Open year round Wednesday through Friday from 2 to 4 p.m. and on Saturday and Sunday from 1 to 4 p.m.

The **New York State Executive Mansion** is a fairly enormous old Victorian mansion set well back from Eagle Street behind a stone wall topped with an iron fence. It was built in 1856 as a private house but has been enlarged and altered by successive governors on an almost-continuous basis ever since. Teddy Roosevelt installed a gym; FDR put in a pool; Al Smith had a zoo; Nelson Rockefeller built a fallout shelter. The mansion is open to the public only on Thursday, and then only by advance reservation. The address is 138 Eagle St., just south of the big ramp that connects I-787 with the Empire State Plaza garage, and the phone number for tour reservations is 518/474-2418.

Hudson and Mohawk River Cruises

An outfit called **Dutch Apple River Cruises** operates excursion boats on the Hudson from the foot of Broadway and Quay Streets (near the old D&H Building). As we went to press, the daily two-hour sightseeing cruises were priced at $7 for adults, $6 for seniors, and $5 for children aged 5 to 12. Also available were daily Sunset Dinner Cruises for about $25 for adults and $12 for kids, the price including a full buffet; Saturday lunch and Sunday brunch cruises ($15 for adults, $9 for kids); and weekend Moonlight Cruises (adults pay $10) with a cash bar and a live band. The new excursions include the Erie Canal Lock Cruise, the Albany to Kingston Cruise, and the four-day Burlington (Vt.) to New York City Cruise though the Champlain Barge Canal. Call 518/463-0220 for current prices and schedules.

Across the Hudson River is the **Capt. JP Cruise Line,** 278 River St., Troy (tel. 518/270-1901). The 600-passenger *Capt. JP* operates daily from April through October 15, with 2-, 3-, and 4-hour cruises priced from $8 for the Port of Albany Cruise to $22 for the Prime Rib Dinner Cruise. Call for more information.

Riverboat Cruises, Inc., 1 Terminal Road, Clifton Park (tel. 518/273-8878), runs the *Nightingale II* on the Mohawk River just north of Albany. Daily with the exception of Monday, there is a three-hour narrated lock cruise at 1:30 p.m. costing $7 for adults and $4 for children. They also have a popular twilight dinner cruise from 6:30 to 9:30 p.m. for $25 per person.

The *Kittie West II* is operated by **Waters Edge Cruise Line, Inc.** from the Community College at Schenectady (tel. 518/371-2387). Afternoon and dinner cruises on the Mohawk River run seven days a week. Call for prices and reservations.

For those interested in a three-day excursion on the old Erie Canal from Albany to Syracuse (or the other way), contact the **Mid-Lakes Navigation Co. Ltd.** (tel. 800/255-3709).

Architectural Side Trip to Schenectady

Albany occupies the southern point of a triangular metropolitan district that includes the industrial cities of Troy and Schenectady. Schenectady, on the western extremity of the tri-city area, is a General Electric company town that is by most measures a fairly modest place. It does contain a sensational restored movie palace called **Proctor's,** now the scene of concerts and theatricals, about which more later. For sightseers interested in architecture and history, Schenectady also contains two intriguing in-city neighborhoods.

The first is called the **Stockade,** a reference to an actual wall that protected (albeit none too successfully) 17th-century settlers from Indian attack. Today's Stockade is an unbelieveably quaint district encompassing perhaps 12 or so downtown blocks between the Mohawk River, Washington Avenue, and State Street. It has all the charm of Georgetown, together with the same wonderful inventory of 18th-century buildings. The streets are narrow and crooked, overarched with trees, and lined with delicious restored houses. It's literally a world apart, and quite a treat for those interested in this sort of thing. An organization called Friends of the Stockade arranges guided tours by reservation for $3 a head; their phone number is 518/393-8622 or 518/322-0280. Alternatively, you can take a self-guided walking tour of the Stockade aided by one of the blue circulars printed and distributed by the **Schenectady Historical Society.** The society maintains quarters in a suitably picturesque building in the Stockade at 32 Washington Ave. They're open Monday through Friday from noon to 5 p.m. (tel. 518/374-5131). Also useful to know about, depending on your plans and interests, is the annual "Walkabout" in the Stockade, which is held on the last Saturday in September. For $6 you can see the interiors of six of these wonderful houses, plus four of the neighborhood's beautiful churches. An alternative source of information on the Stockade is the **Schenectady Chamber of Commerce,** 240 Canal Square, at the corner of Smith and Broadway, near the back wall of Proctor's (tel. 518/372-5656).

Schenectady's other district of architectural note bears the amusing name of **The Plot.** More correctly it's the G.E. Plot, a parcel of land developed by General Electric in the early years of the 20th century for upper-level Schenectady executives. The Plot adjoins the campus of Union College and is only a few minutes' drive, first up Union Street and then Union Avenue from the Stockade. The main streets in The Plot are Lenox, Wendell, Stratford, and Lowell, lying between Nott and Rugby Road. It's a perfectly wonderful collection of big old houses in practically every style imaginable, from Queen Anne to Mediterranean to Georgian. This is good-quality stuff too, set on spacious grounds, along quiet roads lined with mature trees. Most people would probably call them mansions. The Plot is still a neighborhood of beautifully kept private houses whose residents have a high regard for what they've got.

The fastest way to Schenectady from Albany is via I-90 to I-890, the latter road being a spur that cuts through Schenectady's downtown. It's only about a 20-minute drive. To get to the Stockade, take the Washington Avenue exit off I-890, proceed to the end of the ramp, then cut straight across State Street onto narrow Washington Avenue. And there you'll be, right in the middle of it. Better ask directions to get to The Plot. But it's not far via Union Street, which traverses the middle of the Stockade.

WHERE TO EAT IN SCHENECTADY The restaurant landmark in the Stockade is the **Van Dyke,** 237 Union St. (tel. 518/374-2406). The Van Dyke, a family operation since 1947, offers continental cuisine, but for over 30 years has been best known for fine

Friday- and Saturday-night jazz. The formal main dining area overlooks a fountain terrace popular for summer meals. Open Tuesday through Sunday, the Van Dyke serves dinner from 5:30 p.m. to midnight and costs in the $11 to $22 range. Lunch is available from 11 a.m. to 4 p.m., typical entrees costing approximately $4 to $10. Closed Mondays.

For a light meal downtown, try the **Manhattan Exchange,** 605 Union St. (tel. 518/374-5930), halfway between the Stockade and the G.E. Plot. The restaurant, the motto of which is "Our roots are in Schenectady but our heart is in Manhattan," serves great salads, omelets, burgers, and grilled chicken. Open Sunday through Wednesday from 11:30 a.m. to 11 p.m. (to 1 a.m. the rest of the week), and moderately priced from $2.50 to $11.95.

Just one week before the deadline of this book, the **Glen Sanders Mansion** finally came on-line, opening its doors in true 18th-century theatrical style. Housed in an adapted 1670–1713 historic stone riverside mansion located across the Mohawk River from Schenectady at 1 Glen Ave., Scotia (tel. 518/374-7262), it is a definite must for regional dining. The restaurant sports original Dutch doors, fireplace mantels, wide-plank floors, smoothly planed 18-inch-thick beams, chair rails, and low doorways, and has all the real feel of an old-world country inn. The staff is dressed in period outfits and works three separate dining rooms in the historic section of the complex, as well as the large and tastefully decorated Riverside Ballroom (for banquets). The dining rooms are comfortable and elegant, furnished with Oriental rugs, flowering plants, reproduction Queen Anne furniture and lighting fixtures. Lunch is served Monday through Friday from 11 a.m. to 2 p.m.; expect to pay from $6 for sandwiches and burgers to about $9 for hot specials. Dinner is available Wednesday through Saturday from 5 to 10 p.m. and features entrees like steak au poivre, scallops with pesto cream, and lobster pie (my favorite), all priced in the $9 to $25 range.

WHERE TO STAY IN GREATER ALBANY

Though an appealing city to visit, Albany suffers from a real shortage of interesting hotels. What follows is a selection, from deluxe to moderate in cost, chosen from the best of what there is.

Here as elsewhere it's possible to find accommodations with a bit more character in the booming world of **bed-and-breakfasts.** As this cottage industry matures, however, it grows more expensive: $75 to $85 for a double in somebody's house is not my idea of budget lodgings. Even if you're more likely to find doubles priced at $50 to $60, you have to be willing to make somebody else's household at least a limited part of your vacation. Some travelers find this an appealing idea; others definitely do not. The efforts of bed-and-breakfast hosts to be completely unobtrusive are rather poignant, as it's an impossible task.

Nevertheless, those unafflicted by a compulsion for total privacy might well find a bed-and-breakfast an enjoyable alternative to familiar hotels and motels. The **American Country Collection,** operated by Beverly Walsh, acts as a sort of central booking agency for B&Bs all around the Capital District. The address is American Country Collection, 984 Gloucester Pl., Schenectady, NY 12309 (tel. 518/370-4948). Although Ms. Walsh prefers three weeks' notice and a deposit, last-minute reservations are sometimes accepted when possible.

Travelers take note: Many hotels here in Albany, as in other cities, offer **reduced-rate packages,** especially during slack weekends. Sometimes package rates require advance reservations. Sometimes "advance" means nothing more than asking at the desk when you check in, or possibly telephoning ahead. Wherever you go, it never hurts to ask whether any package rates are in effect. They won't tell you unless you ask. Here now are recommended hotels, ranging downward in price from deluxe to moderate:

Best hotel in town is the **Albany Hilton,** State and Lodge Streets, Albany, NY 12207 (tel. 518/462-6611 or 800/445-8667). This is a modern brown-brick and smoked-glass affair with an ideal downtown location in the middle of all that makes Albany so unique. The Hilton has lush modern lobbies, atmospheric restaurants full of plants and brass and rattan chairs, an indoor swimming pool, and free parking for guests. The rooms are big, exceedingly comfortable, full of burled furniture and thick rugs. It's all very new, clean, and modern. Single-room rates range from $105 to $125; doubles run $120 to $140—the different prices depend on where your room is located, and a bit on the state of the market. All rooms, whether they have a high-floor view or not, are very "Hilton-y."

The **Albany Marriott,** 189 Wolf Rd., Albany, NY 12205 (tel. 518/458-8444, or toll free 800/228-9290), is the newest hotel complex in the Capital District. This facility boasts over 300 rooms, 11 multipurpose parlors, 10 banquet rooms, a grand ballroom, 2 restaurants, a bar, a nightclub, a health club, an indoor and an outdoor pool. The coordinated maroon and tan rooms are outfitted with king-size and double beds, climate control, AM/FM radios, color TVs, free HBO and pay movies. For formal dining, try Ashley's, appointed with brass and mirrors, or the more casual Market, open from 6 a.m. to 11 p.m. daily. Flirtations, a high-energy nightclub, features live bands six nights a week and is a local hot spot. Room prices vary according to one's government, military, or corporate affiliation. But if you're a writer with no associations, expect to pay $119 single and $131 double—or only $89 for either one on weekends.

The **Desmond Americana,** 660 Albany Shaker Rd., Albany, NY 12211 (tel. 518/869-8100), may well be called simply the Desmond by the time you arrive. It has nothing to do with other Americana hotels, and evidently the owner has tired of being confused with same. The Desmond, as I'll call it, is located near the north end of Wolf Road, close by the airport and within sight of I-87 (this part of which is called the Northway). From the outside it appears to be an agglomeration of colonial houses mashed together into a sort of condensed village. Inside it's terrifically handsome, full of first-class Colonial Revival decor, hardwood oak floors, beautiful moldings, brass chandeliers, wing chairs, etc. About half the 340 guest rooms face into a pair of roofed interior courtyards, one of which contains a free-form pool. A typical room will have thick rust-colored carpeting, colonial-style wood furniture, mirrored closet doors, a phone in the bathroom, a corduroy wing chair, etc. Rates for these very handsome rooms are about $100 single and $115 double. To get here from downtown (about a ten-minute drive), take I-90 westbound to I-87 (the Northway) and get off at Exit 4. The ramp will deposit you on Albany Shaker Road and the hotel is to your left on the other side of the Northway. This hotel contains an excellent restaurant called the Scrimshaw, described below.

The **Holiday Inn–Turf on Wolf Road,** 205 Wolf Rd., Albany, NY 12205 (tel. 518/458-7250, or toll free 800/HOLIDAY), is the old Turf Inn recently bought and renovated by the Holiday folks. This upgraded facility now features 300-plus rooms, a great indoor pool, an outdoor pool with a café, tennis courts, a Holidome recreation center (family amusement area), two restaurants, and a 1950s theme nightclub. On-site restaurants include the Turfhouse Grill, which serves full meals from 5:30 a.m. to 11 p.m., and Heathers, a bar laden with etched glass and brass, featuring light fare. A nightclub called Fenders is an oldie dance club decorated with 50s paraphernalia. It has a DJ seven nights a week. The rooms, all redecorated with new queen-size beds, cost $83 single and $93 double. Rooms with Jacuzzis are available for $135 nightly.

The **Tom Sawyer Motor Inn,** 1444 Western Ave. (U.S. 20), Albany, NY 12203 (tel. 518/438-3594), is a good-value family-style motor hotel on the western edge of town, very close to Crossgate and Stuyvesant Plazas, and only a few blocks east of where the Northway (I-87) begins. It's a long, low-slung affair whose accommodation wings embrace a large swimming pool set amid lawns overlooking suburban Western Avenue. The decor is pleasant 1950s Turnpike. There are 85 rooms, modestly but attractively decorated with wall-to-wall carpeting, cable color television sets, nice floral spreads, and immaculately clean black-and-white-tiled baths. Adjacent to the lobby is a moderately priced restaurant that serves breakfast, lunch, and dinner. Rates go as low as $39 single and $42 double; rooms with newer decor cost up to $48 double. A good price and a nice informal atmosphere.

All the familiar chains, it should be noted, are well represented in Albany. The Ramada and TraveLodge, for example, are just down Western Avenue from the Tom Sawyer. Others are over on Wolf Road, among them the **Days Inn,** 16 Wolf Rd., Albany, NY 12205 (tel. 518/459-3600, or toll free 800/325-2525). This establishment stands at the start of the Wolf Road shopping strip for which Albany is so well known. It's a flat-roofed, modern construction surrounded by new and immaculate lawns and landscaping. Inside it are 168 brand-new rooms decorated with beige textured-vinyl wallcoverings, brown wall-to-wall carpeting, color TVs, a chair, a desk, perhaps a framed picture of a partridge, and a nice clean functional bathroom. It has a mass-market look but is nonetheless comfortable for that. And rates are very low: $42 for singles, $64 for doubles—except during the month of August, when rooms cost up to $70 nightly, single or double.

Cheaper yet, but quite attractive in spite of its low prices, is the **Red Roof Inn,** 188 Wolf Rd. (next to the Sheraton Airport Inn), Albany, NY 12205 (tel. 518/459-1971, or toll free 800/848-7878). All Red Roofs have a Colorado-ski-lodge look and a huge swooping red roof over the lobby. This one has 116 immaculate rooms with patterned spreads, burgundy-brown-cream color schemes, color TVs, patterned wallpaper, and nice modern baths. Single-room rates range from $37 to $42; doubles pay only $39 to $44. No pool or restaurant, but so what? In fact, Red Roof Inns across New York State offer some of the best travel bargains I've seen. You might want to call the toll-free number above and request a copy of their national directory. Or you could write to them at Red Roof Inns, Inc., 4355 Davidson Rd., Hilliard, OH 43026.

And I'm afraid to say that that, unfortunately, is about as much variety as you're going to find in Albany. Unless you're willing to undertake an 11-mile drive east across the Hudson to the village of Averill Park and try the **Gregory House,** Averill Park, NY 12081 (tel. 518/674-3774). This is a little complex of dark-brown buildings surrounded by pretty flower gardens and sporting an attractive swimming pool. The restaurant, described below, is in a 150-year-old house. The 12 inn rooms are in a new compatible structure adjacent. These rooms have dark floors, private baths with flowery shower curtains, random antiques, hooked rugs, and a most attractive, well-kept air. The place definitely has style, and the presence of the excellent restaurant is further inducement to stay here. Double-occupancy room rates fall mostly between $50 and $70 nightly, and include continental breakfast. Averill Park straddles N.Y. 43, reached via Exit 7 (Washington Avenue) from I-90. I've timed the drive; it's 15 easy minutes from I-787 in downtown Albany.

WHERE TO EAT IN ALBANY

The city has quite a sophisticated assortment of restaurants. First we'll tackle those in the downtown area, starting with the upper bracket and moving down. After that we'll move to the fringes of town.

Restaurants Close to Downtown

La Serre, 14 Green St. (tel. 518/463-6056), is an elegant oasis located just off downtown State Street. A greenhouse overlooks little Green Street from behind trees and a tall iron fence. Inside are several exceedingly elegant rooms, alternately paneled in rich mahogany or mirrors. There are sprays of gorgeous flowers, immaculate white and pink linen, and the tinkle of laughter and piano music. Cuisine is French-continental and quite reasonable at lunch, when entrees like veal meunière, the crêpe du jour, seafood fettuccine, etc., cost in the $7 to $13 range. At dinner expect to pay $18 to $23 for an à la carte entree like veal Oscar, steak bordelaise, bouillabaisse marseillaise, or duckling au poivre. Open from 11:30 a.m. until 2:30

p.m. for lunch and 5:30 to 9 p.m. for dinner; closed Sunday. It's a beautiful place and the food is famous.

Jack's, 42 State St. (tel. 518/465-8854), is a horse of a different color. Opened in 1913, it's a seafood and oyster house with unpretentious decor and a reputation for good food and a unique oldtime Albany atmosphere. The lofty-ceilinged dining room is an institution, filled with red leatherette chairs, gilt-framed pictures of Albany, and boisterous crowds. Huge sandwiches (available only at lunch) cost around $4 to $7, ditto for clams and oysters of almost every description. Seafood entrees like fresh swordfish filet, Boston bluefish, combination seafood grill, etc., run about $12 to $20; chopped sirloin, chef's salad, and omelets are about half that. Open seven days from 11:30 a.m. until 10 p.m. Very typical of Albany. The food is great, so try and include a meal here if you can.

Ogden's, Howard and Lodge Streets (tel. 518/463-6605), is a stylish new restaurant in a former Edwardian-era telephone building. Besides the attractive high-ceilinged dining room there's a wonderful outdoor terrace with a yellow and white awning, hanging plants, and crisp white linen. The lunch menu offers things like ginger chicken, filet of sole, giant combination sandwiches, sophisticated salads, and so on for around $5 to $13. At dinner you might order a New York strip steak, tournedos Rossini, veal japonaise, chicken française, Dover sole, or other faintly nouvelle geographic specials priced mostly from $10 to $20. Ogden's serves lunch Monday through Friday only from 11:30 a.m. to 3 p.m.; dinner is available Monday through Saturday from 5:30 until 10 p.m.; closed Sunday.

The **Quackenbush House,** Clinton Avenue and Broadway (tel. 518/465-0909), occupies an ancient little gable-ended brick house with sky-blue shutters right next door to the Urban Cultural Park. The house is the oldest in Albany, and barely escaped demolition during the construction of I-787. It's airy and modern inside, furnished with rush-seated wooden chairs, blowups of old Albany street scenes, and blue linen cloths with burgundy napkins. Prices are very reasonable. At lunch you can have hamburgers, sandwiches, omelets, and the like for around $4 to $6, served with considerable style in lovely surroundings. Dinner entrees, like broiled haddock, sole amandine, veal Burgoyne, champagne chicken, etc., fall mostly between $10 and $16. Open for lunch Monday through Friday from 11:30 a.m. until 3 p.m.; for dinner Monday through Saturday from 5 until 10 p.m.; closed Sunday.

Quintessence, 11 New Scotland Ave. (tel. 518/343-8186), occupies a 1930s stainless-steel diner that has been renovated with a unique art deco and neon motif. The clientele of this diner, located one block south of the park, is as lively as the decor. Food is served from 8 a.m. to 2 a.m. daily. My last supper there consisted of an appetizer of alligator with papaya glaze ($3.95) and an entree of sautéed scallops in vodka tarragon cream sauce on black squid-ink pasta, also called scallops negro ($8.95). Breakfast, lunch, dinner (with nightly themes), and brunches are priced very moderately. There are a DJ and dancing Wednesday through Saturday, and a live band on Sunday night.

I'm a particular fan of neighborhood tavern/restaurants, especially if good food is combined with a lot of character. Three very excellent Albany establishments fit this description to the proverbial "T." The first is **Lombardo's,** 121 Madison Ave. (tel. 518/462-9180), which is complete with vintage neon sign, white tile floors, booths, and a separate bar room with the original liquor license from 1919. Nobody decorated this place to look old, it just does. Cuisine is Italian—eggplant parmigiana, homemade sausage, lasagne, ravioli, stuffed shells, all sorts of pastas with all sorts of sauces—and prices are moderate. Getting out of here for $10 a head is eminently do-able. Open from 11:30 a.m. until 9 p.m.; closed Monday and Tuesday. The location is just off the intersection of Madison and South Pearl, quite near the Pastures.

A few blocks away is the **Pastures Tavern,** 147 S. Pearl St. (tel. 518/463-

7222), which is a new tavern adjacent to the newly restored Pastures Historic District. It has a natural-wood façade with small-pane tavern windows, a long skinny natural-wood bar inside, plus lofty ceilings, terracotta floors, butcher-block tables, and exposed brick walls. There is rock and roll on the jukebox and an attractive, young-looking crowd. Hot sandwiches, burgers, plus things like chicken wings, onion soup, and taco salad, are served seven days a week from 11:30 a.m. until midnight. The atmosphere is great and everything on the menu costs less than $6.

The third of the trio is **Hurley's,** located on the other side of town on gentrifying (working at it, but not there yet) Clinton Avenue, corner of Quail Street (tel. 518/434-6854). Hurley's is an old corner tavern, modernized unpretentiously, and filled at most hours with a young exuberant crowd watching TV at the bar up front or putting away sandwiches and chicken wings at tables in the back. Nothing fancy here, but great burgers and sandwiches for usually less than $5. Open Monday through Saturday from 11:30 a.m. to 4 a.m., on Sunday from noon until 4 a.m. (food served until 3 a.m.).

Hungry sightseers looking for cafeteria-style sandwich shops in the downtown area should know about **Bruegger's Bagel Bakery,** a local chain (here and in Saratoga Springs) whose various locations feature hi-tech pipe rails, blond wood café chairs, and all sorts of sandwiches in the $3 to $4 range. There's a convenient Bruegger's near the Hilton on North Pearl Street at the corner of Maiden Lane. Practically next door on Maiden Lane is **Sandwiches to Go,** which is bright, clean, attractive, and offers almost any sandwich you can think of for about $3. Both these places are packed at lunchtime with downtown office workers.

Good Suggestions Farther Afield

The **Stone Ends Restaurant,** located one mile south of Thruway Exit 23 on U.S. 9W (tel. 518/465-3178), is only five minutes from downtown Albany and is well worth the trip. Owner/chef Dale Miller is a Culinary Institute of America graduate whose restaurant has received the Escoffier Award of Honor and the Travel-Holiday Award. The building is a modern 50s, Frank Lloyd Wright sort of a place with expansive blue-stone gable walls and floors. The decor is accented with art nouveau light fixtures and leaded glass. The waiters are in black tie and the music is soft and classical. As for the food, it is progressive American with a distinct European influence. Main dishes include prime rib of (Provime) veal, steak (black Angus) Diane, and salmon with seafood sausage (mousse), and they cost in the $16 to $20 range. The Stone Ends is open for dinner only from 4:30 to 10 p.m. Monday through Thursday, and from 4:30 to 11 p.m. on Friday and Saturday. Sunday hours are 3 to 9 p.m. On the weekends there's live piano music in the dining room and the bar.

A most authentic Indian restaurant called **Sitar,** 1929 Central Ave. (tel. 518/456-6670), is only five minutes west of downtown Albany. The owners have been delighting the community on Central Avenue for 14 years and have a very loyal following. A large wood carving at the front door consists of two parts: the top is Kalimata, the goddess of darkness; the bottom is the awe-inspiring Shiva, goddess of goodness. The Sitar's Moorish arches and stuccoed walls are decorated with inlaid wood and ivory. The kebab and tandoori dishes are skewered and charcoal-broiled in clay ovens. Indian bread called "nan" is baked by means of fastening the dough to the under lip of a large clay-pot oven, then watching until it falls. The chef catches the nan before it hits the red-hot coals. This operation can be witnessed through a four-by-eight-foot window opening onto the kitchen from the bar. Lunch is served Tuesday through Saturday from 11:30 a.m. to 2 p.m. and costs in the $5 to $6 range. The Sunday buffet, served from 12 to 3 p.m., costs $9.50. Dinner is available from 5 to 10 p.m. and is priced between $7 and $15. Closed Monday.

The **Scrimshaw** is located in the Desmond Americana, at Exit 4 on the Northway/I-87. The address again is 660 Albany Shaker Rd. (tel. 518/869-8100). Here the staff is in colonial costume and the atmosphere suggests prosperous New

England. As a matter of fact, new though it may be, the Scrimshaw is singularly handsome in a high traditional manner. There are numerous dining rooms, all decorated with curtains on formal swags, Queen Anne armchairs, brass wall sconces, framed paintings of ships, etc. You might have a drink before dinner in the handsome bar with its beams and leather furniture. The luncheon menu offers omelets, seafood, various grills and broils, plus all manner of salads priced mostly from $6 to $8. At dinner you'll pay more like $16 to $22 for entrees such as grilled swordfish, breast of duck, sole en papillote, or roast prime rib. Open for lunch on weekdays only from 11 a.m. to 2 p.m.; dinner is served Monday through Saturday from 5 to 10 p.m.; closed Sunday.

The **Shipyard Restaurant,** 1171 Troy-Schenectady Rd., Latham (tel. 518/785-1711), is located on N.Y. 7 halfway between the Latham Circle (I-87) and the city of Schenectady. This charming early-19th-century brick house features a dining room, an enclosed porch and an intimate and dimly lit bar. The American cuisine has a slight French flair, and for anywhere from $14 to $20, one might try such dishes as roast rack of lamb, braised veal sweetbreads, Long Island duck, etc. Open Monday through Saturday from 5 to 11 p.m.; reservations are a must; closed Sunday.

Located about equidistant from downtown in the exact opposite direction from the Desmond is the restaurant at the **Gregory House** in Averill Park (tel. 518/674-3774). Dinner here truly is a treat, taken in one of several intimate dining rooms by candlelight under beamed ceilings. The place has a very nice old-fashioned country inn atmosphere, and a dinner menu that features entrees like filet mignon, London broil, shrimp scampi, sautéed oysters, lamb chops, and so forth, priced mostly from $11 to $17. Open for dinner only from 5 p.m. until people go home (from 4 p.m. on Sunday); closed Monday and Tuesday. For directions, see the description of the Gregory House under the hotel listings, above.

Back in Albany's western suburbs, in the Stuyvesant Plaza, at Western Avenue and Fuller, is **T.G.I. Friday's** (tel. 518/489-1661). That it looks identical to every other Friday's in the land detracts not one whit from its considerable appeal. Outside are red-and-white awnings to distinguish it from everything else in the plaza. Inside is the familiar raised bar, Tiffany-style colored-glass lamps, brass rails, hanging ferns, etched glass, and crowds of satisfied patrons. Every day from 11:30 a.m. to 1 a.m. you can order things like pasta salads, gourmet burgers, oversize sandwiches, sweet-and-sour chicken, enchiladas, or more elaborate fare like a mixed seafood plate or chicken piccata, mostly priced between $5 and $12. The bar, open daily until 2 a.m., is always busy.

Grandma's, 1273 Central Ave. (tel. 518/459-4585), isn't far from the other end of Fuller Road. The owner studied fast-food techniques, combined it with a family-run atmosphere, and the result is Grandma's, a local family-style fast-food restaurant. It looks rather like a suburban diner, its clean and functional interior softened by Victorian-ish lighting fixtures. It's famous for its pies and baked goods, as well as its reasonable lunches and dinners. Expect to pay between $5 and $10 for things like triple-decker sandwiches, barbecued chicken, special omelets, etc. They're big on breakfasts here too, especially Belgian waffles (under $5). Open every day from 6 a.m. to midnight.

ALBANY AFTER DARK

A variety of pleasures awaits those not tired out by a day's sightseeing. For example:

Drinking and Dancing

Cahoots is the name of the disco in the Albany Hilton, at State and Lodge Streets (tel. 518/462-6611). Somnolent during the week, it comes decidedly to life on Friday and Saturday nights. In the same hotel, on the lobby level is a bar called

Cinnamon's. Nothing so out of the ordinary here, but it's a very good-looking room bathed in soft golden light. Good place for an intimate conversation.

The crowd is (dare I say?) a little "yuppier" at the **Elbo Room,** near Delaware and Morton (tel. 518/465-9001). DJ and jolly drinkers . . . you get the picture. A similar crowd, a shade more elegant, frequents the **Parc V Café,** out in Colonie, close by the Desmond Americana, on Albany Shaker Road and the Northway (tel. 518/869-9976).

As long as you're in the area, the newest and possibly the hottest night spot in town is **Flirtations** at the Albany Marriott, 189 Wolf Rd. (tel. 518/458-8444). Live bands, DJs, and laser light shows line 'em up on weekends. Another good idea, just up the road at the Holliday Inn–Turf, is the 50s-theme nightclub **Fenders** (tel. 518/458-7250).

For rock and roll, try **September's,** also out in Colonie, on Central Avenue just west of Osborne Road (tel. 518/459-8440). Format Top 40; live bands most evenings after 10 p.m. For rock and roll try **288 Lark Street,** on Lark north of Madison (tel. 518/462-9148). Trilevel, new wave, pretty exciting actually.

Theater

Shakespeare in the Park is a regular summer occurence in Albany's Washington Park as it is in Manhattan's Central Park. Most shows are mounted in July at an outdoor theater adjoining the lake house. Perhaps the best way to find out whether shows are planned during your stay is to call the Albany Arts Office at 518/434-2032.

A broad range of theatricals is staged between September and May at the **Egg,** that curiously aerodynamic-looking thingummy that sits midway down the Empire State Plaza. The Empire State Institute for the Performing Arts (ESIPA) is the genius behind the productions; the box office number is 518/473-3750.

Proctor's, the extravagantly elegant restored movie palace in nearby Schenectady, is almost worth a trip just for a glimpse of its Hollywood imperial interiors. This great architectural treasure now features an electric calendar of shows and concerts from contemporary drama to opera, to punk rock, to ballet, to musicals, to symphony orchestras, etc. Call the box office between 10 a.m. and 6 p.m. Monday through Saturday, at 518/346-6204. It's only about a 20-minute drive from downtown Albany, via super-expressway (I-90 and I-890) virtually all the way.

SHOPPING

Albany is famous for its mega-malls, many of which are lined up along Wolf Road to the west of town near the intersection of the Northway (I-87 and I-90). There are so many of these malls, not just on Wolf Road but throughout the area, that it's not practical to try and describe them all. Highlights include:

The **Cohoes Specialty Stores,** 43 Mohawk St., in the nearby city of Cohoes (tel. 518/237-0524). This place is perhaps best known for its premium-quality and designer clothing for men and women at discount prices. In many ways it's a sort of upstate Loehmann's.

The newest mall in town is called **Crossgates,** and it's out on Western Avenue (N.Y. 20) near the start of the Northway. Jordan Marsh, Filene's, and J. C. Penney are the anchors. The **Off-Price Center/Northway Mall,** on Central Avenue (N.Y. 5) between Wolf Road and Fuller Road, sells women's clothing, men's clothing, shoes, electronic equipment, linens, children's wear, you name it, at fairly fabulous discounts. Open seven days a week; the phone number is 518/459-5320.

My favorite place to shop in Albany is **Stuyvesant Plaza,** located at the corner of Western Avenue and Fuller Road (tel. 518/482-8986). They have an exquisite collection of 62 specialty stores and restaurants.

Definitely worth a shopping stroll in atmospheric downtown Albany is **Lark Street** in the 100 to 300 blocks. Here you'll find a small-scale potpourri of boutiques, antiques shops, cafés, bars, jewelry stores, etc., each with its own unique flavor. And let's face it, the in-town atmosphere beats the malls by a long shot.

2. Saratoga Springs

How to convey the vintage luxury and atmosphere of this old resort in a few short paragraphs? This is a problem. Saratoga Springs, 44 miles north of Albany on the Adirondack Northway (I-87), is a small place graced with a famous racetrack at which millions are won and lost by high-rolling gamblers. The season is only four short weeks in August. But during those weeks the restored Victorian streets are clogged with fancy cars and definite urban types (socialites to dese-dem-an-dose guys). The restaurants are packed and hotel prices triple. The swell mansions along North Broadway and Union Street ring to the sound of laughter and popping champagne corks. In the words of Heywood Hale Broun, August in Saratoga is a time when "hopes begin to seem like expectations, where fantasies look like investment opportunities."

What started it all is a series of natural mineral springs that bubble to the earth in various locations around the town. Usually they are sheltered beneath open-air pavilions, described on adjacent plaques, and their various-tasting waters are free for the taking (bring your own glass or cup). During the last century "taking the cure" at Saratoga, which is to say dressing up and drinking a lot of water, fit nicely with the notion of betting heavily at the track, gambling at one of the swank casinos, and eating oneself almost insensate at the opulent restaurants and hotel dining rooms of the day.

The controversial Madame Jumel, once the wife of Aaron Burr (subject of wonderful descriptive passages in Gore Vidal's novel *Burr*), was an early summer resident. Her house on Circular Street still stands. Diamond Jim Brady and Lillian Russell were big fans of Saratoga summers too. So was a fellow named John Morrissey, founder in 1863 of the local thoroughbred racing track (also president of a New York City gang called the Dead Rabbits). Numerous other colorful types inhabit the pages of Saratoga's past. But Jumel, Brady, Russell, and Morrissey epitomize the tone of the place, a heady brew of illicit luxury, fast money, and lots of fun. Interestingly enough, for all the changes wrought by the 120-plus years since the founding of Morrissey's Horse Haven Race Track, for all the wars and upheavals and social changes this country has undergone, August in Saratoga is approximately the same as it always was.

The famous springs, or at least most of them, are now preserved within the confines of a New York state park. Built in the 1930s and occupying 2,000 manicured acres, it's a world of classical pavilions, serene outdoor pools, white-coated staff, etc., all very much in the European spa tradition. Culture has also come to Saratoga with a capital "C" in the form of the Saratoga Performing Arts Center (SPAC), which is a huge open-air shell on the grounds of the Spa State Park.

Notwithstanding all that, the horse remains the object of greatest interest, be he on the thoroughbred track or the harness-racing track, or on the auction block at the famous annual Fasig-Tipton Yearling Sales, or on the field of the Saratoga Polo Association, or on the minds of all the Rolls-Royce and Seville drivers of August.

WHAT TO SEE AND DO IN SARATOGA SPRINGS

The town pretty much closes down during the depths of winter. But there's lots to do in spring, summer, and fall, whether or not you're a particular fancier of horseflesh. First thing to note is the address and phone number of the extremely helpful **Greater Saratoga Chamber of Commerce,** at 494 Broadway (U.S. 9), Saratoga Springs, NY 12866, just south of the big new Ramada Renaissance Hotel (tel. 518/584-3255). The chamber is the source of walking-tour maps, up-to-the-minute information on what's going on around town, advice on hotels and restaurants, etc. They couldn't be nicer, or more readily prepared with good advice for visitors. Alternatively, there's a well-stocked **tourist information booth** open during the summer, located in the middle of town on Broadway at the entrance to Congress Park, as well as the **Urban Cultural Park Visitors Center** across the street at Drink Hall, 297 Broadway, Saratoga Springs, NY 12866 (tel. 518/584-3913).

Now then, on to the local attractions, starting with the one that has greatest seniority.

Saratoga Spa

Saratoga's naturally carbonated mineral springs were discovered by Europeans in 1771. Friendly Indians brought Sir William Johnson up here in a litter, as this worthy agent (for Indian affairs) of the king was too gouty to walk on his own two feet. By 1803 Saratoga had already become sufficiently famous to warrant the erection, by Gideon Putnam, of a hotel strictly for the accommodation of visitors taking "the cure." Fashion smiled on Saratoga throughout the 19th century. But while palatial hotels, restaurants, casinos, and tracks were carefully cultivated, the springs were ironically neglected.

By the beginning of this century Saratoga's booming industry based on extraction of carbon dioxide from the naturally carbonated springs threatened to pump the place dry. A hue and cry was raised in time, the result being a New York State Reservation, created in 1909 and charged with protecting the springs from rapacious commercial development. In 1927 Gov. Franklin D. Roosevelt appointed a further commission to study the possibility of transforming Saratoga Springs into a European-style health spa. The result of that commission's efforts was the erection of an elegant series of buildings that constitute today's state park. Designed by one Joseph Henry Freedlander in a chaste Georgian/Classical Revival style, the new complex was opened to the public on July 26, 1935.

The reservation didn't actually become a state park until 1962, when an 18-hole golf course and an additional pool were added. Today's spa encompasses 2,000 acres, hosts 1½ million visitors each year, includes about ten different natural springs welling up in various locations, plus the deluxe Gideon Putnam Hotel, the outdoor SPAC shell, hot and cold running pools, and pavilions, bathhouses, etc. Despite its heavy use, it's quite a beautiful place.

The Spa State Park is located on the southern edge of Saratoga Springs, bordering U.S. 9 (South Broadway) and N.Y. 50 (Ballston Avenue). The main entrance is on U.S. 9 next door to the Lincoln Baths Building. Probably the best place to get a map of the spa is at the chamber of commerce, 494 Broadway (tel. 518/584-3255).

Within hours of your arrival at Saratoga the chances are you'll hear about something called the **ninety-minute relaxer.** This is a popular treatment at the spa consisting of a soak in a private tub of fizzy mineral water, followed by a professional massage, and topped off by a wrap in warm sheets. It's fairly heavenly and costs only around $20. Reservations are required for this and other bath treatments. The Roosevelt Baths (tel. 518/584-2011) are open all year from Wednesday through Sunday; the Lincoln Baths (tel. 518/584-2010) only operate during the summer months.

You can sample the various **spring waters** just by driving up to them and taking a drink. A visitors' pamphlet titled "The Springs of Saratoga" locates them all and gives a bit of history about each. (The best tasting in town, in my opinion, is the Hathorn No. 1, which isn't in the spa at all but on the northern edge of Congress Park.) The famous **Saratoga Mineral Water,** whose stylish-looking bottles are available in supermarkets everywhere, used to be bottled in the park itself. Now Anheuser-Busch does the honors in a plant on N.Y. 50. On the grounds of the spa itself, next door to the former bottling plant, is one of the state park's more interest-

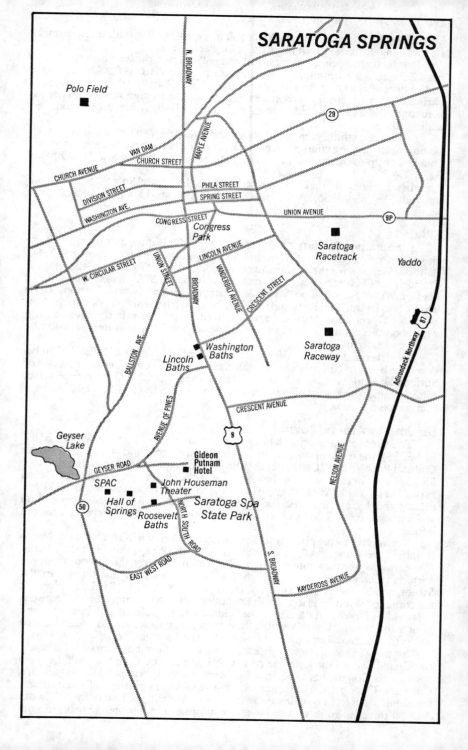

ing springs. Identified as Geyser Well No. 7, it contains enough radium to warrant a sign warning drinkers against more than one glass a week.

Besides baths, springs, picnic areas, and golf courses, the state park sports two beautiful outdoor swimming pools. My favorite is the **Victoria Pool,** an immense and architecturally gorgeous facility surrounded by classical pavilions, comfortable chaises, a snackbar, changing rooms, etc. Adults can laze away a sunny summer day here for a modest $3 (for kids 6 to 12 the tariff is $1.50). Towel rental is but 25¢ additional.

Besides everything mentioned above, the state park also has tennis courts, ice skating rinks, jogging courses, picnic areas, and of course the aforementioned golf course. For up-to-the-minute information on fees, etc., call the Spa Park Office at 518/584-2000.

An interesting alternative to the park baths is the **Crystal Spa,** 92 South Broadway (tel. 518/584-2556). A mineral bath here will cost $11, a massage $22, and a sauna $3.

SPAC

The **Saratoga Performing Arts Center** (SPAC) is quite an ornament to the city of Saratoga. Located on the grounds of the Spa State Park (entrance on N.Y. 50, Ballston Avenue), it's the summer home of both the New York City Ballet *and* the Philadelphia Orchestra. Besides its resident companies, SPAC stages shows by the likes of Willie Nelson, Bob Seger, Manhattan Transfer, George Benson, Twyla Tharp, Bob Dylan, Tom Petty and the Heartbreakers, the Temptations, and the New York City Opera. Lawn seating is available in addition to seats in the covered shell, which occupies a sort of natural amphitheatric hollow. Sight lines and general ambience are wonderful.

For ticket and program information, call the box office at 518/587-3330 between the hours of 10 a.m. and 5 p.m. during the summer only. The adjacent **Hall of Springs,** an immense Classical Revival interior dripping with 1930s elegance, serves a dinner buffet on concert nights. You can call them at 518/584-9330 for information and reservations.

Landmarks Around Town

The **Greater Saratoga Chamber of Commerce,** 494 Broadway (tel. 518/584-3255); the tourist information booth at Commerce Park; and the new **Urban Cultural Park Visitors Center,** at 297 Broadway in the old Drink Hall (tel. 518/584-3913)—all carry a useful brochure titled "Saratoga Springs Urban Cultural Park." For those who'd like to get to know the town and its stock of wonderful 19th-century architecture, this brochure is a must. It will lead you knowledgeably around and among the porticoed and turreted mansions, the public gardens, and the old hotels.

Saratoga isn't a big place; you can easily get the feel of it in an afternoon. Not to be missed are: **Congress Park,** a little enclave filled with splashing fountains, frou-frou pavilions, and elaborate beds of brightly colored flowers; the **Casino,** a restored Victorian memento of the days of high-stakes gaming and high-cost dining; **Circular Street,** notable for various mansions, among them the amazing Batcheller House at the corner of Whitney Place; **North Broadway,** five concentrated blocks, between the middle of town and the campus of Skidmore College, lined with huge trees and great mansions; and **Union Avenue,** location of the famous Race Course and similar to North Broadway, but with a lot more traffic and fewer fine houses.

Saratoga's **Broadway** was once the site of three enormous Victorian-era hotels: the United States Hotel, on the corner of Division; the Congress Hall, between Spring and Congress Streets; and the Grand Central, between Washington and Congress. These palatial old joints were famous for their pillared balconies stretching hundreds of feet along Broadway and rising to a height of four or five full floors. Alas, all three are gone, replaced with the most mundane shopping malls imaginable. The rest of Broadway still retains its classy old brick buildings, most of which have been sensitively restored in recent years, plus handsome shops and restaurants. But the loss of the old hotels is a situation rather akin to a beautiful girl with a few missing teeth.

Horse Racing

Saratoga has three tracks. The **Saratoga Race Course,** oldest active thoroughbred racetrack in the U.S., is the most famous of them all. Dating from 1864, it's a world of striped awnings, gilded cupolas, grassy paddocks, fancy cars, beautiful women, fevered betting, rich owners, and the fastest horses in America. It's open only in August; post time is 1:30 p.m. and there are races every day but Tuesday. Traditional here during race weeks is the "Sunrise Breakfast," available trackside from 7 a.m. You can watch the horses being walked out, even attend a handicap seminar in the Paddock Club. Be advised, the track is formal. No shorts or T-shirts; and in the Clubhouse dining rooms you'll need a jacket and tie. Outdoor food concessions, however, abound.

For further information, call the Race Course General Information number at 518/584-6200, or the chamber of commerce at 518/584-3255. Gates open at 11 a.m.; admission to the grandstand is $2; to the clubhouse it's $5. Go early—it's mobbed. You'll find the track on the eastern edge of town on Union Avenue about half a dozen blocks from Congress Park.

The **Saratoga Harness Raceway** is the standardbred track, where trotters and sulkies replace the more aristocratic thoroughbreds. The trotters run ten months a year. Grandstand admission is $1.75; to the clubhouse it's $3. Post time is typically 7:45 p.m. This establishment recently changed hands, so call them at 515/584-2110 (or the chamber of commerce at 518/584-3255) for up-to-date information.

The third track, visible on all the maps of town, provokes the curiosity of numerous visitors. It's located just the other side of Union Avenue from the famous Race Course, is called the **Oklahoma Track,** and is used only for training and therefore not open to the public.

Interesting to know about, while I'm on the subject of horse racing, is the annual **Fasig-Tipton Yearling Sale,** which usually takes place around the second week in August. The scene is the Finney Pavilion, located on East Avenue (tel. 518/587-2070), where buyers from around the world watch a tuxedo-clad John Finney conduct auctions where prices for untried horses can go into the millions. Potential bidders might possibly be readers of this book, but you don't have to be to attend the auction. The atmosphere is definitely big league and seating is limited, so be sure to call ahead.

The Saratoga Polo Association

Besides thoroughbred racing, the month of August now also witnesses a full schedule of exciting polo matches. For $3 a head you can join the crowd at the field out Seward Avenue on the western edge of town. Call the chamber of commerce at 518/584-3255 for current match schedules.

The National Museum of Racing and Hall of Fame

Located across Union Avenue from the Saratoga Race Course is a state-of-the-art museum dedicated to American thoroughbred horse racing. The exhibits are almost as exciting as the track itself. Upon entering the building you will sense the tension of the track with the sounds of jockeys yelling, horses being handled, and the starting gates flying open. Elsewhere you can trace the history of thoroughbred racing from 17th-century New York and Virginia to the present day. The actual Hall of Fame is much more than a fascinating collection of memorabilia; it is a hi-tech multimedia center where one can actually select and watch any historic race film with the aid of a computer. A wide-screen theater room features a great 20-minute film that is guaranteed to move the most dispassionate tourist. The museum is open from Labor Day to Memorial Day, Tuesday through Saturday, 10 a.m. to 4:30 p.m., and every day in the summer. Admission is $2 for adults (the best bet you'll ever make) and $1 for students and senior citizens.

The National Museum of Dance

Opened in 1986 in a former spa building (the Washington Baths) on South Broadway (U.S. 9), this establishment has the distinction of being the only dance museum in America. Exhibits and demonstrations record the history and development of modern dance. There are photo essays, costume exhibits, and a library/resource center that features lectures and video presentations. Special events are held throughout the season. The museum is presently open from late May through September 4; Tuesday through Saturday from 10 a.m. to 5 p.m., and Sundays from noon to 4 p.m. Closed Mondays and holidays. Beginning in September, the museum will be open Thursday through Saturday from 10 a.m. to 5 p.m., and Sundays from noon to 4 p.m. For additional information, call 518/584-2225.

Yaddo

The former Saratoga estate of industrialist Spencer Trask and his wife, Katrina, has been operated as a retreat for writers and artists since the 1920s. The mansion itself is off-limits to visitors but the lovely gardens are open free to the public during daylight hours. Yaddo (tel. 518/584-0746) is a world of velvety lawns, marble statues, and somber 80-foot-tall pine trees presided over by a majestic (to say the least) stone mansion with a five-story central tower. At the foot of the rose garden is a statue of *Christalan,* dated 1900, and dedicated "to the children of this house" (all four of the Trasks' children perished in a smallpox epidemic). Be sure to see the moody and mysterious woodland garden on the hillside behind the rose garden. Yaddo is located on Union Avenue, past the Race Course and just before the intersection with the Northway.

Antiques

An outfit called the **Regent Street Antiques Center,** 153 Regent St. (tel. 518/584-0107), contains not just a collection of more Hummel figurines than you've ever seen in your life, but also the shops of approximately 30 dealers. Merchandise runs the gamut from rugs and oil paintings to toys and dolls, books and silver, dishes and framed pictures, etc. It's a good browse; open daily from 10 a.m. to 5 p.m.

Saratoga National Historical Park

The Battle of Saratoga was one of Britain's pivotal defeats during the American War of Independence. Two American heroes emerged from the battle: Benedict Arnold, later of West Point infamy; and Colonel Daniel Morgan, forever of Green Mountain Boys fame. Saratoga foiled the British plan to split the colonies in two along the line of the Hudson Valley. And temporarily anyway, it established Arnold as a national figure of great promise.

One looks in vain for the old town of Saratoga on the map these days. That's because it's now called Schuylerville, in honor of the aristocratic Schuyler family whose country seat is part of the National Historical Park (tel. 518/664-9821). Interestingly, General Schuyler had been relieved of command of the Continental troops hereabouts just prior to the battle. To add injury to insult, the retreating General John Burgoyne burned Schuyler's country house to the ground in the course of his retreat. Schuyler's personal loss did not, however, prevent him from later treating the vanquished "Gentleman Johnny" with every courtesy. Subsequent to the debacle at Saratoga, Burgoyne was confined to the Pastures, Schuyler's town residence near Albany, as a combination prisoner/houseguest.

Schuylerville and the Saratoga National Historical Park are located about 14 miles due east of Saratoga Springs via N.Y. 29. The bulk of the park consists of the actual terrain, still rural and undeveloped, on which the famous battle occurred. Students of the Revolution are going to love this place. Besides an informative **visitor center** full of audiovisual exhibits and enlightening brochures, there is a paved one-way loop, nine miles long, at which key points in the course of the battle can be visited much like Stations of the Cross. If anything, there might be rather more here than is possible to absorb in a single day. One does feel a twinge of guilt skipping the odd site along the way.

On the southern edge of Schuylerville, on today's U.S. 4, is the **Schuyler House,** (tel. 518/695-3664), a restored colonial manse built in 30 days on the ruins of the house burned by Burgoyne. All the nails and hardware were salvaged from the ashes of the former house. It's quite a pretty old place, immaculately restored, rather smaller than it looks from the outside, partially furnished with 18th-century pieces and open daily June to Labor Day from 9 a.m. until 5 p.m.

The other site of interest is the **Saratoga Monument,** a Victorian-era obelisk which can be climbed for a breathtaking view of the surrounding mountains. On a clear day the panorama stretches from the Catskills to the Berkshires to the Adirondacks. Fitness buffs won't want to miss this staircase. Like the Schuyler House, the monument is open daily June to Labor Day from 9 a.m. to 5 p.m. The monument is on Burgoyne Street, atop a hill overlooking the center of Schuylerville.

There's no admission charge to any of the historical park attractions.

WHERE TO STAY IN SARATOGA SPRINGS

Instead of starting with the most expensive place in town, I'm starting with the one I think is hands down the best in town. The **Adelphi Hotel,** 365 Broadway, Saratoga Springs, NY 12866 (tel. 518/587-4688), has three-story Victorian columns supporting a porch overlooking the middle of Broadway. Erected in 1877, it has an intricate brown-and-yellow paint job that oozes period charm. Inside is a lobby loaded with Victorian froufrou furniture, a stenciled ceiling, rococo revival sofas, and fringed draperies. A skylit staircase leads to 34 perfectly wonderful rooms, each different, all decorated with antique rugs and furniture, pictures on silk cords, curtains on swags, bordello color schemes, perhaps crystal drips on the bedside lights or involved chandeliers. All have high ceilings and private bathrooms. An upstairs lounge packed with potted plants and appealing Victorian clutter leads to a wicker-filled porch beyond whose blossom-laden flower boxes lies the panorama of Saratoga's famous Broadway. What a place for breakfast. Downstairs is an atmospheric café/bar for drinks and light meals, an outdoor garden with tables and chairs, plus a dining room for heavier fare. Open only May through October; off-season rates (May, June, September, and October), single or double, range from $55 to $95 nightly for the smallest room to the biggest suite. Add another $40 for stays during Skidmore graduation, holiday, and foliage weekends; add about $50 for each night of a July weekend (and figure a two-night minimum too). And during August (gulp), the nightly rate range leaps to $120 to $250, with a two-day weekend minimum.

All the rate structures in Saratoga are similarly complicated. And like all hotel charges, they're quite likely to change. The above description is meant to give you a feel for the local vagaries in price. This is, after all, a seasonal resort. Wherever you decide to stay, phone ahead for precise rates. The Adelphi, though not the costliest place in town, is the most atmospheric and my particular favorite.

The **Ramada Renaissance,** 534 Broadway, Saratoga Springs, NY 12866 (tel. 518/584-4000, or toll free 800/2-RAMADA), sits right in the middle of town contiguous to, and indeed a part of, Saratoga's new convention center. This place has everything—a fancy restaurant called the Sandalwood, an indoor pool, game rooms, exercise rooms, meeting rooms, you name it. It's new (built 1983), huge (190 rooms, which seems huge in Saratoga), modern (brown-brick, squared-off, no-frills architecture), and open all year. Essentially it's just a sexy Ramada Inn with a lot of facilities and a vast lobby filled with colonial furniture and oil paintings beneath acres of acoustic ceiling. The rooms are examples of state-of-the-art motel luxury. They typically have plush rose carpeting, wing chairs, bathrooms equipped with hairdryers and telephones, framed pictures of horses, color TVs, and good-quality fabrics and furnishings. Indeed this place attracts a fair share of comfort and money-oriented sale and racing week heavies. During the off-season (November through April) a room for two costs $82 a night; during the shoulder seasons (May through July and September through October) doubles cost about $92 nightly. In August a double will run you between about $225 a night, and up to $400 for what they call a "king-alcove" (essentially an oversize room with a kitchenette and some living room furniture).

The **Gideon Putnam Hotel,** Saratoga Spa State Park, Saratoga Springs, NY 12866 (tel. 518/584-3000), is a big 132-room Georgian colonial affair right in the middle of the Spa State Park. Built with the rest of the spa in the 1930s (and still owned by the State of New York), it has an elegant sweeping driveway, lofty white columns, a marble-floored lobby with lots of potted plants and a suave beige color scheme, plus lots of restaurants and bars. The hotel has been recently renovated and all rooms are furnished with appropriate-looking Georgian colonial pieces, along with new bedding, carpeting, and drapes. The old Roosevelt Bath House is presently being upgraded in association with the hotel. In addition to traditional mineral baths, it will soon offer a European health spa, including hydrotherapy; massage (Swedish, shiatsu, and sports); herbal wrap; Swiss shower; loofa scrub; various facials; waxing; body, hand, and foot treatments. The above will be supplemented by fitness training, cholesterol testing, body composition analysis, sports programs, and spa cuisine. The Gideon Putnam basks somewhat in its reputation of being the *ne plus ultra* of racing week addresses. There's no question that it's the most famous hotel in town. In the winter (November through April) a standard double room here will cost you about $85 nightly; in the shoulder seasons (May through mid-June and September through October) that same room will be $120; the upward spiral culminates during racing weeks, when double-occupancy rates including three meals (you pay for them whether you take them or not) start at about $260 nightly.

The **Inn at Saratoga,** 231 Broadway, Saratoga Springs, NY 12866 (tel. 518/583-1890, or toll free 800/421-6662), is a brand-new hotel in a fully renovated old gabled wooden building. Its tiny lobby is decorated with tasteful striped paper, oak floors, gilt-framed mirrors, and period pictures on the walls. What was once the porch is now the Ascot Lounge for drinks; a former sitting room is now the Earl Grey Tea Room for breakfast and lunch. Everything in this place is perfect and new and salmon and beige. There is gracious Muzak in the halls, thick patterned rugs, and a definite plush look to things. The rooms feature great old-fashioned wallpapers, wing chairs, floral comforters, curtains on swags, brand-new bathrooms, 25-inch TVs, full-length mirrors, and turn-down service. Nightly rates are your typical Saratoga tangle of dates and categories. The place is open all year and double-occupancy rates vary from about $70 to $90 in the winter, to $160 to $220 or so during the August racing weeks. Suites, of course, cost more. As always, phone ahead to confirm the exact prices.

The **Holiday Inn,** Broadway at Circular Street, Saratoga Springs, NY 12866 (tel. 518/584-4550), looks just the way you'd expect a Holiday Inn to look. The building adjoins Congress Park, and unlike the Victorian concoctions in the neighborhood, it has your basic flat roof, brick walls with random "used" bricks, panels of glass, and neatly clipped shrubs. There's a quite attractive outdoor pool, as well as 150 rooms available year-round. The place has been kept up very nicely and renovated regularly. Accommodations are spacious, equipped with twin queen-size beds, thick rugs, nice pictures, textured wall coverings, phones, and color TVs. Adjacent to the lobby is a closet full of gurgling video games, and a bright restaurant serving breakfast, lunch, and dinner, and doubling as a nightclub. Management provided me with two solid pages of single-spaced rate categories. Basically, doubles seem to hit a winter low of about $60, climb to shoulder highs of about $75, before rocketing into the August racing weeks' stratosphere of $185 a night.

The Washington Inn is located just north of the Spa State Park at 1 South Broadway, Saratoga Springs, NY 12866 (tel. 518/584-9807). Consisting of two large turn-of-the-century boarding houses, the inn offers travelers a budget option for the hectic summer season. Open only during July and August, the Washington offers 19 rooms with private baths, TVs, and phones. The July rate is $45 for a double and $60 for a twin. August rates are $75 and $90, respectively. Reservations are a must.

Numerous motels line Broadway shoulder to shoulder south of Congress Park and the Holiday Inn. Most are 30-odd years old and have rate structures that reflect the extreme bell curve of the Saratoga racing season. My favorite of the bunch is the Turf and Spa, 140 Broadway, Saratoga Springs, NY 12866 (tel. 518/584-2550), whose 42 rooms are open all year long. There's a heated pool here, with a nicer aspect than most. The rooms are contained in a two-story L-shaped building, and decorated with comfy double beds, pool-blue telephones, thick rugs, vinyl chairs, cable color TVs, and immaculate bathrooms. It's very well kept and the prices are reasonable, ranging from an off-season winter low of $35 for two, to a racing weeks high of $105. During July doubles are only $55, and during the months of May, June, September, and October they're only $40. The location is convenient to downtown. All told, it's an excellent value.

WHERE TO EAT

Herewith, a list of my personal favorites, starting with the most expensive.

Deluxe

Ye Olde Wishing Well, on U.S. 9 about four miles north of town (tel. 518/584-7640), is definitely worth the trip. This is the sort of place where rich daddies take their little girls to dinner on Skidmore parents' weekends, where stable owners toast one another over a winning season. Only dinner is served, from 5 to 10 p.m. daily except Monday (to 11 p.m. on Saturday), and the place is closed for three weeks in January. When it's open, it's packed. Diners are distributed in a collection of rustic/elegant old rooms of the stone-fireplace-and-exposed-beam variety. I had the biggest lamb chop I've ever had in my life at the Wishing Well. Also available are things like king crabmeat au gratin, hot seafood platter, sirloin steak, filet mignon, roasted fresh turkey, all of which come with salad and potato and cost between about $11 and $21 per à la carte entree.

The Union Coach House, 139 Union Ave., at the corner of Nelson Avenue (tel. 518/584-6440), occupies an antique blue house located about midway between Circular Street and the Race Course. The interior decor is sleek and modern (gray rugs, hanging ferns, greenhouse walls) with a few Victorian antiques scattered about for accent. Only dinner is served, during which time you might try something like chicken Kiev, Delmonico steak, baked stuffed shrimp, or seafood crêpes, for between $13 and $18. Open pretty much year-round (save for about twelve weeks from Christmas to mid-February) from 5 to 10 p.m.; closed Sunday and Monday except during the racing season, when they're open all week.

Five miles south of Saratoga is a gourmet northern Italian and seafood restaurant called The Elms, 2721 U.S. 9, Malta (tel. 518/587-2277). In 1959 Filomena Viggiani, at the age of 58, opened her first restaurant. Today it's become an institution, run with the help of daughter/hostess Esther and son/chef Michael. Chances are, if you've had a fine pasta plate anywhere in this neck of the woods, it was made in this kitchen. Distributed in eastern New York State, the Viggianis' pastas come in an ever-growing variety of flavors, including egg, spinach, tomato, artichoke, beet, carrot, tomato-basil, tomato-rosemary, lemon–white pepper, egg–black pepper, garlic –white pepper, fennel-lemon, saffron, even chocolate and squid ink. The decor of The Elms, unlike that of so many Saratoga restaurants, has no Victorian frills, antiques, or other gimmicks. But during August, when no reservations are accepted, you may find yourself standing in line with a duchess or a member of the American aristocracy or maybe even a movie star. Dinner entrees like shrimp Fra Diavolo, tagliatelle pescatora (my favorite), and linguine al pesto mostly cost from $9 to $17. Open for dinner only from 5 to 10 p.m.; Sundays from 2 to 9 p.m.; closed Monday in July; open seven days a week in August. The restaurant is closed from Thanksgiving to mid-February and on Mondays and Tuesdays the rest of the year.

About a 15-minute drive south of Saratoga on N.Y. 50 and west on Charlton Road, you'll find the **Charlton Tavern,** 746 Charlton Rd., Charlton (tel. 518/399-9951). The tavern was an 18th-century stagecoach inn, now converted to an intimate restaurant with a large open-hearth fireplace, wood-burning stove, exposed hand-hewn beams, and wide-plank floors. The Maloney family has run the restaurant for more than 20 years and its Continental-American cuisine is well known in the Capital District. Lunch ($3 to $6) and dinner ($10 to $15) are available from 11 a.m. to 9 p.m. Tuesday through Thursday, and to 11 p.m. on Friday and Saturday.

Moderate Prices and Lots of Atmosphere

Eartha's Kitchen, 60 Court St. (tel. 518/583-0602), is famous for mesquite grilling. The new location (since our last edition) is in a quiet residential area between Union Avenue and Spring Street. Eartha's interior has a crisp country look, decorated with traditional Victorian Saratoga colors of bachelor cream, jumel red, and congress green. The wine bar sports wicker furniture and is a great place to taste Eartha's newest vintage. The restaurant, which is a local center for wine-tasting and gourmet-cooking classes, is open for dinner from 5 p.m. to 11 p.m. every night during July and August, only Tuesday through Saturday the rest of the year. There's also a Sunday brunch from 11 a.m. to 3 p.m. The menu changes daily and offers a selection of wonderful grilled and sautéed dishes in the $15 to $18 range.

Lillian's, 408 Broadway (tel. 518/587-7766), is a local favorite serving dependable steaks, seafood, and chicken. The restaurant's Victorian decor combines etched glass, stained-glass panels over the bar, mahogany woodwork, brass fixtures, tin ceilings, and Tiffany-style lamps. Antiques, Laura Ashley wallpaper, and a mauve/dark-green interior color scheme create a comfortable dining environment. Lunches are served Monday through Saturday from 11:30 a.m. to 4 p.m. Hot entrees and sandwiches are mostly in the $4 to $7 range. Dinners cost in the $14 to $18 range and are available Monday through Thursday from 5 to 10 p.m., to 11 p.m. on Friday and Saturday.

The Olde Bryan Inn, 123 Maple Ave. (tel. 518/587-2990), which is just off U.S. 9 a block north of the Ramada Renaissance parking lot, looks from the outside like it might be a luxury restaurant. It occupies a restored stone house dating from 1832, the oldest in Saratoga. The interior is decorated with working fireplaces (three of them), exposed stone walls, church pews, exposed beams, wide-plank floors, hanging ferns, and wooden tables. There is rock and roll on the jukebox and a great friendly ambience. A single menu is available all day and features all manner of hearty sandwiches (corned beef Reuben to BLT club to Canadian grill) priced at about $5 each; "light" items (chili, vegetable wrap, seafood salad, pasta primavera, etc.) ranging from around $4 to $8; and "hearty" selections (such as Cajun blackened steak, seafood kebab, prime rib, Jamaican shrimp sauté, etc.), most of which cost between $9 and $16. Open all year, every day, from 11:30 a.m. until midnight.

Professor Moriarty's, 430 Broadway (tel. 518/587-5981), is at the absolute center of Saratoga Springs. It's in essence a classy bar and burger joint, with a diminutive outdoor terrace on Broadway and a very busy interior decorated with saloon tile floors, brick walls, Victorian woodwork, antique light fixtures, oak tables, café chairs with brown leather seats, and racing paintings. At lunch a burger and fries will run you around $4.50, a Moriarty burger is about $5, and various deli sandwiches run between $4 and $5. At dinner an amusing menu divides courses into the "Plot" (appetizers), the "Crime" (main courses), and the "Verdict" (dessert). Puns abound, chief among them being a dessert called "Death by Chocolate." Most main courses (such as chicken Moriarty, bay scallops, prime rib, etc.) cost between $10 and $17. Open daily, year-round, from 11:30 a.m. to 5 p.m. for lunch, and 5 to 11 p.m. for dinner. The bar is very lively at night and of course stays open much later.

Mother Goldsmith's, 43 Phila St. (tel. 518/584-9772), is a Jewish deli-restaurant serving authentically terrific Jewish deli food. In decor it's not unlike a Manhattan coffeeshop, which is to say nondescript and sort of modern. This is the place for a $5 or $8 sandwich of brisket, turkey, or corned beef that's really worth it. Also blintzes, pancakes, kosher knockwurst, omelets, fresh fish, burgers, even pizza. Open seven days a week from 7 a.m. until 10 p.m. (until midnight in August). A big favorite for breakfast too.

Hattie's, 45 Phila St. (tel. 518/584-4790), is a green-and-white-painted soul-food restaurant with a squeaky screen door and nice oldtime atmosphere. Complete lunch specials cost less than $5 and include soup or juice, a choice of things like chicken liver or fried haddock or maybe a cheese omelet, biscuits, potato, dessert, and coffee. Sandwiches cost $2 to $3, and dinner is usually a $10 ticket, rarely more. Barbecued ribs, sirloin, pork chops, fried shrimp, and the specialty of the house, fried chicken, are among the items available. Indeed, the complete $10 chicken dinner is a Saratoga favorite. And is it good! So much so, in fact, that reservations are usually needed for summer dinners. Lunch is served from 11 a.m. to 3 p.m., dinner from 4 to 11 p.m. Open seven days a week in July and August; closed Tuesday the rest of the year.

Margarita's, 392 Broadway (tel. 518/583-1107), is a sleek and atmospheric place that's the sister establishment of Margarita's on Lark Street in Albany. A pile of sand, a cactus plant, and a neon Margarita glass decorate the plate-glass windows overlooking Broadway. Inside the look is cool and lofty, with rose walls, track lights, chrome-and-black bar stools, and lots of mirrors. There's but one menu, available all day every day from 11:30 a.m. to 1 a.m. Chili con carne, various burritos, a chicken tostada, taco salad, a burger with fries, and chicken salad in a stuffed tomato are but a few of the many items available. Most things on the menu cost between $5 and $11. This bar and that at Moriarty's are particular hot spots on summer nights.

In a Class by Itself

The **Caunterbury,** out Union Avenue past the Race Course and maybe another mile past the Northway (tel. 518/587-9653), is *not* pronounced in any highfalutin manner. It's just plain ole "Canterbury," the spelling resulting from incorrect advice obtained from an Englishman prior to opening. The restaurant occupies a barn complex erected originally, if I've got the story straight, by the famous 19th-century publisher Frank Leslie for his Saratoga estate. Its cavernous interior has been converted into a sort of indoor dinner Disneyland. The Wharf Area features mock colonial façades facing one another across real water and ceilings that look like the sky. The Waterfall Room has a huge free-form pool with (what else?) a waterfall. Diners are distributed hither and yon amid all this. Overhead balconies and catwalks extend all over the place. Only dinner is served, from a menu including selections such as filet mignon, tournedos, chicken Chaucer, seafood marinara, beef Wellington, etc., priced mostly between $15 and $22 per à la carte entree. Certainly an unusual setting, and actually lots of fun. Open every day, except Tuesday in the winter.

Budget

And don't forget **Bruegger's Bagel Bakery,** 451 Broadway, between Caroline and Lake Streets (tel. 518/584-4372), where all manner of sandwiches on all manner of bagels, etc., cost but $2 to $4. It's bright, clean, modern, cafeteria style—even has an outdoor terrace in the summer. The same outfit operates similarly attractive locations in Albany. Open daily from 7 a.m. to 7 p.m. (to 4 p.m. on Sunday).

---

3. The Road West—Cooperstown and Cazenovia

Though somewhat geographically isolated, Cooperstown and Cazenovia are two aristocratic upstate towns with more than luxury real estate to recommend them. They both lie along the natural route between the Capital District and the Finger Lakes which I call "The Road West."

COOPERSTOWN

Only 70 miles west of Albany, at the foot of Otsego Lake, lies Cooperstown (pop. 2,300). This immensely attractive village was founded by 1786 by William Cooper, father of the famous American novelist James Fenimore Cooper. Besides having important literary associations, Cooperstown is where Abner Doubleday is reputed to have invented the game of baseball in 1839. (Actually, a compelling historical case can be made for Hoboken, N.J., and 1846 as the correct place and date, but I won't go into that in a section on Cooperstown.) Regardless of where the game originated, Cooperstown is where the Baseball Hall of Fame is today located. Baseball and Cooper—what could be more American?

For the benefit of those who've never actually read anything by James Fenimore Cooper, here is Mark Twain: "The conversations in the Cooper books have a curious sound in our modern ears. To believe that such talk really came out of people's mouths would be to believe that there was a time when time was of no value to a person who thought he had something to say; when it was the custom to spread a two-minute remark out to ten; when a man's mouth was a rolling-mill, and busied itself all day long in turning four-foot pigs of thought into thirty-foot bars of conversational railroad iron by attenuation . . ." This is from an 1897 essay titled "Fenimore Cooper's Literary Offenses."

Here is Louis C. Jones, author of *Cooperstown*, an informative publication of the New York State Historical Association (headquartered in Cooperstown): "It is easy enough to criticize Cooper's tortuous style, his unrealistic conversations, his fatuous 'females,' his endless descriptions, but he remains one of our literary giants and as much a pioneer in our literature as his father was in the wilderness. More than any other writer until the advent of Mark Twain, Cooper gave Europeans their most convincing picture of our country."

And Cooperstown is a delightful place to explore. It's situated at the foot of a beautiful lake and its physical plant has benefited from generations of attention from one rich and interested family. Its rural elegance is enhanced by a sumptuous lakefront resort hotel called the Otsega, which has been operating here in an essentially unchanged manner since 1909. Filled with huge shade trees, beautiful old houses, a charming late-19th-century business district, good inns and restaurants, and lots of fascinating museums, Cooperstown is an excellent place to stop while en route across upstate New York.

The Sights of Cooperstown

The village has three important museums, whose existence is due in large part to the generosity of the Clark family (of Singer Sewing Machine fame). These museums are the Baseball Hall of Fame, the Fenimore House Museum, and the Farmers' Museum.

Johnny Carson pointed out in a monologue one night that the last two words in America's National Anthem are "Play Ball!" The **Baseball Hall of Fame** is a Georgian brick shrine to those of our fellow countrymen who have most excelled in this most American of pastimes. Superfans won't be disappointed by the collection here. There is a "Great Moments Room" with nine-foot blowups; a collection of over 1,000 artifacts (bats, balls, gloves, etc.) tracing the evolution of the game; the "All-Star Game Display," which is a clever mounting of clippings, programs, and pictures from the past; the "Ballparks Room," memorializing famous parks (complete with old turnstiles, benches, and seats); the "Hall of Fame Gallery," where 200 immortals are fittingly represented by bronze plaques; plus lots more, much of it dealing with players and games of the recent past. Museum admission is $5 for adults, $2 for "juniors" (ages 7 to 15). Summer hours are 9 a.m. to 9 p.m. daily from May through October; during the rest of the year they close at 5 p.m. The museum is located on the corner of Main and Fair Streets, adjacent to the middle of the village (tel. 607/547-9988).

If you elect to visit more than one of the Cooperstown museums, you'll be entitled to a discount combination ticket, available at any one of the three museums. Tuck that bit of knowledge away; I'll return to it shortly.

The **Fenimore House** is the former Georgian Revival mansion of Edward Severin Clark, grandson of Singer partner Edward Clark. Edward S. Clark was the "Squire" of Cooperstown in his day. His white-columned stone mansion was completed in 1932, the year before he died. His heirs saw to its (gentle and tasteful) conversion to a museum, which today contains an important collection of American folk art. Fenimore House's splendid rooms display woodcarvings, paintings, duck decoys, weather vanes, tavern signs, etc. Usually there's an interesting interpretive display mounted at any given time. When I was there the one on deck was called "A Shifting Wind" and demonstrated the different meaning folk art has to the house's various custodians over the passage of years. Fenimore House, which stands on the site of the original Cooper farm, is also the headquarters of the New York State Historical Society. The folk art museum charges $4 for adults and $1.50 for juniors, and is open daily from 9 a.m. to 6 p.m. from May until the end of October. Winter hours vary; call them before you go at 607/547-2533.

Third of the trio is the **Farmers' Museum,** adjacent to which is a reconstructed **Village Crossroads.** These installations occupy the former stable complex and adjacent grounds of the old Clark estate. Endangered buildings from hither and yon have been salvaged, moved to the spot of the Crossroads, and painstakingly restored. Nowadays all manner of colonial and early republican domestic business goes on here—shoeing horses, baking bread, spinning thread, printing broadsides, etc. Besides the demonstrations are all manner of exhibitions and shows held at various times each summer. It's a most attractive and carefully researched (if prettified) view of life on the edge of the frontier. It certainly demonstrates pioneer American ingenuity. Open daily May through October from 9 a.m. to 6 p.m.; during April, November, and December, open Tuesday through Sunday from 10 a.m. to 4 p.m.; closed January through March. Admission is $5 for adults and $2 for juniors (ages 7 to 15); the phone number is 607/547-2533.

As for those reduced-rate tickets: put briefly, you can save about 20% off the individual prices of two, and 25% off the per-museum price of all three.

Other things to do in Cooperstown would include **walking around town** and admiring the prosperous Victorian streetfronts along Main Street and the leafy byways of Pine Boulevard, Lake Street, and Chestnut Street between Main and Lake. The center of the village is at Chestnut (also designated as N.Y. 80 and 28) and Main; more than six or seven blocks in any direction will put you out in the country. You can really get to know the village by taking a self-guided **walking tour of Cooperstown,** directions for which are printed by the New York State Historical Society and available free at both the Fenimore House and the Farmers' Museum.

Perhaps you'd enjoy a **cruise on Lake Otsego,** the famous Glimmerglass of James Fenimore Cooper. The *Chief Uncas* is a vintage lake boat operated during the summer by **Lake Otsego Boat Tours.** For sailing times and prices, call 607/547-9710.

Culture in Cooperstown doesn't stop at just museums. Would anyone have guessed that it's also the home of a flourishing opera company? The **Glimmerglass Opera** celebrated its 15th-anniversary season in 1989, and the third season in the company's new home. The **Alice Busch Opera Theatre** is a 900-seat, partially open-air theater a few miles north of Cooperstown on N.Y. 80. What's more, the performances are all in English. For summer program and ticket information, contact Glimmerglass Opera, P.O. Box 191, Cooperstown, NY 13326, or phone the box office at 607/547-2255.

Actually you could spend quite a few happy days here, unwinding to be sure. A more romantic and out-of-the-way spot is hard to imagine.

Where to Stay in Cooperstown

The places I like best usually are small, old, and charming. The **Cooper Motor Inn,** Lake Street at Chestnut Street (P.O. Box 311), Cooperstown, NY 13326 (tel. 607/547-2567), is all of that and more. The name is misleading; for many years it was just called the Cooper Inn. Now it's owned by the nearby Otesaga, which has rechristened it as a "Motor" inn. Heaven only knows why. It's a handsome early Italianate house with white shutters and elaborate brackets under the eaves, sitting in park-like grounds smack in the middle of town. Inside is a fine central hall with a graceful staircase and assorted lounge rooms filled with lovely antiques and an air of patrician calm. The 20 rooms are located upstairs, some with black marble fireplaces, others with elaborate ceiling rosettes, all with private bath and old-fashioned furnishings, cable color TV, and tons of charm. And guests here can use the plush facilities down the block at the Otesaga. Double-occupancy rates at the Cooper range from about $90 to $100 during the July to Labor Day season. They're about $10 or so less during the rest of the year.

Right across the street, with its own deep lawn and immense maples, is the satisfyingly Victorian façade of the **Inn at Cooperstown,** 16 Chestnut St., Cooperstown, NY 13326 (tel. 607/547-5756). The inn is a three-story, mansard-roofed Second Empire confection whose inviting front porch is filled with rocking chairs. Inside everything has been restored to a level of perfection that one soon comes to expect in Cooperstown. The atmosphere is most appealing, if slightly less gentrified than over at the Cooper Inn. Downstairs is a small lounge with a television, adjacent to which is a breakfast room. All the floors are refinished; all the paint is crisp; every Victorian antique gleams. Each of the 17 newly decorated rooms has a private bath, thick wall-to-wall carpeting, table lamps with pleated shades, gauzy curtains on tie-backs, and dark-stained colonial-reproduction furniture. Double-occupancy rates include a continental breakfast and range from about $65 to $75 nightly, with reduced winter packages available.

One of the architectural and psychological anchors of Cooperstown is the aforementioned **Otesaga Hotel,** Lake Street (P.O. Box 311), Cooperstown, NY 13326 (tel. 607/547-9931). This huge (125 guest rooms) Georgian palace sits right on the lake amid velvety lawns and specimen trees, a block or two from the center of town. There is a formal columned portico (and a formal dress code in the evening), beyond which lie vast traditional public rooms decorated with pale colors, gleaming brass, lots of WASPy floral prints, and sweeping lake views. It's a very fine 1909 building in very fine condition, with not a tacky addition in sight. Besides the lake frontage, there is a big outdoor swimming pool, a bar, a lounge, an adjacent golf course, and a big old-fashioned main-floor dining room worth a visit for lunch or dinner whether or not you stay here. Room decor is more chaste than the Edwardian architecture of the place might suggest. But the rooms are big and the furnishings all seem to be pretty new and of high quality. All rooms have TV sets. They all have private bathrooms and are spanking clean. The Otesaga is open only from May until the end of October, during which time the per-person Modified American Plan (breakfast and dinner included) rate per day per person ranges from about $120 to

$200, depending on the size and location of the room. Take note: This is a resort hotel and as such they offer accommodations on the MAP basis only.

Also good to know about is the string of immaculate little mom-and-pop motels that dot N.Y. 80 along the northern half of Otsego Lake. Prototypical of these is the **Lake View Motel,** on N.Y. 80 (R.D. 2, Box 932), Cooperstown, NY 13326 (tel. 607/547-9740), whose 14 units have thick rugs, cable color TVs, AM/FM radios, direct-dial phones, vaguely traditional-looking furnishings, and gleaming private baths. It was built 25 years ago but looks brand-new. The location is right across the road from a lakefront landing at which you can swim or rent a boat, a canoe, or a Sunfish. From late June until Labor Day double-occupancy rates range from $65 to $75 nightly; there's a $15 to $20 drop in prices during the rest of the year. A number of other motels in the vicinity are just as nice; this one appealed to me the most.

Where to Eat in Cooperstown

A meal at the **Otesaga,** on Lake Street (tel. 607/547-9931), should be a part of any visit because . . . well, just because it's such a part of the town. The hotel dining room is only slightly smaller than a football field—or perhaps more appropriately, a baseball diamond—and features lofty ceilings, lots of moldings, and (if you're lucky) a good view of the water. Lunch and dinner are both sumptuous buffets at which you can have as much as you want of anything you see. The price, which includes tip and tax, is a surprisingly affordable $10 at lunch, $25 at dinner, and $12.50 for Sunday brunch. The dining room is open every day during the hotel's season (May through October) from 7:30 a.m. to 9 a.m. for breakfast, noon to 2 p.m. for lunch, and 6:30 to 8:30 p.m. for dinner.

In the same price bracket, but located eight miles north of the village on N.Y. 80, is a great old-fashioned-looking roadhouse called the **Red Sleigh** (tel. 607/547-5581). Only dinner is served, seven days a week during June, July, and August, from 5 to 11 p.m. The place is full of nooks and angles; the dining room has a low-beamed ceiling and lots of atmosphere; the tap room has more beams and deep-crimson walls. A la carte entrees like beef Stroganoff, veal Oscar, steak au poivre, open steak sandwich, broiled scallops, shrimp scampi, etc., are priced mostly between $9 and $20.

Back in the village is an atmospheric tavern/restaurant called the **Bold Dragoon,** 49 Pioneer St. (tel. 607/547-9800). Half of it's a bar with a regular clientele; the other half is a cozy narrow dining room with pine-paneled booths, dim lighting, and rock and roll on the jukebox. Expect to pay well under $5 for sandwiches and burgers at lunch, and around $6 to $10 for dinners like chicken parmesan, pork chop, broiled scallops, roast beef, etc., all of which include soup or salad, potato, and vegetable. They even have "light" dinner items (honey-dipped chicken, chef's salad, etc.) for $4 to $5. Open daily all year long: 11:30 a.m. to 2:30 p.m. for lunch, and 5 until 9 p.m. for dinner.

People in town love the **Lake Front,** overlooking Otsego Lake at the foot of Fair Street (tel. 607/547-9511). The decor is modern and pleasant (murals, picture windows, acoustic ceilings with iron chandeliers). The extensive and sophisticated lunch menu has elaborate sandwiches (teriyaki turkey, Cooper Special, barbecued beef on a Kaiser, etc.), plus interesting entrees (marinated chicken breast, "spreads" consisting of cold sandwiches served with a grilled stuffed tomato, omelets of all sorts, etc.) almost all of which are priced below $5. At dinner you might have something like filet mignon chasseur, broiled lamb chops, chicken au gratin, sautéed scallops, duck à l'orange, etc., which will likely cost you somewhere between $10 and $15. The chef studied at the famous Culinary Institute of America in Hyde Park. Between Easter and late October, lunch and dinner are served daily from 11 a.m. to 5 p.m., and 5 to 9 p.m. respectively. During the off-season, lunch hours are 11 a.m. to 2 p.m.

Sherry's, at the corner of Main and Chestnut Streets (tel. 607/547-9261), is a bright, friendly, family-style restaurant with good home-cooking, unpretentious decor, and moderate prices. There are two rooms, one containing a counter and a new-ish pseudo-Mediterranean decor, the other being a dining room that looks much as it must have looked for the last 40 or 50 years. The menu lists ice cream parlor treats, burgers and deli sandwiches for $3 and under, dinner entrees (grilled liver, turkey salad platter, fried chicken, sirloin steak, etc.) for $5 to $11, and is available every day all year from 8 a.m. until 8:30 p.m. From late October until Easter, however, they close on Thursday.

Also modest, and located right in town, is **Obies Brot und Bier,** on little Pioneer Alley, a half block down Pioneer Street from Main (tel. 607/547-5601). A sandwich menu running the gamut from franks to barbecue to cold ham to surf and turf (steak and lobster salad) is served daily from April through October. Most things cost between $2 and $5. Open from 7 a.m. to 10 p.m. in the summer, until 10 p.m. in the spring and fall.

CAZENOVIA

About 100 miles west of Albany on N.Y. 20 is Cazenovia. This delectable little upstate village has wonderful inns, a picturesque lake, an abundance of handsome early-19th-century architecture, and a beautiful and historic mansion bequeathed to the State of New York in 1968. The mansion is called Lorenzo and it has been, in its ups and downs, a bellwether of the fortunes of Cazenovia itself. There are other fine estates in the nearby rolling countryside and along the shores of Cazenovia Lake. But Lorenzo is the soul of the town.

Cazenovia was founded in 1793 by one John Linklaen. The founding of the town and the sale of lots were a part of but one of many speculative land subdivisions taking place across upstate New York in those days. Linklaen was the agent of an outfit called the Holland Land Company, and he named his new town after Theophile Cazenove, a sort of T. Boone Pickens of his day and Linklaen's boss.

For about 20 years both Linklaen and Cazenovia prospered. Trouble started when it became known that the Erie Canal was going to bypass Cazenovia. Learning this, the Holland Land Company decided to liquidate its area holdings immediately. And in order to protect the value of his own lands Linklaen felt compelled to buy *all* the company's unsold land in the Cazenovia vicinity. Construction had hardly started on the Erie Canal in 1817 when land prices in Cazenovia, not unexpectedly, crashed.

Linklaen died in 1822, deep in debt. The following year his widow sold Lorenzo, at that time one of the finest estates in America, for $100. She retained only the right to live in the house until she died.

But that was not the end of the Linklaens. Through judicious marriages and adoptions Mrs. Linklaen and her family managed to preserve and indeed enhance their position in Cazenovia. Their name was Fairchild during the late 19th and early 20th centuries. They still ruled at Lorenzo when other mansions, this time for summer people, began rising all around them. They were Remingtons until the 1950s, and Ledyards at the end, when George S. Ledyard, as much of an "aristocrat" as this country is ever likely to produce, died at Lorenzo in October 1967.

Today's visitors to the village can savor its elegant traditions in various ways. You can, for instance, stay at one of its **charming inns,** about which more below. If you fancy colonial, patrician Federal, Greek Revival, and mid-Victorian architecture, you can spend many pleasurable hours on do-it-yourself **walking tours** and **driving tours.** The village is full of elegantly columned Greek Revival houses shaded by huge trees. It's truly a treat to walk around. The Cazenovia Preservation Foundation, Inc., P.O. Box 266, Cazenovia, NY 13035, publishes two pamphlets titled, respectively, "5 Walks in the Village of Cazenovia," and "5 Drives, Town of Cazenovia." These brochures cost 50¢ each, and are usually available at the Linklaen House Hotel, the Town Office, local bookstores and drugstores, or in advance by mail from the Preservation Foundation.

It's worth noting that Cazenovia didn't survive in quite so handsome a condition all on its own. The local Preservation Foundation has been working for over 25 years urging merchants to take down ugly signs and storefronts, and encouraging owners to restore buildings aesthetically. The result is a village without unsightly signage, where the gas stations that do exist actually still wash your windows.

The brick Federal mansion of **Lorenzo** is, of course, the principal attraction in town. It's not huge as mansions go, but it has a fine position looking up the length of Cazenovia Lake, and the lands around it are still rural and bucolic. Inside it looks just like the lived-in house of some rich old family. All the original stuff is still here —paintings, fabulous upholstered furniture, crystal chandeliers, silver, dishes, photographs in silver frames, the lot. Behind the house is a lovely garden bordered by lines of ancient evergreens called the Dark Aisle. Planted in the 1850s to screen the gardens from the surrounding fields, they contain romantically gloomy paths. Lorenzo (tel. 315/655-3200) overlooks the lake and N.Y. 20, but the entrance is on N.Y. 13 going toward DeRuyter. The house is open May to Labor Day from 10 a.m. until 5 p.m. (from 1 p.m. on Sunday). The grounds are open all year from 8 a.m. until sunset; closed Tuesday. Admission is free.

Aside from touring Lorenzo, soaking up the ambience in the streets, and enjoying good meals and atmospheric lodgings, there isn't a lot else to do in Cazenovia. There is, however, the annual **Lorenzo Driving Competition.** This is an exposition of horse-drawn vehicles that takes place on the third weekend in July. There is also **Christmas at Lorenzo,** which is an annual holiday celebration in the old house. You might consider writing to the Cazenovia Business Association, P.O. Box 66, Cazenovia, NY 13035, to inquire whether other special events might be taking place at the time of your proposed visit.

Where to Stay and Eat in Cazenovia

I love the **Linklaen House,** 79 Albany St., N.Y. 20, Cazenovia, NY 13035 (tel. 315/655-3461). In fact, my wife and I spent a night there during our honeymoon. It's a three-story brick building in the middle of town, not too big, with small white-columned porches and dark-green shutters. The lobbies and public rooms on the main floor have a gracious and dignified air. There is old painted paneling, red leather furniture, Oriental rugs, big fireplaces, a graceful old staircase, and a lovely old dining room with painted paneled columns. There are only 21 rooms, all with private bath, and they tend to be small. But they're absolutely immaculate and decorated with pretty wall stencils, chenille spreads, tiny TV sets, tons of fluffy towels, and comfortable armchairs. Double-occupancy room rates vary from about $70 nightly for a small room with a double bed to $130 for larger accommodations and suites. Befitting its status as a local institution (it's been a hotel since 1835), the Linklaen House is open all year long.

The **Brewster Inn,** N.Y. 20 on Cazenovia Lake, Cazenovia, NY 13035 (tel. 315/655-9232), is a fine old shingled manse with velvety lawns that sweep down to the water's edge. Built as a summer home in the late 1880s for a railroad man and sometime Rockefeller partner named Benjamin Brewster, it contains lots of handsome woodwork, a gorgeous three-story staircase, gilt mirrors, Empire antiques, gleaming floors, thick rugs, and eight guest rooms, each with a private bath. Some of the rooms have features like Jacuzzis mounted adjacent to king-size brass beds. Others look like nice old-fashioned guest rooms in your rich grandmother's house. The furnishings are of no precise period, but the effect is certainly good. And the rooms, with their tall ceilings and old moldings, are inherently elegant. Two people will pay anywhere from about $65 to $130 nightly, depending on whether or not they want the Jacuzzi and the fantasy-provoking bed. Five of the eight rooms cost under $80.

The **Brae Loch Inn,** on N.Y. 20 at the corner of Forman Street (tel. 315/655-3431), has 12 great rooms and offers wonderful Scottish hospitality. The Barr family has brought to Casenovia not just a good inn and restaurant, but also the largest Scottish gift shop in New York State. Rooms here are very comfortable, filled with antiques, and have private baths, color TVs, and air conditioning. Prices range from $70 for a room with a double bed, to $90 for a room with a queen/king canopied bed (bridal suite), to $125 for king-size luxury rooms. The Brae Loch is a Victorian barn of a place with modern additions. Best accommodations, in my opinion, are in the old part.

For meals too, the **Brewster Inn** (tel. 315/655-9232) is hard to beat. The original lake-view porch has been enclosed, furnished with tables and chairs, and converted into a singularly smooth operation that dispenses dinner only from 5 until about 9 p.m., seven days a week. Sample menu items include blackened sea bass, Long Island duckling Montmorency, London broil, cape scallops, roast beef, etc., and cost between about $13 and $16 à la carte.

The **Linklaen House,** 79 Albany St. (tel. 315/655-3461), serves both lunch and dinner in its charming white-painted paneled dining room or, if the weather is nice, on a terrace in the back. Lunch is typically a $5 to $10 affair, chosen from selections that include omelets, club sandwiches, inventive salad plates, etc. At dinner you might try country inn chicken, sirloin steak, broiled scallops, baked ham with port wine sauce, etc., priced from about $10 to $18. Lunch hours are noon to 2 p.m.; dinner is served from 5 to 9 p.m.; open daily.

The restaurant at the aforementioned **Brae Loch,** at the corner of Albany Street and Forman Street (tel. 315/655-3431), is rather posh-looking, with a rich dark-wood staircase and crimson wall coverings. Most people eat in the low-ceilinged atmospheric basement, which is a warren of brick-walled, candlelit rooms, all very dim and red. Only dinner is served, daily from 5 to 9 p.m. (to 10 p.m. on weekends). The menu features things like lamb chops, Rock Cornish hen, filet mignon, lobster tail, crabmeat au gratin, mixed grill, etc. for prices between about $12 and $18 per à la carte entree.

For something simpler, try **Alberts,** 52 Albany St. (N.Y. 20) just east of the Square (tel. 315/655-2222). This little old gray-and-white building contains a pair of simple rooms, one with a bar, the other with booths and tables with paper placemats. It's a local spot for sandwich and burger lunches for $3 or less, and dinners that rarely top $9. Breaded veal, deep-fried sea scallops, open steak sandwich, stuffed flounder, chicken in the basket, spaghetti dishes, etc., are typical evening alternatives. Open daily from 11 a.m. until midnight.

SOMETHING IN BETWEEN: THE MUSICAL MUSEUM AT DEANSBORO

About midway between Cooperstown and Cazenovia, some seven miles north of N.Y. 20, is the little village of Deansboro. This otherwise anonymous hamlet is worth a detour for the sake of the Musical Museum, N.Y. 12B, Deansboro (tel. 315/841-8774). Operated by the Sanders family since 1948, this is a delightful and unusual display of antique music boxes, melodions, wildly elaborate player pianos, grind organs, mechanical violin players, band organs, automatic singing birds (real skins on wooden forms!), calliopes, vintage phonographs, etc. There are 17 rooms full of the stuff, much of which you can crank up, switch on, pump up, or trigger yourself. The Sanderses take especial pride in their "hands on" policy, which has allowed almost two generations of visitors to touch and activate some of the most amazing musical gizmos you're ever likely to see. Also on the premises is a shop specializing in old lamps, an ice cream parlor, and a vintage bar room. Open daily from 10 a.m. until 4 p.m., April through December. Definitely a one-of-a-kind place.

THE ADIRONDACKS

Fully one-sixth of New York State lies within the so-called Blue Line of the Adirondack State Park. That's six *million* acres of forest, with 45 mountain peaks over 4,000 feet in height and around 2,000 lakes.

Actually, only about half this acreage is owned by the state and protected by the "forever wild" provisions of the State Constitution. The rest of it belongs to folks like you and me, and contains houses and motels, shops and estates (called "great camps" in this neck of the woods), filling stations, car dealerships, and ski areas. Of course, none of this development is too closely spaced. The Adirondacks are sparsely populated to say the least. Many private holdings up here number in the tens (sometimes in the hundreds) of thousands of acres.

The Indians sensibly avoided the Adirondacks, at least in the winter. It was the white man's lust for timber and fur that led to the first real settlements. By the late 19th century the charms of the mountain wilderness began to attract the attention of America's bursting crop of industrial millionaires. Clever hoteliers like the legendary Paul Smith, and inspired developers like William West Durant, managed to put the stamp of fashion on the place. It was said of Smith, in his 1912 obituary, that "When he went to the Adirondacks many years ago the woods were full of Indians; when he died they were full of millionaires." In 1896, it is interesting to note, undeveloped land around fashionable Upper St. Regis Lake (which is really in the middle of nowhere) was selling for $4,000 an acre.

William West Durant, son of a railroad millionaire, devoted most of his life to promoting the development of the Adirondacks as a vacation preserve for the rich. The rustic/elegant school of architecture and furniture design which we call the "Adirondack style," and which is today an important part of our national cultural heritage, exists largely because of Durant and his tireless promotional efforts. W. W. Durant strove for effect, for opulence in the midst of untamed wilderness, for the "improbable, if not the impossible." People with names like Vanderbilt, Webb, Morgan, Woodruff, Bache, Rockefeller, Lewisohn, Garvan, Stokes, etc., were captivated by the Adirondack style. The name referred not just to massive, rustic architecture, but to an image as well. The Adirondacks were a place where one might see a woman in full evening dress, dripping with diamonds, being paddled to dinner in a canoe by a man in a boiled shirt and tails; where one's dinner might be served in a room with a ceiling of hand-rubbed logs and walls covered with antique French damask; where the "camp" of one's host might contain 60-odd buildings, employ a permanent staff of 80-odd locals, and be visited but three weeks a year.

Besides the great camps were the great hotels, wooden palaces now long vanished where city dudes dropped $20 tips and drank champagne on the piazzas, where society women waltzed to the music of imported orchestras, where grizzled mountain men found new careers as "guides." Of course, intrepid types were hiking into the mountains and roughing it for real even while the "great camp" era was at its peak. The development of the Adirondacks as an outdoor playground for the masses, however, has been a relatively new phenomenon. The state park dates from the late 19th century, but its use by other than millionaires, occasional Teddy Roosevelt types, and lumber companies is a development that is not much more than 30 years old.

1. Deciding Where to Go

I suspect that many people leave the Adirondacks feeling cheated and disappointed because they didn't find the type of experience that would have satisfied their expectations. Therefore, I've divided the balance of this chapter into four sections, each of which corresponds to a distinctly different type of Adirondack vacation.

To start with I'll describe a representative sampling of the most interesting **vacation resorts.** These establishments are destinations unto themselves, where your meals and activities are part of the total package, and where the ambience of the surroundings—mountains, lakes, crystal-clear atmosphere—is the point of the whole trip. The selection ranges from a famous hotel on the shores of Lake George, to a great camp on Upper Saranac Lake that takes in guests, to a couple of old-fashioned family hotels in the mountains, to a gaggle of "dude ranches" where the daily emphasis is on western-style horseback riding.

After that we'll talk about the most famous of the **resort towns,** notably Lake Placid and Lake George Village. These towns are attractions in and of themselves, and each has its own complement of accommodations in various price ranges.

Next we'll discuss the **wilderness experience,** which is to say, hiking, boating, hunting, camping, that sort of thing. This book is not a wilderness guide, but at least this section will point those interested in the right direction for more detailed information.

Last is the part I've called "Just Passing Through." This suggests scenic routes, interesting stops, and famous attractions for people who, while en route somewhere else, don't want to miss a taste of New York State's famous upstate wilderness. Together with the section on resort towns this material will enable you to plan an enjoyable itinerary on your own.

2. Vacation Resorts

Let's start with the most gorgeous of them all, the **Sagamore,** on Lake George at Bolton Landing, NY 12814 (tel. 518/644-9400, or toll free 800/THE-OMNI). The hamlet of Bolton Landing is about ten miles due north of Lake George Village on N.Y. 9N. There's a turnoff in the center of town, clearly marked with Sagamore signs. A short drive takes you to a bridge leading to the Sagamore's private island. Beyond this is a gatehouse and a separate building for guest registration. The historic core of the Sagamore complex is an enormous green-shuttered, white clapboard inn dating from the 1920s. It's surrounded by painstakingly precise formal plantings, sweeping drives, views of the "Queen of American Lakes" (that's Lake George), surmounted by an elaborate white cupola, and listed on the National Register of Historic Places. The hotel was recently renovated to the tune of some $65 million and reopened in 1985. It is very impressive.

Some 53 rooms and 47 suites are contained in the original hotel building. Another 120 rooms and 120 suites occupy seven modern "cottage" complexes distributed around the island. The cottages are quite luxurious, but to my taste the old hotel is more appealing. I could go on for pages describing the Sagamore. It contains beautiful restaurants, a marina with lake swimming, a private launch called the *Morgan* (which can seat 88 for dinner), a nightclub, a health club and spa, indoor and outdoor tennis courts, an indoor pool, a nearby golf course, a shopping promenade, and beautifully decorated rooms with thick rugs, remote-controlled TVs, handsome traditional furniture, and the look and feel of real luxury.

The hotel has a splendid view of Lake George, whose shoreline looks almost uninhabited from this vantage point. I can't think of more aesthetically appealing surroundings for a summer vacation in the mountains. I hasten to note, however, that the Sagamore is open all year long and offers numerous packages (Golf, Fall Foliage, Spa, Classic Romance, Murder Mystery, Culinary Celebration, Easter Weekend, Big Band, etc.) during cool and colder months.

In the height of the summer (June through August) there's a four-night minimum stay at prices that vary from about $120 to $210 per person per night, breakfast and dinner included. The most typical rate is about $175 per person, MAP. Those prices remain the same in May, September, and October, but management drops the four-night minimum. From November through April the MAP rate range descends to between $85 to $135 per person per night, with the most typical rate being about $125. No minimum stay is required in the winter, except on certain special weekends. The package plans mentioned above offer considerably reduced rates throughout the year, excepting the months of June, July, and August.

This is a memorable place, and without question the nicest in the mountains.

A few miles south of the Sagamore is the **Canoe Island Lodge,** on N.Y. 9N (P.O. Box 144), Diamond Point, NY 12824 (tel. 518/668-5592). Though a considerably less pretentious affair than the Sagamore, it has a great deal of charm and a nice warm atmosphere. The 56 units are distributed among a collection of little log cabins and shingled lodges hugging a steep hillside overlooking Lake George. At the center of the complex is an attractive old-fashioned lodge with peeled-beam ceilings, hooked rugs, burlap-shaded lamps, a huge stone fireplace, and a great woodsy-family atmosphere. During July and August management requires a three-day minimum stay. During other months they don't encourage overnighters, but if you present yourself at the door and they have the space, of course they'll take you in.

Rates include breakfast and dinner, and range from about $70 to $130 per person per night. Stay for a week and you'll get a slightly better rate. Stay during the shoulder months (May, June, September, and October) and they'll toss in lunch for no extra charge. Meals are taken in a huge log-walled dining room overlooking the lake. There isn't a pool, but there are 600 feet of private lakefront—plus a dock with all manner of boats—and a private island just offshore. Accommodations are modern, comfortable, and sparkling clean. Closed November through April. I liked it a lot.

Guests at Marjorie Merriweather Post's famous Camp Topridge used to fly up to the mountains on her private prop-jet, be driven by limo to the shores of Upper St. Regis Lake, transfer to Mrs. Post's private boat to cross the water, land at her wonderfully posh Adirondack-style boathouse, walk to the private funicular for the ride up the side of the ridge, and emerge at last on the threshold of a luxurious living room 60 feet long by 70 feet wide. Now that was luxury!

Other great camps were almost as luxurious, among them William Rockefeller's Camp Wonundra. Today Wonundra has been renamed **The Point,** Saranac Lake, NY 12983 (tel. 518/891-5674), and is open to paying guests. Staying here is about the closest you can come to the Adirondack millionaire experience. It's a beautiful place, complete with Adirondack-style main lodge, ancillary buildings, and a boathouse replete with vintage speedboats, canoes, sailboats, etc. (use of which is gratis to guests). Each of the 11 rooms has a name and a distinct character. My favorites are the four in the main lodge—Mohawk, Morningside, Algonquin, and Iroquois. Meals are taken houseparty style in the great hall, a grand interior space with natural-wood walls, zebra rugs, stuffed animal heads, and the obligatory stone fireplace. One of the highlights of my short life was waterskiing on Upper Saranac Lake at what seemed like 50 mph behind an iridescent silver speedboat belonging to The Point.

Rates here include the use of all facilities, plus all meals, and drinks as and when you want them from serve-yourself bars located around the house. A couple will pay between $425 and $650 nightly for this historic luxury. Open all year; advance reservations are a must.

Some 40-odd miles south of Upper Saranac Lake is Blue Mountain Lake, a mountain crossroads that is home to several crafts shops, the famous Adirondack Museum (see Section 5, "Just Passing Through," below), as well as two perfectly wonderful old-fashioned camp-style Adirondack hotels. Now don't forget that around here "camp" means a lot more than a pup tent in a clearing. **The Hedges,** Blue Mountain Lake, NY 12812 (tel. 518/352-7325), was built originally for Brigadier General Hiram B. Duryea. It's a picturesque product of the 1880s, a complex of charmingly asymmetrical log, shingle, and stone buildings on the edge of beautiful Blue Mountain Lake. There are 14 separate cottages, plus another 14 rooms in the main building and an adjacent stone lodge built about 1886 for Duryea's son. The interiors have that great old-fashioned camp look, a product of much stained tongue-and-groove paneling, old photos, gray-blue wicker furniture, big fireplaces, stamped-tin ceilings, and stuffed animal heads. Rooms and cottages are simple, but they all have private baths and lots of rustic character. I liked the accommodations in the stone lodge best, as they're the most formal.

The Hedges is a place to relax, swim, lie in the sun, take out the canoe, hike, visit the nearby Adirondack Museum, enjoy big family-style meals in the hotel dining room, and generally unwind. Most people stay for at least a couple of days but overnight guests are always welcome, even in July and August. MAP (breakfast and dinner included) per-person rates start at about $54 and top out at about $64. All rooms require occupancy by at least two persons. Open from about mid-June to mid-October.

On the other side of the lake is **Hemlock Hall,** Blue Mountain Lake, NY 12812 (tel. 518/352-7706), another wonderful old shingled Victorian house, this time set up on a hillside and enjoying a perfect Adirondack view of lake and mountains. The main house has stone fireplaces, wood paneling, lots of books, a wicker-filled porch, a boathouse with a sandy beach and a full complement of canoes, rowboats, sailboats, etc. The woods adjacent to the house are filled with really pretty little cottages, most of which have fine water views and private baths. Accommodations in the main house share baths. Meals here, as at the Hedges and elsewhere, are included in the room rate. The public rooms are transformed twice daily into dining halls where everyone sits down together, resort style. The atmosphere is friendly and informal; there are usually lots of kids. Between July 1 and Labor Day the MAP daily rate for double occupancy is about $100 in the main house and about $115 in the cottages with private baths. These rates drop about 10% in the shoulder seasons. Open mid-May to mid-October. Both the Hemlock and the Hedges are refreshingly unspoiled.

Near the southern edge of the Adirondack State Park, close to Lake George Village, is the little town of Lake Luzerne, noted for its dude ranches. The most elaborate of these is **Roaring Brook Ranch,** Lake George, NY 12845 (tel. 518/668-5767), whose sign on N.Y. 9N proclaims it to be a "tennis and ranch resort." The property is a large modern campus composed of dark-stained wood-sided buildings set on steep hillsides. There are tennis courts, velvety lawns, swimming pools, gardens, fountains, 600 acres, and 38 horses. While not elegant, it certainly is nice. The 134 accommodations resemble units in a good-quality motel. They have two double beds, TVs, telephones, full tile baths, and nice modern furniture. MAP rates also include a free tennis clinic and riding once a day. From late June until Labor Day you'll pay between about $60 and $70 or so per person per day. Deduct about $5 daily if you don't care to ride. Spring and fall rates are slightly less. The main lodge contains an immense catering-hall-style dining room, a coffeeshop, a bar, and a lobby with barn siding and wagon-wheel chandeliers. There's plenty of family-style entertainment in the evening. Open all year.

Much the same experience can be had at nearby **Hidden Valley,** Lake Luzerne, NY 12846 (tel. 518/696-2431). This complex of log-cabin-style buildings (plus a few new additions) overlooks little Lake Vanare. It has nightclub-type family entertainment, pools (an indoor one too), tennis courts, plus snowmobile trails and a lighted skating rink in the winter. There's even a ski run, plus of course a stable full of horses. Reduced-rate packages abound at Hidden Valley; the base double-occupancy MAP rate in the spring, summer, and fall ranges from close to $110 per night up to about $190 per night; less in the winter. Open all year. Again, the atmosphere is relaxed, unpretentious, and evidently as popular with couples as with families.

---

3. Lake Placid and Lake George

The two most important Adirondack resort communities are Lake Placid in the northern highlands, and Lake George Village in the south, adjoining the famous body of water that bears the same name. We'll start in the north with—

LAKE PLACID AND NEARBY SARANAC LAKE

These communities are nine miles apart on a 55-mph highway. **Lake Placid** is unquestionably the more important of the two. It's a bustling, prosperous resort village with big-time hotels (there's a Hilton smack in the center of the place), lots of good restaurants, and a full range of year-round resort facilities. Lake Placid was the site of two Winter Olympics, in 1932 and 1980. For many people it remains today primarily a ski resort, the slopes being on nearby Whiteface Mountain. Winter is perhaps more of a high season than summer. However, there are plenty of things to see and do in Lake Placid all year long. **Saranac Lake** is a town of about the same size but with far fewer facilities and attractions. It does have a great hotel, however, and a couple of very interesting restaurants, about which more later.

Lake Placid was settled—unless one counts ancient Mohawk Indian summer camps—by miners and lumbermen. Alas, the local ore proved inferior and the winter weather (notably 1816, known as the "year without a summer") too intimidating. In 1845 Lake Placid became the focus of a social experiment conducted by one Gerrit Smith. Free land was given to any free black man who cared to come up here and work it. This was a daunting challenge to say the least, and one that ultimately failed. But not before it attracted John Brown, who came to teach efficient farming techniques to newly arrived black settlers. Lake Placid was the town from which Brown departed in 1859, bound for the U.S. Arsenal at Harpers Ferry, Va. His intention was to arm Southern slaves with arsenal weapons and lead them in an insurrection. Here was where his body was returned after his execution by the Commonwealth of Virginia. His farm and gravesite, a few miles south of town, are now a State Historic Site.

Another of Lake Placid's famous residents was Dr. Melvin Dewey, originator of the Dewey Decimal System and founder of the old Lake Placid Club. This once-exclusive organization (it no longer exists as a private club) is credited with introducing America to winter sports. In the process it had a major impact on the village of Lake Placid. After two Winter Olympics the village now has a highly developed infrastructure geared to everything from tobogganing to bobsledding, to ski-jumping, to snowmobiling, to alpine skiing (almost, if not quite, the equal of the Rockies), to something called the luge (which is a feet-first plunge down a refrigerated bobsled course). In the summer you can hike, swim, boat, listen to outdoor concerts in the village park, and visit the various Olympic sites, one of which is an auto route to the top of Whiteface Mountain. Also during the summer are the prestigious **Lake Placid Horse Show** and the **I Love New York Horse Show,** both of which take place in July.

As mentioned earlier, less is going on over at Saranac Lake. The town has a nice old-fashioned business district, in the middle of which is the Hotel Saranac, run by the students of nearby Paul Smith College and recommended below. Every winter during the second week in February, Saranac Lake hosts a **Winter Carnival,** the oldest in the United States. There are skating races, a hockey tournament, cross-country ski races, torchlight skiing, wrapped up on Sunday night with the "storming of the ice palace," a big fireworks display. The last weekend in January in Saranac Lake witnesses the **International Sled Dog Championships,** sponsored by the manufacturers of Alpo dogfood. This features events like the six-dog, the weight-pull eliminations, the Mushers' Ball, and culminates with a big dance and an awards ceremony.

Both Lake Placid and Saranac have very helpful and efficient visitor information organizations. In Lake Placid you should take your questions to **"I Love New York,"** 90 Main St., Lake Placid, NY 12946 (tel. 518/523-2412), or the **Lake Placid Chamber of Commerce,** Olympic Arena, Lake Placid, NY 12946 (tel. 518/523-2445). In Saranac Lake, inquiries should be directed to the **Saranac Lake Area Chamber of Commerce,** 30 Main St., Saranac Lake, NY 12983 (tel. 518/891-1990).

Here now is a brief overview of attractions in the Lake Placid/Saranac area.

What to See and Do in the Lake Placid Area

There's a lot going on at any given time. Every month the **Lake Placid Chamber of Commerce** mimeographs a sheet for tourists called "Action in Lake Placid," which lists it all. Best place to pick up a copy is either at your hotel or the "I Love New York" office at 90 Main St.

Skiing on Whiteface Mountain is the town's premier attraction. This is a big installation, located a few miles east of Lake Placid on N.Y. 86. All sorts of lift, lesson, and hotel packages are available. Additionally there are competition events of various sorts taking place at the Olympic facilities throughout each winter. Skiers desiring fuller information on Whiteface Mountain can either call Whiteface Information at 518/946-2223, or write to the Lake Placid Chamber of Commerce (see above). They can send you fee schedules, a description of the mountain, a listing of fall and winter events, etc.

Throughout the year visitors can take something called the **Olympic Tour,** which is a self-guided visit to the various sites of former Olympic Games. These include the Olympic Ski Jump Complex (where you can ride to the top of an amazing pair of giant slides looming over the forest), Mount Van Hoevenberg (with bobsled and luge tracks, plus video displays), the Whiteface Memorial Highway (tough on the transmission and the brakes, but an awesome view and a nifty "castle" on top), and the Whiteface Mountain Chair Lift (like the drive, but minus the car). Each of these attractions can be visited separately for between $3 and $5 per adult and $2 and $4 per child. Or you can buy a combination ticket to all four for $12 per adult and $7 per child. Tickets are available at the individual facilities; a descriptive "Olympic Tour" brochure, with a map and a rate schedule, sits in stacks on most hotel desks and is dependably to be found at the "I Love New York" office (see above).

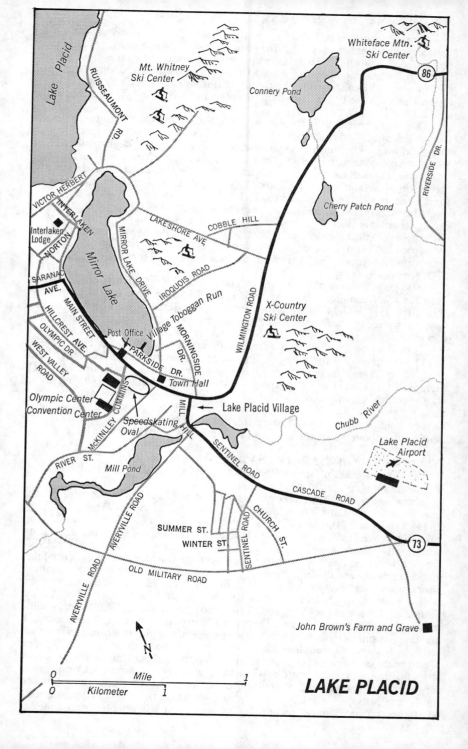

LAKE PLACID

Summer visitors might also like to have a look at the **John Brown Farm,** a New York State Historic Site on John Brown Road, off N.Y. 73 just south of Lake Placid (tel. 518/523-3900). This is a modest place, but evocative of great events. You can take a self-guided tour of the farmhouse, the 244-acre farm, and the adjacent grave of the famous abolitionist Wednesday through Saturday from early May until late October. The hours are 10 a.m. to 5 p.m. (from 1 p.m. on Sunday). There is no admission fee.

Over in Saranac Lake is the **Robert Louis Stevenson Cottage,** where the author of *Treasure Island* took up residence in 1887. Stevenson buffs are going to love this place, which is in totally original condition and contains the largest collection of Stevenson mementos in America. There are old photos, ice skates, a lock of the great man's hair, items of clothing, even cigarette burns on the mantelpiece courtesy of Stevenson's own cigarettes. Open from July 1 until September 15; admission is $1 for adults and 50¢ for kids. Call 518/891-1990 for further information.

Also pleasant in the summer are **Lake Placid Boat Rides,** an hour-long, 16-mile excursion on an enclosed tour boat that wends its way past islands and private estates to the base of Whiteface Mountain. Boats leave the Lake Placid Marina (not far from the Mirror Lake Inn) between two and four times daily from late May until the beginning of November. The fare is about $5 for adults and $3 for kids; call 518/523-9704 for departure times.

Also good to know about are the free weekly **Cushion Concerts** performed in Lake Placid's Main Street Park by the Lake Placid Sinfonietta. Ask "I Love New York" (tel. 518/523-2412) when the next one's scheduled. The Sinfonietta, by the way, was started by the famous Lake Placid Club back in 1919 and offers a full summer musical program in the Lake Placid Center for the Arts.

If you're traveling with kids, take note of **Santa's Workshop** (tel. 518/946-2211), located on the other side of Whiteface Mountain from Lake Placid in (where else?) North Pole, N.Y. (true!), which is west of Wilmington, N.Y., on N.Y. 431. Here you'll find Santa and a full complement of elves making toys, blowing glass, cooking candy, carving plastic, etc. A twice-daily show called *Christmas Capers* features puppets, magic, a band concert, and so forth. Open Memorial Day to mid-October; high-season (July and August) hours are 9:30 a.m. to 4:30 p.m. daily and admission is about $8 for adults and $4 for kids; off-season prices are a bit less.

Where to Stay in the Placid/Saranac Area

Please note that the famous **Point,** described in "Vacation Resorts," is located in this area on Upper Saranac Lake.

For those who want to stay right in the middle of Lake Placid, the most deluxe spot is the **Mirror Lake Inn,** 5 Mirror Lake Dr., Lake Placid, NY (tel. 518/523-2544), a short hop from Main Street on a narrow isthmus of land separating Mirror Lake from Lake Placid itself. The inn is actually a complex of seven buildings centered around a brand-new Main Lodge. The original lodge was destroyed in a 1988 fire, but the owners replaced it with a graceful colonial structure reminiscent of the grand hotels of Lake Placid's yesteryear. The living room is beautiful, with walnut floors, mahogany walls, and a rosewood fireplace. The library, which teems with stuffed animals, also has a huge stone fireplace and comfortable antiques. A cozy lounge is adjacent to the living room, and across the street is The Cottage, a cafe-restaurant recommended below. There are 100 extremely comfortable rooms and 16 suites or minisuites, all of which have two-person whirlpool tubs, and often a lofted bedroom. All rooms have lake views, color TVs, and lots of character. Besides a sand beach on Mirror Lake, there is an outdoor heated pool, an indoor pool and spa, a boathouse, a tennis court, and beautiful gardens in the summer. Complimentary afternoon tea is served every day. Rooms are available either with or without meals, and prices for a double range from high-season peaks of $119 per person, MAP (breakfast and dinner included), down to about $84 double without meals.

Off-season rates are about 40% less; special packages are available too. The main restaurant here is famous.

The **Lake Placid Hilton,** at the head of Main Street at 1 Mirror Lake Dr., Lake Placid, NY 12946 (tel. 518/523-4411), is no grand hotel, but it's very nice, very modern, and very Hiltony. Also it's well planned in that every one of the 176 rooms has a view, either of Mirror Lake or the mountains beyond. There are two indoor pools, two outdoor pools, a big restaurant called the Terrace Room, the Dancing Bear Lounge with live entertainment most nights, a game room, and reciprocal arrangements at a nearby club for the use of tennis courts. Guest rooms are big, furnished with two double beds, color TVs, private phones, mirrored closets, and individual balconies. Double-occupancy room rates range from $102 to $122 in the two high seasons (late December through early January and mid-July through mid-August), down to about $92 to $102 in the low seasons (January through mid-June and late October to mid-December); reduced package plans abound.

Nearby (of course, everything is near everything in little Lake Placid) is the **Holiday Inn,** 1 Olympic Dr., Lake Placid, NY 12946 (tel. 518/523-2556). This is a vast place whose 200 refurbished rooms make it look more youthful than it really is. The views from some of the rooms are absolutely breathtaking. Not all rooms have views, as at the Hilton, nor is there an outdoor pool (only an indoor version). All rooms have a comfortable Holiday Inn familiarity, plus two double beds, color TVs, nice furniture, and plenty of space. Also on the premises are six outdoor tennis courts, a nightclub called Cristy's, and the Greenhouse Restaurant. Double-occupancy room rates change all year long, but range from winter and summer highs of around $80 to $146, to off-season lows of between about $60 and $100.

Whiteface Inn Resort, Whiteface Inn Road (P.O. Box 231), Lake Placid, NY 12946 (tel. 518/523-2551), unfortunately no longer contains the old Adirondack-style Whiteface Inn that once gave it so much character. But it does have its own 18-hole championship golf course, a spectacular outdoor heated pool, tennis courts, a boathouse, 1,200 feet of lakefront on Lake Placid, a restaurant called the Adirondack Room, and an interesting variety of accommodations. The rooms overlooking the pool resemble comfortable motel units; the cottages vary in size from two rooms to four bedrooms, and are painted brown and dotted around the wooded slopes above the pool; the lodge colony is a collection of vintage log cabins right on the lakeshore—the most desirable by my lights. Rates are quoted per unit, not per person. They are so complicated as to defy simple categorization. To give you an idea, one of those great log cabins with a fireplace, a separate bedroom, a TV, a couple of rocking chairs, and a view of the lake, can cost as little as $55 on a winter weekday, as much as $120 on a summer weekend. The motel units cost $90 in the summer and about $70 in the winter. Groups of skiers frequent this place because you can get so many people into the larger cottages. It's a good deal.

Located next to the Whiteface Inn Resort is the **Lake Placid Manor,** Whiteface Inn Road (P.O. Box 870), Lake Placid, NY 12946 (tel. 518/523-2573). The Manor, built in 1882, has glorious views of the lake and Whiteface, and a rustic opulence associated with the great camps of the Adirondacks. The gourmet restaurant is open seven days a week for breakfast, lunch, and dinner. Breakfast includes things like creative omelets and pancakes with real maple syrup and costs $3 to $5; lunch is in the $3 to $8 range; and a dinner of perhaps poached monkfish or sauté of veal might cost you $14 to $20. There are 34 rooms tucked away in various buildings on the property. The decor is Adirondack rustic and includes private bath, phone, and TV. Rates are from $55 to $110 a night per person.

The **Hotel Saranac,** 101 Main St., Saranac Lake, NY 12983 (tel. 518/891-2200), is a big, square, ca. 1930 brick building right in the middle of Saranac Lake. One of its distinctions is that it's run by students of nearby Paul Smith's College School of Hotel Management. Don't think for a moment that this is an amateurish operation. The place has several excellent restaurants and 92 extremely nice rooms, decorated with shag rugs, big beds with wooden headboards, cheerful wallpaper, spotless private baths with stacks of fresh towels, color TVs, and telephones. The rooms are really nice . . . and incredibly cheap. "Bed-and-breakfast" minipackages (any two nights) are available for about $42 to $70 per person, complete. They have all sorts of other package deals as well. The ambience is perfectly wonderful, and the place couldn't be more comfortable.

Of the many motels in and around Lake Placid and Saranac, my favorite was **Schulte's Motor Inn,** on N.Y. 73, Lake Placid, NY 12946 (tel. 518/523-3532). This place has a very Bavarian look, highlighted by painted woodwork, cuckoo clocks, cutout wooden balconies, all extremely immaculate and carefully tended. There are 15 motel units and 15 little cottages, the latter bearing names like Spruce, Birch, Beech, Tamarack, etc. In the center of this complex is a very nice outdoor swimming pool. Accommodations all have color TVs, private baths, and very pleasant modern decor. The motel units have velour bedspreads; the little cottages have miniature kitchenettes and are the definition of the word "cute." In the summer and winter seasons two people will pay from $45 to about $70 for one of the motel rooms, and from $45 for a cottage for two, up to about $80 for a cottage that will accommodate six. Off-season rates are about 20% or so less.

Last but certainly not least is the **Stagecoach Inn,** Old Military Road, Lake Placid, NY 12946 (tel. 518/523-9474). This wonderful old green wooden building has a long, wicker-filled porch, hanging pots of plants, and a country location just outside Lake Placid. It was built as an inn during stagecoach days, and indeed it was the first hotel in Lake Placid. Today it's a sleepy little bed-and-breakfast, filled with tongue-and-groove wood paneling, antique furniture, lace curtains, a vintage organ, fireplaces and wood stoves, and nine extremely charming bedrooms. The most expensive rooms have fireplaces and private baths, and cost $70 nightly for two, including breakfast. For $60 nightly you'll get a room without a fireplace, but with a private bath. Another four rooms share two baths and cost $50 nightly. Open almost (but not quite) all year.

By the way, if you're interested in a bed-and-breakfast contact **North Country B & B Reservation Service** at Box 238, Lake Placid, NY 12946 (tel. 518/523-3739).

Do plan one meal in the **Averil Conwell Room** at the Mirror Lake Inn, 5 Mirror Lake Dr. (tel. 518/523-2544). The dining room is bi-level and provides excellent views of Mirror Lake from all areas. A floral burgundy carpet accents mahogony walls decorated with hanging plants and a series of restored murals by Averil Conwell depicting Lake Placid's history. At least two nights a week there is piano music in the adjacent living room of the inn. Typical à la carte dinners include home-smoked trout, smoked shrimp, or smoked salmon appetizers, rack of lamb, Adirondack mixed grill, stuffed shrimp with crabmeat mousse, plus many daily chef's features. A special low-fat menu is available too. Prices range from $12 to $20. Open every day for breakfast 7 a.m. to 10 a.m. and dinner from 7 p.m. to 10 p.m. Reservations suggested; an awfully nice place.

The Woodshed, opposite the Olympic Speed Skating Oval at 237 Main St. (tel. 518/523-9470), has a couple of intimate dining rooms and an inventive menu. In the front they serve things like broiled haddock, stuffed pork chops, lasagne, chicken Dennison, spaghetti, and burgers, priced at around $8 to $17. In the back, called Lindsay's, the fare consists of things like steak au poivre, rack of lamb, veal chalet, scampi in a cream sauce, poached salmon, etc., which cost between about $14 and $22 à la carte. Open daily for dinner only from 5 p.m. to midnight in the front room (where a "light" menu is also available), and from 6 to 10 p.m. in the romantic back room.

Also across from the Olympic Speed Skating Oval is the **Fireside Steak House,** 229 Main St. (tel. 518/523-2682). Don't be misled by the name; this local favorite offers not only beef but chicken and seafood as well, all at moderate prices. The restaurant has two sections: the Sidewalk Cafe, with greenhouse, flowering plants, and fireplace, features a luncheon menu (from 11 a.m. to midnight) that includes the

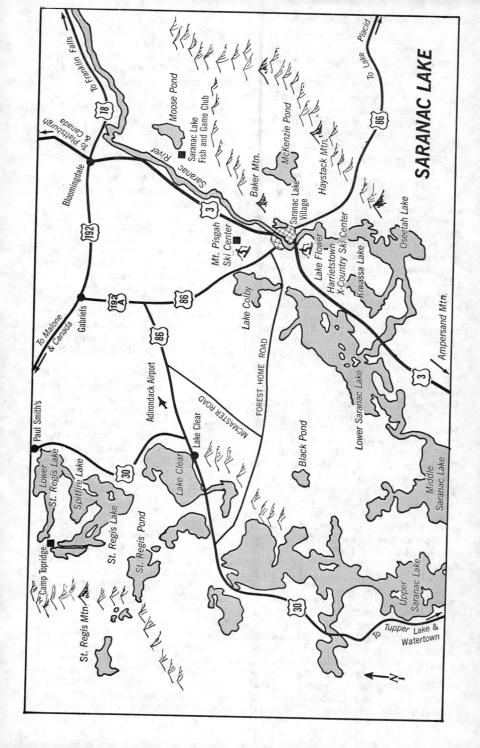

basic burger, Monte Cristo, sizzling fajitas (my favorite), etc., priced from $4 to $7, plus a summer weekend brunch (from 11:30 a.m. to 3:30 p.m.) for $6; the more formal Firehouse Steak Room upstairs has an open-pit charcoal fire, cathedral ceilings, a balcony overlooking the street, and prices between $8 and $15 per entree. The Firehouse Steak Room is open daily for dinner from 5 p.m. to 11 p.m. during the summer, but weekends only in wintertime.

The **Interlaken**, located behind the Mirror Lake Inn at 15 Interlaken Ave. (tel. 518/523-3180), is an old Victorian house with a pleasant dining room paneled in dark oak, with burgundy linens and rugs. The food is great—veal with peaches, pork in mustard sauce, steak au poivre, etc.—and à la carte prices run from about $13 to $21. Open for dinner only from 6:30 until 9:30 p.m.; closed Sunday and Monday.

On the other side of town is the **Villa Vespa,** 85 Saranac Ave. (tel. 518/523-9959), on the road to Saranac Lake. This is an attractive Italian restaurant with stuccoed walls, a beamed ceiling, red leatherette booths, and a statue of a blindfolded Cupid. Try one of the assorted pastas (priced mostly between $10 and $11) or an entree like veal piccata, shrimp marinara, breast of capon, or fried calamari (which cost anywhere from about $12 to $20). Open daily for dinner only, from 5 to 10 p.m.; mandolin music every evening; closed Tuesday in the slow seasons.

Steak and Stinger, 15 Cascade Rd., which is the name for N.Y. 73 hereabouts (tel. 518/523-9927), is a modern and romantically decorated establishment with barn siding, a greenhouse addition, shag rugs, oak chairs, and Tiffany-style hanging lamps. This is the place for beef. New York cut sirloin, beef Wellington, filet mignon, tournedos, and chateaubriand dominate the newspaper-style menu and cost between about $15 and $22. Also on the menu are a vegetarian plate, lamb chops, salmon in pastry, and various fish and chicken dishes, the least of which runs about $9. Open daily for dinner only from 5 until 10:30 p.m.; closed during the month of April, and on Monday during the off-months.

Less expensive fare (and lunch, which doesn't exist at any of the above) can be had in the middle of Lake Placid at three excellent establishments. The first is **The Cottage,** opposite (and owned by) the Mirror Lake Inn, Mirror Lake Drive (tel. 518/523-2544). This is a lively bar, right on the water, with an adjacent deck for warm-weather dining. Inside is a cathedral ceiling, a wall of pictures of regular patrons, a jukebox full of rock and roll, assorted tables, and good-looking female bartenders. Sandwiches with names like the Cottage Club Reuben, and South of the Border cost around $5. There are also chili, salads, quiche, and homemade soup. **Jimmy's** is across the street from the Hilton at 21 Main St. (tel. 518/523-2353). There's a bar up front and a diminutive lake-view dining room with diagonal oak paneling in the back. It's small and very informal, and serves up all manner of sandwiches (club, grilled cheese, burgers, etc.), plus salad platters and omelets, for around $4 to $10. Lunch is served from 11:30 a.m. until 5 p.m.; dinner is from 5 to 9:30 p.m.; closed Monday, plus other nights too in the off-season. Finally, there's the **Artist's Café,** 1 Main St. (tel. 518/523-9493), a cozy and intimate little tavern/restaurant with wood paneling and inviting cushioned booths. Luncheon omelets, burgers, and sandwiches run about $4 to $6; dinner specials like a 16- to 24-ounce T-bone steak, steamed shrimp, seafood platter, king crab legs, etc., cost a reasonable $6 to $19. Open 365 days a year, for lunch from 11:30 a.m. until 3:30 p.m., and for dinner from 5 to 10 p.m.

Lydia's, at the Hotel Saranac, 101 Main St. in Saranac Lake (tel. 518/891-2200), is, I think, definitely worth a visit for lunch or dinner. The students of Paul Smith's College, who run both the hotel and the restaurant, do a crackerjack job and prices are most reasonable. Lunch entrees include a full range of sandwiches, omelets, burgers, crêpes, etc., skillfully cooked and professionally presented. Boy, do they try hard to please! Prices are all under $4. At dinner you might try buttermilk chicken, pork cutlet Dijon, salmon steak, tournedos Rossini, sea scallops, etc., priced from about $8 to $14. Periodically the Regis Room assumes new identities and menus when a graduating class works up a cuisine and a set of meals all its own. The room is modern, thickly carpeted, romantically lit, and looks rather like a lavish coffeeshop. Upstairs in the grand ballroom is a Thursday-night buffet, also designed and cooked by students, and priced at about $9 for adults and $5 for kids. It was an elaborate French affair at the time of my visit. Whatever it is when you get there, I'm sure it'll be good. Breakfast and lunch are served daily in the Regis Room from 7:30 a.m. until 2 p.m.; dinner (including the Thursday-night buffet in the ballroom) starts at 5 p.m. and runs until 9 p.m.

Near the south end of Upper Saranac Lake, maybe 15 or so minutes southwest via N.Y. 3 from the town of Saranac Lake itself, is the **Wawbeek** (tel. 518/359-3777). This Adirondack-style lakefront restaurant deep in its own private forest is about the most atmospheric place imaginable. Built as a private camp in the late 19th century, it has lofty ceilings, old wood paneling, a romantic porch overlooking the lake, and an upstairs bar with old leather and wicker furniture. Only dinner is served, from a menu featuring things like filet mignon, medallions of lobster, sautéed sea scallops, rack of lamb for two, swordfish steak, shrimp in cognac, etc. À la carte prices are mostly in the $12 to $19 vicinity. Open from May through September, daily from 6 to 10 p.m.

LAKE GEORGE VILLAGE

Don't judge Lake George by Lake George Village. The "Queen of American Lakes" really deserves the title. It is crystal clear, entirely spring-fed, surrounded by magnificent mountain scenery, and an altogether appealing place. But Lake George Village, situated at its southern end, is not going to appeal to everybody.

Father Isaac Jogues named it Lac du Saint-Sacrement during an expedition in 1646. Sir William Johnson, royal agent for Indian affairs and an important man in these parts, renamed it in 1755 after King George II. It's typical of the lack of vengefulness in the American spirit that it was never renamed.

Lake George was enormously strategic during colonial and Revolutionary days, as it formed an important part of the water of the water route composed of lakes and rivers connecting Canada with New York City. In 1755 Fort William Henry was erected here by the British with an eye to protecting this route. And herein lies a particularly gruesome tale.

In March of 1757, during the French and Indian War, the fort was attacked by 1,600 French soldiers under the command of General Montcalm. The French had convinced 3,000 Indians from 33 different tribes to make common cause with them against the English. By August it was clear to the English commander, Monro, that even if the fort itself was safe, the people within it (including many women and children from the surrounding settlement) were going to starve. Montcalm arranged a peaceful surrender. The Indians, however, disregarded Montcalm and fell upon the unarmed English. They then proceeded to butcher and scalp each and every one of them, culminating the proceedings by a ritual drinking of blood. Montcalm's horrified Frenchmen, outnumbered two to one by their allies, were unable to stop the massacre. When the Indians withdrew to the forest, the French piled the mutilated victims inside the fort and set fire to it all. This true tale is the basis of James Fenimore Cooper's *Last of the Mohicans*.

By 1810 a peaceful village named Caldwell occupied lands adjacent to the old Fort William Henry. By 1900 the Delaware and Hudson Railroad was depositing summer visitors at an elegant station practically on top of the former earthworks. There is no more railroad, even though the old station still stands alongside the reconstructed fort on Beach Road. Nor is there much of anything else that is "elegant" in Lake George Village.

What to See and Do in Lake George and Vicinity

Useful to know is the location of the **tourist information booth,** where all manner of brochures and helpful advice can be had for the asking. It's on the south side of town, just above the intersection of N.Y. 9N and 9L (near exit 22 of I-87) and at the south end of the village on U.S. 9 opposite Prospect Mountain.

The village itself is today a diminutive strip of tourist trinket shops, T-shirt emporia, and motels that comes alive for the summer season and slumbers the rest of the year. It is Coney Island in the mountains, albeit a very clean and family-oriented Coney Island. The main drag is U.S. 9, also called Canada Street, and in August there is so much traffic on the four blocks that form the heart of Lake George Village that white-gloved traffic cops are required on almost every corner. The lakefront is lined with restaurants, souvenir shops, and docks where you can rent speedboats, aquabikes, wetbikes, minihawks, or paddleboats, arrange parasail excursions, etc. There's also a small beach in **Shepard Park,** which is right in the middle of all this, with a sandy shoreline, a lifeguard, and a pier.

Every inch of downtown Canada Street is devoted to souvenirs, amusement arcades, and establishments like the **House of Frankenstein,** (tel. 518/668-3377), where giggling preteens can be seen on the sidewalk getting their picture taken with the bolt-necked one himself. On the southern edge of town are more elaborate amusement parks like **Gaslight Village** (tel. 518/668-5459), with 45 different rides, an ice show, and all manner of hoopla. It costs about $14 for an adult to spend the day at Gaslight, and about $9-plus for kids. Just down U.S. 9 is **Water Slide World** (tel. 518/668-4407), with a pool featuring four-foot artificial waves, plus bumper boats, hot tubs, you name it. A few miles south of town on U.S. 9 is the biggest of them all, **Great Escape Fun Park** (tel. 518/792-6568), which bills itself as New York's largest theme park. Its 100 different rides have names like the Desperado Plunge Flume, Sea Dragon, Screamer, Steamin' Demon, etc. There are additionally all manner of shows, attractions, and facilities. Great Escape costs about the same as Gaslight Village.

The **Lake George Beach State Park** (tel. 518/668-3352), a short hop from the village on Beach Road, is a world away from all this. Administered by the State of New York, it's a long strand of clean white sand, called the Million Dollar Beach, at the middle of which is a bathhouse. Parking in the adjacent lot costs $3 daily; it's another $1 to get onto the beach; a locker and use of the showers will run you another buck. The view up the length of Lake George is superb.

The **Lake George Steamboat Company,** at the Steel Pier on Beach Road (tel. 518/668-5777), has been carrying passengers on Lake George since 1817. These days it operates three different boats: the *Mohican,* the *Minne-Ha-Ha,* and the *Lac du Saint Sacrement.* All manner of cruises are available, from the basic one-hour shoreline cruise (for about $6.50 for adults and $3 for kids), to the Minne-Ha-Ha Dixieland Moonlight Cruise (about $11 and $6), to various other dinner and island and jazz-band varieties. Call them for further information and departure times. A competing outfit, **Lake George Shoreline Cruise Boats** (tel. 518/668-4644), docks nearby on Beach Road and offers similar services.

The reconstructed **Fort William Henry,** on the grounds of the Fort William Henry Motor Inn between Canada Street and Beach Road (tel. 518/668-5471), is a painstaking reconstruction surrounded by neat lawns and clipped bushes, and containing a museum complete with a costumed acting company. Daily tours and stage shows take place from May 1 to mid-October. Admission is between $6 and $7. Besides blasting muskets, booming cannons, grenadier demonstrations, and musketball molding, you can also catch a slightly edited version of Randolph Scott and Binnie Barnes in the 1936 film version of *The Last of the Mohicans* right here in the fort.

Immediately south of Lake George Village, practically opposite the tourist information office, is the entrance to **Prospect Mountain,** known as **"The 100-Mile View."** This 5½-mile scenic road ascends to the 2,030-foot summit of Prospect Mountain, from which a glorious view can be had. It's open from 9 a.m. until 6:30 p.m. every day from May until October. There's a $4-per-car charge at the gatehouse.

Other things to do in Lake George might include taking in dinner and a Broadway show at the **Lake George Dinner Theater,** in the Holiday Inn on U.S. 9 (tel. 518/668-5781). There's a new production every summer, and nightly performances (except Monday) between late June and mid-October. The price is under $35 per person in the evening and about $20 for the Wednesday lunch matinee.

If you're a nut for antiques, you might enjoy a trip up to the village of **Warrensburg,** about four miles north of Lake George Village on U.S. 9. There are over a dozen different shops on the south side of the town, most of them right on U.S. 9. An atmospheric old inn called the **Merrill Magee House** (tel. 518/623-2449) is located right in the middle of town, is open all year, and serves a dinner consisting of beef Wellington, veal Oscar, roast beef suprême (with melted brie), etc., for about $13 to $17.

The **Warren County Tourism Dept.,** Municipal Center, Lake George, NY 12845 (tel. 518/761-6366), and the **Lake George Chamber of Commerce,** P.O. Box 272, Lake George, NY 12845 (tel. 518/668-5755) publish calendars of events and festivals in the Lake George area, and can also provide you with a copy of the *I Love New York Warren County Travel Guide.* So if you need to know any more, you can direct your questions to them.

Where to Stay in Lake George and Vicinity

In the village itself, my favorite is the **Fort William Henry Motor Inn,** U.S. 9/ Canada Street, Lake George, NY 12845 (tel. 518/668-3081). This place stands in the middle of an 18-acre campus that includes the reconstruction of historic Fort William Henry, several restaurants, various shops, a sometime summer theater, and a pair of motel buildings with 99 rooms between them. There's a big parking lot full of late-model American sedans, an absolutely huge free-form outdoor swimming pool (the largest in the Adirondacks) surrounded with big cement terraces and lots of chairs, acres of rolling lawn, an indoor swimming pool, the Olde Tankard Taverne, a pair of miniature golf courses, etc. Rooms are divided between the new building and the old, but as a practical matter there's not much difference between them. They are spacious, contain color TV's, telephones, nice modern bathrooms, two double beds, and about half have views of Lake George. Double-occupancy rates depend on time of year and view, and range from a low of under $60 to a high of close to $140 nightly. This nice, informal, family-oriented resort motel has the best location in Lake George.

Mass-produced it may be, but the **Holiday Inn,** U.S. 9/Canada Street (P.O. Box 231), Lake George, NY 12845 (tel. 518/668-5781, or toll free 800/356-5625), is still the most aesthetic hotel in town. The location is south of town, adjacent to U.S. 9, atop a little plateau with quite a splendid view of the lake and the nearby village. It's your traditional long, low, flat-roofed, modern-looking Holiday Inn, with lots of terraces and sliding doors and walls accented with used bricks. Inside the lobby the decor is quasi-colonial, with lots of leather furniture, a television permanently on, even a fireplace. There is a coffeeshop, a lounge, and a restaurant, an indoor pool that's actually big enough to swim in, a very nice outdoor pool, laundry facilities, and superlatively nice rooms. Accommodations have thick rugs, color TV's, usually a pair of double beds, colonial-reproduction furniture, and sometimes a truly gorgeous view of Lake George. In the high season (late June to the end of August) a double will cost between about $100 and $140 nightly; the rest of the year that range drops to $50 to $70.

On U.S. 9 immediately north of Lake George Village center is an unbroken line of "resort-type" lakefront motels. I'll be honest: they didn't make a big impression on me. An exception is the **Lake Crest,** 366 Canada St., Lake George, NY 12845 (tel. 518/668-3374), which is sort of cute and cabin-y, has a courtyard/parking lot filled with leafy trees instead of glaring unadorned pavement, a coffeeshop, and 40 attractive motel-style units. The decor consists of shiny varnished pine walls, emerald-green rugs, nice little bathrooms, venetian blinds, and color TVs. The property, like all its neighbors, is long and skinny. At the lake end are seven rooms with water view, as well as a swimming pool and a small private beach. Family operated since 1947, the Lake View is open only from April until October. High-season (end of June to Labor Day) double-occupancy room rates vary from $86 to $135 nightly; the rest of the year the same rooms cost $49 to $98.

There are a zillion other motels in Lake George, but I'm hard-pressed to find much difference among them. Fortunately, other accommodation options exist nearby. The honky-tonk atmosphere stops abruptly as one leaves the village heading north on N.Y. 9N. The road winds through a deep forest dotted with pretty vacation houses and the occasional startlingly grand mansion. The surroundings are considerably more in keeping with the image of Adirondack beauty.

There are a number of attractive motels along 9N between Lake George Village and Bolton Landing, among them the **Melody Manor, N.Y. 9N,** Bolton Landing, NY 12814 (tel. 518/644-9750). This place has a long black macadam drive running down the middle of a velvety lawn, a big pool with a chain-link fence around it, a collection of neat-as-a-pin buildings in motel-Bavarian style, a tennis court, a restaurant/lounge, and a private lakefront with dock and rowboats. The 40 rooms are pretty big, nicely decorated with tables and chairs, usually a pair of double beds, a color TV, and sometimes a view of the famous Sagamore glittering in the distance across Lake George. Open only from May to November, the Melody Manor requires a three-night minimum stay during the months of July and August. The high-season tariff for two ranges from about $70 to $100 nightly; the rest of the season doubles are available for about $40 to $60 a night. The name, incidentally, commemorates the steam organ in a vanished mansion that once occupied the site.

About 15 miles northwest of Lake George Village, via U.S. 9 and N.Y. 28, is Friends Lake and the **Balsam House,** Friends Lake, Chestertown, NY 12817 (tel. 518/494-2828). This is admittedly a little afield from Lake George, but it's a charming place and deserves inclusion. The Balsam is a rambling, Victorian clapboard affair with a mansarded tower, a big porch, 20 guest rooms, and a famous restaurant. There are a private beach and boathouse on Friends Lake, a three-minute walk down a gravelly path. The place has been completely renovated and redecorated in plummy Victorian tones with lots of upholstered furniture and curtains on swags. The rooms all have private bath and phones, pastel carpeting, wicker headboards, and occasional antiques. They're smallish, but very nice. The best part of the place is its congenial and hospitable atmosphere. And of course, its excellent country French restaurant. During weekends and holidays two people will pay $145, MAP, nightly for a room, including dinner and breakfast. During the week that rate drops to $125 nightly. Bed-and-breakfast only costs $50 less. The restaurant is described below.

Recommended Restaurants in Lake George and Vicinity

Lucille's, across from Shepard Park at 259 Canada St. (tel. 518/668-9224), is an altogether-appealing double-level seafood restaurant with a neon lobster out front and rope rails on the terraces. This is a big, convivial place with an antique nickelodeon, piano music on the weekends, a convivial bar, and dining rooms with varnished-wood tables, nautical motif paintings, and views of Lake George. At lunch you can buy steamers, lobster rolls, chowders, chili, and fried oysters, plus "onshore" sandwiches, for between about $5 and $7. Dinner entrees include lobster salad, broiled halibut, shrimp marinara, sautéed brook trout, softshell crabs, plus lamb chops, porterhouse steaks, and veal and pasta specialties. Most dinner entrees cost between about $10 and $13, with some as much as $20. Open from mid-May to the end of October; lunch and light items are served from noon until the midnight closing on the upper level; the downstairs dining room opens at 5 p.m.

The Shoreline Restaurant and Marina, 4 James St. (tel. 518/668-2875), features enclosed and deck dining overlooking a modest fleet of five tour boats (tel. 518/668-4644). The restaurant offers American and continental cooking with an accent on mesquite-grilled specialties. The dining area is on different levels so as to afford everyone a view of the lake. The decor includes light-wood diagonal pine paneling accented by mirrors and lots of glass. Dinners, accompanied by live piano, range from $13 to $22 for things like chicken teriyaki, Cajun jambalaya, veal de Champlain, etc., served from 5 to 11 p.m. daily. Breakfast, from 8 to 11 a.m., includes the usual fare; lunch, served from 12:30 to 4 p.m. and consisting of creative sandwiches and variations on the dinner menu, costs from $5 to $7. Sunday buffet brunch is available from 10:30 a.m. to 2 p.m. for $10; $5 for children. The Shoreline is closed the first two weeks in November.

Mario's is on the north side of town, opposite motel row at 469 Canada St. (tel. 518/668-2665). It's a cheerful, extremely busy, well-kept family-style Italian restaurant. An extensive breakfast, available only July and August, is served from 8 a.m. to 1 p.m. and includes real maple syrup on grilled french toast ($2.95) and old-fashioned hot cakes ($2.50). At dinner, served from 5 to 11 p.m., there's a full complement of pastas, seafood, cacciatores, parmigianas, marinaras, plus veal, steaks, and a few chicken dishes. Typical dinner entrees cost about $10 to $14. The children's menu informs us that "for over 30 years Mario's has been providing the younger set with their own menu. We've also had the pleasure of seeing some of these youngsters returning with children of their own. It was a pleasure then, and it still is." Closed November and the first half of December.

The **Boardwalk,** at the lake end of Amhearst Street, facing Shepard Park (tel. 518/668-3242), is a natural wooden waterside-looking sort of place. The downstairs dining room has a big bar, flocks of red-and-white-clothed tables, beams everywhere, and water views from every table. Upstairs is an outdoor deck overlooking Lake George where light meals are served during the day, and Top 40 dance music is played at night. Outside is a dock where you can rent speedboats, paddleboats, and jet skis. The lunch menu features burgers and all manner of hot and cold sandwiches, priced from about $3 to $5. At dinner you can choose from the catch of the day, king crab legs, New York sirloin, spareribs, seafood platter, shore dinner in a basket, etc., priced from around $9 to $20. Open daily from mid-May until October: lunch is served from 11:30 a.m. to 4:30 p.m.; dinner hours start at 5 p.m. and continue until about 11 p.m. Open in the winter too, but not every day.

Other good places are located in areas nearby, but not in, Lake George Village. For example, **East Cove,** N.Y. 9L and Beach Road (tel. 518/668-5262), is all of a two-minute drive from the center of town down Beach Road past the state beach. It's a log-cabin affair with a wonderful Adirondack-style dining room complete with shiny log walls, thick rugs, and mustard-colored tablecloths. Dinner entrees like center-cut pork chops, prime rib, seafood Newburg, Cornish game hen, New York sirloin, etc., are priced from about $12 to $18. Light meals (burgers, half a chicken, fish and chips, etc.) cost about half that. Open daily for dinner only from 5 to 11 p.m.; Sunday brunch is served from 11 a.m. until 3 p.m.; closed Tuesday during the rest of the year, and for most of November and December.

A couple of good restaurants are up N.Y. 9N in Bolton Landing, among them **The Algonquin,** Bolton Landing (tel. 518/644-9442). This is a sleek and attractive place with gray wash siding, an outdoor terrace with yellow umbrellas, and two dining floors decorated with pine paneling and beamed ceilings, and affording fine lake views from large picture windows. Handsome lunches consisting of elaborate sandwiches (Monte Cristo, French dip, seafood salad, etc.), burgers of every stripe, omelets, and salads, cost between about $5 and $8. Most dinner entrees are in the $12 to $20 range. Open daily from noon until 10 p.m. during the summer (April to Labor Day); closed Tuesday and Wednesday the rest of the year; also closed for two weeks after Thanksgiving.

Definitely worth the 20-minute trip up U.S. 9 and N.Y. 28 from Lake George is the restaurant at the aforementioned **Balsam House,** Friends Lake, Chestertown (tel. 518/494-2828). This is a big, comfortable, thickly carpeted, dimly lit room with a copper-topped island in the middle. The crystal and silver glistens, the linen is immaculate, and food is simply fabulous. Cuisine is French/country and includes stuffed chicken breast, duck à l'orange, baby lamb, poached turbot, fried shrimp in sweet mustard sauce, steak au poivre, etc. Only dinner is served and most entrees cost between $12 and $18. The atmosphere is great; stay in the hotel if you can and take advantage of the excellent MAP room rates (see above). Daily dinner hours are 6 to 9 p.m. (until 8 p.m. in the winter); also on the premises is a very congenial lounge.

4. The Wilderness Experience

The **New York State Department of Environmental Conservation,** Albany, NY 12233 (tel. 518/457-2344), publishes maps and descriptions of trails through-out the Adirondack Park. These publications are usually single sheets folded in four, and are necessarily brief. The DEC also publishes booklets with titles like "Tips for Using State Lands," "Use of New York State's Public Forest Land," "Adirondack Canoe Routes," etc. They'll be glad to send you a selection for free if you write and ask.

Various Adirondack-area chambers of commerce will also send literature that can help do-it-yourself types experience the wilderness. For example, the **Saranac Lake Area Chamber of Commerce,** 30 Main St., Saranac Lake, NY 12983 (tel. 518/891-1990), has a number of interesting folders describing easily accessible parts of the wilderness. These can enable you to savor ancient forests, fern groves, bogs, and silent lakes, all located short distances from public parking areas. Drop them a line and they'll send you what they've got. Other helpful chambers of com-merce are located in Indian Lake, NY 12842 (tel. 518/648-5112); North Creek, NY 12583 (tel. 518/251-2612); Lake Placid, NY 12946 (tel. 518/523-2445); as well as in other north country communities.

Besides local chambers of commerce and the Department of Environmental Conservation publications, there exists a considerable body of other literature on the Adirondack wilderness. Among the most thorough, readable, interesting, and *useable* works are those by Barbara McMartin, who is a recognized expert on the area. Ms. McMartin has published three books that include good maps (better than those in the DEC publications), photos, careful trail descriptions, and historical notes. *Fifty Hikes in the Adirondacks,* published in 1980 by the New Hampshire Pub-lishing Co., Somersworth, N.H., contains detailed directions to the best sights the Adirondack wilderness has to offer. Some of these treks are relatively easy; others aren't. *Discover the Adirondacks, 1* and *Discover the Adirondacks, 2* are companion volumes, also by Ms. McMartin, that describe everything from swimming holes to wilderness fishing grounds, picnic and camping sites to waterfalls and gorges. These latter books are also published by the New Hampshire Publishing Co., and copy-righted 1979 and 1974, respectively. Taken together, these works detail an excep-tionally full range of outdoor wilderness activities for people at all levels of competence.

Fishing is one of the most time-honored of reasons for an Adirondack vacation. In the clear waters of Lake George, as well as in many smaller lakes and rivers through Warren County, are fish of all descriptions, from landlocked salmon to largemouth bass, brook trout to northern pike. The **Warren County Tourism Dept.,** Municipal Center, Lake George, NY 12845 (tel. 518/761-6366), publishes a most informative booklet titled "Grand Slam Fishing," which covers everything from license requirements to the names and addresses of licensed outfitters.

All sorts of other outfitters and guide services exist throughout the Adirondack Park. They can design and arrange hunting trips, canoe trips, bike trips, and trekker trips to virtually any destination, and/or for any length of time. Lists of reputable guides and outfitters are usually available through local chambers of commerce (see the list above). Two good ones are the **Raquette River Bike and Boat Company,** P.O. Box 653, Tupper Lake, NY 12986 (tel. 518/359-3228), and the **St. Regis Ca-**

noe Outfitters, P.O. Box 20, Lake Clear, NY 12945 (tel. 518/891-1838). They'll be glad to send you literature on the sorts of services they provide.

5. "Just Passing Through"

Those traveling to or between the resorts and towns described above will doubtless want to know about additional attractions within the Adirondack Park. This last section will therefore be a sort of "mopping up" operation and/or a reference guide for others who are in transit elsewhere but still want an interesting route.

THE ROAD TO FORT TICONDEROGA

Let it be said from the outset that the **Northway** (I-87), which runs up the eastern flank of the Adirondack Park, is a very beautiful road. I know that interstate highways can be dull. But scenically speaking, this is not the case with the Northway.

An alternative route northward from Lake George Village is N.Y. 9N, which is joined by N.Y. 22 at Ticonderoga on Lake Champlain. The virtue of 9N is that it parallels beautiful Lake George and traverses some fine woodlands. And it's also the road to historic **Fort Ticonderoga,** a restored 18th-century military complex including the fort, a museum, a costumed fife-and-drum corps, and daily July and August firing demonstrations.

The restoration lies two miles east of the town of Ticonderoga, a sleepy place on the LaChute River, and overlooks the strategic outlet from Lake George to Lake Champlain. The former importance of this modest aquatic connection—it was once called "the key to a continent"—is a little hard to grasp in our day of airplanes and superhighways. But two centuries ago considerable blood was let by French, English, and American soldiers so that their masters might control it. It was to Fort Ticonderoga that Montcalm retired after the butchery at Fort William Henry. It was at Ticonderoga, too, that Benedict Arnold demonstrated the bravery and brilliance that would lead him to another and greater victory at Saratoga.

The fort complex is quite an installation, located at the end of a long, tree-shaded approach. It has been preserved due to the efforts of the Pell family, various of whose members began purchasing and protecting the lands here as early as 1820. Admission to four separate sites—the Fort, Mount Hope, Mount Defiance, and Mount Independence (across Lake Champlain on the Vermont side)—is included in the charge: $5 for adults, $3 for kids 10 to 13, free for kids under 10. The fort is open daily mid-May until late October from 9 a.m. until 5 p.m. (until 6 p.m. in July and August). Parking is free and abundant, and there's a lunchroom on the premises. For more information, call 518/585-2821.

Students of 18th-century military history might also like to take a look at **Crown Point State Historic Site,** which is a dozen or so miles north of Ticonderoga, east of N.Y. 9N on the road to the Lake Champlain Bridge. Crown Point is a ruin, and there are no costumed fife-and-drum corps here. But there is an informative visitor center that describes the various battles that once raged in this now-silent place, and the admission is free. The French started the place in 1734, the British took it over subsequently, and the Americans overran it in 1775. Open June through October, Wednesday through Saturday from 10 a.m. to 5 p.m., on Sunday from 1 to 5 p.m. Call 518/597-3666 for further information.

Travelers heading northward on N.Y. 9N/22 may wonder about that strange cutout monster by the road outside **Port Henry.** He's green, wears a large grin, and has a scaly back. Too cute for comfort, perhaps, but this is supposed to be "Champ," the monster of Lake Champlain. Indeed a body of literature (serious or not, I can't tell) exists that cites the various sightings of this supposed creature. Not much else is doing in Port Henry, so criticism of the Champ phenomenon is, if nothing else, uncharitable.

A PAUSE AT WESTPORT

Ten miles north of Port Henry is the very pleasant village of Westport. Established in the last century as a very low-profile resort, this lakefront settlement has manicured summer estates on its southern fringes, capacious Victorian and elegant Greek Revival houses on its streets, lovely lake views, a pretty village green with a shingled clock tower and a nice inn, and a summer-stock theater. It's unhurried, uncrowded, and unspectacular. But while there isn't much to do here, it's an awfully nice place to pass through, and perhaps stay for the night.

If you decide on this latter course, try the **Inn on the Library Lawn,** Westport, NY 12993 (tel. 518/962-8666). This is a pretty Victorian commercial building, painted yellow, situated in the center of the hamlet, equipped with a false front above the second floor, and offering ten rooms. All accommodations have private bath, and some have views of the glittering waters of Lake Champlain at the foot of the hill. Interior decor is quite simple, and clearly the result of recent (late 1970s) structural alterations. But the rooms have big windows, Victorian-pattern wallpaper, the odd antique, and a comfy unpretentious charm. Between mid-May and mid-October a double room costs $55 to $75 a night; the rest of the year it's $50. The restaurant off the little lobby only serves breakfast in the summer, but serves dinner on Friday and Saturday nights in the winter.

For a meal in Westport, try the **Westport Yacht Club,** on Old Arsenal Road (tel. 518/962-8777). This is a very fresh and attractive-looking place located right on the water. It's at the foot of a dirt road that cuts off N.Y. 9N/22 just before the Inn on the Library Lawn. The dining room is furnished with oak captain's chairs, tables with crisp white linens, and wide windows overlooking Lake Champlain and the mountains beyond. The lunch menu has things like quiche, club sandwiches, burgers, tacos, and various salads, priced from about $3 to $6 or so. Dinner entrees include swordfish steak, filet mignon, broiled scallops, trout amandine, chicken Calvados, etc., and cost between about $11 and $16. Luncheon hours are 11:30 a.m. to 3 p.m.; dinner is served from 5:30 to 10 p.m.; open daily from mid-May until the end of September.

And if you do decide to stay over, be sure to check out the **Depot Theater,** located on the north end of town in the former D&H Railroad Station (tel. 518/962-4429). Past summers have seen classic film series in June, and summer-stock productions in July and August. Tickets are a modest $6 a seat.

TWO MAJOR ATTRACTIONS AT THE CENTER OF THE PARK

At the intersection of N.Y. 30 and 28 is a gas station/general store surrounded by a lot of trees. Yet this is a major crossroads in the center of the Adirondacks, adjacent to a hamlet called **Blue Mountain Lake.**

Here is where two recommended resort hotels are located, Hemlock Hall and The Hedges. It's also the hometown of the famous **Adirondack Museum,** "the best of its kind in the world," according to the *New York Times.* The museum houses a fascinating collection that depicts regional history and art. It's set on a sprawling campus, in 25 different buildings, with fine water and mountain views. The collection includes all manner of artifacts and memorabilia such as the famous locomotive that operated from 1900 to 1929 on the three-quarter-mile carry on Raquette Lake (it was the shortest railroad in the world). There are also all manner of freshwater boats, including a rigged sailboat bobbing under a huge glass dome, numerous reconstructed historic buildings and shops, an important collection of paintings, etc. Over two million people have visited this museum since 1957. The average visitor spends three hours here and comes away raving about the place. Open daily mid-June to mid-October from 9:30 a.m. until 5:30 p.m. Admission is $7.50 for adults, $4.50 for kids. Call 518/352-7311 for information.

Some 14 miles west of Blue Mountain Lake on N.Y. 28 is Raquette Lake, a center of Adirondack great camp development. One of the most famous of them all is **Camp Sagamore,** conceived by William West Durant in 1896 as a year-round home in the heart of the wilderness. By 1901 Durant was forced to sell Sagamore at a terrible loss to Alfred G. Vanderbilt. Vanderbilt went down on the *Lusitania* in 1915, but his widow continued to spend summers here until her death in 1954. After a period of ownership by Syracuse University, Sagamore was saved from destruction at the proverbial 11th hour by an alliance of local preservationists. Since 1975 it has been the scene of all manner of creative programs, plus a meticulous ongoing restoration.

Sagamore is currently a conference center whose varied programs include historic tours, personal and professional development workshops, recreational programs, etc. It is also open daily from late June through Labor Day and weekends in the fall for tours. It consists of nine major buildings that constitute some of the best examples of Adirondack-style architecture extant. Although the original furniture was auctioned off in 1975, and the current institutional use is not quite as opulent as intended by former owners, Sagamore is still a fascinating and beautiful place. Its current guardians love it dearly too—all 46 bedrooms and 26 stone fireplaces of it.

Daily summer tours leave at 10 a.m., 1 p.m., and 2 p.m., and cost $5 for adults and $2.50 for kids. If you'd like information on the many programs offered here, contact Sagamore Lodge and Conference Center, Sagamore Road, Raquette Lake, NY 13436 (tel. 315/354-5311).

THE THOUSAND ISLANDS

1. ALEXANDRIA BAY
2. CLAYTON

The Thousand Islands is the name of an archipelago of small (often downright tiny) islands located near the mouth of the St. Lawrence River, at the outflow of Lake Ontario. Indian legend has it that the Master of Life, temporarily away from his shining Sky-lodge, created the islands by accident. He had promised all the tribes of the world an earthly paradise (the tale here parallels the Garden of Eden story pretty closely), if only they would stop quarreling. They promised; he delivered the garden; they broke the promise; he picked the garden up in a blanket and started to carry it back. But just as he parted the Sky-curtain en route home, the blanket broke, the garden tumbled into the St. Lawrence River, and broke into a thousand pieces. And there it is today, the Thousand Islands.

Evidently the garden contained lots of fish. For legendary fishing is what first attracted summer visitors to the region. Originally these were campers who roughed it in an untamed and quite beautiful river wilderness. But by the end of the 19th century newly rich men with names like Pullman, Browning, Emery, and, above all, George C. Boldt, began covering the little islands with high-Victorian summer "cottages." The grandest of them all was a Rhenish castle built by Boldt, president of the Waldorf-Astoria Hotel Corporation in New York, founder of the Thousand Islands Club, and the man most responsible for establishing the Thousand Islands as a fashionable resort.

By the turn of the century Alexandria Bay possessed two fairly spectacular summer hotels. The Crossmon House and the Thousand Island House both had huge porches, elaborate towers, and steeply mansarded roofs from which giant American flags whipped in the wind. The little islands sported literally dozens of elaborate stone-and-shingle vacation houses, mansions really, set on tiny manicured water-girt fiefdoms and accessible only by boat. A large depot at Clayton served New York Central Railroad passengers, who could walk across the platform directly onto elaborate steamers or private yachts.

Today the great hotels are gone, replaced by motels and vacation resorts that for all their facilities have none of the old pizzazz. Alexandria Bay and Clayton are pleasant, smallish, unpretentious summer-resort towns that cater about equally to the summer people in their island mansions, the seasonal fishermen, and the tourists passing through. You couldn't really call the Thousand Islands an American Venice. But it does have a similar dependence on water transportation. In fact, if you don't get out on a boat at least once during your visit, you haven't really seen the place at all.

The season is short in the Thousand Islands—and sometimes a bit cool. Alexandria Bay and Clayton bustle in the high summer, but by late October almost everything closes down. By January it's 40° below zero and those great old houses out there in the river are frozen solid. About the only things moving are the giant supertankers, gliding majestically up and down the St. Lawrence Seaway, between islands a fifth their size.

Can't leave this introduction without a word about the famous salad dressing, can I? Yes, Thousand Islands dressing was invented here (supposedly, anyway). The story goes that George Boldt's steward aboard his yacht whipped it up one day during a luncheon party. Boldt was so pleased that he promoted the man to the kitchens of the Waldorf-Astoria. From there that man rose to fame, ultimately to become known as Oscar of the Waldorf.

---

1. Alexandria Bay

Affectionately abbreviated to Alex Bay, or simply Alex, this is a rather pretty, very unpretentious, upstate summer resort consisting of old buildings on a maze of tree-lined streets. You couldn't call Alex Bay gentrified in any sense. But there are attractive shingled churches, pleasant old houses, handsome 19th-century commercial buildings, and a leisurely uncrowded air. There is also a touch of honky-tonk along James Street in the form of amusement arcades, bars, and souvenir shops. But it's nothing compared to, say, Lake George Village. Many of the people who come to Alex Bay in the summer are modest folk up for a fishing vacation. The waterfront is very active, and crowded with motels, marinas, and incongruous glimpses of those aforementioned supertankers creeping in and out of sight behind the islands offshore.

WHAT TO SEE AND DO IN ALEXANDRIA BAY

A good source of advance information, as well as helpful on-the-scene advice, is an organization called the **Thousand Islands International Council,** P.O. Box 400, Alexandria Bay, NY 13607 (tel. toll free 800/5-ISLAND in New York State, 800/8-ISLAND in the eastern U.S.; from other areas, call 315/482-2520 collect). This agency is devoted to promoting tourism on the St. Lawrence River for the Jefferson County and East Ontario region and is oriented equally toward visiting Canadians and Americans. The office is located between Alex Bay and Clayton adjacent to the Thousand Island Bridge. Actually, it's considerably easier to get to it from the U.S.-bound lanes of the bridge.

Fishing

The principal attraction of the Thousand Islands remains the excellent fishing, and the Thousand Islands Council is a good source of advance fishing information. All manner of booklets listing fishing guides, charterers, marinas, trailer sites, groceries, tackle shops, etc., exist and the council will be glad to send them to you. Other sources of information for fishermen include: the **Alexandria Bay Chamber of Commerce,** Alexandria Bay, NY 13607 (tel. 315/482-9531); the **Clayton 1000 Islands Chamber of Commerce,** Riverside Drive, Clayton, NY 13624 (tel. 315/

686-3771); and the **Cape Vincent Chamber of Commerce,** James Street, (P.O. Box 482), Cape Vincent, NY 13618 (tel. 315/654-2481). New York State's "I Love New York" campaign is responsible for magazine-size travel guides to regions throughout the state. The *I Love New York Seaway Guide,* subtitled the *Chautauqua/ Allegheny Travel Guide,* covers a good many more places than the Thousand Islands. But it does have a fat central "fishing section," consisting of about half the guide and devoted entirely to fishing and fishermen. You can get a copy free of charge by writing to Chautauqua/Allegheny Travel Guide, Dept. SNI, Mayville, NY 14757.

Boldt Castle

This 120-room stone mansion is a melancholy place with a peculiar history. Started in 1900 by hotel magnate George C. Boldt, millions were spent on its construction until work was summarily halted in the beginning of 1904. Mrs. Boldt had died and her husband was too emotionally upset either to have the house completed or to ever again set foot on the island on which it stood.

It was allowed to moulder for three-quarters of a century. During that time, one suspects, a good many of the island houses on "millionaire's row" opposite Alex Bay were either outfitted or at least augmented with architectural fabric from the place. From a distance its complex roofline and multiple towers are picturesque in the extreme. Inside, despite a decade of "stabilization" by the Thousand Islands Bridge Authority (the present owner), the place is a shell. Shreds of original paneling and plaster remain here and there. But mostly it looks like the inside of an immense basement.

Visitors to the island must come either on one of the boat tours (see below) or by water taxi from either the upper or the lower docks on James Street in Alex Bay. Besides the castle, the island includes a five-story stone playhouse, called the Alster Tower, and a triumphal stone water gate intended for arriving yachts. Across a channel on nearby Wellesley Island is a fabulous old shingled boathouse, built by Boldt for his boats and yachts, and listed on the National Register of Historic Places. Every year between mid-May and the beginning of October, about 180,000 people make the trip from Alex to Heart Island to have a look at Boldt Castle. It certainly is a moody place, and evocative of considerable grandeur. A slide show in one of the unfinished rooms helps give one the idea of what the place was, or might have been. Admission is $3 for adults, $2 for kids. For further information, call the Thousand Islands International Council at 315/482-2520.

Boat Tours

James Street, the main business drag of Alex Bay, is all of four blocks long and anchored at either end by a pair of docks. **Empire Boat Tours,** whose parking lot is entered via Church or Fuller Streets (tel. 315/482-9511), operates U.S. Coast Guard–inspected boats from the Upper Dock, at the western end of James Street. In the words of their brochure, the boat tours "make every trip a complete Island tour, showing you the magnificent homes of many of the social and business leaders of the United States and Canada, the undeveloped sections of the Island region which still remain in their primeval state, as well as many hidden bays and channels." Boats will ferry you over to Boldt Castle for about $6 for adults, $3 for kids; take you on a one-hour Sun Set Cruise for around $7, $3.50 for kids; on a two-hour Two-Nation Tour for about $9.50 and $4.75, respectively, etc. You might also inquire about the Island Mansion Tour, costing $10 for adults and $6 for kids, to **Cherry Island,** a typical islet in millionaire's row with a pair of fabulous old mansions.

Empire's competition is called **Uncle Sam Boat Tours** and operates from the dock at the lower (eastern) end of James Street (tel. 315/482-2611 or 315/482-9611). The Uncle Sam boats are a little larger, and from what I can make out the tours seem to be a bit longer (and at least in some cases a bit more expensive too). There are regular departures from May through October, plus ferry service to Boldt Castle.

The Slick of '76

Subtitled *A Musical Catastrophe*, this is an ensemble-theater summer production that takes place each year. The year 1976 brought the largest inland oil spill in North American history. The ensuing mess had a major impact on the Thousand Islands region, and underscored not only the fragility of the local ecology but also the interdependence of formerly unallied groups.

River Barge Productions has a cast of eight that portrays "the march of the summer people," who inhabit the big island houses; "the river rats," who support the islanders; the shoreline people and the tourists; "the muckers," who actually cleaned the stuff up; and the "slick lickers," who arrived from the outside world with things like oil-eating laser guns and the like. In the end the natural antagonism between these various parties evaporates in the face of the new knowledge that the river belongs to them all.

It's very funny and makes a nice night's excursion. You can pick up a water taxi at either of the docks on James Street. Tickets cost $7; for information and show times, call 315/686-3347 or 686-3566.

Excursion to Ogdensburg and the Frederic Remington Museum

About 35 miles east of Alex Bay, via N.Y. 12 and N.Y. 37 (the so-called Seaway Trail), is the little town of Ogdensburg. This was the childhood home of Frederic Remington, one of the most famous artists and sculptors of America's Western frontiers and mountain wildernesses. Remington died in 1909 of a botched appendectomy at the age of 48 (a major malpractice suit would no doubt have ensued had it occurred today), after which his widow returned to Ogdensburg. She rented a fine mansion at the corner of Washington and State Streets, a house that would in time become a museum of her husband's art.

The **Frederic Remington Art Museum** contains marvelous bronzes, oils, watercolors, and pen-and-ink sketches depicting Remington's buckskin-clad frontiersmen, covered wagons, Indians in war paint, birchbark canoes on storm-tossed lakes, and cowboys on bucking broncos. There is even a faithful re-creation of his last studio, plus a good gift shop.

In the summer (May through October) the museum is open daily from 10 a.m. to 5 p.m. (from 1 p.m. on Sunday); the rest of the year it's open only Tuesday through Saturday from 10 a.m. to 5 p.m. Admission is $3 for adults and $1.50 for seniors and youths (ages 13 to 16). The address is 303 Washington St., Ogdensburg (tel. 315/393-2425).

Where to Stay in Alex Bay

The **Thousand Island Club,** Wellesley Island, Alexandria Bay, NY 13607 (tel. 315/482-2551), was originally conceived by George C. Boldt, whose unfinished castle is on the heart-shaped island next to the club. What's great about this place is that it's not in town, but across the river from it. As such, it maintains the feel of a private club. There are 400 manicured riverside acres, a wonderful 1920s stucco Mediterranean-style hotel or clubhouse, an 18-hole USGA golf course, tennis courts, a heated pool, and a full-service deep-water marina. The clubhouse has been recently refurbished, bringing it back to its earlier grandeur with all modern conveniences such as phones, TVs, and HBO. Accommodations in the original clubhouse run between $60 and $80 per night for double occupancy. The newly built villa suites nearby have much larger rooms, some with balconies and kitchenettes, and cost from $100 to $120 nightly. The food here is quite good and is a favorite in the local community, so I advise anyone staying here to consider the meal plan. For those just considering dinner, there is The Commodore Room, which is also open for breakfast and lunch, and serves its evening meal between 6 and 10 p.m. (11 p.m. on weekends). Dinner entrees are in the $13 to $20 range.

A brand-new four-story brick **Riveredge Resort Hotel,** Holland Street, Alexandria Bay, NY 13607 (tel. 315/482-9917), has risen from the ashes of a devastating 1988 fire. No expense has been spared in the construction of this new, state-of-the-art 125-room resort hotel, crowned with 28 split-level suites on the top floor. With majestic views of the St. Lawrence River and Boldt Castle from all the rooms, this year-round hotel also features private balconies, Jacuzzis, cable TV, boat accommodation up to 250 feet, health spa, sauna, exercise room, two restaurants—even indoor and outdoor pools with hot tubs. They even have a separate building for boaters in transit, with bathrooms, showers, laundry, vending machines, water, electric, telephone, and TV. Room and suite rates range between $70 and $130 from May to mid-June; $100 to $190 to Labor Day; $80 to $140 to early November, when winter rates decline to $50 and $100 (highest rates denote Jacuzzi or duplex suites).

The biggest and most elaborate resort in the Thousand Islands is the **Bonnie Castle**, Alexandria Bay, NY 13607 (tel. 315/482-4511, or toll free 800/521-5514). At the heart of this huge place, engulfed by new construction, is an old house built by a 19th-century author referred to as the "great" J.G. Holland (ever heard of him? me neither). The 120 modern guest rooms are really Hilton quality, with their thick rugs, modern tiled baths, good-quality furniture, wet bars, cable color TVs with free HBO, and direct-dial telephones. Some have fantasy bathtubs and mirrored ceilings. Across several acres of blacktopped parking lot is the Bonnie Castle Manor, consisting of the old house and its huge new additions. "The Home of the Stars" says the sign outside. Inside is a glittery/glamorous nightclub that holds 700 people and books acts like the Inkspots, the Platters, Al Martino, and Woody Herman. "Name" or not, there's always somebody there, as management assures me there is entertainment every night of the year. Adjacent is a big lush restaurant with lots of picture windows and water views, and lunch and dinner service every day all year round. Double-occupancy room rates at the peak of the summer season (late May to Labor Day) range from $100 or so to around $150 nightly, the latter rate being for a room with a king-size bed and a Jacuzzi. Rates decline in stages to a deep winter low of about $50 to $80 a night. Also on the premises are an immense outdoor swimming pool, an indoor pool, and several fine new tennis courts.

Of the bunch of other big resorts in town, my favorite is the **Edgewood,** Alexandria Bay, NY 13607 (tel. 315/482-9922). Founded by a group of Cleveland businessmen as a private club in the 1880s, the Edgewood is today a complete modern resort on a beautifully landscaped property immediately west of downtown Alex Bay. In the middle of things is a big old clapboard summer hotel left over from the old days and unused except for special functions. Today's accommodations are located in modern motel buildings that hug the shoreline. Rooms have beamed ceilings (many of them do, anyway), decks overlooking the water, color TVs, telephones, and a nice 1960s contemporary look. There are 160 of them, plus a big outdoor pool, an attractive beach and dock, three lounges, and a resort-type restaurant whose adjacent Gazebo Room offers nightly entertainment. Open from late April until late October, and double-occupancy rates range from a high of $65 to $110 nightly (mid-May to Labor Day) to a low of $55 to $85.

Capt. Thomson's Motor Lodge, P.O. Box 68, Alexandria Bay, NY 13607 (tel. 315/482-9961, or toll free 800/253-9229 in New York State), is located at the lower end of James Street, adjacent to the Uncle Sam Boat Dock. This is a complex of two-story redwood-stained motel-type buildings built on the perimeter of a little point extending out into the river. There's a nice pool, and the 117 reasonably priced units have artificial wood paneling, color TVs (in all but a few village-view rooms), and simple pleasant motel-modern furniture. The most expensive room for two at the peak of the summer season (July and August) is $95 a night; other doubles can be had during that same period for about $55. Prices in the "early" and "off" seasons range from about $50 to $65 nightly. Closed October to May.

Popular with fishermen for its location and good rates is the **Fisherman's Wharf Motel,** 15 Sisson St., Alexandria Bay, NY 13607 (tel. 315/482-2230). This diminutive establishment has but 24 units, all of which overlook the upper harbor and the marina. Rooms are simple but quite pleasant, and all come with cable TV, little refrigerators, and two double beds. If you come with a boat that's less than 25 feet long, you can even tie it up for free right outside your door. Simple, but the ambience is very authentic. Double-occupancy room rates vary from about $60 to $100 during the late June to Labor Day high season. Before and after that you can stay here for about $45 double. Closed from November to May.

RESTAURANTS IN ALEX BAY

The Bonnie Castle and the Riveredge, described above, both have interesting restaurants for either lunch or dinner. The best-known upscale independent restaurant in town is **Cavallario's Steak and Seafood House,** on Church Street near James (tel. 315/482-9867). You can't miss its false-fronted castellated façade. Inside, the castle decor continues with cutout gilded knights mounted on red velvet, crossed lances, wrought iron, and thick rugs. Only dinner is served, from 4 until 11 p.m. (from 2 to 10 p.m. on Sunday), from a menu offering such things as surf and turf, veal Francis, honey orange duckling, snapper "maison," chicken Kiev, etc. À la carte prices are mostly in the $12 to $15 range, but go all the way up to $23. Open from early May until late October.

The **Admiral's Inn,** corner of James and Market Streets (tel. 315/482-2781), is an old wooden house with a pretty covered porch/café furnished with blue plastic tablecloths and white chairs. Inside is a neighborhoody bar and several pleasant, smallish dining rooms with bay windows, plastic-covered chairs, blue tablecloths, and cheerful print curtains. The lunch menu consists of sandwiches, burgers, "tasty tidbits" (which might double as appetizers on a dinner menu), plus soups and salads, priced between about $3 and $7. At dinnertime you can order things like spaghetti, homemade lasagne, fried chicken, pork chop or turkey dinners, trout, scallops, etc., for about $8 to $12, with a few items going as high as $18 or so. Open April to mid-October; meals served daily from 11:30 a.m. until 10 p.m. (until 11 p.m. on weekends).

There are two other good lunch places in downtown Alex. **A Summer Place,** 24 James St. (tel. 315/482-9805), across the street from the Admiral's Inn, is another informal tavern with a very good lunch menu. All sorts of salads, sandwiches, and burgers are available for around $3 to $4. It's dim, friendly, and very informal —and the food is good. Closed November to May. Alternatively, you might try the little **Dock Side,** 17 Market St. (tel. 315/482-9849), which is another vintage small-town tavern with a friendly atmosphere and good bar sandwiches in the $3 to $4 range. Open daily all year from 10 a.m. until 2 a.m. (from noon on Sunday).

---

2. Clayton

About 11 miles west of Alex, via N.Y. 12, is the little riverfront village of Clayton. This is a sleepy place, pretty in its own unpretentious way, well known to fishermen who return year after year and to summer people with island homes in the vicinity. The big resorts, most of the bars, the boat tours, and indeed most of the consciousness of the Thousand Islands is centered on Alex Bay. Yet Clayton has a few attractions of note.

First and foremost I suppose must be the **fishing.** Clayton is, after all, the home of the Muskie Hall of Fame. As fishing has already been described in some detail under Alex Bay, let me (with due respect to Clayton) refer you to that section above.

In the late 19th century Clayton was a famous center of freshwater boat-building, a tradition still honored today. Every year, for example, there's an **antique boat show** that attracts up to 300 antique boaters every August. There's also the famous **Shipyard Museum** at 750 Mary St. (tel. 315/686-4104), the largest freshwater maritime museum of its kind in the world. Here you can see everything from dugout canoes to the sleek varnished commuter boats of the old Thousand Islands millionaires. There are also rare periodicals, old photos, and displays of all manner of power and nonpower boats. Open mid-May to mid-October; admission is $4.

WHERE TO STAY AND EAT IN CLAYTON

Most of the action is in nearby Alex, but several establishments offer good value in Clayton as well. The **Quarterdeck Motel and Restaurant,** east of the village on N.Y. 12, Clayton, NY 13624 (tel. 315/686-5588), is a case in point. The motel is a modest establishment located behind a popular restaurant of the same name. It has but 12 units, with sliding glass doors that lead to little terraces, distant water views, cable color TV, and very attractive modern decor. They are immaculately clean and cost only $40 a night double at the height of the summer. Winter rates are $40 double. The restaurant is a cozy, family-style pine-paneled affair with an adjoining bar. You can get all sorts of sandwiches, a mega dog platter, a Quarterdeck burger, plus French dips, hot sandwiches, pizza, and all sorts of specials, between $3 and $6. At dinner things like fried chicken, veal parmigiana, steak sandwich, plus selected burgers and sandwiches, are priced from $4 to about $14. Open daily at 11 a.m. for lunch, and from 5 to 9 p.m. for dinner (to 10 p.m. for dinner on Friday and Saturday).

Another pleasant and inexpensive place to stay is **Bertrand's Motel,** 229 James St., Clayton, NY 13624 (tel. 315/686-3641). Located in the heart of downtown Clayton, this is a modest, 1963-vintage, two-story motel with 28 rooms and a certain small-town charm. There are pretty gardens outside, and rooms with blond furniture, cable color TV, and a well-kept family-owned air. Double rooms cost about $50 in July and August; that rate drops to about $40 the rest of the season. Closed December through March.

Out on N.Y. 12 again, just east of Clayton, is a very popular restaurant called the **Clipper Inn** (tel. 315/686-3842). This attractive establishment consists of a collection of cheerful contemporary rooms with lots of wood lattice and a vaguely nautical motif. Only dinner is served, the menu offering such selections as sole Oscar, broiled scallops, frogs' legs, seafood scampi, plus Italian pasta dishes and assorted steak and chicken dishes. Prices are in the $10 to $15 range. Open for dinner only, 5 to 10 p.m. daily May through October. Closed Monday and Tuesday in the off-season; closed completely January through March.

Last, but as they say, not least, is the **Koffee Kove,** on James Street opposite Bertrand's Motel. This is the sort of small-town sandwich shop for which I have a soft spot in my heart. It's a cheery, pine-paneled, fluorescent-lit, utterly unpretentious place dispensing delicious sandwiches on homemade bread for around $2 to $3. What could be finer than a piece of homemade pie to follow it all up (available for a modest $1.25)? Open every day, all year long, from 6 a.m. until 3 p.m. On Friday nights, $6 to $8 dinners are available too.

DELUXE FISHING EXCURSION TO CAPE VINCENT

A place called the Riverhead Lodge, located on Carleton Island opposite the village of Cape Vincent, offers an authentic and luxurious experience for serious fishermen and duck hunters. The facility is an old house built in the 1880s, and accessible only by boat from the Anchor Marina in Cape Vincent. There are five guest rooms, a common dining room where gourmet meals are served at the end of the day, and complete facilities for fishing and hunting.

The proprietor, Capt. Jerome LaLonde, acts as guide and organizer. Various hunting and fishing package deals are available, lasting three to five nights and costing up to $650 per person, all inclusive. If you wish, you can also just stay for the night and enjoy meals with the sportsmen for $80 per person including breakfast and dinner.

Carleton Island has 1,300 acres of unspoiled land and only a handful of houses (including a monster of an old mansion decaying picturesquely behind the lodge). Coming out here to this remote spot must constitute about the closest thing possible to the original sporting experience that first drew heavy hitters from the cities to the Thousand Islands. The lodge has big porches, mission-style furniture, picture windows overlooking panoramas of water, and a wonderful air of remoteness. For more information, contact the **Riverhead Lodge,** P.O. Box 142, Cape Vincent, NY 13618 (tel. 315/654-2600).

THE FINGER LAKES

The operative word here is "rural." The Finger Lakes District lies south of Lake Ontario at the very heart of New York State. It's a region of rolling hills, big views, and long valleys, many of which contain deep, narrow lakes. Seneca Lake, for example, is 650 feet deep, its bottom being 250 feet below sea level.

WHAT THE FINGER LAKES ARE LIKE

On the map the Finger Lakes look like the splayed fingers of a multidigited hand. On the ground the area has an agricultural look. Fields and farms and vineyards dominate the landscape between the various towns and cities. There are forests too, but the hand of man lies clearly on the area (appropriate, considering its name) and there's no sense of wilderness. There are, however, quite a few deep ravines and waterfalls in this part of the world. Many are rather impressive, and are preserved on the grounds of state parks we'll visit later.

A great deal of wine is made in the Finger Lakes District. And if you're so inclined, you can spend considerable time vineyard-hopping. "Château" country it ain't, but the roads are pretty and the wine is a great source of local pride.

A BIT OF HISTORY

Until the time of the American Revolution the Finger Lakes were a stronghold of the Iroquois Confederation. After a few particularly bloody raids against white settlers, in which British complicity was suspected, Washington dispatched one General John Sullivan on an expedition to "chastise and humble the Six Nations," as the tribes hereabouts were known. In 1779 Sullivan's men swept through the Finger Lakes, killed just about every Indian there, and utterly destroyed all their settlements. Numerous historic markers commemorate the more bloodcurdling of his successes. Sullivan received the official thanks of Congress in October 1779, despite angry criticism of the campaign. Be that as it may, he did succeed in removing the greatest single impediment to settlement. Interestingly, few people in the area today seem to have any idea who he was or what he did.

The Finger Lakes prospered with the advent of the Erie Canal, and much of the fine Greek Revival architecture of that period remains. So do a lot of Greek place names. Cities, villages, and townships alike bear the most distinguished names imaginable. Your map will reveal not just Ithaca, but Syracuse, Ovid, Pompey, Romulus, Homer, Ulysses, Scipio, even Brutus.

The agricultural and light industrial economy of the area today is quite able to support the population without the help of tourists, thank you very much. Yet the rural charms and tranquility of the Finger Lakes draw a steady stream of visitors every year. In the summer, there are the vineyards and the country roads, the pretty towns and deep, clear lakes. There's also grand-prix racing at Watkins Glen and thoroughbred horse racing at the Finger Lakes Track near Canandaigua. In the fall there's the changing foliage. And any time of year there are attractive and romantic places to eat and stay a night or two. And then there is Rochester, a great little city that's definitely worth a visit.

USEFUL INFORMATION

Although not every town or city in the region is included in this chapter, I have tried to hit the high spots. Surely you'll find enough in the pages ahead to give you what the local tourist organization calls "The Finger Lakes Feeling." That organization, by the way, is called the **Finger Lakes Association,** 309 Lake St., Penn Yan, NY 14527 (tel. 315/536-7488), and has been in business since 1919. They will send you a copy of the encyclopedic *I Love New York Finger Lakes Travel Guide,* if you like, free of charge. They can also provide all manner of other information that might be helpful in planning your trip, so make a note of the number.

And for an extensive listing of bed-and-breakfast establishments in the Finger Lakes region contact the **Finger Lakes Bed & Breakfast Association** at P.O. Box 862, Canandaigua, NY 14424 (tel. 716/394-8132).

HOW THIS CHAPTER IS ORGANIZED

The Finger Lakes cover a large amount of territory, which can be criss-crossed in any number of ways. A majority of the local attractions seem, however, to lie at either the northern or the southern ends of the various lakes. So do the major east-west roads. Therefore, I've divided those attractions into two sections, titled respectively "The Northern Tier" and "The Southern Tier." There are some very nice cities in this part of the world as well, and for the purposes of tourism, I'd have to choose Rochester as the most interesting. Ergo, there's a section devoted to it, and to Syracuse, as well. So without further ado, let's get on the road and take the New York State Thruway to Syracuse (exit 34a to 36).

---

1. Syracuse

Charles Dickens visited Syracuse in 1869 and wrote the following:

I am here in a most wonderful out-of-the-world place, which looks as if it had begun to be built yesterday, and were going to be imperfectly knocked together with a nail or two the day after tomorrow. I am here in the worst inn that was ever seen, and outside is a thaw that places the whole country under water . . . I have tried all the wines in the house and there are only two wines for which you pay six shillings a bottle or 15, according as you feel disposed to change the name of the thing you ask for. (The article never changes.) The bill of fare is in French and the principal article is Paeltie de shay! I asked the Irish waiter what this dish was and he said "it was the name the stewart giv' to oyster patties—

the French name." . . . We had an old buffalo for supper and an old pig for breakfast and we are going to have I don't know what for dinner at 6. In the public room downstairs, a number of men (speechless) with their feet against the window frames, staring out at the window and spitting dolefully at intervals . . . And yet we have taken in considerably over 300 pounds for to-morrow night.

It was a sold-out house for Dickens's reading at the Weiting Opera House. Downtown Syracuse today is a far more civilized place than it was in Dickens's time. Located at the southern end of Onondaga Lake, Syracuse is the approximate geographic center of New York State. With the Thousand Islands to the north, the Adirondacks to the northeast, the Finger Lakes to the south, Lake Ontario to the northwest, and traversed east-west by the Erie Canal, Syracuse is both a destination and a great staging area for holiday trips.

The city supports a population of around 200,000 and is the proud home of **Syracuse University** (tel. 315/423-1870), the **Carrier Dome** (tel. 315/423-4634), and the **State Fair Grounds** (tel. 315/487-7711). It is also the industrial capital of central New York. Nicknamed "Salt City" after its first industry, salt mining, Syracuse is a major regional cultural and recreational center. Although salt may have put the city on the map, it was the Erie Canal that contributed the most to its prosperity. With the canal came boom-town development—horse-and-buggy-clogged streets, thriving businesses, and rowdy canal-house bars. Having attended several unforgettable Syracuse University social functions in my college days, I would venture to speculate that local hospitality may have its roots in an 1870 New Year's celebration thrown by beer baron John Greenway. This gentleman roasted a giant ox in Clinton Square and 20,000 people showed up. The 19th-century reputation of rough-and-tumble Syracuse is today refined to competitive sports, education, and business.

Downtown Syracuse, as was the case with most major Northeastern cities, fell prey to urban-renewel devastation in the 1960s. Then, in the 1970s, insult was added to injury by the construction of a maze of interstate highways. The architectural integrity of Syracuse's downtown center is isolated today in patchwork-quilt fashion by square-block parking lots and elevated highways. As such, the downtown lacks the flavor and style of otherwise comparable cities like Albany and Rochester. Suburban development is rampant around Syracuse. In fact, the suburban shopping center concept of the "miracle mile" or the "franchise strip" is said to have had its roots here. It is perhaps fitting that the home city of the Pyramid Corporation, located in the restored Post Office Building downtown, should be suffering from precisely the plight of other cities where mall builders like Pyramid have eroded the urban retail core. At the time of this writing, Sibley's Department Store, a downtown Syracuse landmark, has just moved to the malls and its building stands abandoned.

WHAT TO SEE AND DO IN SYRACUSE

The **Greater Syracuse Chamber of Commerce's Convention and Visitors Bureau,** 100 East Onondaga St., Syracuse, NY 12302, in the Hotel Syracuse (tel. 315/470-1343), should be your first destination. The bureau has an archive of pamphlets, maps, and brochures, to say nothing of a very attentive and helpful staff. Wonderful downtown architecture exploring, does still exist, and should you have any interest in exploring, stop in at the Hotel Syracuse and pick up "Let's Take a Walk . . ." ($2), a delightful self-tour booklet. This tour includes 36 landmarks and takes about one hour.

The **Everson Museum of Art,** the eighth feature of the tour, is an impressive modern concrete sculpture in itself. You'll find it at 401 Harrison St. (tel. 315/474-6064). The museum is nationally known for its outstanding collection of pottery, ceramics, and porcelain. I noted on a recent visit not only an extraordinary exhibit of

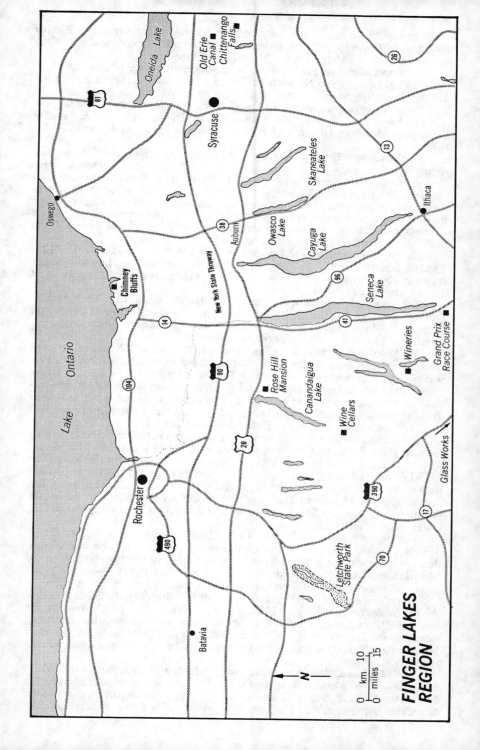

FINGER LAKES
REGION

Hudson River School paintings, but also a fund-raising drive to develop a Stickley furniture collection for permanent display. The museum is open Tuesday through Sunday from noon to 5 p.m., with a $2 suggested donation.

The **Canal Museum,** housed in the Weighlock Building at 318 Erie Blvd. East (tel. 315/471-0593), is a National Register site restored to its appearance in the 1850s, when it functioned as a canal-boat weighing station. You can board a 65-foot-long canal boat to experience life and work on the Erie Canal, and to explore the history of Syracuse as it grew from swamp to city. The museum is open Tuesday through Sunday from 10 a.m. to 5 p.m.; admission is $1 for adults, and 50¢ for children.

The **Landmark Theatre,** 362 South Salina St. (tel. 315/475-7979), was designed by the legendary Thomas W. Lamb in 1928. This totally restored Indo-Persian "fantasy" theater captured in its architecture all the illusion associated with the stage. Featuring a sumptuous lobby, a sweeping grand staircase, a grand promenade, and a gilded vault and fabulous proscenium arch, this theater is one of only a handful left in the country. The Landmark hosts a variety of attractions: symphony concerts, popular singers, Broadway touring companies, and classic movies. Tours of the theater are available by appointment only.

The **Onondaga Historical Association,** 311 Montgomery St. (tel. 315/428-1862), is located in the former New York Telephone Company building and focuses on central New York history. The museum is open Tuesday through Saturday from 12 to 4 p.m., free of charge.

The **Syracuse Symphony Orchestra** (tel. 315/424-8222) and the **Syracuse Opera Company** (tel. 315/475-5915) perform at the **Civic Center of Onondaga County,** 411 Montgomery St. Both these cultural organizations are nationally recognized and are well worth the visitor's attention.

The **Discovery Center,** 321 Clinton St. (tel. 315/425-9068), is a museum of science and technology containing the **Rotary Planetarium.** This is a wonderful experience for adult and child alike, to say nothing of the "Shadow Room," where visitors can observe their permanent shadows created where they stand against a specially treated wall as a strobe light flashes. This hands-on science museum is open Tuesday through Saturday from 10 a.m. to 5 p.m., and on Sunday from noon to 5 p.m., with an admission charge of $2 for adults and $1 for kids.

My favorite kid place in all of Syracuse is the **Burnet Park Zoo,** on South Wilber Avenue, two miles west of downtown Syracuse (tel. 315/478-8516). The "Antiquity Cave" takes the visitor back 600 million years to the age of the dinosaurs. The "Wild Woods" takes you from the arctic tundra to the dusty Western plains. This is a state-of-the-art urban zoo and it will leave you with a real sense of wonderment. You can visit the zoo daily from 10 a.m. to 4:30 p.m. in the winter, to 7 p.m. during the summer. Admission is $2.50 for grown-ups, $1.50 for kids 5 to 14 (bring your ID), and free for the little ones.

The **Onondaga County Parks,** P.O. Box 146, Liverpool, NY 13088 (tel. 315/451-PARK), have no shortage of recreational opportunities for community residents or visitors. Contact their offices for further information. I would suggest the **Old Erie Canal State Park** at Ceder Bay Road in Syracuse (tel. 315/446-4007). The jogger, biker, or canoer will enjoy the 35 miles of canal that end in Rome, N.Y.

If you'd like a beer, stop by the **Anheuser-Busch Brewery,** 2885 Belgium Rd., Baldwinsville (tel. 315/635-4114). From Syracuse, take I-690 west to the Baldwinsville exit, then right on Downer Street, left to Genesee (street not beer), right to the fork, then veer left. If you can find it, a guided tour can be had (by reservation only) Monday through Friday from noon to 2 p.m. Or you may just want to crack a Bud downtown.

The **Mid-Lakes Navigation Co., Ltd.,** 11 Jordan St., Skaneateles (tel. 315/685-8500), offers a delightful maritime travel experience. Mid-Lakes operates the 65-foot double-decked *City of Syracuse,* which docks at Dutchman Landing on the Erie Canal just three miles from downtown Syracuse. The *City of Syracuse* has daily

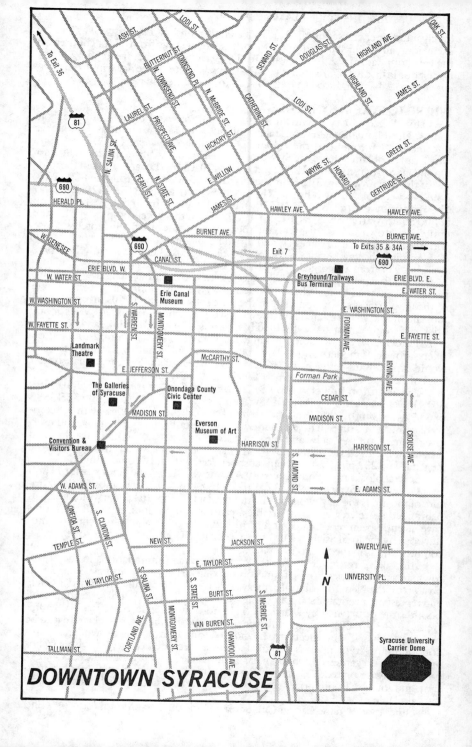

DOWNTOWN SYRACUSE

lunch and dinner cruises on the Erie Canal and Onondaga Lake, as well as Sunday excursions, all of which include great food. The prices range from $3 for children on the two-hour Saturday All-American Hot Dog Cruise to an adult fare of $27 for a three-hour Prime Rib Dinner Cruise. Mid-Lakes also runs three day trips from Syracuse east to Albany and west to Buffalo. Call for schedule and rates.

WHERE TO STAY IN SYRACUSE

This dispersed city is known for its conventions and some 4,000 available rooms. The following suggestions represent only a few of many options. For further information I recommend the *I Love NY, Syracuse/Onondaga Co. Travel Guide,* which can be obtained from the **Syracuse Convention & Visitors Bureau,** 100 East Onondaga St., Syracuse, NY 12302 (tel. 315/470-1343). Located right in the middle of the downtown are **The Hotels at Syracuse Square** (tel. toll free 800/255-3892)—a complex of two hotels, **The Hotel Syracuse** (tel. 315/422-5121) and **The Hilton Towers** (tel. 315/471-7300), linked together by an enclosed esplanade at 500 South Warren St., Syracuse, NY 13202. From this hotel complex one has the entire downtown at one's disposal, and the contrast of the old stately Hotel Syracuse with the modern Hilton offers a grand urban hospitality experience.

Admittedly, my favorite is the old Hotel Syracuse because it truly has style. Built in 1924 from a George B. Post design, the 11-story hotel features a grand lobby with 40-foot ceilings detailed with neoclassical architectural elements. A massive two-story mirrored grand ballroom is located on the tenth floor. The Syracuse is one of the few survivors of its kind left in the state following the 1960s urban renewal movement that so devastated our cities. The very charming rooms have valet doors, Stickley furniture, and grand old tiled bathrooms with pedestal sinks and porcelain tubs. Rates are very reasonable and range from $54 to $78. The contrasting Hilton offers a tower of modern rooms with all the traditional Hiltony features a traveler would expect. Rates range from $69 to $103. The Hotels at Syracuse Square offer a total of 725 rooms and are the center for all major conventions.

The **Sheraton University Inn & Conference Center** at Syracuse University, 801 University Ave., P.O. Box 801, Syracuse, NY 13210-0801 (tel. 800/325-3535 or 315/475-3000), is an ultramodern hotel of steel and tinted glass with the complete gamut of features. These include an indoor pool, whirlpool, sauna, and exercise room, all off the lobby and separated from it by glass. The hotel also has two restaurants, with classical dining at the Pavilion and a more casual atmosphere at the Regatta. The 232 plush guest rooms cost between $86 and $106 per night.

Several blocks north on University Avenue you'll find the **Genesee Inn,** 1060 East Genesee St., Syracuse, NY 13201 (tel. 315/476-4212). The most striking feature of the inn is the airy two-story atrium with its 16-foot Italianate windows. This plant-filled space creates a comfortable area for dining or lounging. All the rooms have recently been redecorated and furnished with colonial-inspired cherry reproductions by the local Stickley Furniture Company. This 98-room hotel offers its accommodations in the $52 to $79 range.

Although I recommend that the traveler seek accommodations in the downtown area, alternatives can be found on the outskirts of town in East Syracuse, at Exit 35 off the New York State Thruway (I-90). This area is called the Carrier Circle and represents a veritable shopping center of motels. The first you'll see from the toll booth is the **Courtyard by Marriott,** 6415 Yorktown Circle, Syracuse, NY 13057 (tel. 315/432-0300). It is not only the newest among the lot, but I believe it to be the best value if one elects to be housed out of the downtown area. This condominium-style motel is designed around a secluded courtyard with gazebos and landscaped gardens. Each room has a queen-size bed, a private terrace, cable TV, and is nicely decorated. The motel also has a small indoor pool, whirlpool, restaurant, and lounge. Room prices range from $39 to $64, with special weekend packages available.

Other motels in the Carrier Circle area include the **Continental Journey's End**

Motel (tel. 315/433-1300, or toll free 800/268-0405), **Days Inn** (tel. 315/325-2525), **Dewitt Inn** (tel. 315/446-3300), **Econo Lodge** (tel. 315/463-0202), **Hampton Inn** (tel. 315/463-6443, or toll free 800/HAMPTON), **Holiday Inn** (tel. 315/437-2761, or toll free 800/238-8000), **Howard Johnson's Motor Lodge** (tel. 315/437-2711, or toll free 800/654-2000), **John Milton Thruway Motel** (tel. 315/463-8555), **Quality Inn** (tel. 315/463-6601, or toll free 800/228-5151), **Red Roof Inn** (tel. 315/437-3309, or toll free 800/848-7878), **Syracuse Marriott** (tel. 315/432-0200, or toll free 800/228-9290), and, last but not least, the **Travelers Motor Inn** (tel. 315/437-0222). All of these are within a stone's throw of one another and are priced from $29 up.

As an alternative you might try **Bed & Breakfast of the Greater Syracuse Area**, 143 Didama St., Syracuse, NY 13224 (tel. 315/446-4199). Rates start at $32 for a single and $42 for a double. These are all in private homes having from one to three well-appointed guest rooms, some with private baths.

RESTAURANTS IN SYRACUSE

There is no shortage of these. The town's best is **Pascale Wine Bar & Restaurant**, 304 Hawley Ave. (tel. 315/471-3040). If you're interested in a truly unusual culinary experience accented with unique and rare international wines, this award-winning restaurant is the place for you. Located in a large 1870s Italianate brick house, Pascale features northern Italian and French cuisine. Open Monday through Saturday for dinner only, from 5 p.m. to midnight, Pascale offers two dining options—a light theater menu downstairs in the lounge, or a formal setting with full menu on the second floor. The upscale upstairs dinner entrees cost in the $10 to $22 range, with such dishes as homard de Maine au vanille (Maine lobster) or danseuse de rivière en chemise verte (rainbow trout with lobster mousse wrapped in lettuce). The theater menu features innovative creations like pizza with duck confit, onion marmelade, and apple, with prices in the $7 to $12 range. Reservations are a must.

Nikki's Downtown, 201 South Salina St. (tel. 315/424-1172), is housed in a National Register–listed building constructed in 1876 in high Victorian Gothic style. The solid mahogany interior of Nikki's was installed for the original H. J. Howe jewelry store, and the old vaults downstairs are now used for intimate dining. Lunch is served Monday through Friday from 11:30 a.m. to 3:30 p.m. and includes sandwiches or options like blackened catfish and chicken tchoupitoulas priced from $3.50 to $9. Dinner, which features continental, French, Cajun, and charbroiled items, is available Monday through Thursday from 5 to 10 p.m., to 11 p.m. on Friday and Saturday, and to 9 p.m. on Sunday. Entrees cost $13 to $22. Sunday brunch is served from 11 a.m. to 3:30 p.m. and reservations are suggested.

The 1865 limestone Gridley Building with its Second Empire mansard-roofed clock tower is the home of **Sterio's Landmark Restaurant** 103 East Water St., (tel. 315/472-8883). This former bank and Erie Canal landmark is a wonderful setting for Sterio's, which is open for breakfast (7 to 10 a.m. Monday through Friday), lunch (11 a.m. to 4:30 p.m. Monday through Saturday), and dinner (4:30 to 11 p.m. Monday through Saturday). Your breakfast will cost in the $3 to $8 range, with lunch from $3 for a salad to $11 for an open-faced steak sandwich. Dinner, served in the continental/French tradition, includes dishes like chicken breast amandine à la Sterio's ($10.95), lamb chops à la touron ($20.75), etc. Reservations suggested.

Down the hill from Syracuse University stands **Phoebe's Garden Cafe**, 900 East Genesee St. (tel. 315/487-2489). Decorated with antiques, large plants, brass light fixtures, and bentwood chairs, this charming restaurant is a local favorite. Between the enclosed porch, the lounge, the secluded dining room, and the terraced atrium, one never gets bored in this lively environment. Lunch is available Monday through Saturday from 11:30 a.m. to 4:30 p.m.; Sunday brunch is served until 3:30 p.m. Midday meal selections include sandwiches, burgers, and entrees like chicken and shrimp jambalaya, and cost between $4 and $10. Evening meals are served daily from 5 to 11 p.m., to midnight on Friday and Saturday, with an 8 p.m. closing on Sunday. The dinner fare is moderate ($8 to $14 range), and reservations are suggested.

Back downtown again, a great restaurant for lighter fare is **Pastabilities,** 311 South Franklin St., next to Armory Square (tel. 315/474-1153). As the name suggests, Pastabilities features and makes its own pasta for a variety of hot dishes and cold salads. Music is played in the courtyard in summer, and inside the restaurant on Saturday night. Open Monday through Saturday, with lunch served cafeteria style from 11 a.m. to 3 p.m.; table-service dinner available from 5 to 10 p.m. on Monday and Tuesday, to 11 p.m. on Wednesday and Thursday, and to midnight on Friday and Saturday.

Ling Ling on The Square, 218 West Genesee St. (tel. 315/422-2800), is a very good Chinese restaurant with an obvious panda bear theme. The pale-gray and mauve decor is accented with an old tin ceiling and shell lanterns. A selection of 25 luncheon specials is served from 11:30 a.m. to 2:30 p.m., Monday through Friday, for $4 to $5. The standard menu contains 150 items costing between $1 and $13, all available from 11:30 a.m. to 9:30 p.m. Monday through Thursday, to 10:30 p.m. on Friday night, from noon to 10:30 p.m. on Saturday, and from noon to 9:30 p.m. on Sunday.

---

2. The Northern Tier

The New York State Thruway runs right across the top of the Finger Lakes. But in order to really see anything of the area, U.S. 20 (joined in places by N.Y. 5) will be your principal east-west route across the northern tier. Much of the road traverses vast rural areas. You climb steadily to the top of a ridge, admire an immense vista, descend to the bottom of a valley, and start all over again. The hills, like the lakes, all seem to run roughly north and south, and all seem about the same height.

Parts of U.S. 20 are pretty built-up, especially the stretch between the northern ends of Seneca and Cayuga Lakes. The north-south roads, however, that wend between the various lakes toward the southern tier are almost all extremely rural. Traffic is light, horizons are wide, the sky is big. The land has a solitary, muscular feel to it, rather like the Midwest. And psychologically that's exactly where it is.

We'll begin on the east and work our way toward Rochester. The first town we'll encounter is:

SKANEATELES

This might well be the prettiest community in the Finger Lakes. It was founded in 1794 and burned to the ground in 1835; many, if not most, of the buildings dating from its reconstruction still stand today.

Things to See and Do

The village is situated at the head of Skaneateles Lake, and it's a trove of white-columned Greek temples, elaborate Victorian summer houses, and manicured country estates. The architecturally handsome **business district** is on U.S. 20. **West Lake Road,** which intersects U.S. 20 within sight of the light at the center of town, consists of a fabulous procession of 19th-century summer houses, some of them quite grand. The surrounding countryside is mostly farmland. The look of the town may be somewhat different, but the atmosphere here is much like that of Cazenovia (described in Chapter XIII, "The Capital District").

There was a time when the denizens of Skaneateles did things like make potash, distill whisky, and grow teazles (a sort of Velcro-like plant used a century ago to raise the nap on woolen cloth). Nowadays they sail on the lake, make prudent investments, and lavish loving attention on their beautiful town.

You can sail on the lake too, on a handsome boat called the *Judge Ben Wiles* (it looks like an antique, but actually it's new). The **Mid-Lakes Navigation Co.** operates the *Judge Ben Wiles* from a dock opposite the Sherwood Inn, right in the middle of town. Various cruises are available, from the Mail Cruise (Mid-Lakes has one of the last water-route mail contracts in the U.S., and you can come along for $15 per person) to the Weekend Village Cruise (which takes about an hour and costs about $7), to the Dinner Cruise ($27, including a full meal). For information and reservations, call them at 315/685-5722 or 800/255-3709; cruises operate only in July and August.

Where to Stay and Eat in Skaneateles

The **Sherwood Inn**, 26 W. Genesee St. Skaneateles, NY 13152 (tel. 315/685-3405), is the nicest inn I saw in the whole Finger Lake District. It's a rambling 19th-century shingled affair with a big screened porch. It's painted blue with black shutters, and overlooks the lake, the *Judge Ben Wiles,* and one of the village's beautiful manicured parks. There's a remodeled colonial look inside, with putty-colored walls, brass chandeliers, wing chairs, and handsome woodwork. To one side of the lobby is a paneled tap room; on the other is an excellent restaurant, about which more in a moment. Upstairs are 13 very attractive rooms, furnished with brass beds, modern bathrooms, assorted antiques, and tasteful color schemes. No color TVs or phones here, but after all, it's a country inn. Open all year. Rates for a double room range from about $60 to $90 a night, depending on room size and location.

The **Sherwood Inn Restaurant** is a really charming and comfortable place, consisting of big, traditional rooms and, in the summer, the screened porch. It has crisp linens, attentive service, and good food. Sample items from the lunch menu include grilled chicken breast à l'orange, swordfish kebabs, etc., and cost about $4 to $8 on the average. The dinner menu features prime rib, crabmeat au gratin, swordfish, New York sirloin, duckling Cointreau, etc., priced from around $12 to $18 à la carte. The lunch menu is available all day in the tap room. Lunch is served daily all year long from 11:30 a.m. to 4 p.m.; dinner is from 5 to 10 p.m. (to 11 p.m. on Saturday).

Another famous place in Skaneateles is the **Krebs** (named after the family that once ran it as a boardinghouse), located on U.S. 20 heading west from the Sherwood Inn (tel. 315/685-5714 or 315/685-7001). This is a pretty little white house in the midst of a residential district. Out front is a small porch with rocking chairs and a neon sign reading "1899." Only dinner is served, a prix-fixe affair with either five or seven courses composed of solid and delicious American cooking. The price per person is about $20 to $27, depending on which meal you take. The first floor is given over to bright, airy dining rooms with flowers on the tables and white covers on the chairs. Upstairs is a little pine-paneled lounge and a couple of Victorian sitting rooms. Open from early May until late October; dinner is served from 4 to 9 p.m.; Sunday brunch is from 10:30 a.m. to 2 p.m.

For something quick, tasty, and cheap, try **Doug's Fish Fry,** which dispenses fries, chowder, clam strips, fried scallops and shrimp, gumbo, franks, fish sandwiches, etc., from a little storefront on Jordan Street (which intersects U.S. 20 at the light). Most things cost $2 or $3; full dinners run $4 to $6. Most of the business is take-out, but there's a counter against the wall, facing the open kitchen. Doug's is extremely popular; it's open all year, and every day in the summer. Hours are 11 a.m. to 9 p.m. (to 10 p.m. on Saturday); closed Sunday in the winter.

AUBURN

This vigorous little city lies but seven miles due west of Skaneateles on U.S. 20. Founded as Hardenbergh Corners at the end of the 18th century, it was renamed in 1803 after a poem by Goldsmith, "Auburn, loveliest village of the plain." Much of its historic loveliness has been sacrificed, however, on the altar of free-flowing traffic. The new "arterials" do carry you around in a hurry. But aesthetically they've done a lot of damage.

What to See

South Street (N.Y. 38) in Auburn is where the former squirearchy built their stately pleasure domes. Architecturally it's much beleaguered, but there are still some great houses along here. A drive down South Street to the city limits is worth it, if only to get Auburn's measure of its own worth in the era when measures were more tangible than they are today.

Also on South Street are two important attractions. The first is the **Seward House**, 33 South St. (tel. 315/252-1283). This was the home of William Henry Seward, one of America's greatest secretaries of state. Seward was the man whose famous speech in 1850 refuted the constitutional "rights" of slaveholders, claiming that there was a "higher law than the Constitution." He was a two-term governor of New York, a founder of the Republican party, and a proponent of the acquisition of Alaska (known as "Seward's Ice Box"). His imposing painted brick house is actually a chaste Federal town house much enlarged. As a matter of fact, it was the first brick house in Auburn. The interior was redecorated with singular lavishness in the mid-Victorian period and it's something to see, especially its sexy staircase and window treatments. The walls of the second-floor hall are covered with pictures of every dignitary Seward ever met (quite a collection). Seward descendants lived here until 1951. Open from 1 to 4 p.m.; closed Sunday, Monday and the months of January and February. Adult admission is $2.50; for seniors it's $2.

"There are two things I've got a right to, and these are liberty or death. One or the other I mean to have. No one will take me back alive." So said Harriet Tubman during her years in the Underground Railroad. Tubman was a black woman who escaped slavery and returned again and again to the South as a "conductor," one who led other black people north to freedom. She is credited with saving at least 300 souls. Her code name was "Moses," and so famous did she become that a bounty was on her head all over the South. Interestingly, few believed the intrepid Moses was really a woman. William Seward, resident of an Auburn mansion at the north end of South Street, sold Harriet Tubman a far more modest house at the south end of that same thoroughfare. Here in the last days of her life she ran a home for aged black people. The house still stands, a simple two-story frame affair set back from the road right at the city line. The historic plaque out front reads as follows: "Harriet Tubman—Moses of her people—served the underground railroad—frequented this site after the Civil War." Although not open to the public on a regular basis, the **Tubman House** can be visited by appointment, Monday through Friday from 11 a.m. to 5 p.m. Those interested should call 315/253-2621 to make arrangements. The exact address is 180 South Rd.

On a lighter note, Auburn also has a **dinner theater,** presented during July and August in the ballroom of the Springside Inn, West Lake Road (N.Y. 38) (tel. 315/252-7247). Productions have included *Evita, Carousel,* and *Fiddler on the Roof.* The total cost for dinner and a show is around $32 on weekends, and $30 during the week. The Springside is an excellent restaurant, and an ambient inn as well; see the description below.

Where to Stay and Eat in Auburn

Right in the middle of town is the **Holiday Inn,** 75 North St., Auburn, NY 13021 (tel. 315/253-4531), with an enclosed atrium that contains a swimming pool and 178 very nice modern rooms distributed on five floors. There's a bar/lounge, a big restaurant, and all the rooms have phones, color TVs, immaculate modern baths, and all the traditional Holiday Inn-type comforts. Double rates range from $55 to about $70 nightly, depending on location and whether or not you want a king-size bed.

The aforementioned **Springside Inn,** West Lake Road (N.Y. 38), Auburn, NY 13021 (tel. 315/252-7247), is a many-gabled red Victorian structure that's out of town, but only by about five minutes (these places don't sprawl too much). It's set back on lovely grounds and is of interest to us equally because of its restaurant and its rooms. First the restaurant: it's big and beamed, and possesses a large stone fireplace and a handsome casual atmosphere. Only dinner is served from a "Bill of Fare" that includes sautéed veal, lobster tail, filet mignon, chicken Cordon Bleu, etc., priced from around $9 to $15 à la carte. Daily hours are 5 to 10 p.m.; Sunday brunch runs from 10:30 a.m. to 2 p.m.; Sunday dinner is from 1 to 6 p.m.

The rooms upstairs are totally idiosyncratic, furnished with stray antiques, thrift-shop pieces, old wallpaper, and the occasional acoustic ceiling. The bathrooms have a summer-camp look and the floors creak. But it's clean, and it does have charm and atmosphere. And at $60 double, including breakfast, you can't go wrong.

A good place for convivial bar room atmosphere, a youthful crowd, rock and roll on the jukebox, and $4 burgers and sandwiches is **Curley's,** adjacent to one of Auburn's swooping arterials at 96 State St. (tel. 315/252-5224). Besides a great, loud, dimly lit bar is a multilevel dining room with dark wood paneling, colored-glass hanging lamps, and a quieter atmosphere. Besides the bar menu you can order evening dinners like fried scallops, stuffed pork chops, all manner of pasta dishes, hot sandwiches, plus steaks and prime rib. Prices for the big entrees are in the $10 to $13 range; hot sandwiches and pastas cost around $5 to $7. Open for lunch from 11 a.m. to 2:30 p.m., and dinner from 5 to 9 p.m. The bar, of course, is open much later; closed Sunday.

SENECA FALLS

This old mill town, about 15 miles west of Auburn on N.Y. 5 and U.S. 20, has wide streets, a comfy ungentrified air, and a 19th-century brick-and-stone downtown area that's eloquent of former wealth and power. Seneca Falls is also a truly historic place, being the site in 1848 of the first Women's Rights Convention. Two local residents, Elizabeth Cady Stanton and Amelia Bloomer, gained national recognition—and suffered a good deal of abuse—for among other things their work drafting a "Declaration of Sentiments" approved by the convention. Although they ultimately eliminated the demand for the vote, the document contained some pretty strong language anyway: "The history of mankind is a history of repeated injuries and usurpations on the part of man towards woman having in direct object the establishment of an absolute tyranny over her." This tyranny is then itemized in a manner that raised the hackles of almost every Victorian gentleman in the land. The document notes that, "in view of this entire disenfranchisement of one-half of the people of this country . . . we insist that they have immediate admission to all the rights and privileges which belong to them as citizens of these United States."

Today in Seneca Falls is something called the **Women's Rights National Historical Park,** which is dedicated to the memory of these very courageous women. There are plenty of men today who would become violent reading the whole Declaration. One can imagine the courage it took to draft it in 1848. The Women's Rights Historical Park is still in its infancy, and as a practical matter, there's not too much as yet that's open to the public. But there is a very informative and, yes, stirring, **Visitors' Center** at 116 Fall St. next door to the Gould Hotel on U.S. 20, plus four historic sites scattered between Seneca Falls and the nearby town of Waterloo. Not all of these sites are open to the public. The building that housed the convention, "The Other Independence Hall," is currently a laundromat, unrecognizable after a century-plus of alterations. The Stanton house has been restored and is open to the public from 9 a.m. to 5 p.m. June to September (and by appointment at other times). Two additional houses that figured prominently in events leading up to the Convention remain in private hands. The park is administered by the U.S. Department of the Interior, and the local address is P.O. Box 70, Seneca Falls, NY 13148 (tel. 315/568-2991). The Visitors' Center is open all year from 9 a.m. to 5 p.m. Monday through Friday, and on weekends too from 9 a.m. to 5 p.m. between April and November. Even if there isn't as yet too much to see, there's lots for us all to learn here, and the place is worthy of a pilgrimage.

Also in Seneca Falls is a converted bank building that is now the home of the **National Women's Hall of Fame,** 76 Fall St. (tel. 315/568-2936). This, too, is a modest attraction, notwithstanding the importance of its mission. So far 38 women have been elected to the Hall of Fame, individuals ranging from Amelia Earhart to Emily Dickinson, from Abigail Adams to Harriet Tubman, and from Eleanor Roosevelt to Elizabeth Cady Stanton. The mission of this institution is to honor women "whose contributions to the arts, athletics, business, education, government, the humanities, philanthropy, and science have been the greatest value for the development of their country." Photos and descriptive text tell the story of each woman honored. Some of these tales are truly amazing. Open Monday through Saturday from 10 a.m. to 4 p.m.; on Sunday, too, May through October from noon to 4 p.m. Admission is $3 for adults and $2 for seniors and students. During my fieldwork I didn't find a single local person who had visited either this or the Women's Rights Historical Park. Too bad—I thought they were very impressive.

Where to Eat (and Maybe Stay)

The **Gould,** at the corner of Fall and State Streets, Seneca Falls, NY 13148 (tel. 315/568-5801), is an old brick building in the center of town right next door to the Visitors' Center of the Women's Rights National Park. It has an opulent, late-Victorian look inside, a function of chandeliers with tinted-glass shades, potted palms, pictures in heavy gilt frames, and rich woodwork. Lunch might be a Monte Cristo, eggs Benedict, fettuccine carbonara, an energy salad, or a Gould burger, priced variously from about $5 to $8. At dinner there is breast of chicken, broiled sea scallops, pork chops, filet mignon, veal chasseur, etc., costing between $10 and $17. Lunch is served on weekdays only from 11:30 a.m. until 2 p.m.; dinner is a daily affair from 4 to about 9 (on Sunday it's from 4 to 8 p.m.). Most of the building is occupied by apartment residents. But at this writing there were ten rooms available to transients, costing between $60 and $65 nightly double occupancy. They have high ceilings, plush carpets, private bathrooms, Victorian furniture, clock radios, color TVs, and lots of space. The $75 suite is perfectly enormous.

GENEVA

Geneva, at the head of Seneca Lake, is among other things the "Lake Trout Capital of the World." It's a moderate-size upstate town with a lakefront boulevard (N.Y. 5 and U.S. 20) behind which lies an elderly downtown business district. **Castle Street** is the main drag, off of which radiate several architecturally interesting side streets. Those who like to explore old towns should peruse both **North and South Main Streets,** and **Genesee Street.** Despite ill-considered modernizations here and there, the place retains a vintage upstate charm. It certainly has a lot of churches too.

South Main Street bends around the top of Seneca Lake, and shortly after crossing a viaduct over N.Y. 5/U.S. 20, comes to **Hobart and William Smith Colleges.** The combined campuses of this pair of liberal arts institutions (one for men, the other for women) constitute a dignified and leafy enclave. South Main hereabouts is lined with elegant houses, many of which belong to the local fraternities and sororities. N.Y. 5/U.S. 20 west of town is lined with shopping centers, a factor in the current condition of Castle Street.

On the east side of Geneva is a splendid restored Greek Revival mansion that's the pride of the entire region. This is **Rose Hill,** on N.Y. 96A a mile south of N.Y. 5/U.S. 20 (tel. 315/789-3848). Dating from the 1840s, the house was once the center of a large model farm. Its magnificent pillared portico overlooks Seneca Lake and is a landmark visible from Geneva. The entire house has been painstakingly restored and furnished through the generosity of an anonymous donor. Wallpapers, chandeliers, silver, Empire antiques, etc., are all of museum quality. Tours start with a slide show that tells the tale of Rose Hill's ups and downs (like many such estates, it too once teetered on the edge of demolition). Outside is an exquisite formal garden. Surely one of the most beautiful sites in the Finger Lakes, Rose Hill is open May through October, Monday through Saturday from 10 a.m. to 4 p.m. and on Sunday from 1 to 5 p.m. Admission is $2 for adults and $1 for kids.

This town is graced with not one but two exceedingly splendid former mansions now operating as true country inns. The first is called **Geneva on the Lake**, N.Y. 14 (an extension of South Main Street), P.O. Box 929, Geneva, NY 14456 (tel. 1-800-3GENEVA). This place was an absolutely first-class private house in its day. It was completed in 1914 for one Byron M. Nester, to plans drawn by Lewis Albro and the famous Harrie T. Lindeberg. In 1949 the Catholic church, which then owned the property, added a pair of modern flanking wings to the central section, which Albro and Lindeberg had closely modeled on an Italian Renaissance palace.

The present owners, the Schickel family, at first altered the building into luxury apartments, each with a full kitchen and usually one or two bedrooms. They later decided to operate it as a resort hotel wherein the original apartments would become luxurious suites. Those in the Catholic wings are quite lush and modern, but those in the old house have sumptuous architectural details. They all have first-class traditional reproduction furniture, color TVs, and private telephones. Between the house and the lakefront are elaborate gardens with clipped ornamental hedges and a knockout of a swimming pool, and down by the lake itself is a private boathouse. There's no big lobby or restaurant here, but throughout the year dinner is served on Friday, Saturday, and Sunday evenings in what was formerly the main hall and is now called the Villa Lancellotti Dining Room, to the accompaniment of live musical entertainment each evening. Also served is the master chef's magnificent Sunday brunch, as well as breakfast each morning throughout the year. Typical main courses cost between $25 and $30. Double-occupancy rates depend on size and location of the various rooms and range from about $167 to $318 between May 15 and October 31, $127 to $278 between November 1 and May 14; discounts for longer stays. My favorite rooms are in the original house, but I hasten to add that every unit really is beautiful and the Schickel family bring a new meaning to the word hospitality.

A bit farther south on N.Y. 14 is **Belhurst Castle**, P.O. Box 609, Geneva, NY 14456 (tel. 315/781-0201). This place is a perfectly immense stone Victorian mansion with ivy-clad walls and a huge slate roof. It sits brooding in the middle of a park of mature trees overlooking Seneca Lake. Built in 1885, it is the very definition of the term "white elephant." And yet it's also quite wonderful, and mercifully quite unspoiled. Inside are lots and *lots* of dark shiny paneling, immense fireplaces, and ornate light fixtures. This place is as satisfyingly elaborate as one could wish. The entire downstairs—conservatory, porches, drawing rooms, dining room, the lot— is now a huge atmospheric restaurant. Lunch is a buffet affair priced at about $7. Dinner is à la carte, chosen from a menu that contains such things as veal Oscar, scallops au gratin, poached salmon, lobster thermidor, duck à l'orange, prime rib, filet mignon, etc. Prices are in the $15 to $20 range for entrees.

Upstairs are 12 great old-fashioned mansion bedrooms, each with a modern private bath, most with natural woodwork, some with ornate mantelpieces, all with lofty ceilings and oodles of atmosphere. Among other things this place was once a casino operated by a high-liver called "Red" Dwyer. Today on the second-floor landing it still has a gravity-fed spigot that dispenses gratis glasses of wine.

The Belhurst is open all year and charges between $80 and $115 a night for two people, depending on the room. A few elaborate suites are available for $160 to $200, double. The restaurant is open daily for lunch from 11:30 a.m. to 2 p.m., and for dinner from 5 to 9:30 p.m. Sunday brunch is served from 11 a.m. to 2 p.m.

For more moderate fare in modern and very appealing surroundings, try the

Crow's Nest, located on the lake beside a small marina off N.Y. 96A (tel. 315/ 781-0600). Take the first right turn on 96A below N.Y. 5/U.S. 20, cross the tracks, and turn immediately right again (I found it; I suppose you can too). This trim little gray-shingled place has a pretty water-view terrace shaded by locust trees, and an airy dining room with gray industrial carpeting and white walls. Lunch (or "launch," as the menu terms it) might be something like an open steak sandwich, crabmeat salad plate, chicken in the nest, beer-boiled cold shrimp, etc., which might cost anywhere from $4 to $8. Sample dinner entrees include broiled scallops, broiled haddock, veal parmigiana, baked chicken, fantail shrimp, plus steak and duckling, priced mostly between $8 and $18. Lighter items are also available at dinner. Open every day, all year: lunch is served from 11 a.m. to 4 p.m.; dinner is from 4 to 9 p.m. (to 10 p.m. on weekends).

CANANDAIGUA

Although settled in the late 18th century, Canandaigua has a decidedly late-Victorian look to it. Main Street, a very broad four-lane thoroughfare, runs perpendicular to the shore of Canandaigua Lake, gradually ascending a gentle hill and (oddly) becoming more handsome the farther it gets from the water. Rising above the center of Main Street, and dominating the entire skyline, is the dome of the Ontario County Courthouse. Everything is very straight and orderly in this town: even the land is fairly flat. Canandaigua has the decided look and feel of the Midwest.

What to See and Do

The name Canandaigua is a corruption of the Indian term for "chosen place." In 1863 a New York City banker by the name of Frederick Ferris Thompson chose it for the site of an elaborate Victorian country estate which he called **Sonnenberg** ("Sunny Hill" in German). After Thompson's death in 1902, his wife, Mary Clark Thompson, proceeded to create a great garden in his memory. The Smithsonian calls Sonnenberg "one of the most magnificent late Victorian gardens ever created in America." And this is no understatement.

After 40 years of neglect under U.S. government ownership, Sonnenberg was purchased by a preservation-oriented foundation that has undertaken the restoration of the Versailles-like gardens, plus the task of restoring and refurnishing the main house. The estate sits on a 50-acre superblock right in the middle of Canandaigua. It feels like you're off in the country, but really you aren't. The mansion, designed by one Francis Allen, is a great big gloomy Queen Anne Victorian monster, its roof spikey with towers and pinnacles and chimneys, and its interior a bit vast and cold.

The gardens, however, are beautiful and elaborate almost beyond belief. There are shaped yews, formal axes, geometric beds of annuals, marble fountains, statues of lions, putti, goddesses, magnificent retaining walls, a rose garden with elaborate semicircular beds, a Japanese Garden with tea house and tumbling brook, a colonial garden with a quarter mile of boxwood hedge and a formal aviary, even an outdoor Roman bath (the as-yet-unrestored estate swimming pool). And this is just a partial list. Also on the premises is a lunchroom, located in a wing of the greenhouse complex and called the Peach House. You can get sandwiches and quiches here for between $5 and $6 every day that Sonnenberg is open.

Admission is $5 for adults, $2 for kids. Open every day mid-May until mid-October from 9:30 a.m. to 5:30 p.m. It's truly something to see. There are signs on Main Street directing you to the main gate of Sonnenberg. If you need any further information, call them at 716/924-5420.

If you're not up to your gills yet with historic houses, have a look at the **Granger Homestead** and its adjacent **Carriage Museum,** 295 N. Main St. (tel. 716/394-1472). Gideon Granger (1767–1822) was both a founder of Canandaigua and United States postmaster for both Presidents Jefferson and Madison. When completed in 1816, his elegant three-story Federal mansion was, in his own words, "unrivaled in all the Nation." After Sonnenberg, it's almost simple. Yet this is a magnificent example of early American architecture, one that would look quite at home on some patrician street in Salem or Providence. The adjacent Carriage Museum has sleighs and surreys and buckboards and barouches, and introduces visitors to the use of horse-drawn vehicles in Victorian society.

The charge to visit both the house and the carriage museum is $2.50 for adults and $1 for kids. Combination tickets admitting one to both Sonnenberg and Granger are available at both sites and cost $6 per person. The Granger House is open May through October, Tuesday through Saturday from 10 a.m. to 5 p.m., and on Sunday from 1 to 5 p.m.

About ten miles from Canandaigua, off Exit 44 of the New York State Thruway, is the **Finger Lakes Race Track,** home of the $125,000 New York State Breeders' Futurity. There's space for 4,000 cars, and you can wager on two daily doubles, seven exactas, and two trifectas. Post time is 1:30 p.m. from April through November. Between May and late June there's also Twilight Racing with a 4 p.m. post time. General admission is $2; call 716/924-3232 for further information.

The newest attraction in the area is the **Finger Lakes Performing Arts Center** at the Community College of the Finger Lakes (tel. 716/454-2620), which is now the summer home of the **Rochester Philharmonic Orchestra** (tel. 716/222-5000). The center features outdoor classical, pops, and superstar concerts from June to September. Call them for schedules and prices.

To appreciate the Finger Lakes one has to get on the water, so try **Captain Gray's Boat Tours** (tel. 716/394-5270). These one-hour lecture tours of Canandaigua Lake originate at the Sheraton Inn dock at the foot of Main Street at 2, 4, 6 and 8 p.m. daily between June and September.

Where to Eat and Stay

In the historic Main Street area of downtown Canandaigua are two great restaurants in the same National Register 1886 brick building. On the first floor is the more formal **Cricketts,** 169 So. Main St. (tel. 716/394-7990), with a country-style decor consisting of fine print wallpaper, chair rails, and polished wood floors. A lunch of creative sandwiches or perhaps broiled swordfish is served Monday through Saturday between 11:30 a.m. and 2:30 p.m., and costs in the $4 to $7 range. Dinners are available Tuesday through Saturday from 5:30 to 10 p.m. (summer Sundays from 3:30 to 9 p.m.) and feature such dishes as chicken with champagne and raspberry sauce, beef Wellington, etc., priced from $9 to $18.

On the second floor you'll find **Burk's Tavern and Oyster Bar** (tel. 716/394-7990) for more casual dining. There is an open-hearth fireplace, and the mood is San Francisco jazz and swing. Thick deli-style sandwiches and seafood at the oyster bar are served Monday through Saturday from 11 a.m. to 11 p.m. with a buffet between 5:30 and 8 p.m. The cost is from $4 to $12. Live entertainment on weekends.

For more stylish dining, try the **Lincoln Hill Inn,** 3365 E. Lake Rd. (tel. 716/394-8254), located in an old brick farmhouse on the outskirts of town. The Lincoln Hill consists of a pleasant collection of rooms on two levels, decorated with exposed brick walls, crisp linens, deep-burgundy accents, and lots of candlelight. At dinner you can choose from a list of entrees that includes whisky chicken, prime rib, tournedos, broiled pork chops, pasta primavera, coquilles St. Jacques, etc., and costs between $10 and $18. Dinner is served every day from 4 to 10 p.m. (until 11 p.m. on Friday and Saturday, and 9 p.m. on Sunday). Open all year.

The best place to stay in town is the lakeside **Thendara Inn and Restaurant,** which is actually four miles south of U.S. 20 at 4356 East Lake Rd., Canandaigua, NY 14424 (tel. 716/394-4868). The restaurant is elegantly detailed with breathtaking views of the lake. Dinner only is served Monday through Saturday from 6 to 10 p.m. and on Sunday from noon to 7 p.m. These gourmet meals cost from $10 to $19; lighter fare is available at the **Boathouse** on the lake every day in the summer (May to October) from 11 a.m. to 2 a.m. Burgers and fish fries cost from $4 to $8.

The inn has five rooms, all with private baths and one with a skylit Jacuzzi, priced from $75 to $115 a night including a continental breakfast. Closed from January to mid-March.

Budget accommodations abound along the N.Y. 5/U.S. 20 strip east of town. Alternatively, you might try the **Sheraton-Canandaigua Inn on the Lake,** 770 S. Main St., Canandaigua, NY 14424 (tel. 716/394-7800, or toll free 800/325-3535). This is a big, deluxe lakefront motel at the end of a long landscaped drive. Low wings flare this way and that and a big illuminated "S" graces the side of a dramatic stone wall. There are 147 rooms, a big beautiful outdoor pool, a restaurant, bar, lakefront gardens, and a busy resort atmosphere. The entire place is undergoing refurbishment/redecoration. As it happens, the 1970s-vintage room decor isn't bad at all. Accommodations all have color TVs, private phones, and nice Sheraton-quality furnishings. By the time you read this, they'll be even spiffier. Rates vary according to the season and the view from the room. Doubles will pay anywhere from a summertime high of about $75 to $95 nightly, down to a midwinter low of around $45 to $60.

You can save money and stay in very comfortable and attractive surroundings at the **Budget Host-Heritage Motor Inn,** N.Y. 5/U.S. 20, Canandaigua, NY 14424 (tel. 716/394-6170). This little motel, situated opposite Nichols Discount City, contains but two dozen immaculately clean rooms, each with cable color TV, shiny black built-in furniture, 1960s-moderne lamps, and private baths. The year-round double rate is $36, and that's a bargain. No pool, no private phones in the rooms, no restaurant. But so what? Or there's an **Econo Lodge,** Canandaigua, NY 14424 (tel. toll free 800/446-6900), just down the road. This establishment offers quite nice modern rooms, each with private bath, wall-to-wall carpeting, color TV, telephone, plus a lobby full of vending machines. Double-occupancy rates for the 65 rooms range between about $44 and $48 in the summer, and $39 and $47 in the winter, the higher rates being for a room with a king-size bed.

Kellogg's Pan-Tree Inn, 130 Lake Shore Dr., Canandaigua, NY 14424 (tel. 716/394-3909), is a modest, modernish motel-restaurant opposite Canandaigua's lakefront park. Luncheon sandwiches and salads are in the $3 to $4 range mostly; dinner entrees like chicken pie, fish fry, ham steak, french-fried shrimp, etc., cost about $7 to $10. Hours are 7 a.m. to 7:30 p.m. daily. Behind the bright, 1950s-looking restaurant is a collection of little flat-roofed buildings, each of which contains a trio of motel units. Rooms have shag rugs, twin double beds, private baths, cable color TVs, color-tiled baths, and an appealing vintage motel look. They're cheap too: $42 to $46 nightly per double in the late-June to Labor Day peak, $34 to $38 the rest of the open season. The entire establishment closes from late October until the beginning of May.

3. Rochester

Everybody told me I'd like Rochester, and they were right. This appealing old city of about a quarter million inhabitants has lots of architecturally important neighborhoods to explore, plenty of exciting and unusual restaurants, places to stay with character, and a number of unique and interesting sightseeing attractions. There are even a lively nightlife and abundant good shopping.

Rochester straddles the Genesee River, which fact is not immediately apparent. You can zip back and forth across the many downtown bridges without even noticing that you're on top of dramatic rapids, and adjacent to a waterfall with a 100-foot drop. The power of this falling water fueled early sawmills and nurtured later industries that would eventually become international giants. Rochester was the cradle of Eastman Kodak, Bausch and Lomb, Sybron, and even Xerox. It's a city whose native industrialists have poured millions upon millions of dollars into local philanthropies. Paramount among them was George Eastman, the bachelor industrialist whose dry plate and film company founded in 1882 now employs 50,000 people here. Eastman donated the money for the University of Rochester, the famous Eastman School of Music, the Rochester Philharmonic, even for the construction of a number of local parks.

Rochester is also the town where Western Union was founded, where the escaped slave Frederick Douglass printed his famous newspaper *The North Star,* where the famous anarchist Emma Goldman took her first American factory job at the age of 17, and where Susan B. Anthony was arrested while trying to vote. So much milling was once done within the city limits that Rochester was called for a time the "Flour City." Nurseries and horticultural establishments eventually became so prevalent that the nickname was changed to the "Flower City."

Of course, everything has not been roses in Rochester's past. Urban decline, riots in the early 1960s, flight to the suburbs, the growth of the Sunbelt—all took their toll hereabouts. But the city today is active, vital, livable, and terribly efficient. There is a downtown core of glass high-rises, looped and relooped by a perhaps overly efficient system of expressways. There is a high consciousness of the value of old buildings and these are being restored and refurbished all over town. It's an easy place to get around too, and parking is convenient.

WHAT TO SEE AND DO IN ROCHESTER

Be advised of the existence of the very helpful **Rochester Convention and Visitors Bureau,** 126 Andrews St., Rochester, NY 14604 (tel. 716/546-3070). The office is staffed by trained professionals who are not only anxious but also quite able to help visitors with all sorts of suggestions and advice. The bureau is a source for maps, brochures on historic walking tours (see below), and all manner of additional touristic publications. They maintain a 24-hour telephone number too, with a recorded message listing current events and activities around town. Called the **Surprise Line,** the number is 716/546-6810.

GeVa, which is institutionalized shorthand for the Genesee Valley Arts Association, is a residential professional theater in Rochester. It mounts between six and eight Broadway-type productions every year. The theater, in a restored brick-and-limestone building at the corner of Woodbury and Clinton Avenues, has a wonderful period interior. For ticket and program information you can write in advance to GeVa, 75 Woodbury Ave., Rochester, NY 14604, or phone them at 716/232-1363.

On the south side of Rochester, down Mount Hope Avenue, is **Highland Park,** the scene each May of the annual Festival of Lilacs. Laid out in 1888 by a pioneer local nurseryman named Ellwanger, Highland Park's 20 acres of nothing but lilacs (not counting the 10,000 hand-planted pansies and the 15,000 tulip bulbs in the borders) are something to see. There are 1,200 bushes and 500 varieties, plus festival events under a big tent. Lots of fun, and the aroma of all those lilacs is unforgettable.

George Eastman's house, on Rochester's millionaires' row called East Avenue, has been carefully preserved as the **International Museum of Photography at George Eastman House,** 900 East Ave. (tel. 716/271-3361). This is a very big and elaborate mansion, in a Colonial Revival style, with imposing fluted Corinthian columns overlooking East Avenue. Inside is a unique museum that is divided into displays showing the evolution of cameras and photography, and a collection of famous photographs by past and present masters of the art. In the rear section of the building are huge galleries filled with zillions of cameras, plus curious contraptions like a zoetrope (a spinning slitted drum with pictures mounted on the inside) and a mutoscope (crank it and it flips a pack of cards) that were the forerunners of motion pictures. Upstairs are galleries full of prints by everyone from Weegee to Cecil Beaton to Henri Cartier-Bresson. You could spend an entire day looking at these pictures, some of which are quite haunting. Eastman's house is something to see as well. In 1932 Eastman himself, having contracted a degenerative disease and already in his 70s, put all his affairs in order, went up to his room one evening, and shot himself. He left a note which read, "I have done all I set out to do. Why wait any longer?" The Museum of Photography is open Tuesday through Sunday from 10 a.m. to 4:30 p.m.; admission is $2 for adults and $1.50 for students.

Another important Rochester philanthropist was Margaret Woodbury Strong, whose gift to Rochester was the **Strong Museum,** One Manhattan Square (actually Woodbury Avenue; tel. 716/263-2700). Opened in 1982, this is a huge, low-slung, ultramodern downtown installation with great expanses of smoked glass and cast concrete, set among clipped lawns dotted with overscale modern sculpture. The setting is ironic, since the collection itself consists of domestic artifacts from the 19th and early 20th centuries that taken together illustrate changes in American traditions, styles, and pastimes from a middle-class living room point of view. There really is a lot of nifty stuff here, organized in changing displays with names like "Light of the Home: Middle Class Women, 1870 to 1910," "Changing Patterns: Household Furnishings, 1820 to 1929," "The Great Transformation," etc. The permanent collection contains something like 20,000 dolls, plus all manner of textiles, furniture, ceramics, old toys, etc. Open Monday through Saturday from 10 a.m. to 5 p.m., on Sunday from 1 to 5 p.m. Admission is $2 for adults, $1.50 for seniors and students, and 75¢ for kids.

One of the Kodak Plants in Rochester is also open to visitors during the summer. **Kodak Park,** 200 Ridge Rd. West, off I-390, is the company's largest and employs 28,000 people. It's a self-contained city with its own power plants, fire department, railroad, and 200 different buildings in which photographic films, papers, and chemicals are manufactured. Tours are free and take about an hour apiece. They're offered from mid-May to mid-September, Monday through Friday at 9:30 a.m. and 1:30 p.m. For tour information, call 716/722-2465.

Looking around town is a source of considerable pleasure in Rochester. Indeed, this town has more buildings listed on the National Register of Historic Places than any other municipality of equivalent size. For an informative strolling tour of downtown, go to the Convention and Visitors Bureau at 126 Andrews St. and ask for the brochure titled "170 Years in One Square Mile." There's enough detail in this little illustrated booklet to satisfy the most eager of architectural historians. Even if you don't tour the downtown pavements on foot, try and have a look at **City Hall,** 30 Church St., a superb, late-1880s Romanesque structure with a vintage three-story interior atrium. The building is open to the public on weekdays from 9 a.m. to 5 p.m. And while you're in the area, be sure to look up at the wings on top of the **Times Square Building,** off Main and State—very Flash Gordon.

Rochester's millionaire's row was along **East Avenue.** Although most of the great mansions built in the late 19th and early 20th centuries have been converted to either apartments or offices, the good news is that practically all of them are still standing. East Avenue very much preserves its original air of opulence and privilege. Almost every late-Victorian architectural style is represented, culminating in the restrained magnificence of the Eastman House. Be sure to drive down it.

Before the era of East Avenue, Rochester's elite were ensconced on the west side of town in what's called Corn Hill. The **Campbell-Whittlesey House,** at 123 S. Fitzhugh St., is an 1835 veteran of a neighborhood that has been rioted, expresswayed, abandoned, and finally reclaimed and gentrified. Many wonderful early-Victorian and Greek Revival houses exist hereabouts, and a meander through its streets will be just to the taste of architecturally/historically oriented travelers. The Campbell-Whittlesey House is one of those places that survived all manner of social and neighborhood upheavals, original furniture intact. Although modest by East Avenue standards, it's still chock-a-block with polychrome ceilings, gold cornices, and great period furniture. Most interesting is a set of "musical glasses," in their original box, and made to be played by rubbing a moistened finger on their respective rims. You can take a tour of the house any Tuesday through Friday from

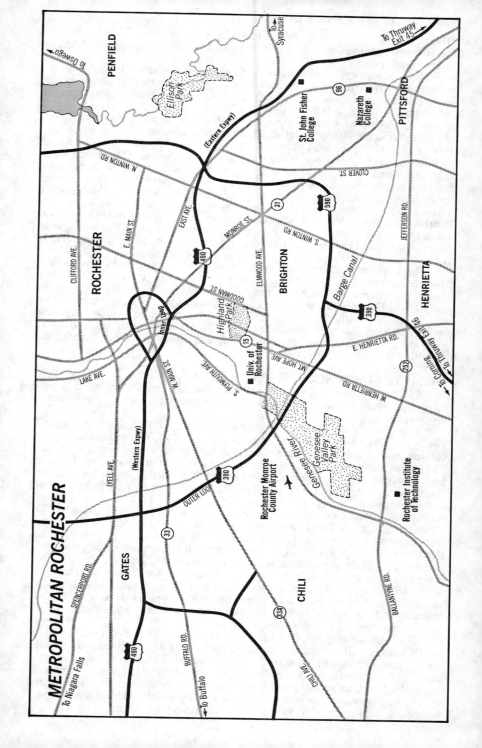

METROPOLITAN ROCHESTER

To Niagara Falls

PENFIELD

To Oswego

Ellison Park

To Syracuse

To Thruway Exit 45

ROCHESTER

St. John Fisher College

96

Nazareth College

PITTSFORD

(Eastern Expwy)

N WINTON RD.

CLIFFORD AVE.

E. MAIN ST.

EAST AVE.

CLOVER ST.

MONROE ST.

31

590

JEFFERSON RD.

490

ELMWOOD AVE.

S. WINTON RD.

BRIGHTON

GOODMAN ST.

Highland Park

15

Barge Canal

390

HENRIETTA

Inner Loop

Univ. of Rochester

MT HOPE AVE.

E. HENRIETTA RD.

LAKE AVE.

S PLYMOUTH AVE.

252

W. MAIN ST.

W HENRIETTA RD.

To Corning Thruway Expwy

(Western Expwy)

LYELL AVE.

Genesee River

Genesee Valley Park

390

Rochester Monroe County Airport

OUTER LOOP

SPENCERPORT RD.

33

GATES

Rochester Institute of Technology

BUFFALO RD.

To Buffalo

33A

CHILI

CHILI AVE.

BALLANTINE RD.

490

10 a.m. to 4 p.m., or on Sunday from 1 to 4 p.m. Admission is $1.50 for adults, 50¢ for students, and one thin dime for the kids. (P.S.: Take a look at nearby Atkinson Street for other good Corn Hill houses.)

There are all sorts of other things to ferret out in Rochester. If you've got the time, ask the Convention and Visitors Bureau for a copy of their tabloid-size visitor's guide called "You're Gonna Love Rochester," which goes into far more detail on local attractions than I can here.

But before we leave the field, you should also know about the **Genesee Country Village and Museum,** located about 20 miles southwest of Rochester on Flint Hill Road in Mumford, off Thruway Exit 46 (tel. 716/538-6822). This is a midwestern version of Sturbridge Village, a collection of 55 restored historical buildings, all moved to the site from other parts of the area. There are farmhouses, blacksmith shops, carriages, barns, old stores, and costumed denizens cooking soup, throwing pots, shoeing horses, staging parades, and organizing country fairs. There's also a carriage barn with 40 horse-drawn vehicles, as well as a gallery that contains the nation's largest collection of wildlife art. It's quite a place, very educational and very beautiful—120,000 visitors come here every year. Open daily mid-May through mid-October from 10 a.m. to 5 p.m. (to 4 p.m. in the spring and fall). Admission is $8 for adults, $7 for seniors, and $3.50 for kids.

The *Spirit of Rochester* (tel. 716/865-4930) is a triple-decked cruise ship, 150 feet long and 30 feet wide, that can accommodate 525 passengers. Docked on the Genesee River at the **Riverview Yacht Basin,** 18 Petten St., the *Spirit of Rochester* cruises Lake Ontario May through October. The ship's decks can be enclosed for foul weather, so it is therefore popular for celebration cruises on New Year's Eve and St. Patrick's Day. This vessel is regionally noted for the daily lunch cruise (noon to 2 p.m.) at $20 per person and for the chef's choice dinner buffet cruises (6 to 9 p.m.) for $35.

WHERE TO STAY IN ROCHESTER

This is a sizable town and there are many places to stay. Be reminded that the following suggestions constitute a much-abbreviated list, ranging from deluxe to moderate in price.

In the heart of downtown is the **Rochester Plaza,** 70 State St., Rochester, NY 14614 (tel. 716/546-3450, or toll free 800/468-3571). This ultramodern, rose-colored, hi-tech box is set on square columns and contains 364 luxurious rooms. The lobby level has lots of smoked glass and a vaguely art deco detailing. There are brass bands set into the buff-colored walls, dramatic floral arrangements, tailored contemporary furniture, and an air of low-key, big-city prosperity. The center of the building is an open courtyard with a beautiful swimming pool overlooked by mirrored walls. Rooms are very blond, pale buff, and rose. They all have cable color TVs, phones, clocks, thick rugs, plush headboards, upholstered armchairs, and an overall first-class look. Downstairs are all manner of bars and restaurants, appealingly decorated, and not cheap. Room rates are a bit of a tangle and depend entirely on supply and demand. The basic double rate seems to be about $100 nightly. But if you reserve a room in advance at the "supersaver" rate, you'll pay $69 double during the week and as low as $49 nightly on weekends. All manner of packages exist as well, and basically boil down to reduced room rates plus a few extras in return for advance reservations. The key to all of this is to call in advance. There's a slight surcharge for pool-view rooms, but city views are usually just as nice.

The **East Avenue Inn,** 384 East Ave., Rochester, NY 14607 (tel. 716/325-5010), has an excellent location that is both on the edge of downtown and also at the start of East Avenue's millionaires' row. It's a suave brick low-rise dating from the early 1950s. It is quiet, moderately priced, and friendly, and has plenty of free parking and 135 attractive and comfortable rooms. Accommodations are decorated with vintage photos of Rochester, and come with color TVs, phones, and white-tile bathrooms with stacks of fluffy towels. There's no pool, but there is an adjoining restaurant, called the Tavern and connected to the lobby by an open-air porte cochere. Double rooms cost between about $65 and $80, depending mostly on whether you want a double, two twins, or a king-size bed.

There are hot and cold running Holiday Inns all over Rochester, but the **Holiday Inn Rochester South,** 1111 Jefferson Rd., Rochester, NY 14623 (tel. 716/ 475-1510), is surely the state-of-the-art Holiday Inn of them all. The location is on the southern, suburban edge of Rochester, on a private triangular island completely surrounded by expressways. There are 250 rooms contained on six floors of brown brick. The place is turned in upon itself and focuses on an elaborate indoor atrium, a sort of Hanging Gardens of Babylon revisited, complete with pool, kiddy playground, and palm trees in planters. It looks quite good, and certainly dramatic. So do the guest rooms, which are decorated in fashionably pale shades of buff and blue, and contain color TVs, thick rugs, and plush furniture. Most doubles cost between $80 and $100 nightly; there are much better deals on weekend packages, some of which require as little as one night's stay.

The **Wellesey Inn,** East Henrietta Road, N.Y. 15E (adjacent to I-390 Exit 16), Rochester, NY 14623 (tel. 716/427-0130, or toll free 800/441-4479), has neither pool nor restaurant. But it does have rooms so new and so nice that you wonder how other people can charge so much for such similar accommodations. Rooms with king-size beds, color TVs, free parking, and very attractive tweedy/tailored furniture cost but $40 to $45 nightly. Next door is an outpost of the ubiquitous T.G.I. Friday's chain of bar-restaurants.

Closer to downtown, in the vicinity of the aforementioned Highland Park, is **Rose Mansion,** 625 Mount Hope Ave., Rochester, NY 14620 (tel. 716/546-5424). This is a delectable old house, mansionized in the mid-19th century by George Ellwanger, donor of all those lilac-covered acres in nearby Highland Park. The place is embowered in lush old trees and shrubbery, and contains very handsome public rooms on the main floor and eight perfectly lovely guest rooms upstairs. No phones or pool or TV, but instead the gracious atmosphere you can only find in a big old house. The rooms have names like Talisman, Medallion, Carousel, etc. (all different types of roses), and are furnished with rosewood antiques, the occasional brass bed, some handsome mantelpieces, period wallpaper, and private bathrooms. Rates: $90 a night buys an atmospheric double room plus two breakfasts in the morning.

And lastly, for not just a place to stay but also some local hospitality, try **Bed & Breakfast Rochester,** Box 444, Rochester, NY 14450 (tel. 716/223-8877). They represent over 16 B&B's in the area, have singles starting at $40, doubles at $45, and even a secluded cabin in the woods for $75 a night.

ROCHESTER RESTAURANTS

The old Gothic-style city hall of Rochester, built in 1873, now houses in its former jail cells **Chapel's,** 30 West Broad St. (tel. 716/232-2300), one of New York State's best French restaurants. The elegant conversion of these old prison cells into three distinct dining areas makes "doing time" nowadays an absolute culinary delight. Award-winning chef/owner Greg Broman and his wife/manager Colleen present "cuisine du marché" (food of the market) in superb French nouvelle style. The restaurant is decorated with a number of Margret Strong's antiques (see Strong Museum) and also has a 19th-century lounge area. A really great bargain and treat is lunch, available from 11:30 a.m. to 2 p.m. Tuesday through Friday, and priced in the $4 to $9 range. A true dining experience is the five-course dinner, perhaps starting with an oyster stew, after which one might choose the escargots "aux nouilles fraîches," move on to the salad with hazelnut vinaigrette, then to the entree, possibly a "feuillette of quail with spinach salpicon & deux sauces," and wind up with a dessert made daily by the pastry chef. Dinner is served from 5:30 to 9 p.m. Tuesday through Friday and on Sunday, and to 10 p.m. on Saturday. The cost of à la carte entrees is between $15 and $23.

Another luxury choice with a wholly different atmosphere is **Edward's,** just off Main Street at 13 S. Fitzhugh St. (tel. 716/423-0140). Considered by many to be the best restaurant in town, it occupies a rich Edwardian-accented suite of rooms in the basement of the 1873 Academy Building. Inside, all is dim and lush, with faux marble and mirrored accents, black flowered chintz pillows, walls covered with books and pictures, the tinkle of piano music, and the low music of cultivated laughter and clinking crystal. Lunch might be tournedos with wild rice, fresh pasta primavera in cream, poached chicken, vegetable quiche, etc., costing between $5 and $11. Dinners change daily, but might include à la carte entrees like coquilles St. Jacques, medallions of veal, sautéed chicken breast, tournedos, etc., priced between $15 and $29. Open for lunch from 11:30 a.m. to 2 p.m., for dinner from 6 to about 9 p.m. (until 10 p.m. on Friday and Saturday); closed Sunday.

Park Avenue, especially in those blocks near the intersection of Berkeley and Park, is a particularly appealing neighborhood about 20-odd blocks from downtown. It's an old residential area, a block away from the architectural glories of East Avenue, but possessing a distinct charm of its own. Park Avenue is a fine place to browse through little shops, stroll the tree-shaded streets on summer evenings, and catch a bite to eat at any of numerous inexpensive restaurants. A neighborhood standby is **Hogan's Hideaway,** which is located behind 197 Park Ave. (tel. 716/ 442-4293). This place is a local favorite and offers a great light menu with daily specials like quiches, omelets, and a vegetarian stir fry. Hogan's features a small bar/ lounge, greenhouse, and a café dining room, all of which are open Monday through Saturday from 11:30 a.m. to 11 p.m.

Nearby is **Charlie's Frog Pond,** 652 Park Ave. (tel. 716/271-1970). This place is cute, cheap, and decorated with frog motifs all over the place, plus booths, brass rails, and a jukebox full of rock and roll. Menu placemats list all manner of hot and cold sandwiches, eggs, omelets, homemade soups, salads, etc., most of which cost between about $2 and $5. Open Monday through Friday from 7 a.m. to 9 p.m., on Saturday from 8 a.m. to 7 p.m., and on Sunday from 9 a.m. to 3 p.m.

Between Park and East Avenues, is another restaurant row. There are lots of attractive places along here for moderately priced meals. For one of life's kinder and gentler experiences, try **Crème de la Crème,** located in an old Victorian townhouse at 295 Alexander St. (tel. 716/263-3580). After entering the canopied doorway and passing the stairway to several second-floor dining rooms, one is confronted with gigantic glass display cases filled with the most sinful selection of tortes, tarts, trifles, and truffles, to say nothing of the éclairs, mousses, napoleons, baklava, cheesecakes, pies, and cakes. If this doesn't have your tastebuds screaming for satisfaction, try a quiche or a seafood pita with cappuccino or perhaps some champagne. Open Monday through Saturday from 11 a.m. to 1 a.m. for light dining, and on Sunday from 9 a.m. to midnight. An English afternoon tea is served daily from 2 to 6 p.m., and a champagne brunch is offered on Saturday and Sunday until 3 p.m. All the desserts are priced at $2.95, with sandwiches and hot entrees in the $4 to $6 range.

A popular place for those still young at heart is the plumber dream theme restaurant **J. Wellington's Waterworks,** located "down-under" 315 Alexander St. (tel. 716/546-5770). This basement eatery is decorated with two-inch copper plumbing fixtures incorporated into the railings, coatracks, partitions, and the circular staircase to the bathrooms. Noted for its pizzas, hamburgers, potato skins, and ("for fowl food fanciers") chicken wings, the Waterworks is truly an American experience. The last time I dropped in, one could not help but notice a local businessman entertaining an entire table of Japanese dignitaries, who, despite obvious culture shock, were all having fun. With the exception of pizza, the individual menu prices are between $1.30 and $6.95. The restaurant is open seven days a week: from 11:30 a.m. to midnight Monday through Thursday, to 2 a.m. on Friday and Saturday. It opens at 5 p.m. on weekends and closes at midnight on Sunday.

Perhaps the best moderately priced restaurant in Rochester is the **Kopper Ket-**

tle, 976 Chili Ave. (tel. 716/235-8060). Chili (pronounced *Chy*-lye) Avenue is a major artery that runs west from the downtown area. The Kettle is large, modern, family run, and nicely decorated with wood paneling, stained-glass accents, thick rugs, and hanging plants. At either the counter area or the spacious dining room you can enjoy the usual gamut of salad-and-sandwich lunches, plus full meals like broiled pork chops, chicken croquettes, New York strip steak, grilled liver, shrimp and ham jambalaya, broiled rainbow trout, etc., priced from around $7 to $12. There are new specials almost every day. And on Monday and Tuesday there's even piano music in the dining room. Open for lunch ($4 to $5) from 11:30 a.m. to 2 p.m., and for dinner from 4:30 to 8:30 p.m. Closed Saturday and Sunday.

Rochester's suburban ring is full of good restaurants too. One of the most unusual is the **Red Creek Inn,** 300 Jefferson Rd. (tel. 716/424-1080), a barn-sided roadhouse in shopping-center land whose sign proclaims "Fine Food—Music—Drink—Friends." It's pretty big inside, and filled with tables in the greenhouse room, a big bar with a color TV, and lots of room for late-night dancing and entertainment. This might be anything from untried comedians to bands like the Skycoasters ("the partying-est band in town"), to Duke Robillart and the Pleasure Kings, to midweek DJ dance nights. A very extensive menu includes lunches like the incredible burrito, mucho macho nacho, chicken wings, hot pastrami, mozzarella burger, grilled cheese ("what can we say . . . it's very nice"), etc., most of which seem to cost between $2 and $6. The "Cajun Cookin'" menu offers dinners like blackened chicken, red snapper with pecan butter sauce, blackened sirloin steak, barbecued shrimp, etc., priced around $10 to $15. The kitchen is open Monday through Thursday from 11 a.m. to midnight, on Friday and Saturday to 1:30 a.m., and on Sunday to midnight.

The Filling Station, 30 Mount Hope Ave. (tel. 716/454-3416), is an innovative café converted from an oldtime automobile service station. The menu reflects the environment: "starters & tune ups" (appetizers), "fuels" (drinks), "lubricants" (salad dressings), "T-bird" sandwiches, and "customized" burgers. Decorated with a neon car motif and old automobile posters, the café has an airy California feel. The Filling Station is open every day of the week: from 7 a.m. to 10 p.m. Monday through Thursday, to 11 p.m. on Friday, from 9 a.m. to 11 p.m. on Saturday, and from 9 a.m. to 8 p.m. on Sunday. The Filling Station is known for its sandwiches, light dinners and desserts. Breakfast costs between $2 and $5; lunch is in the $4 to $7.50 range; dinner will cost you from $7.50 to $13.

About ten expressway minutes east of downtown Rochester is the **Daisy Flour Mill,** 1880 Blossom Rd. (tel. 716/381-1880). This indeed is a real mill, although it looks considerably more glamorous today than it did when Rochester was known as the "Flour City" and a succession of millers kept it running 24 hours a day. The interior is dim, multileveled, still equipped with a dizzying array of huge belts, silent machines, beams, and catwalks. There are exposed stone walls, a basement lounge called the Mill Race Bar, and all manner of atmospheric nooks and crannies furnished with tables and chairs. Dinner might be chicken Louisiana, veal picatta, prime rib, veal Rochester, Long Island duck, etc., the majority of which are priced between $8 and $16 à la carte. Weekday dinners are served from 5:30 to 10 p.m.; hours on Friday and Saturday are 5 to 11 p.m.; Sunday hours are 2 to 9 p.m. Open all week, year-round. There is no lunch service available. To get there, take the Blossom Road exit eastbound from I-590.

ROCHESTER MISCELLANY

There's an abundance of good bars in town, an unusual one being **Blades,** 1290 University Ave. (tel. 716/442-6979), in a former sawblade factory on the south side of town. It's a particularly popular and atmospheric spot, as is **Law's,** 689 South Ave. (tel. 716/461-0310), which features Victorian ambience and dancing at night. Other good places to dance include the aforementioned **Red Creek Inn,** 300 Jefferson Rd. (tel. 716/424-1080); **Shnozz'z,** in the Village Gate Square complex at

302 N. Goodman St. (tel. 716/271-8334); and a glittery disco called the **Glass Onion,** 81 Marshall St. (tel. 716/454-4538). And for laughs, try your luck at **Yuk Yuk's Komedy Kabaret,** 150 Andrews St., near St. Paul Street (tel. 716/325-9857), whose Thursday-, Friday-, and Saturday-night shows features four comedians apiece.

Rochester naturally has its complement of big **shopping malls,** most of which aren't particularly different from their counterparts elsewhere. With, however, two exceptions. The first is **Midtown Plaza,** a stone's throw from the Strong Museum in downtown Rochester (tel. 716/454-2070). Despite its up-to-date look, this was the very first enclosed downtown shopping plaza in the United States, and is now something like 25 years old. There are about 100 shops and services here, plus parking for 2,000 cars in adjacent underground lots. Also worth a visit is the converted factory building on the near east side, now called the **Village Gate Square,** 274 N. Goodman St. (tel.716/442-9168). Lots of unpretentious antiques/secondhand stores in here, plus Schnozz'z (a bar described above), plus hair cutters, ice cream stands, booksellers, basket stores, and a courtyard with all manner of outdoor summertime activities.

Last of all, I'll mention Rochester's least visited sight, the **Upper Falls** of the Genesee River. If this thing were sitting in the middle of the countryside, it would no doubt be the centerpiece of a state park. As it is, the falls thunder away unnoticed in the very heart of Rochester, bypassed by major roads and overlooked by unused factory buildings. The best vantage point is from the east bank of the Genesee, at a clifftop parklet on St. Paul Street. There are but half a dozen parking places here, but don't worry, there's always a spot. True, it's no Niagara, but a 100-foot-high waterfall is still a fine sight. Here was the power source of early Rochester's first wealth. And here too was where some fool daredevil named Sam Patch plunged to his death in the last century. And beyond that, there's not much more to say.

4. The Southern Tier

A number of attractive communities anchor the southern tips of the Finger Lakes. Foremost among them is the famous college town of:

ITHACA
Referred to variously in the past as Storm Country, The Pit, and Sodom, this attractive small city was eventually named Ithaca in the late 18th century by one Simeon DeWitt, surveyor-general of New York State. It sits on the southernmost shore of 38-mile-long Cayuga Lake, in a region of steep hills and picturesque chasms. There are about 30,000 full-time residents in Ithaca, plus another 22,000 college students who attend either Cornell University or the much-smaller Ithaca College.

In 1779 a colonel on the staff of General John Sullivan named Henry Dearborn swept through the Ithaca area. The Continental Army's mission, as mentioned earlier, was to eliminate the threat of pro-British Indians, a task they accomplished with sobering thoroughness. But once the Indians were gone, Ithaca flourished. It was a mill and manufacturing town throughout the 19th century. And then in 1912 the movies arrived. In 1913 Essenay Studios released its first Ithaca production, *The Hermit of Lonely Gulch,* starring Francis X. Bushman. Serials like *The Exploits of Elaine* (not to be confused with *The Perils of Pauline*) were filmed here throughout the 1910s. Some still remember Irene Castle's arrival in town to work on a serial titled *Patria.* She is supposed to have arrived with two servants, 20 trunks, and a pet monkey.

The movies were a short-lived phenomenon, petering out by the end of the 1920s. The business of education, however, has grown to become Ithaca's mainstay.

Cornell was founded in 1868; what is today's Ithaca College started in 1892. These two institutions dominate the town and give it a great deal of its vitality and dimension.

The old 19th-century city center has been restored and rediscovered of late. Two blocks of downtown State Street have been closed to traffic, planted with trees, and transformed into a pedestrian shopping mall called **Ithaca Commons.** This might well be the most successful and aesthetically appealing project of this sort in New York State. Ithaca Commons is not an isolated island amid a wasteland of parking lots. Instead it's part of the fabric of downtown, surrounded by other streets with shops and cars and plenty of on-street parking.

Looming to the east over the compact downtown is a steep hill crowned by the campus of **Cornell University.** The streets are so steep on the uphill slope that the second floor at one end of a house is at ground level at the other. This area, with its late-19th-century architecture, looks a great deal like a miniature San Francisco. To the north of town is a separate municipality called **Cayuga Heights,** which is a densely wooded bedroom community to adjoining Ithaca. Immediately south of downtown is another hill, atop which is the modern campus of **Ithaca College.** The campus isn't much architecturally, but the view up Cayuga Lake is memorable.

What to See and Do in Ithaca

Known as the "Little Apple", Ithaca and the surrounding area have all the cultural, recreational, and culinary resources worthy of this nickname. Well worth a visit or a call is the Ithaca/Tompkins County Convention and Visitors Bureau, 904 East Shore Dr., Ithaca, NY 14850 (tel. 607/272-1313), at the foot of Cayuga Lake. The staff, particularly Ms. Jane Lawrence, are very enthusiastic and even showed a jaded old-time Ithaca visitor such as myself many new and exciting sites.

Ithaca has a businesslike air to it. There's nothing unduly sumptuous or ornate about its architectural heritage, and yet as 19th-century American cities go it's an appealing specimen. At the heart of the downtown area, on the corner of Cayuga and Seneca Streets, is the **Clinton House,** formerly a hotel and the center of civic life. Its rescue and restoration constituted the first and perhaps most important effort of an organization called Historic Ithaca. This pioneering local preservation organization maintains an office in the corner of the old Clinton House, at which you can pick up a **walking-tour brochure** titled "The Rebirth of Downtown Ithaca." Upstairs on the Clinton House's former lobby floor is a museum dedicated to local history, which, depending on your interests, might well be worth a stop. Whether you're into walking tours or not, do take a drive through the **East Hill Historic District,** which is the mini-San Francisco mentioned above. The main drag is Buffalo Street, uphill toward Cornell, between Parker and Quarry.

There are abundant **waterfalls** around Ithaca, including Cascadilla Creek, which is practically downtown. The Cascadilla tumbles most picturesquely from the heights of the Cornell campus to within four blocks of Ithaca Commons. The entrance to the footpath up the gorge is adjacent to the intersection of Court and Linn Streets.

Just outside town are two really lovely natural attractions. Just south of town is **Buttermilk Falls State Park,** on N.Y. 13 (tel. 607/273-5761), a series of cascades and rapids with ten waterfalls, two glens, and a natural swimming pool. Eight miles to the north of Ithaca is **Taughannock Falls State Park,** on N.Y. 89 in Trumansburg (tel. 607/387-6739), with both a swimming beach on Cayuga Lake and a 215-foot-high waterfall, the highest fall east of the Rockies. Very impressive, especially the steep-walled gorge down which Taughannock Creek rushes toward Cayuga Lake. Both parks are open all year.

Other things to do in Ithaca? What about a dinner cruise aboard the historic 60-foot *M-V Manhattan* (tel. 607/272-4868)? This attractive Port of New York cruiser was built in Manhattan in 1917. For about $30 per person, you can enjoy a full dinner with the panoramic view of Cayuga Lake outside. There are daily 6 p.m.

departures between May and September. The dock is at the **Old Port Harbor** restaurant (see below). Call for information and reservations.

You might also like to take a spin through the campus of **Cornell University,** located on the heights overlooking the city from the east. You can pick up a copy of the "Cornell Campus Guide" at the Tourist Information Booth, near N.Y. 13 in Stewart Park on the shore of Cayuga Lake, and also at the Ithaca Chamber of Commerce, on Court Street between North Cayuga and North Geneva Streets. Among other things on campus are the **Cornell Plantations** (tel. 607/255-3020), a pretty theme garden in a bosky dell, and the **Herbert F. Johnson Museum of Art** (tel. 607/255-6464), an ultramodern and architecturally arresting building with a famous collection and a great view of the lake. The museum is open every day but Monday from 10 a.m. to 5 p.m. Like the Cornell Plantations, it's free. If you're an explorer like me, you'll at least want to have a quick look at **Ithaca College** too. Its square gray towers, located south on N.Y. 96B, are clearly visible from downtown. Better to be up here looking at Ithaca than the other way around.

And of course there's **Ithaca Commons,** the downtown pedestrian shopping mall composed of restored 19th-century buildings and occupying two blocks of State Street. Besides being an attractive place to stroll and browse, summer visitors might also enjoy the free Thursday-night concerts held here. The Ithaca Concert Band is the backbone of this annual series which also includes jazz, soul, and country groups.

Where to Stay In and Around Ithaca

The **Statler Hotel,** Cornell University, Ithaca, NY 14853 (tel. 607/257-2500, or toll free 800/541-2501), is a spanking new hotel facility located right in the center of Cornell University. The nine-story complex of 150 deluxe rooms with panoramic views of the campus and Cayuga Lake is accented with a first-rate restaurant, Banfi's. From the valet parking to classic rooms equipped with dual-line telephones for PC hookups, TVs with VCR hookups, refrigerators, minibars, and twice-daily maid service, the Statler offers a full-service hotel experience and then some. The hotel is also a functional classroom for Cornell's world-renowned Hotel Administration School. Accommodations cost about $95 for a standard room with a queen-sized bed, up to $150 for the suites. There is no need to tip.

N.Y. 13 north of Ithaca is an expressway that curves up and over the top of Cayuga Heights. At the intersection of Triphammer Road is a concentration of suburban culture that includes major chain-motel installations, huge shopping malls, etc. The **Sheraton Inn,** Triphammer Road and Hwy. 13, Ithaca, NY 14850 (tel. 607/257-2000), is by far the nicest of this group. There are 106 rather posh rooms, decorated with tweedy sofas, brass moldings, rice-paper-like vinyl wall coverings, luxurious baths, private phones, color TVs, and subtle color schemes. On premises is an indoor pool of proper proportions (it used to be an outdoor pool before they enclosed it), a restaurant, and a lounge. Doubles pay between about $70 and $90 nightly.

In the immediate vicinity are a huge Holiday Inn and a Howard Johnson's Motor Lodge, both offering similar, if not quite as attractive, accommodations for about $10 or so less per night.

Right next to Cornell is an excellent-value family-run motel called the **Collegetown Motor Lodge,** 312 College Ave., Ithaca, NY 14850 (tel. 607/273-3542). This place contains 41 units, was built in 1960, and is located in an alpine section of town whose streets are full of college kids. Inside, it's very spiffy indeed. There is no pool, no restaurant, and only a tiny lobby (with reddish marble desk nonetheless, plus track lights and potted plants). But rooms are of a quality that normally costs much more. They have thick rugs, oak furniture, color TVs, clock radios, stacks of oversize towels, even little baskets of bathroom amenities. Doubles pay between $60 and $90 nightly, depending on size and location of the room.

For an alternative to downtown accommodations, you might want to try **La**

Tourelle, 1150 Danby Rd. (south of town on N.Y. 98B), Ithaca, NY 14850 (tel. 607/273-2734). Located behind L'Auberge du Cochon Rouge (see restaurants), this country inn is a fanciful version of a European alpine "auberge." It's new, nicely detailed, decorated with bleached French-influenced furniture and heavier Mexican carved pieces. The views from the western rooms are spectacular, overlooking the valley and Lake Cayuga. An all-year tennis facility is located on the property. Tasteful fireplace suites are available, as are tower suites with bright red interiors, ten-foot diameter circular beds, Jacuzzis (small), mirrored ceilings, color TV with VCRs (video tapes available at front desk), and nonisolated bathroom fixtures. The per-room tariff is $75 to $95 for a room with one queen- or king-sized bed, $95 to $110 if you need two queen- or king-sized beds, and $100 to $125 for the fireplace and tower suites.

Eight miles north of Ithaca, adjacent to the famous Taughannock Falls State Park, is a really handsome old Victorian manse called the **Taughannock Farms Inn,** N.Y. 89, Trumansburg, NY 14886 (tel. 607/387-7711). This is a great big cream-colored clapboard establishment with a lantern on top and spacious porches on the bottom, and sweeping views of the lake from within. The interior is filled with beautiful painted woodwork, crystal sconces, and Victorian wallpapers. Much of the main floor is given over to a handsome and popular restaurant. Upstairs are five elegant, perfectly restored guest rooms, graced with lofty molded ceilings, enjoying splendid lake views from big windows, and furnished with good-looking antiques. The rooms have private baths and rent for $85 to $100 double, including a continental breakfast. Its adjacent guesthouse costs $125 for two, or $145 for four. The restaurant overlooks Cayuga Lake and offers full dinners for between $17 and $28. This is a good-looking place.

About an equal distance from town, but this time on the eastern side of Cayuga, is the **Rose Inn,** N.Y. 34 (P.O. Box 6576), Ithaca, NY 14851 (tel. 607/533-4202). This terribly elegant place occupies a fine early Italianate mansion set amid farm country with distant views to the hills beyond Cayuga Lake. There is a country kitchen where breakfast is prepared, a handsome dining room where gourmet feasts are served on china and crystal (for $50 per person), and a really terrific circular staircase that climbs up to a lantern on the roof. This is one of those truly unique establishments where the new rooms are actually just as nice as the old ones. They're all very luxurious, furnished with thick carpets, very good antiques, handsome woodwork, and lamps and wallpapers. No phone, TV, or pool, but lots of country elegance. Double rates for bed-and-breakfast vary from $95 to $140 for doubles and $175 to $225 for suites. Of the 14 rooms, all have private baths, and large Jacuzzis are featured in the suites.

Where to Eat in Ithaca

Best place in town is the terribly quaint and charming **Auberge du Cochon Rouge,** which is south of town past Ithaca College on N.Y. 96B (tel. 607/273-3464). The Auberge is housed in a diminutive yellow farmhouse whose numerous little rooms have wide-plank floors, beamed ceilings, and elaborate place settings. Cuisine is classical French, and divine: pasta with lobster and smoked salmon, filet mignon with béarnaise sauce, rack of lamb, confit of duck with Cassis sauce, stuffed quails, etc., cost around $15 to $25 à la carte. Open daily for dinner only from 6 to 10 p.m.; Sunday brunch is served from 11 a.m. to 2 p.m.

The Station, Taughannock Boulevard, at the foot of West Buffalo Street (tel. 607/272-2609), is an ivy-clad brick-and-stone Edwardian-era railroad station. No trains come here anymore, but a few vintage railroad cars are permanently parked on the tracks outside, where they have been converted into dining rooms. The station itself is a dignified place, with lofty ceilings, clusters of tables, and a long bar. The cars are furnished with velvet curtains, thick rugs, tasseled shades, and vintage photos on the walls. The menu is a book of "tickets," each of which describes a different meal. You tear off the one you want and hand it to your waiter, who then punches out vegetables and beverages. Prime ribs, duckling with orange sauce, lamb chops, breast of capon, seafood platter, boeuf bourguignon, etc., cost mostly $9 to $19 or so. Open for dinner only from 4 until 9:30 p.m. Tuesday through Saturday, and from noon until 9 p.m. on Sunday; closed Monday.

Joe's Restaurant, 602 West Buffalo St. (tel. 607/273-2693) has been recently restored to its original 1930s look: neon, a Wurlitzer jukebox, a monitor-top refrigerator, and an old Coke machine. The atmosphere is set for fine Italian dining. The veal is organic, homemade sauces accompany all pasta dishes, and fresh seafood is offered daily; dinner fare runs between $7 and $14. Open all week for dinner only from 4 to 10 p.m. Sunday through Thursday, and to 11 p.m. on Friday and Saturday.

On the Cayuga Lake Inlet is **Old Port Harbour,** 702 West Buffalo St. (tel. 607/272-4868), which bills itself as "a little piece of Europe" on the water. Decorated in a nautical theme with lots of glass overlooking the canal, the restaurant, featuring cuisine ranging from Cajun to continental; serves lunch from 11:30 a.m. to 3 p.m. (Sunday brunch from 11 a.m. to 3 p.m. with music) and dinner from 5:30 to 10 p.m. Lunch will cost between $5 and $7, with the dinner fare in the $13 to $18 range.

Ithaca's downtown **restaurant row** is located adjacent to Ithaca Commons on North Aurora Street, between State and Seneca Streets. On this single block are half a dozen different restaurants, ranging from **Hal's Deli** (deli sandwiches; tel. 607/273-7765), to **Plums'** (brass fixtures and mahogany, serving hamburgers and hot entrees; tel. 607/274-8422), to **Simeons on the Common** (plush sandwiches and evening entertainment; tel. 607/273-2212), to **Ragmann's** (bar burgers with atmosphere; tel. 607/273-5326), to the **Fisherman** (brick walls, blond furniture, and very fresh seafood; tel. 607/273-9108), plus numerous others. Everything's moderately priced, and they're never all closed at once.

Those in the mood for mesquite should take themselves to **Abby's,** in the little Hancock Plaza Shopping Center at 309 3rd St. (tel. 607/273-1999). The interior is gray and curvy, and contains considerable rattan and chromium accents. There are various multicourse prix-fixe dinner deals, ranging from about $16 to $20 and featuring main courses like mesquite-grilled chicken, duck, steak, or swordfish, etc. The kitchen also turns out things like shrimp brochette, yellowfin tuna, lasagne with duck breast, herbed crepes filled with leeks and cheese, etc. À la carte prices run about $9 to $16. Open daily for dinner only from 5:30 to 9 p.m. (to 10 p.m. on Friday and Saturday).

Five minutes south of Ithaca on N.Y. 13 is a flamboyantly Gothic house with steep gables and painted bargeboard. This is **Turback's,** N.Y. 13 (tel. 607/272-6484), a Victorian setting for New York State cuisine. In its various dining rooms, amid plants, a book-lined bar, hanging forests of Tiffany-glass shades, and racks of wine, you can enjoy things like Empire apple chicken, Long Island duckling, Cornell barbecued chicken, pasta primavera, Dutchess County ham steak, etc., which cost around $10 to $19. Lunch in the $8 to $14 range is available from 11:30 a.m. to 4:30 p.m., and dinner is served daily from 5 to 10 p.m. (to 11 p.m. on Friday, Saturday, and Sunday).

CORNING

This small and tidy industrial town houses one of the largest tourist attractions in New York State: specifically, the **Corning Glass Center.** This well-designed series of exhibits, all pertaining to glass and its unusual history, is housed in a glittering museum with sensually sculpted reflective walls. It's easy to find, fun to visit, intellectually exciting, and really something that no visitor to this part of the world should miss. Most don't—a half million people went through the Corning Glass Center last year alone.

It's divided into three parts, connected in sequence and tourable at your own speed. The first, called the "Corning Museum of Glass," contains unbelievably fabulous and precious objects made of glass, and arranged chronologically. I remember particularly a solid-glass banquet table, made in 1878, surmounted by a cut-glass and ormolu punchbowl the size of my wife. The "Hall of Science and Industry" is full of pushbutton exhibits and screening rooms where formerly inexplicable things like binary coding and fiber optics suddenly become quite clear and simple. Don't think for one moment that it's either too complex or too intellectually demanding. It isn't. You could easily wander around here all day with an expression of uncritical wonder on your face. Last is the "Steuben Glass Factory," presumably named after Baron von Steuben and Steuben County. This is an actual working factory, a place full of glowing ovens and glass in every condition, from molten blob to etched vase. You can watch the entire process from grandstand seats and from along a glass-walled corridor. Beyond is a gift shop, where glass is for sale.

The Corning Glass Center is open every day from 9 a.m. to 5 p.m. Admission is $4 for adults and $2 for youths (ages 6 to 17). They tell me the average visit lasts two hours, but you could easily spend a day. For further information, the phone number is 607/974-8271.

Corning itself is kind of an interesting place. "The Crystal City," as it has been styled, is obviously a company town, and just as obviously the company cares what it looks like. In 1972 the Cheming River rose above its banks and made a total wreck of **Market Street,** Corning's busy main business thoroughfare. The event was seized upon by the powers-that-be as an opportunity to "restore" the entire downtown with an eye to re-creating its brick Victorian charm.

As a result, Corning doesn't look like many other places. It has *very* many brick sidewalks and lots and lots of planted locust trees. There are hardly any commercial signs that stick out. The original 19th-century streetscape was probably a lot less smooth, filled as it must have been with signs, clocks, sheds, railings, and all the other necessary furniture of a busy sidewalk. The present-day Corning is also probably prettier, whatever its historic veracity.

Market Street, which is listed on the National Register of Historic Places, is a fun place to browse and stroll. It's full of shops and cars and people, and anchored at its very center by **Baron Steuben Place.** This is a six-story brick hotel from the '20s that closed down in 1974 and has been renovated into a complex of boutiques and galleries that includes a gourmet snackbar, a restaurant, and the **Wine Center.** This latter is a display of wines made in the Finger Lakes, samples of which are there for the tasting. And you can taste them almost any day, from 11 a.m. to 8 p.m. May through October (closed Sunday), to 6 p.m. November through April (closed Sunday and Monday).

Also in Corning is the largest collection of Western art (that's cowboys and Indians I'm talking) in the East. The **Rockwell American Museum,** Denison Parkway (N.Y. 17) and Cedar Street (tel. 607/937-5386), occupies Corning's former City Hall, now (naturally) restored. The excellent collection includes works by New York's own Frederic Remington, Albert Bierstadt, W. R. Leigh, and many others. Good gift shop too. During July and August the museum is open weekdays from 9 a.m. to 7 p.m., to 5 p.m. on Saturday, and from noon to 5 p.m. on Sunday. During the rest of the year hours are 9 a.m. to 5 p.m. daily (from noon on Sunday).

Hotels In and Around Corning

There are some interesting ones at least, if no great bargains. The **Corning Hilton Inn,** Denison Parkway/N.Y. 17, Corning, NY 14830 (tel. 607/962-5000), is a sleek, low-slung channeled cement-block affair surrounded with landscaped parking lots full of shady locust trees. Inside is a hushed modern lobby with an indoor atrium complete with fountain, multiple levels, leather furniture, contemporary tapestries, and an adjacent atmospheric restaurant called the Garden Court. The 180 rooms are, well, just like you hope they'll be in an upstate Hilton. Those in the new wing truly exemplify up-to-the-minute hotel luxury in terms of equipment and muted pastel color schemes. Besides color TVs, private phones, and marble sinktops, guests at the Hilton enjoy an on-premises health club and an indoor pool. A double room costs about $80 to $85 nightly.

A few miles west of Corning via N.Y. 17 is a small neighboring community called Painted Post. Several hotels are located here, the best being the **Best Western Lodge on the Green**, P.O. Box 150, Painted Post, NY 14870 (tel. 607/962-2456). This is a big, luxurious motel in excellent repair that's well on its way to becoming a high-1960s period piece. There are 135 units, housed in low modern buildings on a manicured campus of lawns and trees and flower beds. Outside the lobby is a covered porte cochere with slim steel columns; inside are cathedral ceilings and two-story glass walls. The rooms are big, and come equipped with thick carpets, padded headboards, cable color TVs, digital clocks, radios, direct-dial phones, and good-quality furniture. A large number have views across a grassy inner lawn toward a handsome outdoor pool. Minimum-rate rooms face a parking lot, but otherwise they're just as nice. From May through October a double room will cost between $65 and $85 nightly; the rest of the year those same rooms cost $50 to $55. Also on the premises are a lounge and a restaurant. The lodge is located adjacent to N.Y. 17 and U.S. 15. Take the Gang Mills exit off U.S. 15; you'll see it from the ramp.

Where to Eat in Corning

Baron Steuben Place, the restored gallery/boutique/restaurant complex in the middle of Corning at Market Street and the Centerway, contains two eating establishments of note. The first is the **Ice Cream Works** (tel. 607/962-8481), which has marble-topped tables, a white tile floor, an old-fashioned carved-wood bar with a marble-topped counter, fans on the ceilings, and an overall 19th-century ice cream parlor look. You can get sandwiches of every description here, plus burgers, soups, salads, melts, sundaes, fancy sundaes, etc., priced mostly between $2 and $10, and available all day long. Open daily in the summer from 10 a.m. to 6 p.m., winter hours are 11 a.m. to 5 p.m. Under the same roof is the **Epicurean Café** (tel. 607/ 962-6553), which offers high-class sandwiches with names like Classic, All American Kid, Elite, etc., plus Savory Entree Croissants and other inventive fare. Most prices are under $5. Open all year from 8 a.m. to 6 p.m.; closed Sunday.

On Bridge Street off the western end of Market is a pair of distinctively different restaurants operated under the same roof by the same management. **Rojo's**, 36 Bridge St. (tel. 607/936-9683), is a dim and atmospheric tavern with a central bar, green-shaded hanging lights, lots of dark woodwork, and dark-green walls covered with pictures, street signs, and old photos. Burgers, big combination sandwiches, quiches, all manner of snacks, plus hot entrees and even pizza cost between about $4 and $8 each, or $10 to $20 for dinners. Anything on the menu is available Monday through Saturday from 11:30 a.m. to 10 p.m. (to 1 a.m. in the summer); closed Sunday.

Beyond a door in the back of Rojo's is the **Greenhouse**, 36 Bridge St. (tel. 607/962-6243), a world of mint green and peach, where the walls are made of glass and furniture is painted wicker. Those walls that aren't made of glass are adorned with artistic botanical prints; there's an appealing outdoor terrace in the back for warm-weather al fresco dining. Lunch might be seafood crêpes, a club sandwich, a Monte Cristo, the quiche du jour, broiled sole, etc., and cost anywhere from about $5 to $8. At dinner the list of entrees includes things like bluefish Kennebec, grilled New York strip steak, sautéed shrimp with pecans, lemon-herb chicken, etc., priced from about $10 to $18. Lunch is served Monday through Friday from 11:30 a.m. to 1:30 p.m.; dinner hours are Monday through Thursday from 5 to 9:30 p.m., to 10 p.m. on Friday and Saturday; closed Sunday.

For dependable family-style Italian cuisine at moderate prices, try **Sorge's**, 66-68 W. Market St. (tel. 607/937-5422). This modern, brightly lit establishment has a long counter along one wall and an adjoining dining room filled with tables. Sorge's has all manner of sandwich, egg, and salad lunches, plus a full range of Italian dishes, children's portions, daily specials, etc. Even for the full-course dinners, prices rarely exceed $12; lunch looks like about a $4 ticket. Open from 7 a.m. to 11 p.m. seven days a week.

WATKINS GLEN

This unassuming little village, founded in 1863, sits at the southernmost tip of Seneca Lake. It's famous for two not-very-compatible attractions: international auto racing, and a silent and spectacular natural glen.

In 1986, after a hiatus of several years, **Watkins Glen International** resumed a full schedule of summer auto races. The track is about four miles from the village of Watkins Glen. At least once a month it hosts a major racing weekend, filling the country air with the scream and whine of high-speed engines. Everything—from stockcars to factory prototypes, from GTOs to vintage cars, from "pony cars" to sports cars—races here, sometimes for big money. The approximately 3½-mile-long track is adjoined by campsites, club areas, and a new spectator/photo stand. For ticket and program information, contact Watkins Glen International, P.O. Box 500, Watkins Glen, NY 14891 (tel. 607/974-7162).

Adjoining the village itself is **Watkins Glen State Park** (tel. 607/535-4511), whose centerpiece is a 1½-mile-long gorge filled with waterfalls, grottos, and caverns. It's very deep and accessible by unobtrusive stone paths and staircases. There must be approximately one stair for every year nature took to form this place. Watkins Glen is no Grand Canyon, but it is very beautiful, and very sensitively accessed and protected. Elsewhere on the park's 800 acres are campsites, toilets, parking fields, and a splendid big outdoor pool (50¢ for adults and 25¢ for kids). The park itself is free; parking costs $2.50 per car ($1.50 after 4 p.m. on weekdays). Open daily from 8 a.m. to 10 p.m.; the Gorge Trail is open only from mid-May to late October.

Also in the state park is a jazzy outdoor sound-and-light show called **Timespell,** which takes place in the gorge every night from May through October. Lots of eerie music, artificial rushing winds, and vivid lights and images projected on the walls of the gorge. The whole thing takes about half an hour and costs $4. For program and ticket information, call Timespell at 607/535-4960 or 607/535-2466.

Where to Stay and Eat

The **Glen Motor Inn,** N.Y. 14 (P.O. Box 44), Watkins Glen, NY 14891 (tel. 607/535-2706), sits on a hillside north of town, overlooking Seneca Lake. It has a restaurant and bar at the top of the hill, and 40 units plus an outdoor pool on the lower slopes. Rooms have color TVs, tiled bathrooms, nice-quality furniture, and fine lake views. The charge for a double room is about $50 to $80 nightly, the latter price being the one you're most likely to encounter. It's simple, but quite comfortable. Open April 1 to the beginning of November.

A variety of light snacks are available in the village, at a restored brick factory building now called **Seneca Market.** Snack counters with names like Clam Shack and Sen Fu Chan dispense varying cuisines. You eat at picnic tables on a gravel court overlooking the lake. An adjacent building is filled with boutiques and souvenir stands. Open May through October.

Alternatively, you might try a meal at the **Seneca Lodge,** at the south end of Watkins Glen State Park (tel. 607/535-2014). The dining room here is in a big Adirondack-type building with log walls, heavy beams, a stone fireplace, and flocks of green-clothed tables with paper placemats. At lunchtime (11:30 a.m. to 2 p.m.), salads and sandwiches run from about $2 to $6. Dinner entrees like broiled scallops, rainbow trout amandine, pork chops, chicken Kiev, T-bone steak, and London broil, cost between $8 and $18 (most being right in the middle of that spread) and is served from 6 p.m. to 9 p.m. Open May through November. Look for the sign on N.Y. 14 just south of the main entrance to the Watkins Glen State Park.

HAMMONDSPORT

The village square here could have been painted by Norman Rockwell. It has a little gazebo and mature shade trees, and is overlooked by stolid two-story 19th-century commercial buildings, many in the throes of restoration. Hammondsport, on the southern shore of Keuka Lake, has a decidedly somnolent air, notwithstanding numerous interesting shops along Sheather Street and a few comfortable small-town restaurants and taverns overlooking the square.

The biggest attraction in town is the local **wine.** In fact, this is a good time to talk about Finger Lakes wines in general. The industry started near Hammondsport in 1860 in what is today the Taylor/Great Western/Gold Seal complex in nearby Pleasant Valley. Today there are 34 different wineries in the region, all but four of which are adjacent to Keuka, Seneca, and Cayuga Lakes. The wineries are grouped in three associations: the Keuka Lake Winery Association, the Seneca Lake Winery Association, and the Cayuga Wine Trail. Brochures exist with maps locating various member wineries. The idea is to tour around the region at your own speed, stopping at whichever winery you've either heard of or that simply catches your attention along the road.

The facilities at the different wineries vary considerably. The big ones, notably Taylor (described below), have visitor centers, gift shops, bus tours, and all sorts of glitz. The little ones are just vineyards where someone will appear from behind a barn, show you around, and offer you a glass of wine before you leave. None charges admission, and all take a great deal of pride in their product. To get a copy of the brochure titled "Keuka Lake Winery Route," write the **Keuka Lake Winery Association,** R.D. 1, Box 45, Hammondsport, NY 14840. This will direct you through 43 miles of vineyards surrounding Keuka Lake. "The Wines and Wineries of Seneca Lake" is published by the **Seneca Lake Winery Association,** P.O. Box 91, Hector, NY 14841, and it, too, will lead you on a thorough vinous tour of the area.

Tours of the Taylor Wine Company (not to be confused with an unrelated operation called the Wine Museum of Greyton H. Taylor) constitute the second-largest tourist attraction in the area after the Corning Glass Center. The Taylor Wine Company (tel. 607/569-2111) operates daily tours from 10 a.m. to 4 p.m. between May and the end of October (the rest of the year they close at 3 p.m. and all day Sunday). The winery is a large modern complex set amid cornfields and vineyards just west of N.Y. 54 in Pleasant Valley. There's a big modern visitor center filled with displays pertaining to wine-making and Taylor's various products. A 35,000-gallon former wine tank has been converted to a theater for wine industry films, and a horseshoe bar dispenses gratis samples to whoever bellies up. The free tour takes about an hour, covers the entire process of wine-making, and ends up in a gift shop.

Also in Hammondsport is the **Curtiss Museum,** which presently shares an old ivy-clad building on the corner of Lake and Main Streets with the Village of Hammondsport and the local police. Curtiss was an aviation pioneer, credited, among other things, with founding naval aviation. The tour here starts with a video that shows a succession of wild-looking antique planes. In 1907 these things were puddle-jumping at 1,000 feet or so at a time. By 1908 Curtiss kept the *June Bug* off the ground for a whole mile. Already by 1910 he was demonstrating the feasibility of aerial bombing. And in 1911 he performed the historic act of taking off and landing from the deck of the U.S.S. *Pennsylvania*. He became rich during the First World War, and a major local employer. By 1919 he was able to cross the Atlantic via Nova Scotia and the Azores in a flying boat. In 1930, at the age of 52, he died during a routine appendectomy in Buffalo.

The museum is a great old place full of stamped-tin ceilings and creaky floors. It's filled with fragile-looking antique airplanes and motorcycles, plus a considerable amount of early-20th-century miscellany (toys, tools, uniforms, etc.). The setting is entirely appropriate to the exhibits; however, by the time you read this everything will probably be relocated to a new warehouse by the lake. Currently the museum is open mid-April to the end of October, Monday through Saturday from 9 a.m. to 5 p.m. Admission is $3 for adults, $2.50 for seniors, and $1.50 for kids.

Where to Stay and Eat Near Hammondsport

The area is not strong on accommodations. The best I found (from the standpoint of comfort and value) was the **Steuben Inn,** 330 W. Morris St., Bath, NY 14810 (tel. 607/776-7644). This five-story modern motor inn has variously been a Ramada Inn, a Quality Inn, an independent operation, and as we go to press it's about to become a Days Inn. I don't know why it has been sleeping around so much, as it's a very nice little place. There is a restaurant with moderately priced daily specials, a bar with a happy hour, and bright, pleasant modern rooms furnished with thick rugs, white vinyl swivel chairs, color TVs, textured wall coverings, and direct-dial phones. The atmosphere is like a modest Holiday Inn, which is what it might become next for all I know. Doubles pay between $55 and $65 a night depending on whether the room has a queen-size, two doubles, or a king-size bed.

The **Village Tavern,** overlooking Hammondsport's village square at the corner of Mechanic and Pulteney Streets (tel. 607/569-2528), has booths, a bar filled with locals, and a nice friendly atmosphere. Sandwiches, burgers, and super sandwiches go for about $2 to $4 at lunchtime. In the evening they offer dinners like broiled haddock, fried clam strips, lasagne, chicken parmesan, shrimp basket, etc., for between $5 and $15. On Saturday night there's even piano music. Open daily for lunch from 11 a.m. to 3 p.m., and for dinner from 5 to 9 p.m. The bar, of course, stays open longer.

Across the square is the **Crooked Lake Ice Cream Co.,** on Sheather Street (tel. 607/569-2751), which serves sandwiches and luncheon specials in the $2 to $3 range, plus a broad selection of ice cream concoctions, every day of the year. This is a small-town luncheonette; no dinner is served.

The nicest restaurant in the area is the **Pleasant Valley Inn,** on N.Y. 54 (Bath–Hammondsport Road); (tel. 607/569-2282), located in a pink and white Victorian house quite near the Taylor Wine Co. The inn is divided into a series of very pretty rooms decorated with involved period wallpapers, lofty ceilings, crystal chandeliers, spotless white linens, and elaborate curtains. There's also an informal bar with low ceiling beams and a congenial older crowd. Luncheons like seafood Newburg, liver and onions, omelets, and various sandwiches cost from about $3 to $6. Dinner entrees such as New York sirloin, broiled sole, tenderloin tips marsala, veal à la crème, and duckling are priced from about $9 to $16 à la carte. Open daily during the summer from 11:30 a.m. to 3 p.m. for lunch, and from 5 to 9 p.m. for dinner (to 10 p.m. on weekends). During the cooler seasons they're closed on Monday.

THE NIAGARA FRONTIER

The western extremity of New York State is best known for Niagara Falls, a mighty cataract on the Niagara River connecting Lakes Erie and Ontario. But there are other attractions hereabouts, notably the somewhat battered but still magnificent city of Buffalo, and a cultural institution whose name has entered into the language itself, Chautauqua.

1. Buffalo

New York State's second-largest city is a blue-collar town that amassed considerable wealth and power before hard times began in the 1960s. Today it's a city for connoisseurs, both of former urban magnificence and of present-day urban hopes.

Buffalo is filled with 19th- and 20th-century architectural treasures. And if some are still boarded up and in distressed condition, or hemmed in by the incredible number of downtown parking lots, many others are in gorgeous shape. Since the adoption of the 1975 Buffalo Landmark and Preservation Code, there's been a great new awareness of the local architectural resources. Things are being renovated everywhere.

Buffalo is well along on an ambitious plan to rejuvenate its downtown core around Niagara and Lafayette Squares. Main Street, for example, has been converted to a combination pedestrial mall/streetcar route. The "streetcar" is a sleek new surface train called the **Metro,** whose fare is gratis throughout the downtown area. The route isn't long but the idea is good. And it seems to be bringing renewed life and activity back to the city's core.

Buffalo grew rich on trade between the Midwest and the East. It was the terminus of the Erie Canal, a fact whose impact is hard for many of us to really understand these days. Back in the 1820s, before railroads, the canal was the only practicable means of transporting goods. It had the most tremendous impact on trade imaginable. People in Buffalo became immensely rich through the commerce of that day because everything went through their town. Then when the age of rails arrived, the tracks went through Buffalo too.

After the Civil War, Buffalo became an even greater boom town. Immigrants poured in. Smokestack industries rose along the lakefront and the southern edge of town. By 1901 Buffalo was a world-class city with magnificent banks, office towers, and municipal buildings, splendid mansions along famous Delaware Avenue, a park system designed by Frederick Law Olmsted, and endless tracts of wooden houses filled with immigrant laborers.

That year, 1901, was also the year of the famous Pan-American Exposition, a wonderland of columned white temples, ornamental lakes, and triumphal ways erected in Delaware Park. The exposition brought exotic exhibits and famous visitors from around the world. It was a truly glamorous event. And in the middle of it, while attending a reception, President William McKinley was shot. At first they thought he'd survive. But a week later he was dead, a victim of gangrene that set in after his wounds were prematurely sewed up. Vice-President Teddy Roosevelt was summoned from the Adirondacks back to the Delaware Avenue mansion of Ansley Wilcox, where he'd been staying at the time of the attack. After paying his respects to Mrs. McKinley, he returned to the Wilcox house, where after a short ceremony he became America's youngest president.

The McKinley assassination did not shadow Buffalo's continued prosperity. Heavy industry continued to grow. The great Pierce-Arrow automobile was produced entirely in Buffalo, as were all the Curtiss Wright airplanes manufactured during the Second World War. Plenty of big industries remain, despite the economic travails of the last quarter century.

If exploring interesting old cities appeals to you, by all means take a look at Buffalo. It's also an interesting alternative to staying in nearby Niagara Falls. Buffalo is not at all a typical tourist town, of course. Most visitors come here on business, and depart without much of a look around. Useful tourist maps are unknown. The helpful **Greater Buffalo Convention and Visitors Bureau,** in the former Statler Hotel building at 107 Delaware Ave., Buffalo, NY 14202 (tel. 716/852-0510, or toll free 800/283-3256), will give you a map of the downtown which is better than nothing, but still woefully limited in scope. There's something called the "New Map of Greater Buffalo" too, but the print is so small that it might as well be on microfilm. The bureau has numerous other useful publications, however, so anybody planning to explore Buffalo is well advised to write ahead and/or contact them upon arrival.

The bureau can also inform you of local sports events. Buffalo is a big team town, and between the **Buffalo Bisons** in the new Pilot Field (baseball), the **Buffalo Bills** (football), and the **Buffalo Sabres** (hockey), there may well be an exciting game scheduled during the time of your visit. There's also a vigorous cultural life in Buffalo, much of which centers on the reemerging theater district (about which more below). The Arts Council in Buffalo and Erie County maintains a 24-hour **ARTSline** with information on all area events. The number is 716/847-1444.

So now let's take a look around town.

WHAT TO SEE AND DO IN BUFFALO

Exploring the city is a definite adventure for those who like that sort of thing. A thoroughly detailed and illustrated handbook titled *Seeing Buffalo,* by Maggie Headrick and Celia Ehrlich (Ivyhall, 1978), describes neighborhoods, the Olmsted parks, and the great public, private, and commercial buildings. It locates and illustrates the works of Frank Lloyd Wright (five houses of his are still in private hands in Buffalo), Louis Sullivan (his Prudential Building at Pearl and Church Streets is one of the great structures in America), Stanford White (a few palatial mansions on Delaware Avenue), Carrere and Hastings, Henry Hobson Richardson, and all those other good names that architectural/historian types love to read about. You can get a copy of *Seeing Buffalo* at the Information Desk of the Convention Center (main entrance on Franklin Street), or by writing to Ivyhall, 43 Ivyhurst Rd., Amherst, NY 14226 (tel. 716/832-5146). Or possibly the chamber of commerce will have copies too. The cost is $4.95 per book.

Another way to see the city is on one of the **Architectural Walking Tours** sponsored by the Theodore Roosevelt Inaugural National Historical Site, 641 Delaware Ave. (tel. 716/884-0095). "Reflections of the Past . . . Visions of the Future" is their title for the downtown tour. There are also excursions down Delaware Avenue, another in and around Allentown (a well-preserved in-town neighborhood), and another along Main and North Pearl Streets. The tours usually cost about $2 per person. Call the number above for schedules and further information.

Admittedly, this degree of detail is not going to interest all visitors. But casual sightseers should at least admire the following: the **Lafayette Hotel** (on the southwest corner of Lafayette Square; now closed; designed by Louise Blanchard, the first woman architect in the U.S.); the **Old Post Office** (a fantastical stone Victorian concoction on Ellicott and Swan Streets, which is now the downtown campus of Erie Community College); the **Prudential Building** (Louis Sullivan's wondrous 1896 office tower covered entirely with sculpted terracotta); the **Buffalo City Hall** (a 1932-vintage art deco opus which out–Radio City's Radio City Music Hall); the **Buffalo Savings Bank** (a lavish expression of the aesthetic that gave rise to the Pan-American Exposition, located at the confluence of Main, Huron, Genesee, and Washington Street and now called the Goldome Center); **Delaware Avenue** (the former millionaires' mile, now bereft of its elm trees and most of its mansions; some palatial Newport-type survivors still stand in the blocks immediately north of North Street); and the **Elmwood Strip** (a stretch of Elmwood Avenue, between Bidwell Parkway and Forest Avenue, noted for trendy bars and interesting shops and restaurants). This is a very minimal itinerary, but one that will give a quick idea of what's here.

The **Theater District** occupies a short stretch of Main Street (the present Metro route) just north of the Hyatt Regency Buffalo Hotel. It's a surprised-looking group of old buildings (surprised because, unlike most of the surrounding blocks, they haven't been bulldozed), containing almost half a dozen legitimate theaters, plus shops and restaurants. The restoration of the Theater District is just completed at this writing and there's clearly a future here. There are lots of pink granite paving blocks and newly planted trees. Shops are opening up, and fine old buildings have been restored. People clearly care.

Centerpiece of the Theater District is **Shea's Buffalo Theater,** one of the last intact vaudeville house/movie palaces in the country. Shea's is a satisfyingly baroque confection dating from 1926. It's full of Italian marble, gilded moldings, Czechoslovakian crystal, and opulent murals. George Burns and Gracie Allen, Bob Hope, the Marx Brothers, Red Skelton, Duke Ellington, Benny Goodman—the list of famous names who have appeared here goes on indefinitely. In 1975, after failing to get even an upset bid of $100,000, the city decided to tear the place down for yet another parking lot. Volunteers barricaded the doors. Nonprofit organizations went to work. The entire theater was restored and today it boasts a full calendar of Broadway shows, top-name entertainers, rock concerts, etc. Call the ARTSline at 716/847-1444 to see what's playing here, or at the other district theaters. Tours of the interior are available by appointment only; call 716/847-0850 for information.

The **Buffalo and Erie County Naval and Servicemen's Park** is a long name for a small park containing two famous navy ships. The official address is 1 Naval Park Cove (tel. 716/847-1773), a waterfront area that has been separated from downtown by the elevated lanes of the New York State Thruway. The road that takes you there (and to the nearby Erie Basin Marina) is located two blocks south of the Hilton Hotel. The U.S.S. *Croaker* (one of 17 serving Second World War submarines), the U.S.S. *The Sullivans,* and the U.S.S. *Little Rock* are on loan from the U.S. Navy and open to visitors daily from April through November. *The Sullivans* was named in memory of five young Sullivan brothers, all of whom died on November 13, 1942,

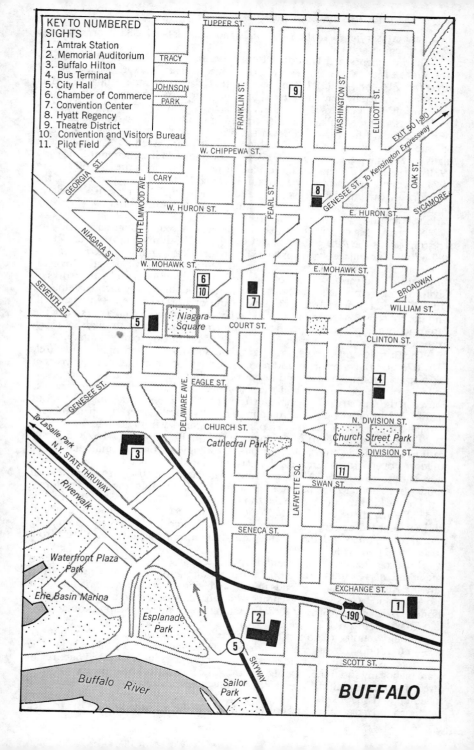

KEY TO NUMBERED
SIGHTS
1. Amtrak Station
2. Memorial Auditorium
3. Buffalo Hilton
4. Bus Terminal
5. City Hall
6. Chamber of Commerce
7. Convention Center
8. Hyatt Regency
9. Theatre District
10. Convention and Visitors Bureau
11. Pilot Field

BUFFALO

aboard the cruiser *Juneau* in the Solomon Islands. Admission is $3.50 for adults and $2.50 for seniors and kids.

The aforementioned **Theodore Roosevelt Inaugural National Historic Site (the Wilcox Mansion)** occupies a big old house at 641 Delaware Ave., at North Street (tel. 716/884-0095). It's modest by later Delaware Avenue standards, and its location, hemmed by new commercial buildings and across the street from a Howard Johnson's, exaggerates this modesty. Parts of the house were originally the officers' quarters for the Buffalo Barracks, erected in 1838 during the socalled Patriots' War in Canada. After that died down the property passed into private hands and became a part of the march of fashion up Delaware Avenue. Ansley Wilcox mansionized the place, and he and his wife continued to live there until the early 1930s. Concerned citizens saved the house from demolition in the late '60s and in 1971 it was opened as a historic site administered by the U.S. Department of the Interior. You can prowl its elegant halls and get the whole McKinley/Roosevelt inaugural tale any day from 10 a.m. to 5 p.m. (from noon on Saturday and Sunday). Parking is around back on Franklin Street.

Naturally a big city like Buffalo has its share of museums. But a particularly interesting one is the **Albright-Knox Art Gallery,** 1285 Elmwood Ave. (tel. 716/882-8700). The gallery is perhaps best known for its outstanding collection of contemporary art of the last 30 years. Pop, op, conceptualism, kinetic art and color field, minimalism, and various trends of the late 1970s are represented by the works of Clyfford Still, Frank Stella, Jackson Pollock, Jean Dubuffet, Roy Lichtenstein, etc. Other historical periods, from antiquity to impressionism, are represented as well. And the collection is housed in a splendid Greek temple adjacent to the side of the Pan-American Exposition. Open from 11 a.m. to 5 p.m. Tuesday through Saturday, from noon to 5 p.m. on Sunday; closed Monday. Admission fee is voluntary.

The **Buffalo and Erie County Historical Society,** 25 Nottingham Ave. (tel. 716/873-9644), is a museum and research library documenting over 125 years of the Niagara Frontier history and heritage. Exhibits cover American Indians, the building of the Erie Canal, and the Pan-American Exhibition. The museum is housed in the only structure remaining from the 1901 Exposition, built of Vermont marble and inspired by the Parthenon. The Historical Society is open Tuesday through Saturday from 10 a.m. to 5 p.m., and on Sunday from noon to 5 p.m.

The **Buffalo Museum of Science,** Humbolt Parkway (tel. 716/896-5200) features exhibits on anthropology, geology, zoology, astronomy, and botany. The **Kellogg Observatory** is great for the stargazer, and the dinosaur room will facinate kids. The museum is open Monday through Saturday from 10 a.m. to 5 p.m. and on Sunday from noon to 5 p.m. The admission is $2.50 for adults and $1 for children.

For the kid in all of us go to the zoo. The **Buffalo Zoological Gardens** are situated in Delaware Park (tel. 716/837-3900) and are part of the original 1875 Frederick Law Olmsted design. The zoo contains sculptured landscapes and fascinating animal collection in both indoor and outdoor interpretive areas. Open all year from 10 a.m. to 5 p.m. daily.

It's also possible to cruise around Lake Erie, taking in the sights of Buffalo from one of the **Miss Buffalo Cruise Boats.** Afternoon sightseeing cruises leave daily in July and August, and on weekends in June and September. The fare is $8 for adults and $6 for kids. On summer evenings additional cruises combine sightseeing with dinner, Dixieland, or "50s to '60s." For sailing times and reservations, contact **Buffalo Charters, Inc.** (tel. 716/856-6696).

Should you like to go to **Cristal Beach Park** in Canada, try the one-hour or two-hour round trip on the cruise ship *Americana* (tel. 716/883-3311). The *Americana* is one of those grand old ships of a more gracious era, decked out in elaborate mahogany and full of nostalgic charm. The boat is docked at the foot of Main Street in downtown Buffalo and takes six cruises a day, with a round-trip fare of $10 for adults and $5 for kids.

For a three-day Erie Canal cruise, contact **Mid-Lakes Navigation Co. Ltd.** (tel.

800/255-3709) for a trip between Buffalo and Syracuse on the cruise boat *Emita II*. This lazy jaunt on the Érie Canal includes bus transportation, all meals, and two nights in hotels for around $400 per person.

WHERE TO STAY IN BUFFALO

This is not a very long list, because frankly I doubt that many people will stay here. But those who do have the opportunity to combine an exciting hotel experience with easy accessibility to both Niagara Falls and the charms of old Buffalo herself. That aforesaid "hotel experience" is the **Hyatt Regency Buffalo,** Two Fountain Plaza (which is the corner of Main and West Huron Streets), Buffalo, NY 14202 (tel. 716/856-1234, or toll free 800/228-9000). The Hyatt occupies the 15-story Genesee Building, a brick-and-limestone office tower built in 1923 and converted to a hotel in 1984. It's a gorgeous place with an attached sun garden whose many levels are filled with fountains, potted trees, and restaurants. Rooms are particularly luxurious, with their tall ceilings, buff and beige palettes, pleated shades, thick rugs, marble bathrooms, padded headboards, cable color TVs, direct-dial phones, and deluxe-looking modern furniture. Standard-double room rates vary from about $80 to $120 nightly, which is a bargain for what you're getting. There are three restaurants on the premises, plus an indoor pool on a high floor with a great view, plus a health club, plus the Genesee Sports Bar, accessible from the atrium lobby on Main Street via the Genesee Building's original marble-framed doorway. Parking is extra at a park/lock across the street.

Moderately priced accommodations in luxurious surroundings can also be had at the **Buffalo Hilton,** 120 Church St., Buffalo, NY 14202 (tel. 716/845-5100). This cast-concrete behemoth at the edge of the downtown core was built in 1980 and played an important role in local redevelopment efforts. It's connected to an immense brick sports complex, which includes six indoor tennis courts. The lobby is a vast marble-floored atrium where buffet lunches are served amid tree-size ficus plants. Standard rooms have vaguely French provincial–looking furniture, marble-topped sinks, thick rugs, cable color TVs, direct-dial phones, and cost mostly between $80 and $90 a night, double occupancy. Actually, 95% of available rooms are likely to be at the low end of that range, making this a superlative bargain. Even parking is free. And guests also have the use of an indoor pool, plus the tennis, squash, and racquetball facilities next door. In addition to the Atrium, there is another pair of on-site restaurants, plus a couple of atmospheric hotel bars.

There are all sorts of other hotels in Buffalo, but these two make staying here a particular pleasure. A highly recommended budget alternative on the edge of the expressway loop that rings Buffalo is either of the two area **Red Roof Inns.** The first is adjacent to New York State Thruway Exit 49, Bowmansville, NY 14026 (tel. 716/ 633-1100, or toll free 800/843-7663). The second is at the Millersport Highway exit of I-290, which is a beltway through the northeast quadrant of greater Buffalo. Both interchanges are equally convenient for travelers heading either into Buffalo or north to Niagara Falls. As such they each have gaggles of motels located nearby. The Red Roofs belong to a chain I've recommended elsewhere. They are brand-new, very attractive, and offer 109 rooms (the same at each location) decorated with wall-to-wall carpeting, a table with chairs, color TVs, vinyl textured wall coverings, and direct-dial phones. There are no pools, no restaurants, and no fancy lobbies. But for $40 double, who's complaining? Mass production and volume marketing have served the Red Roof well—it's a great buy for the money. For a copy of the Red Roof Inns directory, write to them at 4355 Davidson Rd., Hilliard, OH 43026 (tel. 614/876-3200).

WHERE TO EAT IN BUFFALO

Herewith, a half dozen suggestions culled from a long roster of good local places. In the downtown area, next to the Convention Center and across the street from the Hyatt, is the **Macaroni Co.,** 320 Pearl St. (tel. 716/856-1081). This is a big, dimly lit space, filled with rock music and lots of atmosphere, thanks to brass rails, intimate booths, exposed brick walls, Tiffany-style shades, etched-glass partitions, and big blowups of Charlie Chaplin as the Little Tramp. Lunch might be chopped beef with melted cheese, meatballs, a triple-decker club, linguine with clam sauce, beer-batter fish fry, baked lasagne, etc., priced from about $4 to $11. The dinner menu features many of the same items, plus a few more pasta and meat dishes, for almost the same prices. Open for lunch Monday through Saturday from 11 a.m. to 3 p.m.; dinner is served Monday through Thursday until 10 p.m., and until midnight on Friday and Saturday; closed Sunday.

On the next street over is the **Bean Alley Cafe,** 166 Franklin St. (tel. 716/852-3665), featuring continental dining. The decor is light and airy, with bentwood chairs, several large plants, platters that are displayed around the dining area, and French doors that connect to the taproom. Lunch is available Monday through Friday from 11:30 a.m. to 2:30 p.m., with salad plates, sandwiches, and croissants all in the $4 to $7 range. More sumptuous dinners are served Monday through Saturday from 5 to 10:30 p.m. and include dishes like stuffed breast of chicken in phyllo or curried shrimp for around $8 to $14.

Over on the pedestrian mall in the Theater District is the **Bijou Grill,** 643 Main St. (tel. 716/847-1512). The grill has an art deco feel with its neon clocks, hanging Saturn glass lamps, stage-set lighting, and the salmon and turquoise color scheme. Nouvelle cuisine delights like Florentine burger, grilled souvlaki, quattro formaggio pizza, and spinach salad giambotta, are all priced in the $4 to $5 range. The restaurant has a summer sidewalk café and is open from 11:30 a.m. to midnight Sunday through Thursday, and to 2 a.m. on Friday and Saturday; Sunday brunch is served until 3 p.m.

Around the corner off Tupper Street is the best French restaurant in town. The **Rue Franklin,** 341 Franklin St. (tel. 716/852-4416), is a quaint place with balloon curtains in the garden room (overlooking a small rock garden), and a full bar covered with marble. With over 100 choices of wine, the menu ranges from pheasant and duck foie gras pâté at $6.50 up to roast filet of lamb with stewed vegetables at $19.50. The restaurant serves dinner only, Tuesday through Saturday from 5:30 to 10 p.m.; dessert is available until midnight.

Up in the Allen Street area is a great Greek restaurant called **Yianni's,** 581 Delaware Ave. (tel. 716/883-6033). Housed in an old brick building with Italianate Victorian detailing, the interior has exposed-brick walls in the front dining room, and stained glass and a marbleized fireplace with wainscotting in the back. Offering the usual Greek delights, the restaurant also has several continental options available for lunch, all in the $2 to $6.50 range (Monday through Friday from 11:30 a.m. to 2 p.m.). Dinner costs between $10 and $13 (Monday through Friday from 5 to 10 p.m., to 11 p.m. on Saturday). Patio dining is available in the summer months out front.

My favorite lunch and light dinner spot is **Preservation Hall,** 752 Elmwood Ave. (tel. 716/884-4242). This vegetarian restaurant serves pita sandwiches, pasta and grain salads, fruit salads, hot and cold soups, and an endless array of daily specials. This very comfortable place, decorated with antiques, possesses that homey feeling so seldom found. Since it's located not far from the park and zoo, you might try aordering basket lunch and enjoying some of Frederick Law Olmsted's fine work. The standard menu items are priced in the $3 to $4 range, with dinner specials in the $5 to $6 area.

Crawdaddy's, 2 Templeton Terrace (tel. 716/856-9191), is a big new place out by the Erie Basin Marina, near the Sailors and Servicemen's Park. Pieces of driftwood and wooden pilings out front set a nautical mood. Inside are numerous atmospheric dining rooms decorated with acres of weathered barn siding, plush flowered rugs, paisley upholstered booths, Tiffany-style colored-glass shades. A lower-level bar has a sunken dance floor presided over by a screen showing rock videos. In the separate dining rooms you may well have a view of the marina and the skyline beyond. Lunch consists of club sandwiches, chef's salads, fruit plates, steak sandwiches, omelets, burgers, broiled fish, etc. The entrees cost between $6 and $12. At dinner you get a huge full meal with main courses like filet mignon, prime rib, pork tenderloin, seafood linguine, fresh brook trout, lobster tails, etc. And that will cost you anywhere from $10 to about $20. Open for lunch Monday through Saturday from 11 a.m. to 3 p.m.; dinner is from 5 to 11 p.m., until midnight on Saturday; on Sunday they serve a brunch from 10:30 a.m. until 3 p.m., then dinner from 5 to 10 p.m.

The **Anchor Bar,** 1047 Main St., at the corner of North (tel. 716/886-8920), is reputed to be where Buffalo-style chicken wings were invented. It's a very friendly, family-style Italian restaurant, with a dimly lit bar full of regulars and a comfortable modern dining room adjacent. There are all sorts of special lunches like the Greek salad, hot dog and a cup of soup, beef buckshots, vegetarian lasagne, plus omelets, sandwiches, meatballs, spaghetti, not forgetting the famous chicken wings (in strengths up to "suicidal if you're daring") for between about $4 and $6. At dinner you'll choose from chicken cacciatore, homemade ravioli, various pasta dishes, barbecued ribs, or chicken livers, plus many lunch items (not forgetting the famous chicken wings) for prices ranging from about $4 (at the sandwich end) to $14 (at the specialties-of-the-house end). Open daily for lunch from 10:30 a.m. to 3 p.m., and for dinner from 3 p.m. to 12:30 a.m.

The Elmwood Avenue strip has lots of interesting places to eat, plus a collegiate/yuppie atmosphere that one encounters in certain parts of many cities these days. Two good places with lots of atmosphere and reasonably priced food (plenty of things between $5 and $10 anytime, and cheaper at lunch) are **Cole's,** just south of Forest Avenue at 1104 Elmwood (tel. 716/886-1449), and **Jimmy Mac's** at 555 Elmwood on the corner of Anderson St. (tel. 716/886-9112). Both are open every day, and serve food from 11 a.m. to 11 p.m.

2. Niagara Falls

Oscar Wilde said he'd have been more impressed if the falls plunged uphill. Surely the drive through the dreary industrial outskirts of the city of Niagara Falls, N.Y., is not much encouragement. Neither is the matter of tourist disinformation, which seems to be a pastime among one sector of the community. "Tourist Information! Motels!" crows one strategically placed sign, which also bears a fat red arrow pointing in the *opposite* direction from the falls and the principal motels.

Let's trust you won't fall prey to any of this. Take I-190 north from Buffalo (there are no pretty backroad routes). Then take the first exit after the toll bridge that crosses the east branch of the Niagara River, and get right onto the **Robert Moses Parkway.** This four-lane expressway, at the moment, leads right to the center of Niagara Falls, although other sections might be in service by the time you read this. Even if they are, just follow the (dependable in this area) signs that say "Tourist Information and Convention Center."

For the tourist, the city is quite compact. Your first stop should be at the tourist information office. Look for the huge Quonset-hut roof of the modernistic **Convention Center.** This place does extra duty as a bus station too, and as a nesting place for innumerable birds.

A two-block-long pedestrian mall, the **Falls Mall,** connects the Convention Center with the **Wintergarden.** This is a ten-story greenhouse, angular in shape, totally glazed, supported by fat cement columns, and filled with exotic plantings, stone-bordered pools, full-size trees, and a restaurant. Niagara Falls has the same democratic atmosphere you find in places like Lake George Village, except that there's a real city attached. Built in 1978, the Wintergarden is the focus of Niagara Falls' annual winter **Festival of Light.** For 44 days, between the end of November and the first week in January, the city is decorated with millions of lights, the Convention Center is filled with animated displays, and the Wintergarden looks like an immense multicolored jewel. Many private businesses along the Convention Center/Wintergarden axis join in the spirit. The effect, on a winter's night, is quite wondrous. Besides decorations, there's a daily schedule of free events and music in and around the Wintergarden, plus concerts in the Convention Center by the likes of Bill Cosby and Judy Collins. A free daily calendar of events is available throughout the festival area during festival time.

Adjacent to the Convention Center, you will find the **Niagara Falls Convention and Visitors Bureau,** 345 Third St., Niagara Falls, NY 14303 (tel. 716/285-2400 or 285-8727).

The falls themselves are only about as distant from the Wintergarden as the Wintergarden is from the Convention Center. The problem is, we Americans seem to be awkwardly positioned right on top of them, while our Canadian friends across the river have the fine unobstructed view. It's quite possible, let me hasten to say, to get great views of Niagara Falls from the American side. But it does take more doing.

In pursuit of the ideal view, plus general orientation, you might also try the new **Niagara Falls Official Information Center,** Fourth and Niagara Streets (tel. 716/285-8711). Don't hesitate to assert yourself; the lack of tourist information in this area of international prominence is astonishing. For other information you might also try **Niagara County Tourism,** 59 Park Ave., Lockport, NY 14094 (toll free 800/338-7890), or the regional **I Love New York** office of the State of New York Department of Economic Development, 135 Delaware Ave., Buffalo, NY 14202 (tel. 716/847-3625).

SEEING NIAGARA FALLS

There are a number of worthy attractions in the vicinity of the falls themselves. But we'll start, of course, with the purpose of the trip, to wit,

The Falls

A bit of orientation first. The Niagara River is flowing northward at this point, and its course is not direct. There are two cities of Niagara Falls, one on the Canadian side of the river and one on the eastern, American, side. Because of vagaries in the course of the river, the falls are immediately adjacent to, and somehow on the same side of the river as, the American city. We've done all sorts of things to crane our collective neck over the edge for a better view. The most successful was the erection of the **Prospect Park Observation Tower,** which stands perhaps 100 feet away from the cliffs, thus permitting an excellent view of the falls.

Just as there are two cities called Niagara Falls, so there are two cataracts as well, with a bit of parkland called Goat Island in between. The **Horseshoe Falls** (called also the **Canadian Falls**) joins the Canadian city on one side and Goat Island on the other. It's shaped in a horseshoe curve, hence the name. The **American Falls** are comparatively straight and join Goat Island on one end and the American city on the other. Goat Island is nearer to the American side, which is perhaps the reason it belongs to us.

The falls themselves, plus a certain amount of shoreline on both sides, are public parks. Niagara Falls State Park (created in 1885, and the first park of its kind at the time) is on our side, and Queen Elizabeth Park is on theirs. There's a considerable skyline on the Canadian side, obviously devoted to the resort industry. The American city is smaller, no doubt because our hotels don't have views of the falls.

There's a simple, do-it-yourself sequence for seeing the best of the Falls from the American side.

First: Take the car to **Goat Island.** The road over the bridge starts at the former Niagara Hotel, which is now Days Inn, on Rainbow Boulevard. From Goat Island you can see the river rapids as the water approaches the lip of the falls. There's park-

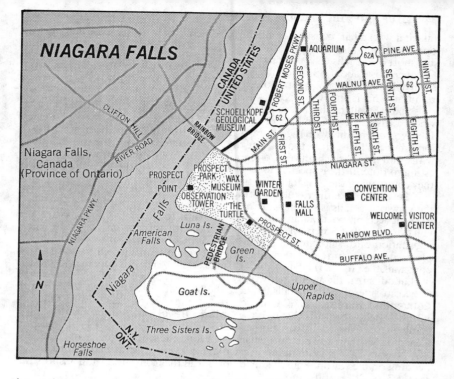

NIAGARA FALLS

ing at the upstream end, and a path to the **Three Sisters Islands,** mere rocks in the torrent hurtling toward the lip of the Horseshoe Falls.

Second: Drive the car to the lot ($3 charge) at the other end of the island, adjacent to the Top of the Falls cafeteria restaurant (tel. 716/285-3316). Then proceed on foot to the respective tops of the **Horseshoe Falls** and the **American Falls.** It's a pleasant and easy walk, of only a few minutes' duration. All that thundering water is fairly intimidating. Everything's safe, of course, but it seems as if you could reach out and touch the water. There was a time when Goat Island and all the land along the shore was privately owned. High fences were erected and people paid for the right to squint through peepholes.

Third: Visit the **Cave of the Winds,** if you're so inclined. An elevator on Goat Island will take you to within 25 feet of the foot of the American Falls. Admission is $4 for adults and $3 for kids. The loan of a thick yellow slicker comes with the deal.

Fourth: Drive the car back across the Goat Island Bridge and park in the Rainbow Shopping Center lot adjacent to the Wintergarden. At the end of the Falls Mall, in line from the Convention Center through the middle of the Wintergarden, is the **Niagara Reservation Information Center** (tel. 716/278–1770) and the **Prospect Park Observation Tower.** A footbridge (25¢ at the turnstile) connects the tower with the clifftop itself. It contains an elevator (free) that will take you either up or down. The upper-level observation decks belie the notion that there's no good view from the American side. The panorama is awesome, and it's also the best available on this side. At night you can admire colored lights trained on the thundering waters from the Canadian side, as well as the brilliantly lit hotels and amusement parks of Niagara Falls, Canada.

Fifth: Take the Prospect elevator down to the **Maid of the Mist** (office tel. 716/284-8897; dock phone 716/284-4233). This boat ride to the base of the falls is Niagara Falls' No. 1 tourist attraction, and has been since 1846. It's an exciting (albeit a wet) affair, consisting of being clad in a yellow slicker, crowded onto an open boat, and piloted apparently toward destruction until the boat turns around just short of the falls. The trip takes about half an hour, operates from mid-May to October, costs about $5 for adults, and half as much for kids. Niagara Falls often seems like a lion in a zoo—no longer dangerous. Being right at the base of it reminds us what it once was.

Sixth: Stroll the short distance from the Observation Tower to **Prospect Point,** where a ring of American flags commemorates the ordeal of the Iranian hostages. Here you can meditate on the surging white froth that spills over the adjacent top of the American Falls. Here, too, despite the coin-operated viewers, the lawn-bordered paths, and the nearby high-rises, one still has a sense of nature untrammeled. Interesting to note: If the respective local power companies together drew all the water they could out of the Niagara River, the falls would dry up.

Seventh: Take the **Rainbow Bridge** (tel. 416/354-6043) to Canada, where the view of the falls is significantly more spectacular and—that historically being so—the accommodations are of a higher standard. To cross into Canada, make sure you bring proof of American citizenship such as birth or baptismal certificate, voters registration card, state firearm permit, FAA or FCC license, draft card with birthplace, citizenship card, or papers. Should you be from a foreign country, have a passport available. To see the falls from Canada is well worth this paperwork, and the likelihood is that the authorities won't request any papers. For information on the Canadian side of Niagara Falls, contact the **Niagara Falls/Canada Visitors and Convention Bureau,** 4673 Ontario Ave., Suite 202, Niagara Falls, Ontario, L2E3R1 (tel. 416/358-3221), or the **Ontario Travel Information Center,** 5355 Stanley Ave., Niagara Falls, Ontario, L2E7C2 (tel. 416/356-6061). The trip to Canada is worth it; however, the details lie beyond the scope of this book.

Niagara Falls is **illuminated** every night, all year long, at different times depending on the season. For scheduled hours, call the Convention and Visitors Bureau at 716/285-2400.

Niagara Power Project

Located a few minutes north of Niagara Falls at 5777 Lewiston Rd., in Lewiston (tel. 716/285-3211, ext. 6660), this is one of the largest electric power projects in the world. About 14% of all the electricity used in New York State is produced here. The water that turns the 13 immense waterwheels is drawn (carefully) from the river, upstream from the falls, then delivered here to the plant via four miles of underground tunnels. The **Visitor Center** consists of all sorts of play-with-'em displays, plus historical museums and a grand view of the Niagara Gorge. Open all year, admission free; call for exact hours.

The Aquarium of Niagara Falls

Located just north of the downtown area at 701 Whirlpool St. (tel. 716/285-3575 or 716/692-2665), the aquarium is a major tourist attraction, as well as an important research and educational facility. Here, for example, was where artificial seawater was developed. It's lots of fun to visit. There are hourly trained-dolphin shows, plus all sorts of changing exhibits (on endangered species, different habitats in the sea, birds of prey, etc.). It's not too erudite, but it's very enlightening. Open daily from 9 a.m. to 7 p.m. (to 5 p.m. in the winter); admission is $5.50 for adults and $3.50 for kids.

Native American Center (The Turtle)

This unusual organization occupies quarters that are shaped like a giant turtle, a reference to Indian legends concerning the origin of the world. It's more of a center for North American Indian culture than a tourist attraction per se. But it's so interesting that visitors flock here. The central round body of the turtle is a big arena for dancing exhibitions, shows, and theatrical productions Adjoining this are galleries devoted to Indian history, culture, and art, plus an excellent craft-cum-gift shop. Hours are 9 a.m. to 6 p.m. daily in the summer, and 9 a.m. to 5 p.m. (noon to 5 p.m. on Saturday and Sunday; closed Monday) in the winter. Admission is $3 for adults, $2.50 for seniors, and $1.50 for kids.

An Excursion to the Artpark in Lewiston

About seven miles north of Niagara Falls, on the banks of the Niagara River, is the village of **Lewiston.** This is a pleasant suburb with old stone and wood buildings facing a very wide main street, and subdivisions in the background.

Every summer Lewiston hosts a sort of Saratoga West called the **Artpark,** which is centered around a 2,400-seat auditorium at which ballet, musicals, opera, children's theater, and symphony are staged. All manner of arts and crafts, offered for sale by the artists themselves, are available as well. For current or upcoming schedules, you can contact Artpark at P.O. Box 371, Lewiston, NY 14092 (tel. 716/754-9001).

Hungry in Lewiston? Try **Apple Granny,** 433 Center St. (tel. 716/754-8037), which is in an old historic-looking building in the middle of the village. There's a bar on one side and a family-style dining room on the other. The menu features ribs, sandwiches, burgers, seafood, charbroiled chicken, plus late-night snacks, for about $5 to $9 in the main. Open daily from 11:30 a.m. until 1:30 a.m. Even dancing, nightly after 10 p.m.

Old Fort Niagara

Another seven miles north of Lewiston is historic Old Fort Niagara. And if reconstructed forts with military reenactments, fife-and-drum corps, tent camps, archeological digs, and the lot are your cup of tea, here's another one. Old Fort Niagara overlooks Lake Ontario from the mouth of the Niagara River. It was enormously strategic in earlier centuries, and an ocean of French, British, Colonial, and American Indian blood was shed in order to control it. The present buildings date from the early part of the 18th century and are in a fine state of preservation. Open daily from 9 a.m. to 7:30 p.m. between July and Labor Day; open after that too, but you'd better call for exact hours. The address and telephone number are: Old Fort Niagara Assn., Inc., P.O. Box 169, Youngstown, NY 14174 (tel. 716/745-7611).

WHERE TO STAY IN NIAGARA FALLS

The most appealing place in town is the **Niagara Hilton,** Third and Old Falls, Niagara Falls, NY 14303 (tel. 716/285-3361). There are 400 rooms here, contained in a modern brown-brick building with rounded edges. Inside you'll find the requisite complement of restaurants, bars, and lounges, plus an indoor/outdoor swimming pool and a health club. Accommodations have color TVs, plush furniture, and lots of space, and cost between $115 and $160 nightly for a double in the summer (mid-May to mid-September) and about $75 to $100 in the winter. The hotel is connected to the Convention Center and to the huge and ultramodern Rainbow Shopping Mall by an all-weather walkway.

The classic standby with the best American views of the falls is the former Niagara Hotel, now called the **Niagara Falls-Days Inn,** 201 Rainbow Blvd., Niagara Falls, NY 14303 (tel. 716/285-9321). With the exception of the marquee, this landmark hotel is still recognizable with its grand lobby, notable mezzanine, dining room, and ballroom. If the building and lobby were really restored, it would put American side accommodations back in style and revitalize the tradition of honeymooning at the falls. For those of you who experienced the Niagara Hotel in its heyday, I'm sure the memories and the fact that it still stands will at least be reassuring. The rooms have been redecorated with modern mauve and gray furniture. The White Parrot cocktail lounge has an all-new sound and light system, with a DJ on weekends. The Portofino Restaurant serves from 7 a.m. to 10 p.m. The double-occupancy room rates are $59 to $108 from June to September, and $36 to $59 the rest of the year.

All the chains are in town, and they all offer essentially the same good motel-quality accommodations at similar prices. The **Holiday Inn,** 114 Buffalo Ave., Niagara Falls, NY 14303 (tel. 716/285-2521); the **Quality Inn,** 443 Main St., Niagara Falls, NY 14303 (tel. 716/284-8801); and the **Ramada Inn,** 401 Buffalo Ave., Niagara Falls, NY 14303 (tel. 716/285-2541), all have pools. The **Howard Johnson's Motor Lodge Downtown,** 454 Main St., Niagara Falls, NY 14303 (tel. 716/285-5261); and the **TraveLodge,** 200 Rainbow Blvd., Niagara Falls, NY 14303 (tel. 716/285-7316), do not. Room rates collectively are higher in the summer, and range from about $75 to $130 or so for two persons.

Double rooms at the **Best Western Red Jacket Inn,** five Moses-expressway minutes east of the Convention Center at 7001 Buffalo Ave., Niagara Falls, NY 14303 (tel. 716/283-7612), are as nice as many of those in town, and a bit cheaper. This place has a nice big outdoor pool overlooking the I-190 toll bridge across the Niagara River, plus a bar and a reasonably priced restaurant. From mid-May until the end of September doubles cost $75 to $85 nightly; the rest of the year you'll pay $60 to $70 for the same room.

For something rather different, you might investigate a bed-and-breakfast through **Rainbow Hospitality,** 9348 Hennepin Ave., Niagara Falls, NY (tel. 716/283-4794 or 283-0228).

WHERE TO EAT IN NIAGARA FALLS

Starting at the top, there's the **Red Coach Inn,** next to the Turtle at 2 Buffalo Ave. (tel. 716/282-1459). This is a 1920s Tudor building with leaded windows, iron chandeliers, stone fireplaces, oak tables, comfortable armchairs, and costumed waiters and waitresses. Lunch consists of omelets, salads, and entrees like London broil, baked scrod, fish and chips, eggs Benedict, etc. The cost for most of these dishes is somewhere between $4 and $7. At dinner you can choose from prime rib, broiled haddock, crisp glazed duckling, chopped tenderloin, and mixed grill, to name only a few, priced from around $10 to $15 or so. Open daily for summer lunches from 11:30 a.m. to 5 p.m., and for dinner from 5 to 10 p.m. (until 11 p.m. on weekends, and only for dinner from 5 to 9 p.m. on Sunday). Winter hours are a little shorter.

The Como, 2220 Pine Ave., near 22nd Street (tel. 716/285-9341), is a local Italian restaurant with thick rugs, mirrored walls, Mediterranean stucco arches, white cloths, and huge portions. Almost every pasta, veal, and chicken dish imaginable is available, plus low-priced luncheon specials, meatball sandwiches, and traditional entrees like lamb chops, roast beef, Porterhouse steak, etc. Typical lunchtime selections cost about $5; at dinner the range is from about $6 to $14. Open Monday through Saturday for lunch from 11:30 a.m. to 2:30 p.m., and for dinner from 2:30 p.m. until midnight (to 1 a.m. on weekends); Sunday hours are noon to midnight.

The **Wintergarden Restaurant,** located inside the famous Wintergarden itself (tel. 716/282-1215), is separated from the public areas by a tall iron fence. It's a pretty spot, furnished with white wicker pergolas, potted plants, and a little pool, all set against a jungly backdrop. Lunch is a $5 to $8 ticket, chosen from such items as a chicken salad plate, shrimp Créole, haddock filet, triple-decker sandwiches, burgers of all sorts, etc. At dinnertime, things like mesquite-broiled fish, baby back ribs, ginger chicken, and beer-battered fish, plus a selection of light dinner items, are available for between about $8 and $20. Open for lunch Monday through Saturday from 11:30 a.m. to 2 p.m., and for dinner daily from 5 to 10 p.m. Sunday brunch hours are 9:30 a.m. to 2 p.m.

Located next to the Hilton and across from the Convention Center is **The Cataract House Restaurant,** 225 Rainbow Mall (tel. 716/282-5635). Housed in part of a 19th-century granite bank, this Greek restaurant's interior is decorated in royal green and ivory colors, with etched-glass entry doors. The first things you'll notice upon entering is a vast display of desserts and an espresso coffee bar, followed by the lounge and a large dining room. A canopied terrace is open in the summer, with lunch served from 11 a.m. to 3 p.m. Monday through Saturday. Beef-ka-bab, moussaka, sandwiches, and pizza are all in the $3 to $8 range. Dinners are available, with the exception of Sunday and Monday, from 3 to 10 p.m. and include not just the traditional Greek treats but several continental dishes as well, priced between $9 and $14. A lighter menu has items in the $4 to $7 range.

Last, but certainly not least, is a combination restaurant/nightclub called respectively **Ports of Call** and the **Bakery**, 3004 Niagara St., at 30th Street (tel. 716/282-9498). The former consists of a multilevel dining room decorated with mooseheads, artificial hanging plants, quilted tablecloths, and an overall atmospheric clutter. The adjoining bar/disco is dim and glittery and equipped with telephones atop its little tables, so that you can call from one end of the room to the other. The restaurant serves full dinners only, chosen from a menu that lists Italian favorites (veal cutlet parmigiana, spaghetti, etc.), Greek favorites (moussaka, stuffed grape leaves, etc.), French favorites (poulet à la crème, coquilles St-Jacques), German favorites, Spanish favorites, etc. Fare from these various ports of call costs about $8 to $18. Open daily from 4 to 10 p.m. (from 2 p.m. on Sunday); the Bakery's DJ spins top-40s and oldies every weekend until 3 a.m. (no DJ during the week but you can still dance until 2 a.m.).

---

3. Chautauqua

About 65 miles southwest of Buffalo is the lakeside village of Chautauqua, famous since 1874 as the home of the **Chautauqua Institution.** Dedicated to the pursuit of culture and the arts, Chautauqua sent bands of performers and artists into rural America throughout the late 19th and early 20th centuries. As a result, the word "chautauqua" came to mean a summer series of lectures, concerts, or performances.

But the institution's focus was ever on the village itself, where every July and August there is a full schedule of lectures on pertinent topics, instruction in arts and languages, concerts, opera, musical performances, etc. A typical season might include appearances by the likes of Jeb Magruder, Dinah Shore, Albert Shanker, and Neil Sedaka. In addition to the rich cultural fare, the village offers sailing and swimming on Chautauqua Lake, golf, tennis, instruction in dance, music, or theater, plus the pleasure of being in a near idyllic village setting.

Cars are restricted in Chautauqua, which is filled with leafy trees, narrow streets, and delightful Victorian buildings. Although it's a real village, complete with hotels, restaurants, a post office, shops, and all the expected services, it's also a preserve with a gate that bars all but holders of valid passes. These are available on a daily basis at the gate for between $10 and $20 for adults. The price depends on the day of the week you come, and on who's appearing that night (the pass entitles you to attend whatever's scheduled).

Although it is possible to visit Chautauqua as a day-tripper, most people plan longer stays. All manner of packages—from "Weekend Getaways," to periods of seven nights or longer—are available. They include passes plus accommodations in all price categories. The hotels are overwhelmingly Victorian and good-looking, and range from the deluxe **Athenaeum** ($100 per person and up, including all meals) to an array of inns and guesthouses where two can stay for $250 a week or less.

You can request full particulars of current or upcoming seasons by writing to the Chautauqua Institution, Chautauqua, NY 14722 (tel. 716/357-6200). "Certainly the best 'Whole Package' you'll find anywhere," says the *Smithsonian* magazine. "An unusual blend of intellectual stimulation and summertime fun," adds the *New York Times.* And one of the ornaments of New York State, add I.

And that's the end of the *Frommer's New York State,* as well as another year of my life. I was born in Manhattan and have spent most of the succeeding years in various parts of the state. Yet I think few native sons have ever had such an opportunity to explore. The pay wasn't extravagant, but I'd be lying if I said I didn't enjoy it. My 1973 Cadillac convertible is still running, and has indeed been repainted since the first edition of this book. My daughter is a year older; my wife and I still remain married. I've heard that even great writers, Poe and Dickens among them, have had to turn to travel writing from time to time. Once again, it was my turn. I hope you will find the product of these efforts to be both useful and entertaining. Even after two editions, I can still say "I Love New York."

INDEX

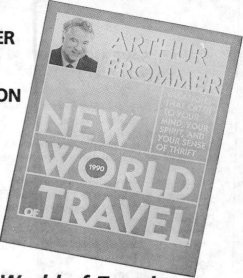

NOW, SAVE MONEY ON ALL YOUR TRAVELS!
Join Frommer's™ Dollarwise® Travel Club

Saving money while traveling is never a simple matter, which is why, over 29 years ago, the **Dollarwise Travel Club** was formed. Actually, the idea came from readers of the Frommer publications who felt that such an organization could bring financial benefits, continuing travel information, and a sense of community to value-conscious travelers all over the world.

In keeping with the money-saving concept, the annual membership fee is low—$18 (U.S. residents) or $20 U.S. (Canadian, Mexican, and other foreign residents)—and is immediately exceeded by the value of your benefits which include:

1. The latest edition of any TWO of the books listed on the following pages.
2. A copy of any one Frommer City Guide.
3. An annual subscription to an 8-page quarterly newspaper, *The Dollarwise Traveler,* which keeps you up-to-date on fast-breaking developments in good-value travel in all parts of the world—bringing you the kind of information you'd have to pay over $35 a year to obtain elsewhere. This consumer-conscious publication also includes the following columns:
    Hospitality Exchange—members all over the world who are willing to provide hospitality to other members as they pass through their home cities.
    Share-a-Trip—requests from members for travel companions who can share costs and help avoid the burdensome single supplement.
    Readers Ask . . . Readers Reply—travel questions from members to which other members reply with authentic firsthand information.
4. Your personal membership card, which entitles you to purchase through the club all Frommer publications for a third to a half off their regular retail prices during the term of your membership.

So why not join this hardy band of international Dollarwise travelers now and participate in its exchange of information and hospitality? Simply send $18 (U.S. residents) or $20 U.S. (Canadian, Mexican, and other foreign residents) along with your name and address to: Frommer's Dollarwise Travel Club, Inc., 15 Columbus Circle, New York, NY 10023. Remember to specify which *two* of the books in section (1) and which *one* in section (2) above you wish to receive in your initial package of member's benefits. Or tear out the next page, check off your choices, and send the page to us with your membership fee.

FROMMER BOOKS
PRENTICE HALL TRAVEL
15 COLUMBUS CIRCLE
NEW YORK, NY 10023

Date_____

Friends:
Please send me the books checked below:

FROMMER™ GUIDES

(Guides to sightseeing and tourist accommodations and facilities from budget to deluxe, with emphasis on the medium-priced.)

☐ Alaska $14.95	☐ Japan & Hong Kong $13.95
☐ Australia. $14.95	☐ Mid-Atlantic States. $14.95
☐ Austria & Hungary $14.95	☐ New England. $14.95
☐ Belgium, Holland & Luxembourg. $14.95	☐ New York State $14.95
☐ Bermuda & The Bahamas. $14.95	☐ Northwest $14.95
☐ Brazil $14.95	☐ Portugal, Madeira & the Azores $13.95
☐ Canada. $14.95	☐ Skiing Europe. $14.95
☐ Caribbean. $14.95	☐ Skiing USA—East. $13.95
☐ Cruises (incl. Alaska, Carib, Mex, Hawaii,	☐ Skiing USA—West. $13.95
Panama, Canada & US) $14.95	☐ South Pacific $14.95
☐ California & Las Vegas. $14.95	☐ Southeast Asia. $14.95
☐ England & Scotland. $14.95	☐ Southern Atlantic States $14.95
☐ Egypt $13.95	☐ Southwest. $14.95
☐ Florida $14.95	☐ Switzerland & Liechtenstein $14.95
☐ France $14.95	☐ Texas $13.95
☐ Germany. $14.95	☐ USA $15.95
☐ Italy $14.95	

FROMMER $-A-DAY® GUIDES

(In-depth guides to sightseeing and low-cost tourist accommodations and facilities.)

☐ Europe on $40 a Day. $15.95	☐ New York on $60 a Day. $13.95
☐ Australia on $30 a Day $12.95	☐ New Zealand on $40 a Day $13.95
☐ Eastern Europe on $25 a Day $13.95	☐ Scandinavia on $60 a Day $13.95
☐ England on $50 a Day $13.95	☐ Scotland & Wales on $40 a Day. $13.95
☐ Greece on $30 a Day. $13.95	☐ South America on $35 a Day $13.95
☐ Hawaii on $60 a Day $13.95	☐ Spain & Morocco on $40 a Day. $13.95
☐ India on $25 a Day $12.95	☐ Turkey on $30 a Day $13.95
☐ Ireland on $35 a Day $13.95	☐ Washington, D.C. & Historic Va. on
☐ Israel on $40 a Day $13.95	$40 a Day $13.95
☐ Mexico on $35 a Day $13.95	

FROMMER TOURING GUIDES

(Color illustrated guides that include walking tours, cultural & historic sites, and other vital travel information.)

☐ Australia. $9.95	☐ Paris. $8.95
☐ Egypt $8.95	☐ Scotland $9.95
☐ Florence $8.95	☐ Thailand $9.95
☐ London. $8.95	☐ Venice $8.95

TURN PAGE FOR ADDITONAL BOOKS AND ORDER FORM.

A

FROMMER CITY GUIDES

(Pocket-size guides to sightseeing and tourist accommodations and facilities in all price ranges.)

☐ Amsterdam/Holland	$5.95	☐ Minneapolis/St. Paul	$5.95
☐ Athens	$5.95	☐ Montréal/Québec City	$5.95
☐ Atlantic City/Cape May	$5.95	☐ New Orleans	$5.95
☐ Belgium	$5.95	☐ New York	$5.95
☐ Boston	$5.95	☐ Orlando/Disney World/EPCOT	$5.95
☐ Cancún/Cozumel/Yucatán	$5.95	☐ Paris	$5.95
☐ Chicago	$5.95	☐ Philadelphia	$5.95
☐ Dublin/Ireland	$5.95	☐ Rio	$5.95
☐ Hawaii	$5.95	☐ Rome	$5.95
☐ Las Vegas	$5.95	☐ San Francisco	$5.95
☐ Lisbon/Madrid/Costa del Sol	$5.95	☐ Santa Fe/Taos/Albuquerque	$5.95
☐ London	$5.95	☐ Sydney	$5.95
☐ Los Angeles	$5.95	☐ Washington, D.C.	$5.95
☐ Mexico City/Acapulco	$5.95		

SPECIAL EDITIONS

☐ A Shopper's Guide to the Caribbean	$12.95	☐ Manhattan's Outdoor Sculpture	$15.95
☐ Beat the High Cost of Travel	$6.95	☐ Motorist's Phrase Book (Fr/Ger/Sp)	$4.95
☐ Bed & Breakfast—N. America	$11.95	☐ Paris Rendez-Vous	$10.95
☐ California with Kids	$14.95	☐ Swap and Go (Home Exchanging)	$10.95
☐ Caribbean Hideaways	$14.95	☐ The Candy Apple (NY with Kids)	$12.95
☐ Guide to Honeymoon Destinations		☐ Travel Diary and Record Book	$5.95
(US, Canada, Mexico & Carib).	$12.95		

☐ Where to Stay USA (Lodging from $3 to $30 a night) $10.95

☐ Marilyn Wood's Wonderful Weekends (NY, Conn, Mass, RI, Vt, NH, NJ, Del,Pa) $11.95

☐ The New World of Travel (Annual sourcebook by Arthur Frommer previewing: new travel trends, new modes of travel, and the latest cost-cutting strategies for savvy travelers.) $14.95

SERIOUS SHOPPER'S GUIDES

(Illustrated guides listing hundreds of stores, conveniently organized alphabetically by category.)

☐ Italy	$15.95	☐ Los Angeles	$14.95
☐ London	$15.95	☐ Paris	$15.95

GAULT MILLAU

(The only guides that distinguish the truly superlative from the merely overrated.)

☐ The Best of Chicago	$15.95	☐ The Best of Los Angeles	$14.95
☐ The Best of France	$16.95	☐ The Best of New England	$15.95
☐ The Best of Hong Kong	$16.95	☐ The Best of New York	$14.95
☐ The Best of Italy	$16.95	☐ The Best of San Francisco	$14.95

☐ The Best of Washington, D.C. $14.95

ORDER NOW!

In U.S. include $2 shipping UPS for 1st book; $1 ea. add'l book. Outside U.S. $3 and $1, respectively.

Allow four to six weeks for delivery in U.S., longer outside U.S.

Enclosed is my check or money order for $_____

NAME _____

ADDRESS _____

CITY _____ STATE _____ ZIP _____

A